ENGLISH PLACE-NAME SOCIETY

The English Place-Name Society was founded in 1924 to carry out the survey of English place-names and to issue annual volumes to members who subscribe to the work of the Society. The Society has issued the following volumes:

The volumes for the following counties are in preparation: *Berkshire, Cheshire* (Parts 4–5), *Dorset, Kent, Leicestershire & Rutland, Lincolnshire, the City of London, Shropshire, Staffordshire.*

All communications with regard to the Society and membership should be addressed to:

THE HON. SECRETARY, English Place-Name Society, University College, Gower Street, London W.C. 1.

ENGLISH PLACE-NAME SOCIETY. VOLUME XLVI
FOR 1968–9

GENERAL EDITOR
K. CAMERON

THE PLACE-NAMES OF
CHESHIRE

PART III

ENGLISH PLACE-NAME SOCIETY. VOLUME XLVI

THE PLACE-NAMES OF CHESHIRE

By

J. McN. DODGSON

PART III
THE PLACE-NAMES OF
NANTWICH HUNDRED AND
EDDISBURY HUNDRED

CAMBRIDGE
AT THE UNIVERSITY PRESS
1971

Published by the Syndics of the Cambridge University Press
Bentley House, 200 Euston Road, London, N.W.1
American Branch: 32 East 57th Street, New York, N.Y.10022

© English Place-Name Society 1971

Library of Congress Catalogue Card Number: 77–96085

ISBN: 0 521 08049 5

Printed in Great Britain
at the University Printing House, Cambridge
(Brooke Crutchley, University Printer)

The collection from unpublished documents of material for the Cheshire volumes has been greatly assisted by grants received from the British Academy

CONTENTS

[ix]

PREFACE

IN THE preface to Part I of *The Place-Names of Cheshire*, I thanked many people who had helped me in the preparation of these volumes. I omitted some names which ought to have been there. In this volume, which contains the results of their help, I hope I can appropriately thank Miss Mary C. Hill, M.A., County Archivist of the County of Salop, Mr J. L. Hobbs, F.L.A., Borough Librarian of Shrewsbury, and Miss Margaret Coggin, B.A., sometime of the Dept. of English, University College London, for assistance with the material for Tittenley and other information.

Since this volume is the half-way mark in a long course, I am glad to acknowledge the patient assistance of Mr R. Turner of Knott End, sometime of Bolton le Moors, La.

Yet again, for the many evidences of erudite assistance and prudent correction which these volumes contain, my thanks and the gratitude of the Society, are right willingly paid to Dr O. von Feilitzen and Professors M. T. Löfvenberg, J. K. Sørensen, K. H. Jackson, G. Melville Richards and Bruce Dickins, and not least, to the Hon. Director of the Survey.

JOHN MCNEAL DODGSON

University College London
Corpus Christi 1970

ADDENDA AND CORRIGENDA

VOL. XLIV

THE PLACE-NAMES OF CHESHIRE, PART I

p. xxiv. Add 'Brad   *List of the Muniments of the Earl of Bradford at Weston Park, Shifnal*, NRA 0403.'.

p. xxviii, s.v. Hogan. For *tribium* read *tribuum*.

p. xxix. Add 'ex inf.   From information privately communicated by the person named'.

p. xxxi. Add 'IEW   J. Pokorny, *Indogermanisches etymologisches Wörterbuch*, Bern 1948—'.

Add 'Jackson   K. H. Jackson, *Language and History in Early Britain*, Edinburgh 1953, occasionally referred to as LHEB'.

Add 'JEPN   *The Journal of the English Place-Name Society*, 1 (1969) *et seq*, occasionally referred to as Journal'.

Add 'Journal   *v.* JEPN'.

p. xxxii. Add 'LHEB   *v.* Jackson'.

p. xl. Add 'StRO   Staffordshire Record Office'.

'*StRO*   Unpublished document in Staffordshire Record Office'.

p. xli. Add 'VKG   H. Pedersen, *Vergleichende Grammatik der keltischen Sprachen*, Göttingen 1909–13'.

p. xlii. Add ' >   becomes, becoming, changing to, giving rise to'.

Add ' <   coming from, derived from, originating as, changing from'.

p. 5, l. 2 from foot. For *lomm* read *lom*.

p. 10, last line. For 'Mondrem' read 'Mondrum'.

p. 11, l. 7. For 'Aston iuxta Mondrem' read 'Aston iuxta Mondrum'.

p. 21, l. 5 from foot. For *Dēua* read *Dēu̯a*.

p. 22, s.n. DUCKOW. For **Duboglassio-* read **Duboglassi̯o-*.

p. 25, l. 8 from foot, s.n. FLUELLENS. For *Llewellyn* read *Llewelyn*.

p. 26, s.n. R. GOWY. Professor Jackson says, 'I think there must be some misapprehension somewhere here. Gowy could come from an IE **u̯ei-* 'to bend, twist' etc., but since there is no evidence that the Celtic languages had such a form this must be regarded as at least highly doubtful. The *r*-extension of **u̯ei-* referred to is of IE date (Irish *fiar*, OE *wīr*, etc., derived from **u̯eiro-*; see IEW 1122 and Pedersen, VKG II 59), and it does not of itself provide evidence for the existence of a more primary *r*-less form in Celtic. In any case if Gowy was derived from this root the name must have been given during the British period, and not in the later Middle Ages, when the supposed **gwy* would long have ceased to have any identifiable meaning to the Welsh speakers who are supposed to have called the river by it.'

p. 28, l. 11 from foot, and p. 332. For 'Latch Cote Fd' read '*Latchcote*'.

p. 36, s.n. R. TAME, and p. 31, s.n. R. MERSEY. Professor Jackson points out that the Brit name for R. Mersey was *Belisama*. He observes, '*Belisama* is given by Ptolemy in a position which seems to identify it with the Mersey; and most writers have agreed with this. The older edition of the *Map of Roman Britain* did not mark it, but the new edition now identifies it with the Ribble, which I think is wrong. It is the name of the Gaulish (and doubtless British) goddess *Belisama*, which is probably a superlative adj., fem., from the root **bhel-* "to be brilliant, to flash, etc.", therefore "she who is brightest" (Brit *beli-+-isamā* fem. superl. suffix).'

p. 37, l. 9. Insert space between 'or' and 'Walvern'.

[xiii]

p. 67, s.n. SHIPLEY. *TA* location 110–915695.

p. 71, s.n. Thorpe. Two fields at 110–865678, close to HIGHER MUTLOW 1 81.

p. 87, s.n. Burying Fd. Location 110–849710.

s.n. Gallows Hill. Location 110–833713.

p. 94, s.n. ALDERLEY. Add 'Cf. *Aldredelie* in Kingsley, **3** 239'.

p. 118, s.n. GALLOWS FD. *TA* location 110–911738, the site of Longacre St. and Hope St.

p. 120, s.n. SWILLINDITCH. *TA* location 110–907736, between Holly Bank Fm and Chester Rd, west of Clowes St.

p. 129, l. 8 from foot. For 'Mankin' read 'Maukin'.

p. 138, s.n. HARROP. Professor Jackson sensibly objects, that the hare is a common indigenous creature, and that 'hare valley, hare hollow' would have been a commonplace allusion to places frequented by this animal. He draws attention to the fairly common p.n. *Harehope* for valleys in SE Scotland in hilly districts where hares abound. In view of this, substitute 'Probably' for 'Possibly' at the beginning of the discussion.

p. 151, s.n. ROSSEN CLOUGH. I misunderstood Professor Jackson's notes on the discussion of this p.n. He does *not* object to the proposal of ModWelsh *-yn*. He accepts the meaning 'a particular piece of moorland in a general area of moors'. I regret the impression of controversy which arises from my construction of his notes.

p. 188, s.n. KERRIDGE. To the example Cabus La, Professor Jackson adds the analogous *the Caiy Stane*, a menhir standing in a street at Fairmilehead in SW Edinburgh.

p. 193, l. 8. For "from' read 'from'.

p. 197, s.n. FALLIBROOME. Add 'Cf. Botterley **3** 142'.

p. 198, l. 12 from foot. For *Hanle y* read *Hanley*.

p. 210, l. 18. Insert comma after *Pou-*. For *Minacct* read *MinAcct*.

p. 234, s.n. NORTHENDEN. For '[ˈnɔːrðəndən, older nourðin, -ən]' read '[ˈnɔːrðəndən] older [nourðin, -ən]'.

p. 238, l. 9. For *Crymbaltʒ* read *Crymbaltʒ*.

p. 239, l. 14. For eā-mōt read ēa-mōt.

p. 244, s.n. GATLEY. Add 'Cf. Botterley **3** 142'.

p. 282, s.n. WYBERSLEY. Add [ˈwibəzli].

p. 292, s.n. ROMILEY. Add 'Cf. Botterley **3** 142'.

p. 305, under (*b*). For *Seisill* read *Seisyll*.

p. 310, l. 9. For 'would' read 'could'.

p. 311, under (*a*). For 'Besso' Cotton's' read 'Bess o' Cotton's'.

p. 320–1, s.n. TINTWISTLE. Professor Jackson observes something amiss with Ekwall's derivation of this p.n. from a r.n. *Teign*. The *-ge-* in the *Tenge-* spellings is not explained. The *g* cannot come from Brit **tagnā* since the *g* in this word must have been vocalised long before the name could have been borrowed. **Tagnā* would give PrWelsh **tain*, with *ai* diphthong. There would be no consonantal [g] nor even consonantal [j]. In view of this objection it is necessary to look at an alternative etymology for this p.n., i.e. 'the prince's (place at a) river-fork', taking the first el. to be the rare (archaic and poetic) OE þengel (*v.* EPN s.v.) as in Finglesham K 570 (KPN 169), Dinglesden Sx 531.

p. 330. Add 'Botterley Hill (Faddiley), 197, 244, 292: **3**'.

p. 337, s.v. Bosden. Delete '54,'.

VOL. XLV

THE PLACE-NAMES OF CHESHIRE, Part II

p. viii, s.v. p. 119. Professor Dickins notes that WHALEBONE FM was probably named from whale's ribs set up as an arch.

p. 12, s.n. BAGULEY. Add 'Cf. Botterley **3** 142'.

p. 48, s.n. Ashby Mdw. Location 101–684825.

p. 60, s.n. TABLEY. Add 'Cf. Botterley **3** 142'.

p. 115, s.n. Sandyway. A group of fields 101–600789 to 603785.

p. 135, s.n. STREET LANE. *Street Field* is at 101–626786.

    s.n. Raby Lights. Location 101–605791.

p. 181, s.n. ROSAM GRAVE. Location 109–542843.

p. 182, s.n. Duck Lake. Location 109–544803.

    p. 193, l. 4. After '*AddCh.*' add 'Professor Richards notes the fifteenth-century Welsh allusion, by Lewis Glyn Cothi, to *y tair Heledd* "the three salt-springs", i.e. Nantwich, Middlewich and Northwich'.

p. 200, s.n. Hunts Hey. *TA* location 110–682716.

    s.n. Lady Hey. *TA* location 110–678718.

    s.n. Long Acre. *TA* location 110–694703, at Drakelow Fm, irrelevant to the older material.

p. 201, s.n. Pear Tree Fd. *TA* location 110–717697.

p. 209, s.n. Marstow. Location 110–674717.

    s.n. Moss Fd. Location 110–683706.

p. 211, s.n. Gooseledge. Location 110–676729.

p. 223, s.n. Rogery Fd. Location 110–794702.

p. 229, s.n. Rooley Fd. Location 110–728682.

    s.n. Whishaw. Location 110–737684.

p. 231, s.n. SALTERSFORD BRIDGE. *Salter's Hay* 1839 *TA* is at 110–783687.

p. 270, s.n. ETTILEY. Add 'Cf. Botterley **3** 142'.

p. 325, Index of Cross references. Add 'Botterley Hill (Faddiley), 12, 60, 270: **3** '.

VOL. XLVI

THE PLACE-NAMES OF CHESHIRE, PART III

    p. 16, s.n. Road Fd. All the numerous instances of this f.n. in Haslington township lie adjacent to roads, lanes or tracks. *v.* rād.

    p. 17, s.n. Street Fd. Located 110–738558, beside Waterloo Rd. The ref. to **1** 44 may be irrelevant.

    p. 19, s.n. STANNERHOUSE LANE. Near *Stannier House* 1841 *TA*, at 110–776588, was *Stanways Croft* 1841 *TA*.

    p. 20, s.n. Stangate Fd. Location 110–782583.

    p. 31, s.n. NANTWICH. Professor Richards adds *Heledd Wen caerll.* 1612 from *Y Llyfr Plygain 1612* (ed. Cardiff, 1931) 42, i.e. '*Heledd Wen* Cheshire'. Similarly, op. cit. 38, 41, 44, the name *Heledd ddu* 'black salt-pit', presumably for Middlewich or Northwich.

    p. 37, discussion of LOTHBURNE. Professor Dickins draws attention to Free School Lane (Cambridge) C 45 and other instances listed there.

    p. 50, s.n. Street Fd. Located 110–717518, adjacent to The Sutch, parallel with Casey Lane.

    p. 55, s.n. Mollingham Fd. Location 110–722453.

    s.n. Street Fd. Location 110–720448 and 724438.

    p. 66, s.n. PEPPERSTREET MOSS. The *TA* shows this name extending 110–699475 to 703464.

    p. 67, s.n. Old Lane. The enclosed site of a disused roadway, 110–698453.

    p. 77, s.n. Cae Hyn. Professor Richards takes *Cae Hyn* to represent Welsh *cae ynn* 'ash field', from Welsh *onnen*, pl. *ynn*, 'ash-tree'.

    p. 82, s.n. Street Croft. The location is in the village street at 110–696498.

p. 84, l. 8 from foot, p. 109, l. 7 from foot. The references 'Brad' and 'NRA 0430' are to *List of the Muniments of the Earl of Bradford at Weston Park, Shifnal*, NRA 0430.

p. 86, s.n. WOOLFALL FM. Professor Richards points out that *Pentre Cloud* means '*pentre* at the dyke' rather than 'stockaded or moated village', and compares the Welsh p.ns. Trefarclawdd (Oswestry) 'farm on the dyke', and Trefyclawdd (Radnorshire) 'farm at the dyke', alluding to Offa's Dyke.

p. 109, s.n. HOLTRIDGE. Professor Jackson points out that the slight elevation of ground south of this place does not conform to the meaning of allt 'steep hill-side' etc. A different el. should be sought. The spellings suggest that the first el. might be the ODan pers.n. *Auti* (*Alti* (St), *Outi* (Ch) DB, v. Feilitzen 169), with vocalised *l* for *u*.

p. 117, l. 3, s.n. Eight Shilling Mdw. Add '*v. 325 infra*'.

p. 150, s.n. Street Fd. Location 110–641548.

p. 151, s.n. The Bury, Bury Fd. Location 110–661557 to 662552.

p. 157, s.n. Pavement Fd. Location 110–664623 and 651615.

p. 176, s.n. Street Fd. A group of three fields at 110–632667.

p. 181, s.n. Stanways Moss. Location 110–625663.

p. 205, s.n. Castle Hill. Location 109–595742.

p. 209, s.n. Halloway Cross Fd. Location 110–622738.

     s.n. Pavement End. Location 110–615739.

p. 212, l. 3 from foot, s.n. Brock's Road; p. 299, l. 6 from foot, s.n. Brock's Gate. These refer to the same access to the forest of Delamere.

p. 220, s.n. EDGIN COTES (lost), ABBOT'S CLOUGH. The location of Edgin Cotes, a f.n. in 1844 *TA* 13, is 109–485725, on the east bank of Peckmill Brook. Abbot's Clough is at 109–493729 half a mile ENE.

p. 223, s.n. BROOK FURLONG LANE. Location 109–511780 to 508790.

p. 223, s.n. FLUIN LANE. Professor Jackson queries the first el., in that English *fl-* for Welsh *ll-* is a very late substitution, and *Fluhen* c.1290 would be an instance unique in his experience. 'So far from the Welsh border, it seems highly unlikely.' The explanation given must be taken as only tentative.

p. 224, s.n. SINEPOOL (lost). The *TA* f.ns. appear about 109–503779.

pp. 224–5, s.n. SNIDLEY MOOR. The place is about 109–513752, in a detached part of Frodsham township lying in Frodsham Lordship township, which led to the explanation 'detached, cut off', from sniŏ.

p. 226, s.n. Rapdowl(e)s. The name of four fields at 109–514788.

p. 243, l. 6 from foot, s.n. Handkerchief Fd. Add '(*v. 325 infra*)'.

p. 265, s.n. Banford Croft etc. The location of these fields is 109–478692 to 481694.

p. 288, discussion of Iddinshall. Professor Dickins concurs with Löfvenberg (as elsewhere).

p. 292, s.n. (Y)EANLEY. The *TA* names occur at 109–567654, the location of Hare Hill 300 *infra*, in Utkinton.

p. 296, s.n. HERMITAGE. The *TA* f.ns. occur at 109–544628 to 545624.

p. 300, s.n. Hare Hill. The location was 109–567654, v. addendum to p. 292 (Y)EANLEY *supra*.

p. 300, s.n. Ollerton Mdw. Location 109–565659.

p. 314, s.n. Hubback Fd. Professor Dickins observes that there is a surname *Hubbock*.

p. 323, s.n. WATFIELD PAVEMENT. *Pavement Fd* 1840 *TA* is at 109–593583, probably extending to the road before the canal cut it off.

IV. NANTWICH HUNDRED

NANTWICH HUNDRED

Warmundestrou Hd' 1086 DB, *Warmondstrow* 1086 (1380) IpmR
hundred' de Wich Malbanc', -*Maubanc* 1260 Court *et freq* with
forms and spellings as for Nantwich 30 *infra*.

'The hundred of Wǣrmund's tree', later 'of Nantwich', from the
OE pers.n. *Wǣrmund*, which may appear also in Warmingham 2 262,
and trēow. The location of the original meeting-place is unknown,
but cf. Rope 68 *infra*. The DB hundred comprised the area of the
modern one, less Alsager, Betchton, Church Minshull and Hassall
2, 18, 154, 21 *infra*, which were all in *Mildestuic* (Northwich)
hundred. The new hundred of Nantwich, created at some time
between 1086 and 1260, seems to have been organized to include in
one hundred all the manors of the Nantwich barony, cf. The Barony
36 *infra*, Saga Book XIV, 311 and *Tunendune* 2 1. Nantwich is the
southernmost hundred of the county. It is bounded by Northwich
hundred to the north-east, Eddisbury hundred to the north-west,
Broxton hundred to the west, Sa and St to the south-west and south-
east. It contains the greater part of the upper basin of the R. Weaver,
bounded to the east by the end of the east-Cheshire slopes of the
Pennines, south of Mow Cop hill 2 308, and, to the west, by the foot
of the central ridge of hills south of Peckforton Hill 311 *infra*. To the
south, the broken country east and north of the Ellesmere moraine
lies along the county boundary. Except for small areas of the Lower
Trias formations near Doddington and the Lias near Dodcott cum
Wilkesley, extending into St and Sa respectively, the geology of the
hundred is the usual Triassic structure of Rhætic Beds, Keuper Marls
and Sandstone, and the whole area is overlaid by a drift of glacial sand
and gravel and boulder-clay. Salt beds in the Triassic rocks cause
brine-springs along the Weaver and its tributary streams, the basis of
the salt industry at Nantwich.

LOST PLACES IN NANTWICH HUNDRED: *Claytone* 1338 *CampbCh*
XXXVIII, 2 ('clay farm', *v.* clæg, tūn); *Drakelond* 1347 *AddCh* 27408
('dragon land', perhaps an allusion to folklore, cf. Drakelow 2 198,
v. draca, land); *Newton's Bridge, Old Bridge, Sandiland Bridge* 1621
Sheaf[3] 22 (5255) (bridges over R. Weaver, from the surname *Newton*,

the p.n. *Sandiland* (*v.* sandig, land), and ald with brycg); *Smallegh* 1340, 1352 *Eyre* (p) ('narrow glade', smæl, lēah); *Soughill Bridge* 1621 Sheaf³ 22 (5255) (from brycg and a p.n. *Soughill,* perhaps 'hill at a bog' or 'sow's hill', from sogh or sugu and hyll); *Stretehay* 1393 ChRR (p), 1411 ib (p) ('enclosure at a paved road', *v.* strǣt, (ge)hæg. This surname is associated with Newhall 101 *infra*); *Sutton's Bridge, Warton's Bridge* 1621 Sheaf³ 22 (5255) (bridges over R. Weaver, from the surnames *Sutton* and *Warton* and brycg).

i. Barthomley

The ancient parish of Barthomley comprised the township of Balterley (110–7650) in St, and in Ch the townships 1. Alsager (now a c.p. including parts of Linley and Talke in St), 2. Barthomley (now a c.p. including part of Radway Green and Engleseabrook from Haslington and Weston townships 7, 75 infra), 3. Crewe (part now included in Monks Coppenhall 26 *infra*, the rest a c.p. in Nantwich Rural District), 4. Haslington. A small part of Hassall 21 *infra* is reported to have belonged to this parish, cf. Orm² III 299.

1. ALSAGER (110–8055) [ˈɔːlseidʒər] older local [ˈɔːdʒər]

Eleacier 1086 DB

Al(l)esacher e13 *Vern,* c.1240 Dieul, *-is-* 1260, 1286 Court, *Allas-* 1307 Plea (p), *Alleshacher* 1288 Court (p)

Alzachyr, -ir H3 *AddCh, -er* 1304 Chamb (p)

Alsacher 1285 AD *et freq* with variant spellings *-ach(e)re* to 1621 Orm², *Alsache* 1418 Plea

Aldsacher 1289 Court (p)

Alesager c.1300 AD

Alsacre 1307 Plea, *Alsacer* 1724 NotCestr

Alsager 1342 (1438) ChRR, 1350 *Eyre et freq, Alsagere* 1500 Plea, *-agir* c.1360 *BW* (p)

Alesecher 1360 *BW* (p)

Alsecher 1399 *AddCh,* 1508 Orm²

Alsegre 1419 Plea, *Alseger* 1422 *AddCh et freq, Alsege* 1549 Pat

Alsynger 1489 Orm² (p), *A(l)singer* 1650 *ParlSurv*

Alger 1568 *AddCh, Awger* 1572 Chol, *Auger* 1602 ib, *-alias Alsager* 1663 *BW*

Aulsager 1571 *AddCh, Aus-* c.1602 Chol

Alsiger 1598 Orm²

'Ælle's plot of arable land', from the OE pers.n. *Ælle* and æcer. For the palatalized form of æcer, cf. Cliviger La 84. The forms

-ynger, -inger, -iger are analogous with those of certain Ch p.ns. in *-ingham*, cf. **2** 8. Alsager was originally in *Mildestuic* (Northwich) hundred, cf. 1 *supra*.

STREET-NAMES. ASHMORE'S LANE (cf. *Ashmore Meadow* 1576 Cre, 9 *infra*); BROOKHOUSE RD (*v.* Brookhouse Fm *infra*); CHANCERY LANE; CROSS ST.; THE FIELDS (*v.* feld); WELL LANE (*v.* wella).

CRESSWELLSHAWE (FM), CRESSWELLSHAW BROOK (lost), *Crossewelle-schawe* 1285 *Eyre* (p) (Court 210 reads *-walleshawe*), *Creswalleshawe* 1290 Court (p), *-schagh* 1374 *BW*, *-wals(c)hawe* 1400, 1402 *ib*, *-wallshaw* 1567 Orm[2], *Cressewalleschawe*, *Cresseweschawe* 1305 Tab (p), (*-Brook*) 1842 OS, '(wood near) the spring or stream where cress grows', *v.* cresse, wælla, sceaga, brōc. The farm was *Brook House* 1831 Bry. The brook becomes R. Wheelock.

ALSAGER HEATH, 1831 Bry, cf. *Hethcroft* c.1300 AD, *Heath Place* 1688 *BW*, *Heath House* 1842 OS, *v.* hæð, croft, place. ALSAGER HALL. ALSAGER OLD HALL, *Alsager Hall* 1831 Bry. ALSAGER LODGE (lost), 1834 *EnclA*. ALSAGER MILL, 1831 Bry. ALSAGER SPRINK, 1839 *TA*, *Sprink Wood* 1831 Bry, *Alsager Wood* 1842 OS, *v.* spring 'a copse'. ASH BANK FM. AUDLEY RD, leading towards Audley St. BANK FM. BANKHOUSE FM, *Bank House* 1831 Bry. BEECHWOOD. BOTTOMLESS MERE, *v.* botm-les, mere[1], cf. 21 *infra*. BROOKHOUSE FM, *Brook House* 1842 OS, *v.* brōc, cf. William de *le Broc* H3 *AddCh*. BRUND'S FM, cf. *Big & Little Brun*, *Brund* 1839 *TA*, probably land cleared by burning, *v.* brand. CHAPEL LANE. CRANBERRY MOSS, 1831 Bry, 'bog where cranberries grow', *v.* cranberry, mos. DAISYBANK FM. DAYGREEN FM, cf. *Day Green End* 1842 OS, named from Day Green 21 *infra*, *v.* ende[1]. FANNY'S CROFT, *Fannings (Croft)* 1839 *TA*. FARFIELD, cf. *Far Field* 1839 *ib*. GROVE HO. HEATH END, HEATHFIELDS, HEATHFIELD COTTAGES, cf. *Big & Little Heathfield* 1839 *TA*, Hall o' the Heath 13 *infra*, Alsager Heath *supra*, *v.* ende[1], feld. THE HILL, cf. *Hill Field (Meadow)* 1839 *ib*. HOLEHOUSE FM, *Hole House* 1831 Bry, *v.* hol[1]. HOOZE HOLLOW, 1842 OS, *v.* holh. The first el. is unintelligible. LANE-ENDS FM, *Lane End Farm* 1830 *BW*, *Lane Ends* 1831 Bry. LINLEY LANE, 1831 *ib*, leading to Linley St. LONGSTILE, cf. *Long Stile Meadow & Field* 1839 *TA*, *v.* lang, stigel. MANOR FM, *Manor House* 1831 Bry. MAPLE HAYES. THE MERE, 1831 *ib*, *v.* mere[1] 'a pool, a lake'. MERE-LAKE, *Mere Lake* 1839 *TA*, 'boundary watercourse', *v.* (ge)mǣre,

lacu. This place is on the county boundary. It might be *Merebroc* 13
Dieul 30, *v.* brōc.   MOORHOUSE FM, *v.* mōr[1], hūs.   OAK FM,
Great Oak Farm 1831 Bry, *The Oak* 1842 OS.   RADWAY HO, cf.
Radway Green 7 *infra.*   SUNNYSIDE.   SWALLOWMOOR WOOD,
1839 *TA*, *Swalomore* 1384, 1399 *AddCh*, 'marsh frequented by
swallows', *v.* swalwe, mōr[1].   TOWNEND FM, TOWNHOUSE FM,
Alsager Town 1831 Bry, 1842 OS, *v.* toun, ende[1].   THE WOOD-
LANDS.   WOODSIDE.

FIELD-NAMES

The undated forms are 1839 *TA* 11. Of the others, 1285, c.1300, 1322 are
AD, 1289 Court, 1297 Orm[2], 1301–3 *Vern*, 1688 *BW*, 1834 *EnclA*, and the
rest *AddCh.*

(*a*) Ashenhurst (*v.* æscen, hyrst); Big & Little Beech (cf. Thomas de *la
Bache* 1297 (p), from bece[1], bæce 'a stream, a valley'); Bentley (*v.* beonet,
lēah); Big Mdw (cf. *Great Meadow* 1688, *v.* big, grēat); Birchen Fd (*v.*
bircen[2]); Black Croft (cf. *Blake Field, Blackfield Meadow* 1688, *v.* blæc);
Bottoms (*v.* botm); Broad Rain (*v.* rein); Brook Croft (cf. *Broccroft* 1322, *v.*
brōc, croft); Broomy Bank & Ridding (*v.* brōmig, banke, ryding); Bug Hall
(*v.* bugge); Bustard Hill; Churn Moor Fd ('marsh field frequented by the
churn (EDD)', the Ch dial. name for the long-tailed titmouse *Parus caudatus*,
v. mōr[1]); Cocksheads, Cockshutt (*v.* cocc-scyte); Crappilow (cf. Crappilous
Mdw **2** 322); Dunnocks Fold 1834 (*v.* dunnoc, fald); Dingle (*v.* dingle);
Eddish (*v.* edisc); Falling Croft (perhaps from fælging 'ploughed or fallow
land'); Fender Mdw (*v.* fender); Ferney Heys, Ferny Hill (cf. *Fernileg*
c.1300, *v.* fearnig, lēah); Foxley Fd (*v.* fox, lēah); Gill Pleck (*v.* gil, plek);
Hand Mdw; Harboro' Flat (*v.* here-beorg); Heathering Bank (*v.* hǣddre,
-ing[1]); Heys Lane (*v.* (ge)hæg); The Holt (cf. *Little Hoult Field* 1688, *v.*
holt); Hough (*v.* hōh); Innage Fd (*v.* inheche); Ireland Fd (*v.* 325 *infra*);
Knowl; Langot (*v.* langet); Big & Little Lodge Fd (*the great Lodge Field*
1834, cf. Alsager Lodge *supra*); Lunt (*v.* land); Marl Hole (*v.* marle, hol[1]);
Meer Hill (*v.* (ge)mǣre, cf. Merelake *supra*); The Moat (*v.* mote); Moor
Fd; Moss Fd; Mow Fd (*v.* mūga); Nook Fd; Over Lane (*v.* uferra); Ox Hay;
The Paddock 1834 (*v.* pearroc); Patch Mdw (*v.* pacche); Peck-, Pick Mdw,
Picklunt (from pīc[1], but in what sense is not apparent, *v.* mǣd, land);
Pickmere-, Pike Mere Fd (*Pike Meer* 1834, 'pike pool', *v.* pīc[1], mere[1]);
Pingot (*v.* pingot); Plech (*v.* plek); Pool Ring (a ring-fenced field at a pool,
v. hring); Prison Bars Fd (*v.* prison-bars); Rakes Fd (*v.* rake); Randle; Rye
Sitch (apparently from ryge 'rye' and sīc, but perhaps *Russisich* 13 Dieul 30,
cf. Rushy Lake 9 *infra*, *v.* riscig, sīc); Short Butts (*v.* butte); Shoulder of
Mutton (*v.* 325 *infra*); Slang (*v.* slang); Slum (cf. Slum Wood **2** 321–2, *v.*
slump); Spa-Well Mdw, Spar (Mdw) (presumably named from a medicinal
spring, *v.* spa); Little Spatch, Spatch Bank & Mdw (*v.* spatch); Stately
Mdw, Far & Near Steakley ('stake clearing', *v.* staca, lēah); Steen Fd
(*v.* stǣne 'a stony place'); Sweet & Sour Fd (*v.* 325 *infra*); Tester Fd;

Three Nooks (cf. three-nooked); Tip Ridding (*v.* ryding); Townfield; Twenty Day (cf. day-work); Wichhouse Fd (*v.* wych(e)-hous(e)); Yarwood (perhaps analogous with Yarwoodheath 2 58, *v.* earn, wudu, but the first el. could be gear 'a fish-weir').

(*b*) *le Aspenehurste* 1301–3 ('aspen wood', *v.* æspen, hyrst); *le broc iuxta le Bothumforde* H3 ('the brook next to the ford in the hollow', *v.* brōc, botm, ford. The location appears to be 110–798540); *le Brodemeduwe* 1322 (*v.* brād, mǣd); *Bromdon* c.1300 ('broom hill', *v.* brōm, dūn); *Cartelache* 1301–3 ('boggy stream in rough ground', *v.* kartr, læcc, cf. *Cartelache* 1 17); *Cartereslake* H3 ('the carter's watercourse', from the ME occupational surname *Carter* and lacu. This stream runs 110–786550 to 778545, cf. Valley Brook 1 37); *Cherluslowe* c.1300 ('peasant's mound', from ceorl, perhaps here a pers.n. and hlāw); *the Clif style* 1289 ('stile near a cliff', *v.* clif, stigel); *Colynnesheye* 1356 ('Colin's enclosure', from the ME pers.n. *Colin* (*Nicholas*) and (ge)hæg, cf. *Nicholas de Birthimleg* (Barthomley 5 *infra*) 1289 Court 134); *le dedemonnesbruche* H3 ('the dead man's intake' perhaps named from the discovery of a corpse or burial when new ground was being broken in, *v.* dede-man, bryce, cf. Deadman's Fd 8 *infra*. Professor Sørenson observes that corresponding Dan words (*dødning, døding, dødmand*) used as p.n. els. sometimes allude to a belief in ghosts); *Dunneiggeslond* 1285 (perhaps 'Dunning's selion' from the OE pers.n. *Dunning* and land. A *Dunning* was tenant of Sandbach 2 269 and elsewhere in Ch in 1066); *Great & Little Harratt* 1688 (*v.* here-geatu); *Hempbutts* 1688 (*v.* hænep, butte); *le hersichecliff(3)* 1384, *-cluf* 1399 ('cliffs near the higher watercourse', from hēah (comp. (Angl) hēr(r)a) and sīc, with clif (nom.pl. cleofu)); *le Myrehey* 1289 ('dirty enclosure', *v.* mýrr, (ge)hæg); *le Narewesicheheued* H3, *le Nareuseceheued* 1311, *le Narwesecheheued* 1329, *Narewsete heued* 1301–3 ('(the head or source of) the narrow watercourse', from nearu and sīc, with hēafod); *Pease Croft* 1688 (*v.* pise); *Salingecroft, Salinchecroft* c.1300 (the first el. is not identified, but its form shows the familiar assibilated palatalization in *-inge, -inche-*, which may indicate an *-ing*[2] derivative of *salh, salig* 'a willow', cf. 2 7, 136. The final el. is croft); *Schit(h)raweford(e)* c.1300 (perhaps 'ford with a row of posts', from skíð or scīd, *v.* rāw, ford); *le Waterlade, -laud* (Court 134 reads *-land*) 1289 ('the watercourse', *v.* wæter, (ge)lād); *le Witemere* c.1300 (probably from mere[1] 'a lake, a pool'. The first el. appears to be OE *wīte* (ME *wīte*) 'a punishment, a penalty', rather than hwīt 'white').

2. BARTHOMLEY (110–7652) [ˈbɑːtəmli]

Bertemeleu 1086 DB

Bertamelegh H3 *AddCh*, *-leg'* E2 *ib* (p)

Bertumleg' e13 *Vern et freq* with variant spellings *-lega, -lehga, -ley(e) (freq), -legh(e) (freq), -le, -leigh* to 1516 Plea, *Berthumlegh* 1288 Court, *Bertumeley* 1419 Plea

Birchinley 13 Dieul, *-l(egh)* 1289 Court

Bircheley 13 Dieul, *Birchell'* 1289 Court (p)

Berthon(eleg') l13 *Chol* (p), 1287 Court, *Bertonelegh* 1289 ib, *Bertunnleg'* 1291–1301 *AddCh*, *Bertonleye* 1305 *ib*, *-legh* 1353 ChRR, BPR, 1394 *Chol*, *Bertonile* 1307 Pap, *Bertunlegh* 1332 Cl, 1362 *AddCh* 37226 (BM reads *-tum-*), 1498 Sheaf, *Bertonnlegh* 1351 *Eyre*, *Bertenlegh* 1374 *BW*

Bertoveleye 1282 Court, *Bertovile* 1308 Pap

Bartumilegh 1287 Court, *Bartumlegh* 1338 Cre, *-ley* 1507 AD *et freq* to 1653 Sheaf, *Barth-* 1592 *AddCh*

Birthumlegh 1288, 1289 Court (once written *Birch-*), *Byrth-* 1345 ChRR (p)

Birthimleg' 1289 Court (p)

Bertomlegh 1290 Ipm (lit. *Berc-*), 1295 ChF *et freq* with variant spellings *-leg'*, *-ley* to 1528 *Dow*, *Bertomelegh* 1296 Plea, *-l(eg)'* 1302, 1305 *Vern*, *-ley* 1415 Orm[2]

Bertmil' 1291 Tax

Bertymleg' 1297 Cre

Beritunleg' c.1300 *Chol* (p)

Barptonile 1307 Pap

Birthomleye 1308 Plea (p) (lit. *Birch-*), *Birthomele'* E2 *AddCh*

Bartomelegh 1325 Orm[2], *-ly* 1635 Sheaf, *Bartomlegh* 1337 ChRR, *-ley* 1541 ib *et freq* with variant spellings *-ly*, *-leye* to 1724 NotCestr

Burtumlegh 1459 ChRR

Bartonley 1534 Cre, *Bartenle* 1545 Sheaf

Barthomley 1549 Pat *et freq*, *Barthomeley* 1588 Cre

This is a difficult place-name. It is probably OE **Bert-hǣma-lēah* 'wood of the dwellers at a bere-tūn', from lēah and a compound of hǣme with a lost p.n. *Berton* (bere-tūn), as suggested by WRY 1 248, where the analogy with Mortomley YW and Marchamley Sa is discussed. A similar process is found in Marchington St, *æt Mærcham* 951, *Merchametone* DB, and in Walkhampton D 243. Some spellings for Marchamley contain *-s-*, supposing a gen.sg., whereas hǣme is plural, which would support Ekwall's proposal that the first el. of that p.n. is a pers.n. But the early forms now available for Barthomley make the pers.n. basis proposed in DEPN unlikely. As with Mortomley, there is a good deal of scribal confusion in the forms of Barthomley. The spelling *-c(h)-* for *-t(h)-* leads to a form which looks like a distinct place-name in bircen[1] and lēah, especially in the alternation of *Birchinley* > *Bircheley* and *Birthimleg, Birthom-,* etc. *Bertove-* is probably due to *-v-* for *-u-* for *-n-*; *Bertovile* is probably for *-omle, Bertmil'* for *Bertunl'* or *-iml'*; *Barptonile* may be for *Barptomle.* The name also appears in Bartomley **1** 168, but there is no evidence to show whether that is a derivative or a parallel instance; cf. also Millhill **1** 308.

MONNELEY MERE (110–749531), *Monnerley-* 1831 Bry, cf. *Monilee* 1260 Court (p), *-legh* 13 VR (p), *-lg'* E1 *AddCh, Monileweyord* 1295 *Vern* and Monnerley Mdw 11, 77 *infra*. The form *Mannelegh* 1296 Plea (DKR XXVI 45, Orm² III 306, 363) may belong here and not to Manley 245 *infra*. The lake is on the boundary of Barthomley, Crewe and Weston townships. The name may be 'Monn(a)'s woodland glade', from the OE pers.n. *Monn(a)* and lēah, perhaps with -ing-⁴, *v.* **mere¹** and **geard**. The **geard** was probably a fisc-geard 'a fish-pond, a fish-trap'. The place now gives name to Smiths Green Fm *infra*.

RADWAY GREEN (110–7754) ['rædə], 1831 Bry. This seems to be an old compound, though no early spellings have been found. The name appears to mean 'green at a road-way', from rād and weg (cf. **rode-way**), with grēne², cf. Radway Wa 272, Rodey Lane 241 *infra*. It may be that the wide lane through this hamlet was a major road in former times, cf. **1** 44.

BANKTOP FM, cf. *Bank (Field)* 1839 *TA*.   BARTHOMLEY MILL, 1831 Bry, *-mylne* 1580 *Rental, v.* **myln.**   BASFORD COPPICE, *Church Field Wood* 1831 Bry, cf. *Church Field (Meadow)* 1839 *TA*, cf. Basford 48 *infra*, Churchfield Fm *infra*.   BLUEMIRE FM, *Blew-mires tenement* 1709 Cre, cf. *Blumire Croft* 1839 *TA*, presumably from a surname such as *Blamire*, but cf. Bloomer Hill YW 6 20, from blēo and mýrr.   CHERRYTREE FM.   CHURCH BANK, cf. *Church Hill Croft* 1839 *TA*.   CHURCHFIELD FM, 1842 OS, *(the) Church Field* 1778, 1829 Cre, cf. Basford Coppice *supra*.   CRANBERRY MOSS, cf. 3 *supra, v.* **cranberry.**   DAISYBANK, *Daisey-* 1831 Bry. DEAN BROOK & ROUGH, cf. *Dean Brook Bridge, Dean Lane* 1831 ib, 'brook in a valley', *v.* **denu, brōc, rūh, lane.** The brook forms the county boundary between Barthomley and Balterley St. It becomes Englesea Brook **1** 22.   ENGLESEA-BROOK, *Inglesea Brook (Lane & Bridge)* 1831 ib, *Inglesey Brook (Croft & Tenement)* 1839 *TA*, 1842 OS, a hamlet in this and Weston township, 76 *infra*, named from Englesea Brook **1** 22.   FLASH HO, 1842 ib. *v.* **flasshe.**   FOXLEY

FM, 1831 Bry, v. fox, lēah.   LIMES FM, *Lime Trees* 1831 Bry, *The Limes* 1842 OS.   MILL LANE (FM), cf. *Mill Lane & Bank* 1831 Bry, and Barthomley Mill *supra*, v. myln, lane, banke.   NEW FM. OLD HALL FM.   SMITH'S GREEN (FM), 1831 Bry, from smiδ or the surname *Smith* and grēne[2]. The farm is now *Monneley Farm* 1″ OS, cf. Monneley Mere *supra*.   SMITHY LANE, cf. *Smithy Croft* 1779 Cre, 1839 *TA*, named from a smithy here 1831 Bry, v. smiδδe, lane, croft.   TODHOLES, *Toadhole Farms* 1831 ib, *Toad Hole* 1839 *TA*, 'fox-holes', v. tod-hole.   TOWNHOUSE FM, *Town House* 1831 Bry. VALLEY FM.   WALNUT TREE FM, *Walnut Tree* 1839 *TA*.

FIELD-NAMES

The undated forms are 1839 *TA* 39. Of the others, e13, 1295, 1355, 17 are *Vern*, 1289 Court, 13 Dieul, 1356 *AddCh*, 1724 NotCestr, 1831 Bry, 1842 OS, and the rest Cre.

(a) Back Lane 1831 (v. back); Barrow Hill (v. bearu or bearg); Black- & White Bear; Little Bent (v. beonet); Birchen Croft (v. bircen[1]); Black Croft; Black Shaw Croft (v. blæc, sceaga, croft); Blake Lawn (v. blæc, launde); Boosy Fd (v. bōsig); Bottoms (v. botm); Breach Mdw (v. brēc); Brook Limb (cf. Way Limb *infra*); Browhurst (v. brū, hyrst); Butts Lane (v. butte); Camp Foot Hill, Camp Hill (apparently from camp[2] 'a camp', v. hyll, fōt); Causeway Croft (v. caucie); The Chapel Fd 1765; Clay Hill; Clumley Park (v. park, cf. Clemley 47 *infra*); Cock pit mdw (v. cockpit); Cockshead (v. cocc-scyte); Colley Croft (v. colig); Coney Greave (v. coningre); Cow Hay; Crow Lake ('crow stream', v. crāwe, lacu); Day(s) Work (v. day-work); Deadmans Fd (cf. *le dedemonnesbruche* 5 *supra*); Dumble Fd (v. dumbel); Furlongs (v. furlang); Glade Floor; Griffage; Hand Fd; Heads Bank (v. hēafod 'a headland'); Heath Hay(e)s (cf. Alsager Heath 3 *supra*, Hall o' the Heath 13 *infra*); Hernes Lane (*Horns Lane* 1831, v. hyrne); Hob Dale, Hob Dane (from hob or hobbe and dæl[1], denu); Hoff Mdw (v. hōh); Hop Yard (v. hoppe, geard); Hot Crofts (v. hāt); Hunger Hill (v. hungor); Intake (v. inntak); Kent Acre; Kiln Acre; Kiln Croft; Lake Fd (v. lacu); Lime Fd (v. līm); Long Acre; Long Shoot (v. scēat); Lucky Croft (v. 325 *infra*); Lunt Mdw, Lunts Croft & Moss (cf. *Lunt's Cottage* 1766, 1829, from a surname *Lunt*); Madge Fd (v. madge); Marl Fd; Mile Croft; Milking Bank (v. milking); Missick ('boggy place', v. mizzick); Moor Hill; Motish Yard (perhaps 'full of bits of straw', from OE *mot* 'a mote, a speck, a bit' (ModEdial, 'a scrap of straw or chaff') and the adj. suffix -isc (ModE -*ish*), v. geard); Oulton Coppice 1842; Overley (Moss) (probably from uferra and lēah, with mos); Ox Hey; Paddocks Moss ('frog's marsh', v. paddock, mos); Par Field Bank, Par Flatt (v. pearr(e)); Park (v. park); Patch; Pinfold Croft (v. pynd-fald); Pingle (v. pingel); Pit Hole Fd (*the Pitt Hole Field* 1776, v. pytt, hol[1]); Poolstead Mdw (v. pōl-stede); Preston Hill (v. prēost, tūn); (Great) Priest Hay (*the Priest Hays* 1809, v. prēost); The

Puff; Pye Moor ('magpie moor', v. pīe², mōr¹); Ravens Nest (le Rauenisnist 1295, 'the raven's nest', v. hræfn, nest); Riddings (v. ryding); Ridley Irons (v. (ge)ryd(d), lēah, hyrne); Rope Croft (v. rāp, cf. Rapdowl(e)s 226 infra); Rushy Lake (cf. Russisich 13 and Rye Sitch 4 supra, v. riscig, sīc, lacu); Ryders Rough 1831 (v. rūh; Ryder is probably the surname); Rye Moor (v. ryge, mōr¹); Sandy Knowl; Seven Butts (v. seofon, butte); Sinderhill (v. sinder, hyll); Sloppy Lane 1831 (v. sloppy); Slum (v. slump, cf. Slum Wood 2 321–2); Spout Fd (v. spoute); Sprinks (v. spring 'a young wood'); Starch Fd & Moss (probably named from starch-corn, i.e. spelt-corn, v. starch, spelt NED); Steeles oth Hatch ('land belonging to one Steele who lives at the Hatch', v. hæcc); Styers; Swine Trough (v. swīn¹, trog); Tentry Croft (v. tentour); Tie Lunt (perhaps 'selion at a water-meadow', from land and a place-name Tie 'at the water-meadow', v. atte, ēg); Titch Fd; Town Croft, Fd & Mdw (le tounfeld 1355, Townfield (Croft) 1778, Great Town Field 1829, 'the communal field', v. toun, feld); Turf Brook ('brook running in peaty soil', v. turf); Turf Cote Fd (v. turf, cot); Wainhouse Croft & Fd ('wagon-shed', v. wain-house); Walkers Pool (v. walcere, pōl¹); Wall Hay & Spring (v. wælla, (ge)hæg, spring); Way Butts, Fd & Limb (v. weg 'a right of way', butte. Limb here and in Brook Limb supra seems to allude to a projecting or outlying part of a field, v. limb NED); Wheat Fd, Hill & Marsh (le Whetecroft 1355, v. hwǣte, croft); Whiteley Hill ('white wood', v. hwīt, lēah).

(b) Ashmore Meadow 1576 (either from a surname or from a p.n. 'ash moor', v. æsc, mōr¹, cf. Ashmore's Lane 3 supra, Ashemorepoole 12 infra); Bertumleymere 1356 (v. mere¹ 'a pool'); Booth Lane 1632 (cf. Booth's Cottage 1775, probably from a surname Booth); Grenesich 13 (v. grēne¹, sīc); Hospiteler(e)scroft e13, le- 1355, hospitall croft 17 ('croft belonging to an hospitaller, or to the Knights Hospitallers', v. hospiteler, cf. hospitaller c.1330 NED); Munestanescloch 13 (apparently 'Mundstān's dell', from an OE pers.n. Mundstān and clōh; but in view of the source, this might be a form of 'mill-stone dell' from mylen-stān); Sondes 13 ('the sands', v. sand); Wicheleg 1289 (p) ('wych-elm wood', v. wice, lēah).

3. CREWE (110–7354) [kruː]

> Creu 1086 DB, Crewe 1297 Cre (p) et freq with variant spellings Crew, Creue
> Criwa c.1150 Orm² (p)
> Crue 1220–40 Whall (p), AddCh (p) et freq to 1586 ChRR, with variant spellings Cruwe 1290 to 1472, Cruue, Crwe 1288 to 1572, Crwue, Cure, le Crue 1398 ChRR (p), Crue juxta Weston 1314 Orm², -Haselynton 1337 Plea, -Bertumley 1440 ChRR
> Crowe 1330, 1391 MidCh (p), 1351 BPR

'The fish-trap, the weir', from PrWelsh *criu, Welsh cryw, glossed in EPN 1 118 s.v. cryw 'a ford', corrected in JEPN 1 46 s.v.

*criu 'a weir'. This el. also appears in Crewe 326 *infra* and possibly in Crewood, *Crufaughis* (Frodsham) 195, 227 *infra*. Professor Jackson and Professor Richards point out that the fundamental meaning of **cryw** is probably 'basket', whence it seems to have been extended to the kind of wicker-work woven fence across a river to catch fish, hence the meaning 'weir'. But it occurs in NW p.ns. in the sense 'stepping-stones', whence the idea that **cryw** means 'ford'. That **cryw** does not primarily mean 'ford' is indicated by the p.n. *Rhyd-cryw* in Llane-gryn, Merionethshire, 'ford of the weir' (*v.* **rhyd, rid** EPN **2** 82, 83, JEPN **1** 50). Nevertheless, it seems likely that a structure such as a fish-weir might often have been built near a convenient ford, or that the structure itself might have offered a means of crossing the stream in which it stood. The meaning 'stepping-stones' probably developed from a row of large stones used to reinforce a wicker-work weir. The fish-weir from which this township took its name was, presumably, on Valley Brook or Englesea Brook at Crewe Bridge *infra*, or perhaps at Stowford 76 *infra*. The modern borough of Crewe takes its name from this township.

THE BANK, BANK FM, *the banke* 1580 *Rental, Bank Farm* 1831 Bry, *v.* banke 'a bank, a hillside'.   BARTHOMLEY RD FM.   BRIDGE-HOUSE FM, *Knights Green* 1831 Bry, *Wrights Tenement* 1842 OS, from the surnames *Knight* and *Wright, v.* grēne², tenement, later named from a nearby railway bridge.   BROOK COTTAGE, named from Valley Brook **1** 37.   CREWE BRIDGE, *Crew-bridge* 1621 Sheaf, *v.* brycg, cf. Crewe *supra*.   CREWE GATE, -*Gates* 1831 Bry, the entrance to Crewe Park, *v.* geat.   CREWE GREEN, 1831 ib, *Little Crewe* 1573, 1578 Cre.   CREWE HALL, 1579 ib. *Great Crewe* 1573, 1578 ib.   CREWE MILL, -*Mylne* 1580 *Rental*.   CREWE PARK, cf. *Park Side* 1839 *TA*, and foll.   CREWEHALL FM, *Park Farm* 1831 Bry, *Crewe Farm* 1842 OS.   ENGLESEA HO, named from Englesea Brook **1** 22.   THE FIELDS, 1831 Bry.   GRAVEL FM, cf. *Gravel Hole Plantation* 1839 *TA, v.* gravel.   HOLLOW BRIDGE (lost, 110-749543), 1831 Bry, 'bridge at a hollow', *v.* holh.   OAK COPPICE. OAK FM, *Clapgate* 1831 ib, *v.* clap-gate.   OFFLEY LEY, probably from dial. *ley* 'a piece of pasture' (cf. lēah), with the Ch surname *Offley*.   PHILIP'S HILL, *Phillips hills* 1580 *Rental, Phellips Hill* 1711 Cre, from the ME pers.n. *Philip* and hyll.   QUAKER'S COPPICE, 1839 *TA*.   ROOKERY WOOD.   SLAUGHTER HILL (BRIDGE) [slɔː-tər] older local [slɑːðər], *Sloderhilbroke* 1536 Sheaf, *Slatherhill* 1580

Rental, Slaughter Hill 1831 Bry, (*-Bridge*) 1842 OS, (*-Field & -Lodge*)
1839 *TA, Slather-Hill Bridge* 1883 Sheaf, 'black-thorn hill', *v.* slāh-
þorn, hyll, brycg, brōc, cf. Valley Brook 1 37, *Bromhale feld infra.*
TEMPLE OF PEACE WOOD, named after a park folly.   TOLLGATE
FM, *v.* toll-gate.   WESTON ROAD (FM).   WOODNETS GREEN
(lost, 110–711548), 1842 OS, *Woodnettes Greene* 1580 *Rental, Wood-
netts green(e)* 1703 Cre, 1831 Bry, from the Ch surname *Woodnoth* or
Woodnett (cf. 70 *infra*) and grēne². The site is occupied by Crewe
railway station (26 *infra*).

FIELD-NAMES

The undated forms are 1839 *TA* 135. Of the others, E1, l13, E2, 1311, 1317
and 1657 are *AddCh*, 1288 Plea and Court, 1439 Orm², 1536 Sheaf, 1580
Rental, 1582 (1630) *Chol*, 1724 NotCestr, 1831 Bry, 1842 OS, and the rest Cre.

(a) Adderhill Croft (*v.* hǣddre, hyll); Bellaston (*v.* tūn); Great & Little
Bent (*the Bent* 1580, *v.* beonet); Birchton Hill (*v.* birce, tūn or dūn);
Blakelow (*blakelowfeld* E1, 'black mound (field)', *v.* blæc, hlāw, feld);
Blakeney ('black water-meadow', *v.* blæc (wk. dat. blacan), ēg); Boosy
Pasture (*v.* bōsig); Brain Fd; Brick Yard, Brickkiln Fd (*the Brick field* 1579,
Brickefielde 1580, *v.* bryke); Cat Moor (*v.* cat(t), mōr¹); Claycroft 1724 (1571,
Cley(e) Croft(e) 1579, 1580, 1582 (1630), *v.* clǣg, croft); Cockshoot, -shut
(*Cockshotte field* 1576, *the Cockeshiute* 1580, cf. *uolatum Thome de Mora de
Crue* E1, *v.* cocc-scyte); Cow Fd (*Cowfield Close* 1657); Cow Pasture (*the-*
1579, *v.* cū, pasture); Crewe Hay (*Greate Crewhayes* 1580, *Little Crewe hey*
1714, *v.* (ge)hæg, cf. Crewe *supra*); Cross Fd (*Crossefield* 1580, 'field at a
cross', *v.* cros, feld); Daw Hayes (*-hey(e)s* 1579, 1580, 1582 (1630), 'enclo-
sures frequented by jackdaws', *v.* daw(e), (ge)hæg); Day Math (*v.* day-
math); Dicky Danes Bank; Eyes (*v.* ēg); Fender Croft & Mdw (*v.* fender);
Ferny Lee (*v.* lēah); Five shillings (*v.* 325 *infra*); Gamestalls; Glade Fd (*the
Glade* 1580, from ModE *glade, v.* glæd³); Graystile (*v.* stigel. The first el.
may be either grǣg¹ or grēat); Great Mdw (*the-* 1571, 1579, *The greate
Meadowe* 1580, 1582 (1630)); Hazle Barrow ('hazel grove', *v.* hǣsel, bearu);
Healer; Heath Croft; Hemp Butts (*v.* hænep, butte); Hibborn Fd; Horse
Coppice 1842; Hudhouse; Jack Fd (*v.* jack); Jake Hill Mdw; Laggoon Mdw;
Long Fd ((*the*) *Long field(e)* 1579, 1580, *v.* lang, feld); Long Wd; Lower Lay
('lower pasture', *v.* lēah); Lownds Bottoms (*v.* botm, cf. *lownes bache* 18
infra); Marl Fd (*marldefield* 1580, *v.* marle, marlede); The Marsh; Milking
Bank (*v.* milking); Monnerley Mdw (cf. Monneley Mere 7 *supra*);
Moor(s) ((*la*) *Mora* E1, l13, *the more* 1580, *v.* mōr¹); Moseley Fd (*Moseley*
1579, 1580, *Greate Mosley* 1579, *New Maslefield* 1579, *v.* mos, lēah);
Narrow Lane 1831; New Fd & Piece (cf. *the New(e) Me(a)dow(e)* 1579, 1580,
Lyttle Newhayes 1580, *v.* nīwe, mǣd, (ge)hæg); New River (a watercourse);
Outlet (*v.* outlet); Oven Yard (cf. *Oven Croft* 1577, 1580, *v.* ofen, geard,
croft); Pinfold Mdw (cf. *the Pinfold tenement* 1707, *v.* pynd-fald, tenement);

Rails Fd (*v.* rail(e)); Rangs (*v.* range); Ridding (*Reddinge Lande* 1580, *v.* ryding, land); Rye Croft; Sandy Croft (*the Sandyfielde* 1580, *v.* sandig, feld); Servants Fd (*Servan(n)tes Field(e)* 1579, 1580, *v.* servant); Shukers Croft; Sinder Hill Fd & Mdw (*Sinderhills* 1571, 1580, *Syndrelles* 1579, *v.* sinder, hyll); Sludge Croft (*v.* sludge); The Slum (*v.* slump, cf. Slum Wood **2** 321–2); Spout Mdw (*v.* spoute); Swines Mdw (1573, *Swine Meadow* 1579, *Swynes medowe* 1580, *v.* swin[1], mæd); The Tettons (probably belonging to Tetton **2** 260); Twynyfer; Wall Croft & Fd (*v.* wælla); Way Croft (*v.* weg); White Gate Fd; Wood Fd.

(*b*) *Ashemorepoole* 1580 ('(pool at) ash-tree-moor', *v.* æsc, mōr[1], pōl[1], cf. *Ashmore Mdw* 9 *supra*); *Blacke Erthe* 1580 ('black ground', *v.* blæc, eorðe or erð); *le brodehet* E1, E2 ('broad heath', *v.* brād, hǣð); *Brom(h)ale feld* E1, *Broomhall* 1536, *Lees Bromehale* 1576, *-Broomhall* 1579, *Leys-* 1590, *Great Browmall* 1577, *-Bromale* 1578, *Greate-, Slatherhill- & Lez Bromall* 1580 ('broom corner', *v.* brōm, halh, a medieval common field, later parcelled out into closes, cf. Slaughter Hill *supra*, *v.* grēat, lǣs); *the Conyegree* 1580 ('rabbit warren', *v.* coningre); *le Eclis* E1, E2 (an assart, *v.* ēcels, cf. *le Hetheles infra*); *Filbarnes* 1580 ('fill-barns', probably a good field, cf. 325 *infra*); *Godithye* E1 (a meadow, 'Godgȳð's water-meadow', from the OE fem. pers.n. *Godgȳð* and ēg); *Graystef', Graystyfyld* 1439 ('Gresty field', *v.* feld, Gresty 69 *infra*); (*the*) *Thorney-, Rough-, Rowghe- & Cowe Heathall* 1579, 1580 ('heath-nook', *v.* hǣð, halh, þornig, rūh, cū); *le Hetheles* E2 (perhaps a form of *le Eclis supra*, otherwise 'heath clearings', *v.* hǣð, lēah); *le long(g)eheye* E1, E2 (*v.* lang, (ge)hæg); *Nurse Croft* 1579, *Nurcroftes* 1580, *the nurse croftes* 1582 (1630) ('nurse's croft', *v.* nurse, croft); *Otwode* 1288, (*H*)*Odwodecroft* E1 ('outlying wood', *v.* ūt, wudu, cf. Oat Wd 27 *infra*. It lay between Crewe and Coppenhall); (*the*) *Ox(e)hey(e)s* 1579, 1580, 1582 (1630) (*v.* oxa, (ge)hæg); *Snelsons Haye* 1580 (from (ge)hæg, with the surname from Snelson **1** 93); (*le*) *Sponnehet(h)* E1, E2, 1311, *Sponheeth* 1318 (*v.* spann[1], hǣð, *v.* Sponds **1** 200).

4. HASLINGTON (110–7456) [hæzliŋ-]

Hasillinton e13 *AddCh*, *-ellyn-* E1 Orm[2]

Haselin(g)ton(e) H3, l13, c.1293 *AddCh*, 1288 Court, *-yn(g)-* l13 ChF, 1325 Plea *et freq* to 1516 Plea, *Haslyn(g)ton(e)* 1330 Fine, 1351 BPR, 1407 ChRR *et freq* to 1586 Cre, *-intone, -toun* 1330 Ipm, IpmR, *-ington* 1425 MidCh, 1568 Cre *et freq*

Hesinglinton 1256 AD

Halinton 1292 *AddCh*, *-yng-* 1536 Dugd

Hasselynton 1307–27 *JRC*, *-in-* 1380 Eyre (p), *Hasslyngton* 1432 *AddCh*

'Enclosure growing with hazels', *v.* hæslen, tūn. The form has been influenced by -ing-[4].

STREET-NAMES. CROSS ST. (cf. *fountain of St Helena by the Cross* 1536 Sheaf[1]
3 130, *v.* cros); FIELDS RD (*v.* feld); HIGH ST. (*v.* hēah); MERE ST. (cf.
Merebank, etc. *infra*).

BRADELEY HALL (110–726565), *Bradeley* 14 Tab, 1621 Orm[2], a place
of land called *Braddeley* 1412 *JRC*, *Bradely Howse* 1571 *AddCh*,
Bradley (*Milne*) 1601 *ib*, 1629 Sheaf, *Bradley Hall* 1724 NotCestr,
'broad clearing', *v.* brād, lēah, hall, hūs, myln.

CLAYHANGER HALL (110–729575)

> *Clayhung*(*er*) 1268, 1318 Rich, *Clehungre* 1315 Plea (p), *Cleyhunger*
> 1621 Orm[2], 1650 *AddRoll*, *Clayhunder House* 1629 Sheaf
> *Clehongur* 1432 *AddCh*, *Cleyhonger* 1577 *AddRoll*, 1621 *ChCert*,
> *Cle*(*y*)*onger* 1621 *ib*, *Clayhonger Hall* 1724 NotCestr
> *Clayhanger* 1614 Cre, *Cleyhanger* (*Hall*) 1668 *Vern*

'Wood on a clayey hill-side', *v.* clæg, hangra, hongra, hall, hūs.
A variant upon this type is Clamhunger 2 52.

HALL O' THE HEATH, HEATH HO (110–752553), *maner' de le Heth*
1422 *AddCh*, *the Hall of the Heth* 1500 *ib*, *Hall o' Heath* 1621 Orm[2],
(*the*) *Hall of Heath* 1686 *AddCh*, 1697 *ib*, *Hall-a-Heath* 1724 NotCestr,
named from (*la*) *Bruer*(*ia*) e13 *AddCh*, 1322 Orm[2] (p), (*le*) *heth* l13
AddCh et freq, *le Heet* 1335 *ib*, *Hethe* 1343 Cl (p), *the Heath* 1630
Sheaf, *Hasling-*, *-yngton Heath*(*e*) 1571–1598 *AddRoll*, '(the hall on)
the heath', *v.* hǣð, hall, cf. Heath End, Heath Hay(s) 3, 8 *supra*.

HOMESHAW LANE (110–753556 to 758552), *Horn Shaw Lane* 1831
Bry, cf. *Homeshaw* 1840 *TA*, a group of nine fields probably identical
with *Ormeshull* 1288 Court (p), *Ormeshalg*(*h*) 1299 Plea (p), *-shaae*
1521 Comb (p), *Hermeshagh* 1408 ChRR (p), *Ormeswode vel Orme-
shalgh* 1419 Plea, (*-shalge*) 1528 *Dow*, 'Orm's wood', from the ODan
pers.n. *Orm. v.* sceaga, wudu, hyll, halh. Cf. *Ormelegh*, *Ormesty* 1 53,
271.

OAKHANGER HALL, MERE (lost) & MOSS (110–7655)

> *Okehungurmos* 1351 *AddCh*, *Okehungur* 1621 Orm[2]
> *Okehongermosse* 1433 ChRR, *Okehonger*, *Woke-*, *Ooak-*, *Oake-*,
> (*-wood*, *-mere*, *-heath*, *-mosse*) 1571–1601 *AddRoll* 6284–6, *le*
> *Woconger Wood* 1599 *ib*, *Oakhonger* 1649 Sheaf, *-Hall* 1724
> NotCestr
> *a moss called Okehenger* 1444 ChRR, *Oakenger Hall* 1720 Sheaf

Okehanger Wood 1572 *AddRoll*, *O(a)kehangermere*, *-mear* 1621
(1656), 1656 Orm², *Oakhanger* 1692 Sheaf
Oteconger Mosse 1598 *AddRoll*

'Hill-side grown with oaks', from āc and hangra, hongra, with
mos, mere¹, hǣð, wudu, hall. The spellings *Woke-* 1571, *Woc-* 1599
are due to stress-shifting in a diphthongized form of *Oak-*. The mere
no longer exists. It was on Oakhanger Moss at 110–767550. It was
le Meare 1577 *AddRoll*, *The Mere* 1831 Bry, and gave name to
Me(a)re Hethe 1536 Sheaf, *Meere-*, *Meyre Heathe* 1589, 1597 *AddRoll*
and *le Mere-Crofte* 1575 *ib*, *Mere Corner*, *Croft & Field* 1840 *TA*, *v.*
hǣð, croft, corner.

WINTERLEY (MILL & POOL) (110–747571)

Wyntanelegh 1329 Plea (p)
Wyntanlegh 1344 *Eyre* (p)
Wyntenley 1435 *Eyre*, *-ton-* 1536 Dugd
Witaneleg 14 Tab
Wyntomeley 1538 *AOMB* 399
Wi-, *Wynteley* 1570 Orm², *-Heath(e)* & *-Mylne*, *-Milne*) 1571–1601
    AddRoll, *Wintley* 1621 Orm²
Winterley Pool 1840 *TA*, *Winterly Mill* 1842 OS

From an unidentified dithematic p.n. or pers.n. or a disyllabic cpd.
and lēah 'a wood, a glade, a clearing', with myln, hǣð, pōl¹. Professor
Löfvenberg suggests an OE cpd. *wīn-tān* 'vine-shoot', referring to
some wild climbing or trailing plant, analogous with OE *mistel-tān*
'mistletoe'. The pool is a mill-dam, and gives its name to POOL FM,
and to POOL HEAD (lost, 110–753570), 1831 Bry, *le poole heade* 1598
AddRoll, cf. *Pool* (*Field & Meadow*) 1840 *TA*, *pratum Poole*, *Pooles
Mead* 1588 *AddRoll*, *le greate pooles*, *le litle poole* 1600 *ib*, *v.* pōl¹,
hēafod, mǣd.

BRIDGEHOUSE FM, *Bridge House* 1831 Bry, near a crossing of Fowle
Brook **1** 25, *v.* brycg.   BROOK HO, 1831 *ib*, named from Fowle
Brook **1** 25.   BUTTERTON LANE, *Batterton's Lane* 1831 Bry,
probably from the surname from Batherton 50 *infra* and lane.
BUTTERTON LANE FM, *The Such* 1831 Bry, *The Suck* 1842 OS, 'the
drain', *v.* sīc, cf. prec.   CLAY LANE, CLAYLANES FM, *Clay Lane*
(*Farms*) 1831 Bry, cf. *le Claye fyeld(e)*, *le Claye(s)*, *Betchtons Cley*, *the
Ould Clayes* 1573–1608 *AddRoll*, *v.* clǣg 'clay', feld, lane.   CREWE
RD, leading to Crewe 9 *supra*.   FERNY BANK.   FIELD FM.

Fox Covert, 1842 OS, *Bradley Hall Gorse Cover* 1831 Bry, cf.
Bradeley Hall *supra*. Fox Holme Covert, *v.* fox-hol. Grove
Fm, *v.* grāf. Haslington Hall, 1629 Sheaf. Haslington
Ho, 1842 OS, *Crab Tree Hill* 1831 Bry, cf. (*le*) *Crabtree-, -trie-,
-fyelde, -fieldes* 1573, 1588 *AddRoll, Crabtree Field* 1840 *TA*, *v.*
crabbe, trēow, hyll. Hooterhall, *Hooters Hall or Birchen Fields*
1831 Bry, *le Byrchyn Fieldes* 1575 *AddRoll, Owl Hole* 1842 OS, *v.*
bircen[1], feld, ūle, hol[1], hall. 'Hooter' is an epithet for the owl. 'Hole'
is a derogatory substitution for the pretentious 'hall'. Kent's
Green Fm, 1831 Bry, cf. *Kentes Croft(e)* 1573, 1596, 1598 *AddRoll,
Kents Meadow* 1840 *TA*, probably named from the family of Amita
Kent 1573 *AddRoll, v.* grēne[2], croft, cf. Amos Fd *infra*. Lane
Ends Fm, cf. *Lane Ends* (lost) 1831 Bry, 1842 OS. Manor Ho.
Maw Lane, cf. *le Mowe Brooke* 1588 *AddRoll*, perhaps from mūga
'a stack, a heap, a mound', but the first el. may be māwe 'a meadow',
v. brōc, lane. Merebank, Merefield Ho, houses in Haslington
village. Merebank overlooked an ancient moat, cf. mere[1]. Moss
Cottage & Fm, *Moss Farm & Lane, Pasture Moss* 1831 Bry, cf. *le
Mosse* 1608, 1611 *AddRoll, v.* mos, pasture. Nevitt's Lane, cf.
Knevitts Field & Meadow 1840 *TA*, from the surname *Knevitt* or
Nevitt, v. Reaney s.n. *Knivett*. New Fm. Park Rd.
Ragged Castle, an ironic name alluding to proud poverty.
Higher Richards, *le Rexes yardes meadowe, Rexes Fields* 1608, 1609
AddRoll, Rick Yard (Field) 1840 *TA*, 'the ricks, the rick-yard', from
ME *rek*, pl. *rekes* (OE hrēac) and geard. Sandfield Ho, cf.
Sondfield Knowe 1585 *AddRoll, Sand Field, Bank & Hole* 1840 *TA*,
v. sand, feld, cnoll. Sydney Ho, cf. *Sydnall Field* 1585 *AddRoll,
Sidnall Fielde* 1603 *ib, New Sidney Wood* 1840 *TA*, *v.* Sydney 24
infra. White Moss, 1831 Bry, *v.* hwīt, mos. Woodshutts,
cf. *Woodside* 1570, 1621 Orm[2], 1629 Sheaf, *le wood dyche* 1607
AddRoll, v. wudu, sīde, dīc, scēat.

FIELD-NAMES

The undated forms are 1840 *TA* 192. Of the others, H3, l13, 1293, c.1293,
1297, 1351, 1362, 1420, 1783 are *AddCh*, 1391 *AddRoll* 5230, 1536, 1606[2]
Sheaf, 1751 Cre, 1831 Bry, and the rest *AddRoll* 6278–88.

(*a*) Acres, Acre (Fd) (cf. *le(z) Acres* 1588, 1611, *le Acre* 1575, 1592, 1603,
1650, *v.* æcer); Amos Fd (*Amesfield* 1609, *le Amies felde* 1611, probably
named from *Amice* or *Amita* Kent, cf. Kent's Green *supra*); Ash Coppy
(*v.* æsc, copis); Barn Fd (*freq*, cf. *barnefield meadowe* 1585, *v.* bere-ærn);

Barrow Dashes ((*le*) *bar*(*r*)*o*(*w*)*di*(*s*)*sh*(*e*), (*-lane*) 1571, 1596, 1609, (*le*) *Borrow*(*e*)*dishe*, (*-lane*), *-dyche* 1588, 1590, 1592, 'enclosure at a wood', *v.* bearu, edisc); Birch (*le Birche* 1609, either from birce 'a birch-tree', or brēc 'a breaking-in of ground'); Black Fd (*le-* 1596, *v.* blæc, feld); Bone Fd (*v.* bān, cf. bone-dust); Bottoms (*v.* botm); Brook Croft & Fd (*le Brooke field* 1592, cf. *Brook Meadowe* 1596); Brown Ley (cf. *lyttel browneleyes* 1575, *v.* brūn[1], lēah); Cabin Piece (*v.* cabin, pece); Calvelong ((*the*) *Calverlonde* (*fielde*), *Calvarlonde yate*, *Calverlondes*, *Cawver-*, *Calverlonge* 1571, 1572, 1596, *Cofferlonge* 1588, *Calvelong Lane* 1831, 'calves' selion', from calf (gen.pl. calfra) and land, with feld, geat, lane. The final el. has been confused with furlang by metanalysis); Chapel Croft & Fd (cf. *capella de Haselynton*(*e*) 1325 (1420), 1420, *the Chappell dyngle* 1578, *v.* chapel(e), dingle); Cinder Fd (*v.* sinder); Coal Ridding (*v.* col[1], ryding); Cooks Fd ((*le*)*Cookes Fielde* 1575, 1588, 1603, 1611, from cōc, ME cōk 'a cook', perhaps as a surname); Cow Pasture & Piece (*Cowe fielde* 1606, *le Cow Ridding* 1649, *v.* cū, ryding); Dales Fd (cf. *terra Hugonis Dale* 1596); (Eight-, Five-) Days Math (*v.* daymath); Dob Heath (*v.* daube); Elton Croft & Fd; Fallow Fd (*v.* fealu); The Field (*v.* feld); Four Lane Ends; Foxlow Fd (*v.* fox, hlāw); Glade Bank (*v.* gleoda or glæd[3]); Goose Fd (*-field*(*e*) 1590, 1592, *v.* gōs, feld); Goose Mdw (1783, (*le*) *Goose meadowe* 1596, 1598, cf. *Goose Crew* 1783, *v.* gōs, mæd, crew); Gravel Pit Fd (cf. *lez Gravelye Croftes* 1585, *v.* gravel); Big Greggs-, Little Graggs Croft (*le Gregcrofts* 1650, *v.* greg(g)e); Grimshaw (from the ON pers.n. *Grímr*, *v.* sceaga); Hall Bank & Fd (cf. *le hall meadowe* 1585, *v.* hall); Hanging Fd (*v.* hangende); Hassalls Crofts (*-Croftes* 1575, probably from the surname from Hassall 21 *infra*); Hay Knowl (*v.* (ge)hæg, cnoll); Hazel Tree Mdw (*v.* hæsel, cf. Haslington *supra*); Hench (*v.* hencg); Hermit Fd (*heremytes Croftes* 1575, *v.* ermite); Herring Pasture; Higher Fd (*the higher fyelde* 1572, *le Highefield*(*e*) 1598, 1606, *v.* hēah); Hillock (*v.* hylloc); Hop Moss, Hope Fd & Mdw (*le ho*(*o*)*pe* (*meadowe*) 1585, 1596, 1606, *le hopes* 1606, *v.* hop[1] 'a piece of enclosed land in a marsh'); House Fd ('field near a house'); Hunts Croft (cf. (*le*) *Hunt*(*e*) *Riddinge*(*s*), *-ryddynge* 1574, 1575, 1588, 1596, probably from a surname *Hunt*, *v.* ryding); Intake (*le Intack*(*e*) 1575, 1603, *v.* inntak); Big- & Little Keddles (*le litle Kyddels* 1585, *v.* kid(d)e(l)l); King-tree Fd; Knowl (Bank) (*le Knowle* 1649, *v.* cnoll); Lampers Hill (*Lympittes hill* 1611, 'lime-pits hill', *v.* līm, pytt, hyll); Leech Fd; Long Fd (*le longe fielde* 1596, *v.* lang, feld); Marl Fd(s) (cf. *le marled hay meadowe* 1585, *v.* marle, marlede, (ge)hæg, mæd); Marsh; Meadow Piece (cf. *le medowe flatt* 1577, 1611, *v.* mæd, flat); Mill Fd & Mdw (cf. *the mylne streame* 1572, *le mylne* 1575, *le Mylne-*, *-milne Brooke* 1585, 1588, 1590, 1601, *le myllne lane end* 1598, *the Myll hill* 1606[2], *v.* myln. The stream is Fowle Brook I 25); Mixen Fd (*v.* mixen); Moor Mdw (*le more field* (*medowe*) 1574, 1585, *le more crofte* 1577, *v.* mōr[1]); New Lane 1831 (*le newe lane* 1590, *v.* nīwe, lane); Outcast Moss (*v.* out(e)-cast, mos); Ox Pasture (*le-* 1650, *v.* oxa, pasture); Park (*v.* park); Patch (*v.* pacche); Pigcourt Fd (*v.* pigga, cot); Pinfold Croft (*v.* pynd-fald); Rag Nook; Rail Fd (*v.* rail(e)); Long Rein (*le longe reane* 1574, *v.* lang, rein); The Riddings, Little & Near Ridding (*le Rydyng* c.1293, (*le*) *Riddinge* 1572, 1573, *Little Riddinge* 1609, *v.* ryding); Road Fd (*freq*, probably from rod[1] 'a clearing'); Rollicks Moor; Rope Field (*v.* rāp, cf. Rapdowl(e)s 226 *infra*); Sandy Lane Fd (*v.* sandig, lane); Sheep-Cot(e) Fd (*v.* scēp, cot); Sheet Hays; Shilling Croft (*v.* scilling); Spring Fd (cf. *le Sprynke* 1585, *the Sprink* 1783, *v.* spring 'a young wood'); Staney Hays, Stoney Heys (perhaps 'stony enclosures', *v.* stānig, (ge)hæg, but cf. *Stanway's Crofts* 1751 Cre, and Robert *Stanway* 1616 ib, a cottager in Crewe 9 *supra*); Street Fd (*v.* strǣt, cf. 1 44); Sun Fd (*v.* sunne); Ten Pound (probably the rent or purchase price, *v.* 325 *infra*); Tetton (cf. *Tettonlewe* l13, *v.* lēah, Tetton 2 260); Tongue Fd (*v.* tunge); Townsend (*v.* toun, ende[1]); Twenty Oaks; Village Fd; Walleys Bank 1831 (cf. *le Walle heys* 1362, 'enclosures at a spring', *v.* wælla, (ge)hæg); Widows Acre (*le Widdowes acre* 1606, *v.* widuwe, æcer); Wind-Mill Fd (*v.* wind-mylne); Winney Hill (*v.* hvin, hyll); Yard Fd (*v.* geard).

(*b*) *Alis fielde* 1574, *Alys-* 1575, *leʒ Ales fielde* 1606, cf. *le Ayles bothoms* 1596 (perhaps 'Alice's field and bottoms', from the ME pers.n. *Alis* (ModE *Alice*), *v.* feld, botm); *le Army croftes* 1575; *Barkhowse meadowe* 1609 ('meadow near a tan-house', *v.* bark-howse, mǣd cf. *Tanne howse infra*); *le Bentley Crofte* 1596 ('(croft at) the grassy clearing', *v.* beonet, lēah, croft); *Bridgefielde lake* 1571, (*lacus vocatus*) *Bridgefyelde* 1572, 1573, *-fielde* 1603 ('(watercourse at) the field near a bridge', *v.* brycg, feld, lacu); *leʒ Broomelies* 1606 ('broomy clearings', *v.* brōmig, lēah); *le Bushie Croftes Yate* 1585 ('(gate at) the bushy crofts', *v.* busshi, croft, geat); *le butte* 1575 (*v.* butte); *le Calke-, le Cark dore* 1603 from duru or dor 'a door, a gateway', with an unidentified first el.); *Calvercrofte* 1572 ('calves' croft', *v.* calf (gen.pl. calfra), croft); *le Cart Gapp* 1598 ('gap for carts', *v.* carte, gap); *le Cawder Crofte* 1608; *le Cawsey* 1578 (*v.* caucie); *Cobb(e)heath poole* 1585 (*v.* cobb(e) 'a round lump, a cob', hǣð, pol[1]. Dicklow Cob 1 90 is a tumulus); *Cold Moss* 1606[2] (*v.* cald, mos); *le Davenport acre* 1603 (probably an acre belonging to the *Davenport* family, *v.* æcer); (*le*) *Day(e)heies, -heyes, -hayes* 1577, 1588 ('dairy enclosures', *v.* dey, (ge)hæg); *Deepe mosse* 1606 (*v.* dēop, mos); *Doggelane* 1606[2] (*v.* dogga, lane); *le Ele arke in Wynteley* 1577 (probably an eel-trap or stew, from ēl[2] 'an eel', with ME *arke* (OE earc), ModE and dial. *ark* 'a chest, a receptacle, a bin; a hutch' cf. *Eelearke* (from 1570) Cu 393, Eel Ark We 1 143, xv); *le Fernileg*' 1297 ('ferny clearing', *v.* fearnig, lēah); *Goldhordesmos* 1293, *Golt-* 1351 ('moss where a hoard of gold has been found', *v.* gold-hord, mos); *le Hack ryddynge* 1596 ('clearing at a hook of land', *v.* haca, ryding); *le Hall Ashe* 1601 ('ash-tree near a hall', *v.* hall, æsc); (*the-, le-*) *Han(d)fyeld, -field(e), (-yordes), -fieldes* 1573, 1574, 1575,1588 (perhaps 'cock field', from hana 'a cock', and feld with geard); *le Haughe meadowe* 1574 (*v.* halh); *Headesse Lane* 1598 (*v.* edisc); *le Hethevesin* 1297 ('land cut off the edge of a heath', from hǣð and an el. which is either ME *evesen*, a pl. form of *evese* from OE *efes* 'an eaves, an edge or border', or ME *evesinge, -unge* 'the eavesing of a house', cf. OE *efesung* 'a hair-cutting' and *The Isinge* 1 119); *Hokynfyelde lakes* 1571, *Hocknisfield* 1585; *Kynsye Crofte* 1571 (from a pers.n. or surname *Kinsey* (OE *Cynesige*) and croft); *the Lake heade* 1575, *the Lake* 1606[2] ('(the top end of) the watercourse', *v.* lacu, hēafod); *le Leasowe medowe* 1575 (*v.* lǣs); *le Leighe fylde* 1571 (*v.* lēah, feld); *le Lee lackes* 1585, *le Lie lakes* 1588 ('watercourses at a clearing', *v.* lēah, lacu); (*the*) *Lynge fyelde* 1571, 1573, *Linge field*(*e*) 1574, 1598 (*v.* lyng, feld); *Longe flatt* 1571 (*v.* lang, flat); *le Lordshides* 1606 ('the lord of the manor's sheds', *v.* hláford, scydd); *Lownes bache, le Lownes Springe* 1585 (from bæce[1] 'a stream, a valley', and spring 'a young wood', with either a pers.n. or launde 'a glade, a woodland pasture', cf. Lownds Bottoms 11 *supra*); *Newetley, le New'they* 113 ('new heath-clearing and heath-enclosure', *v.* nīwe, lēah, (ge)hæg, cf. *le Oldethey infra*); *le Neyther hey end* 1606 (*v.* neoðera, (ge)hæg, ende[1]); *le Newe Poole* 1585 (*v.* nīwe, pōl[1]); *Olde Fieldes* 1575 (*v.* ald, feld); *the Olderleyes* 1577 ('alder woods', *v.* alor, lēah); *le Oldethey, Holdetley* 113 (*v.* ald, hǣð, (ge)hæg, lēah, cf. *Newetley supra*); *Oldlandeschawe* c.1293, 113 ('(wood at) the old selion', *v.* ald, land, sceaga); *Over Crofte* 1608 ('higher croft', *v.* uferra, croft); *Pagebroke* 1575, 1589 (*v.* brōc); *the Plumpe* 1606[2]; *le Roule-, le Rowele*(*s*)*mor* 1293, c.1293 ('moor at rough-clearing', *v.* rūh, lēah, mōr[1]); *le Salion Crofte* 1588 (*v.* selion, croft); *Senewaldeschawe* 113 (from sceaga 'a wood', with either an OE pers.n. *Scēn(*e*)*wald*, of a rare type with the prototheme *sc*(*i*)*ēne* recorded only in *Scenuulf* LVD (OET 156, 556), or a p.n. 'bright forest', from scēne and wald); *le Small More Bridge* 1585 ('(bridge at) the narrow moor', or 'narrow bridge at a moor', *v.* smæl, mōr[1], brycg); *le Sturchfflat* 1608 ('stirk flat', *v.* stirc, styrc, flat); *the Tanne howse* 1578 (*v.* tan-hous, cf. *Barkhowse meadowe supra*); *le Tibfielde* 1574, *Tib*(*b*)*field*(*e*) 1590, 1592, cf. *Tibbet Flat* 1608 (from the ME pers.n. *Tibb, Tibbet, v.* feld, flat); *le Wilkemore* 1588, 1606 (probably refers to Wheelock 2 273, *v.* mōr[1]); *le Wynchurche fielde* 1598, *Winchurchfeild* 1649 ('gorsy churchfield', from cirice and feld, with hvin).

ii. Sandbach

The greater part of Sandbach parish lies in Northwich Hundred, *v.* 2 264, but two of its townships are in Nantwich Hundred, 5. Betchton, 6. Hassall (part of this township was in Barthomley parish 2 *supra*). Hassall was in *Mildestuic* (Northwich) Hundred in 1086, the same hundred as its parent parish, and so, probably, was Betchton, though not mentioned in DB.

5. BETCHTON (110–7859) ['betʃtən]

> *Bechetona* H2 (17) Orm², *Parua Becheton*' 1256 Cl, *Bech*(*e*)*ton* 1260 Court (p) *et freq* with variant spellings -*tone*, -*do*(*u*)*n* to 1696 Wil, *Beachton* 1602 Wil, *Beech-* 1724 NotCestr
> *Bechinton, -yn-* c.1277 AD (p), 1305 ChF (p) *et freq* to 1398 ChRR, -*en-* 1294 ChF (p), 1344 ChRR (p); *Bechynaton* 1342 *BW* (p), *Bechyngton, -ing-* 1353, 1356 BPR (p) *et freq* ib to 1359
> *Becheston* 1327 *BW* (p), 1328 ChRR (p), 1393 Cl (p), 1417 Plea
> *Berchynton, -in-* 1333, 1345 *AddCh*
> *Bechinson* 1344 MidCh (p)
> *Bekynton* 1361 BPR (p)

Betcheton 1441 Cre (p), *Betchton* 1699 Wil, cf. *Bitchton Field* 1841
TA

'Farm at a valley with a stream', *v.* bece[1], tūn, hǣð. The forms are of
three types, one with the first el. uninflected, another with the first el. in
gen.sg. inflexion, a third with -ing-[4]. This last makes Sx 421 irrelevant.

BANK FM, *Bank* 1842 OS.   BETCHTON HEATH & HO, 1831 Bry, *v.*
hǣð.   BOULTS GREEN, *Bolts-* 1831 ib, from the surname *Bo(u)lt*
and grēne[2].   BROOK FM, *The Brooke* Eliz Orm[2], *Brook House* 1762
Wil, *v.* brōc.   CAPPERS LANE, 1841 *TA, Cappurs-* 1831 Bry,
probably from a surname.   CHELLSHILL, *Chells Hill* 1831 Bry, *v.*
hyll. The first el. may be a surname from Chell St.   COLLEY LANE,
cf. *Colley Croft & Field* 1841 *TA, the Cole Croft* 1689 Cre, *v.* col[1],
colig, croft, lane.   THE CROSS, *Betchton Cross* 1831 Bry, *v.* cros.
CROSS FM, *Crossehowse* 1444 AddCh, *Hassall Cross* 1831 Bry, *v.* cros,
hūs, cf. Hassall 21 *infra.*   DEAN HILL, 1796 Wil, *Deane-* 1657 ib,
from denu 'a valley', or the surname *Dean, v.* hyll.   DRUMBER FM,
dial. *drumble* 'a wooded ravine', cf. dumbel.   DUBTHORN, 1831
Bry, 'dubbed thorn-tree', *v.* dubbed, þorn.   THE FIELDS, FIELDS
FM, *Betchtons Fields* 1831 ib, *v.* feld.   FOURLANES END, *Smallwood
Four Lane Ends* 1831 ib, cf. *Four Lane Ends* 1831 ib (110–780588) and
Smallwood 2 316, *v.* lane, ende[1].   GRAVEL BANK FM, *v.* gravel,
banke.   HASSALL GREEN, 1831 ib. *v.* grēne[2] 'a green', cf. Hassall
21 *infra.*   LADY'S WELL, cf. *Lady Acre* 1841 *TA, v.* hlǣfdige,
wella, æcer.   LAWTON HEATH END, *Lawton Heath* 1831 Bry, cf. 2
321, *v.* ende[1].   LOVE LANE (FM), *Love Lane* 1598 AddCh, (*-Farms*)
1831 Bry, *v.* lufu, lane.   LYNNHOUSE BRIDGE & FM, ['lin-], *Lynn-
hurst-* 1831 Bry, *Lyn House* 1842 OS, cf. *Big & Little Linnias, Linnias
Meadow* 1841 *TA*, 'maple-wood hill', *v.* hlin, hyrst.   MALKIN'S
BANK (FM & WORKS), *Malkin's Bank, Malkin Bank Salt Works* 1831
Bry, 'scarecrow bank', *v.* malkin, banke. The salt-works may be
associated with Salters Acre *infra.*   MANOR HOUSE (FM).   OAK-
TREE FM.   PEARTREE FM, 1842 OS, *-House* 1831 Bry.   ROUGH-
WOOD BRIDGE, FM, HILL FM, & (HIGHER & LOWER) MILL, *Roughwood* (*New Mill*) 1831 ib, *Roughwood, New & Upper Mill* 1842 OS,
v. rūh, wudu.   SANT FM (lost, 110–776583), 1831 Bry, possibly
from sand 'sand'.   STANNERHOUSE LANE, cf. *Stanner Houses* 1831
ib, *Stannier House* 1841 *TA, Stonners House* 1842 OS, from the
occupational surname *Stonehewer* or *Sto-, Stanier.*   THURLWOOD
FM, cf. Thurlwood 2 309.

FIELD-NAMES

The undated forms are 1841 *TA* 46. Of the others, 1270–1300 and E1 are *JRC*, 1404 *AddCh*, 1498 (1511) ChRR, 1689 Cre, 1696 Wil, 1831 Bry, 1842 OS.

(*a*) Acre(s); Ashmoor, -more (*v.* æsc, mōr[1]); Bakehouse Fd; Barn Fd (*the*- 1689); Bent (*v.* beonet); Birchen head ('hill growing with birch-trees', *v.* bircen[2], hēafod); Black Acre; Blunders; Breach-, Breech (Fd) (*v.* brēc); Broad Moor; Broom(e) Fd, Brooms (*v.* brōm); Broomleyfield 1696 (*v.* brōm, lēah); the Bryery Croft 1689 (*v.* brērig); The Buttons (named from 'blue-buttons', the devil's bit); Five-, Long- & Seven Butts (*v.* butte); By flatts ('flat pieces of ground in a bend of a stream', *v.* byge[1], flat); Cartricks Fd (probably representing *Cartridge*, a form of *Cartlache*, cf. *Cartelache*, Cartlidge Wood 1 17, 54, *v.* kartr, læc(c)); Cash'd-, Casha Bank (*v.* banke, cf. Cassia Green 182 *infra*); Chill Moss; Church Field Bank; Clough Fd (*v.* clōh); Cock(e)las; Cock Pit Fd (*v.* cockpit); Cow Hay, Coe Hey & Lane (*v.* cū, (ge)hæg, lane); Cranberry Moss (*v.* cranberry, mos); Craplow Mdw (cf. Crappilous Mdw 2 322); Crow Barrow ('crow wood', *v.* crāwe, bearu); Daw Fd (*v.* daw(e)); (Eight-, Four-, Half-, etc.) Day Math, Day Work (*v.* day-math, day-work); Devonshire Banks; Dick Acre, Croft, How (*v.* dīc, æcer, croft, hōh); Dingle Mdw (*v.* dingle); Down Clough (*v.* dūn, clōh); Fender Fd (*v.* fender); Finny (cf. Finney 240 *infra*); Flatts (*v.* flat); Fox Knole, -Knoll (*v.* fox, cnoll); Foxley (*v.* fox, lēah); Galley Field (*v.* gagel, lēah); Gorsley Bank (*v.* gorst, lēah); Gorst Hey (*v.* gorst, (ge)hæg); Gorsty Croft & Hay (-*Hey* 1689, *v.* gorstig); Green Lane Fd; Hall Fd & Heys (cf. *le Hall Yerds* 1498 (1511), *v.* hall, geard); Hand Ridding (*v.* ryding); Hewitts Lane 1831; Hill Fd; Holl(e)y Bank (*v.* holegn, banke); Hood Lane 1831; Hook (*v.* hōc); House Green (*v.* hūs, grēne[2]); Intake (*v.* inntak); Kiln Fd & Yard (*v.* cyln, geard); Knowl, Knoll (*v.* cnoll); Land Croft (*v.* land); Linnicars ('flax acres', *v.* līn, æcer); Little Mdw (*the*- 1698, *v.* lȳtel, mæd); Long Shoot(s) (*v.* lang, scēat); Loses (*v.* hlōse); Madge Acre (*v.* madge, æcer); Mansion(s); Mare acre (*v.* mere[2]); Marl Fd (*v.* marle); Mill Hey (*v.* myln, (ge)hæg); Minacre (Wood) (*v.* (ge)mǣne); Mor(r)sley, Moseley (*v.* mos, mōr[1], lēah); Moslin (obscure, perhaps from mos 'a bog', cf. Moslin, Moslin Wood 2 313, 285); Newland (*v.* nīwe, land); Nick Acre (*v.* nick(e)); Nook Fd (*v.* nōk); Oakless (*v.* āc, lǣs); the Oak Stubble 1689 (*v.* āc, stubbil); Ol(l)ery Croft & Fd (*v.* alor); Out Broom ('outlying broomy land', *v.* ūt, brōm); Ox Hey(s) (*v.* oxa, (ge)hæg); Oxen Grass (cf. prec., *v.* gærs); Penny Croft (*v.* peni(n)g); Phlegm Mdw (perhaps from flem 'a mill-stream'); Pinfold Fd (*v.* pynd-fald); Pingle (*v.* pingel); Pingot (*v.* pingot); Qui Croft (probably from cȳ, pl. of cū, but cf. ME *qui* 'a heifer' (NED)); Rabbit Burrow; Randle Rode 1842 (from rod[1] 'a clearing' and the pers.n. *Randle*, for *Randolph*); Ridding (*freq, v.* ryding); Rough (*freq, v.* rūh); Round Fd (cf. *the Round Croft* 1689, *v.* rond); Rush Acres (*v.* risc, æcer); Salters Acre (*v.* saltere, æcer, cf. Malkin's Bank *supra*); Sand Flatt (*v.* sand, flat); Shew Thorn; Sleen Fd (*v.* slinu 'a slope'); Slum (*v.* slump, cf. Slum Wood 2 321–2); Stangate Fd (significance uncertain, *v.* stān, gata, geat); Stean Fd

(*v.* stǽne); Stone Wall Bank (1831, *v.* stān, **wall**, **banke**); Swan Flatt (Wd);
The Sweet Fd (*v.* swēte); Tin Fd; Tom Fd & Moss, Town Fd (*v.* toun,
feld, mos); Tyrant (cf. Tyrant **2** 278); the Washing Meat field 1689; Wet
Close (*v.* wēt); White Edge, Whiteidge (*v.* hwīt, ecg); White Stones (*v.*
hwīt, stān); Wizzard Fd; Wolven Fd (*v.* **wylfen**); Wood Bank.

(*b*) *Haselden*(*e*) 1270–1300, E1, 1404 (*v.* hǽsel, denu); the two *snapes* E1
('the two boggy pieces of land', *v.* snǽp, or 'the two pieces of poor pasture',
v. snap, cf. Snape 76 *infra*, La 17); *Walse-*, *Vasse-*, *Wassedene* 1270–1300
('swamp valley', *v.* wǽsse, denu); *Wildecathisheuede* (lit. *Gilde-*) E1 (p)
('wild-cat's hill', or perhaps a place where the head of one of these animals
was displayed, *v.* wild-catt, hēafod. The *G-* spelling is due to French
influence; in this deed (*JRC* 1315) the p.n. Wheelock and the pers.n.
Walter appear as *Geloke* and *Galter*).

6. HASSALL (110–760570) ['(h)æsɔːl]

Eteshale 1086 DB, *Htesh'* 13 Seal (Orm² III 294n.), *Hatishale* 13
    Orm², *Hattesale* l13 AddCh, *Hatteshall* 1318 Orm², *Hatsale* 1425
    Plea (lit. *Hac-*), *Hatesall* 1581 ChRR
Hassale l13 *JRC*, 1293 *AddCh et freq* with variant spellings
    Ha(*s*)*s*(*h*)*ale* to 1472 ChRR (p), (*-iuxta Whelok*) 1288 Court
Hashall, *Hasshal* 1299 Ipm, *Hassalle* 1331 *AddCh*, *Hassall* 1408
    ChRR *et freq* with variant spellings *-al*, *-ell*, *Hassehall* 1488 *Vern*
    (p), *Little Hassall* 1592 *AddCh*, 1662 Orm², 1831 Bry, (*the town-
    ship of Hassall otherwise-*) 1840 *TA*

'The witch's nook', *v.* hǽgtesse (in a reduced form *hǽtse*), halh.
Cf. Wheelock **2** 273, Hassall Green 19 *supra*. Hassall Hall *infra* is
identified with *Little Hassall* (*v.* lȳtel) in some references.

BANK FM, cf. *Little Bank* 1840 *TA*, *v.* banke.   BOSTOCK HO,
-alias Bostock House Farm 1784 *BW*, probably derived from the
surname from Bostock **2** 202.   BOTTOMLESS MERE, *v.* 3 *supra*.
BUTCHER'S BANK, 1831 Bry, *v.* bocher.   DAISY BANK.   DAY
GREEN, 1831 ib, *Dawgrem* 1610 Cre, cf. Daygreen Fm 3 *supra*, *Day
Green Field* 1840 *TA*, 'dairy green', *v.* dey, grēne².   DUNNOCK'S
FOLD FM, *Dunnock Fold or Pool Farm* 1831 Bry, *v.* dunnoc, fald, cf.
Hassall Pool *infra*.   FINGERPOST FM, *Fingerpost House* 1831 ib.
HASSALL HALL, 1831 ib, *the hall, commonly called Little Hassall* 1662
Orm², cf. Hassall *supra*.   HASSALL MOSS, 1831 Bry, *v.* mos.
HASSALL POOL, cf. Dunnock's Fold *supra*, and *Pool Hay* 1784 *BW*,
Pool (*Field*), *Pool Head* (*Bank*) 1840 *TA*, *v.* pōl¹ 'a pool', hēafod,
banke, (ge)hæg.   ROUGHWOOD BRIDGE, *v.* 19 *supra*.   SCHOOL
FM.   WALNUT TREE FM.

FIELD-NAMES

The undated forms are 1840 *TA* 193. Of the others, 1293 is *AddCh*, 1337 Orm², 1784 *BW*, 1831 Bry.

(*a*) Baddeley (cf. Baddiley 124 *infra*); Bednal Fd & Mdw (*the Bedna Meadow* 1784, perhaps named after Ranulph de *Budenale* E1 *JRC* 1315 and his son Richard de *Budenhal* 1288 Court 89 (lit. *Dud*-), who held an assart in Betchton, cf. Boden Hall 2 307); Bent Bank (*v.* beonet); Biddence Fd; Birchall Moor Fd (probably 'marsh at birch-nook', from birce and halh, with mōr¹); Birchen Croft 1784 (*v.* bircen²); Bitter Sweet (*v.* 325 *infra*); Blake Fd (*v.* blæc); Bleak Flatt (*v.* bleak); The Bottoms (*v.* botm); Broadbent (*v.* brād, beonet); Broken Hurds; Broom Fd 1784 (*v.* brōm); Brown Fd (*v.* brūn¹); Calvey Croft 1784 (*v.* calf, (ge)hæg); Clemlie Park (cf. Clemley 47 *infra*, *v.* park); Clerks Croft; Coal Fd (*v.* col¹); Cock Shed (*v.* cocc-scyte); Colley Fd (*v.* colig); Cushey; Dung Fd (*v.* dung); Fender Mdw (*v.* fender); Footroad Fd; Foxley Hill ('fox clearing', *v.* fox, lēah, hyll); Grass Gate ('grassy pasture', *v.* gærs, gata); Green Hay, -Hey (*v.* grēne¹, (ge)hæg); Hassall Fd & Moor (*v.* feld, mōr¹); Heavens; Hitchcroft Mdw (Bank) 1784 ('(meadow and bank at) the hurdled croft', *v.* hiche, croft); Hoggy Riddings (*v.* ryding); Hollins (cf. *Holin*(*i*)*schaue* 1293, 'holly wood', *v.* holegn, sceaga); Hooler Fd (*v.* alor); (The) Knowl, Knowl Bank; Lidiam Fd 1784; Lodley Bank, Fd & Mdw; Long Moor; Megg Fd 1784 (*v.* meg); Mere Mdw (*v.* mere¹); Merry Hill (*v.* myrge); Moon Acres; Moor Mdw 1784; Ox Pasture; Pasture Lane; The Patch; Riccardine Fd (perhaps a lost p.n. in worðign); Rye Roost (*v.* ryge, root); Sand Fd; Shaw Croft (*v.* sceaga); Shipley Wd (*v.* scēp, lēah); Long Shoot(s) (*v.* scēat); Sount Fd (*v.* sand); (Far & Near) Spring Fd & Mdw (*Far, Lower, & Upper Sprink, Sprink Meadow* 1784, *Sprink Wood* 1831, *v.* spring 'a young wood'); Thorn-hurst Fd & Wd (*Thorn Hurst* 1784, 'thorn wood', *v.* þorn, hyrst); Town Fd, Big & Little Town Ridding otherwise Large & Little Tom Fd (*v.* toun, ryding); Wall Hill (*v.* wælla); Whittal Wd, Whittnall Fd (probably 'at the white nook', *v.* hwīt (wk.dat.sg. hwītan), halh); Whittley ('white wood', *v.* hwīt, lēah); Witch Croft Bank & Mdw (from either wīc or wīce 'a wych-elm'); Big & Little Withen(s) (*v.* wīðegn); Wood Mdw (cf. *de Bosco* 1293 (p), *del Wode* 1337 (p), *v.* wudu).

(*b*) *le Bruche* 1293 ('the breaking-in of land', *v.* bryce); *Holewemede* 1293 ('meadow in a hollow', *v.* holh (ME dat.sg. holwe), mæd).

iii. Coppenhall

The parish of Coppenhall contained two townships, 1. Church Coppenhall, 2. Monks Coppenhall. It was originally a chapelry of Wybunbury parish, and became a separate parish in 1373 (Orm² III 326). The whole is now included in Monks Coppenhall c.p., which comprises the municipal borough of Crewe 26 *infra*.

1. CHURCH COPPENHALL (110–7057) ['kɔpŋɔːl] older local ['kɔpŋəl]

Copehale 1086 DB

Chopenhale H3 *HarlCh*

Copenhale c.1249, 1253 MRA, 1288 Ch *et freq* to 1478 ChRR,
(*Church(e)-*) 1303–5 AddCh, (*Chirch(e)-*) 1321, 1337 Plea *et freq*
to 1447 ChRR, (*Cherche-*) 1403 Pat, (*Chyrche-*) 1423 Rich,
(*Chirches-*) 1444 Adl, *Copenale* 1294 Imp, (*Chirche-*) e14 AddCh

Copinhale H3 AddCh, -*yn-* 1296 (1524) Comb (p)

Copynal H3 AddCh, *Copinhal* 1288, 1289 Court, Plea, -*hall* 1319
MidCh

Coppenhal 1243 Cl, (*Church-*) *Coppenhall* 1317 AddCh, 1399 ChRR,
1581 Cre *et freq*, (*Church(e)-*) 1567 ChRR

Copenhal E1 AddCh, 1289 Court, (*Chirche-*) 1288 Court, -*hall* 1293
IpmR, 1454 ChRR, (*Chirche-*) E1 AddCh, (*Church(e)-*) 1514,
1515 *ChEx*, -*haull* 1554 Pat, *Chirchecopenal* 1316 AddCh,
(*Churche*)*copenall* 1514 *ChEx*, 1550 ChRR

Chirchecopunnale 1310 Rich

Chyrchecapenale 1316 AddCh

Coponhale 1317 Rich

Copnall 1417 Rich, (*Chirche(e)-*) 15, 1477 ChRR, (*Church(e)-*) 1477
(1581) ib, 1510 Plea

Copnale H6 AddCh

Capnal 1562 ChRR

Church Coppenhale 1616, 1629 Cre

'Coppa's nook', from an OE pers.n. *Coppa* and **halh** (dat.sg. **hale**),
cf. *Copenhaleeues(e)* 247 *infra*. The affix is **ciric**e 'a church', this being
the church township, cf. *Chirchetonfeld infra*. Cf. Monks Coppenhall
26 *infra*.

HALL O' SHAW (110–713563)

Shahe John (1622) Orm[2]

Schawe H3 AddCh (p), (*la-*, *le-*) 1290, 1311 Ipm (p), l13 Sheaf (p),
-*schaw* 1316 MidCh (p), *Schaue* 1330 Ipm (p), (*le*) *Shaw(e)* 1313,
1316, 1317 MidCh (p) *et freq* to 1466 ChRR (p), *the Hall of (the)*
Shaw(e) 1621 (1656) Orm[2], 1663, 1668 *Vern*, *Hall o' th' Shaw*
1831 Bry

le Sagh(e) 1287 Court (p), 1327 ChRR (p)

(*le*) *Shagh(e)* 1289 Cre (p), 1307, 1319, c.1320 MidCh (p) *et freq*
with variant spellings *Sc(h)agh* to 1456 Rich (p)

(*le*) *Swagh* 1329 MidCh (p)

(*le*) *Schaugh* 1362 *Vern* (p)

'(Hall at) the wood', *v.* sc(e)aga, hall. This is the origin of a wide-spread Ch family, and much of the material is derived from the forms of the local surname used by the Coppenhall and Middlewich houses.

SYDNEY (110–722563), [sid-], *Sidenhale* 1260 Court (p), *-hal* 1289 ib, *Sydenhale* 1387, 1478, 1541 ChRR, *-hall* 1433 ib, *Sidney Meadow &* *Orchard* 1841 *TA*, and cf. *the Sidneys, -Sydnes, -Sidnes* 1681 to 1731 Cre (the local surname of a branch of the Shaw family (cf. Hall o' Shaw *supra*) at Sandbach, *v.* **2** 273), and cf. also the forms given under Sydney Ho 15 *supra*, which suggest the identification with Sydney of the p.n. forms given in Court. The identification is also suggested by the appearance, in the action in Court 149, of the Knights Hospitallers, and of Richard Underwood, local tenants (cf. Underwood Fm *infra*). The name means 'at the wide nook', *v.* sīd (wk.dat. sg. sīdan) 'spacious, roomy, wide', halh (dat.sg. hale). It may recur at Faddiley Bank 143 *infra*.

UNDERWOOD FM & LANE (110–696568), *Wndir-, Undir-, Undrewode* 1288, 1289 Court (p), *Under-* 1399 (p), 1408 ChRR, *Underwood* 1289 Court (p), (*-Farms*) 1831 Bry, 'near the wood', *v.* under, wudu. Cf. the notes under Sydney *supra*.

ALDERLEY HO.   BRADFIELD RD.   BROOKLANDS.   CHURCH HOUSE FM, *Church House* 1831 Bry, *v.* cirice, hūs.   COPPENHALL HO, *Moss House* 1831 ib, cf. foll.   COPPENHALL MOSS, 1831 ib, *Copinhale Mos* 113 *AddCh, le Mos* 1318 Rich, *Chirchecopenhale Moss* 1361 ib, *Coppenhall Mosse* 1668 *Vern*, cf. *mora de Chirchecopenhale* 1348 Orm², *le Mor* 1358 Rich, *le Moor(e)* 1423, 1456 ib, *v.* mos, mōr¹. The moor was enclosed in 1456 (Rich 162).   CROSS GREEN (lost, 110–705572), 1831 Bry, 1842 OS, *Cross Green* (*at the Moreland Crosse*) 1566 *AddCh*, 'green at a cross', *v.* cros, grēne². The cross seems to have been on a boundary of Coppenhall Moss *supra, v.* mōr¹, land.   DONKINSON'S OAK, 1840 Chaloner, *Donkinson Oak* 1831 Bry, a tree on the boundary with Warmingham, *v.* **2** 262, from the surname *Donkinson* (cf. Reaney, Bardsley, s.n. *Dunkin(son)*) with āc, cf. *Donkinsons* (*Oak*) *Croft* 1841 *TA.*   FREE GREEN (lost, 110–700569), 1842 OS, *Free Green Farm* 1831 Bry, 'a hamlet or piece of land free of rents or services', *v.* frēo, grēne².   GROBY CROFTS, FM & RD, perhaps from a surname *Groby*, cf. Groby Lei.   KENT'S LANE, cf. *Kents Field* 1841 *TA*, and Kent's Green Fm 15 *supra.* MABLINS LANE, *Maplin Moss Lane* 1831 Bry, cf. *Maplins Croft &*

Moss 1841 *TA*, *Mable Mosse* 1541 ChRR, 'maple-tree marsh', *v.* mapel, mos. The modern form contains an *-en* derivative adj. **maplen* 'of maple; growing with maple', cf. ModEdial. *maplin-tree* EDD. MAW GREEN, 1842 OS, *Maul Green* 1831 Bry, cf. *Maul Barn Field, Maul Field & Yard* 1841 *TA*, probably from dial. *maul* 'clayey or marly soil', *v.* grēne². MOUNT PLEASANT. PARKER'S RD. PUMP HO, 1831 Bry, *v.* pumpe. SHANDON HO. STONELEY RD, *Drury Lane* and *Stoneley's Green* 1831 ib. The modern name is that of a hamlet, from a surname *Stoneley* (cf. Stoneley Green 135 *infra*), *v.* grēne². If not an allusion to Drury Lane (Westminster) Mx 178, the old name of the road would mean 'love lane', *v.* druerie 'courtship, love'. THORNEYFIELD, 1831 Bry, *The Thornefield* 1668 *Vern*, *v.* þorn, feld. WALDRON'S LANE, *Moss Lane* 1831 Bry, *v.* mos, lane, cf. Valley Brook 1 37. WARMINGHAM RD, leading to Warmingham 2 262. YEW TREE HO (lost, 110–722563), 1831 ib.

FIELD-NAMES

The undated forms are 1841 *TA* 114. Of the others, c.1275–8 (18) is Sheaf, 1310, 1440 Rich, 1354 *Indict*, 1383, 1668 *Vern*, 1507 *MinAcct*, 1566, 1570 Orm², Eliz 1 *Rental*, and the rest *AddCh*.

(a) Bargains Mdw (*v.* 325 *infra*); Beans Fd; Bennett's Croft (*Bennettuscroft* 1310, 'Benedict's croft', from the ME pers.n. *Bennett* (OFr *Beneit*, Lat *Benedictus*) and croft); Black Fd; Boosey Pasture (*v.* bōsig); Bowling Green; Bradley Fd (*v.* brād, lēah); Brook Fd; Two Butts (cf. *le Hedbutt* E2, *v.* hēafod, butte); Church Fd; Cliffe Ground (*v.* clif); Cooley Croft (*v.* cū, lēah); Cow Leasow (*v.* lǣs); The Crime (*v.* cryme, cf. *le Crymbe* 2 171); Cross Fd ('field at a cross', *v.* cros); Davenport(s) Fd (the *Davenport* family held land at Sydney *supra*, in 1478 and 1571 ChRR, *v.* DKR xxxvii 188, xxxix 89); Fallow Fd; Fords Lane Fd (cf. Ford Lane 27 *infra*); Gunners Close; Hanging Fd (*v.* hangende); Hatch Fd (*v.* hæc(c)); Hoo Grove Mdw (*v.* hōh, grāf); Hunger Hill (*v.* hungor); Intake (*v.* inntak); Kitchen Fd; The Knowl (*v.* cnoll); Markers Wd; Marl Fd (cf. *le marledefeld* 1303–5, *le marlidecroft*, -ed- e14, *v.* marlede, feld, croft); Mill Fd; Long & Short Oakes (*v.* āc); Outlett (*v.* outlet); Pingott (*v.* pingot); Purse End (*v.* purs, ende¹); Ridding(s) (*v.* ryding); Rough Green; Sand Fd; Spiggot; Tom Ridding, Town Fd (*v.* toun); Way Fd (*v.* weg); Whettenhall Fd (Richard de *Wettenhall* (Wettenhall 166 *infra*) died 1369 in possession of land at Sydney *supra*, *v.* DKR xxxvi 44); White Fd; Withins (*v.* wīðegn); Within Lake (*v.* wīðigen, lacu).

(b) *Banecroft* e14, *Bancroft* 1440 ('bean croft', *v.* bēan, croft, cf. *Bannemore* 1440, 'poor land where beans are grown', *v.* bēanen, mōr¹); By-, Birches 1566, 1570 (*v.* birce); *le Bothileghe* 1386 ('clearing where booths stand', v. bōth, lēah); le Chirchetonfeld 1383 ('(field at) the church-enclosure or churchyard', v. cirice, tūn, feld); le Docfeld 1383 ('field where the dock grows', v. docce, feld); Dolle lawne Eliz 1 (v. launde); Gleuesrudyng 1321 AddCh 43304 (from ryding 'a clearing of land' and a ME pers.n. Gleu, cf. OE glēaw 'wise, prudent', v. Reaney s.n. Glew. Barnes[1] 692 reads Olewes- and derives it from the pers.n. ODan Olaf, ON Ólafr); Hasulbache 1331 ('valley-stream where hazels grow', v. hæsel, bæce[1]); Midelhurst 1354 (p), Medul- 1507 ('middle wooded-hill', v. middel, hyrst); Le Prestes Ruding E1, -yng 1383 (v. prēost, ryding); Tabaldes rydyng 1383 (probably 'Theobald's clearing', from the ME pers.n. Tebald (OFr Theobald) and ryding); le Weracokesflatte E2, Verkocfelde e14, the three Warcock Crofts 1668, Warwicke feilds 17 ('flat piece of ground frequented by the wer-cok (a small bird)', v. flat, cf. Warcockhill La 44); le Wode E1 (p) (v. wudu); Wlueshall c.1275–8 (18) ('wolf's nook', v. wulf, halh).

2. MONKS COPPENHALL (110–6955), Monkescopenhall 1294 Ipm, Munkescopenhale 1295 Cl et freq with other spellings as for Church Coppenhall 22 supra (except le Munkescopenhale 1366 Vern, Monkes-kopnale H6 AddCh), and variant spellings of the affix as Monkes- 1294 Ipm et freq to 1583 ChRR, Monkis- 1295 Ipm, Monks- 1400 ChRR et freq, Monces- 1439 AddCh, Munkes- 1295 Cl et freq to 1583 ChRR, Munck(e)s- 1523 AddCh, 1685 Sheaf, Munks- 1608 ChRR, Monekes- 1308 Ipm, 1316 Plea, Moonkes- 1579 Chol, 'Coppenhall belonging to the monks', v. munuc. The township was owned by Combermere Abbey 93 infra (Orm[2] III 328).

CREWE (110–6955) [kru:], 1837 Chaloner, 1860 White, a municipal borough which now includes Monks Coppenhall, Church Coppen-hall 22 supra, and parts of Crewe 9 supra and Shavington cum Gresty 69 infra. A railway town, it took its name from the railway station of Crewe built in 1837 at Woodnets Green 11 supra in Crewe township. The station remained in Crewe township until 1892, the town named from it being in Monks Coppenhall, whose boundaries formed those of the borough until that date.

STREET-NAMES. HIGHTOWN, 1842 OS, v. hēah, toun, cf. 2 241, 269; FLAG LANE, 1831 Bry, 'reedy lane', v. flagge, lane; GRESTY RD, Gresty Lane 1831 ib, cf. Gresty 69 infra; HALL O' SHAW ST., v. Hall o' Shaw 23 supra; OAK ST., site of The Oak Farm 1831 ib, The Oak 1842 OS, v. āc.

ASHBANK (FM), 'ash-tree hill', v. æsc, banke. COPPENHALL HEYES, -Heys 1831 Bry, cf. le Heye 1310, 1406 Rich, Coppenhall Hey Field 1840 TA, v. (ge)hæg 'a fenced-in enclosure'. DAIRY HO (lost), 1831 Bry, 1842 OS, cf. Dairy Field 1840 TA, v. deierie. The site

is about Pedley St. in Crewe borough.   FORD LANE, cf. Fords
Lane Fd 25 *supra*, v. ford, lane.   HILLOCK HO (lost), 1842 OS,
cf. *Hillockesfeldes, Hillokkesfyldes, Hillokke fylde, -fild* 1541 *AddCh, v.*
hylloc, feld.   PEARTREE FM.   PYM'S LANE, *Narrow Lane* 1831
Bry, 1840 *TA, v.* nearu, lane.   ROCKWOOD FM, 'rook wood', *v.*
hrōc, wudu.   SOUND OAK (lost, 110–685560), 1842 OS, *Sounds-*
1831 Bry, from sand or the surname from Sound 121 *infra* with āc.
THE VALLEY, VALLEY FM, cf. Valley Brook 1 37.

FIELD-NAMES

The undated forms are 1840 *TA* 271. Of the others, 1275–8 (18) is Sheaf,
1295 Cl, E1, 1317 Orm[2], 1318 *Eyre*, 1349, 1406 Rich, 1359, 1368 *Tourn*, 1384,
1392, 1398, 1399, 1408, 1409 ChRR, 1400 Pat, Eliz 1 *Rental*, and the rest
AddCh.

   (a) Bottom- and Top Beech (*v.* bece[1]); Bent (*v.* beonet); Bone (Waste)
Feild (cf. bone-dust); Top Boo Bridge (cf. *Boghbrugge* 1359, *le Bogthbrugge*
1368, 'the arched bridge', *v.* boga, brycg); Big & Little Bootherson (this
probably represents *Bootherston*, which could be 'enclosure belonging to a
booth-dweller or booth-keeper, herdsman', from tūn and ME *bothere, an
-ere[1] derivative of bōth); Bottoms (*v.* botm); Brassey Fd (*Bressyes field* 1579,
after the *Brescy, Brassey* family, cf. Brassey Hall 43 *infra*); Briery Fd (*le
Brerefelde* 1439, *the Brerefeld* 1541, *v.* brēr, feld); Calves Green; Captains
Croft & Fd; Cote Fd; Cross Fd (*v.* cros 'a cross'); Four- & Eight Daymath
(*v.* day-math); Friday Croft (*v.* Frīgedæg); Good for nothing (*v.* 325 *infra*);
Little Grew; Hatch Fd (*v.* hæc(c)); Hemp Flatts (*v.* hænep, flat); Big-, Cote-
& Little Hodge, Hodge Mdw (*Hogefield* c.1275–8 (18), *v.* Hodg Croft 1 158,
hocg, hogg); (H)Oldershaw (*Oldershawe* H6, 'alder wood', *v.* alor, sceaga);
Howe Croft (*v.* hōh); Hunger Hill (*v.* hungor); Intake Head ('the top end of
an intake', *v.* inntak, hēafod); Knoll; Little Lont (*v.* land); Mill Fd (cf. 'a
water mill in *Munkescopenhale*' 1295, and *le Mulneheye* 1406, *v.* myln,
(ge)hæg); Moors; Oat Edditch (*v.* āte, edisc); Oat Wd (*Odwood* E1, *Otewode
flatte* H6, *þe Outewoud* Eliz 1, the later forms show the name interpreted as
'the outlying wood', *v.* ūt, wudu, but the earliest one may be from ād 'a fire'
(cf. *Otwode* 12 *supra*). This may have been the site of a bonfire; but the
significance is not known, for it is perhaps dangerous to allude to ād in the
sense 'funeral pyre'. EPN suggests 'ash heap' but the word is also used of a
beacon. Dr von Feilitzen takes the first el. to be āte 'oats' with $t > d$ due to
attraction from final *d*); Rail Croft (*v.* rail(e)); Big Scout; Sprinks (*v.*
spring); Stubbins (*v.* stubbing); Swine Cote Fd (*v.* swīn[1], cot); Weelock Fd
(cf. Wheelock 2 273); Wood Fd (cf. *le Wodefeld* e14, *v.* wudu, feld).

   (b) *le bruche* 1406 ('land broken in for cultivation', *v.* bryce); *Fellefeld* 1419
(perhaps 'ploughed land', *v.* felh, feld); *Garne(r)sfeldes, -fyldes* 1541 ('granary
fields', *v.* garner, feld); *the Hyll Croft* 1579 (*v.* hyll, croft); *the Littlors Crofts*
1697 (from the surname from Littler 172 *infra*);); *Toodeholecroft* 1419 (either

'fox-hole croft' or '(croft at) the toad hollow' from tod-hole or tāde, hol¹);
(*le*) *Wodehouses* 1317 (p), 1318 (p), *-house* 1349 (p), *-hous* 1384 ('house(s) at
a wood', *v.* wudu, hūs); *Wortyorn' bonk* 15 (cf. Valley Brook 1 37, *v.* banke);
Yatesfeldes 1541 ('fields belonging to the *Yate* family', *v.* feld, cf. (*le*) *Yate*
1399 (p), 1400 (p), *v.* geat 'a gateway').

iv. Nantwich

Nantwich became a separate parish in 1677. It was formerly a parochial
chapelry of Acton 126 *infra*, containing the townships 1. Alvaston (now
included in Nantwich and Worleston c.ps. *infra* and 151 *infra*), 2. Leighton,
3. Nantwich (now a c.p. including part of Alvaston *supra*), 4. part of Willaston
(*v.* 41 *infra*), 5. Woolstanwood.

1. ALVASTON (110–6654) ['alvəstən]

Alfualdest' e13 *AddCh*
Alualdiston 1260 *Plea* (p) (Court 28 reads *Alv-*) *et freq* with variant
    spellings *Alv-*, *Alw-*, *-es-* to 1342 (1438) ChRR
Aluaston 1304 Chamb (p), *Alv-* 1380 Plea *et freq* with variant
    spellings *Alu-*, *Alw-*, *-es-*
Alvandeston 1393, 1420 Plea, 1407, 1428, 1430 (p), 1435, 1446
    ChRR, 1428 Orm² III 451, 665, all probably mistakes for *Alvaudes-*
'Ælfwald's farm', from the OE pers.n. *Ælfwald* and tūn.

BEAM HEATH (lost, 110–655532 to 663559), 1831 Bry, *v.* Beam Heath
36 *infra*.

ALVASTON HALL, *The Grove* 1831 Bry, *Alvaston House* 1842 OS, cf.
Alvaston *supra*, *v.* grāf, hūs.   BEAMBRIDGE, *v.* 153 *infra*.   COL-
LEYS BRIDGE.   MARSHFIELD BRIDGE, *v.* 45 *infra*.   WHITEHOUSE
LANE, *v.* 43 *infra*.   WINDY ARBOUR FM, *Windy Harbor* 1831 Bry,
'windy shelter', *v.* windig, here-beorg.

FIELD-NAMES

The undated forms are 1841 *TA* 14.

(*a*) Bache House Fd (cf. Bachehouse, etc. 147 *infra*); Carrs Croft (*v.*
kjarr); Pinfold Croft (*v.* pynd-fald); Ridding (*v.* ryding); Roberts Eye Mdw
(*v.* ēg).

2. LEIGHTON (HALL) (110–6757) [lɛtən, leitən]

Lekton John (18) Orm², *Lecton(a)* H3 *AddCh*, Orm² (p), l13 *AddCh*,
    Chol (p), AD, 1311 Orm², *-tun* l13 *AddCh*, *-tan* l13 *ib*
Lechton e13 *AddCh* (p), 1259 Plea (p), l13 *AddCh*

Legthon 1270–80 *AddCh* (p), *Legton* 1342–53 *Attorn* (p), *Leghton* 1289 Court *et freq* with variant spellings *Legthtone, Legh'ton(n)* to 1544 Cre, (*-iuxta Copinhal*) 1289 Court, (*-iuxta Chirchecopenhale*) 1344 *ChGaol*

Leyhton 1294 Ipm, *Leyghton* 1304 ib, 1312 Plea, c.1550 *Surv*, *Leighton* 1316 ChRR *et freq*, (*-iuxta Copinhall*) 1319 MidCh, (*-Green & Hall*) 1831 Bry

Leytton 1295 Ipm, *Leittone* 1342 *AddCh* (p)

Layton 1559 Pat

Laighton 1821 Cre

'Herb-garden', perhaps 'vegetable garden', *v.* lēac-tūn. It adjoins Church Coppenhall 22 *supra*. A form of this p.n. may appear in *Leccon strete* 35 *infra*.

MAYOWSE (lost), 1529 ChRR, *Mayouesegh* (lit. *-one-*) 1394, 1395 ChRR, Orm², *Mayowes-* 1424 ChRR, *AddCh, Mayowese(e)* 1421 Orm², 1424 ChRR, *AddCh*, 1455 ChRR, Orm², *Mayow(e)see* 1424, 1455 ChRR, *Mayoegh* 1454 *AddRoll, Mayswesee* 1455 ChRR. This was a piece of pasture land belonging to and lying in both Leighton and Eardswick in Minshull Vernon 2 247. The name is 'Matthew's water-meadow', from the OFr pers.n. *Mahieu* (for *Matthew*, cf. the surname *Mayhew*) and ēg. The same pers.n. appears in Childer Thornton 325 *infra*.

BARROWS GREEN, 1831 Bry, *v.* grēne². DODD'S LANE, *Dods-* 1831 ib. FLOWERS LANE, 1831 ib, cf. *Floureslane* 40 *infra*. THE GRANGE. LEIGHTON BROOK (R. Weaver), *Leighton* (*or South*) *Brook* 1950 Chaloner, cf. *de la Brook, de Doito* 1277 (1666) Orm² (p) *et freq* with spellings (*le*) *Broc, Broke*, etc., the surname of the manorial lords of Leighton, *v.* brōc, sūð. MABLINS LANE, *v.* 24 *supra*. MANOR HO, *v.* maner. MILE HO, at a milestone, *v.* mīl. MOSS FM & LANE, cf. *le mos* (*de Legh'ton*), *le mosfeld* c.1315 *AddCh*, *Leighton Moss* 1831 Bry, *Moss Side* 1842 OS, *v.* mos, sīde, lane, feld. RED HALL, 1831 Bry, *v.* rēad, hall. TOTTY'S HALL, 1831 ib, *Tatty's* 1842 OS, *v.* hall.

FIELD-NAMES

The undated forms are 1845 *TA* 239, and 1831 is Bry.

(*a*) Ash Bank; Broom Croft (*v.* brōm); Bullocks Bache (*v.* bæce¹); Coal Pit Lane 1831; Far & Near Deans (*v.* denu); Gate House Croft (cf. *Gate Field Lane* 1831); Hob Ridding (*v.* hobb(e) 'a tussock', ryding); Onion Croft; Road Fd (*v.* rād); Smithy Lane 1831.

(b) *Leghtoneseye* 1344 *AddCh* ('water-meadow belonging to Leighton', *v.* ēg); *Wyslies Medowe* 1570 *AddCh* (*v.* mǣd. The first component may be a pers.n.).

3. NANTWICH (110–6552) [ˈnæn?witʃ, ˈnæntwitʃ] older local [-weitʃ, -waitʃ]

Wich 1086 DB *et freq* with variant spellings (in, de) *Wicho, Wic, Wiche, Wyke,* (in, de) *wico,* (in, de) *Wycho, Wicus,* (apud) *Wicum,* (*le*) *Wiz,* (*le*) *Wych, Wycus, Wyci* (gen.), (de) *Wyco, Wick,* (*the*) *Wyche,* (*le*) *Whiche* to 1527 *AddCh, Wicche in the parisshe of Acton* 16 *AOMB* 397, *The Wyche towne* Eliz 1 *Rental*

Wike Malb' c.1130 (1479) *Cott.* Faust. B VIII (Dugd V 324, reads *Wyche Malbanc*), (in) *Wico Maubanc* 1136–76 Chest *et freq* with variant spellings *Wi-, Wyke-, Wi-, Wych(e)-, Which(us)-, Wi-, Wyc(us, -um, -i, -o)-, Wi(c)k-, Wy- Wich(us, -um, etc.)-,* (in) *Wiko-, Vi-, Vycus-, (-o)-, Wycii-* (gen.), *Wi-, Wychius (-um,* etc.), *Wi-, Wyz-, Wis-, Wi-, Wyce-,* and *-Malban (-us, -um,* etc.), *-ane(us), -ain(e), -aun, -anc (-us,* etc.), *-an(c)k(e), -on(o), -Malebanke, -Mauban, -aunk, -aunc, -anc(us,* etc.), *-ank, -ancii* (gen.), *-anch, -en, -ayn, -un, -Maban, -Mabonke, -Melbank, -Mil-, -Mulbank* to 1679 *AddCh,* (*le-, la-, the-*) from 1359 BPR, (*-alias Namptwych, -wich,* etc.) from 1397, 1398 Pat, *Wecumalbang* 1272–1307 *AddCh, Wymabank* 1256–7 AD, *-mauban* 1309 Cl, *Wychic Maubanc* 1288 Ch, *the Quiche Malbanke* 1492 *AddCh, Wico Malbus* 1535 VE, *Wicus Malwini, Wicomalba* 1556 Pat

Nametwihc 1194 *AddCh,* (de) *Nametwico* (lit. *Ram-*) 1193 Dugd, *-wich* 12–13 (14) *Harl.* 3868, *le Namtewych(e) Maban(k)* 1301 ChancW, 1452 Sheaf, *La Namt(e)wich, -wych* 1360, 1361 BPR, (*le*) *Nampt(e)wich(e), -wych* 1322 Fine, ChancW *et freq* with variant spellings *-wyche, -wiz, -witch, -wick, Namp-* to 1775 Sheaf, (*-alias Wich Malbank*) from 1397 Pat

Nonewich 1208–29 Dieul

Nantwich 1257 Pat (but see note *infra*) *et freq* with variant spellings *Nan(n)t(e)-, -wiche, -wych(e), (the-, -apon Wiver)* c.1536 Leland, (*-Malbanke*) 1553 Pat, (*-alias Wychemalbanke*) 1560 Chol

Namntthwych 1349 *Eyre*

(de) *Wycombe Albano* 1359 Pat, *Wycombmalban* 1387 Trev, *Wycumalban* 1482 Trev(Cx), (in) *Wicom Albano* 1527 *ChCert,* (in) *Wico Albano* 1560 Sheaf

Wychenmabank 1479 BM

the Nomptwich 1514 Sheaf

(the) Nuntwich 1516, 1517 Sheaf

Nauntwiche 1517 AD *et freq* in Pat, Tab, Sheaf, *AddCh* with variant spellings *(le) Nawnt(e)-*, *-wyche* to 1583 Sheaf, *(-alias Wich Malbain)* 1559 Pat

Nawnewiche 1553 Pat

Wich-banke 1655 Sheaf

Nanptwich 1658 Sheaf

Namwich 1744 Sheaf

'The wīc', later 'the famous wīc' from wīc 'an industrial- or trading-settlement', and ME *named* 'well-known, renowned'. The manorial suffix *-Malbanc*, etc. is taken from the surname *Malbanc* (Tengvik 349) of the post-Conquest barons of Nantwich. The el. wīc is used in the sense 'a collection of buildings for a particular purpose' —here the manufacture of salt, cf. **2** 192–3, 242–3, *v.* Wych House Bank *infra*. For the p.n. *Salinis* RavGeog, often identified with Nantwich, *v.* **2** 238. Nantwich was noted for the excellence and the whiteness of its salt, which is alluded to in an epitaph of 1637 'apud Wici Malbani candidissimas salinas' (Orm[2] III 446), and in the Welsh name for Nantwich, *Nant yr Heledd Wen* 'stream of the white salt-pit' (Hewitt 112, ArchCamb IV, vii, 91–93 and n. 3), cf. 'the Britons called the town *Hellath-wen*, the White-pit', 1621 (1656) Orm[2] III 290 (Webb's *Itinerary* in King's *Vale Royal*). Professor Richards observes a reference to Nantwich in *o dir yr helet* 'from the land of the salt-springs', in a poem of Prydydd y Moch (1160–1220) to Gruffudd ap Hywel ab Owain Gwynedd (*The Myvyrian Archaiology*, 206a). The modern form of the p.n., Nantwich, appears from 1257 in Pat, Misc, Ipm, AD, ChRR, Fine, BPR, Cl, all printed calendars. In MS. sources the earliest instance noted is *Nantewich* 1340 *Sotheby*. It appears that editors of documents have often supposed it necessary to translate *Wich Malbank* into *Nantwich*, as if the former were in a foreign language. Perhaps this is the result of the prevalence, in the Latin contexts of official and legal documents, of the series *Wicus Malbanus* (< *Wich Malbank*) which led to its being regarded as the peculiar Latin version of the vernacular series *Namet-*, *Nantwich*. Cf. Addenda xv *supra* (2x).

STREET-NAMES

BARKER ST., *le Barkereslone* 1421, 1425 Rich, *Barkers lane* 1448 ib, 1625 *AddCh, Barkerstrete* 1464 Rich, *Le Barker Strete* 1526 *AddCh*, *(the) Barkers Strete* 15 Rich, *le Barkers Streete* c.1606 Orm², *Barkers-street or Mills-street* 1621 (1656) ib, *Barker's Street* 1749 Sheaf, 'the tanner's street', *v.* barkere, lane, strǣt, cf. Mill St. *infra.*

BEAM ST., *(le) Bemstrete* E1, 1319 *AddCh, Bemmstrete* 1395 Rich, *the Bemstret* 1526 Comb, *le Bemestrete* 1289 Comb *et freq* ib to 1526 (with variant spellings -*stre(e)t(e)*, with *the*- from 1465, and without def.art. from 1469), (vicus de-) 1483 *AddCh*, (forum animalium vocatum-) 1482 Comb, *le Beinstrete* 1339 AD, *le Beemstrete* 1429 ib, *the Beaymstret* 1526 Comb, *Beam Strete* 1550 *MinAcct*, -*street* 1621 (1656) Orm², *(the) Beamestreet(e)* 1581 AD, 1590 Sheaf, 1672 *AddCh, Bamstreate* 1560 Sheaf, *Beane streete* c.1662 *Surv*, 'street leading to, or lying towards, Beam Bridge', *v.* strǣt and Beam Bridge *infra*, cf. Beam Heath *infra*. Beam St. was the site of a cattle-market, cf. *le Rethermarket infra.*

BEAVERHOLD (lost), 1711, 1712, 1743 *AddCh, Baywardesholt* 1454 Comb, *et freq* ib and *AddCh*, with variant spellings *Bey*-, *Bowardes*-, -*hold*, -*holte*, to 1630 *AddCh*, (alta strata vocata-) 1464 *ib, le Bowardesholt* 1479 *ib, Baywarsholt* 1545 *ib, Ballardesholt* 1455 *ib, Bayartesholt* (high road called-) 1468, 1515 Comb, *le Boyhardesholt* 1479 *AddCh, Baires*-, *Bayresholt*, -*holde* 15 Rich, 1520 *Sotheby*, (high street called) *Bersalt* 1491 *AddCh*, 1526 Comb, perhaps 'Bēagweard's wood', from an OE pers.n. *Bēagweard* and holt, but Professor Löfvenberg suggests that the first el. may be an unrecorded ME cpd. **bayward* 'a weir-keeper' (cf. ME *wereward*, Thuresson 110), pointing out that ME *bay* 'a weir' is recorded from St in 1283 and from Ch in 1359.

CART LAKE, a short, crooked street at the west end of Beam St. The name may be the fairly common stream-name *Cart(e)lache*, cf. 1 17, and refer to some old watercourse here, *v.* kartr, læc(c).

CASTLE ST., 1860 White, *Castell Lone* 1489 *AddCh, Pudding Lane* 1794 Atlas, cf. *castrum Wici Malbani* 1288 Orm², *de*-, *du Chastel* 1347 BPR (p), ChRR (p), Pat (p), *del Castell* 1398 ChRR (p), *Chastelyord* 1341 ib, *le Castelhull'* 1344 *ChEss*, -*hul* 1583 Sotheby, *via ad Castelhull* 1442 Rich, named from a castle here, of which no trace remains, *v.* castel(l), lane, strǣt, geard, hyll. The alternative name is from pudding, and may refer to 'puddings' i.e. 'entrails, butchers' offal'.

CHURCH LANE, 1860 White, 'the lane leading to the Church' 1336 AD, *(the) Church(e) Lane* 1385, 1485, 1487 Comb, -*lone* 1445 ib, *Le Chyrchelone* 1416 *AddCh, Church Street* 1728 *ib*, cf. *(the) church(e)stele* 1465, 1479, 1485, 1487 Comb, -*stell* 1526 ib, 'lane or street leading to the Church'; 'stile near the church', *v.* cirice, lane, strǣt, stigel; named from the parish church (*capella de Wike Malb'* c.1130 (1479) *Cott.* Faust. B VIII, *the Wych chyrche* 1426 AD), cf. foll.

CHURCHYARD SIDE, *the church syde* 1465 Comb, *Chirch yorde* 15 Rich, *the churche yorde* 1485, 1519 Comb, *the churchyorde syde* 1485 ib, cf. *le Chuirchehouses* 1451 Orm² (p), *Chirchehouses* 1454 Comb (p), *-ez* 1470 ib (p), *-house* 1452 AD (p), 'the side of the church(yard)', 'houses beside the church', v. cirice, geard, sīde, hūs, cf. *the Churchyard side* 2 242.

COW FIELDS, probably named from the common pasturing of cattle here, cf. Beam Heath *infra*, v. cū, feld.

CROWFOOTS LANE, 1794 Atlas.

DOG LANE, *Doglane* 1467 *AddCh*, 'lane infested with dogs', v. dogga, lane.

HIGH ST., *alta strata* 1260 *Plea et freq*, (*-ducens versus Acton*) 1443 *Dav*, *-regia* (*que ducit versus le Mylne street*) 1456 Comb, *the kynges hegh strete* 1468 *Sotheby*, *the* (*kynges*) *hye stre*(*e*)*te* 1487, 1519 Comb, *-heʒ strete* 1520 *Sotheby*, *-high strete* 1538 *AddCh*, *the High Street* 1597 AD, *High Street alias Corn Market Street* 1600 AD, *Highstreet Street* 1637 *Chol*, *the Highestreete* 1648 *Corp*; *the hye town* 1465, 1485 Comb, *-Hiegh-* 1526 *AddCh*, *Hightowne* c.1550 *Surv*, (*le-*) 1605–6 Orm², *highton* 16 *AOMB* 397, *the highe towne* (*in Wiche Malbanke*) 1584 *AddCh*, 1605 Orm², *High Town* 1794 Atlas, 'the main street', 'the upper and more important part of the town', v. hēah, strǣt, toun. Cf. Hightown 2 241. The corn market was *le Corne Markett* 1604–5 Orm², v. corn¹, market, cf. *le Rethermarket infra*.

HILLFIELD PLACE, cf. Hillfield *infra*, v. place.

HOSPITAL ST., *in vico* (*H*)*Ospitalis* H3, E1 *AddCh*, 1285 *ChFine*, *-Hospitali* 1454, 1458, 1474 Comb, *Hospitalstrete* 1319 *AddCh et freq* with variant spellings (*le-*, *the-*) *Hospitel*(*l*)-, *-all-*, *-ull-*, *Hospetyl-*, *Hospitle-*, *-street*(*e*), *Thosptle strte* 15 Rich, *Hospell Streete* 1385 Comb *et freq* with variant spellings (*le-*, *the-*) (*H*)*Ospel*(*l*)-, *-stre*(*e*)*t*(*e*) to 1648 *Sotheby*, *the hospell alias Hospytall Streete* 1625 ib, *The Aspell Street*(*e*) 1598 Orm², Sheaf, 'street in which a hospital stands', v. hospital, strǣt. It is named after the hospital of St Nicholas which stood in or near this street (Orm² III 436), an eleventh-century foundation (*op. cit.*, 448–9). Cf. *terra ospitali, -hospitalis,* (*-in villa de Wico Maubanco*) H3 *AddCh* 43377–8, *-386*, also referred to but not named in 1194 *AddCh* 43371; cf. also *the chantry of St Nicholas* 1353 BPR, *church of St Nicholas* 1455 ChRR, *capella de Nicolo* 1465 ib, *St Nicholas chapel* 1489 Pat, *the Hospitall or Free Chapell of St Nicholas* 1506 (1724) NotCestr, *hospital of St Nicholas* 1507 Pat, *libera capella Sancti Nicholai* 1535 VE, 1550 *MinAcct*, *the chapel or house called the chapel of St Nicholas* 1548 Pat, and *the Hospytall Croft* 1548 Pat, *in hospitali platea* 1550 *MinAcct*, (*the*) *Hospital*(*l*) *place* 1560 Sheaf, c.1662 *Surv*, v. croft, place, chapel(e).

KING'S LANE, *Fulleshurst Lane* 1593 *Sotheby*, from lane and the surname from Fullhurst 122 *infra*. The modern name is due to analogy with King's Ley *infra*, to which the lane leads.   LOVE LANE, 1674 *AddCh*, 'lane where courting is done', v. lufu, lane.   MARKET ST., v. market.   MASON'S LANE, 1788 Sheaf, 1879 Sheaf¹ 1 361, a lane off Love Lane, cf. *Masons Yords* 1549, 1605 Orm², 'lane, and yards or enclosures, belonging to one Mason', v. lane, geard.

MILL ST., 1646 *Corp*, *le Mylne street* 1456 Comb, *-Streete* 1626 *Corp*, *-Miln-* 1466 Rich, *Milstrette* 16 *AOMB* 397, (*Barkers-street or*) *Mills-Street* 1621 (1656) Orm², leading to Nantwich Mill *infra*, *v.* myln, stræt, cf. Barker St. *supra*.

MILLSTONE LANE, 1842 OS, *v.* 43 *infra*.   OATMARKET, 1794 Atlas, *v.* āte, market.   PALL MALL.   PARK RD, cf. *Park* 1846 *TA*, *v.* park.

PEPPER ST., 1794 Atlas, *peper strete* 15 Rich, *Pepperstreete* 1604–5 Orm², cf. Pepper St. (Chester) 326 *infra*. Here may belong *Ratunrowe infra*.

PILLORY ST., *Pillorestrete* 1314–15 ChRR, (*the*) *Pyllery Str(e)te* 1479, 1520 Comb, (*the*) *Pyllere stre(e)te* 1485 ib, 1550 *MinAcct*, *Pyllerystret* 1550 *ib*, Le *Pillery Strete* 1554 *AddCh*, *Pillery Street*, *Pyllery Streate* 1560 Sheaf, *the Pyllorye strete* 1487 Comb, *Pillory Street* H8 Plea, 1574 *AddCh*, (*the-*) 1621 (1656) Orm², *v.* pillori, stræt.

PRATCHITT'S ROW, *v.* rāw.   RED LION LANE, 1794 Atlas.   SOUTH CROFTS, *Tynkers croft* 1439 Orm², *-Crofts* 1499 ib, *-Croftes* 1516 Comb, *Tinker's-croft* 1643 Orm², *Tinkers Crofts* 1690 *Dep*, 1794 Atlas, 1846 *TA*, *v.* tink(l)ere, croft.   SWINEMARKET, 1794 Atlas, *v.* swīn, market.   WALL LANE, 1574 *AddCh*, (*le-*) 1579 *ib*, *v.* wælla 'a well, a spring', lane, cf. Wall Fields Fm *infra*, which is adjacent.

WELSH ROW, *Frog(ge) Rowe* 1412 *AddCh*, 1427 *MainwB*, (*le-*) 1440 Rich and five other instances with variant spellings *Roo*, *Row* to *Welsh Row alias Frog Row* 1597 AD, (*le*) *Frogstrete* 1438, 1490 *MainwB*, *le Walsch Row yrde* 15 Rich, *the Walssh Roo* 1520 Sotheby *et freq* with variant spellings (*the-*, *le-*) *Walshe-* (to 1554), *Walche-* (to 1560), *Welch(e)-* (from 1540), *Welsh(e)-* (from 1593), *-Row(e)*, *-Rewe*, 'row of houses, street, infested with frogs', later 'row of houses owned or used by the Welsh', *v.* frogga, rāw, ræw, stræt, Welisc. This street is on the west bank of R. Weaver opposite Nantwich. The earlier name is probably due to the proximity of the houses to the river, cf. *Froggemulne* 128 *infra*. The later name arises from the presence of Welsh business men in Nantwich for the salt-trade, and the Row was probably an ancient lodging for Welsh salt-merchants. One Llewellyn *Walshmon* held a croft in Nantwich 1439 Orm² III 478. Welsh Row is also at the eastern terminus of a great salt-way into Wales, *v.* I 48. Cf. Welshmen's Green & Lane 145 *infra*.

FIRST & SECOND WOOD ST., *le Wodestrete* 1353 AD, *the-* 15 Rich, *Wodestrete* 1470 *AddCh*, *Woodstrete* 1548 Pat, *the-, -streete* 1602 Sotheby, *le Ouerwode-strete* 1477 *AddCh*, *Gret & Litle Wode strete* 1520 Sotheby, (*the- le-*) *Little & (the-) Great Wood(e) Street(e)* 1573 *AddCh*, 1611–12 Orm², 1650 *ParlSurv*, 1692 *AddCh*, 'the (great-, little-, higher-) streets where wood was kept', from the stocks of wood fuel for the salt-boiling industry, *v.* wudu, stræt, lȳtel, grēat, uferra. Cf. Snow Hill *infra*.

LOST STREET-NAMES: *le Barberslone* 1440 Rich ('barber's lane', *v.* barber, lane); *le Crosse Pament* 1447, 1455, 1465 *AddCh* ('pavement near a cross',

v. cros, pavement. The cross was probably 'the greate stonne crosse...
standing...in the Churche Yarde of Wiche Malbanke' 1577 *AddCh* 43778);
Flessherowe 1394 Rich (either 'row of houses where meat is sold', or 'butchers'
row', from rāw with either flǣsc or flesshewer); *Floureslane* (*v. Flourescroft
infra*); *Heth Strete* 1526 *AddCh* ('heath street', *v.* hǣð, strǣt, probably near
Beam Heath *infra*, perhaps part of Beam St. *supra*); *Leccon strete* 14 *Sotheby*
(perhaps *Lecton*, for Leighton 29 *supra*, *v.* strǣt); (*le) Melestret(e)* 1434,
1465, 1467 *AddCh*, 1456, 1459 Rich, *Mole-* 1456, 1459 ib ('meal street',
v. me(o)lu, strǣt. Here was *le Melehall* 1467 *AddCh*, *-hill* 1469 *ib*, *v.* hall,
cf. *Meelhall* in Congleton 2 296); *Monkyslone* 1466 Rich, *le Munkeslone* 1468
Dav, (*le) Monk(e)s lone* 1470, 1516 Comb, *-lane* 1512 ib, 1597 AD, *le
Mounkeslane* 1604-5 Orm² ('monk's lane', *v.* munuc, lane, alluding to the
convent of Combermere Abbey 93 *infra*, which held land and salt-works in
Nantwich, cf. (*the) Munkes orchard infra*, and Monk's Lane 127 *infra*);
Ratunrowe 1445 Comb, *Raton-* 1449 Rich, 1454 Comb *et freq* with variant
spellings (*le-*), *-row*, *Ratten-*, to 1526 Comb, *Rotton Rowe* 1597 AD ('row
of houses infested with rats', *v.* raton, rāw. It was described in 1454 (Comb
22) as a street from the Churchyard to the beast-market in Beam St., and
Comb 4 identifies it with Pepper St. *supra*); *le Rethermarket* 1317 *AddCh*,
forum animalium 1454 Comb, (*-vocatum le Beme Street*) 1482 ib ('the cattle-
market', in Beam St. *supra*, *v.* hrīðer, market); *le Tayntre Yord* 1447 *Mainw*
('yard with a fuller's stretching-frame', *v.* tentour, geard); *Thevis lane*
1488-9 Orm² ('thief's lane', *v.* þeof, lane); (*le) Twych(h)ull* 1473, 1476, 1491
AddCh, *the Twichull lawne* 1520 *Sotheby*, *greate Twichill* 1625 *ib* ('the
narrow passage', from twychell, with grēat, lane).

LOST NAMES OF BUILDINGS: *le Boothall or le Courthowse* 1579 *Chol*, *le Booth
Hall alias dicto le Court Howse* e17 Orm² ('hall with booths in it', *v.* bōth,
hall, court, hūs. For *booth-hall* 'a great hall in which assizes are held, a town-
hall' Professor Löfvenberg cites *La Bothhall* (Shrewsbury Sa) 1324 Cl 79);
Cheney Hall (*v. infra*); *Dysart Buildings* 1794 Atlas, 1846 *TAMap* (between
Churchyard Side and South Crofts); *the Escheators Halle* 17 Orm² (*v.* hall);
the Gilde Hall of the Wich Malbank 1497 Rich, cf. *aula in cimiterio* 1445
Comb (*v.* gild-hall. ChetOS VIII 225, n.9, observes it was named R2 and
1461, was in the churchyard, and was made a school-house t. Eliz 1 after the
guild was suppressed); *le Gothehall* 1459 Rich; *le Hole howses* 1554 *MinAcct*
('houses in a hollow', *v.* hol¹, hūs); *the Hors Mylne* 1465, 1485, 1487 Comb,
-mele 1526 ib, *a horse mylne* 1578 *AddCh* ('mill driven by a horse', *v.* horse-
myln); *le Melehall* (*v. Melestrete supra*); *Ratunrowe* (*v. supra*); *capella Sancte
Anna super pontem* 1398 Orm² III 450, *St Anne's Chapel near the Bridge* 17 ib,
(cf. 'four shops which lately were on the bridge, with the Chapel' 1438-9 ib,
and 'There hath been a little chapel situate near this brine-seth, dedicated,
as some say, to St Anne' 1621 (1656) Orm² III 291. This appears to have
been an oratory on Nantwich Bridge, *v.* chapel(e)); *unum hospitium Sancti
Laurentii* 1354 Orm², *St Lawrence Chapel* 1489 Pat, *free chapel of St Lawrence*,
-Laurence, (*libera capella Sancti Laurentii, -enci*) 1499 ib, 1535 VE, 1548 Pat,
1556 Orm² (Sheaf¹ 38, describes it as a lazar-house in Welsh Row *supra*);
St Nicholas's Hospital (*v.* Hospital St. *supra*); *The Swan* (*in the highe town*)

1465, 1526 Comb (an inn destroyed in the great fire of Nantwich 1583, along with *The Ship*, *The Cock*, *The Bell*, *The Crane*, *The Hart's Horn* and *The Bear*, v. Sheaf[1] 1 346).

THE BARONY, BARONY RD, *Baronee* 1493 ChRR, cf. *le Barones medew(e)* 1363 *MinAcct*, 1439 Orm[2], 'land of the barony of Nantwich', 'the Baron's meadow', v. baronie, baroun, mǣd. This is the last trace of the extensive fee of the Malbanc family, *baronia Wichi Maubanci* 1252 RBE, *et freq passim* with variant spellings as for Nantwich *supra*. This great fee, almost co-extensive with Nantwich hundred (v. 1 *supra*), was shared out among three co-heiresses in 1342 (DKR xxxvii, Appendix ii, 478), and so disintegrated.

BEAM BRIDGE, v. 153 *infra*, cf. foll., and Beam St. *supra*.

BEAM HEATH (110–656526) [biːm]

> *boscus de Creche* c.1130 (1479) *Cott.* Faust. B VIII, H3 (1331) Ch, 1266 Dugd, (the common of Wich Malbanc called) *Creche* 1472 *AddCh*, *the Croach* 1621 (1656) Orm[2]
> *le Bem(e)heth* 1442 *Dav*, 1478, 1545 *AddCh*, *le beame heth(e)* 15 Rich, 1579 *AddCh*, *Beam Heath* 1719 Sheaf

'The mound, hill or barrow', v. crŭc[1] (Pr Welsh *crŭg*). The later name is 'heath at the Beam', from hǣð and Beam Bridge *supra*, cf. Beam St. *supra*. Beam Heath is now a district at the end of Beam St., but the name formerly described a considerable area in which Nantwich had common rights. Webb, 1621, describes 'a fine common, called *the Croach*, extending from the end of Beam-street by Weaver side to the length of a mile and a half...in breadth a quarter of a mile, where the inhabitants summer their cattle' (Orm[2] III 292), cf. Cow Fields *supra*. This extent is approximately that shown in Bry, 1831, including the northern and eastern parts of Alvaston township (v. 28 *supra*). The boundary of Beam Heath in Alvaston township was probably settled in the agreement of 1285 printed in Orm[2] III 451. The heath also extended into Wistaston township, cf. Critch Fd 48 *infra*.

LOTHBURNE (lost)

> *Lortebourn(e)* 1332, 1349 AD, *Lort(e)burne* 1397 Rich, (fons vocata) 1412 *AddCh*, (quadam cisterna vocata) 1456 *ib*, *Lortborn* 1422 *ib*, *Lorkborne* 1466 Rich

Le Lotheburne 1385 Comb *et freq* ib with variant spellings (*le-*, *the-*) *Loth(e)burn(e)* to 1525, (communis cisterna vocata-) 1516 Comb

Lottebarne 1547 *MinAcct*

'Dirty stream', *v.* lort(e), burna. This was a common drain running from near the churchyard into R. Weaver (cf. *the Commyn Syche* 1520 Comb, 'public watercourse', *v.* commun, sīc), and probably carried away the town's sewage. Cf. *Lorteburne* 193 *infra*.

SNOW HILL 1725 *AddCh*. *Snorehill* 1463 *ib et freq* with variant spelling *-hyll* to 1732 *ib*, *the Town Green or Snower-Hill* 1715 *ib*, *Snore alias Snow Hill* 1781 *ib*. As originally drafted, in terms of EPN and the Society's earlier volumes, the explanation of this p.n. was '"brushwood hill", *v.* snār, hyll, cf. Snower Hill Sr 284, Snow Hill StNLn 180, Snoreham Ess 217. Like Wood St. *supra* and Gorse Stacks (Chester) 326 *infra*, this was probably a fuel dump.' However, Professor Löfvenberg, and the correction of EPN 2 132 in JEPN 1 36 s.v. *snār, require that this etymology be rejected. Löfvenberg observes, 'As is shown by Ekwall StNLn 180–1 and DEPN s.n. Snoreham Ess, the OE word must have been *snor or *snōr, probably the latter in view of spellings with *-ou-*, *-ow-*. The origin of this word is not clear, but I am inclined to believe that the etymology suggested by Ekwall in StNLn is correct. The original meaning would be "something twisted or knotted", in a transferred sense "hill, hillock". For the sense-development cf. OE *wrǣst "something twisted" in Wrest Park Bd 162 (DEPN s.n.) and OE *wrāse "a knot, something twisted" in Wrose YW 3 267.' It seems likely that the el. *snār in EPN requires investigation or cancellation. An entry should be added to EPN 2 133 for *snōr OE 'something twisted or knotted', hence 'a (rough) hill', and then the series of p.ns. for which *snār has been adduced should be listed under *snōr.

WALL FIELDS FM, (*le*) *Wall(e)field*, *-fyld(e)*, *-filde* 1445, 1479 Comb, 1455, 1502, 1511 *AddCh*, *Walfyld* 1465 *ib*, *the Wallesfildes* 1470 *ib*, *le Lyttul-* & *le Morewalfield*, *-feild* 1474 Rich, 'field at a spring', *v.* wælla, feld, lȳtel, māra, cf. *William de Fonte* E1 *AddCh*, *William Attewalle* 1313 *ib*.

WYCH HOUSE BANK, [witʃ], 'hill where a "wich-house" stood', *v.* wych(e)-hous(e), banke, cf. *Wich(e) House Street(e)* (Middlewich, Northwich) 2 193, 242. The description 'wich-house', meaning 'a building in a wīc' is used here, as at Northwich and Middlewich, for a salt-boiling factory in a manufacturing town, cf. *Wychehous* 1356 *CampbCh, tres tenementa salina vocata Wychehowses* 1527 *ChCert, domus vocata Wychehouse* 1541 Dugd, and 'a cite, wich-house place, peice of ground or walling land commonly called or known by the name of an eighteene leads walling ground, with the wood-Roome thereunto belonging' 1692 *AddCh* 43831 (between Great & Little Wood St., i.e. First and Second Wood St. *supra*, where the 'wood-rooms' (*v.* rūm[1]) were, and cf. Walling Mdw *infra*). Brine from a central brine-pit (*le Brynseth* 1473 *AddCh, the Brine-seth* 1621 (1656) Orm[2], *v.* brīne, sēað), later known as *the old Biat* (1774 Orm[2] III 437, an account of well-dressing, *v.* biʒeate, cf. Byatts Ho 325 *infra*) was conduited to wich-houses and to open-air 'walling grounds' where stood the 'leads' (leaden 'walling'-pans, cf. dial. *wall* 'to boil (salt), to seethe'), cf. *le leede-, le leade ground* 1548 Pat, from OE lēad 'lead'. The other salt-wiches also had lead-smithies for the repairing of these pans, *v. le Leadsmythye*, Lead Smithy Street **2** 193, 241. DB mentions eight salt-pans in Nantwich, TRE, shared between the king and earl Edwin, and several others owned by men of the county. The abbeys of Chester and Combermere had salt-works here a.1093 and c.1130. Very few names of the eventually numerous wich-houses in Nantwich have been noted—*a wich house in Baywardesholt* 1454 Comb, *a wychhouse called Baywardesholt* 1470 ib, *a wych in-* 1499 ib, *a half wychhouse of six leads...adjoining the high road which is called Bayartesholt* 1468 ib (cf. Beaverhold *supra*); *salina quondam Johannis de Brodefeld* 1382 Chol; *le Courtwichehouse* 1511, 1513 Plea ('salt-factory belonging to, or making salt for use at, the court', *v.* court, wych(e)-hous(e)); *Hordernesalt* 1275 Misc ('salt for the store-house', *v.* hord-ærn, salt); *Le Owlewychehous* 1402 *AddCh* (perhaps 'the old wich-house', from ald); *St Mary Wyche-house* 1404 Sheaf, *the wych-house of St Mary* 1445, 1469 Comb (belonging to *the chapel of St Mary* 1410, 1466 ChRR, this factory was near *the bridge-end* 1469 Comb (Nantwich Bridge), which puts it near Wych House Bank). A *salina de Schavinton* is mentioned 1276 Ipm II 122, No. 196, but whether this was in Nantwich or at Shavington 69 *infra* is not clear. It may have been in Nantwich and belonged to Shavington manor, an arrangement found in the other salt-wiches, cf. **2** 193–4, 242–3. In DB the wīc at Nantwich was an enclave included between R. Weaver and a ditch (*fossa oppidi de Wico* c.1200 Facs 5 (2)). It is possible that this enclave was originally part of one of the adjacent townships, and

that its economic importance gave it independence, as Northwich
from Witton, or Middlewich from Newton, *v.* **2** 193, 243–4.

BROOKFIELD HO, 1846 *TA*.   CHENEY HALL (lost), *Chanuez hall in
Wixsterston* 1530 Orm² III 489, *Chayne Hall* (in *Wixstaston*) c.1557–8
ib 490, *Cheynye Halle* 1590 Sheaf (in Beam St.), *Cheyney Hall* 1590
Orm², *Cheney Hall* (*Barn*) 1788, 1797 Sheaf, 'hall of the *Cheyney*
(*Chanu*) family', *v.* hall, bere-ærn. This family were lords of
Wisterson 42 *infra*. The location of this house is doubtful. Whereas
the earlier references put it in Beam St. *supra*, the later ones (Sheaf¹
1 344, 361) place it near Love Lane and Barker St. *supra*. It is likely
that the Love Lane site was that of a barn belonging to Cheney Hall,
and that the hall itself, although in Nantwich township, was part of
Wisterson manor.   CLAN HO, *Clanhurst(e)* 1420, 1478, 1482
AddCh, (two fields called) *Clanhurstis* 1493 *ib*, *Great-* & *Little
Clanhurste* 1671 *ib*, 'clean wood-hill', i.e. free of undergrowth, *v.*
clæne, hyrst.   DAISY BANK.   DOVEHOUSE CROFT, cf. *le Dove-
hous Yarde* 1561 MainwB, *v.* dove-house, geard.   ELM HO.
FARFIELD HO, cf. *Far Field* 1846 *TA*.   HEATH COTTAGE (lost),
1831 Bry, named from Beam Heath *supra*.   HILLFIELD.   MARSH
LANE, *via que ducit versus Edlaston* 1439 Orm², *March Lane* 1643 ib,
Marsh Lane (*Field*) 1846 *TA*, cf. *the martchside* 1646 Sheaf, and
Marsh Fm 141 *infra*, *v.* mersc, lane, side, cf. Edleston 140 *supra*. In
1794 Atlas, the northern end of Marsh Lane is called *Marine Lane*.
NANTWICH BRIDGE, *le Wechebrugge* 1382 Chol, *the bridge end* 1445,
1469 Comb, *-brige*, *-brege* 1487, 1526 ib, *the bridge of Wich Malbank*
1479 *Chol*, *the brigge* 1538 *AddCh*, *Namptwich Bridge* 1621 Sheaf,
'the bridge at the wīc', *v.* wīc, brycg, ende¹, Nantwich *supra*.
NANTWICH MILL, *molendina de Wico Malbano* 1363 *MinAcct*, *v.*
myln, cf. Mill St. *supra*.   NEW TOWN, *v.* nīwe, toun.   PARK-
FIELD HO, *The Lodge* 1831 Bry, 1842 OS, *v.* loge.   SHREWBRIDGE
HALL FM, SHREWBRIDGE RD, cf. *Shrew Bridge House* 1831 Bry, 1842
OS, shown as Brine Baths Hotel 6″ OS, *v.* Shrewbridge 131 *infra*.
TOWNEND HO (lost), 1831 Bry, *the town's-end* 1621 (1656) Orm²,
Namptwich townes end 1646 Sheaf, *Townesend* 1711 ib, *Towns End*
1794 Atlas, *Townsend* 1819 Orm¹, at Welsh Row, near the boundary
with Acton 126 *infra*, 'at the end of the town', *v.* toun, ende¹.
VAUXHALL (HO), *Vauxhall* 1831 Bry, probably named from Vauxhall
Sr 24.   WILBRAHAMS ALMSHOUSES, *the Almshouses* 1671 *AddCh*,
cf. 'the late charitable erection of an alms-house for six poor aged

men, which Sir Roger Wilbraham, knight,. . .at the town's end, there new built. . .' 1621 (1656) Orm[2] III 292, cf. also Townend Ho *supra*, and *Wilbrahams Piece* 1846 *TA*, *v.* pece. The surname is pronounced [ˈwilbrəm]. WOODSIDE, 'the side of the wood', *v.* wudu, sīde.

FIELD-NAMES

The undated forms are 1846 *TA* 281. Of the others, 1286 is Cre, 1294 Ipm, 1330 Fine, 1363 *MinAcct*, 1369 *Tourn*, 1372 AD, 1382, 1695 *Chol*, 1400, 15, 1440, 1460 Rich, 1400[2], 1447 MainwB, 1428 ChRR, 1439, 1492, 1499, 1509, 1549, 1583, 1605, 1639, 1643 Orm[2], 1443[1], 1445, 1453, 1645, 1470, 1479, 1485, 1487, 1516, 1525 Comb, 1446, 1520, 1537, 1583, 1593 *Sotheby*, 1548 Pat, 1607 *Vern*, 1634, 1638, 1750 Sheaf, 1650 *ParlSurv*, 1690 *Dep*, 1731 *BW*, 1794 Atlas, 1831 Bry, 1842 OS, and the rest *AddCh*.

(*a*) Boosy Pasture (*v.* bōsig); Broad Lane Mdw (from brād 'broad', with either leyne 'a tract of land', or lane 'a lane'); Brown Hill(s) (*le Bromehull* 1439, cf. *Brom crofte* 1428, *v.* brōm, hyll, croft, cf. *le Brunehul(l)* 142 *infra*); Calf Croft (*v.* calf, croft); Causeway Mdw ('meadow at, or with, a causeway', *v.* caucie, mǣd); Clean Fd (*v.* clǣne); Eating House or Salt Lee Mdw (*Heatyng house yorde* 1545, *le heyting house* 1556, *Heatinge house meadowe* 1662, *Heating-House Meadow* 1750, perhaps named from a building in which brine was heated for evaporation, from *heating* (NED), and hūs, with geard, mǣd. The alternative name is from salt and lēah, cf. Salt or Walling Mdw *infra*); Footway Fd; Kingsley Fd (1794, *Kyngerley fielde* 1593, *Kings Ley* 1842, 'the king's meadow', *v.* cyning, lēah, cf. Kingsleyfield 145 *infra*); Leech Fd & Mdw (*v.* lǣc(c)); Mill Mdw (*the Mill Eye* 1695, *v.* myln, ēg, mǣd, cf. Nantwich Mill *supra*); The Moat Fd (cf. *the Motts* 1731, *v.* mote); Orchard Fd (*v.* orceard, cf. (*the*) *Munkes orchard infra*); Ox Pasture (*v.* oxa, pasture); Park (*v.* park); Pear Tree Fd & Mdw (*le Peartree Feilde* 1605, *Pearetree field and meadow* 1638); Ridley Fd (*Rideley field* 1400[2], *Rydleyfylde* 1439, 1549, *Ry-*, *Riddeleyfylde* 1440, 1460, *Ridley feld* 1509, '(field at) the cleared wood', *v.* (ge)ryd(d), lēah); St Anne's Croft (cf. *St Anne's chapel supra*); Salt Lee Mdw (cf. Eating House Mdw *supra*); Salt or Walling Mdw (probably a 'walling ground' where brine was 'walled' or seethed, cf. dial. *wall* 'to seethe'); Sea Pipe Mdw; Shoulder of Mutton Fd (*v.* 325 *infra*); Town Mdw (*v.* toun); Volunteers Fd; Walling Mdw (*v.* Salt or- *supra*).

(*b*) (*le*) *Mykule barne-place* 1445, 1479, *the berne yard* 1502 ('site of, and yard at, a barn', *v.* mikill, bere-ærn, place, geard); (*the*) *Beame medowe* (*v.* Beam Bridge 153 *infra*); *le Brodemed(we)*, *-medowe*, *-ewe* E1 (*v.* brād, mǣd); *Choucheresfeld* 1310 ('coucher's field', from the ME trade-name and surname *Couchur* 'a coucher' (NED, cf. Fransson 97) and feld); *Duneley Hill* 1639; *Flourescroft & -lane* H3 (*v.* croft, lane. Professor Löfvenberg notes the *-ou-* spelling and suggests the ME surname *Flour* (< OFr *flour*, *flur* 'flower') perhaps in the sense 'a maker of flour', *v.* Reaney s.n. *Flower*. Cf. Flowers Lane 29 *supra*, to which this, from *AddCh* 43385, may refer); *Foullake hull*

1369 ('(hill near) the foul watercourse', v. fūl, lacu, hyll); *Frensemonnes-ruydyng* 1286 ('Frenchman's clearing', v. Frenscheman, ryding); *Friday Cheste* 1492 (probably the name of a piece of ground in which some disputed manorial service was due on a Friday, v. Frīgedæg, cēast); *le forgge-, le frogg chanell* 1537, cf. *Frog Pooles* 1731 ('ditch, and pools, full of frogs', v. frogga, chanel, pōl¹, cf. Welsh Row *supra*); *Gigg-Hill* 1607 (v. gigge, hyll); *Godwynsley croft* 1439 (v. croft, cf, Gonsley Green 52 *infra*, here used manorially); *the Heathside* 1634 (v. hǣð, sīde); *Laueraunce-wall* l13, *Saynt Laurence Croft* 1548 ('well and croft belonging to St Lawrence' cf. *St Lawrence's chapel supra*, v. wælla, croft); *Lombercote* 1382 ('lambs' shed', v. lamb (gen. pl. lambra), cot); *le loode* (v. *Waterlode infra*); *le Mayfield* 1447; *le Medeynde* 1443, *le Medoende* 1448, *le Medowe ende* 1478 (v. mǣd, ende¹); *Meresichfeld* 1309 ('(field at) the boundary stream', v. (ge)mǣre, sīc, feld); *the mylnefield* 1578 (referring to the *Horse Mill supra*); *Mistelsich* (a certain ryuer called) 1520, *Missellsich* 1650 (from sīc, probably with mistal 'a cowshed'); *(the) Munkes orchard* 1443¹, 1453, *le Monkesorchard* 1498, 1525, cf *(le-, the-) Munkes-, Monkesyorde(s), -yardes* 1445, 1465, 1470, 1485 ('the monk's enclosures and orchard', v. munuc, geard, orceard, named from the monks of Combermere Abbey 93 *infra*, cf. *Monkyslone* st.n. *supra*); *le Nyne Buttes* 1548 (v. nigon, butte); *le Oldecroft* 1344, cf. *le Ooldeʒort* 1402 (v. ald, croft, geard); *Partriche Croft* 1502, 1511 ('partridge field', v. pertriche); *Prestham* c.1236, H3, (*inferior & superior*) *Prest(h)am* H3, 1318, *le Prestahameʒ* 1323, *Prestames* 1328 ('the priests' meadow(s)', v. prēost and hamm. The name is that of a group of fields in Nantwich adjoining Batherton 50 *infra & partly in Stapeley 73 infra*, about 110–658509); *Scratʒord* 1417 (a piece of land in Hospital St. *supra*, v. geard 'a yard, an enclosure', and scrætte 'a harlot', scratta 'an hermaphrodite', or skratti 'a goblin, a devil'); *Shoteshaws* (v. 1 6); *Stenkelescroft* 1338 (named after Thomas *Stenkel* of Nantwich, E1, 1338 *AddCh*, v. croft. The surname is from the ON pers.n. *Steinkell, -ketill*); *Stodleycross* 1363 ('(cross at) the clearing where there is a stud', v. stōd, lēah, cros); *Thakers croft* 15 ('thatcher's croft', from the ME trade-name *thak(k)er* 'a thatcher', cf. þak, þæc); *Tobuttes* 1309 ('two selions', v. twā, butte); *le Tolstok* 1294 (v. tol-stok, cf. *le Tolstok* 1316–17 Plea, quoted in NED s.v. *toll-stock*, for which this is an earlier instance. NED conjectures that this is the same as *toll-pin* 'a handle for a toll-dish'. It could have been a stocc 'a stump, a pillar', at which tolls were levied on salters at the Nantwich wīc, v. toln, cf. *Banners Stoope* 2 246); *Tomkynesfeld* 1372 ('Tomkin's field', from the ME pers.n. *Tomkin* (for *Thomas*) and feld); *Waterdelake* 1347, *Waterdeslake* 1400 ('Hwætrēd's stream', from the OE pers.n. *Hwætrēd* and lacu); *the Waterlode, le loode* 1583 ('the conduit', v. wæter, (ge)lād); *le Yheifeld* 1363, *le ʒayefeld* 1392, *le Yaefylde* 1446 (perhaps '(field at) the yew enclosure', from īw and (ge)hæg, with feld).

4. WILLASTON (110–6752).

This township was divided between Nantwich and Wybunbury parishes, v. 78 *infra*, cf. *Wisterson infra*. The arrangement of the material follows the boundaries given in Bry (1831).

WISTERSON (lost), approx. [ˈwistəsən]

Wistetestune 1086 DB

Wichtrichestona, Wythticheston 1096–1101 (1280) Chest, *Witrecheston* 1096–1101 ib

Wihcdrest' 1175 Facs 3 (Chest No. 487 reads *Woderstone*)

Wictredest' 1194 AddCh (p), *Wict(e)riddiston* c.1230–40, c.1250–60 Orm²

Wiarediston c.1230–40 Orm²

Wicretaist' c.1230–40 Orm²

Wicliddiston c.1230–40 Orm²

Wictreest' 1241 MRA (p)

Wyctristun c.1260 Orm², *Wictruston* 1316 ib, *-is-* 1515 Plea

Wystglteston 1260–72 (14) AddCh

Wit'ruston E1 Orm²

Wyghterston 1303 Orm² *et freq* with variant spellings *Wighters-, -urs-, Wyght(t)urs-, Wyghteres-, Wygthtres-, Wyghtres-, Wightres-, Whightres-, -ton(e)* to 1579 Dugd

Wisturnston 1316 Orm²

Wyzterston 1343 Orm², *Wys-* 1414 ib, *Wis-* 1606 Sheaf

Whigtreston 1350 Orm²

Wyterston(e) 1400 ChRR, CampbCh, *Wytereston* 1422 Orm²

Wyghtreton 1409 Plea, *Wigh-* 1468 MinAcct, *Whi-* 1507 *ib*

Wyghtreson 1418 Plea, *-terson* 1450 AddCh

Wyghterton other ways called Wyksterston 1442 Orm², *Wexturston* 1489 AddCh, *Wixsterston* 1505 ChRR, *Wiksterston alias Wyxtersterston* 1532 Plea

Wighstretton 1471, 1486 MinAcct, 1553 Pat, *Whistretton* 1488 MinAcct

Wightstretton 1486 MinAcct, *Whit(e)stretton* 1487, 1488 ib

Whitetreton 1507 MinAcct

Wixstaston 1511 AddCh, 1516 ChEx, 1553, 1557, 1559 Orm², *Wixtaston* 1557 ib, *Wigstaston* 1628 ib, 1702, AddCh, 1724 NotCestr

Wixs'ton 1512 Orm²

Wighsterston 1513 ChEx

Wighsterton 1513, 1515 ChEx

Wy- Wixsterton 1515, 1522 Plea, 1516 ChEx, *Wixterton* 1542 AddCh

Wictrison 1528 Plea

Wygsterston 1551 ChRR, *Wi-* 1579 Dugd
Wisterson 1819 Orm[1], 1860 White

'Wihtrēd's farm', from the OE pers.n. *Wihtrēd* and tūn. OE *Wihtrēdestūn, by numerous combinations of AN and ME assimilation, dissimilation, metathesis and elision in the groups *-htr(e)-*, *-r(e)d(e)s-*, *-(e)d(e)st-*, leads to a variety of forms. In some of them, the first el. has been identified with the OE pers.n. *Wihtrīc*. Orm[2] III 487 states that Willaston township, 'variously written Willaston, Wightreston, Wisterson, Wigstanton and Wistaston', is divided between Nantwich and Wybunbury parishes, and that it was originally two manors. The name of this part has been confused with that of the other, Willaston 78 *infra*, and of Wistaston 45 *infra*. *Wisterson* is here identified with the northern, Nantwich, half of Willaston township, because Birchin Lane *infra* was in *Wisterson* manor, and so was *Cheney Hall* 39 *supra* (near Beam St. in Nantwich). Moreover, the proximity of this half of Willaston to Wistaston 45 *infra* makes confusion of their names the more likely. Under Willaston 78 *infra*, the suffix '*-iuxta Alvandeston* (Alvaston)' may denote that part of the township which was in the manor of *Wisterson*.

BADDILEY GRANGE (lost), *Badileghgraunge* 1355 BRP (III 205, in the manor of *Badilegh*), 1357 ib (III 262, in *Wilaston*), *Badiley Grange* 1384 Chol, *Badyley Gra(u)nge* (in *Wylaston iuxta Alvandeston*) 1435, 1446 ChRR, *Badeley-* 1466, 1474, 1505 ib, *Badley-* 1471, 1507 MinAcct, 1547 Plea, 1553 Pat, 'grange belonging to the manor of Baddiley', *v*. grange, cf. Baddiley 124 *infra*.

ASHFIELDS. BIRCHEN LANE, 1831 Bry, *Birchenlane* (within the lordship of *Wixsterton*) 1542 AddCh, 'lane growing with birch-trees', *v*. bircen[2], lane. BRASSEY HALL, 1831 Bry, *v*. hall. This house appears to have been the home of a branch of the *Brescy* family, called 'of Moorfields', cf. Moorfields 79 *infra*, variously described as 'of Wisterson', 'of Willaston', and 'of Wistaston', *v*. Orm[2] III 494. CARTWRIGHT'S ROW, *v*. rāw. COLLEYS LANE, 1842 OS, *College Lane* 1831 Bry. CREWE RD, *Millstone Lane* 1842 OS, *Milstone-* 1845 *TA*, from either mylen-stān 'a millstone' or ModE *mile-stone*, with lane. DAIRY HOUSE FM, *v*. deierie, hūs. MILLSTONE LANE, *v*. Crewe Rd *supra*. WHITE HOUSE (LANE), *v*. hwīt, hūs. WILLOW FM.

FIELD-NAMES

The undated forms are 1845 *TA* 433. Of the others, 1314 is Barnes[1] 740, 1342 *Eyre*, 1343 Orm[2], 1348 ChRR, 1403 AD, 1697 *AddCh*.

(*a*) Bache (*v.* bæce[1]); Bully Wall Fd (*Bullwall Lands* 1697, apparently '(selions at) bull's-well', from bula and wælla, with land); Dunstall (probably from tūn-stall 'site of an enclosure or farmstead'); Kitchen Fd (*v.* cycene); Malpas Butts (*v.* butte, cf. Malpas 326 *infra*. There may have been a manorial interest); Marl Pit Fd (*v.* marle-pytt); The Park (*v.* park); Pratchit's Fd (cf. Pratchitt's Row 34 *supra*); Sand Croft; Way Fd (*v.* weg); (The) Webb (cf. *Quelbe* (? for *Quebbe*) c.1250–60 Orm[2] III 488, probably 'bog, marsh', from a side-form of OE cwabba, cf. MLG *quebbe* 'marsh, bog'); Windmill Fd (*Wyndmulnefeld* 1403, *v.* wind-mylne, feld).

(*b*) *Adgarescroft* 1342, 1348, *At'hgaves croft* 1343 ('Ēadgār's croft', from the OE pers.n. *Ēadgār* and croft); *Chanyeslee* 1314 ('wood or clearing belonging to one Cheney', from lēah and the surname *Chanu*, *Cheney*, cf. *Cheney Hall* 39 *supra*. This family were lords of *Wisterson*).

5. WOOLSTANWOOD (110–6756) ['wulsten-, 'wustən 'wud] older local ['uːstən-]

Wolfstanwod 1283 Pat (wood of-)

Wolstanwode a.1292 (1331) Plea, *Wlstanwod* 1292 Cl (park at), *Wulstonwode* 1292 Ipm, *Wolstanewod* 1294 ib *et freq* with variant spellings *Wolston(e)-*, *Woolstan-* (from 1428 ChRR), *-ston-*, *-Wod(d)e*, *-wo(o)d*, *-wounde*; *Wolston* 1393 ChRR, *Wolstanwood* called *Wostonwoode alias Oustonwoode* 1597 Orm[2]

Wolsta(u)neswode, -stones- 1294 Ipm

Woluestoneswod 1507 *MinAcct*

Westonwode alias Wolstonewode 1529 ChRR

Owstenwood 1550 ChRR, *Owestenwoodde* 1560 *Chol*, *Owston-wod* 1566 ChRR, *Owsteonwood* 1567 ib, *Oustonwoode* 1597 Orm[2]

Wostonwoode 1579 *Chol*, 1597 Orm[2], *Woostonwood* 1657 *AddCh* (*Woolston Wood alias*) *Oulston Wood* 1629 Orm[2]

'Wulfstān's wood', from the OE pers.n. *Wulfstān* and wudu. Cf. Wood Fm *infra* (*messuage called Woolstanwood* 1624 ChRR, *Woolstan Wood* 1831 Bry). The same pers.n. appears, with tūn, in *Wlfstaneston* 1286 *AddCh* 43971, *Wilstaneston* 1290 Court (p), a lost place in or near Wistaston 45 *infra*. The *Ow(e)st-*, *Oust-* spellings are due to the vocalization of *-l-* and *w-* with stress-shifting in the resultant diphthongs.

MARSHFIELD (BANK & BRIDGE) (110–674552), *Marchesford* E1 *AddCh*, *Marshford bridge* 1621 Sheaf, *Marchford-* 1656 Orm², *Marshfield Bridge* 1831 Bry, *-Bank* 1842 OS, probably 'ford at a boundary-mark', *v.* mercels, ford, banke, brycg. The *Marches-* form seems analogous with *Marchesden* 1246 for Marsden La 86.

BRASSEY BANK BRIDGE, cf. *Brassey Croft* 1839 *TA*, and Brassey Hall 43 *supra*. BUCKLEY MILL COTTAGE, *Leather or Buckley Mill* 1831 Bry, *Buckley Mill* 1842 OS, cf. 'the new mill of *Wolstanewode*' 1294 Ipm III 122, *v.* myln. *Buckley* is probably the surname from Bulkeley 325 *infra*. COPPENHALL LANE, leading to Monks Coppenhall 26 *supra*. FIELD FM. LODGEFIELD, cf. *Big-*, *Little Lodge* 1839 *TA*, *v.* loge. PYM'S LANE, *Narrow Lane* 1831 Bry, *v.* nearu, lane. WOOD FM, *v.* Woolstanwood *supra*. WOODLANDS.

FIELD-NAMES

The undated forms are 1839 *TA* 448.

(*a*) Broom Croft (*v.* brōm); Brush Fd (*v.* brusshe); Butty Fd (*v.* butty); Carriers Fd; Copthorn Fd (*v.* coppod, þorn); Crimmer Lane; Crutch Fd; Flat Fd(s) (*v.* flatr); Glade Fd; Hatch Croft (*v.* hæc(c)); Intake (*v.* inntak); Kiln Croft; Lady Fd (*v.* hlǣfdige); Leighton Fd (cf. Leighton 28 *supra*); Marl Croft & Fd; Mill Croft, Fd & Mdw; Moat Bank (*v.* mote); Pave Lake ('water-course with a paved bottom', *v.* paued(e), lacu); Pin Croft & Fd; Little Rough (*v.* rūh); Sand Fd; Stack Fd (*v.* stakkr); Stock Fd (*v.* stocc); Straw Fd (*v.* strēaw); Stubbs Fd (*v.* stubbe); Weaver Fd (from R. Weaver 1 38); Wood Bank (*v.* wudu, banke).

(*b*) *Huggeruydin* 1394 ChRR ('Hugge's cleared-land', from the ME pers.n. *Hugge* (Reaney s.n. *Hug*, from 1180), *v.* ryding, cf. *Huggeruding* 55 *infra*, Hug Bridge 1 55. Professor Löfvenberg and Dr von Feilitzen concur in rejecting Reaney's derivation of *Hugge* from OE *Ūhtrēd*. It is a pet-form of *Hugh*, *Hugo*, cf. Reaney s.nn. *Huggard*, *Huget*, *Huggin*, *Huggon*).

v. Wistaston

Wistaston was originally part of Wybunbury parish 48 *infra*, and became independent c.1299–1300 (NotCestr, *v.* ChetOS VIII 230).

1. WISTASTON (110–6853) ['wistastən] older local ['wistisn̩]

Wistanestune 1086 DB, *Wistaniston* 12 Dieul, c.1180 *AddCh et freq* with variant spellings *-tona*, *-tun*, *-don*, *Wy-* to 1355 *ib* (p), *Wi-*, *Wystan(e)ston* 1230 *ib* (p), *Chol* (p), 1249–65 Chest (p), 1289

Court (p) *et freq* with variant spellings *-tun, -stams-* (for *-stanis-*?),
-stauns- (for *-stanns-*?), *-stann(e)s-* to 1535 VE
Wystoneston 1220–40 Whall (p), *Vistonstun* c.1291 *AddCh*
Wystanton H3 (14) *AddCh et freq* to 1400 ChRR, *Wi-* 1469 Rich,
   Wistenton 1518 Orm²
Wytstaniston' 1270–80 *AddCh* (p)
Wynstaneston 1307 ChRR (p), *Winstanston* 1331 ib, *Wyn-* 1387
   Eyre
Wistastun 1314 *AddCh*, *-ton* 1421 ChRR *et freq*, *Wy-* 1396 ChRR
   et freq to 1653 Sheaf, *-tone* 1558 (1582) *AddCh*, *Whistaston* 1629
   Cre
Wynstanton 1348 ChRR (p), *Win-* 1515 Orm²
Wystalston 1516 Sheaf
Wystatston 1517 Sheaf
Wistason 1548 Pat, 1550 *MinAcct*, 1554, 1557 Pat, *Wisterson* 1660
   Sheaf, 1722 *AddCh*
Wigstanton 1601 ChRR, *Wigstaston* 1646 Sheaf
Whitaston 1616 Cre
Wisterton 1673 Sheaf
Whistonson 1804 Sheaf

'Wīgstān's farm', from the OE pers.n. *Wīgstān* and tūn. Certain
forms of this p.n. are confused with those of *Wisterson* 42 *supra*, and
this has led to mistaken identifications, cf. Orm² III 330 n. The
development of the *Wisterson* form is analogous with that of Austerson, Hunsterson 130, 65 *infra*.

WILCOTT'S HEATH (lost), 1860 White, *Wildecattesheth* 1354, 1375
Eyre, 1403 ChRR, *Wy-* 1444 Orm², *Wil(d)cat(t)s Heath* 1674 Sheaf,
'wild-cat's heath', *v.* wild-catt, hǣð. This place gave another local
surname to the Brescy family of Moorfields 79 *infra*, and in 1673
was described in the parish of *Wisterton* (Wistaston).

CHURCH HOUSE FM, *Church House* 1831 Bry, *v.* cirice.   GREEN
END FM, *v.* grēne², ende¹, cf. Wistaston Green *infra*.   HINGING
BANK, *v.* hangende.   HUNTSBANK FM, *Hunts Bank* 1831 Bry, from
banke, probably with a surname.   MANOR HO, *Mill Farm* 1831
Bry, *Mill House* 1839 *TA*, *Wistaston Old Hall* 1842 OS, cf. Wistaston
Hall & Mill *infra*.   MARSHFIELD BRIDGE, *v.* 45 *supra*.   MOAT-
HOUSE FM, near a moated site, cf. *Moat* 1839 *TA*, *v.* mote.   MOOR-
FIELDS, cf. *le moor* 1362 *AddCh*, *Moor Field* 1839 *TA*, *v.* mōr¹, feld,

cf. 79 *infra.* THE OAKLANDS. OLD COVERT, *Wistaston Rough*
1842 OS, *v.* rūh. OLD GORSE COVERT & FM, *Whin Cover* 1831
Bry, *Gorse Covert* 1842 OS, *v.* hvin, covert, gorst. RED HALL,
1831 Bry, probably from the colour of the brickwork, *v.* rēad, hall.
RIDDING LANE, cf. (*Big-, Far-, Little-*) *Ridding* 1839 *TA, v.* ryding.
ROBINSON'S CORNER, 1831 Bry. ROOKERYBANK COVERT.
SALANDER COVERT, cf. *Great & Little Sallinder* 1839 *TA,* 'wood
where the celandine grows', from dial. *sallender, saladine* 'the greater
celandine' and covert. SHOULDER OF MUTTON COVERT, cf.
Shoulder of Mutton 1839 *ib,* named from its shape, *v.* 325 *infra.*
TOLLGATE FM, cf. *Toll House* 1839 *ib,* a turnpike, *v.* toll-gate.
VALLEY RD, cf. The Valley 27 *supra,* Valley Brook 1 37. VINE-
TREE FM. WELLS GREEN (BRIDGE & BROOK), *Wells Green* 1831
Bry, 'green at the springs', *v.* wella, grēne[2], with brycg, brōc. The
brook joins Wistaston Brook *supra.* (LITTLE) WEST END, *West
End* 1766 *AddCh, v.* west, ende[1]. WHITEHOUSE FM, *v.* hwīt, hūs.
WISTASTON BRIDGE, 1621 Sheaf, *Winstanstonbrugge* 1368 *Tourn.*
WISTASTON BROOK, joins Valley Brook 1 37. WISTASTON GREEN,
1831 Bry. WISTASTON HALL, 1724 NotCestr. WISTASTON
MILL, 1831 Bry, *Wynstanston milne* 1429 *AddCh.* WISTASTON
VILLA, *The Rockwood* 1831 Bry (the house and a wood nearby), 'rook
wood', *v.* hrōc, wudu. YEWTREE FM.

FIELD-NAMES

The undated forms are 1839 *TA* 441. Of the others, l13 is *Chol,* 1286 Cre,
1303 Orm[2], 1336 Plea, 1356 *Eyre,* 1385 (1524) Comb, 1460 ChRR, 1550
MinAcct, 1831 Bry, and the rest *AddCh.*

(*a*) Bache (*v.* bæce[1]); Bank(s); Beach (*v.* bece[1]); Bearfotts; Beverlong
(probably 'bean furlong', from bēan and furlang); Bone Fd (*v.* bān, cf. bone-
dust); Burnt Mdw (*v.* brende[2]); Causeway Mdw (*v.* caucie); Clemley (*Clemly
Park* 1744. This is a type of f.n. which appears frequently in the *TA* lists for
central and west Ch, as Cleml(e)y-, -lie (Park, Heys, Field) (15 examples),
with variants Clemn- (2), Clum- (3), Clom- (2), Clomn- (1). The -*n*- seems
epenthetic. The same first el. appears in Clam Croft (1), Clem Park (3),
Clemn Patch (1) and in Clemhunger 175 *infra,* Clamhunger, -hanger,
Clemonga 2 52, 85, 70. Similar names appear in Db, cf. Clemley Park, Clam
Park Db 142, 305, 759, for which a derivation from ModEdial. *clam, clem*
'to starve' is suggested. But the forms *clam-, clem-, clom-, clum-* in the Ch
series suggests clām (cf. *cloam* NED) 'mud, clay', or a derivative OE
*clǽme 'a muddy, damp, clayey place', or OE **clǽmig* (cf. *clammy* NED)
'muddy, clayey, damp', cf. ModEdial. *cleam, clame* 'to daub', *clam* 'wet,
cold, sticky, clammy' (NED, EDD); *v.* lēah (cf. ModEdial. *ley* 'a pasture'),

park (cf. pearroc 'a paddock, a small enclosure'), (ge)hæg, feld, croft, pacche); College Fd; Common Fd; The Coppy (*v.* copis); Cote Fd (*v.* cot); Critch Fd (*Creche in parochia de Wystaston* 1550, *v.* cruc[1] (Pr Welsh *crūg*) and Beam Heath 36 *supra*); Day(s) Math (*v.* day-math); Dyers Croft (cf. *Dye House* 1831); Fallow Fd (*v.* fealu); Flax Croft (cf. *les flax yordes* 1498, *the Flaxeyardes Landes* 1550, *v.* fleax, geard); Goody Moors; Hall Fd; the Holmes heys 1728 (probably from the surname *Holmes* and (ge)hæg); Long Humbless; Illages; Intake (*v.* inntak); Kitchen Fd; Long Butts; Marl Fd; Marsh; Mill Pool (cf. *piscarium apud le Flodegates* 1429, *v.* flōd-yate, myln, pōl[1]); Minshull's Wood 1700 (cf. Richard *Minshull* of Wistaston 1716 *AddCh*); Old Road (*v.* ald, rād); Ox Fd; Patch; Peaseall Fd (*v.* pise, halh); Rabbit Fds; Rail Fd (*v.* rail(e)); Big- & Little Rough (*v.* rūh); Slang (*v.* slang); Sprink ('a young wood', *v.* spring); Swan Fd (*the Swanground* 1690, -*Swann-* 1729, *v.* swān[2]); Three Penny Fd (named from a rent or a purchase, *v.* peni(n)g); Willston Fd (cf. Willaston 78 *infra*); Within Fd (*v.* wiðegn); Wood (Fd) (cf. *de Bosco* l13 (p), *del Wode* 1336 (p) *et freq, v.* wudu).

(*b*) *Bradefeld* H3, 1295 (p), *-feld* c.1287, 1291, (*-in Wy-, Wistan(e)ston*) 1302, 1353, *Morebradefeld* 1318, *Brodefield* 1385 (1524) (p), *-felde* 1460 (p), ('broad field' or 'broad tract of open land', *v.* brād, feld); *Cochenardeshay* 1329, 1337, *Cochin-* 1434 (*v.* (ge)hæg 'an enclosure'; the first el. may be either a personal description or a surname, e.g. ME **Cokaygnard*, OFr **Coquaignard* 'a cockney', from cokaygne and the adj. suffix *-ard* NED, but it could be of French origin, cf. the French surname *Cochinart, v.* A. Dauzat, *Dictionnaire des noms de famille* 145); *Gillecroft* c.1287 ('Gilli's croft', from the ON pers.n. *Gilli* (OIr **Gilla*) and croft); *Hanewelle* E1 (p), *Hanewall* (lit. *Haue-*) 1286 (p) ('cock's well or spring', *v.* hana, wella, wælla); *Haywardes Ruydinges* 1337 ('the hayward's clearing', *v.* hei-ward, ryding); *le Oldelee* 1303 ('the old clearing', *v.* ald, lēah); *parcum de Wystanton* H3 (14), 1329, *le park(e)* 1362, 1434 (*v.* park); *Wlfstaneston* (*v.* Woolstanwood 44 *supra*).

vi. Wybunbury

The ecclesiastical parish of Wybunbury originally included Audlem, Coppenhall and Wistaston parishes 82 *infra*, 22, 45 *supra*, and perhaps Baddiley 124 *infra*, as well as the following townships, 1. Basford, 2. Batherton, 3. Blakenhall, 4. Bridgemere, 5. Checkley cum Wrinehill (most of Wrinehill is in St), 6. Chorlton, 7. Doddington, 8. Hatherton, 9. Hough, 10. Hunsterson, 11. Lea, 12. Rope, 13. Shavington cum Gresty, 14. Stapeley, 15. Walgherton, 16. Weston, 17. part of Willaston (the other part is in Nantwich parish 41 *supra*), 18. Wybunbury.

1. BASFORD (HALL) (110–718522) ['basfəd]

Berchesford 1086 DB

Barkis-, Barkesford 1260 Court (p), l13 *Chol*, 1296 Plea *et freq* with variant spellings *-ys-, -fort, -forde* to 1579 *Chol, Barksford*

1296 Plea (p), *Barxeford* 1457 *Chol*, (*le manoire de Barkesford*) 1398 *ib*

Barkeford 1307 Plea, E3 *Rental* (p), 1546 Dugd, *Barcford* 1315 Plea, 16 Barnes[1]

Basforth 1392 Pat (p), *-forde* 1488 ChRR, (*Barkesforde alias-*) 1579 *Chol*, *-ford* 1521 *ib*, (*-bridge*) 1621 Sheaf, (*-Hall*) 1724 NotCestr

Barsford 1466 Comb (p), 1478 *Chol*, 1488, 1490 ChRR, *-forde* 1512 *Chol*

Baronsford (for *Barcus-*?) 1479 *Chol*

Backisford, Backes-, Bakkesforde 1508, 1518, 1528 *Chol*

The final el. is ford 'a ford'. The first el. is obscure. It may represent the same OE pers.n. *Beorcol* as appears in Basford and Baswich St. In those p.ns., Dr J. P. Oakden reports forms without -*l*- appearing amongst those with it. In the Ch material -*l*- never appears, and this supports Ekwall's suggestion (DEPN) for Basford Ch, i.e. **beorc** (gen.sg. **beorce**) 'a birch tree', with an intrusive -*s*-, as in Berkesden Hrt 171. However, the early and persistent -*a*- spelling is against **beorc**, and the ON pers.n. *Bǫrkr, Barkr*, with ME gen.sg. -*es*, might well explain this Ch p.n., cf. Barkisland WRY 3 57. If this is so, Basford (and possibly also Batherton 50 *infra*) is to be interpreted as an instance of Scand influence.

BACK LANE, 'outlying lane', *v.* **back, lane**. It is the boundary with Shavington cum Gresty 69 *infra*.   BASFORD BROOK (> Gresty Brook 69 *infra*), cf. Brook Fd *infra*, Mere Gutter 1 31.   BURROW COPPICE, *Barrow Gorse* 1831 Bry, *The Burrough* 1838 *TA*, *The Burrow Rough* 1842 OS, cf. *Borowehopis* H8 *Surv*, 'burrow hollows', *v.* **borow, hop**[1], cf. *Hopton infra*.   CASEY LANE, *The Casey* 1831 Bry, 'the causeway', *v.* **caucie**.   DAIRY HO, *v.* **deierie**.   DUNGE COTTAGES, *The Dunge* 1831 ib, 'manured land', *v.* **dyncge**.   THE SUTCH, *The Such* 1831 ib, cf. *Sych Croft* 1838 *TA*, 'the drain', *v.* **sīc**.

FIELD-NAMES

The undated forms are 1838 *TA* 42. Of the others, 1260 is Court, 1308, 1391 ChRR, 1371, 1398 *Chol*, H8 *Surv*, 1831 Bry, 1842 OS.

(a) Basford Wd (1842, *Basford Heath Wood* 1831, cf. *le Dychetheth infra*, *v.* **hǣð, wudu**); Black Croft; Brook Fd (*Brokefyld* 1398, *v.* **brōc, feld**); Clay Fd; Common Fd; Dirty Mdw; Dog Lawn; Feuellens, -ans ('a few elder-trees', *v.* **fēawe, ellern**); Finger Post Croft; The Five Shillings (named from a rent or a purchase, *v.* 325 *infra*); Gresty Mdw, Long Gresty (cf. *Graysty-*

heth 1398, *v.* hǣð, cf. Gresty 69 *infra*); Old Intack (*v.* inntak); Lea Fd; Long Butts; Marl Fd; Mill Fd (*le Mulnefeld* 1371, *v.* myln, feld); Moat Fd (*v.* mote); New England (*v.* 325 *infra*); Patch; Penlingtons Wd; Pool Fd; Sand Fd; Shoulder of Mutton (*v.* 325 *infra*); Sloppy Fd (*v.* sloppy); Spring Fd; Street Fd (*v.* strǣt); Way Fd (*v.* weg); White Fd Mdw; Wood Fd.

(*b*) *Annottusfyld* 1398 ('Annott's field', from the ME fem. pers.n. *Annott*, diminutive of *Anne*, and feld); *le Blomeresfeld* 1371, *le Blom'fyld* 1398 ('the ironworker's field', from the ME occupation-name blomere (cf. Fransson 144) and feld); *Bolyntones Acres* 1398 ('ploughlands belonging to one Bollington', *v.* æcer, cf. Bollington 1 187, 2 43); *le Bothefyld* 1398 ('field at a herdsman's booth', *v.* bōth, feld); *Brouestres croft* 1398 ('Brewster's, or the brewster's croft', from the ME occupation-name brewstere, fem. of brewere, and croft); *Caluerhey* 1398 ('calves' enclosure', *v.* calf (gen.pl. calfra), (ge)hæg); *Clarotuscroft* 1398 ('Clarot's croft', from the ME fem. pers.n. *Clarot*, diminutive of *Clara*, *Clare*, and croft); *le Cowehey* 1398 (*v.* cū, (ge)hæg); *le Dychetheth* 1398 ('heath with ditches', *v.* diched, hǣð); *la Forde* H8 (p) (*v.* ford); *le halis* 1260 ('the nooks', *v.* halh); *Harecourt terres* 1398 (lands belonging to one Harcourt); *Herdemonescroft* 1398 ('herdsman's croft', *v.* heorde-mon, croft); *la hom* H8 (p) (*v.* hamm 'a paddock'); *Hopton* H8 ('farm or enclosure in a hollow', *v.* hop¹, tūn, cf. Burrow Coppice *supra*); *le houer Flat* 1398 ('the higher plot of ground', *v.* uferra, flat); *le Hoxhey* 1398 (*v.* oxa, (ge)hæg); *Mydulfyld* 1398 (*v.* middel, feld); *le Parrok* 1398 (*v.* pearroc); *Platteforlong'* 1398 ('furlong near a footbridge', *v.* plat¹, furlang); *Rohecroft, le Roherudyng* 1398 ('rough croft and clearing', *v.* rūh, croft, ryding); *le moleyn de Schawe* 1398 (*v.* sceaga, Crotia Mill 76 *infra*); *Schaynton'fyld* 1398 ('field near, or belonging to, Shavington 69 *infra*', *v.* feld); *Stillerydyng* 1398 (apparently 'peaceful clearing', from stille and ryding); *le Wall* 1308 (p), *atte Wall* 1391 (p) (*v.* wælla 'a well, a spring'); *le Quyteleche Flat, le Quitesechemewdo* 1398 ('(flat piece of ground, meadow, at) the white watercourse', from hwīt and lece, sīc, with flat, mǣd).

2. BATHERTON (HALL & MILL) (110–6650) [ˈbaþə(r)tn̩]

Berdeltune 1086 DB

Bertherton l12 *AddCh* (p), H3 *ib* et freq with variant spellings *-ir-*, *-ur-*, *-tun* to 1522 Plea, (*-iuxta Stapelegh*) 1312 Plea, (molendinum de-) 1354 *Eyre*, Berterton 1400 Pat, Berderton 1522 Plea

Bartherton H3 *AddCh*, 1621 (1656) Orm², 1624 ChRR, 1724 NotCestr, 1838 *TA*, Barterton 1600 Sheaf, (*-Hall*) 1845 ChetOS VIII, *Barderton* 1605 *Chol*

Betherton 1283 Ipm, 1293 Plea, 1309 Pat, 1310 Cl

Bertheringtone 1283 Sheaf³ 26 (5877) (lit. *Berch-*)

Berdynton 1293 Plea

Bethtirton 1299 Pat

Bertheton (molendinum de) 1351 *Eyre*

Bretherton 1468 *MinAcct*
Batherton 1831 Bry, 1842 OS

The final el. is tūn 'an enclosure, a farm'. The first el. is probably a pers.n., but the original form is uncertain. DEPN suggests the OE fem. pers.n. *Beornþrȳþ*, but ON fem. *Bergþóra* would equally well account for the lack of a genitive inflexion in *-es*. Barnes[1] 673 suggests an uninflected-genitive construction from the OE pers.n. *Beorhthere*, but ON *Bergþórr* would do as well here, and either would make this p.n. analogous with Barnton & Bartington 2 105, 106. In fact, the material for Bartington, Batherton and Barnton is similar in many respects. The forms *Bertheringtone, Berdynton* are evidence of an alternative -ingtūn construction for Batherton. The *-l-* in the DB spelling is AN substitution for *-r-*. In Batherton, the forms are rather more representative of the ON fem. pers.n. *Bergþóra* than are those in the other p.ns. However, this district, unlike that of Bartington and Barnton, does not contain many other Anglo-Norse p.ns. (cf. Basford 48 *supra*), and it might be rash to suppose an ON pers.n. here. Ekwall's suggestion of the OE fem. pers.n. *Beornþrȳþ* seems very probable.

BATHERTON DAIRY HO, *The Dairy* 1831 Bry.   BROAD LANE, cf. 72 *infra*.

FIELD-NAMES

The undated forms are 1838 *TA* 38.

(*a*) Artle Mdw (cf. Artle Brook **1** 13); Bail Fd & Lane; Bell Lane; Brook Mdw; Broomy Wd (*v.* brōmig); The Coppy (*v.* copis); Flash Mdw (*v.* flasshe); Goldsmiths Croft; Intack (*v.* inntak); Lady Hill (*v.* hlǣfdige); Lamb Fd (*v.* lamb); Milking Bank (*v.* milking); Moat Croft (*v.* mote); Nants Fd ('aunt's field', *v.* aunt); Ox Pasture; Weaver Mdw (cf. R. Weaver **1** 38); White Fd & Lane; Wood Fd.

(*b*) *Holthemedwe* H3 *AddCh* ('meadow at a wood', *v.* holt, mǣd); *Sparchemedue* c.1236 *ib* ('meadow at the brush-wood', *v.* spearca, mǣd).

3. BLAKENHALL (110–7247) [ˈblækənɔːl, ˈblæknɔːl]

Blachenhale 1086 DB, 1316, 1581 Orm[2], *Blakenhale* c.1200 Facs
 (p) *et freq* with variant spelling *Blakenale* to 1510 Plea
Blaken(h)all c.1188–1216 MidCh (p) *et freq* with variant spellings
 -(*h*)*al*, -*hall(e)*, *Blakin-*, *Blachen-*, *Blacken-*
Blaginghale 13 Dieul
le Blake Halch 1260 Court 24
Blakenald 1378 ChRR

Blaknall 1188 (17) Tab, 1396 Pat, 1468 *Outl*, 1527 *ChCert*, 1561
Orm², 1584 ChRR, *Blaknoll* 1695 *Chol*

'At the black nook', *v.* blæc (wk.dat.sg. blacan), halh (dat.sg.
hale). The place lies in a valley opening into that of Checkley Brook.

GONSLEY GREEN (110–730488)

Godewyneslegh 1311 Orm² *et freq* with variant spellings *God(e)-*
wyn(e)s-, -win(e)s-, -wen(e)s-, -ley(e), -leghe to 1583 ib, *Goodwin's*
ley 1646 Sheaf
Codwynesleye 1341 *Eyre*
Goddenesley 1429 MainwB, *Godunsley* 1445 Plea
Gonsley Green 1831 Bry

'Gōdwine's wood or clearing', from the OE pers.n. *Gōdwine* and
lēah, with grēne² 'a green'. Cf. *Godwynsley Croft* 41 *supra*.

ASH COPPICE, *Ash Rough* 1831 Bry, *v.* æsc, copis, rūh.   BETLEY
(LITTLE) MERE, *Betley Great-* & *-Little Mere* 1831 Bry, named from
Betley St, *v.* grēat, lȳtel, mere¹.   BLAKENHALL MOSS, 1831 ib, *v.*
mos.   CHECKLEY BRIDGE, 1831 ib, cf. Checkley 56 *infra*.   COPP-
ICE BANK, 1813 ib.   DEN COPPICE, FM & LANE, HIGHER DEN, (*The*)
Den 1831 ib, 1842 OS, *The Dens*, *Den Farm* & *Cottage* 1842 *TA*,
probably from denu 'a valley', but denn 'a den' is possible.
DODDINGTON MILL FM, cf. Doddington Mill 61 *infra*.   THE
FIELDS, 1831 Bry, *v.* feld.   GRANGE FM, *v.* grange.   HALFMOON
FM, *Shortley Cross* 1831 ib, *Shortleys Cross* 1844 *TAMap*, from either
a surname *Shortley* or a p.n. 'short clearing' (*v.* sc(e)ort, lēah), with
cros.   HAREHILL ROUGH, 1831 Bry, *Herons Rough* 1842 OS, from
hara and hyll, with rūh.   MANOR FM.   MILL COVERT & HO, cf.
Doddington Mill 61 *infra*.   ROBIN KNIGHT'S (LITTLE) ROUGH, *v.* rūh.

FIELD-NAMES

The undated forms are 1842 *TA* 56.

(*a*) Acre; Annuity Mdw (probably a meadow endowing a pension); Bake-
house Croft; Bargans Fd; Bean Yard (*v.* bēan, geard); Big-, Far- Near- &
Great Birch (apparently from birce 'a birch-tree', but possibly from bryce
'land broken-in for cultivation', and the same as *le Mukele Bruche* 1288 AD,
Mucklebruche 113 (18) Sheaf, *v.* mycel, bryce); Black Acre; Blakenhall Moor
(*v.* mōr¹, cf. Blakenhall Moss *supra*); Blythe Fd; Branley Fd; Broad Fd(s);
Broom Fds (*v.* brōm); The Burnt Earth (*v.* brende², eorðe); The Butts;
Chorlton Mdw (cf. Chorlton 59 *infra*); Church End, Fd & Mead (*v.*
cirice, ende¹); Claimers; Cote Fd (*v.* cot); Cymet Mdw; Doghurst Mdw
('dog's wood', *v.* dogga, hyrst); The Drains (*v.* drain); Drumble Plantation
(dial. *drumble* 'a wooded ravine', cf. dumbel); Five Shillingsworth (probably

named from a rent or purchase, cf. 325 *infra*, *v.* shilling-worth); The Flatts; Footmans Way; Foxley Fd ('fox wood', *v.* fox, lēah); Furndol (probably 'ferny dole', *v.* fearn, dāl); Glade Bank (*v.* glǣd³); Greasty (cf. Gresty 69 *infra*); Green Lane; Hales (*v.* halh); Higher Hayward 1844 *TAMap*; Hemp Butts (*v.* hænep, butte); High Lane; Hob Fd (*v.* hobb(e)); Hunger Hill (*v.* hungor); Intack, Intake (*v.* inntak); Island; James Reins Heath (*v.* rein, hǣð); Kiln Fd (*v.* cyln); Luggraves, Luzgraves (*v.* grǣfe 'a grove'. The first el. might be lūs 'a louse', with the *s* voiced or elided before *-g*); Mablet; Marl Fd(s) (*v.* marle); The Moor(s) (*v.* mōr¹); New Hay (*v.* nīwe, (ge)hǣg); Old Ditch; Old Hill; Pannel; Patch; Pentie Yard; Pinfold Croft (*v.* pyndfald); Plain Hill; Plex Fd (*v.* plek); Plymbarrows ('plum-tree wood', *v.* plȳme, bearu); Pool Stead (*v.* pōl-stede); Randelow Mdw (cf. Randilow Fm 58 *infra* in the adjoining township); Raven Fd (*v.* hræfn); Round Crop (*v.* cropp(a)); Sand Hills; Sheep Shaw (*v.* scēp, sceaga); Shut Hay (*v.* scēat, (ge)hæg); Slam, Slam Bank (*v.* slump, banke, cf. Slum Wd 2 321–2); Slang (*v.* slang); Small Lane ('narrow lane', *v.* smæl, lane); Snape (*v.* snæp or snap); Snow Fd (*v.* snōr); Sprink (*v.* spring 'a young wood'); Stockings (*v.* stoccing); Swine Bank (*v.* swīn¹, banke); Town Barn Mdw, Town Fd(s), Townsend (*v.* toun, bere-ærn, feld, ende¹); Way Fd (*v.* weg); Well Crofts (*v.* wella); White Butts (*v.* hwīt, butte); Winter Corn Fd; Withy Mdw (*v.* wīðig); Far-, Little-, Middle- & Near Wd (cf. *Higher Woods* 1831 Bry); Big & Little Yell (*v.* helde 'a slope, a declivity').

(*b*) *le Mukele Bruche* (*v.* Birch *supra*).

4. BRIDGEMERE (FM & HALL) (110–7145) [¹bridʒmiːə(r)]

> *Bridesmere* H3 *AddCh*, 1372, 1413 Plea, 1429 Tab, -*meire* 1560
> Orm², *Brydesmere* 1481 ChRR
> *Briddesmere* 1234 Tab *et freq* with variant spellings *Briddis*-,
> *Bryddes*-, -*ys*-, -*mer'*, -*meyre*, -*meire*, -*meare* to 1584 ChRR
> *Bryddemere* 1241 MRA (p), *Bridmere mara* 1299 IpmR
> *Brisdismere* 1287 Court (p)
> *Bridsmere* 1296 Plea, *Bryds*- 1558 *AddCh*
> *Bridgmeir* 1589 Orm², *Bridgemere* 1621 (1656) Orm² *et freq* with
> variant spellings *Bridg(e)*-, -*meare*, -*meyre*, -*meire*
> *Bridgemore* 1594 Plea

'Lake frequented by birds', *v.* bridd (gen.sg. briddes, gen.pl. bridda), mere¹. The mere no longer exists.

BRUNESHURST (lost)

> *Bruneshurst* H3 *AddCh*, 1275, 1296, 1299 Cl, 1341 *Eyre* (p), -*e* 1299
> Cl, *Brunnes*- 1295 Ipm, *Brounes*- 1274, 1299 ib, 1316 Plea (p),
> *Brones*- 1276 Ipm, 1316 Plea, *Brounhurst* 1304 Chamb (p)
> *Bromshurst* 1260 Court, *Bromes*- 1308 Ipm

'Brūn's wooded hill', from the OE pers.n. *Brūn* and **hyrst**. This was the site of a toll-passage usually held in conjunction with that at Swanbach in Audlem 84 *infra*, and the similarity of the names might suggest Brown's Bank 103 *infra*, in Newhall but not far from Swanbach. However, *Bruneshurst* might well have been some distance from Swanbach, as the toll-passage of Lawton-Gate **2** 320, in Church Lawton, was held in conjunction with those of *Huggebrugge* (cf. Hug Bridge **1** 55) and Nantwich 30 *supra*, *v.* Hewitt 71. Moreover, Brown's Bank is a name of fairly recent origin, analogous with *Bruneshurst*, but not identical. Cf. Brownmoss 66 *infra*. The location of *Bruneshurst* near or in Bridgemere is suggested by their association in H3 *AddCh* 51455 'the house at the clough between Bridgemere and *Bruneshurst*', and in 1316 Plea (DKR XXVII 111) where the two surnames appear together, cf. *Donnington*, under Doddington 61 *infra*. Further, in 1313 *AddCh* 51457 a road *Lymestrete* is the boundary of a piece of land in Bridgemere. This is 'main road to the Lyme' from **strǣt** and *The Lyme* **1** 2, cf. Street Fd *infra*, *v.* **1** 48 (route XXVII). The road is that from Woore Sa towards Nantwich, cf. Pepperstreet Moss 66 *infra*. Such a road, from the border of the palatine county to a salt-wich, would be a likely place for a toll-passage. Swanbach, the toll-passage complementary to *Bruneshurst*, would cover the road from Market Drayton Sa to Nantwich, *v.* **1** 48 (route XXVI).

HARROW'S WOOD, 1842 OS, *Harwars Wood* 1831 Bry, 1842 *TA*. LEA'S WOOD, *Leas Wood* 1842 OS.   LEY GROUND FM, cf. *Doddington Ley*, *Ley Ground* 1842 *TA* 146, 62 *infra*, from ModE *ley* (cf. lēah, lǣs) 'a pasture'.   PARRAH GREEN [para], (*Croft*) 1842 *TA*, *Parah Croft* 1600 Vern, *Parry Green* 1831 Bry, -*Field* 1842 *TA*, perhaps from **pearroc** 'a fence enclosing a piece of ground, a paddock', *v.* **grēne**[2], **croft**, **feld**.   PRINCE HILL, *Prince's Hill* 1831 Bry, from **hyll**, perhaps with a surname *Prince*.   THREEPER'S DRUMBLE, cf. *Thrippers Lane* 1831 Bry, *Threapers Field, Meadow & Wood* 1842 *TA*, from either ModE and dial. *threeper, threaper,* 'one who disputes' (*v.* **prēapere**, cf. **prēap**, -**ere**[1]), or a p.n. 'disputed hill' from **prēap** and **hyrst** (cf. Threaphurst **1** 288) and dial. *drumble* 'a wooded ravine' (cf. **dumbel**).   WHEEL GREEN, 1673 Vern, *Will Green* 1831 Bry, *v.* **hwēol**, **grēne**[2]. The allusion may be to a turning of the road here below the exit from Threeper's Drumble *supra*.   YEWTREE FM, cf. *Yew Tree Hey* 1842 *TA*.

FIELD-NAMES

The undated forms are 1842 *TA* 70. Of the others, 1673 is *Vern*, 1831 Bry, and the rest *AddCh*.

(*a*) Bache Bank (*v.* bæce¹); Back Lane 1831; the Barons Yards 1673 (*v.* baroun, geard); Big Beach Bank (*v.* bece¹); Birch Wd; Black Acre; Blake Fd (*v.* blæc); Breach Mdw (*v.* brēc); Breezes Green 1831 (*v.* brēosa); Brinshall; Clinton Park; Cote Croft (*v.* cot); Cow Wd, Cow Wood Moss (*v.* cū, wudu, mos, cf. Ox Wd *infra*); Cross Gate; Dearnhall, Darnhill (perhaps 'secluded nook', from derne and halh, cf. Darnhall 168 *infra*); Demberley; Downfall (*v.* 325 *infra*); Ermer(s) Green; Flash Mdw (cf. *Woore Flash* 1831, and Flash Fm in Woore Sa, *v.* flasshe 'a swamp', dial. *flash* 'a shallow water'. The name refers to the low ground and the stream at 110–725435); Green Moor; Hanmer Mdw; Hare Croft & Hill (*v.* hara); Hell Hole (*v.* hell, hol¹); Hemp Butts; Big & Little Hey (*v.* (ge)hæg); Hollins Bank (*v.* holegn); Howcroft Rough (*v.* hol¹, croft, rūh); Intake (*v.* inntak); Kiln Croft; Lane Patch; Leamoor (*v.* lēah, mōr¹); Long Butts; Marl Fd; Mollingham Fd (it is not evident whether this represents a surname or a lost p.n. in -ingahām); Moody Wall (perhaps 'muddy spring', *v.* muddig, wælla); Moseley Moss, Moss Croft, Mossley Mdw ((*le*) *Mosileg'* 1313, 1322, *mossa de Briddesmere* 1322, 'mossy clearing', *v.* mos, mosig, lēah); Ox Wd & Yard (*v.* oxa, wudu, geard. The significance of *Wood* here and in Cow Wd *supra* is not clear, since neither is near woodland); Patch; Pentongue ('projecting piece of ground with a fold on it', *v.* penn², tunge); Pinfold Croft (*v.* pynd-fald); Poolstead (*v.* pōl-stede); Sheep Walk; Slough Croft (*v.* slōh); Smithy Crofts (cf. *le Smithiford* 1313, 'ford near a smithy', *v.* smiððe, ford); Sprink Wd (*v.* spring 'a young wood'); Star(s)field (*v.* storr²); Street Fd (*v.* strǣt, cf. *Bruneshurst supra*); Swinley (*v.* swīn¹, lēah); Wall Bank & Flatt (*v.* wælla); Wash Brook Croft (*v.* wæsce, brōc); Way Wd (*v.* weg, but this is not woodland, cf. Ox Wd *supra*); White Fd; Wood Fd.

(*b*) *campus de Bolewik* 1322 ('wīc where bulls, or a bull, stand(s)', *v.* boli, ME *bole*); *cloh inter bridesmere et bruneshurst* H3 ('the dell between Bridgemere and *Bruneshurst*', cf. *Bruneshurst supra*, *v.* clōh); *le Hetruding* 1317 ('the heath clearing', *v.* hǣð, ryding); *Huggeruding* 1322 (from the ME pers.n. *Hugge* and ryding, cf. *Huggeruydin* 45 *supra*); *Loueruding'* 1322 ('clearing at a mound', *v.* hlāw, ryding); *Lymestrete* (*v.* 1 49 (route XXVII), *Bruneshurst supra*); *le Newetunyng'* 1322 ('the new fencing', *v.* nīwe, tȳning); *le Slacruding* 1317 ('clearing at a hollow', *v.* slakki, ryding); *le Stokking'* 1313, *le Spencerstokkyng* 1322 (from stoccing 'a piece of ground cleared of stumps', and the surname *Spencer*); *Weselmosse* 1343 ('weasel's moss', *v.* wesle, mos).

5. CHECKLEY CUM WRINEHILL (110–7345), 1724 NotCestr, *Chatkylegh cum Wrymhull* 1518 AD, (lit. *Chalk-*) 1518 Plea, cf. Checkley, Wrinehill *infra*.

CHECKLEY

Chackileg 1252 Ch, *-ylegh* 1329 Plea, *-lee* 1378 AD, *-ley* 1440
  AddCh, *-eleg'* 1274 Ipm, *-legh* 1363 *AddCh*
Chadkeleg' 1275 Cl
Chakkeleye 1299 Ipm, *Chakele* 1308 ib, *Chacculey* 1431 *AddCh*
Chatkileg, (*boscus de-*) c.1300 AD, *Chattkylegh* 1308 ChRR, *Chatk-*
  1323 Plea *et freq* with variant spellings *Schat-*, *-ley* to 1510 Plea,
  (*-iuxta Briddesmere*) 1437 ChRR, *Chatkeley* 1417 AD, 1418
  ChRR
Chekkeleye, *Checke-* 1321, 1322 Fine and four forms with variant
  spellings *Cheche-*, *Cheke-*, *-ley* to 1584 ChRR, *Chekylegh* 1581 ib
Chekleghe 1396 Cl, 1429 Tab, *-ley* 1437 AD, 1482 *Chol*, 1517
  ChRR, *Checkley* 1519 AD *et freq*, *Checley* 1600 AD
Cheickley 1560 Orm[2]
Chetley 1740 Cre

'Ceaddica's wood', from an OE pers.n. *Ceaddica* and lēah. No such
pers.n. form is recorded, but it is a possible *-ica* derivative of the OE
pers.n. *Ceadda*. The first el. of this p.n. is usually taken to be the same
as that in Checkley He, St, either ceacce 'a lump, a hill' or an OE
pers.n. *Ceacca* (cf. DEPN s.n. Checkendon, EPN s.v. ceacce). This
supposes the *Chatk-* spellings represent *Chack-*, but the *Chadk-*,
Chattk- forms argue for the originality of *-d-*, *-t-* in the first syllable.
OE **Ceaddican-lēah* would become *Chadkeleg'*, hence *Chatk-*, *Chak-*,
with the unvoicing of *-d-* before *-k-*. For the *-i-*, *-y-* in *-ilegh*, *-ylegh*,
cf. Botterley (in Faddiley) 142 *infra*.

WRINEHILL (BRIDGE) (110–755467) [ˈrainil], WRYNEFORD (lost), THE
WRYME (lost)

Wriman ford 975 (11) BCS 1312, *Wrimeford* 1240–50 *AddCh* (p),
  Wryme- 1354 Chamb, *-fforde* 1392 AD, *-forde* 1505 ChRR (in *le
  Wrymehill*), *Wrymford* 1517 ib (*Wrymhill in-*)
Wrynehull 1225 Cl, 1404 *MinAcct*, 1442 ChRR, (*-alias Wryneford*)
  1527 *ChCert*, *-hill* 15 Rich, 1454 *AddCh*, 1503 *ChFor et freq* to
  1603 *Surv*, *the-* 1550 AD, *Wrynhull* 1340 *ChFor*, 1378 Eyre, *-hul*
  1513 Sheaf, *-hill* 1589 AD, *Wrinhull* 1386 *Chol*, *Wrine Hill* 1552
  AddCh et freq, *-hull* 1588 AD, *Wrinehill Bridge* 1831 Bry,
  Rinehill 1698 *Chol*
Wryme 1299, 1308 Ipm, 14 AD, 1342 *Eyre* (p), 1430 Cl, 1452 AD,
  le- 1404 *MinAcct*, *the-* 1563 AD, cf. *the Rimes* 1842 *TA*

le Wrineford 1322 Ipm, *Wryneford* 1364 AD, (*Wrynehull-, -hill alias*) 1527 ChCert, 1589 AD, 1686 *Chol, -forde* 1404 *MinAcct,* (*Wrynhill alias*) *Wrynefourde* 1558 (1582) *AddCh, Wrynford* 1517 ChRR

Wrymehille 1418 Cl, (*the-, le-*), *-hill* 1486, 1496 AD, 1492 *AddCh,* 1505 ChRR, *le Wryme Hull* 1429 AD, *-Wrime-* 1486 ib, *Wrymhill* 1481 ChRR, 1515, 1531 AD, (*-in Wrymford*) 1517 ChRR, *-hull* 1518 Plea, AD, *Whrymhylle* 1492 *Chol*

le Wryme Syche 1429 AD

le Wryenhyll 1550 *AddCh*

The Wrynque 1564 AD

Worme-hill 1621 (1656) Orm[2]

'Ford, hill, bridge and watercourse at *The Wryme*', from **ford, hyll, brycg** and **sīc**, with a p.n. theme appearing in 1299 as *Wryme,* the name of the whole district, cf. The Rimes *infra*. Wrinehill village is partly in Betley St. Wrinehill Hall, Mill and Wood are in Madeley St. Wrinehill (110–7547) is named from its position on a slight ridge between Cracow Moss and Checkley Brook. Wrinehill Bridge (110– 755466), probably the site of the ford, crosses Checkley Brook at the county boundary. Wrinehill Hall and Mill (110–753460) are in a low-lying position beside R. Lea. Wrinehill Wood (110–750450) lies between the 300 ft and 400 ft contours, half a mile south of, and from 50 to 100 ft higher than the hall. *le Wryme Syche* alludes to some water-course running into Cracow Moss (110–7447). *The Wrynque* was a pasture at Ravenshall in Betley St, but it may not be pertinent here. Ekwall (DEPN) suggests that *Wryme* is an old name for Checkley Brook or the hill at Wrinehill, and rejects the proposal in Duignan 176 of an OE pers.n. *Wrim(a)* for *Wriman ford*. But the tract called *Wryme* appears to have been all the low-lying land about the confluence of Checkley Brook (from Heighley St) and R. Lea (from Madeley St), about 110–750460. These streams are deflected from their westward course by the high ground at Randilow *infra* (110–7446), to run south-westward to 110–744456 where they resume their line. It seems very likely that this deflection gives rise to the name. Ekwall derives the theme appearing as *Wriman-, Wryme, Wrime, Wryne, Wrine,* from the stem *wrīg-* of the OE verb *wrīgian* 'to tend, go forward, bend' (cf. **wrēo** and ModE *wry*) with the PrGerm concrete-noun forming suffix *-ma(n)* (Kluge §88). This could produce an OE form **wrīma* 'a bend', whence a p.n. **Wrīma,*

*(æt) *Wrīman*, '(at) The Bend', of which the gen.sg. would be represented in *Wriman ford*, and which would develop naturally into ME
Wryme, Wrime. The *Wrine, Wryne* forms, with *n* for *m*, may be due
to scribal confusion, the interchange of nasals in final position, or
the influence of the inflexional -*n* of the dat.sg. in *(æt) *Wrīman* or of
the gen.sg. in *Wrīman*-compositions.

Another explanation of *Wryme* is offered in LCHS 119, 12 where
the name is taken as analogous with the *of wryoheme* of BCS 606 (*v*.
EPN s.v. wrēo, DEPN s.n. Wrington So), which is from hǣme
'dwellers at', with the r.n. Wring, (OE *wrīo-ing* from wrīo and
-ing²). This attempt to derive the Ch and St p.n. *Wryme* from an
OE *wrīohǣme*, 'dwellers at the twisting-place', or 'at the bend(s)',
must be forsaken in the face of criticism, that the name appears as
Wriman in *Wriman ford* BCS 1312, an early eleventh-century MS.,
a form which is hard to reconcile at that date with the morphological
changes required by a *hǣme* compound.

HEYWOOD BARNES (lost), *Heywode* 1260 Court *et freq* with variant
spellings *Hay*- (from 1308 Ipm), -*wo(o)d* to 1665 Cre, *Heywood
Barnes* 1519 AD *et freq* with variant spellings *Hay*-, -*wood(e)*-,
-*woodes*-, -*wod*- to 1817 Orm², (*Heywood(es*) *Barnes alias vocat*'
Hay-, *Heywood*) 1547 MinAcct, *Ha*-, *Hewood Barnes* 1547 *ib*, 1558
AddCh, '(barns at) the fenced-in wood', *v*. (ge)hæg, wudu, bere-ærn.

BUNKERS HILL, the name of a railway cutting, probably an ironic
commemoration of the American battle of 1775, cf. Db 756.
CHECKLEY BRIDGE, GREEN, WOOD & WOOD FM, 1831 Bry.
CHECKLEY HALL, 1611 Orm².   CRACOW MOSS, *Crakalmosse* 1429
AD, *Creka Moss* 1842 *TA*, 'moss at raven's nook', *v*. crake, halh,
mos, cf. the nearby Ravenshall St.   DEN LANE, cf. The Den 52
supra.   MALTKIN FM, *v*. malte-kylne.   RANDILOW FM, *Randilow* (*Lane*) 1831 Bry, *Randilo Farm* 1842 *TA*, cf. Randelow Mdw 53
supra, named from the hill on which the place stands, probably
'round hill', *v*. rondel, hlāw, but the name might have been originally
Wrinehill-low, from Wrinehill *supra*.

FIELD-NAMES

The undated forms are 1842 *TA* 98. Of the others, 1505 is ChRR, 1518,
1593 AD.

(*a*) Abbey Croft; Berks Fd; Bickerton Fd (cf. Bickerton 325 *infra*); Black
Pit Fd; Brickkiln Fd; Big Broom (*v*. brōm); Butter Tree Bank; Causeway Fd

(*v.* caucie); Close (*v.* clos); Cote Fd; Eating House Mdw; Fin Coins Hayes; Forge Fd; Foxley (cf. *Foxewood* 1593, *v.* fox, lēah, wudu); Gowders Bank; Hayes, Heyes (*v.* (ge)hæg); Hill Fd; Horse Wash Fd; Lady Mdw (*v.* hlǣfdige); Lockpost Croft; Long Ridding (*v.* ryding); Long Slang (*v.* slang); Marl Fd (*Marlefeild* 1593, *v.* marle); Pay May; Rail Fd (*v.* rail(e)); Range Pool (*v.* range); The Rimes (cf. Wrinehill *supra*); Round Bank; Shaw Bank & Rough (*v.* sc(e)aga); Shire Fd (near the county boundary, *v.* scīr[1]); The Shutts (*v.* scēat); Sprink (*v.* spring 'a young wood'); Stocking(s) (*v.* stoccing); Sweet Wd; Ten Acres Coppice; Town Fd, Townsend (*v.* toun, ende[1]); Turnpike Fd (*v.* turnepike); White Fd; Withey Croft (*v.* wīðig); Wood Fd; Yellow Fd (*v.* geolu);

(*b*) *Brastoneffyd* 1518 (probably 'field at a broad stone', *v.* brād, stān, feld); *le Conyngre Smythffyld* 1518 ('Smith's-field with a rabbit warren', *v.* coningre, smið, feld); *le Ladywod* 1518 (*v.* hlǣfdige, wudu); lands and tenements called *Lucas thyngez* 1505 ('Lucas's property', from the ME pers.n. *Lucas* and ModE *thing* 'an object, a piece of property'); *Oneyleywaye Field* 1593 (*v.* weg, cf. Onneley, in Madeley, St).

6. CHORLTON (110–7250) ['tʃɔːrltən] older local ['tʃɔːrtn̩]

Cerletune 1086 DB, *Cherleton* 13 *Vern*, *Cherl(e)ton*, (*-iuxta Wyben-biryhagh*, *-Wybunbury*) 1295 ChancW, 1296 Plea (p), 1298 ib, 1308 Ipm, 1342 (1438) ChRR

Jorleton l12 *AddCh* (p)

Chorl(e)ton, (*-iuxta Wib(b)enbury*) 1288 Court, c.1295 Sheaf, 1312 Plea, 1348 *Eyre*, (*-iuxta Godwynesley*) 1364 (1484) ChRR

Charlton 1646 Sheaf

'Peasants' farm', *v.* ceorl (gen.pl. ceorla), tūn. It is adjacent to Wybunbury (cf. *Wybenbiryhagh* 82 *infra*), and Gonsley Green 52 *supra*. For *Jorle- v.* 116 *infra*.

BASFORD HO. CHORLTON LANE, *Green Lane* 1831 Bry, *v.* grēne[1], lane. CHORLTON MOSS, *Chorlton Wood Moss* 1831 ib, *v.* wudu, mos. HEATH FM, cf. *Chorlton Heath* 1831 ib, *v.* hǣð. WAY-BUTT LANE ['wɛibət], *Wyberts Lane* 1831 ib, cf. *Way Butt Bank & Meadow* 1842 *TA*, perhaps 'Wibert's lane', from the ME pers.n. *Wibert* (OE *Wīgbeorht*, OGer *Wigbert*) and lane, later forms showing confusion with weg, butte.

FIELD-NAMES

The undated forms are 1842 *TA* 111. Of the others, c.1295 is Sheaf, H8 *Surv*, and 1831 Bry.

(*a*) Bar Moor; Barn Moor ('waste land with a barn', *v.* bere-ærn, mōr[1]); The Chair, Chair Chair; Cote Fds (*v.* cot); Cow Hayes (*v.* (ge)hæg); Dung

Fd (v. dung[2]); Flax Butts & Pool (le Flaxpull c.1295, 'pool where flax is soaked', 'selions where flax is grown', v. fleax, pull, butte); Flower Flunt; Gleade (perhaps ground cleared by burning, v. glēd(e)); Gonsley Fd (cf. Gonsley Green 52 supra); Gutter Mdw (v. goter, cf. Mere Gutter 1 31); Hammer Head; Heath Fd & Plex ('field and plots of land, at a heath', v. hǣð, plek); Hemp Butts & Flat (v. hænep, butte, flat); Hob Riddings (v. hobbe, ryding); Hot Croft (v. hāt); The Leach (v. lece 'a boggy place or stream'); Lee Crofts, Gate, Hole & Moor (from Lea 67 infra, v. geat, hol[1], mōr[1]); Madge Brook(s) (v. madge, brōc); Maidenhead (v. 325 infra); Mall Mdw; Marl Fd; Milking Bank & Patch (v. milking); Moat Buildings (v. mote); Monk House Spring; Ox Pasture; Patches; Pingo (v. pingot); Ridding (v. ryding); Rough Moor; Rousing Fd, Mdw, Moor & Wd; Rushey Moor; Sandy Fd; Span Fd (v. spann[1]); Steel Ridding ('clearing at a stile', v. stigel, ryding); Tom Croft, Town Fd & Mdw (v. toun, croft, feld, mǣd); Wall Fd (v. wælla); Far & Near Wood (cf. Wood Hollow 1831); Woodcock Hey (v. wodecok, (ge)hæg); Yellow Hill (v. geolu).

(b) le Bere Furlong c.1295 ('barley furlong', v. bere, furlang); Brangayn-land c.1295 (v. land 'a selion'). The first el. appears to be a pers.n. resembling the MWelsh fem. pers.n. Brangwain (whence the ME surname Brangwayn 1300 (from London), v. Reaney s.n. Brangwin), or even an anglicisation of a MIrish form of the Irish surname Ó Branagáin (v. Woulfe 440, Reaney s.n. Branaghan); le Cheplade c.1295 ('the sheep stream', v. scēp, lād, probably a sheep-wash); Hakhaldisland c.1295 (from land 'a selion', perhaps with a p.n. Hakhald, 'shelter at a hook of land', v. haca, hald); le Holthe Meadow plek c.1295 ('(plot of land at) wood-meadow', v. holt, mǣd, plek); the Mulneway c.1295 (v. myln, weg); Nethirhowse H8 (v. neoðera, hūs); le Peascroft c.1295 (v. pise, croft).

7. DODDINGTON (110–710470)

> Dudinton(a) 1198–1216 Facs, H3 AddCh (p), Dudynton 1342 (1438) ChRR, Duddynton alias- 1581 ib, Duddyngton 1531 AD, -ing-, (-alias Derrington) 1622 ib
>
> Dodinton 1241 MRA (p), 1280 P (p), -yn(g)- 1312 Plea, 1315 Misc et freq to 1531 AD, (-alias Dorungton) 1481 Chol, -ing- 1365 Tab, 1663 ChRR, 1719 Sheaf, Doddington 1365 BRP, 1403 ChRR, 1831 Bry
>
> Derynton 1380 Eyre, (Duddington alias) Derrington 1622 AD (Dodyngton alias) Dorungton 1481 Chol
>
> Dunnyngton 1574 Dow

'Farm called after Dudda', from the OE pers.n. Dudda, v. -ingtūn. The interchange of Dud-, Dod- with Der-, Dor-, Dun- in some of the forms suggests confusion or analogy with Dorrington Sa, near Woore four miles south of Doddington, (Derintune DB, Derynton 1285, Deorintone 1327), and analogy with Dorrington Sa, near Condover

(*Dodinton* 1198), and Donnington Sa, near Newport (*Derintune* DB, *-ton* 1255). The change *-d-* > *-r-* is noted as a NWMidl dialect feature EDGr §299. A form *Dorinton* (p) 1351 Chamb 172 may belong to Dorrington near Woore, as may a series *Deryn(g)ton* (p) 1341 to 1356 *Eyre*, ChRR, Plea, BPR, Chamb, but this series appears to be alternative to the *Dod(d)in(g)-*, *-yn(g)-* surname, and the *Der-Dor-* forms quoted in the examples *supra* are certainly the Ch place. The form *Dunnyngton* 1574 is identified with Doddington Ch by association with the Delves family. It might indicate connexion with another series of forms, *Donynton'* 1311 *Eyre*, *passagium de Donyngton* 1468, 1471 *MinAcct*, 1505 ChRR, *-Donnington* 1560 Sheaf. It has been suggested that this is Castle Donington Lei, which was indeed part of the duchy of Chester, but which seems rather remote from Ch. The reference is to a toll-passage held of the earls of Chester, but it was part of the barony of Nantwich. The passage was reported to be non-existent by 1471 (*DuLaMinAcct* 3, 22). In 1311 (*Eyre* 3, m.11) it is associated with the surname *Bruneshurst*, (*v.* 54 *supra*), which suggests a location in this district of Ch, and probably on the Woore–Nantwich road like Doddington, *v.* 1 48 (route XXVII), Pepperstreet Moss 66 *infra*. *Donynton*, etc., could well be a form of Doddington, derived from a form *Dorin(g)-*, *Dorung-*, with assimilation of *-r-* to following *-n-*. It could also be from the OE pers.n. *Dunna* with *-ingtūn*, so a connection of the *Donynton'* series with Doddington is not proven.

BLACK MERE, 'dark pool', *v.* blæc, mere[1].   THE CASTLE, *Castle Ruins* 1831 Bry, cf. *Castle Pool* 1842 *TA* (Doddington Pool *infra*), the site of a mansion crenellated c.1364 and destroyed during the Civil War, cf. BPR III 469 and Orm[2] III 519, *v.* castel(l)   THE COTTAGE, 1831 Bry, *v.* cottage.   DEMESNE FM, *George's Wood Farm* 1831 Bry, *The Farm* 1842 OS, cf. George's Wood *infra*, *v.* demeyn. DODDINGTON HALL, 1719 Sheaf.   DODDINGTON MILL, *molendinum de Derynton* 1380 *Eyre*.   DODDINGTON PARK, 1842 OS.   DOD-DINGTON POOL, *Doddington (Castle) Pool* 1842 *TA*, 1843 *TAMap*, cf. The Castle *supra*.   FURNACE BANK, 1842 OS, *v.* furneis 'a kiln, a furnace', banke.   GEORGE'S WOOD, 1831 Bry, also 74 *infra*. SHAW'S ROUGH, *Shaw Rough* 1842 OS, 'rough ground at a wood', *v.* sceaga, rūh.   WHISPEY HILL, *Wisby-*, *Wispy Hill* 1842 *TA*, *v.* wisp 'a wisp', hyll.   WILBRAHAM'S WALK, from ModE walk 'a promen-ade, an avenue of trees', with the Ch surname *Wilbraham* ['wilbrəm].

FIELD-NAMES

The principal forms are 1842 *TA* 146.

(*a*) Doddington Ley, Ley Ground (cf. Ley Ground Fm 54 *supra*); Mere Fd (*v.* mere¹, cf. Black Mere *supra*); Mill Mdw (after Doddington Mill *supra*); Moss Mdw (*v.* mos); Stockdale Croft (*v.* stocc, dæl¹).

8. HATHERTON (110–6847) [ˈhaðətən]

> Haretone 1086 DB
> Hatherton 1262 *JRC* (p) *et freq* with variant spellings -*tona* c.1310
>   Chest, *Ath*- 1325 (1420) *AddRoll* (p), 1364 BPR to 1559 *Chol*,
>   -*ir*- 1396 Fine, 1434 ChRR (p), -*ur*- 1398 ChRR, 1470 Comb (p),
>   Hatherton alias Had(d)erton 1567, 1577 ChRR
> Hathyerton 1341 *AddCh*
> Hartherton 1400 ChRR
> (*H*)Ad(d)erton 1473, 1536 ChRR, 1514 *ChEx* (p), 1543 Plea, 1567,
>   1577 ChRR

'Hawthorn farm or enclosure', *v.* hagu-þorn, tūn.

BIRCHALL BRIDGE & MOSS (FM) (110–680460), BIRCHALL BROOK [ˈbəːtʃɔː(l)]

> Birchowre (lit. *Hirch*-) c. 1300 Sheaf (p)
> Birchoure, -*overe* (p) 1304 Chamb *et freq* ib, ChRR, *AddCh*, Orm²
>   with variant spellings -*ouer*, -*ovre*, *Byrche*- to 1348
> Birchore 1353 BPR (p), *By*- 1357 ChRR (p)
> Burchar(e) 1529 Plea, 1549 ChRR
> Bircher 1573 ChRR
> Berchall Bridge 1621 Sheaf, *Birchall Brook & the ville of Birchall*
>   1831 Bry, *Birchall Moss, Birchall Brook Bridge* 1842 OS

'Birch slope', from birce and ofer², with brycg and mos. Cf. Birchover Db 45. The moss was *The Heath* 1831 Bry, *v.* hǣð. The brook joins R. Weaver.

ACTON'S GORSE & ROUGH, *Lunt's Rough* 1831 Bry, from the surnames *Acton* and *Lunt*.   ARTLEBROOK BRIDGE, *v.* 72 *infra*.   ASH-FIELDS, 1831 ib.   BANKTOP FM, cf. *Bank (Head)* 1842 *TA*, *v.* banke, topp, hēafod.   BLACKTHORN WOOD.   BROOMLANDS, (*The*-) 1831 Bry, *v.* brōm, land.   CHESTNUT WOOD.   FIELD FM. GLOVER'S MOSS, *Moss* 1831 Bry, *v.* mos.   GORSE WOOD. HATHERTON FM, *Twemlows Farm* 1831 ib, cf. *Twemlows Bank* 1842

TA, probably from the surname from Twemlow **2** 230.   HATHER-
TON HALL, *the hall of Hatherton alias Had(d)erton* 1567, 1577 ChRR.
HATHERTON HEATH, HO & LODGE, 1831 Bry.   HATHERTON
WOOD, *The Grig* 1831 ib, cf. *Grig Piece* 1842 *TA* and Richard *del
Wode* 1352 *Chol*, *v.* wudu, grig² 'heather, heath'.   HEATHFIELD,
cf. *Heath Field* 1842 *TA*, *v.* hǣð.   HILL HO (twice), cf. William
del Hull 1352 *Chol* (p), *Hilles Grovende* 1515 *MinAcct*, 'grove and
house belonging to the Hill family, or at a hill', *v.* hyll, grāf, ende¹.
KILN COTTAGE, cf. *Brick Kiln Bank* 1842 *TA*.   LANE WOOD, cf.
Lane Croft, Field & Meadow 1842 *ib*, from either **lane** 'a lane', or
leyne 'a plot of land'.   LAURELS FM.   MANOR HO, 1831 Bry.
PARK HO & LANE, *Park Lane* 1831 Bry, *Park House* 1842 OS (called
The Moss 1831 Bry), cf. *parcum de Hatherton* 1297 Sheaf, *v.* park.
RIVER WOOD, beside R. Weaver.   YEWTREE HO, 1842 OS.

FIELD-NAMES

The undated forms are 1842 *TA* 194. Of the others, 1297 is Sheaf, 1342
AddCh, 1436, 1440 ChRR, 1515 *MinAcct*.

(*a*) Acres; Artle Brook Mdw (cf. Artle Brook **1** 13); Bache Fd (*v.* bæce¹);
Bead Hey; Big Betton, Sandy Field Betton (*v.* tūn. The first el. is unintelligible); Birch Fd; Black Brook; Blue Cap; The Two Bottoms (*v.* botm);
Brine Pit Mead or Water Mead (*v.* brīne, pytt, wæter, mǣd); Broomy Bank
(*v.* brōmig); Cart House Fd; Clapper Bank, Clappers Fd (*v.* clapere); Clay
Hill; Cow Lane; Cross Lane Park; Diddle; Dirty Fd; Drumble Field (dial.
drumble, 'a wooded ravine', cf. dumbel); Farther Slade (*v.* slæd); Fearney
Heys; Fish Pool Hill; Flash (Moor) Mdw (*v.* flasshe); Gorsty Bank (*v.*
gorstig); Big- & Hanging Hold, Little- & Near Holt (*v.* holt, hangende);
Hop Yard; Hough (*v.* hōh); Hyson-, Isen Bridge (probably a back-formation
from a form *Hyron-*, *Iren-* from hyrne 'a corner', construed as OE īren
'iron', cf. Heronbridge 326 *infra*); Intake (*v.* inntak); Kitchen Fd; Lady Pool
Mdw (*v.* hlǣfdige, pōl¹); Lawn (*v.* launde); Leg and Foot (*v.* 326 *infra*);
Ley (*v.* lǣge); Marl Pit Bank (*v.* marle-pytt); Mill Hill; Moat Bank (*v.* mote,
though there is no moat mapped here); Moor; Moss; Off Mdw (*v.* hōh);
Otter Down Mdw; Oulton Brow & Fd (*v.* ald, tūn, brū, cf. Oulton 185
infra); Ox Leasow (*v.* lǣs); Paper Mill Fd; Pingle (*v.* pingel); Pool End;
Prestbury Fd (cf. Prestbury **1** 212); Big- & Long Ridding (cf. *le Ryddyng*
1515, *v.* ryding); Ridley (perhaps 'cleared wood' *v.* (ge)ryd(d), lēah, or
named from Ridley 313 *infra*); Sand Fd; Scrap Riddings (*v.* ryding); Slade
(*v.* slæd); Broad- & Long Sneyd (*v.* snǣd); Spring Bank ('hillside at a
spring', *v.* spring); Sprink ('young wood', *v.* spring); Three Day Math (*v.*
day-math); Toll Gate Ho; Town Fd; Traffinch Lake; Under Ship; Warriors
Fd & Mdw; Wat Fd; Way Patch (*v.* weg); Weaver Bank (from R. Weaver);
White Moss Mdw.

(b) *via ecclesiastica* 1297 ('the church-way' v. cirice, weg); *Dogcrofte* 1436, 1440 (v. dogga, croft); *le Lyttulhegh* 1342 ('the little fenced-in enclosure', v. lȳtel, (ge)hæg).

9. HOUGH (110–710510) [hʌf, ʌf]

le Hothg 13 *Vern*
Hohc 1241 MRA
le Ho 1241, 1278 MRA, *Ho* c.1255 ib
Houth 1241 MRA, *Houth(t)* 1288 Court (p)
Hoc 1260 Court (p)
(*le*) *Hogh* 1287 Court, 1312 Ipm, 1361 MRA *et freq* to 1517 Plea,
    (*-iuxta Wi-, Wybbenbury*) 1288 Court, 1315 Plea, 1316 MRA, *le
    Hoghe* 1399–1413 Orm², *the-* 1561 Cre
Hough 1287 Court (p), 1393, 1404, 1601 ChRR *et freq* with variant
    spelling *-e* 1535 VE, (*le-*) 1412 ChRR (p), (*the-*) 1621 (1656)
    Orm², 1625 Sheaf
Houcht (*iuxta Wybunbury*), *le Houcht* (p) 1287 Court
le How, Houw (p) 1287 Court
le Houh 1288 Court (p)
Hoo 1328 MRA
(*le*) *Hugh* 1351 BPR (p), 1403, 1434, 1453 ChRR

'The spur or ridge', v. hōh. The situation is on high ground north of Wybunbury. Cf. Hough **1** 221, Hoo Green **2** 51. In some spellings *-c-* has been read *-t-*.

BROOKLANDS, named from Swill Brook **1** 36.   THE CLIFF, 1842 OS,
Cliff House 1831 Bry, 'steep hillside', v. clif.   COBB'S LANE &
MOSS, v. cobb(e), lane, mos.   COCKSHADES, *Cockshead Farm* 1831
ib, 'cock-shoot', v. cocc-scyte.   DOVE HO, 1831 ib, v. dove-
house.   ELLESMERE FM, *Ellesmere* 1831 ib, perhaps called after
Ellesmere Sa.   HEATHFIELD HO.   HIGHFIELD COTTAGE, cf. *High
Field* 1838 *TA*.   HOUGH COMMON, HALL, HO & MILL FM, *Hough
Heath, Hall & Mill* 1831 Bry, *-House* 1860 White. The mill-site was
created c.1241, MRA 531 p. 254.   JERUSALEM, cf. Jericho 67
infra, v. 325 *infra*.   PIT LANE.   STOCK LANE, 1838 *TA*, v.
stocc.   WOOD COTTAGES.   YEWTREE FM.

FIELD-NAMES

The undated forms are 1838 *TA* 210, 1241, c.1255, 1278, 1328 are MRA, 1583 Orm².

(*a*) Baltershaw (perhaps 'Baldŏrȳð's wood', from the OE fem. pers.n. *Baldðrȳð*, *v.* sceaga, cf. Balterley St); The Bank; Birchlays, -leys (*v.* birce, lēah); Blake Fd (*v.* blæc); Chorlton Fd (cf. Chorlton 59 *supra*); Church Mdw; Coat Fd (*v.* cot); Copy Fd (*v.* copis); Finger Post Fd; Hob Ridding (*v.* hobbe, ryding); Kitchen Mdw; Lady Fd (*v.* hlæfdige); Lumpy Fd (*v.* lump); Mill Edge Mdw (from Hough Mill *supra*, *v.* ecg 'a bank, the edge of a hill'); Moss Bank (*v.* mos, banke); Old House Mdw (probably named from the site of the former hall, ruined in the seventeenth-century); Pool Side (*v.* pōl¹, sīde); Little Ridding (*v.* ryding); Little Rough (*v.* rūh); Sitch Fd (*v.* sīc); Spath Mdw (*v.* sparð); Spout Mdw (*v.* spoute); Statute Croft; Stoneley Fd (*v.* stān, lēah); Thorn Tree Moss; Walk Mdw (*v.* walk); Way Fd; Willow Yard (*v.* wilig, geard).

(*b*) *Barnhill* 1583 (*v.* bere-ærn, hyll); *the Haye of Hohc, -at-, -of Houth, -Ho, -del Ho* 1241, c.1255, 1278, *boscus* (*Haye*) *de Ho*(*o*) 1328 ('the fenced-in wood-enclosure', *v.* (ge)hæg).

10. HUNSTERSON (110–7045) [¹(h)unstəsn̩]

Hunsterton 1188–1209 MidCh (p), 1241 MRA (p) *et freq* with variant spellings *-tona, -ir-, -ur-, Hus-* to 1724 NotCestr, *Honsterton*' 1272–90 *ChFor* (p), 1316 Chamb, 1326 Pat (p), 1460 *AddCh*

Hunsterston 1188–1209 Tab, 1294 ChF (p), 1307 ChRR, *-ur-* 1380 *ChCal* (p), *Hum-* 1503 Plea, *Hunstristun* 1241 MRA (p), *Honstreston* 1307 ChRR (p)

Huntirtun H3 *AddCh* (p)

Hunteston 1241 MRA (p)

Hunstraton' 1280 P (p), *-streton* 1346 *ChGaol* (p), 1352 BPR (p), *Hon*(*e*)*stretton*(*e*) c.1311 *AddCh*

Hunsterson 1319, 1321 *AddCh*, 1719 Sheaf *et freq*

Hunstrinton 1328 *AddCh*

Honstrerton 1348 *ChFor* (p) (Barnes¹ 712)

Hunston 1653 Sheaf

Hunterson 1831 Bry

The final el. is tūn 'an enclosure, a farmstead'. The first el. is difficult. Ekwall (DEPN) suggests the name may be *Stretton* (from stræt and tūn) with a prefixed pers.n., OE *Hūn*, or alternatively, analogous with Houndstreet So, from steort 'a tail' and either an OE pers.n. *Hund*, or hund 'a dog, a hound', with tūn. Dr Barnes

proposes 'farm at a tail of land, belonging to Hunna', from the OE
pers.n. *Hun(n)a* and a p.n. from steort and tūn. There may be
historical grounds for *strǣt-tūn* (cf. Pepperstreet Moss *infra*) but the
topography supports steort, for Hunsterson is on a low spur of land.
Professor Löfvenberg proposes that the first el. is either hund 'a dog'
or hūne 'horehound', and the second is steort 'a tail', and that the
p.n. means either 'farmstead on the dog's tail (owing to a fancied
likeness of a piece of land to such a thing)', or more likely 'farmstead
on the tail of land overgrown with horehound'.

BADGER'S BANK, *v.* bagga.   BIRCHENHILL WOOD, *Birchen Hill* 1842
TA, v. bircen², hyll.   BLACK COVERT.   BROWNMOSS, 1842 OS,
Browns Moss 1831 Bry, *v.* brūn¹, mos. Lack of evidence prevents a
connection of this place with *Bruneshurst* 53 *supra*.   CHAPEL
WOOD, 1831 ib, probably named from St John's Church, not far off.
FOXES BANK, 1831 ib.   GREENFIELDS, *Green Fields* 1831 ib.
HUNSTERSON FOUR LANE END.   LEMON POOL, *v.* pōl¹.   MALTKIN
FM.   MANOR HO, *Broomfields Farm* 1831 Bry, cf. *Broom Field*,
Demberley late Bromfield 1842 *TA* and Demberley *infra, v.* brōm,
feld.   OLD FIELDS LODGE, cf. *Old Fields* 1842 *TA*, commemo-
rating fields lost by inclusion in Doddington Park 61 *supra*.
PEPPERSTREET MOSS (110–702465), 1842 OS, *v.* mos, cf. Pepper St.
(Chester) 326 *infra*. If this p.n. alludes to an ancient road, it would
support one of Ekwall's explanations of Hunsterson, *v. supra*. There
was probably an old line of road hereabouts, on the route from Woore
Sa, to Nantwich, cf. **1** 48 (route XXVII), *Bruneshurst* 53 *supra*,
Donnington 61 *supra*, (Pepperstreet Moss is on a line between Broad
Lane 72 *infra* and *Bruneshurst*). It would be lost or diverted at some
time by inclusion in Doddington Park, cf. Old Fields Lodge *supra*.
There may have been a 'street' at Doddington, for the surname *le
Streteward* 1312 Plea (DKR XXXVII 100) appears there, *v.* strǣt,
strete-ward.   PEWIT GORSE & HALL, *Pewit Gorse, Hunterson or
Pewit Hall* 1831 Bry, from pewit 'a pewit', with gorst and hall.
THE REED, 'the reed-bed', *v.* hrēod.   RIDLEY'S POOL, *Hunterson
Pool* 1831 Bry, *Hunsterson Pool* 1842 *TA, v.* pōl¹.   SLADE COTTAGE,
cf. *Slade Yards, Slades (Garden)* 1842 *ib, v.* slæd.   WEIGHBRIDGE
COTTAGES.   WHITTAKER'S GREEN, *Whitaker Green* 1831 Bry,
probably from the surname *Whittaker*, but possibly from hwīt and
æcer, and grēne².   WOODEND, *-s* 1831 Bry.

FIELD-NAMES

The undated forms are 1842 *TA* 213. Of the others, c.1311, 1328 are *AddCh*.

(*a*) Barnetts Pleck (*v.* plek); Bath Mdw (*v.* bæð); Beech Mdw (*v.* bece[1]); Bill Blake; Little Birchen (*v.* bircen[1]); Blackhurst (*v.* hyrst); Breeges (*v.* brēc); Broe Croft; Bro(o)mfield (*v.* Manor Ho *supra*, Demberley *infra*); Brown Sprink (*v.* brūn[1], spring); Butt Mdw (*v.* butte); Cinder Bank (*v.* sinder); Cockshead, Cockshut (*v.* cocc-scyte); Coldhurst Mdw, Colthurst, Cothurst Wd (probably 'cold wooded-hill', from cald and hyrst); Cote Fd (*v.* cot); Cow(s) Hey(s); Cross Fd (*v.* cros); Dawry Bank & Wd (*v.* dowarie); Big Demberley, Demberley late Bromfield (*Demburleghmedue* 1328, '(meadow at) Deneburh's clearing', from the OE fem. pers.n. *Deneburh* and lēah, with mǣd, cf. Manor Ho, Bro(o)mfield *supra*); The Diddle; Dreary Wd; Gad Fd; Gumminger; Gunners; Hall Leasow (*v.* lǣs); The Hays (*v.* (ge)hæg); Heady Leys (*v.* hǣðig); Heath Pleck (cf. *le Heeth* c.1311 (p), *le Het* 1328 (p), *v.* hǣð, plek); Highurst (*v.* hēah, hyrst); Lady Pool (*v.* hlǣfdige); Long Hill; Love Croft (*v.* lufu); Marl Fd; Mill Hay & Ridding (*v.* (ge)hæg, ryding); Moss Bank, Croft & Fd; Mowing Piece & Sprink (*v.* spring); Old Lane; Patch; Peas Land; Pinfold Bank (*v.* pynd-fald); Pingle, Pingo (*v.* pingel, pingot); Big- & Little Quarters (*v.* quarter); Rains Hat; Riddings (*v.* ryding); Rough Moss; The Round (*v.* rond); Shut Ridding (*v.* scēat, ryding); Slane Hurst (*v.* hyrst); Big Sprink (*v.* spring 'a young wood'); Stockings (*v.* stoccing); Stonery Fd (*v.* stonery); Surfeets Mdw (*v.* 325 *infra*); Three Brooks (*v.* þrēo, brōc); Town Fd & Piece; Tunstall Fd (*v.* tūn-stall); Turn Hurst (*v.* trun, hyrst); Wadding Lake Mdw; Wet Land; Wheat Furlong; White Fd.

(*b*) *le Bulwemedue* 1328 (*v.* mǣd); *le Wallebuttus* 1328 ('headlands near a spring or well', *v.* wælla, butte).

11. LEA (110–7148) [liː]

Lee 1241 MRA (p), (*le*) *Lee* 1281, 1287 Court *et freq* to *the Lee* 1621 (1656) Orm[2], *Lee by Berterton* 1400 Pat, *-juxta Wybunburye* 1581 Orm[2]

Ley 1515 ChEx

Lea 1558–79 ChancP, (*-iuxta Wybunbury*) 1584 ChRR, *Lea or Lee* 1860 White

'At the clearing', *v.* lēah (dat.sg. lēa). Lea is near Batherton 50 *supra*, Wybunbury 80 *infra*.

FORGE BROOK (Wybunbury Brook 82 *infra*), cf. Lea Forge *infra*. HUNTER'S HILL, 1838 *TA*. JERICHO, cf. Jerusalem 64 *supra*, *v.* 325 *infra*. LEA FM. LEA FORGE (MILL), *Lea Forge* 1780 Sheaf,

The Forge 1860 White. There was a notable iron-forge here, de-molished about 1820, cf. Forge Brook *supra*, Mill Pond, Hamer Mdw *infra*.   LEA HALL, 1719 Sheaf.   LEA PARK, 1842 OS.   LEA WOODS, 1831 Bry.   MILL POND, *Lea Pool* 1831 ib, *Forge Pool* 1838 *TA*, *v.* pōl¹, cf. Lea Forge *supra*.

FIELD-NAMES

The undated forms are 1838 *TA* 232.

(a) The Acres; The Bank; Beach (*v.* bece¹); Beating Pasture; Blakenhall Hatches (*v.* hæcc, cf. Blakenhall 51 *supra*. Lea was part of the manor of Blakenhall); Broom Fd (*v.* brōm); Ferny Bent (*v.* beonet); Greasly; Hamer Mdw (probably from hamor 'a hammer', alluding to Lea Forge *supra*); Kitchen Hill; Little Loomons, Loomons Lane; Marl Fd; Ox Pasture; Patch; Pool Sits; Big-, Far- & Middle Ridding (*v.* ryding); Rough; Royal Bank (from banke 'a hillside, a slope', perhaps with an older f.n., 'rye-hill', *v.* ryge, hyll, cf. Royal's Green, The Royals, Royalswood 97, 102, 102 *infra*, Royle Green 1 237); Way Fd.

(b) *nemus de Bradeie* 13 AD ('wood of broad island' or 'of broad-enclo-sure', from brād, with either ēg or (ge)hæg); *Leefeld* 1308 Ipm ('the field of Lea', *v.* feld).

12. ROPE (110–6952) [roup]

    Rap c. 1180, 1259, 1322 *AddCh*, 12 (17), l13 *Chol*
    Rape 1259 *AddCh*, 1308 ChRR
    Rop H3 (14) *AddCh*, 1280 P (p), *Ropp* 1584 Sheaf, *-e* 1621 (1656) Orm²
    Roop 1311 *AddCh* (p), *-e* 1449 Sheaf (p)
    R(o)ep 1359 BPR (p)
    Rope 1416 ChRR (p), 1842 OS, *le Rope* 1432 *AddCh* (p)

'The rope', from rāp. This unusual p.n. may be analogous with the Rapes of Sussex, alluding to a space roped off for a meeting-place, cf. Sx 8–9. From its central position in the Hundred, Rope could have been the location of 'Wǣrmund's tree', cf. 1 *supra*. However, a 'rope' was an ancient land-measure and the el. appears elsewhere in Ch, *v. Rapdowl(e)s* 226 *infra*, so this p.n. may be simply 'a rope of land', *v.* NED, *rope* sb¹, 2a.

BRIDGE FM, named from a railway bridge.   OWL HO.   PUSEY-DALE (110–6951) ['puːsi-], *Pucey Dale* 1831 Bry, *Pussey Dale* 1842 OS, cf. *Poosa Rails* 1838 *TA*, from dæl¹ 'a valley', and rail(e) 'a railing', with an undetermined name, perhaps that of a watercourse running past the place to Rope Hall, e.g. 'stream at a pool', from pōl[1] and ēa. ROPE BANK, 1842 OS, *Bank Farm* 1831 Bry. ROPE FM. ROPE GREEN & HALL, 1831 ib. ROPE LANE.

FIELD-NAMES

The undated forms are 1838 *TA* 339, 1831 is Bry, 1842 OS.

(a) Ambert (perhaps the same name as Ambutt 73 *infra*); Cross Fd; Cyderope Fd (cf. Rope *supra*, *Rapdowl(e)s* 226 *infra*, v. sīd, rāp); Five-, Three days Math (v. day-math); Flash Fd (v. flasshe); Gold Lake (v. golde, lacu); Greasty Fd (cf. Gresty 69 *infra*); Heath Piece; Hunger Hill (v. hungor); Kiln Mdw; Long Shoot (v. scēat); Mill Fd; The Moor; Owlery Lane 1831 (v. alor, cf. 71 *infra*); The Patch; Rye Bank; Sprink (v. spring 'a young wood'); Sweet Fd; Tanners Green 1831, 1842; Turning (v. turning(e)); Two Year Old Croft; Way Fd; Witches Croft; Witch House Fd (v. wych(e)-hous(e), cf. 2 193-4); Yolk of Egg (v. 325 *infra*);

13. SHAVINGTON CUM GRESTY, *Greasty cum Shavington* 1739 Sheaf, *Shavington cum Greastey* (lit. *Greasby*) 1724 NotCestr, *Shavinton cum Gresty or Shavinton Woodnoth* 1819, 1882 Orm[2] III 505, v. Gresty, Shavington *infra*.

GRESTY BRIDGE, BROOK & GREEN (110–7053) [gresti]

Graysty 1308 ChRR, 1418 Plea, (-*in Shawynton'*) 1395 *CampbCh*, (-*heth*) 1398 *Chol*, *Graisty* 1515 Plea

Greysty 1312, 1316 Plea (p), 1322 *AddCh* (p) *et freq* to (-*in Shavyngton*) 1400 ChRR, *CampbCh*, -*sti* 1341 *Eyre* (p), 1350 ChRR (p), *Greisty* 1519 ChRR (p), 1380 *Eyre*, -*stie* 1528 Plea

Gresty 1327 ChRR (p), (-*Green*) 1831 Bry, -*e* 1518 *AddCh*, *Gressty in Shavington* 1400 Orm[2]

Grayste 1418 ChRR, *Graiste* 1447 Tab

Graystoue 1437 Orm[2], -*stowe* 1443 ChRR, *Grestowe* (lit. -*scowe*) 1478 ib

Grasty 1512 *ChEx*

Greasty 1604 Cre, -*stey* (lit. -*sby*) 1724 NotCestr

'Badger-run', from grǣg[2] and stīg, with brycg, brōc and grēne[2]. The brook becomes Wistaston Brook 47 *supra*.

SHAVINGTON (FM, GREEN, HALL & MILL), formerly SHAVINTON WOODNOTH (110–700520) ['ʃævintən] locally ['ʃentən]

Santune 1086 DB

Shawynton 1260 Court (p), 1395 *CampbCh*, 1421 Orm², (-*in Hogh*) 1436, 1440 ChRR

Schavinton 1276 Ipm, *Shavinton* 1287 Court *et freq* with variant spellings *S(c)hau-*, *S(c)hav-*, -*en*-, -*yn*- to 1882 Orm², (-*iuxta Barcford*) 1315 Plea, (-*iuxta Wybenbury*) 1362 Orm², (-*iuxta le Hogh*) 1377 Plea, (-*alias Sheynton*) 1496 ChRR, *Shavinton Hall* 1845 ChetOS VIII

Schavyngton c.1298 *Chol* (p), *Shavington* 1299 Plea *et freq* with variant spellings *Shau-*, *Schav-*, -*yng*-, (-*iuxta Wybenbury*) 1362 Plea, (-*alias Shenton*) 1802 Sheaf, *Shavington Hall* 1724 NotCestr, -*Green Farm* 1831 Bry

Schayntonfyld 1398 *Chol*, *Shaynton* 1400 ChRR, *Sheynton* 1496 ib, 1515 Plea

Shevington c.1415 Sheaf (p), 1567 ChRR, *Chevington* 1573 ib, *Sheavington* 1575 Sheaf

Shenton 1514 *ChEx*, 1666 Orm², (-*alias Shavington*) 1699 *AddCh*, (*Shavington alias*-) 1802 Sheaf, *Sheneton* 1531 AD

Shaventon-Woodnoth 1621 Orm², *Shavington Woodnote*, -*Woodneth* 1621 *ChCert*, *Shavinton Woodnoth* 1819 Orm¹, 1845 ChetOS VIII, 1882 Orm²

'Farm called after Scēafa', from the OE pers.n. *Scēafa* and -*ingtūn*, with feld, grēne², hall, and myln. Cf. Shavington Sa (DEPN), where this pers.n. also occurs, and Shannock **1** 64, *Shauintonfeld* **2** 192. The location is near Basford, Hough and Wybunbury 48, 64 *supra*, 80 *infra*. The manorial suffix *Woodnoth* is the surname of a family settled here from the thirteenth to the seventeenth centuries, cf. William & Randle *Wodenot* 1298–9 Orm² III 506, and it distinguishes this place from the other Shavington, ten miles away. The DB form has been ascribed to Sound, but it suits Shavington better, cf. Tait 155 n.133.

BACK LANE, on the boundary with Basford 48 *supra*.   BROOK HO, 1831 Bry, named from Gresty Brook *supra*.   GREEN BANK. GRESTY LANE, *Shavington Lane* 1831 ib.   GRESTY RD, now in Crewe borough, 26 *supra*, *Gresty Lane* 1831 ib, cf. prec.   THE GROVE, GROVE FM, cf. *Grove Field* 1839 *TA*, *v*. grāf.   HEN LANE, 1839 *ib*, cf. *Hen Heath* 1831 Bry, 1839 *TA*, from henn, perhaps a 'moor-hen'.   HOLLY MOUNT.   MOUNT PLEASANT.   OAK FM. SPRINGBANK.

FIELD-NAMES

The undated forms are 1839 *TA* 351, 1831 is Bry, 1842 OS.

(*a*) Alderley Fd (*v.* alor, lēah); Beggars Croft (*v.* beggere); Black Patch; Br(o)ad Shawes (*v.* brād, sceaga); Brick Kiln Fd; Coat Fd (*v.* cot); Cockshead (*v.* cocc-scyte); Copy Fd (cf. *Gresty Coppice* 1842, *v.* copis); Crow Lake ('crow's watercourse', *v.* crāwe, lacu); Dove House Mdw; Duckers Lane; Five Pound Piece (cf. foll., *v.* 325 *infra*); Five Shillings (*v.* scilling, cf. 325 *infra*); Flax Fd; Flood Gate (*v.* flōd-yate); Glabe Pieces ('pieces of glebe land', *v.* glebe, pece); Gold Lake (*v.* 69 *supra*); Greaves (*v.* grǣfe); Intake (*v.* inntak); Lee Moor (*v.* lēah, mōr¹); Long Butts; Long Foot (*v.* lang, fōt, but the significance is not apparent); Marl Pit Fd; New Ditch; Oat Eddage (*v.* āte, edisc); Ollen Croft (*v.* alren); The Outlet (*v.* outlet); Owlery Lane 1831 (cf. 69 *supra*); Ox Pasture; Patch; Pinfold Fd (*v.* pynd-fald); Poosy Dale Croft (*v.* Puseydale 68 *supra*); Red Hay (*v.* rēad, (ge)hæg); Ridding(s) (*v.* ryding); Rough Hey; Sandy Hill; Slang (*v.* slang); Sprink (*v.* spring 'a young wood'); Wale Fd; Wall Fd (*v.* wælla); Welchmans Fd (*v.* Wels(c)hman); Wheat Eddage (*v.* hwǣte, edisc, cf. Oat Eddage *supra*); White Fd; Willow Moor; Wimping Fd; Yolk of Egg (*v.* 325 *infra*); Yords (*v.* geard).

14. STAPELEY (BANK, FM, GRANGE, HALL & HO) (110–6749) ['steipəli, 'steipli]

> *Steple* 1086 DB, *Stepeley* 1414 ChRR
>
> *Stapeleg'* 1216–72 *AddCh et freq* with variant spellings -*le(e)*, -*ley* (from c.1240 Dieul, 1340 Chamb (p)), -*lehe*, -*legh*; (*maner of Stapeley*) 1330 Plea, (*Stapeley Hall*) 1622 Sheaf, (-*House*) 1842 OS
>
> *Stapelleya* c.1250 CASNS X (p), -*leg'* 1287 Court (p), -*ley* c.1298 *Chol* (p), -*le* c.1300 Sheaf (p), -*legh* 1308, 1316 ChRR
>
> *Stapilegh* 1312 Ipm
>
> *Staple* 1366 *ChCal* (p), 1367 *Tourn* (p), -*ley* 1445 *AddCh*, and seven instances to 1775 Sheaf

Either 'wood or clearing at a post', or 'wood where posts are got', from stapol and lēah (cf. Stapleford 326 *infra*), with banke, grange, hall, hūs. For the -*i*- spelling, cf. Botterley (in Faddiley) 142 *infra*.

HOWBECK BANK (110–6849), BRIDGE (74 *infra*) & FM (81 *infra*) ['houbek]

> *Holebag(ge)* 1259 Plea (p), 1260 Court, *Holbagg'* 1355 *Eyre* (p), -*bache* 1416 ChRR (p)
>
> *Hollebeke* 1304 Chamb (p), 1547 Orm²

Holebek 1330 Plea, 1331 Orm², *(le) Holebec(ke)* 1347 *AddCh* (p),
1349, 1358 *Eyre*, *(Holebeck Hall)* 1719 Sheaf, *Holbech(e)* 1359,
1360 BPR (p), 1397 ChRR (p), *Holbeck* 1558–79 *ChancP*,
(-Bridge) 1621 Sheaf
Howbecke 1508 *AddCh*, *Howbeck Bank & Bridge* 1831 Bry,
-House 1838 *TA*

'Hollow valley', or 'deep valley-stream', from hol² and bece¹,
bæce (with -*k*- due to influence from bekkr), with banke, brycg, hūs,
hall. Cf. Howbeck Brook 1 30.

THE ALOES.   ARTLEBROOK BRIDGE & FM, ['artḷ-], *Arteley bridge*
1621 Sheaf, *Artle or Harthill Bridge* 1831 Bry, named from Artle
Brook 1 13. The bridge carries Broad Lane over the brook, and is
probably the limit of the grant recorded 1357 ChRR (DKR xxxvi 282)
of the toll-passage rights for Church Lawton and Nantwich between
Arthull and *Huggebrugge* (Hug Bridge 1 55), cf. foll. and 1 48 (route
XXVII).   BROAD LANE, 1842 OS, (-*Green*) 1831 Bry (*v.* grēne²).
This road runs along the Batherton boundary (51 *supra*), leads from
Nantwich to Hatherton (110–508658 to 678482), and would seem to
continue the line of the lost road at Pepperstreet Moss 66 *supra*,
v. 1 49 (route XXVII).   BROOK BANK, *Cheer Brook* 1831 ib,
named from Cheer Brook 1 18, cf. Cheerbrook Bridge *infra*.   BUTT
GREEN, 1831 ib, *v.* butte, grēne².   CHEERBROOK BRIDGE, cf. *Salt-
ford infra, v.* 79 *infra*.   CRONKINSON FM.   CROSSLANDS,
'selions which run athwart', *v.* cros, land.   GREENFIELD HO.
HAYMOOR GREEN (FM), *Eimer-* 1831 Bry, *Haymoor Green* 1842 OS.
This hamlet is partly in Wybunbury township, cf. 81 *infra*.
LONDON RD, *-Roade* 1621 Sheaf, 'the road to London', *v.* rād.
MANOR HO, 1831 Bry, *Brick House* 1842 OS, *v.* maner, bryke.
MILE HO, 1842 ib, *The Mill House* 1831 Bry, cf. *molendinum de
Stapeley* 1347 *AddCh, v.* myln, mīl.   OAK FM.   OAKFIELD.
PIT HO, *v.* pytt.   RAVEN'S OAK, cf. *Ravens Oak Field* 1838 *TA, v.*
āc.   SPEWTREE FM, perhaps named from a swarming of bees, from
ModEdial *spew* (EDD, NED) 'the fourth swarm in a season' and
trēow.   WOODLANDS.   WYBUNBURY LANE, 1831 Bry, leading to
Wybunbury 80 *infra*.   YEWTREE FM.

FIELD-NAMES

The undated forms are 1838 *TA* 366. Of the others, 1309 is ChRR, 1330 Plea, 1387 Rich, 1437, 1447, 1522 *AddCh*, 1602 Sheaf, 1831 Bry.

(a) Ambutt (*Ambolt* 1522, cf. *Ambaldeside* 1330. The latter (DKR xxvIII 24) alludes to a place on the east side of Stapeley Hall, where the road from Howbeck *supra* to Nantwich 30 *supra* was to be closed. The name probably contains bold 'a house, a dwelling', with sīde 'the side of'. The first el. is obscure. Professor Löfvenberg suggests ān 'lonely', cf. OE ān-seld 'lonely dwelling, hermitage', also One House 1 140. The name may also appear in Ambert 69 *supra*); Bradley (v. brād, lēah); Brook Piece (named from Cheer Brook 1 18); Broom Fd (v. brōm); Brown Field Mdw (v. brūn¹); Bush and Whip Fd (cf. Bush O'Whip Fd 80 *infra*); Hand- & Long Butts (v. butte); Corncastle; Cross Fd (cf. *Bartons Cross* 80 *infra*); Five-, Four Day Math (v. day-math); Deakins Lake (v. lacu); Dig Lane 1831 (v. dīc); Flash Mdw (v. flasshe); Hanging Fd (v. hangende); Hedgrew Fd ('a hedgerow', v. hecg-rǣw); Hob Ridding (v. hobb(e), ryding); Horse Pasture (cf. *the Horsecroft* (*meadowes*) 1602, v. hors, croft, mǣd); Intake (v. inntak); Big- & Little Leason; The Lumps (v. lump); Marl (Pit) Fd; Far- & Near Marsh (*le Merssche* 1387, v. mersc); May Moor; Big & Little Moors (cf. *the morefildes otherwise called the heth fildes lying nygh Ambolt* 1522 and *le Heth* 1309 (p), v. mor¹, hǣð, cf. Ambutt *supra*); Mucked Fd (v. muked); Ox Pasture; Pale Fd (v. pale); Round Mdw; Sedge Mdw (v. secg); Stadmoral; Stall Mdw (v. stall); Walk Mdw (v. walk); Wary Croft; Winter Fd (v. winter); Wolfs Fd.

(b) the *Clayfeildes*, *Clayfeilde meadow* 1602 (v. clǣg, feld, mǣd); *the Croftes in Wichefilde* 1522 (v. croft, cf. *Wychefeld* 1 6); *Frapsance* 1522; *Prestham* (partly in Stapeley, v. 41 *supra*); *Safern garden* (lit. *Sasern*) 1602 ('saffron garden', v. saffroun, gardin); *Saltersich* (v. 79 *infra*, cf. foll.); *Saltford* 1447 (p) ('ford where salt is transported', perhaps at Cheerbrook Bridge *supra*, cf. prec., v. salt, ford); *le town orchart* 1387, *the Towne Orchard* 1523, 1622 ('the communal orchard or vegetable plot', v. toun, orceard); *Wallfylde* 1437, *the Wallfeilde* 1602 ('the spring or well field', v. wælla, feld, cf. Wall Fields 37 *supra*).

15. WALGHERTON (110–6948) [ˈwɔldʒərtən] older [ˈwɔːkər-]

Walcretune 1086 DB, *Walcerton(a)* 1260 *Plea*, Court (p), *Walquerton* 1272–1307 *AddCh*, *Walkerton* l13 MRA, 1297 Sheaf, 1307 *Eyre* (p), 1328 MRA, 1346 BPR, 1351 Plea, 1412, MainwB, 1429 Tab, 1453 *Chol*, *Walchirton* (lit. *Walth-*) 1308 ChRR
Walhreton c.1275 *Shav*
Walgherton 1295 ChF, 1315 Plea *et freq*, -ar- 1317 Plea (p), *Whalg(h)erton* 1404, 1408 ChRR
Walguerton 1309 Rich
Halgherton 1395 ChRR

Walhalgherton 1542 Plea
Wallessherton- 1549, *v.* 82 *infra*
Waukerton 1719 Sheaf
Wolgherton 1724 NotCestr
'Wealhhere's farm', from the OE pers.n. *Wealhhere* and tūn.

OAT EDDISH (110–689486), 1831 Bry, *Atedis* (lit. *Ac-*), *Hotedia*, *Othed(e)ys* 113, 1297, c.1300 Sheaf (p), *Otedhis* (*nova acra de*) 1297 ib, *Otesdissh*, *Hoteesdihs* 1307 *Eyre* (p), *Otedishe* 1318 *ib* (p), *-dyshe*, *-dische* 1532 Plea, *Oteedishe* 1543 *AddCh*, 'enclosed land where oats are grown', *v.* āte, edisc.

BACK LANE, 'lane at the back of the village', by-passing the hamlet, lying out towards the Hough and Lea boundaries.   BANK COTTAGE. BROOK HO, 1831 Bry, named from Wybunbury Brook 82 *infra*. DAGFIELDS, 1831 ib.   HOWBECK BRIDGE, cf. *Great & Little Howbeck*, *Howbeck Meadow* 1842 *TA*, *v.* 71 *supra*.   HUSSEY'S NOOK, 1842 OS, from the surname *Hussey*, *v.* nōk.   LODGE FM, cf. Walgherton Lodge *infra*.   MANOR HO, *Waukerton Hall* 1719 Sheaf, *Walgherton Hall* 1831 Bry, cf. Walgherton *supra*.   THE OAKS. PERRY'S ROUGH, from the surname *Perry*.   POOLBANK, 1831 Bry, cf. Walgherton Pool *infra*.   SHEEPWALK COTTAGE, cf. *Sheep Walk(s)* 1842 *TA*, 1843 *TAMap*, *v.* scēp, walk cf. *sheep-walk* NED 'a range of pasture for sheep'.   SPEAKMAN'S MOSS, from the surname *Speakman*, *v.* mos.   SPRINKS, *Far- & Near Sprink* 1842 *TA*, *v.* spring 'a young wood'.   WALGHERTON LODGE & POOL, 1831 Bry.

FIELD-NAMES

The undated forms are 1842 *TA* 408. Of the others, 113 is MRA, 1297 Sheaf, 1515 *MinAcct*, H8 Plea.

(a) The Acre; Backside (*v.* ba(c)k-syde); Bank Fd; Bessy Green Fd; Bowling Bank; Broomy Leasow (*v.* brōmig, lǣs); Bunkers Hill (*v.* 325 *infra*); Church Mdw; Cockshut (*v.* cocc-scyte); Counter Patch; Cranmere ('crane's pool', *v.* cran, mere¹); Duck Lake (*v.* dūce, lacu); Ferney Heys (*v.* fearnig, (ge)hæg); The Flatt (*v.* flat); Georges Wd (cf. 61 *supra*); Gibbiting Fd (*v.* gibet 'a gibbet'); Gorsty Lane and Wd (*v.* gorstig); Hammerhead (*v.* 325 *infra*); Hatherton Heath Croft (*v.* Hatherton 62 *supra*); Hen Hill; Intake (*v.* inntak); Killn Croft & Mdw (*v.* cyln); Long Wd; Mark Ridding (*v.* ryding); Marl Fd; The Mill Hills; The Moor; Moss Fd; Mott Mdw (this adjoins Oat Eddish *supra*, and may refer to some lost motte, cf. mote); Nine Days (cf. day-math, day-work); Ox Pasture; Poors Croft (probably

land devoted to poor-relief); Sand Hill; Sir Thomas's Fd; Six Butts; Slang
(v. slang); Townsend (v. toun, ende[1]); Walgherton Moss; Wall Gates (v.
wælla, gata); Well Bottoms (v. botm); White Fd; Wood Roas (v. rāw);
Woodwas (v. wudu, wæsse).

(b) *Beteleslegh* 1297 ('Bettel's clearing or wood', from an OE pers.n.
Bet(t)el and lēah); *Dovefeld* 1ı3 ('field where doves flock', v. dūfe, feld);
Hallewall Moore H8 ('(moor at) the holy well', v. hālig, wælla, mōr[1]);
Haptonhill' 1515 (v. hyll. The first el. may be Hatherton 62 *supra*, with
Haþ(er)- mistaken for *Hap*-, but the name may be analogous with Hapton
La 8o, 'enclosure at a hill', v. hēap, tūn); *Waterlode* 1ı3 ('the watercourse',
v. wæter, (ge)lād).

16. WESTON (110–7352) ['westṇ] older local ['wessṇ]

> *Westun* 13 Cre (p), *Weston* 1260 Court *et freq, passim* with variant
> spelling *-tone* 1290 Ipm, (*-iuxta Bertumleg'*) 1281 Court *et freq,*
> (*-Berel*) 1293 Plea, (*-Crue*) 1313 ib, (*-Barkesford*) 1338 Cre,
> (*-Chorleton*) 1348 *Eyre*, (*-Dodynton*) 1438 Plea, (*-Webunbury*)
> 1481 Orm[2]
>
> *Waston* 1551 ChRR

'Western farm', v. west, tūn. The place is west of Barthomley 5
supra, and adjoins Basford, Chorlton, Crewe 48, 59, 9 *supra*, and
Wybunbury 80 *infra*. Doddington 60 *supra* is four miles away.
For *-iuxta Berel*, v. foll.

CROKEMERESHO (lost)

> *Crokemeresle* 1216–72 *Harl.* 83 D19
> *Cn-, Knok(e)maresho* (passagium de) 1237 to 1242 P *freq*, *-mer(e)s-*
> 1245, 1247, 1250 ib
> *Crekemeresho* (passagium de) 1245 P
> *Croke(s)mersch* (passagium de) 1275, 1276 P
> *Crokemeresho* (a place called, in *Weston iuxta Berel'*) 1293 Plea
> (Orm[2] III 509 reads *-she*)

'(Wood, and spur of land, at) a pool at a corner', from krókr and
mere[1], with lēah and hōh. The form *-mersho* has been confused with
-mershe (from mersc), and a form *Cn-, Kn-* results from dissimilation
of *-r-* to *-n-*. The identification of *Weston iuxta Berel* 1293 Plea
(DKR xxvi, 42) with this Ch place is not certain. Moreover, the
context concerns the rights of Geoffrey son of Geoffrey Griffin in land
here. The Griffins were of Batherton 50 *supra*, four miles from
Weston, and Weston adjoins Barthomley 5 *supra*. Since there is no
p.n. in the area with a form like *Berel*, it could be a mistaken form of

Barthomley or Batherton. The location of the toll-passage of *Croke-meresho* in this Weston would make it analogous with *Bruneshurst* and *Donnington* 53, 61 *supra*, on a road to the salt-wich at Nantwich. Sheaf³ 23 (5357) suggests that P refers to a fee in the earldom of Chester at Crakemarsh St. Crakemarsh is at a ford of R. Dove on the Db border north of Uttoxeter, and such a place might have had a toll-passage, but it is not on a major route, and there does not appear to be a Weston near it.

SNAPE FM, BANK & HOLLOW [sneip], *le Snape* 1433, 1541 ChRR, *les Snape* 1443 ib, *Snape* 1585 Cre, (*-Farms*) 1831 Bry, cf. *Dinger-, Long-& Rushy Snape* 1845 *TA* 'poor pasturage', from snap, with banke and holh. *Dinger-* in the f.n. is from dingle 'a dell'. Cf. *snapes* 21 *supra*.

STOWFORD (110–733534) ['stou-], *-Farm* 1831 Bry, may be associated with *de Stowhet* 1260 Court, *del Stowhet* 1260 ib, E1 *AddCh, de Stou(e)heth* 1281, 1287 Court, a surname in this district. The names would be from stōw 'place of assembly', with ford 'a ford' and hǣð 'a heath'. The significance is not known.

BALTERLEY MERE, *Inglesea Mere* 1831 the head of Englesea Brook **1** 22, cf. Balterley St and Englesea-Brook *infra*, *v*. mere¹.   CARTER'S GREEN, 1845 *TA*, *v*. grēne². CROTIA MILL [krouʃə], *Cowshall Mill* 1831 Bry, *Crowfall Mill* 1847 *TAMap*, cf. *Further- & Middle Crowshall, Near Crowshall inclosure* 1845 *TA*. If this is *le moleyn de schawe* 1398 *Chol* referred to under Basford 50 *supra* the second el. is sc(e)aga 'a wood' with crāwe 'a crow', and myln.   ENGLESEA-BROOK *v*. 7 *supra*.   THE FLASH, *Flash* 1845 *TA*, *v*. flasshe 'a swamp', dial. 'a shallow water'.   GORSTY HILL, 1831 Bry, *v*. gorstig.   GREEN FM (lost) 1831 ib *v*. grēne² 'a green'.   HENBURY LEE, LEES WOOD, *Henbury Leys Wood* 1831 ib, *Henbury Lees* 1845 *TA*, perhaps from the surname from Henbury **1** 78, with either lǣs 'a pasture', or the plural of lēah 'a wood, a clearing'.   HOLLY-HEDGE FM, *Holly Hedge* 1831 Bry.   JACK LANE, 1831 ib, *v*. jack. LAGGERS BANK [lagəz], *Laghouse Bank* 1831 ib, perhaps 'wild-goose hill', from dial. lag-goose 'the wild grey goose' and banke.   LEES WOOD *v*. Henbury Lee *supra*.   MEREMOOR (MOSS), 1831 ib, probably named from Monneley Mere *infra*, which would have been more extensive formerly than now, *v*. mere¹, mōr¹, mos.   MILL LANE cf. *the Milne Crofte* 1605, *Mill Croft* 1656 Cre, 1845 *TA*,

named from Crotia Mill *supra* *v.* **croft.** MONNELEY MERE *v.* 7
supra. REDLION FM, *Red Lion* 1831 Bry, a p.h. name. WESTON-
COMMON, *Weston Heath (Farm)* 1831 ib, *v.* hǣð, commun. WESTON
GATE cf. *Toll Bar* 1847 *TAMap* a turnpike, *v.* **toll-bar, toll-gate.**
WESTON GREEN, 1831 Bry. WESTON HALL, 1724 NotCestr.
WESTON MERE, 1845 *TA.* WESTON MILL HILL BRIDGE. YEW-
TREE FM, 1831 Bry.

FIELD-NAMES

The undated forms are 1845 *TA* 421. Of the others, 1293 is Plea, 1324
AddCh, 1433, 1443, 1541 ChRR, 1470, 1572, 1602, 1670, 1744 Cre, 1752,
1777 Sheaf, 1831 Bry.

(*a*) Acres; Addershill; Backside (*v.* ba(c)ksyde); Bank; Barn Croft (*the*
1752); Big- & Little Birch (*Great-* & *Little-* 1752, *v.* birce); Blackamoor Fd;
Blake Fd (*v.* blæc); Boat House Fd; Boosy Pasture (*v.* bōsig); Brick Kiln Fd;
Broom Fd (1752, *v.* brōm); The Butcher's Fd; Butter Fd (*v.* butere); Cae
Hyn (a Welsh f.n., 'older field', from cae 'a field', and *hŷn*, comp. of hên
'old'); Clay Hill, Clays (*v.* clǣg); Clover Bank; Cock Walk Fd (*the cocke
walke* 1670, a 'cock-walk', where game-cocks are reared, *v.* cocc², walk);
Coppice Fd (cf. *Further-, Middle- & Nether Coppy* 1752, *v.* copis); Cow
Brook & Moor (*v.* cū, brōc, mōr¹); Crab Tree Fd; Cross Croft & Fd (*v.*
cros); Dredge Fd; Eccles Mdw & Yard (cf. *Eccles tenement* 1744, from the
surname *Eccles*); Fishpool Fd; Big Flatts (*v.* flat); Fox Yards (*-Yard* 1752,
v. fox, geard); Galacre (*v.* gagel, æcer); Giant Fd; Green Fd & Mdw (1752);
Grout; Hall Bank Moor (*v.* hall, banke, mōr¹); Hather Hill (cf. *Hatherhill
Moss* 1831, 'moss at heather-hill', *v.* hǣddre, hyll, mos); Hemp Yard 1752
(*v.* hemp-yard); Highland Fd; Hodge Lane Croft (cf. *Hodge Lane* 1831, *v.*
hocg, hogg, lane, cf. *Hodg Croft* 1 158); Holin Hurst, Hollen Fd & Mdw
('holly wood', *v.* holegn, hyrst); Hot(t)croft 1752 (*v.* hāt); Hough Fd
(*v.* hōh); Intake (*v.* inntak); Island Fd (cf. Highland Fd *supra*, *v.* ēg-land);
Kiln Fd; Kitchen Croft (*Kitchen's Croft* 1752, belonging to Weston Hall, *v.*
cycene, croft); Ley Fd (*v.* lǣge); Maltkiln Orchard (*v.* malte-kylne); Marl
Fd (1752); Marshy Bank, Far Marshy Bank Moor (*Martial-Banks* 1752,
Marshall Bank 1777, 'marsh corner', *v.* mersc, halh, banke); Molder Such
(*Mould Estick* 1752); Monnerley Mdw (cf. Monneley Mere *supra*); Moors;
Big- & Little Morrey ('moor enclosure', *v.* mōr¹, (ge)hæg); Moss Fd; Moss
Lane 1831; Mossy Horn (*v.* horn 'a horn of land'); Muck Fd (*v.* muk);
Oat Eddish (*Oat-Edish* 1752, *v.* āte, edisc, cf. Oat Eddish 74 *supra*); Ostrich
Fd; Ox Hay (1752, *v.* oxa, (ge)hæg); Packsaddle Bank (*v.* pakke-sadil); The
Part (*v.* part); Patch; Pickenhill (Fd), Picken Hill (Rough), Pickhill (Moor)
(perhaps 'Pica's hill', from an OE pers.n. *Pīca* and hyll, cf. Tickenhill *infra*);
Pinfold (*v.* pynd-fald); Pool Sitch & Mdw (cf. *the Pool-Place* 1752, *v.* pōl¹,
sīc, mǣd, place); Ridding (*v.* ryding); Rye Stubble (*v.* ryge, stubbil); Sand
Fd; Seven Shillings (*v.* 325 *infra*, *v.* scilling); Shoulder of Mutton (*v.* 325
infra); Slang (*v.* slang); Smooth Hat Croft; Sprink (*v.* spring 'a young

wood'); Stocking Mdw (1752, *v.* stoccing); Swan Fd (1752, *v.* swān²); Tickenhill (perhaps 'Tica's hill', from the OE pers.n. *Tica* and hyll, cf. Pickenhill *supra*); Timmis's Living (*Timmyes living* 1752, *v.* living); Town Fd (*Tom-Field* 1752, *v.* toun); Turnpike Fd; Wall-, Well Fd (*v.* wælla, wella); Weston Wd (1831); White Fd (1752); Withen (*v.* wīðegn).

(*b*) *le Hewkerd* 1324; *Latham in Weston* 1602, cf. *Lathom* 1470 (p), *-am* 1572 (p) (probably 'the lands or property of the *Latham* family', cf. Latham-hall 2 29); *Werfurd Mulne* 1433, *-ford Milne* 1443, *-mylne* 1541 (probably '(mill at) the weir ford', from wer and ford, with myln, but possibly 'Warford's mill', from the surname from Warford 1 104, 2 82–3).

17. WILLASTON (110–6752). Cf. 41 *supra*.

This township, composed of two ancient manors, *Wisterson* 42 *supra* and Willaston, was divided between Nantwich and Wybunbury parishes. The arrangement of the material here and at 41–4 *supra* follows the boundaries of this division down to 1831 (Bry) and 1845 (*TA*).

WILLASTON (HALL) (110–674525) ['wiləstən]

Wilavestune 1086 DB, *Wlaveston* 12 Dugd (p), *Wylaveston, -tun* c.1250 Orm², *Willawestun* c.1250–60 ib, *Wilawiston* 1272–1307 ib
Wilast(on) c.1180 *AddCh*, (17) *Chol*, *Wy-*, *Wilaston* H3 (14) *AddCh*, 1287 Court (p) *et freq* with variant spellings *-tone* to 1250 Plea, (*-iuxta Wich-Malbank*) 1311 Plea, (*-iuxta Wyghtreston*) 1337 Orm², (*Magna-, Great-*) 1373 *JRC*, 1374 Pat, (*-iuxta Wistanston*) 1383 Plea, (*-iuxta Alvandeston*) 1393 Orm², *Wyll-* 1340 Plea, *Will-* 1466 Comb *et freq*, (*-Hall*) 1831 Bry
Wolaston 1216–72 MainwB (p), (*-alias Wollaueston*) 1295 Ipm (p) (Barnes¹ 738), *Woll-* 1550 *AddCh*, 1574 ChRR, 1590 Sheaf
Wi, Wylaxton 1287 Court (p)
Welaston 1349, 1409 Orm²
Wileston 1359 BPR, *Wylestone* 1400 *CampbCh*, *Willeston* 1560 Sheaf
Wuleston 1350 BPR (Barnes¹ 739)
Wy-, Willason 1554, 1557 Pat, 1602 Sheaf
Waddelston 1563 Pat
Wallaston 1705 ChetOS VIII

'Wīglāf's farm', from the OE pers.n. *Wīglāf* and tūn, cf. Willaston 327 *infra*. The place adjoins Nantwich, *Wisterson* and Wistaston 30, 42, 45 *supra*. For the location *-iuxta Alvandeston* (Alvaston 28 *supra*) *v.* 43 *supra*. The forms of this p.n. have often been confused with those of Wistaston and *Wisterson*, cf. Orm² III 487.

BLAKELOW (110–680517), 1735 Tab, (*Farm*) 1752 Sheaf, *-e* 1307 *Eyre* (p), 1363, 1549 Pat, *Blaklowe* 1548 ib, *-lawe* 1550 *MinAcct*, 'black mound', *v.* blæc, hlǣw.

MOORFIELDS (110–679526), *Morefeld* 1326 ChRR, (*le-, the-*) 1391 ib, *the morefelds in Wixterston* 1531 Orm², *Morfeld* 1352 *Eyre*, 1353 *AddCh, Mores-* 1354 *Indict*, 1359 BPR, *Moor-* 1375 *Eyre*, 'field(s), or open land, at a moor', *v.* mor¹, feld, cf. 46 *supra*. This is now the name of a hamlet in this and Wistaston townships. It was formerly the name of a district including Brassey Hall 43 *supra*, which gave the Brescy family a local surname, cf. *Wilcott's Heath* 46 *supra*.

SALTERSICH (lost)

> *Salteressiche* 1194 *AddCh*
> *Saltersych* E1 *AddCh, -syche* 1338 *CampbCh et freq* with variant spellings *-sych, -sich*(e) to 1646 Sheaf (lit. *Saller-*), *Saltersyche in Wylaston and Wyghtrestone* 1395 *CampbCh*, 1400 ChRR, (*Wichefild*(e) *nigh*) *Saltersich* 1522 *AddCh*
> *Saltherysseche* (in *Wylestone*) 1400 *CampbCh*
> *Saltersoche* 1445 *AddCh*
> *Salter-such bridge* 1621 Sheaf

'Salter's stream', *v.* saltere, sīc. It may be possible to identify this place. The name applies to a stream and a place or district upon it. It is found in contexts associating it with Stapeley, *Wisterson* 71, 42 *supra, Wychefeld* 1 6, and Willaston. It had a ruined bridge in 1621 (Sheaf³ 22 (5255)). The only stream which runs through Stapeley, Willaston, Wisterson and Nantwich is that variously called Cheer- and Cheney Brook (1 18). The hamlet on this stream is at Cheerbrook Bridge, etc. *infra*. It would seem that the stream was *Saltersich*, and the bridge and the hamlet were named from it. Cheerbrook Bridge may then be the site of *Saltford* 73 *supra*. This would be on the Nantwich–Woore route, *v.* 1 48 (route XXVII).

ASHFIELD COTTAGES & HO. BROOK BUILDINGS, named from Cheney Brook 1 18. CHEERBROOK BRIDGE, FM, HO & LANE (110–672518), *Chearbrooke or Chear brooke house* 1602 Sheaf, *Cheer Brook* 1831 Bry, cf. Brook Bank 72 *supra*, all from Cheer Brook 1 18, *v. Saltersich supra*. The bridge is on the Stapeley boundary, cf. 72 *supra*. CHENEYBROOK BRIDGE, cf. *Cheny Brook Meadow* 1845 *TA* and Willaston Cottage *infra*, named from Cheney Brook 1 18, cf.

Saltersich supra.   COPPICE RD, *v.* copis.   CROSSLANDS, cf. Cross Field *infra*, *v.* cros, land.   GREEN LANE.   LONDON RD & NEWCASTLE RD, leading to London, and Newcastle under Lyne St. OAKBANK.   PARK RD.   WARREN HO, 1842 OS.   WILLASTON COTTAGE, *China Brook House* 1831 Bry, cf. Cheneybrook Bridge *supra.*   WYBUNBURY RD, leading to Wybunbury *infra.*

FIELD-NAMES

The undated forms are 1845 *TA* 434. Of the others, H3, 1250–60, 1260, E1, 1440 are Orm², 1357 BPR, 1522, 1526, 1697 *AddCh*, 1831 Bry, 1842 OS.

(a) Aspers Close (cf. *Asphale* 1260, 'aspen nook', *v.* æspe, halh); Beach (*v.* bece¹); Broom Fd (*v.* brōm); Burrow Fd (*v.* borow); Bush O' Whip Fd (cf. Bush and Whip Field 73 *supra*); Cheer- & Cheny Brook Mdw (cf. Cheer-, Cheney Brook 1 18); Coney Greave (*v.* coningre); Cross Fd & Mdw (cf. *Bartons Cross* 1842, -*Crosse* 1522, from cros 'a cross', probably with a surname *Barton*, though this may be a p.n. from beretūn, cf. Barthomley 5 *supra*); Day Math (*v.* day-math); Hammer Wood Fd (*v.* amore); Heath Fd (cf. *Willaston Heath* 1831, 1842); Higherland; Johnsons field 1697; Laundry Fd; Malpas Butts (from butte with the surname from Malpas 326 *infra*); Moat Fd (*v.* mote); The Moor (cf. Moorfields *supra*); Norcops Fd; Outlet (*v.* outlet); the two Ox pastures 1697; Pack Horse Fd; Big- & Little Piece; Pole Fd; Queen Ann's Bounty Fd; Slang (*v.* slang); Swan Mdw; Thieves Lane Fd (*v.* þēof); Water Piece ('piece of ground by a stream', *v.* wæter, pece); Well Mdw; White Fd.

(b) *Bexcros* H3 (from cros 'a cross', with an obscure first el., perhaps the gen.sg. *Bēaces of an OE pers.n. *Bēac* as in Beswick La 35, Bexwell Nf (DEPN), Bexton 2 72); *le Fridle* E1 (perhaps 'woodland glade', *v.* (ge)fyrhð(e), lēah); *Hough'hull* c.1250–60 ('spur hill', *v.* hōh, hyll); *Mylnefeld* 1526 (*v.* myln, feld); *Munstelmor* E1 (apparently '(marsh at) the fish-pond at the mouth of a stream', *v.* munnr, stell, with mōr¹); *Les Rydyngges* 1357, *Ryddingessfeld* 1526 ('the cleared lands', *v.* ryding, cf. foll. and The Riddings 81 *infra*); *Rosseryding* 1440 ('horses' clearing', *v.* hross, ryding); *tuntainlmor* H3 (Orm² III 493, unintelligible).

18. WYBUNBURY (110–700500) [ˈwibṃbri, ˈwinbəri, ˈwibənbəri] older local [ˈwidṇbəri, ˈwimbəri]

Wimeberie 1086 DB

Wybbunberi 1199–1216 *AddCh et freq* with variant spellings
Wyb(b)-, Wib(b)-, Whyb-, -en- (*freq*, e13 Dieul to 1516 Plea),
-in- & -yn- (*freq*, 1234 Orm² to 1467 *Chol*), *-on-* (1243 Cl), *-em-*
(1291 Tax), *-um-* (1452 Comb), *-ym-* (1452, 1464 *BodlCh*),
-bur(e), -buri(e), -buria, -bury(e), -bir(y)

Westbenburi e13 Dieul
Wibibr 1208–26 Adl
Webbenburi H3 *JRC*, *-bury* 1358 BPR, *Webunbury* 1380 *Eyre* (p),
   -bery 1478 AD, *Webnury* 1479 AD
Wilbinbur' c.1280 *Dow* (p), *Wylbenbury* 1352 *Eyre*
Wymbinbur' c.1280 *Dow* (p)
Wylbrisbur' 1288 *Eyre* (p), *-bury* 1290 Court (p), *-biry* 1290 *Eyre*
Wyb(b)risbur(y) 1288, 1290 Court, *Eyre* (p), *Wybresbur(y)*,
   Wib(i)ris-, *Wybrysbir(y)* 1290 *Eyre*, Court (p)
Woddunbury 1509–47 AD, *Wooden-* 1547 *MinAcct*
Wedenbyre 1526 Comb (p), *-burye* 1549 Pat, *Wednebury* 1550
   MinAcct, *Wedden-* 1698 Sheaf
Widenbury 1536, 1682 Sheaf, *Wyd(d)en-*, *Wydnebury(e)* 1549 Pat,
   1550 *MinAcct*, 1551 ChRR, *Widden-* 1660 Sheaf
Winbury 1646 Sheaf
Winburn Bury 1775 Sheaf

'Wīgbeorn's stronghold or manor-house', from the OE pers.n.
Wīgbeorn and burh (cf. Studies[1] 93).

THE RIDDINGS (110–690498)

Rudinges 1260 Court (p), 1283 Pat, *-ynges* 1364 *AddCh* (p), *-inggs*
   1304 Chamb (p), *(le) Rudyngges* 1330 Fine, 1355 BPR, *Rudding(g)s*
   1331 IpmR, *-yng(g)es* 1352 BPR, *the Ruddynges* 1367 Orm[2], *(le)*
   -yngus 1379 *AddCh* (p)
le Rudingh 1281 Court (p)
Rydingges 1330 Ipm, *Riddings* 1846 *TA*

'The cleared lands', *v.* **ryding.**

BRIDGE HO, named from Howbeck Bridge 74 *supra.*   CLANNOR
HEATH, 1842 OS, *Clonner Heath* 1831 Bry, from hǣð 'a heath', with
an unexplained first el.   DAISY HILL.   GROVE HO, *The Groves,*
Grove's Meadow, Grove Field 1846 *TA*, *v.* grāf.   HALL BANK, &
Field 1846 *ib*, *v.* hall, banke.   HAYMOOR GREEN, cf. *Haymore*
Green Meadow 1846 *ib*, *v.* 72 *supra.*   HOLLIN HO, 1831 Bry, cf.
Holly Housefield 1846 *TA*, *v.* holegn, hūs.   HOWBECK FM, *v.* 71
supra.   MOSS LANE, cf. Wybunbury Moss *infra, The Moss* 1831
Bry, *le Mossefelde* 1549 Pat, *v.* mos.   PINFOLD HO, *The Pinfold*
1831 Bry, *Penfold House* 1842 OS, *v.* pynd-fald.   THE POPLARS.
SPRINGFIELD HO.   TOMWALL WELL, *Tam Wall* 1846 *TA*, 'the
town well', from toun and wælla, with wella.   WYBUNBURY

BRIDGE, *Wibunbury-* 1621 Sheaf.   WYBUNBURY BROOK (Artle
Brook).   WYBUNBURY GRANGE.   WYBUNBURY LANE, MERE &
MOSS, 1831 Bry, *v.* mere[1], mos.   YEWTREE HO, 1831 ib.

FIELD-NAMES

The undated forms are 1846 *TA* 451. Of the others, l13, 1241 are MRA, 1295
ChancW, 1549 Pat, 1646 Sheaf, 1831 Bry, and the rest ChRR.

(*a*) The Acres; Back Lane Croft; Birch Fd; Black Fd; Boughlay Cottage;
Brick Kiln Fd; Church Bank; Dead Croft (*v.* dēad); Diglake Mdw (cf.
Diglake 1831 Bry, a watercourse, *v.* dīc, lacu); Flash (*v.* flasshe); Footway
Croft (*v.* fote-waye); Gorsty Bank (*v.* gorstig); Hospital Bank (*v.* hospital);
Hunger Hill (*v.* hungor); Kitchen Mdw; Long Shoot (*v.* scēat); Marl Fd;
Means (*v.* main); Millfield (*le Mylnefelde* 1549, *v.* myln, feld); Pasture Fd;
Pillow Stitch Croft (perhaps associated with Adam de *Pillee*, *-Pillileg'* 1241,
v. pīl, lēah); Pingle (*v.* pingel); Pleck (*v.* plek); Podmore Fd ('toad-marsh,
v. pode, mōr[1]); Roundabout (*v.* 325 *infra*); Sandfords Brook (from brōc,
probably with a surname); Street Croft (*v.* strǣt); Town Fd (cf. Tomwall
Well *supra*); Unnions Lane Fd; Way Fd; Way-go (*Wygall* 1549, perhaps
v. wīc, halh); Whitening Yard.

(*b*) *Bradenaker* 1241 (*v.* brād, æcer); *Dee house* 1646 (*v.* dey-hūs); *Grene*
1459 (p) (*v.* grēne[2]); *the Lady House* 1549 (a house at Blakelow *supra*, perhaps
'Our Lady's House' and part of the property of Combermere Abbey 93
infra, *v.* hlǣfdige, hūs); (*le*) *Lowe* 1399 (p), 1402 (p), 1407 (p), 1408 (p),
(*v.* hlāw); *Olenwrthug* 1241 ('curtilage growing with alders', *v.* alren,
worðign); *Tentercrofte* 1549 (*v.* tentour, croft); *Wallessherton Felde* 1549, cf.
the Walkerton field l13 MRA p.298 ('field near, or belonging to, Walgherton
(73 *supra*)', *v.* feld); *Wybenbiryhagh* 1295 (this p.n. occurs in the context
Cherlton by- (Chorlton 59 *supra*) and is either a form of the p.n. Wybunbury
supra, or the same with haga 'a hedge');

vii. Audlem

The ecclesiastical parish of Audlem contained 1. Audlem, 2. Buerton,
3. Hankelow, 4. Tittenley (transferred to Salop in 1895, now included in
Adderley Sa), and also parts of Dodcott cum Wilkesley 92 *infra*, Newhall
101 *infra*, and Coole Pilate 138 *infra*. There is no mention of a church at
Audlem in DB, the first reference noted being *ecclesia de Aldelyme* John
AddCh 875. The parish was probably formed out of Wybunbury parish 48
supra, cf. Tait 20.

1. AUDLEM (110–6643) ['ɔːdləm] locally dial. ['ɔːləm]

   Aldelime 1086 DB, *-lim(e)* c.1180 *AddCh* (p), *-lyme* John ib *et freq*
   with variant spellings *-lim(e)*, *-lima*, *-limu* (1291 Tax), *-lym* to
   1527 ChRR

Aldelyn 1220–40 Whall (p), Dieul, 1342 (1438) ChRR, -*lyne* 1281
  Court (p), 1327 Pat (p), -*lin* 1486 MidCh (p), -*line* 1621 (1656)
  Orm²

Audelime c.1280 (17) *Chol* (p), -*lym(e)* 1281 Cl, 1285 *Chol*, 1301
  AddCh (p)

Audeline 1282 Court (p)

Aldelune 1304 Chamb

Aldeleme 1348 *Eyre*, -*lem* 1388 Pat (p) *et freq* to 1724 NotCestr,
  -*leym(e)* 1393 *ChCal*, 1421, Plea, -*leem* 1469 Cre

Aldlim 1425 MidCh, -*lyme* 1485 Plea

Aldlem 1496, 1621 Orm², 1724 NotCestr

Audelem 1527 ChCert, 1592 Orm², 1646 Sheaf, 1687 *Chol*, *Awd*-
  c.1550 *Surv*, *Audilem* 1577 Cre

Audeleyn 1547 *MinAcct*, -*len* 1549 Pat

Aldelam 1548 Pat

Aldelen 1549, 1550 Pat

Awlame c.1550 *Surv*, *Awlam* 1565 Wil

Awlem 1558 *AddCh*, 1619 Sheaf, *Aulem* 1656 Orm², 1708 Sheaf,
  (-*alias Audlem*) 1721 *Chol*, *Awleme alias Awlam alias Audelam*
  1565 Wil

Audelam 1565 Wil

Audlem 1575 Cre, 1646 Sheaf *et freq*, (-*alias Aldelem*, -*Aldlem*,
  -*Aulym*) 1724 NotCestr

Auldlim 1579 *Chol*

Adelem 1644 Sheaf

Audlim 1652 Sheaf

Audla-, *Audleham* 1685 *Chol*

Aulme 1719 Sheaf

Aulym 1724 NotCestr

Audlan 1769 Wil

The second el. of this p.n. is *The Lyme* 1 2. The formation of this
p.n. may be analogous with that of Burslem St which is 'Burgweard's
or Burgheard's part of *The Lyme*' (DEPN, Duignan). In that case, the
first el. of Audlem would be the OE pers.n. *Alda*, *Ealda*. However,
the forms of Audlem would support derivation from a first el. ald
'old, former', and the p.n. probably means 'formerly in *The Lyme*,
former *Lyme* territory'. This raises unanswered questions of the
history and geography of *The Lyme*, and in particular, of the time and
and cause of Audlem's removal from it.

GORSECROFT FM ['gɔːskrɔft], *Gosecroft* 1348 ChRR, (*le*) *Goscroft* 1403 Orm², 1421 ChRR, *-e* 1440 ib, *Gorse Croft* 1831 Bry, 'geese's croft', *v.* gōs (gen. pl. gōsa), croft. The first el. has been confused with gorst.

SWANBACH BRIDGE, FM & GRANGE (110–655422) ['swɔnbatʃ]

> *Swanesbache* (passagium de) 1274 Ipm, *-bach* 1295 ib, Cl, *Scuanes-bache* 1276 Ipm, *Swannes-* 1299 ib
> *Swanebache* (passagium de) 1275 Cl, 1369 Plea (p), 1584 *Chol*, *Swanbache* 1348 ChRR (p), 1539 *MinAcct*, (*-alias Szyanbache*) 1393 Pat (p), *-bach* 1515 Plea, 1831 Bry, *Swannebache* 1438 *AddCh* (p)
> *Szyanbache* 1393 Pat (p)
> *Swanbeach* 1781 Sheaf
> *Swanback* 1860 White

Probably 'valley-stream frequented by swans', from swan¹ and bæce¹, with brycg and grange, though the first el. could be an OE pers.n. *Swān* or swān² 'a herdsman, a peasant'. This was the site of a toll-passage held of the earls of Chester in the barony of Nantwich, usually in conjunction with that of *Bruneshurst* 53 *supra*, e.g. *passagia de Brunneshurst et Swanesbach* 1295 Ipm III 177. Swanbach Bridge crosses Coxbank Brook *infra* into Adderley Sa, on the way from Market Drayton Sa, to Nantwich 30 *supra*, *v.* 1 48 (route XXVI), and the p.n. probably alludes to that stream. Swanbach Grange is *Grange Farm* 1860 White, *v.* grange.

WOOD ORCHARD HO & LANE, *Le Wodeorchard* 1421 ChRR, *Wood Orchard* 1831 Bry, (*-House*) 1842 *TA*, perhaps named from the family of John *del Wode* 1348 ChRR, *v.* orceard.

WOOLFALL (110–678450) ['wulfɔː], WOOLFALL-HALL FM (88 *infra*, 100–682545) ['wulfə-]

> *Wolfhill* 13 Brad (p), *-hull* 1281 Court (p), (*molendinum de-*) 1444 Sheaf, *-hul* c.1311 *AddCh* (p), *Wolfull* 1595 Sheaf, *Vulfhull'* 1280 P (p), *W(u)lfhul(l)*, *Wlfull*, (*-iuxta Aldelyme*) 1282, 1288, 1289 Court
> *Vulfshull'* 1280 P (p)
> *Wolfhall* 1281 Court (p), *Wulfhal* 1283 Cl (p)
> *Wolfall* 1400 ChRR (p), 1430 *Chol* (p), *Wofall* 1577 ChRR, *Woolfall* (*Pool & Hall*) 1831 Bry

'Wolf hill', from **wulf** and **hyll**, with **pōl**[1], **hall**, and **myln**. Cf. Woolfall Fm *infra*. The development of the *-(h)all* form may be due to substitution of ON **hallr** 'a slope, a hill for **hyll**. The hall is in Buerton township.

AUDLEM BRIDGE, *Aldelem Bridge* 1621 Sheaf.   AUDLEM MILL, 1831 Bry.   BAGLEY LANE, *Cow Lane* 1831 ib, cf. *Baggeley's Croft, Cowlane Field* 1842 *TA*, from **cū** and **lane**, with the surname from Baguley **2** 12.   BATH FM & LANE, cf. *Bath Field & Meadow* 1842 *ib*, *v.* **bæð** 'a bath'.   BLACKWATER MOSS, 1831 Bry, *v.* **blæc**, **wæter**, mos.   BRIDGE FM, cf. *Bridge Meadow* 1842 *TA*, named from Swanbach Bridge *supra*.   BROOK HO, from an unnamed stream joining R. Weaver near Swanbach Mill *infra*.   BUNSLEY BANK, 1842 OS, *Bansley Bank* 1831 Bry, *Bu(r)nsley-* 1842 *TA*, cf. *Bansley Bridge* 1621 Sheaf, and *Far- & Near Bunsley* 1843 *TA* 61 (89 *infra*), *v.* **brycg**, **banke**. The origin of the name is uncertain. CHAPEL END, *v.* 87 *infra*.   COPTHORNE (HO), *Copthorne* 1831 Bry, *Copthorn Bank* 1842 *TA*, 'polled thorn', *v.* **coppod**, **þorn**.   COR-BROOK HO, *Cor Brook* 1831 Bry, presumably named from the stream on the boundary with Hankelow 89 *infra*, *v.* **brōc**. The stream-name is obscure.   COXBANK (BROOK), *Coxbank* 1831 Bry, *Cock Bank* 1842 OS, cf. Coxbank Wood in Adderley Sa, presumably 'wood-cock's hill', *v.* **cocc**[2], **banke**. The stream joins R. Duckow.   DAISY BANK, cf. *Daisy Field* 1842 *TA*.   FIELD FM, *Fields* 1860 White. GORSE COTTAGE.   GREEN BANK, *-Cottage* 1860 White, *Green End Cottage* 1831 Bry, *v.* **grēne**[2] 'a green', **banke**, **ende**[1].   GREEN LANE, 1774 Wil, 'lane leading to a green', *v.* **grēne**[2], **lane**, cf. prec. GREY'S BRIDGE.   HANKELOW HO, cf. *Hankelow Mill Meadow, Hankelow Park* 1842 *TA*, cf. Hankelow 89 *infra*.   HEN LANE, *v.* **henn**.   HILLSIDE.   THE HOLLIES.   HOLLYBANK.   THE HOLMES, *le-* 1540 Dugd, 'the marshes', *v.* **holmr**.   KETTLE LANE, on the boundary with Buerton 87 *infra*, perhaps a tinkers' camping place, from **ketill** 'a kettle', but cf. **keddle-dock**.   KINSELL FM, cf. foll. and Kynsall Lodge 88 *infra*.   KINSEY HEATH (FM), *Kinsley Heath* 1831 Bry, *Kinsey Heath* 1842 OS, *v.* **hǣð** 'a heath', cf. prec. This may be the same as *Kynstanley* 1398 Orm[2] III 488, 'Cynestān's wood', from the OE pers.n. *Cynestān* and **lēah**. LITTLE HEATH, 1831 Bry.   LONGHILL LANE, leading to Longhill 88 *infra*.   MAYBANK.   MEADOWS FM.   MILL LANE, cf. Audlem Mill *supra*.   MILL PLANTATION, near Hankelow Mill 90 *infra.* MONK'S LANE, 1831 Bry, from munuc 'a monk', or the surname *Monk*.   MOSS HALL, 1831 ib, *le Mosse* 1534 *Chol, Mosse* 1673 Sheaf, *Mossehouse* 1620 Sheaf, *le Mossehowse* 1621 Orm², *the Moss-house* 1643 Orm², *Audlem Hall, called the Moss Hall* 1882 Orm², cf. *Mosse Bridge* 1621 Sheaf, from mos 'a bog, a marsh', and hall, brycg.   PADDOCK LANE, 1842 *TA, Audlem Lane* 1831 Bry, leading to Audlem, *v.* pearroc, lane.   PARK'S FARM, *The Parks* 1831 ib, *v.* park, cf. pearroc.   RAVEN'S BANK, older local ['raːnz-], 1842 OS, *Ransbank* 1860 White, *v.* hræfn, banke.   ROPEBANK FM, cf. *Rope Walk* 1842 *TA*, 'bank where rope is made', *v.* rāp, banke.   SANDY LANE, 1842 *ib.*   SPRINGFIELD, 1842 OS, *v.* spring 'a spring', feld.   SWANBACH MILL, *New Mill* 1831 Bry, *Audlem New Mill* 1842 OS, *v.* nīwe, myln, cf. Swanbach *supra*.   WOOLFALL FM, *Pentry Cloud* 1831 Bry, *Pentre Cloud* 1842 OS, apparently 'hill hamlet', from Welsh pentref 'village' and clūd 'a hill', but the second el. may also be Welsh, e.g. *clawdd* 'a dyke, a hedge, a ditch', and the name may mean 'moated house' or 'stockaded settlement'. Cf. The Cloud **2** 291, Woolfall *supra*.

FIELD-NAMES

The undated forms are 1842 *TA* 28. Of the others, 1300 is Plea, 1550 Pat, 1831 Bry.

(a) Acres; Audlem Wake Mdw (probably the place where the Wakes sports took place); Bache (*v.* bæce¹); Backstone Hill (*v.* bæc-stān); The Bank; Bantree-, Bantry Fd; Birchall Mdw (cf. Birchall 62 *supra*); Black-, Blake Flatts (*v.* blæc, flat); Blackstone Hill (*v.* Backstone Hill *supra*); Blusty Bank 1831; Boos-, Booz(e)y Croft & Pasture (*v.* bōsig); Broomy Bank (*v.* brōmig); Butts (*v.* butte); Butty Fd (*v.* butty); Clutmans Dale; Cocksheads, Cockshutt Fd (*v.* cocc-scyte); Coppice Hole (*v.* copis, hol¹); Cordway Fd; Cote (*v.* cot); Cranberry (*v.* cranberry); Cross Barn Fd; Crow Pleck (*v.* crāwe, plek); Drumble, Rumble (dial. *drumble*, cf. dumbel 'a wooded ravine'); Duckow Fd (cf. R. Duckow **1** 22); Excisemans Fd; Fasacre; Fern(e)y Hayes (*v.* fearnig, (ge)hæg); Flash Fd (*v.* flasshe); Flatts (*v.* flat); Foul Heath (*v.* fūl); Foxhole Fd (*v.* fox-hol); Glade Fd (*v.* glæd³); Hang Hill; Harpsley (perhaps *Herteplawe* 1300, 'hart's play, place where the hart ruts', *v.* heorot, plega); Harrow Field Bank (*v.* harwe); Heath Leasow (*v.* læs); Hempbutt (*v.* hænep, butte); Hollinhurst (*v.* holegn, hyrst); Holly Wd; Horse Hay; Intake (*v.* inntak); Lady('s) Fd, Lady Hill (*v.* hlǣfdige); (Heath- & Pool-) Levy; Lidgates (hlid-geat); Long Butts; Long Shoot(s) (*v.* scēat); Malpas Croft, Malpasses's (from the surname *Malpas*); Marl pit croft; Milking Bank (*v.* milking); Mill Fd, Fleam, Hay(e)s & Mdw (cf. Audlem Mill *supra*); Morrey's Bank Fd; Old Park; Orchard Fd; Outlett (*v.* outlet); Ox Leasow (*v.* læs); Pavement Lane Fd (*v.* pavement); Pearl Fd (*v.* pyrl(e)); Pool Bank

& Slang (*v.* slang); Raven Fd (*v.* hræfn); Riddings (*v.* ryding); Ring Fd (*v.* hring); Rood Fd (*v.* rōd²); Rough Fd & Moor; Round Robin (*v.* 325 *infra*); Rye Croft; Sinacre (*v.* seofon, æcer); Six Acres; Slang (*v.* slang); Sparrow Bank (*v.* spearwe); Spoil Bank (*v.* spoil-bank); Spout Fd (*v.* spoute 'a spring'); Sprink (*v.* spring 'a young wood'); Big Stocking, Stocking Mdw (*v.* stoccing); Taintree Fd, Ten Tree Field (*v.* tentour); Ten Butts; Tinker's Croft (*v.* tink(l)ere, cf. Kettle Lane *supra*); Town Fd; Trows (perhaps the pl. of trog, but Professor Löfvenberg suggests the pl. of trēow 'a tree', with shift of stress, or an OE **trēo-hūs* 'wooden house' as in Trowse Newton Nf (DEPN)); Turf Moor (*v.* turf); Turnpike Fd (*v.* turnepike); Water Mdw; Weaver Mdw (cf. R. Weaver 1 38); White Fd (cf. *la Wyteridinge* 1300, *v.* hwīt, ryding); Windmill Fd (*v.* wind-mylne); Wood Ground (cf. Wood Orchard *supra*); Wooler(e)y Mdw (probably *owlery* 'full of alders', from dial. *owler*, *v.* alor); Wyche Fd.

(*b*) *The Churchehouse* 1550 (*v.* cirice, hūs); *Redith* 1300 (probably for *Redich*, 'reed ditch' *v.* hrēod, dīc).

2. BUERTON (110–6843), ['bjuːǝrtǝn, 'buːǝrtǝn]

> *Burtune* 1086 DB, *Burtun* c.1200 Facs (p), *Burton* 1260 Court
> *Buerton* 1272–1327 *JRC* 1405 (Barnes¹ 679), 1535 VE *et freq*,
>   (*-within Aldelem parish*) 1548 Pat, (*Aldelem-Buerton*) 1577 ChRR
> *Bureton* 1290 Ipm, 1610 Speed
> *Buyrton* 1312 (1348) Pat, 1316 Plea *et freq* to 1491 ChRR, (*-iuxta Aldelym(e)*)) 1321 Plea *et freq* to 1372
> *Boerton* 1349 Orm² (p)
> *Bewerton* 1724 NotCestr
> *Brewerton* 1724 NotCestr

'An enclosure belonging to a **burh**', *v.* byrh-tūn. There is no trace of earth-works here, and the *burh* may have been a fortified house. Cf. Buerton 325 *infra*.

THE ASH. BITHEL'S FM, from the surname *Bithel.* BRICK-KILN WOOD, cf. *Brick Kiln Field & Meadow* 1843 *TA.* BUERTON BRIDGE. BUERTON FM, *The Fields* 1831 Bry. BUERTON GORSE, GRANGE, HALL & MOSS, 1831 ib. CHAPEL END, cf. *Buerton Chapel* 1842 OS, *Chapel Croft & Field* 1843 *TA*, *v.* chapel(e), ende¹. COLLEGE FIELDS, 1831 Bry, cf. College Field 99 *infra*, *v.* college. The advowson of Audlem church belonged to the priory of St Thomas, Stafford, and this land may have been theirs. GAMBLERS FIELD FM, *Gamblers Field* 1843 *TA.* HANKINS HEYS, -*Hays* 1844 *TAMap, Hankeys Heys or Goblins Hole* 1831 Bry, from the pers.n. or

surname *Hankin*, and **gobelin** 'a goblin', *v.* (ge)hæg, hol[1].   HIGH-
FIELDS (FM), *High Fields* 1831 ib. This is a seventeenth-century house,
but no records of it have come to hand.   HOLLY FM.   KETTLE
LANE, 1831 ib, *v.* 85 *supra*.   KYNSALL LODGE, cf. *Kinsey Heath
Field* 1843 *TA* and Kinsey Heath 85 *supra*.   LONGHILL, 1844
TAMap.   LONG WOOD.   MANOR FM.   MERE FM, *Mere Hall*
1831 Bry, cf. perhaps *Meyrhowse* 1519 Orm[2] III 374. There is a pool
here, but the place is on the county boundary with Sa, and the name
is probably from (ge)mǣre 'a boundary' rather than mere[1] 'a pool',
v. hūs.   MOBLAKE, 1831 Bry, *Moblock tenement* 1706 Sheaf, cf.
Mob Field 1843 *TA*. The second el. is probably lacu 'a watercourse',
but the first is obscure.   THE OX LEASOW, 1843 *ib*, *v.* læs.
PARKFIELDS, *Parkfields tenement* 1706 Sheaf, cf. *Buerton parke, the
Parke Poole* 1615 Orm[2], and *Park* (*Field*) 1843 *TA*, *v.* park, feld,
pōl[1].   PINDAR'S END, *Penders End* 1831 Bry, 1843 *TA*, from either
OE **pyndere* 'a pinder', or the derived surname (Thuresson 108,
Reaney s.n. *Pindar*), *v.* ende[1].   THE SULLENS, 1842 OS, *Sullins*
1831 Bry. This is probably analogous with Sillins Wo 320, explained
in EPN as ME *sulhene*, wk.pl. of sulh 'a plough, a plough-land',
and in Wo 320 as from OE *sulum*, dat. pl. of sulh. Syllenhurst,
in Woore, Sa, (110–725428) a mile or so from The Sullens, may be
analogous.   THREEBROOKS WOOD, *Buerton New Gorse* 1831 Bry,
named from Three Brooks, a wood in Woore Sa, where three brooks
meet.   THE THREE-WELLS, *Three Well*(*s*) 1843 *TA*, a place with
three wells.   TOP FM, *v.* top.   TOWNHOUSE, *v.* toun, hūs.
OLD WINDMILL, *The Mill* 1831 Bry, *Buerton Mill* 1842 OS, cf. *Wind
Mill Field* 1843 *TA*, *v.* wind-mylne, myln.   WOODHOUSE FM &
LANE (FM), *Woodhouselane* 1590 Sheaf, 1842 OS, *Woodhouse or
Widows Lane*, *Woodhouse Farm* 1831 Bry, 'house at a wood', *v.* wudu,
hūs, lane.   WOOLFALL-HALL FM, *Woolfall Hall* 1831 ib, *v.* 84
supra.   YEWTREE FM, cf. *Yew Tree Field & Leasow* 1843 *TA*, *v.*
læs.

FIELD-NAMES

The undated forms are 1843 *TA* 81.

(*a*) Ack Croft; The Acres; Ashy Moor (*v.* æsc, -ig[3], mōr[1]); Backside (*v.*
ba(c)ksyde); Ball Fd; Bare Ridge (*v.* bær[1] 'bare', hrycg); Bastard Fd (*v.* 325
infra); The Beach (*v.* bece[1]); The Bents (*v.* beonet); Bickerton Moss (*v.* mos,
cf. Bickerton 325 *infra*); Black Fd; Boat Ridding (*v.* bōt, ryding); Bone Fd
(*v.* bān, cf. bone-dust); Boosey Pasture (*v.* bōsig); Boxley Bank ('box-wood
hill', *v.* box, lēah); Brand Pool; Briery Moor (*Briery Moors* 1831 Bry);

Britains Bank; Broad Leasow (*v.* lǣs); Buggins Croft (from boggin 'a boggart', probably a scarecrow here); Bullace Tree Croft ('wild plum tree croft', *v.* bolace, cf. Plum Tree Hill *infra*); Far- & Near Bunsley (cf. Bunsley Bank 85 *supra*); Bye Flatt (*v.* byge[1], flat); Chaise (perhaps for *Shays,* from sc(e)aga 'a wood'); Cold Corner; Coney Greave, Coney Green Croft (*v.* coningre); Old Far- & -Near Corn Field (*v.* corn[1]); Cote Fd (*v.* cot); Cuckholes Fd ('cuckold's field', *v.* cukewald); Three Day Math (*v.* day-math); Drumble (dial. 'a wooded dell', cf. dumbel); Eight Butts (*v.* eahta, butte); Far News; Fine Yard; Fisherman's Nook; Flag Brook Fd & Mdw (*v.* flagge); Frog Moor (*v.* frogga, mōr[1]); Gill Pleck (*v.* plek); Gun Moors; Hales Fd (cf. Norton in Hales Sa, the adjacent township); Halfpennys Mdw (*v.* halfpeny, cf. 325 *infra*); Harbour Ridding (*v.* here-beorg, ryding); Hare Butts (*v.* hara, butte); Hodge Ridding, Hodgkin Hill (probably from the ME pers.n. *Hodge,* dimin. *Hodgkin,* but cf. *Hodg Croft* 1 158); Intake (*v.* inntak); Jack Ridding (*v.* jack, ryding); Kiln Croft; Lady Croft, Fd & Hill (*v.* hlǣfdige); The Little Lawn (*v.* launde); Leasow (*v.* lǣs); Leatherly Mdw; Marl Croft; Milking Bank (*v.* milking); The Moor; Morass; Moss Cob, Croft, Fd, Mdw, Piece & Room (cf. Buerton Moss *supra, v.* mos, cobb(e) 'a hill, a hump, a tumulus', rūm[1]); Mountain Piece; Patch; Piles; Pinfold Fd (*v.* pynd-fald); The Pleck (*v.* plek); Plum Tree Hill(s) (cf. Bullace Tree Croft *supra*); Pool Fd; Prickden, Pricken; Rake Brook (*v.* hraca, brōc); Reins (*v.* rein); Road Slang ('long narrow strip of land alongside a road', *v.* rād, slang); Roundabout (*v.* 325 *infra*); Rushy Moor; Rye Hill (*v.* ryge); Sand(y) Fd; Sidlane Fd; Site Fd; Slang (*v.* slang); Slaughter Moor (*v.* slōhtre); Sprink (*v.* spring 'a young wood'); Stocking (*v.* stoccing); Stonery ('place where stones are to be had', *v.* stonery); Thrawl Moor; Threap Wd ('disputed wood' or 'wood where disputes take place', *v.* þrēap, wudu); Town Croft, Fd & Mdw (cf. *Town End Lane* 1831 Bry, *v.* toun, ende[1]); Trickts Bank; Trie Croft; Twin Hole; Wall Mill Patch (probably for *Walk Mill-, v.* walke-milne, pacche); Way Field Bank (from weg and feld, with banke); White Moor; Wicksteads Fd (from the surname from Wicksted 112 *infra*); Within Mdw, Withing Croft (*v.* wīðegn); Woore Lane Fd (named from the adjacent township of Woore Sa).

3. HANKELOW (110–6745) ['hæŋkəlou, 'hæŋkələː]

Honcolawe 112 *AddCh* (p)

Honkelawe H3 *AddCh* (p), *Honkilawe, Honkylowe* 1260 Court *et freq* with variant spellings *Honke-, Hunki-, -low(e)* (all from 1281, 1282 Court), *Hunky-, Huncke-, -lay, -le* to *Honkylowe* 1513 *ChEx, Hunkelowe* 1542 ChRR

Hunkenelowe 1281 Court

Hunekelow(e) 1281 Plea, Court (p), *Hon-* 1282 ib (p)

Hankylowe 1520 Plea, *-low* 1745 Sheaf, *Hankilowe Bridge* 1621 ib, *Hanckelow* 1570 Cre, *Hankelowe* 1577 ChRR, *-low* 1621 (1656) Orm[2], 1724 NotCestr, *Hanculoe* 1599 Orm[2]

'Haneca's mound', from an OE pers.n. *Haneca* and **hlāw**. The form *Hunkene-* arises from confusion of OE gen.sg. *-an* (ME *-en*) with OE gen.pl. *-ena* (ME *-ene*). For the *-y-*, *-i-* spellings see Botterley (in Faddiley) 143 *infra*. The pers.n. appears in Hankerton W 59, Hankford D 92, Hankham Sx 447. Coole Hall 139 *infra* was part of this township.

CHURCH LEYS (lost), 1543 Orm² III 295, *Chircheleges* 13 *AddCh* (p), *-leg'* 13 Orm² (p), 1308 *Vern* (p), *-leghe* 1293 *AddCh* (p), *-leghs'* 1379 *Eyre* (p), *-leye* 1447 Orm² III 366, *Schurcheslegh* 1304 Chamb (p), *Church-Leys* 1520 ChRR, *Churchleys*, *Church Leys* 1521 Orm² III 295, 367, *Churcheleis* 1542 ChRR, presumably in Hankelow since it was an estate belonging to the *Hassall* and *Wettenhall* families of Hankelow, perhaps 'church clearing(s), woodland glades at, or belonging to, a church', *v.* cirice, lēah. There is, however, no ancient church on record at Hankelow, nor connected with it, and the first el. could be an OWelsh el., **cruc¹** (PrWelsh *crūg) 'a barrow, a hill, a mount', cf. OE **hlāw** in Hankelow *supra*.

BIRCHALL BRIDGE, *v.* 62 *supra*.   BRINEPITS WOOD, cf. Brinepits 139 *infra*.   CHAPEL HO.   COOLE HALL FM, *v.* 139 *infra*. CRIMEA WOOD, *v.* 325 *infra*.   THE DELL, *v.* dell.   HANKELOW COURT, *v.* court.   HANKELOW GREEN.   HANKELOW HALL & MILL, 1831 Bry, cf. Manor Fm *infra*.   LODGE WOOD.   MANOR FM, *Old Hall* 1831 Bry.   MONKS HALL FM.   ROOKERY WOOD.

FIELD-NAMES

The undated forms are 1838 *TA* 188.

(a) Ambrey Mdw (*v.* almarie); Broomy Lane Croft (*v.* brōmig); Bruch (*v.* bryce); Corbrook Fd (cf. Corbrook 85 *supra*); Crime Fd (*v.* cryme, cf. *le Crymbe* 2 171); Dithering Fd; Finnacres (*v.* finn 'coarse grass', æcer, cf. Finney 240 *infra*); Gutter Fd (*v.* goter); Hoult Hill (*v.* holt); Milking Bank Fd (*v.* milking); Moss Fd; Rye Hay (*v.* ryge, (ge)hæg); Sand Croft; Town Lake ('public watercourse', *v.* toun, lacu); Weaver Mdw (named from R. Weaver 1 38); Windmill Fd.

4. TITTENLEY (FM) (110–648378) ['titṇli] older local ['titli]

Titesle 1086 DB, 1286 Orm² (p)
Titneleg', *-leia*, *-leya* 1257, c.1275 Shav, *Tytnelegh* 1295 ChF
Titeneleg' c.1275 Shav

Tyttinleg' c.1275 *Shav*, *Tyttenlegh* 1286 Orm² (p), 1528 Orm²,
  Tyttenn' 1304 Chamb (p), *Tittenleye* 1313 Eyton (p), *Tittenley*
  1631 Sheaf *et freq*, (*Bridge*) 1621 Sheaf, (*Green, House*) 1846 *TA*
Teteneleg' l13 *AddCh* (p)
Tittelegh 1286 Ch (p), 1287 ChRR (p), -*ley* 1290 Orm² (p), 1313
  Eyton (p), *Tyttelegh* 1355, 1356 *Indict*, 1398 ChRR (p) *et freq*
  with variant spellings *Ti-*, *Tytty-*, *Ty-*, *Ti(t)t(e)ley(e)*, -*le(gh)*
  from 1418 *Shav*, ChRR, Orm², *Titley Hall* 1656 Orm², *Titley or*
  Tittenley 1842 OS
Tutenl(egh) 1304 Chamb
(*le*) *Ty-*, *Tintenlegh* 1304 Chamb (p)
Tittumlegh 1354 *Indict*, 1364 (1454) ChRR, 1373 Orm², 1404 ChRR

'Titta's clearing or wood', from an OE pers.n. *Titta*, as in Tid-
combe W 356, and lēah, with **brycg**, **grēne²**, and **loge**.

BANKHOUSE FM, *Bank House* 1831 Bry.   DRY POOL PLANTATION,
the drained site of *Titley Pool* 1842 OS, *Tittenley Pool* 1846 *TA*, cf.
foll. and Tittenley Pool *infra*.   LONG POOL, *New Pool* 1842 OS,
cf. prec. and Tittenley Pool *infra*.   PEPPERHILL, 1831 Bry,
Pepperhyll 1579 Orm² II 435, cf. Pepper St. (Chester) 326 *infra*.
TITTENLEY BELT, a plantation, *v*. **belt**.   TITTENLEY LODGE, 1846
TA.   TITTENLEY POOL, 1831 Bry, *Old Pool* 1842 OS, cf. Dry- and
Long Pool *supra*, *v*. **pōl¹**.   TURBINE SPINNEY, presumably named
from an engine-house here.

FIELD-NAMES

The undated forms are 1846 *TA* 399; c.1275 is *Shav*, 1481 (1581), 1538
Sheaf, 1842 OS.

(*a*) Blackhurst Fd (*v*. **blæc**, **hyrst**); Kingtree Fd; The Loon (*v*. **land**);
Mill House Plantation (cf. *Mill House* 1842, *Miln of Title* 1481 (1581), *Tytle*
Milne 1538, *v*. **myln**); Moat Fd (*v*. **mote**); Big- & Little Moor; Pale Mdw
(probably a park-pale, *v*. **pale**, cf. foll.); Park, Park Fd (cf. *Titley or Tittenley*
Park 1842, the park is referred to in 1666, Orm² III 476); Shavington Park
(from Shavington Sa); Slang (*v*. **slang**); Water Mdws.

(*b*) *Goderichislewe* c.1275 ('Gōdrīc's mound', from the OE pers.n. *Gōdrīc*
and hlǣw); *le Hummedewe* c.1275 (perhaps 'marsh meadow', *v*. **hulm**, **mǣd**,
cf. Water Mdws *supra*, but *hum-* may represent ME *homm* from hamm ' a
water-meadow').

viii. Audlem and Wrenbury

The township of Dodcott cum Wilkesley was partly in Audlem parish and partly in the Wrenbury chapelry of Acton parish. White (1860) puts it in Audlem following the 1841 Census, but local authorities in 1860 had it as in Wrenbury save for one house in Acton. It is now a c.p. including part of Shavington in Moreton Say Sa. The township contains the several hamlets of Dodcott and Wilkesley in Audlem parish, and of Smeatonwood (including Combermere) in Wrenbury chapelry. It represents the old demesne lands of Combermere abbey. Bryant's map (1831) shows the parochial boundary from the Sa border to Burleydam along Barnett Brook. St Michael's Church at Burleydam was a chapel-of-ease to Wrenbury, and NotCestr (1724) describes it in the Wrenbury township of Smeatonwood. There is a small detached portion of Dodcott cum Wilkesley in Acton township, *v.* 126 *infra*.

DODCOTT CUM WILKESLEY, *Dodcot and Wilksley* 1621 (1656) Orm², *Dodcott cum Wilslea* 1692 *Chol et freq* with spellings as for Dodcott, Wilkesley *infra*.

DODCOTT FM (110–619414)

> *Doddecote* c.1130 (1479) *Cott.* Faust. B VIII, 1260 Court, *-cota in Feld* 1266 (1331) Dugd
> *boscus de Dodcote* c.1130 (1479) *Cott.* Faust. B VIII, *Dodcote* 1437, 1560 Sheaf, 1882 Orm², *Dodcott Wood* c.1130 (18) Sheaf³ 28 (6118), *Dodcott* 1664 Wil, (*-Hall*) 1831 Bry, (*-Field*, *-Green*, *-Heys*) 1842 *TA*, *Dodcot* 1535 VE, 1621 (1656) Orm², (the grange called) 1581 Sheaf, *Dodcothey* 1538 (1581) ib, *-haye* c.1550 *Surv*, *Dodcotte*(*hey*) 1547 *MinAcct*, *Dodcoat* 1724 NotCestr
> *Dottecote* 12 Dugd v 326 (p)
> *Dodecote* 1201 Sheaf, 1253 Ch, 1291 Dugd
> *graungia de Dedcott* 1535 VE
> *Dodicot in Wilksley* 1727 Sheaf

'Dodda's cottage' from the OE pers.n. *Dod(d)a*, **Dodd*, and cot, with wudu, grēne², (ge)hæg and hall. 'Dodcott in the Field' 1266 distinguishes the hamlet from the wood, *v.* feld. A certain *Dot* was tenant of Wilkesley *infra* in 1086 DB (*v.* Feilitzen 226). *Dot* and *Dodda* may have been alternative names for the same man. However, Dr von Feilitzen observes that *Dot* and *Dodda* are not formal alternatives of the same name, and that the spelling *Dottecote* is due to unvoicing of *d* before *k*, and does not contain the pers.n. *Dot*.

WILKESLEY (110–628410) ['wilksli]

Wiuelesde 1086 DB, 12–13 Dugd v 326, *Wivelescle* 1230 & 1282
(1331) Ch IV 204, 205, (Dugd v 325 reads *Winelestele, Winelesde*),
Wyv- 1253 Ch, *Wivelesce* 1266 (1331) ib

Winclestle c.1130 (1479) *Cott.* Faust.B VIII (Dugd v 323 reads
Wynclesle, Winkasle)

Winelesthe c.1130 (18) Sheaf³ 28 (6118), *-de, Winelestele* 1230
(1331) Dugd v 325, *Wynelescle* 1253 Ch, *Winelesele* 1266 Dugd,
Wynelestr' 1291 Tax

Willescle 12 (14) *Harl.* 3868 (Orm² III 418 reads *Wilkesle*), *Willesley*
1437 Sheaf, 1547 *MinAcct, Wilslea, -ley* 1692, 1695 *Chol*

Wiveslee 1245 Sheaf, *Wyvescle* 1253 Ch

Wilskelegh 1404 ChRR, *Wilskley* 1724 NotCestr

Wylseley 1408 (1422) Plea

Wencsley 1499 Sheaf

Wylkeley 1534 Dugd

Wilkesley, Wy- 1535 VE *et freq, (New) Wilkesley* 1831 Bry,
Wilksley 1621 (1656) Orm², 1842 OS

Wylkesbye 1547 *MinAcct*

'Wīfel's claw' from an OE pers.n. *Wifel* (cf. ON *Vifill*, and
Wilcote O 274, Wilsford W 326) and clēa 'a claw', alluding to the
tongue of land between R. Duckow and the stream forming the
county boundary near Shavington Sa, at 110–6439, cf. *Spritlewithrintle infra*. The forms are confusing and confused. *Wiuel-* is often
miscopied as *Winel-, Wincl-* and *-cle* as *-de, -tle, -the*. The final el. has
been replaced by lēah.

COMBER MERE, COMBERMERE ABBEY & PARK (118–590440) ['kumbə-,
'kʌmbə-]

Cumbermere 1119–1128 (1285) Ch (p), *Combermere* c.1130 (1479)
Cott. Faust.B VIII *et freq* with variant spellings *Cumber-, -bur-,
-bir-, -byr-, -bar-, Coumber-, -mar(a), -mare, -mer', -mora, -more,
-meyre, -meire, -Mear*

Combremara c.1170 Dieul, *Cumbremara, -mar(e)* 1181, 1182, 1184
P, *Com-, Cumbremere* 1271, 1285 Pat, *Cumbremer* c.1536 Leland

Crumbremare 1182 P

Cumremara 1185 P

Cunnbremar' 1245 Cl

Cumbresmare 1253 Ch

Cambermere 1385 Comb *et freq* ib with variant spelling -*bir*- to 1524, -*mer* c.1550 *Surv.*

The lake is *aqua de Combermere* c.1130 *Cott.* Faust. B VIII, *the water of-* c.1130 (18) Sheaf³ 28 (6118), *Cumbermere* c.1536 Leland, *Comber-lake*, *Comber-mere* 1621 (1656) Orm², -*Mear* 1656 ib, *Combermere Mere* 1842 OS. It gave name to the Abbey of St Mary and St Michael there a.1130, *locus et situs qui vocatur Combermere ad fundandum et construendum quendam Abbatiam* c.1130 *Cott.* Faust. B VIII, *abbatia de Cumbermere* 1133 Dugd v 323, *monasterium de-* 1232 ib 324, 1235 (1353) *ChFor*, *ecclesia beate Marie de Cumbermere* 1357 ib, *monasterium-* 1466 *Dav*, *Cumbremere Abbay* c.1536 Leland, 'the late monastery of *Cum-*, *Cambermer(e)*' 1548 Pat, 1550 *Surv*, *scitus nuper monasterii infra parochiam de Wrenbery* 1540 Dugd v 327. The p.n. is 'Welshmen's lake', from Cumbre (gen.pl. Cumbra) and mere¹, with park, abbaye and lake.

BARN WOOD FIELD 1842 *TA*, *boscus qui vocatur Breidwood* c.1130 (1479) *Cott.* Faust. B VIII (Orm² III 417 reads *Brend-*, Dugd v 323 reads *Brende-*), *Brandwood* 13 (18), *Barndwood*, *Barndwood ford by Weever* 1334 (18) Sheaf³ 28 (6138, 6156), 'burnt wood' *v.* brende², wudu.

BRANKELOW (118–581442) [ˈbræŋkəlou]

    Bromkelawa c.1130 (1479) *Cott.* Faust. B VIII
    Broncelow 12 (18) Sheaf³ 28 (6124)
    Bronchelau 12 Dugd v 326
    Branchelow 12 (18) Sheaf³ (6124)
    Brankelow 1133 and 1577 (18) Sheaf³ (6118), 1831 Bry
    Branchehillaue 1540 Dugd v 327 (lit. -*lane*), -*awe* c.1550 *Surv*

The final el. is hlāw 'a hill, a mound'. *Branch of Wood* (109–588455), 1831 Bry, 1842 OS, is probably another form of the same name, with wudu 'a wood', in which an alternative, assibilated [tʃ] is preserved. Barnes¹ 698 suggests a Welsh pers.n. *Branoc* for the first el. It might also be a PrW p.n., 'wood on the breast of a hill', from the antecedent of Welsh *bron(n)* 'a breast, a hill' (cf. Corn bron EPN s.v.) and cēto-. However, Professor Löfvenberg notes that, if the form with -*m*- is correct, the first el. may be an OE **brōmuc* 'a clump of broom', which he also takes as the first el. of Branksome 2 31.

BRANKELOW MOSS (118–579444), 1842 OS, (*le*) *Haremos* c.1130 (1479) *Cott.* Faust. B. VIII, (18) Sheaf³ 28 (6118), *Hare Moss* 18 ib (6138), 'the old moss', *v.* hār[2], mos. It is on the county boundary, and the boundary with Marbury 106 *infra*. The later name is from Brankelow *supra*.

BROOKS MILL (110–632437), OLDMILL BRIDGE (110–642429), *molendinum de Cholley* c.1130 (1479) *Cott*. Faust. B VIII (Dugd v 323 reads *Chel-*), *molendinum de Chekley* c.1130 (1479) *ib* (Dugd v 323 reads *Check-*), *-Chelyleye* 12 (14) *Harl*. 3868 (Orm[2] III 418 reads *Cheky-*), *-legh* 1266 (1331) Ch, *Chelileie* 1253 ib, *Chelel(e)y Millne* 1133 (18) Sheaf, *Chelley milne alias Brooks milne* 17 Sheaf, *Brooks Mill, Oldmill Bridge* 1831 Bry, *Cheley Bridge* 1842 OS, cf. *Cheely-, Chelley Field* 1845 *TA* 285 (104 *infra*), 'Cēola's clearing or wood', from the OE pers.n. *Cēola* and lēah (cf. Chowley 326 *infra*), with ald, myln and brycg. *Brooks* is probably from the surname *Brook(s)*.

BURLEYDAM (BRIDGE & FM), ST MICHAEL'S CHURCH (110–6042)

    Burleya c.1130 (1479) *Cott*. Faust. B VIII, *-ley* c.1130 Dugd v 323, (*milne*) 13 (18) Sheaf, 17 ib, *Burle* 1253 Ch, (*Mill*) 1287 Court *Burldame* 1621 (1656) Orm[2] III 289 ('wherein is a little chapel of ease'), *Burleydam* (*Chapel*) 1643 Orm[2], 1724 NotCestr, 1831 Bry, *Burledam* 1751 Sheaf
Sandfitch Green in Lodmore Lane 1582 Sheaf, *Sandfitch* 1831 Bry
Chapel Farm 1831 Bry
Burleydam alias Sandwich Green 1843 *TAMap*

    'Peasant's clearing', *v.* (ge)būr, lēah. The later names are taken from an old mill-dam here (*v.* myln, damme) and a chapel-of-ease to Wrenbury, *v.* chapel(e), cf. 92 *supra*. The place gave name to Barnett Brook 1 14. No explanation has been found for *Sandfitch-*, popularly corrupted to *Sandwich Green* (*v.* grēne[2]). It may be a form of a p.n. *Sandbache* 'sandy valley-stream', from sand and bece[1], bæce[1], cf. Sandbach 2 269.

BUTTERLEY HEYS (110–648419)

    (*boscus qui vocatur*) *Buterlehey* c.1130 (1479) *Cott*. Faust. B VIII (Dugd v 323 reads *Buterlhey*), *Butreleyheye* 1342 ChRR, *Butterleyhay(e)* 1553, 1567 *Chol*
Butterly heare 1133 (18) Sheaf[3] 28 (6118), *-hease* 18 ib (6138), *Butterley Hease* 1537 (1581) Sheaf, *-Heys* 1831 Bry
Buterleishay 1362 BPR

Boturlehay 1377 Orm[2], 1383 ChRR (lit. *Rot-*), *Bot(h)erleyhay* 1400 ChRR, *Boterley* 1406 ib (p), 1417 *Chol* (p)

'(Fenced-in place(s) at) the butter clearing' (probably a rich pasturage), *v.* butere, lēah, with (ge)hæg.

CHESHIRE FIELDS (110–611401), 1503 (18) Sheaf, *-Field* 1831 Bry, cf. *Cheshire Beach* 1842 *TA*, 'fields, and valley-stream, lying in Cheshire', *v.* feld, bece[1]. These are on the Sa county boundary. It seems very likely that this locality was *boscus de Trepwodde, le Trepwood* c.1130 (1479) *Cott.* Faust. B VIII (Dugd v 323 reads *Trepewode, le Trepewood*), *Trep(e)wood* c.1130 (18) Sheaf[3] 28 (6118), *Trepwood in Wynesele* 12 (18) ib (6122), *le Trepwode* 1266 (1331) Ch, *pars nemoris de Wivelesde quae dicitur Threpwode* 12 Dugd v 326, 'wood in dispute', *v.* þrēap, wudu, cf. Threap Wood 89 *supra*, Threapwood 326 *infra*. This land was not included in Wilkesley manor by the bounds stated in *Cott.* Faust. B VIII ('the watercourse which runs between the wood of Dodcote and the wood of Trepwodde'). It was subsequently granted to Combermere abbey by Roger lord of Ightfield (Dugd v 326, Sheaf[3] 28 (6162)) as that part of the woods of Wilkesley which belonged to his manor of Ightfield Sa[1] At that time, it was probably disputed which county this wood was in—geographically Ch but manorially Sa, hence the name. The later name alludes to its detachment from the Sa territory of the Ightfield manor, cf. Northwoods *infra* which is named in relation to Shavington Sa.

BIG & LITTLE DITCHLEY 1842 *TA, quadam terra que vocatur Dicheley* c.1130 (1479) *Cott.* Faust. B VIII (Dugd v 323 reads *Sycheleya*), (a land called) *Dycheley* 12 (14) *Harl.* 3868, *-Magna* 1540 Dugd, *Ditch ley* c.1130 (18) Sheaf[3] 28 (6118), *the Ditchley* 1293 (18) Sheaf, *Ditchleys*

---

[1] The twelfth-century bounds of *T(h)repwode*, given fully in Sheaf, partly in Dugd, loc. cit., are 'from the entrance from *Fotemor* (*Oxefotemor* Dugd, '(marsh-land at) the foot of a hill where oxen graze', *v.* oxa, fōt, mōr[1]), to *the head of Grenhull* (*caput de Grenehul* Dugd, 'the top of the green hill', *v.* hēafod, grēne[1], hyll), then to *Spritlewithrintle* (*Spritlewithimle* Dugd, 'claw of land where the twiggy willow grows', from clēa (cf. Wilkesley *supra*), wīðegn (cf. Withymoor *infra*) and OE **sprytele* 'a twig, a chip' (BT)) then to *Riscwich brooke* (*Risewithbroc* Dugd, '(brook at) the rush factory or at the wīc at the rushes', *v.* risc, wīc, brōc), and again 'from *Greenhull* downward by *the siche* (*v.* sīc) to *the head of Fotemore*, thence to *Gosepoole* ('goose pool', *v.* gōs, pōl[1]), thence to *Cartlake* ('watercourse flowing through stony ground', *v.* kartr, lacu cf. Cart Lake 32 *supra*, *Cartelache* 1 17), thence to *the sych*, thence to *Riscwich brook*, thence to *Spritlewithrintle*, thence to the said *Greenhull*'.

18 ib, (*grangia de*) *Dyghleg'* 1287 Court 68, 69, 'clearing at a ditch', *v.* dīc, lēah, cf. *Dychefeld* c.1550 *Surv. v.* feld. In DEPN the 1287 Court form is wrongly connected with Disley **1** 269, cf. Diglee **1** 178.

LIGHTWOOD GREEN (110–632428) ['lait-], *boscus qui vocatur Bichewood* c.1130 (1479) *Cott.* Faust. B VIII (Dugd v 323 has *Lightbirchwood*), *Lightwood* 13 (18), 1538, 1581 Sheaf, (*Green*) 1831 Bry, 'light (birch-) wood', *v.* birce, lēoht (līht), wudu, with grēne².

LODMORE LANE (110–615421), *Lodmore* c.1130 (1479) *Cott.* Faust. B VIII, (18) Sheaf³ 28 (6118), 1416 ChRR, *-Lane* 1536 (1581) Sheaf, *Lodmere-* 1843 *TAMap*, *Ladmore near Newhall* 1454 Morris, cf. *The Lodmore* 1845 *TA* 154 (105 *infra*) and (a pasture called) *Lodheath* 1536 (1581), 1547 (18), 18 Sheaf, 1842 *TA*, *Lodhethe* 1547 *MinAcct*, *Lodeheth* c.1550 *Surv*, 'moor-, heath with a track over it', from (ge)lād and mōr¹, hǣð, cf. *Ladmor* 317 *infra*.

ROYAL'S GREEN (110–622427) [rɔilz] older local [raiəlz]
> *villa de Ruhull* c.1130 (1479) *Cott.* Faust. B VIII (Dugd v 323 reads *-hall*), *Ruehull* 1287 Court (p)
> town of *Ruhall* c.1130 (18) Sheaf³ 28 (6118)
> *Ryehull* 1287 Court (p), *Ruy-* c.1300 AD (p), *-hul* 1321 City (p)
> *Royal* 18 Sheaf³ 28 (6138)
> *Royles Green* 1831 Bry, 1842 OS

'Rye hill', from ryge and hyll, with grēne² 'a green'. Cf. Royalswood, The Royals 102, 102 *infra*.

SMEATON HALL, SMEATONWOOD FM, THE GRANGE (109–587470, 594465, 110–600468) [smiːtṇ]
> terra-, *molendinum de Smetheton* 1266 (1331) Ch, *Smethetonwode* 1359 ChRR, *Smethton* 1408 (1422) Plea
> grange of *Smeaton or the wood thereof* 1296 (18) Sheaf³ 28 (6144), *Smeaton Wood* 1536 and 1538 (1581), 1727 Sheaf, (*-Farms &* *-Grange*) 1831 Bry, *Smeton Woode* 1547 *MinAcct*

'Smiths' farm', from smið (gen.pl. *smeoða) 'a smith' and tūn, with wudu, hall, grange and myln.

ADAMLEY POOL, 1842 *TA*, cf. 103 *infra*. BARNETTBROOK BRIDGE, *-brooke-* 1621 Sheaf, cf. Barnett Brook **1** 14. BIG WOOD, *v.* Royalswood Fm 102 *infra*. BLACKHURST FM, *Blackhurst* 1503 (18) ib, 'dark wooded hill', v. blæc, hyrst. CHAPEL COVERT, cf. *Chapel Croft, Field & Meadow* 1842 *TA*, cf. Burleydam *supra*. COCKED HAT PLANTATION, 1842 OS. COMBERMERE WOOD, *Boundary Fence Plantation* 1842 ib. DODCOTT BROOK (Walkmill Brook *infra*). DUCKOW BRIDGE, cf. R. Duckow 1 22. FERNY HEYS, 1842 ib, *Ferneyheys* 1667 Sheaf, 'ferny enclosures', v. fearnig, (ge)hæg. GOLDSMITH'S HOUSE, 1842 OS, *Goldsmith House* 1831 Bry, perhaps from the surname *Goldsmith*. THE GRANGE, v. Smeaton Hall *supra*. HEWITT'S MOSS, *Hewetts Moor* 1842 *TA*, either 'moss where trees have been cut down', from hīewet and mōr[1], mos, or from the surname *Hewitt*. HEYFIELDS FM, *graung' de Hayfyld* 1535 VE, *Heyfeldes* 1547 *MinAcct*, c.1550 *Surv*, 1560 Sheaf, *Highfelde* 1554 *MinAcct*, 'fields at a fenced-in place', v. (ge)hæg, feld, cf. foll. HEYWOOD FM & LANE, *Heywood Coppie* 1542 (1571) Sheaf, *Heywoode Coppye* 1547 *MinAcct*, *Heywode* c.1550 *Surv*, *Hewod Copie* 1560 Sheaf, *Hay-* 1843 *TAMap*, 'fenced-in wood', from (ge)hæg and wudu (cf. prec.), with copis and lane. KENT'S ROUGH, 1831 Bry. LONG WALK COVERT, v. walk. MANOR FM. NEWHALL LANE, leading to Newhall 101 *infra*. This and Shropshire Lane *infra* are approximately on the line of 'a certain road which leads towards the town of *Wiche* (Nantwich)' c.1130 (1479) *Cott*. Faust. B VIII. NEWTON FM, *Newtown* 1831 Bry, v. nīwe, toun (cf. tūn). NORTHWOODS FM, *the Hall of Northwoods*, (land taken out of) *Great Northwoods* 1528 (1581) Sheaf, *Northwoods* 1581 ib, *Northwood* 1831 Bry, 'northern wood', from norð and wudu. This place, in the southeast corner of Wilkesley hamlet (110–646401), is north of Shavington Sa, cf. Cheshire Fields *supra*. OLDMILL BRIDGE, v. Brooks Mill *supra*. PARKVIEW FM, *Park View* 1831 Bry, on the edge of Combermere Park. PINSLEY GREEN, 1831 ib, *Pennesley* 1341 Plea, 1342 (1438) ChRR, 'clearing with a pen or fold in it', v. penn[2], -es[2], lēah, grēne[2]. POOLE'S RIDING WOOD, v. pōl[1] 'a pool', ryding 'a piece of cleared land'. THE ROOKERY, ROOKERY FM, *Rookery* 1831 Bry. SHROPSHIRE LANE, 1831 ib, leading to the county boundary, cf. Newhall Lane *supra*. THE STAIRS, *The Staires* 1707 Wil, *Stairs* 1831 Bry, v. stæger 'a stair', but the significance is uncertain. The house here may have had an external staircase. STONELODGE WOOD, named from Stone Lodge, a nearby gatehouse, v. loge. THE STEWS, fishponds in Combermere, v. stewe, stuwe. WALKMILL BRIDGE, BROOK, COVERT & FM, *Walke Milne bridge* 1621 Sheaf, *Walk Mill House & Covert* 1831 Bry, 'fulling mill', v. walke-milne.

The brook joins Barnett Brook 1 14. WILKESLEY COVERT, *Wilksley Cover* 1842 *TA*. WILKESLEY LODGE, *Morrey Lodge* 1842 OS, cf. (boscus de) *Morehey* c.1130 (1479) *Cott.* Faust. B VIII, *Morray* 1437 Sheaf, represented by Morrey, in Moreton Say, Sa (110–6240), *v.* mōr¹, (ge)hæg. WITHYMOOR FM, (110–609409), *Withy Moor* 1831 Bry, 'willow marsh', *v.* wīðig, mōr¹, cf. *Spritle-withrintle* at Cheshire Fields *supra*, which was not far distant. WORKHOUSE COTTAGES, *Poor House* 1831 ib, *v.* poorhouse, workhouse. YEWTREE FM, *Yewtree House* 1831 ib.

FIELD-NAMES

The undated forms are 1842 *TA* 145, 1843 *TAMap*. Of the others c.1130 (1479) is *Cott.* Faust. B VIII, n.d., c.1130, 12, 13, 1293, 1575 all (18) Sheaf, 1528, 1530, 1536 all (1581) ib, 1560, 1581, 1582, 17, 18 ib, 12 (18), 1540 Dugd, 1283¹ Pat, E1 Orm², 1283² IpmR, 1547 *MinAcct*, c.1550 *Surv.*

(a) Abbey Fd (cf. Combermere Abbey *supra*); Adams Croft & Hill (cf. Adamley Pool *supra*); Anchor Croft (*v.* ancra); Aston Fd & Mdw (cf. Aston in Newhall 102 *infra*); The Bache (*v.* bæce¹); The Banks; Barnacle (*Banacre* 1547, 1582, 17, *Bannaker* c.1550, *Barnacre* 18, 'bean-field', *v.* bēan, æcer); Near Barnett (cf. Barnett Brook 1 14); Bassoe Fd; Beach (*v.* bece¹); Beancroft (*v.* bēan); Beech (*v.* bece¹); Beggars Fd (*v.* beggere); Birchen Fd (*v.* bircen²); Bitch Fd (*v.* bicce or bece¹); Black Butts (*v.* butte); Great Block Ditch (*Blackditch Meadow* 13 (18), *Blakedychmedowe* 1540, *Blackedycche-medowe* c.1550, *v.* blæc, dīc, mæd); Boozy Fd (*v.* bōsig); The Bottoms (*v.* botm); Breech's Mill (cf. *The Breach* 1528 (1581), *v.* brēc); Brine Pit Fd (*v.* brīne); Carthouse Fd (*v.* carte-hows); Castle Fd & Mdw (*v.* castel(l) 'a castle', but no traces have been found); Cat Hurst (*v.* cat(t), hyrst); Chesters Mdw (this may refer to the property of the hospital of St John without Northgate, Chester, which held land at Pinsley Green *supra* in 1341); Clay Fd; Coal Fax (perhaps colefox 'the brant fox, the colefox'); College Fd (*Colledge Fields* 1536 (1581) Sheaf³ 49 (9814, an unexpired lease from the abbot and convent of Combermere), *v.* college); Coral Fallow and Fd; Cranberry Moss (*v.* cranberry, mos); Dale Acre (*v.* dæl¹); Day Math (*v.* day-math); Dodcott Fd, Green & Heys (*Dodcothey* 1538 (1581), *Dodcottehey* 1547, *Dodcothaye* c.1550, *v.* (ge)hæg, Dodcott *supra*); Dry Pit Fd; Big- & Little Dunstall, Dunstall Mdw (*v.* tūn-stall, cf. 104 *infra*); Fig Fd; Figure of Seven (*v.* 325 *infra*); Finger Post(s) Fd; Ford Fd (*v.* ford); French Hill Mdw; Glade Fd (*v.* glæd³); Handley (*v.* hēah, lēah); Hare Hind Fd; The Heath; Hedge Bank (*v.* hecg); Hobs Green; Holmes (*le holmes* c.1550, *v.* holmr); Horse Heys (*v.* (ge)hæg); Horse Mill Fd (*v.* horse-myln); Little Ightfield (named from Ightfield Sa, cf. *Ightfield Fd* 140 *infra*, Cheshire Fields *supra*); Intake (*v.* inntak); Iron Fd(s) (*v.* hyrne); Jack Acre (*v.* jack); Kiln Fd; Kitchen Mdw; Knoughs ([nouz], *v.* cnoll); Lady Fd (*v.* hlæfdige); Lanthorn Fd; Cote-, Cow-, Ox-, Rough- & Wood Leasow (cf. *The Lees* 1540, *le Lees* c.1550, *v.* cot, cū, oxa, rūh, wudu and læs); Long Shoots (*v.*

scēat); Main Fd (v. main); Marl (Pit) Fd; Merrytree Fd; Milk(ing) Bank (v. milking); Mill Fd (cf. Weir Croft infra); Moat Fd (v. mote); The Moor; The Moss; Moss Mere (Mossemere 1530 (1581), 'pool at a bog', v. mos, mere[1]); New Heys (v. (ge)hæg); New Mdw (cf. le Newemedowe 1540, -medwe c.1550, v. nīwe, mǣd); Nine Butts (v. butte); Outlet(t) (v. outlet); Ox Hey, Leasow & Pasture (v. (ge)hæg, lǣs); Pan Croft; Paradise Fd (v. paradis); Patch; Pinfold Bank & Fd (v. pynd-fald); Platt Bridge Mdw (cf. Platt bridge 1621, v. plat[1]); Primrose Hill; Rabbit Borrow (cf. Conyger 1540, le Conygar c.1550, v. borow, coningre); Radmoor, Radmoor Fd (Radmores 1538 (1581), Redmores 1547, c.1550, 1560, Rod- 1581, 'red moor(s)', v. rēad, mōr[1]); The Riddings (le (Parva) Ryddyng(e) 1540, c.1550, the Rid(d)ing(s) 1575, Riddings 18, v. ryding); Big- & Little Rough; (Big-, Further-, etc.) Rough Field (Rough Fields 1530 (1581), v. rūh); Rye Bank (cf. Royal's Green supra); Sandhole Fd; Scratley Fd (cf. 121 infra); Shavington Park (part of the park at Shavington Hall Sa); Sheep Cote Fd; Slang (v. slang); Squinting Mdw (v. squint); Sweet Fd; Swine Fd; Town Fd; Water Fd (v. wæter); Way Field (v. weg); Weir Croft (the milnfield or Were crofft 1528 (1581), v. myln, wer, cf. Mill Fd supra); Welch's Bank; Well Fd(s); Westerley (v. westerra, lēah); Wild Goose Mdw; Woller Croft; Wrenbury Fd (cf. Wrenbury 119 infra).

(b) Blakepulles 12 (18), Blackpules 12 ('dark pools', v. blæc, pull); Brymsey coppie 1547, Brymesey c.1550, Brymsley Copie 1560; Deyhowsse-crofte 1540, Deyhousse crofte c.1550 ('dairy-house croft', v. dey-hūs, croft. This and Bakehouse Field 104 infra refer to offices of Combermere abbey); Dintesmere 12 (18), Duntsmere 12 (the name of a pool near Combermere or of an arm of that lake, cf. le Nonnepoole infra, v. mere[1]. The first el. may be a pers.n. such as PrWelsh *Dūnǭd < BritLat Dōnātus), the name of Bede's Dinoot(h) abbot of Bangor Iscoed in 603, v. Jackson 295, 41); Farreburres Medowe 1540, Furburres c.1550; Grundelsmore n.d. (Barnes[1] 700 quotes Grandlesmore 1299 Sheaf[3] 28. The name is from mōr[1] 'a marsh' perhaps with grendel 'a gravelly place or stream', but grundleās 'bottomless, very deep' is more likely. Professor Sørensen notes the Dan p.n. Grundløse 'the bottom-less one', a lake in the island of Langeland); Groueford(e)ley, -fordsley c.1130 (1479) Cott. Faust. B VIII (Orm[2] III 417 reads Grovefordley, Dugd v 323 reads Gre(e)nefordeley, Greenefordes-), Gronford Ley c.1130 (18) Sheaf[3] 28 (6118), Gronfordley 13, 1293, Grenefordlegh 1283[1], Grenfordley E1, Granfordeleye 1283[2] ('(wood at) the green ford', v. grēne[1], ford, lēah, cf. Grandford 103 infra. This wood was about 110–605420); Havecthesmos 12 (18), Hanethmos 12 (perhaps 'hawk's moss', from hafoc and mos, cf. foll.); Hevetthelbeche 12 (18), Hanethebeche 12 (perhaps 'hawk's valley', from hafoc and bece[1], with -el- miscopied for -es- (v. -es[2]), cf. prec.); Hawkescopie 1547, Hawkys Copye c.1550, Hawkesope 1560 ('hawk's coppice', v. hafoc, copis); pons de Hortalebroc 12 (18), 'the bridge of Hortal brook' 12 (perhaps '(brook in) the nook where whortleberries grow', from horte and halh with brōc, brycg); Lacie Coppie 1547 (from copis 'a coppice' and the surname Lacy); Lefdi-ac 12 (18), Lesdiat 12 ('Lady's Oak', probably 'Our Lady's Oak', since Combermere abbey was dedicated to St Mary, v. hlǣfdige, āc);

Leviethelcote 12 (18) (probably 'Lēofgēat's cottage', from the OE pers.n. *Lēofgēat* and cot, with *-el-* for *-es-*, cf. *Hevetthelbeche supra*); *Mosseney* 1540, *Mosseuis* c.1550 ('the edge of a moss', *v.* mos, efes); *le Nonnepoole* c.1130 (1479) (Dugd v 323 reads *Nonepulle*), *-pole* c.1130 (the name of the small lake at the east end of Combermere (110–599445), 'Nunna's pool', from the OE pers.n. *Nunna* and pōl[1]. Cf. *Dintesmere* and Combermere *supra*); *le Okes* c.1550 (a wood, *v.* āc); *Pereorcheyarde* 1540, *Pere Orcheyard* c.1550 ('pear orchard', *v.* peru, orceard); *Ravenhill Ruding* 13 ('(clearing at) raven's hill' from hræfn and hyll, with ryding); *Rysingfeld* 1540, *Ryfyngfelde* c.1550 ('field which slopes upward', from rising and feld, though Barnes[1] 700 suggests hrīsen, 'growing with brushwood'); *le Sparthisshe* c.1130 (1479) (Dugd v 323 reads *-ishe*), *the Sparchitche* c.1130 ('the fold at the brushwood', *v.* spearca, hiche. The order of the bounds of Wilkesley in *Cott.* Faust B VIII would locate this at 110–625406); *Wyndmyllfelds* 1540 (*v.* wind-mylne, cf. Windmill Bank & Fd 105 *infra*); *Wytmylle Polefeld* 1540, *Whyte Mylne pulfeld* c.1550 ('(field at the pool of) the white mill', *v.* hwīt, myln, pōl[1], feld).

ix. Audlem, Acton & Wrenbury

The township of Newhall was partly in Audlem parish, and Wrenbury chapelry, and Acton parish proper.

NEWHALL (110–6145)

> *Nova Aula* 1227 Ch *et freq* in Lat texts to 1430 ChRR (p)
> *La Nouehall* 1252 Ch, 1378 Pat
> *Newhall* 1256–7 AD *et freq* with variant spellings (*la- le-, the-*), *Newe-, Neu(e)-, -halle, -(h)all, -haule*; (*-iuxta Cumbermere*) 1336 Plea, (*-iuxta Aston*) 1354 *Eyre*, (*-iuxta Merbury*) 1621 (1656) Orm[2], (*-in Wrenbury*) 1573 BM, *Niewehall* 1330 Pat, *Nywe-* 1337 AddCh, *Nuhall* 1540 *Chol*
> *la Neuhalle alias la Wodehalle* 1312 Cl
> *Newehal* 1321 Fine, *Neuhale* 1358 BPR (p)
> *Newnhall* 1745 Wil

'The new hall', 'hall in a wood', *v.* nīwe, hall, wudu. This was a new house built by the lords Audley c.1227. It was fortified, probably with a peel-tower. Leland v 25 states 'There was a place of the Lorde Audelays in Chestreshire betwixt Cumbremere and Nantwiche caullid *Newhaule Tower*. It is now downe. There be motes', cf. *Moat Meadow* 1845 *TA*, (*v.* mote), and *castrum de Nova Aula* 1276, 1283 Ipm, *tower of Newehalle* 1322 ChancW (*v.* tour 'a turret, a castle-tower'). Combermere 93 *supra* and Aston *infra* are adjacent, but Marbury 106 *infra* is beyond Wrenbury 119 *infra*. The additions distinguish this from Newall 2 208.

ASTON (HEATH) (110–610470), *Estune* 1086 DB (*v.* Tait 151, n.129), *Aston* 1252 Ch, 1287 Court *et freq passim*, (*-iuxta Sonde*) 1287 Court, (*-iuxta Neuehalle*) 1330 Fine, (*-iuxta Bromhall, -Bromale*) 1389 ChRR, (*-iuxta Wrennebury*) 1437 Sheaf, *Astoun by Neuehalle* 1330 Ipm, *Aston Hethe* 15 Rich, *-Green* 1831 Bry, 'eastern farm', from ēast and tūn, with hǣð and grēne². This place is east of Wrenbury 119 *infra*, in which parish it lies. Newhall *supra*, Sound and Broomhall 121, 114 *infra*, are adjacent.

COOLE LANE (110–647457 to 643435), BACK COOLE LANE (110–643435 to 622448), HALL O'COOLE (110–628456) & COOS FM (110–637443), *Cool Lane, Hall a Coole* 1831 Bry, cf. *The Coo, Great Coo, Cool Meadow, Coole Field* 1845 *TA, Coulesfeld, -medowe* & *-mosse* 1358 ChRR, from lane, hall, mǣd, feld and mos, with the p.n. *Coole, v.* Coole Pilate, Coole Hall Fm, Coole Lane 138, 139, 139 *infra*. Part of this district was in Audlem parish.

GRINDLEY GREEN (lost, 110–605435), 1842 OS, *Grenley, Grendele* 1408 ChRR (p), *Greenl(e)ys-, Greenles(s) Green* 1609 Sheaf, *Grindleys Green* 1831 Bry, cf. *Grendleys Croft* 1845 *TA*, 'green wood', from grēne¹ and lēah, with grēne² 'a green', as Grindley 326 *infra*.

THE ROYALS (110–605461) [rɔiəlz] older local [raiəlz], 1751 Sheaf, *le Ryalth, the Ryalls* 1547 *MinAcct, le Ryalles* 1553 Pat, *Ryalls House* 1609 Sheaf, *the Royalls* 1615 ib, 'the rye nooks', *v.* ryge, halh, cf. foll. and Royal's Green 97 *supra*.

ROYALSWOOD FM (110–601456) [rɔiəlz-] older local [raiəlz-], BIG WOOD (118–595448), *boscus de Ruhale* c.1130 (1479) *Cott.* Faust. B VIII, *the Royall Wood* c.1130 (18), 1577 (18) Sheaf³ 28 (6118), (*the*) *Royal(l) Wo(o)de, -Wood* 1547 *MinAcct*, c.1550 *Surv*, 1560, 18 Sheaf, *Royals Wood* & *Farm* 1831 Bry, *Big Wood* 1842 *TA* 145, 'the rye-nook', from ryge and halh, with wudu. Cf. prec.

SANDFORD BRIDGE & FM (110–619469)

Soundfort e13 (17) Tab (p), *Sontford* 1300 Sheaf, *Sond-* 1368 *Dow* (p), *Sonford bridde* 15 Rich, *Sonford* 1326, 1368 ChRR (p)

Saunford(e) 1252 RBE (p), 1257 AD (p) *et freq* to 1344 Pat (p), *Sauntford* 1294 Ipm (p), *Saund-* 1386 ChRR (p)

Samford 1281 Court (p), *Sampford* 1292 Ipm (p)

Sanford 1282 Court (p), 1299 Ipm (p)
Sandford 1359 *Dow* (p), (-*e*) 1621, 1640 Sheaf, *Sandford(e) bridge*
1547 (18), 1621 ib, *Sandford tenement lying near Sandford Bridge*
1709 ib
Stanford-Bridge 1621 (1656) Orm² III 289
'Sandy ford', from **sand** and **ford**, with **brycg**. This is a crossing
of R. Weaver from Aston *supra* into Sound 121 *infra*. The forms show
the same over-rounding of *a* > *o* > *ou* as in the p.n. Sound.

WILD HEATH (lost), 1845 *TA, Wy-, Wildeheth* 1355 *Eyre* (p), 1361
ChRR, *Wilde- Wyldhethe* 1547 *MinAcct, Wyldheathe* 1590 Sheaf,
(land in Audlem called) *Wildheath* 1724 NotCestr, 'wild heath', *v.*
wilde, hǣð.

ADAMLEY POOL, 1845 *TA*, cf. 97 *supra*.   AUDLEM BRIDGE, *v.* 85
supra.   BARNETTBROOK, *Barnett Brooke* 1609 Sheaf³ 39 (8442), a
hamlet named from Barnett Brook 1 14. The 1609 reference may be
the brook itself.   BIG WOOD, cf. Big Wood 97 *supra, v.* Royalswood *supra*.   BLEAK HO.   BLUE BACHE FM, [-bætʃ], *Blue Beech*
1831 Bry, 1842 OS, *Blew Bache* 1880 Sheaf, 'dark, or blue valley-
stream', from ME *blew* (< OFr *bleu*) 'blue', cf. **blāw, blá(r)**, with
bece¹, bæce¹. The name probably means 'cold, dark hollow', but
may refer to some natural characteristic e.g. blue flowers.   BRICK-
BANK WOOD, cf. *Brick Bank Field, Brick (Kiln) Field* 1845 *TA, v.*
bryke, banke, bryke-kyl.   BRICKWALL FM, *Brick Wall* 1831 Bry,
v. **bryke, wall**.   BROWN'S BANK, 1831 ib, named after the family of
John *Brown* of Coole Lane 1546 Sheaf, cf. Coole Lane *supra*, and
Bruneshurst 53 *supra, v.* **banke**.   BURLEYDAM, *v.* 95 *supra*.
DODD'S GREEN (LANE), *Dodds Green* 1609 Sheaf, *Dodd's-* 1842 OS,
probably from the surname *Dod(d)* and **grēne²**, cf. foll.   DODDS-
GREEN FM, *Boldridding* 1842 OS, cf. *Ball Moor & Ridding, Bell
Ridding Field* 1845 *TA, v.* **mōr¹, ryding**, cf. prec. The significance of
Bold-, Ball-, Bell- is not apparent.   EAGLE HALL COTTAGES, *the
Hall of Eagle* 1609 Sheaf, *Eagle Hall* 1644 ib, *Eagleshall* 1691 Wil.
The origin of this name is not found, *v.* **hall**.   FERNEYBANK, 1831
Bry.   GRANDFORD (LANE) (110–619465), *Grandford Lane* 1831 ib.
If this is an old name it could be derived from **grand** 'gravel' and
ford, cf. the nearby Sandford *supra*. But there is a *Gran-* form in the
spellings of *Groueford(e)ley* 100 *supra*, and the first el. of Grandford
may be **grēne¹**.   HOLLINGREEN (LANE), HOLLIN LANE (FM),

Hollin Green 1831 ib, *Hollins Green & Lane* 1842 OS, 'holly-tree green', *v.* holegn, grēne². KINGSWOODGREEN BRIDGE, *Knowles Bridge* 1621 Sheaf, *Nows Bridge* 1831 Bry, cf. *atte Knoll, le Knolle* 1408 ChRR (p), *le Knolles* 1423 ib (p), *v.* cnoll 'a hillock', cf. foll. KINGSWOODGREEN FM, *Kings Wood Green* 1609 Sheaf, *v.* cyning, wudu, grēne². LOWER HOUSE FM, *New House* 1842 OS, *v.* Top House Fm 139 *infra*. MANOR HOUSE, *Will Yate* 1831 Bry, perhaps 'well gate', *v.* wella, geat. MOORHALL FM, *Moor Hall* 1831 ib, *v.* mōr¹, hall. NEWBRIDGE, 1609 Sheaf, *Newe-* 1621 ib, *v.* nīwe, brycg. NEWHALL LANE, *v.* 98 *supra*. NEWHALL MILL (FM), *Newhall myll* 1547 *MinAcct*, the water mill called *Newhall mylle* 1553 Pat, *-Milne* 1566 (18) Sheaf, *-Mill* 1609 ib, *v.* myln. OAK FM. OLDMILL BRIDGE, *v.* Brooks Mill 95 *supra*, cf. *Cheely Field, Chelley Field* 1845 *TA*. PARADISE BRIDGE, *v.* paradis. PARK HO, cf. *Little Park by Coulesfeld* 1358 ChRR, *Newhall Park* 1609 Sheaf, *-es* 1622 ib, *Old Park, Park Field* 1845 *TA*, *v.* park, lȳtel, ald, cf. Coole Lane *supra*. PINNACLE FM, cf. *pynnacle* 15 Rich, probably 'hill with a little fold on it', from pinnok and hyll. SALESBROOK BRIDGE & FM, *Sales Brook* 1842 OS, named from Sales Brook 1 34. SHEPPENHALL HALL, *Shapnall Green* 1609 Sheaf, *Shepnall* 1657 ib, *Sheppenhall* 1831 Bry, *Shepen Hall* 1842 OS, cf. *Shippenhall Field* 1845 *TA*, perhaps 'cow-shed nook', *v.* scypen, halh, grēne², hall. SHEPPENHALL LANE, *White Moor Lane* 1831 Bry, *Whitemoor* 1845 *TA*, *v.* hwīt, mōr¹, cf. prec. SUMMERFIELD HO.

FIELD-NAMES

The undated forms are 1845 *TA* 285. Of the others, 1287 is Court, 15 Rich, 1436 ChRR, 1540 Dugd, 1547 *MinAcct*, 1543, 1553 Pat, c.1550 *Surv*, 1831 Bry, and the others Sheaf.

(a) Amblebury Mdw (cf. Ambleberry 118 *infra*); Audlam Fd (cf. Audlem 82 *supra*); Audley Mdw (from the lords *Audley*, ancient owners of Newhall); The Bache (*v.* bæce¹); Bakehouse Fd (cf. *Bakhowsse* 1540, *le Bakhouse clos* c.1550, *v.* bæc-hūs, and cf. *Deyhowssecrofte* 100 *supra*); Barleys Wd; Beggars Fd (*v.* beggere); Black-, Blake Croft (*v.* blæc); Blackwater (*v.* blæc, wæter); Blitchley Fd; Boozey Pasture (*v.* bōsig); Brindley ('burnt clearing', *v.* brende², lēah, cf. Brindley 133 *infra*); Broomy Knowl (*v.* brōmig, cnoll); Cheely-, Chelley Field (cf. Brooks Mill 95 *supra*); Cow Flatt; Cross (Lane) Fd (cf. *Newhall Cross* 1831 Bry, 1845 *TA* (a p.h.), *v.* cros); Cunge Croft; Cupids Alley (*v.* 325 *infra*); Day Math (*v.* day-math); Dingle (*v.* dingle); Dunstall (*Dinestall* 1658, cf. Dunstall 99 *supra*. This is probably tūn-stall 'the site of a farmyard'. For the form *Dun-* cf. Townfield 117 *infra*. For the vowel in the form *Dine-*, cf. Danes Moss 1 67); Fingerpost Fd; Fishers Fear (a field beside a brook); Flatt Lowe (either 'a flat-topped hillock' or 'a mound in a flat piece of ground', *v.* flatr, flat, hlāw); Footway Fd; Glead Green Fd (*v.* gleoda); Gollinge; Hall Fd & Mdw (cf. *the hall orchard* 15, *v.* hall, orceard); Hands Fd; Hanes Fd & Lane; Hatch Fd (*v.* hæcc); Hewitts Moor (*v.* 98 *supra*); High Cop (*v.* copp); The Hole; Humberry Bank; Idle Bank (*v.* īdel); Intake (*v.* inntak); Key Fd & Mdw (cf. *Key Lane* 1898, 'cows' field, meadow and lane', from ME kye, pl. of cou (*v.* cū) 'a cow'); Kitchen Fd & Piece; Ladyhill (*v.* hlǣfdige, hyll); Lees (*v.* lǣs); The Lodmore (*v.* 97 *supra*); Long Butts, -Shoot & -Slang (*v.* butte, scēat, slang); Lumfoot Mdw ('meadow at the lower end of a pool', *v.* lumm, fōt); Market Fd (*v.* market); Marl Fd; Marsh Fd; Middenhole Fd (*v.* midding, hol[1]); Milking Bank (*v.* milking); Moor; Moss; Office Field (probably named from a 'house of office', i.e. a lavatory); Outlet(t) (*v.* outlet); Ox Hay & -Ley (cf. *le oxhall, le oxhay* 1547, (*le*) *Ox Medowe* 1547, 1553, *the Oxe Meadow* 1615, *v.* oxa, (ge)hæg, mæd); Pavement Fd (*v.* pavement); Pingott (*v.* pingot); Poorhouse Fd (named from the village workhouse, *Poor House* 1831); Rabbit Burrow Fd; Rick Field (*v.* hrēac); Round Moss (*v.* rond); Rye Croft, Eddish & Fd (1694, *v.* ryge, croft, edisc); Sand Hole Fd (cf. *Sand pitt green* 1609, *v.* sand, pytt); Shirley ('bright glade', *v.* scīr[2], lēah); Sidderdine (if this is an old name, the final el. could be worðign); Sling Fd (*The Sling* 1898, dial. sling 'a strip of land', cf. slang); The Spinks, Sprink (*v.* spring 'a young wood'); Sterling Heath; Styche Fd (*v.* sticce[1]); Swan; Tinkers Fd; Tom Fd, Town Fd (*v.* toun); Trig(g) Lane Fd; Turnips Moor; Upton Stairs (*v.* stæger, cf. The Stairs 98 *supra*); Way Fd (*v.* weg); Weaver Mdw (*v.* R. Weaver 1 38); Wier Ground, Wire Croft (*v.* wire); Windmill Bank & Fd (cf. *Wyndmyllfelds* 101 *supra*); Wood Fd (cf. *Newhall Wood* 1609, *v.* wudu); Works Fd; Long- & Short Yard (*v.* geard).

(*b*) *the byflett* 15 ('flat piece of ground in the bend of a stream', *v.* byge[1], flat); *the Cokys grounde* 15 ('the cook's land', *v.* cōc, grund); *le Curte* 1547, *le Courte* 1553, *the-* 1615 ('the yard, the courtyard', *v.* court, perhaps with the castle at Newhall *supra*); *Malkynfeld* 1436 ('Malkin's field', perhaps from the ME pers.n. *Malkin*, often used of a hare or a cat, *v.* malkin, and feld); *Newbacke* 1609; *the Ninepennyworthe of Ground* 15 (*v.* 325 *infra*); *Rodlandes, Rotland* 1547 ('selions of one rood', *v.* rōd[2], land); *the late free chapel of St James in Newall in the parish of Acton* 1548, *the seyte...of the late free Chappell of St James in þe parish of Acton within the lordship of Newhall* 1615 (*v.* chapel(e)); *Stretehay* (*v.* 2 *supra*); *Grene Wethale* 1287 ('the green wet nook', *v.* grēne[1], wēt, halh).

x. Marbury Chapelry

Marbury was made a parish in 1870. Previously it was a parochial chapelry of Whitchurch Sa, cf. Wirswall 112 *infra*. In 1291 Tax it is treated as a parish, and c.1536 Leland IV 2 calls it *Merb'y paroche*. The chapelry contained two townships, 1. Marbury cum Quoisley, 2. Norbury.

1. MARBURY CUM QUOISLEY, 1837 *TA*, *v.* Marbury, Quoisley *infra*.
MARBURY (HALL) (109–5645) [mɑːbəri]

> *Merberie* 1086 DB, *-bere* 1470 *Chol*, *-bury* 1260 Court *et freq* with
> variant spellings *Mere-*, *-burye*, *-buri*, *-bur(e)* to 1656 Orm²,
> (*-iuxta Wyreswall*) 1348–50 Orm², (*-iuxta Wrennebury*) 1351
> ChRR, (*-iuxta Norbury*) 1436 Plea
> *Marburia* c.1130 (1479) *Cott*. Faust. B VIII, *-bury* 1289 Court, 1621
> Sheaf *et freq*, *-burye* 1595 ChRR, *Marbury Hall* 1819 Orm¹

'Fortified place near a lake', *v.* mere¹, burh (dat. sg. byrig), hall.
Cf. Big- & Little Mere *infra*. It is distinguished from Marbury 2 117
by relation to Wirswall, Wrenbury and Norbury 112, 119, 109 *infra*.

QUOISLEY, MERE FM (109–5445) [ˈkɔizli]

> *Cuselegh'* 1350, 1353 *Eyre*
> *Kuyseley* 1440 ChRR (lit. *Kny-* DKR XXXVII 290, Orm² III 307),
> *Kuysley* 1499 Orm² 308 (lit. *Kny-*), 1515 *MinAcct*, 1516 Plea
> *Covsley* 1535 VE
> *Coyseley* 1599 *Chol*, *-ly* 1685 Sheaf, *Coysley* 1576 Saxton, 1621,
> 1633 *Chol*, *Coisl(e)y* 1598, 1700 *ib*, 1656 Orm²
> *Quoisley* 1724 NotCestr

'Cūsa's clearing', from the OE pers.n. *Cūsa* (Feilitzen 219) or a
derivative **Cȳsa*, and lēah. Mere Fm is *Quoisley* 1831 Bry, 1842 OS,
cf. Quoisley Big- & -Little Mere *infra*, and *Quoisley Field* 1837 *TA*,
Coisley Field, Little Coisley Croft 1598 *Chol*, and Bickley Brook 325
infra.

HADLEY HALL (109–557460)

> *Hadeleg'* c.1258 *Chol* (p), *-ley* c.1280 (17) *ib* (p), *-legh* 1298 ChF
> (p) *et freq* to 1380 *Eyre* (p), *Hadde-* 1402 ChRR
> *Hadleg'* 1260 Court, *-legh* 1302 *Chol* (p), 1402, 1418 ChRR, *-leigh*
> 1396 ib (p), *-ley* (*within Coisley*), *Hadley Hayth* 1598 *Chol*,
> *Hadley Hall* 1842 OS
> *Hadileg'* 1280 P (p), *-le* 1288 Court (p), *-legh* 1334 ChRR (p),
> *Hadylegh* 1320 ib (p), *Over Hadyley* 1420 Plea
> *Hanley Hall* 1831 Bry

'Hadda's wood or clearing', from the OE pers.n. *Had(d)a* and
lēah, with hǣð 'a heath', hall, lȳtel, uferra. In Bry the name is
confused with Handley Park 110 *infra*.

HURST HALL (109–570462)

Horshale 1304 Chamb (p), Horsale 1312 Plea (p), Horshal 1335 ChRR (p)

Horsall 1330 Chol (p), 1624 Wil, 1845 ChetOS VIII, Horshall 1595 ChRR, Horhshall 1673 Sheaf, cf. Horsehall Field, Horse Hall Field 1837 TA

Hurst Hall 1842 OS

'Horse nook', v. hors, halh (dat.sg. hale). The two els. have been replaced by hyrst and hall. The identification is suggested in Sheaf[3] 39 (8411), because Hurst Hall and Horshall were seats of the Bickerton family.

TOWNLEY FM (109–573462), Tunleg', Tounlegh 1287 Court (p), Townley 1593 Orm[2], 1619 Sheaf, (-Hall) 1820 ib, Townly 1724 NotCestr, 'woodland clearing with a farmstead or belonging to one', v. tūn, lēah, hall. A surname, perhaps from this place, appears as Tunlegh 1288 Court, Tounelegh 1342 Eyre, 1344, 1399 ChRR, Tounley 1394 ib. Cf. Towneley La 84.

BANK FM. BIG WOOD. BRANKELOW MOSS, v. 94 supra. BUTTERMILK BANK, the site of Buttermilk Hall 1831 Bry, v. buttermilk, banke. Presumably a good place for butter. CHURCH BRIDGE, 1831 ib, cf. Marbury Bridge 1621 Sheaf. The bridge is named after Marbury Church. CROSSHILL FM, v. cros 'a cross', hyll. FOX HALL. GLEBE COVERT, v. glebe. THE GRANGE. HEATH LANE. HOLLINS LANE, 1842 OS, Hollin- 1831 Bry, 'holly-tree lane', v. holegn. HOLLYHURST, 1831 ib, Holy- 1724 NotCestr, 'holly wood', v. holegn, hyrst. HOLLY ROUGH, 1837 TA, v. holegn, rūh. THE KNOWLES, 1842 OS, 'the hillocks', v. cnoll. LIMEPITS, cf. Lime Pit Field 1837 TA. MARBURY BROOK (R. Weaver), v. brōc, cf. Steer Brook 1 35. MARBURY HEYS, 1831 Bry, Marley Heys 1842 OS, from the p.ns. Marbury supra, Marley infra and (ge)hæg 'a fenced-in enclosure'. MARBURY MILL (lost), 1842 ib, cf. Mill Field 1837 TA. MARLEY GREEN, HALL & MOSS, (109–5845), Marley 1621 (1656) Orm[2], -Green & -Hall, Marbury Moss 1831 Bry, Marley Moss 1837 TA, probably 'boundary wood or clearing', v. (ge)mære, lēah, grēne[2], hall, mos. These, and Marbury Heys, are near the Wrenbury boundary. There is confusion of Marley and Marbury in all these names. BIG- & LITTLE MERE, 1837 ib, too goodly meres or pooles c.1536 Leland. Big Mere is Marbury Meare 1656 Orm[2], -Mere 1837 TA, The Mere 1831 Bry, v. mere[1].

MERE FM, v. Quoisley *supra*, mere[1].   MOSSBANK, cf. *Moss Head* 1837 *TA*, v. mos, banke, hēafod.   POOLE GORSE, cf. *Old Pool* (*Land*) 1837 *ib*, v. pōl[1], gorst.   POOLE HOOK, -*Hoo*(*c*)*ke* 1570, 1585 *Chol*, 'nook of land at a pool', v. pōl[1], hōc.   QUOISLEY BIG- & -LITTLE MERE, 1842 OS, *The Meres* 1831 Bry, *Quoisley Meres* 1837 *TA*, v. mere[1], Quoisley *supra*.   STEER BRIDGE, 1842 OS, *Steep Bridge* 1831 Bry, from Steer Brook 1 35.

FIELD-NAMES

The undated forms are 1837 *TA* 252. Of the others, 1831 is Bry, 1842 OS, and the rest *Chol*.

(*a*) Acre Bank; The Anchor(s) (*v.* ancra); Ashley (*v.* æsc, lēah); Badgers Bank (*v.* bagga); Beany Furlong (*v.* bēan, furlang); Bottle Mdw; Broom Fd (cf. *the bromye field* 1598, *v.* brōm, brōmig); Coe Fd (*v.* cū); Cote Fd (*v.* cot); Cranks; Creamer; Dacepit Fd; Damage Croft (*v.* demming); Four- & Six Daymath (*v.* day-math); Dovery Bank; Drade Low (perhaps a form of *Drake Low*, *v.* draca, hlāw, cf. Drakelow 2 198); Farralls Fosse (*v.* foss[1]); Flash Fd (*v.* flasshe); The Flatts (*v.* flat); The Gales, Galey Mdw (cf. *Gale Moor* 1598, 'bog-myrtle marsh', *v.* gagel, mōr[1]); Hanging Fd (*v.* hangende); The Harries; Big- & Little Heath; Herbage Mdw; Hole Mdw (cf. *The Hole* 1831, 1842, *v.* hol[1]); Intake (*v.* inntak); Jack Moor (*v.* jack, mōr[1]); Kettle Bank 1842 (*Kettles-* 1831, *v.* keddle-dock, banke); Kitchen Mdw; The Lees (*v.* lǣs); Long Shoot (*v.* scēat); Lyn Croft (*v.* līn); Marlpit Croft & Moor (*v.* marle-pytt); Milking Bank (*v.* milking); Moat Fd (*v.* mote); The Moor; Mud Croft (*v.* mudde); Old House Fd ('field where a house used to stand', *v.* ald, hūs); Outlet (*v.* outlet); Ox Moor; Ridge (*v.* hrycg); Ridley Fd & Mdw (*Rydley fieldes, -fyeldes* 1570, 1585, *le Ridley fieldes* 1598, cf. Ridley 313 *infra*); Little Rough; Round Bank (*v.* rond); Rye Bank; Saint John's Bank; Sand(hole) Fd; Sawpit Fd (*v.* saw-pytt); Shooter or Shooting Butts; Sibby-hough; Sling Fd (dial. sling 'a long, narrow field', cf. slang); Sour Fd; Stannydale ('stony valley', *v.* stānig, dæl[1]); Stocking (cf. *Gylstokkyng* 1447, *Gyllt Stokkyngeʒ* 1540, 'grounds cleared of tree-stumps, where marigolds grow', *v.* gylde, stoccing); Town Fd; Wann Bank; Weir Mdw (*Weer Meadowe* 1598, *v.* wer); White Fd; Willow Moor Fd ('willow marsh', *v.* wilig, mōr[1]); Yoke Ho.

(*b*) *le Held Moores* 1570, 1585, *Helde-* 1598 ('moors at a hill', *v.* helde, mōr[1]); *le Hew*(*e*)*stoke*(*s*) c.1280 (17) ('the servant's farmstead', from the ME sg. *hewe* from OE hīwan, and stoc); (*le*) *Parrocke Me*(*a*)*d*(*d*)*owe* 1570, 1585, 1598 ('paddock meadow', *v.* pearroc, mǣd); *le Stonriforde* c.1280 (17) ('ford at a stony place', *v.* stanry, stæner, ford, cf. Stoneley Mdw 111 *infra*. Professor Löfvenberg also suggests that the first el. could be the ME adj. *stanry* 'stony, gravelly' (c.1440 NED), also written *stonri* owing to the influence of the ME form *ston*, and draws attention to ModEdial. *stannery* 'gravelly' (Scottish, EDD). Cf. Dunham on the Hill 253 *infra*).

2. NORBURY (109–5547) [-bəri]

> *Norberie* 1086 DB, *-bery* 1562, 1567 ChRR, *-bur(ia)* e13, 1259 *Chol*,
> *-bury* 1305 *ib et freq* with variant spelling *-burye*, *-bur'*, *-burie*;
> (*-iuxta Merbury*) 1337 Plea, (*Althurst &-*) 1411 ChRR, (*-&*
> *Althurst*) 1486 ib, (*-cum Althurst*) 1597 Orm[2]
> *Northburi* 12 (17) *Chol*, H3 (14) *AddCh*, *-bur'* 1250–60 *Chol*, *-bury*
> 1287 Court (p) *et freq* with variant spellings *Nort(he)-*, *Northt-*,
> *-bur'*, *-bure*, *-burie* to 1492 *Chol*, (*Nort(he)bury iuxta Mer-*,
> *Marbury*) 1289 Court
> *Norhbur'* c.1180 *AddCh*, *Norhebur* c.1260 *Chol*

'Northern manor-house or stronghold', *v.* norð, burh. This was
the most northerly part of the parish of Whitchurch Sa, *v.* 112 *infra*,
105 *supra*. Cf. Marbury 106 *supra*, Holtridge *infra*.

HOLTRIDGE (109–563484) [ˈɔːtridʒ]

> *Althurst* 1380 Pat, 1411 ChRR *et freq* with variant spelling *Alte-*
> to 1597 ChRR, *-or Altridge* (*Hall*) 1860 White, 1882 Orm[2]
> *Alhurst(e)* 1559, 1562 ChRR, 1567 ib, *Chol*
> *Altwyche* (*Mylne*) 1587 *Chol*
> *Altrich* 1630 *Chol*, the *Altridge tenement & Mill* 1693 *ib*, *-Hall* 1860
> White
> *Holtridge Greene* 1630 *Chol*
> *Ortridge Meadow* 1778 *Chol*
> *Outridge Green* 1831 Bry, 1842 OS

Barnes[1] 726 proposes Welsh allt (cf. Corn alt) 'steep hill-side,
(rocky) hill, cliff, mountain-woodland', as in Alt La 29, to which have
been added the English equivalents hyrst 'a hill, a wood' and hrycg
'a ridge', *v.* also grēne[2], hall, myln, mǣd. The place lies on the north
side of a slight eminence. *v.* Addenda.

SWANWICK GREEN (190–547478) [ˈswɔnik, ˈswɔniʔ-, ˈswɔnə-ˈgriːn]

> *Squanewic* 13 NRA 0430 (p)
> *Swanewik* 1250–6 *Chol* (bruera de), 1325 ChRR (p), *-wyk* c.1300
> *Chol* (bruera de), *-wike* 1311–13 Orm[2] (p)
> *Swanwyk* 1319 ChRR (p) *et freq* with variant spellings *-wik(e)* to
> 1575 *Chol*, *-wyck* 1568 Orm[2], *-wycke Greene* 1575 *Chol*, *-wicke*
> 1579 *ib*
> *Swanway Greene* 1630 *Chol*

Swanhow Green 1831 Bry
Swanna or *Swanwick Green* 1842 OS, 1882 Orm²

'Peasants' dairy-farm or work-settlement', *v.* swān² (gen.pl.
swāna), wīc, and grēne². Cf. Swanwick, Swannick 2 228, 208, 256.

WENSLEY (lost), 1837 *TA, Wennesll', Wennelleg'* 1209–28, *Wennisleg'*
1250–6, *Wenis-, Wenes* c.1258, *Wennes-* c.1300, *Wensleys* 1703 all
Chol, 'clearing or wood at a tumulus or a hillock', *v.* wenn, -es², lēah.

CANAL COVERT.   CHURCH BRIDGE, *v.* 107 *supra.*   COMMON FM,
cf. Norbury Common *infra.*   GAUNTONS BANK, 1842 OS, -*or
Hollybush* 1831 Bry.   LOWER HALL, 1831 ib, cf. *Upper Hall* 1831
ib.   HANDLEY HILL & PARK *the Handley hill & croft* 1598,
Handley Hill, Long Handley 1731, *Handley Park* 1753, *the Big Rough
Henley* 1778 all *Chol, the little Handley* 1623 Sheaf, *Hanley Park* 1831
Bry, -*Hall* 1842 OS, probably 'high clearing', *v.* hēah (wk.dat.sg.
hēan), lēah.   HORSE GREEN, 1778 *Chol, le hurst grene iuxta
Merbury* 1496 *Chol, (the) Hurst Green(e)* 1598, 1713 *ib, the Hurste
greave* 1581 Sheaf, 'green at a wooded hill', *v.* hyrst, grēne².   THE
MOUNT.   NORBURY COMMON, 1831 Bry, *Norburie Mosse* 1593
Chol, v. mos, commun.   OAK COTTAGE, *The Oak* 1831 Bry, *Oak
House* 1842 OS, *v.* āc.   PEARTREE FM, *Wood House* 1831 Bry,
'house at a wood', *v.* wudu, hūs.   RYEBANK, 1831 ib, *v.* ryge,
banke.   LOWER SNAB, -*Snabb* 1842 OS, cf. *the Snab poole* 1693
Chol, Snab Croft 1837 *TA, v.* Higher Snab 326 *infra,* pōl¹, croft.
STEER BRIDGE, *v.* 108 *supra.*

FIELD-NAMES

The undated forms are 1837 *TA* 296. Of the others, 1380 (1399) is Pat, 1610,
1623 Sheaf, 1831 Bry, and the rest *Chol.*

(*a*) Annuals Fd; The Banks (*v.* banke); Barne Meere 1703 (*v.* bere-ærn,
mere¹); Black-, Blake Lake (*Black Lake* 1709, 1744, 1831, cf. *Blake Pul*
1250–6, c.1300, 'dark pool or stream', *v.* blæc, pull, lacu); Briery Fd (cf. *le
breres* 1451, *v.* brēr); Brow Fd (cf. *Brow Croft Stile* 1700, *v.* brū, croft,
stigel); Butter Croft (*v.* butere, croft); Clap Gate Meadow 1703 (*v.* clap-
gate); Coat Fd (*v.* cot); Colefox Mdw 1735 (*v.* colefox); Cote Fd (cf. *Cote
Croft* 1703, 1744, *v.* cot, croft); Cribby; Cross Lane Fd (cf. *the Crosse Field*
1598, *v.* cros); Cunnerin Town Fd, Curney Croft (cf. *Conerie Banke* 1598,
the Conigree 1623, *Cunny greame* 1709, -*greave* 1726, *Cunney Greave* 1744,
Cunering Croft 1736, *v.* coningre, banke, croft, cf. Town Fd *infra*); the
Damage Pitts 1700 (cf. *the Dammage craft* 1693, *v.* damming. The -*ing* is

assibilated); Daymath (*v.* day-math); Dockey Mdw (*the Dockameadowe*
1598, *v.* docce, mǣd); Bottom Dows (*v.* dāl); Edges Intake & Mdw (cf. *the
Eddishes* 1598, *v.* edisc); Flashes (*v.* flasshe); Green Bank 1700; Green Fd
(*Great & Little greene field* 1595, *v.* grēne¹); the Green Lane 1700; Hadley
(cf. Hadley 106 *supra*); Halla Mdw 1706 (*the Hallameadows* 1693, *v.* halh,
mǣd); Hough Bottom & Fd (*v.* halh, botm); Intake (*v.* inntak); Long Butts
(*v.* lang, butte); the Maine Brooke 1700 ('the common brook', *v.* (ge)mǣne,
brōc, cf. *Meane Brooke* 118 *infra*); Marl Fd; Meg Fd (*the great- & -Little
Megge field* 1598, *Megg-Fields* 1731, *v.* meg); Milking Bank Fd (*v.* milking);
The Molts (*the Mottes* 1598, *v.* mote); Moor Mdw (cf. *Myddell Moore* 1588,
the Moorefield 1598, *v.* mōr¹, middel); Moss, Moss Head (*v.* hēafod); the
Newtown in Norbury 1721 (*v.* nīwe, toun); Old Feilde 1700; Outlet (*v.*
outlet); Oven Fd (*v.* ofen); Ox Pasture (*Oxpasher* 1700, *v.* oxa, pasture);
Padock 1703 (*v.* pearroc); Park Fd; Pease Mdw (*v.* pise); Pingo (*v.* pingot);
Poole Mdw 1700 (*v.* pōl¹); Ridding (*v.* ryding); Rough Moor (*Rughe Moore*
1588, *v.* rūh, mōr¹); Round Fd (1831); Rush Fd 1777 (*v.* risc); Shear Croft
(*Shaw Croft* 1588, *Sha-Fields* 1731, *v.* scaga, sceaga); Slang (*v.* slang); Bigg-,
Little- & Nearer Smithsfield 1753 (*Smythfelds* 1593, cf. *Smithy Craft* 1700,
v. smiδ, smiδδe); Soapwater Fd; Stoneley Mdw (*Stonery Meadows* 1693,
cf. *Stonriforde* 108 *supra*, *v.* stǣner, stanry, stonery); Stript Mdw; Swans
Lake (*v.* lacu); (Butty) Town Fd (*the towne feild* 1623, *v.* toun, feld, butty);
Turf Coat Field, Turf Meadow (*v.* turf 'peat', cot); the Twitchoofields &
-lane 1721 (*v.* twychell); Water Fd (cf. *the Water Furrow Field* 1778, *v.*
wæter, furh); Weir Mdw; Welchmans Yard (*v.* Wels(c)h-mann, geard);
Winkley (*Wynkeleg*' c.1260, perhaps 'Wineca's wood or clearing', from an
OE pers.n. *Wineca* and lēah, cf. Winkleigh, Winkley D 373, 588)); Within
Croft 1703 (*v.* wīδegn).

(b) *Bardeleg Broc* 1250–6, c.1300, *Barndeleg*' c.1258, *-More* c.1260
('(brook and moor at) the burned clearing', from berned and lēah, with
brōc, mōr¹); *Daysie Croft* 1588 (*v.* dægesege, croft); *Fluaiggescrofte* 1347
(*v.* croft. The first el. is unidentified); *the Greene Yate* 1598, *the greene-yate*
1610 ('gateway to a green', *v.* grēne², geat); *Hulles* c.1258 ('the hills', *v.*
hyll); *Knafhalewey* c.1260 ('(way to, by, or at) the youth's nook', *v.* cnafa,
halh, weg); *the Melhurst* 1598 ('dappled wooded hill', *v.* mǣle, hyrst);
Mosileg' *Mor* 1250–6, *-More* c.1300 ('(moor at) the mossy clearing', *v.*
mosig, lēah, mōr¹); *the Orchard crofte* 1598 (*v.* orceard, croft); *Perdooe
meadowe* 1598 (apparently from ModE *perdu(e)* (NED) and mǣd. The sense
is not clear, perhaps 'hopeless meadow' or 'outlying meadow'); *Solengak*
1250–6, *Solinhac* c.1300 (a boundary-point. The same name appears in
Solinhac c.1260–70 2 316, also as a boundary-point. It is probably 'lonely,
solitary, oak', from āc with ME solein (NED from 1369) 'lonely, solitary,
apart'); *Wyldemore* 1250–6 ('desolate marsh', *v.* wilde, mōr¹); *Yeamorre*
1588 ('high moor', *v.* hēah, mōr¹).

xi. Whitchurch

In addition to the parochial Chapelry of Marbury 105 *supra*, the parish of Whitchurch Sa contained the township of Wirswall. Wirswall, Norbury and Marbury are described in DB as berewicks (*v.* bere-wīc) of Whitchurch Sa, as also was Stoneley Green 135 *infra*, *v.* Tait 153.

1. WIRSWALL (HALL) (118–5444) [ˈwəːzwɔːl] locally [-wəl, -(w)əl]

> *Wireswelle, -uelle* 1086 DB, *Wyreswell(e)* 1276, 1308 Ipm, 1324 Orm², *Wierswell* 1831 Bry
>
> *Wyriswall* c.1180 AddCh, *Wy-, Wiriswall(e)* 1260 Court, 1283 Ipm, *Wyreswall* 1288 Court (p) *et freq* with variant spellings *Wires-, -wall(e)* to 1526 Plea, (*Over Wireswall*) 1499 Orm²
>
> *Wyrswall' iuxta Album monasterium* 12 (17) Chol, *Wy-, Wirswall* 1321, 1322 Fine, Pat, 1342 (1435) ChRR, *Wyrs(e)wall* 1493 Chol, *Wirswall* 1727 Sheaf
>
> *Wyswall(e)* H3 (14) AddCh
>
> *Wereswall* 1357 BPR, *Werres-* 1507 (1571) ChRR, *Werswall* 1660 LCWills
>
> *Wyreswale* 1358 AddCh
>
> *Worswall* 1488, 1490 ChRR, 1597 Orm², 1679 Chol, *Worse-* 1724 NotCestr
>
> *Wyrsal* 1621 (1656) Orm²

'Wīghere's spring', from the OE pers.n. *Wīghere* and wella, wælla, with uferra. *Album Monasterium* is Whitchurch Sa.

BRADELEY GREEN, 1837 *TA*, *Bradeley* 1463 Orm², 1493 Chol, *Bradley Green* 1831 Bry, 1842 OS, '(green at) the broad clearing', *v.* brād, lēah, grēne².

WICKSTED FM (118–551442)

> *Wyckestede* 1315 AddCh (p), 1360 Chamb (p), *Wykkested* 1358 ChRR (p), *Wickestude* 1358 BPR (p)
>
> *Whicksteed* 1315 (17) Sheaf (p), *-sted* 1499 Eyre (p), *Whikstid* 1490 ChRR (p), *Whickstide* 1629 Sheaf
>
> *Wicstede* 1348 Eyre (p) *et freq* with variant spellings *Wi(c)k- Wyk-, Wic-, -sted* to 1513 Chol, *-stud* (1409 ChRR), *-styd* (1436 Plea), *-stid(e)* (1477 Chol, 1519 Orm²) to *Wyckstead* 1588 Sheaf (p), *Wick-* 1724 NotCestr (p), (*-Hall*) 1831 Bry
>
> *Wyxted* 1493 Chol, *W(h)ixsted* 1512, 1514 ChEx (p)

Either 'place where a dairy farm stands', from wīc and stede, styde, with hall, or 'dwelling-place, habitation', from wīc-stede, -styde. The compound and the p.n. are discussed in Sandred 80, 93, 293.

THE DELL. ELLYMAS COTTAGE, cf. *Ellymoss Close, Croft & Field* 1837 *TA*, 'elder-tree marsh', v. elle, -ig[3], mos, cf. Ellis Bank **1** 133. GRANGE FM. MERE COTTAGE, named from Quoisley Big Mere 108 *supra*. PEEL'S GORSE. WICKSTED HALL, *Belvedere* 1831 Bry, *Belvidere (House)* 1837 *TA*, 1842 OS, a modern residence which has assumed the old name of Wicksted Fm *supra*. WILLEYMOOR COTTAGE, cf. *le Wyldeley morr syde* 1493 *Chol, Willymoor Meadow* 1837 *TA*, from Willey Moor 327 *infra*, v. sīde. WOOD FM, *The-* 1831 Bry, *The Wood* 1781 Sheaf, 1842 OS, cf. *Big-, Further- & Higher Wood, Wood Ridding* 1837 *TA, le Wodruddynges* 1493 *Chol* v. wudu, ryding.

FIELD-NAMES

The undated forms are 1837 *TA* 440.

(a) The acre; Barley Eddish (v. edisc); Bog; Brewhouse Fd; Brickkiln Fd; Broad Fd; Broomy Bank (v. brōmig); (Hanging) Bytham (v. byðme, hangende); Carthouse Fd (v. carte-hows); Cheshire Acre (the Ch acre was almost twice the area of the standard English acre, v. æcer); The Close; Cockshut, -sheet (v. cocc-scyte); Cranberry Moss (v. cranberry); Cranmere Mdw ('crane pool', v. cran, mere[1]); Dingle Hill ('hill with a dell under it', v. dingle); Dole Back Hill; Dun Ridding (v. dunn, ryding); Green Fd (*le grenefelde* 1493 *Chol*, v. grēne[1], feld); Hand Croft; Hayes Croft (v. (ge)hæg); Hedge Close (v. hecg); Hinton Fd; Hodgil a Man; The Kease; Kill Cow (v. 325 *infra*); Lady Hill (v. hlǣfdige); Mere Greaves (v. mere[1], grǣfe); Miram; Osmere (Croft) (cf. Oss Mere Sa, a lake); The Paddock (v. pearroc); Park Hill; Quickin (v. cwicen 'a mountain ash'); The Shardes (v. sceard); Sheep Walk; Springs (v. spring 'a well-spring'); Sprinks (v. spring 'a young wood'); Stocking Bank (cf. *le hye felde vel le Stockyng* 1493 *Chol*, v. hēah, feld, stoccing); Tom Ridding, Town Fd ('public clearing and field', v. toun); White Gate Fd; Windle Tree Croft; Windmill Fd.

xii. Wrenbury

Wrenbury was a parochial chapelry of Acton parish 126 *infra*. It contained the townships 1. Broomhall, 2. Chorley, 3. Woodcott, 4. Wrenbury cum Frith, and also parts of Dodcott cum Wilkesley and Newhall, 92, 101 *supra*, and of Sound 121 *infra*.

8

1. BROOMHALL (GREEN), (110–6347) ['bruːmɔːl]

Brunhala 1086 DB, 1175 Facs (ed. reads *Brim-*)

Bromhale 1096–1101 (1280), 1150 Chester *et freq* with variant
   spellings *-hal(a)* from p.1266 Chest, *Bromale* from 1308 AD to
   1475 *Chol*, (*-iuxta Cowel*) 1328 Plea, (*-iuxta Sonde*) 1348 *AddCh*,
   (*-iuxta Batynton*) 1475 *Chol*

Brumhale 1260 Court (p)

Bromhall 1303 Chamb (p), 1334 VR (p), 1389 ChRR, 1623 Sheaf,
   1882 Orm², *Bromall* 1400 Pat, 1463 Plea

Bromhull 1348 ChRR

Bromehale 1355 BPR, 1463 ChRR, 1480 AD (p), 1486 *AddCh*,
   Bromeale 1379 Orm²

Bromehall 1379 (1574) ChRR, 1454 ib, 1514 *Chol*, 1552 ChRR,
   1623 Sheaf

Broomhull 1389 ChRR

Bromhole 1391 Pat

Broomhall 1462, 1508 ChRR, (*-Heath*) 1831 Bry, *Broomall Green*
   1695 *Chol*

Bromold c.1536 Leland

Bromham 1554 Pat (*Aston iuxta-*)

'Nook where broom grows' from **brōm** and **halh** (dat.sg. **hale**),
with **grēne²** and **hǣð**. Broomhall adjoins Coole Pilate, Sound,
Baddington 138, 121, 131 *infra* and Aston in Newhall 102 *supra*.

MICKLEY HALL (110–637473) *Myckeley* 1558, 1580 *AddCh*, *Myckley*
(*in Wrenbury*) 1565 ib, *Mickley* 1590 Sheaf, (*the hall of-*) 1621 (1656)
Orm², 'big clearing', from **micel** and **lēah**, with **hall**. This house was
the ancient seat of a family surnamed *de Schesewis* 1352 *Chol*,
-Cheseuys 1353 Eyre, *-wis* 1421 ChRR, *-wyce* 1375 Eyre, *-Cheswys*
1410 *Chol*, 1434 ChRR *et freq* to 1512 *ChEx*, *-wis* 1468 ChRR,
-Cheswise 1515 *ChEx*, *Cheswes* 1558 *AddCh*, *-wycs* 1443 ChRR,
-Chesewis 1410 *Chol*. This surname is a p.n. 'cheese farm' *v.* **cēse**,
wīc. It may represent an older name of Mickley, but it is also found
with an original p.n. at *Schesewys* 317 *infra*.

BROOMHALL WOOD, 1841 *TA*, cf. Hugh *del Wode* 1418 ChRR, *v.*
wudu.   CORONERAGE FM, *Coronerage* 1831 Bry, perhaps sometime
the subject of a coroner's inquest, *v.* **coroner**.   DEVIL'S NEST, *The-*
1831 ib, *v.* **dēofol**, **nest**.   GREEN HO, at Broomhall Green *supra*, *v.*

grēne², hūs.   HEATLEY, 1718 Sheaf, *Haytle* 1599 ChRR, 'heath clearing', *v.* hǣð, lēah.   OAK FM, *Oak* 1718 Sheaf, *The Oak* 1831 Bry, *v.* āc.   PRITCH FM, *Pritch* 1831 ib.   SANDFORD BRIDGE, *v.* 102 *supra.*   TOP OF THE TOWN, 1831 ib, *v.* topp, toun.

FIELD-NAMES

The undated forms are 1841 *TA* 76.

(a) Body Hay; The Bottoms (*v.* botm); Brathertons Fd (from the *Brereton* family (cf. Brereton 2 274), which owned land at Heatley in 1559 ChRR); Brick Bank & Kiln; Bromley Fd (*v.* brōm, lēah, cf. Broomhall *supra*); Broomy Knoll (*v.* brōmig, cnoll); Cherry tree Croft (cf. *a Smithie in Bromehall at or near the lane end called Cherytree Lane* 1623 Sheaf, *v.* chiri, trēow); Chiplakes, Chiplake Mdw (probably from scēp 'a sheep', and lacu 'a stream, a watercourse', though cipp 'a beam, a log' is possible); Cock Croft; Colley's Croft, Colliers Fd (*v.* colig, colere); Cool Hayes (cf. Coole Pilate 138 *infra v.* (ge)hæg); Day Math (*v.* day-math); Depth Moor; Drumble Fd (dial. *drumble*, cf. dumbel); Dunster (perhaps tūn-stall); Gorsecote Mdw (*v.* gorst, cot); Hacks't House Bank; Hank Ridding (*v.* ryding); Hazle Hurst (*v.* hæsel, hyrst); Holly Bank & Moor; The Hurst (*v.* hyrst); Jocunds Fd; Langot (*v.* langot); Lean Fd; Long Shoot (*v.* scēat); Marl Fd; Mean Field (*v.* (ge)mǣne); Milking Bank (*v.* milking); Moat Fd (*v.* mote); Moseley (*v.* mos, lēah, cf. Mosley's Head 121 *infra*); New Bridge House 1718; Oat(s) Acre (*v.* āte); Oozey Croft (*v.* wōsig); Outlett (*v.* outlet); Ox Pasture; Patch; Poolhurst (*v.* pōl¹, hyrst); Priors Fd; Sandhole Fd; Six Butts (*v.* butte); Spoil Bank; Spot House Fd, Spout Fd (*v.* spoute); Sprinky Hill (*v.* spring 'a young wood'); Stockings, Stocking Cotes (*v.* stoccing, cot); Sycamore Tree Ho 1831 Bry; Tadpole (probably named from its shape); Tag Ridding Mdw (*v.* tagga, ryding); Town Fd & Mdw (*v.* toun); White Fd, Far Yard (*v.* geard).

2. CHORLEY (GREEN (FM) & HALL) (109–5750) ['tʃɔːli]

> *Cerlere* 1086 DB, *Cherlegh* 1307 Plea, 1342 (1438) ChRR, 1371 *Chol*, *-le* 1308 Ipm, 1310 Cl, *-ley* 1398 ChRR
>
> *Chorleg'* 1280 P (p), *-legh* 1305 Chol et freq with variant spellings *-ley*, *freq* from 1398 ChRR, *-leye*; (*Chorlegh iuxta Wrennebur'*) 1307 Plea, (*Chorley iuxta Badleigh*) 1379 (1574) ChRR (lit. *Rad-*), (*-Badiley*) 1419 Plea, (*-ioust Cholmeley*) 1410 *Chol*, (*-negh-*, *-neere Wrenbury*) 1508, 1599 *ib*, *Chorley Grene* 1454 *ib*, *-Green* 1732 *ib*, *Chorley Hall* 1831 Bry, *Chorley Green Farm* 1841 *TA*

Jorley 1404 *Chol*
Corley c.1550 *Surv*
Chourley 1579 Orm²

Cholley 1702 Cre
Charley 1703 *Chol*
Chawley 1704 *Chol*

'Peasants' clearing', from ceorl and lēah, with grēne², hall. The form *Jorley* is from the context 'Johannes *jolmonney* dominus de *jorley* and de *jolmonney*' (*Chol* A 113), and represents French orthographic influence, cf. Cholmondeley 325 *infra*, and the forms of Chorley 1 225, Chorlton 59 *supra*.

Bank Ho, Chorley Bank, cf. *The Bank Field* 1750 *Chol*, v. banke. Breeze Hill, 'gad-fly hill', v. brēosa, hyll. Brook Ho, 1831 Bry, *the Brookhouse tenement* 1686 *Chol*, named from Black Brook³ 1 15, v. brōc, hūs. Caldecott Fm, 'cold cottage', v. cald, cot. Chorleystock, *Chorley Stock tenement* 1732 *Chol*, v. stocc. Fir-tree Ho, 1831 Bry. Roseground [rɔːz-], *Rowe Grounds* 1831 ib, *Rowes Ground* 1842 OS, (& *Field*) 1841 *TA*, 'ground belonging to one Rowe', from ModE *ground* (cf. grund) and the surname *Rowe*. Wallstone, 1831 Bry, 1842 OS, *Horstone Farm, Higher- & Lower Horstone Croft* 1786 *Chol*, 'hoar stone', v. hār², stān. Wood Barn Fm (lost, 109–585506), 1851 *EnclA*, *Wood Barn* 1831 Bry, 'wooden barn', v. wudu, bere-ærn.

FIELD-NAMES

The undated forms are 1841 *TA* 109. Of the others, 1433 is *AddCh*, 1645 Cre, 1831 Bry, and the rest *Chol*.

(a) Bakehouse Fd (*the-, & croft* 1750); Bar Croft (*Barcroft Lane* 1693, 1831, *The Higher- & Lower Bar Croft* 1750, 'barley croft', v. bere, croft); The Bare Fd 1750; Big Mdw 1733 (*magnum pratum* 1447, *le grete medowe* 1454, *the greate medowe* 1637, *Chorley meadow* 1670, v. grēat, mǣd); Black Acre (1717, *the blacke acre* 1638); Bottoms (v. botm); Brickiln Fd; (Little) Broad Fd 1786; Brook Fd (*the-* 1750); Broomy Fd 1786 (v. brōmig); Bulls Yard (1733, v. bula, geard); Burley Fds 1728 (*-Fe(e)ilds* 1648, 1717, *the Bigg Burley field* 1717, v. burh, lēah); Butty Mdw (*the-* 1700, *-medow* 1693, *the Booty Meadow* 1749, 1767, v. butty, bōtye); Caldwell ('cold well or spring', v. cald, wella, cf. *Calday* 1385 (1619), perhaps 'cold stream', v. cald, ēa); Chorley Hey Mdw (*heya de Cherlegh* 1371, *Chorlegh Hay* 1496, *Chorleyhey(e)* 1454, 1479, 1508, 1518, *-Hay(e)* 1515, 1536, *-Hays* 1724, *-Heyes* 1727, 1754, 'the enclosure(s)', v. (ge)hæg); Clay Fd (*the* 1714); Corey; Corloose 1733; Far- & Near Cow Fd (*the farther- & -nearer Cow Field* 1786); Cranks Moor (*Crounks Moore* 1703, *Cronks Moor* 1733, 'crane's march', v. cranuc, mōr¹); the Crooked Fd 1732; Cross Fd & Flat(t) (*the Cross(e) Flat(t)* 1700, 1767, v. cros 'a cross'); Five-, Four-, Ten-, Three Daymath (cf. *Eight Days Math*

1733, *v.* day-math); Eardleys (*the three Yardleyes* 1637, *-yard leyes* 1639, 'pastures in enclosures', *v.* geard, ModE dial. *ley* (cf. lēah, lǣs)); Eight Shilling Mdw (named from its rent or purchase); Flash Mdw (*v.* flasshe); Glade Fd (*the-* 1733, *v.* glæd³); the Gorst(e)y Field 1732, 1733 (*v.* gorstig); Granary Fd; Grass Yard (lit. *Graff-*) 1733 (*v.* gærs, geard); Green Fd (*Great-* & *Little-* 1786, *-Feild* 1700); Half Acre (*the-* 1750); Hand Fd (1733, *þe Han'feld* 1559, *the Hamfelde* 1601); Little Harper's Fd 1786; Lower- & Near Harry's Croft (*The Higher-* & *-Lower-* 1750, *Harry Crofte* 1536); Big & Little Harthill Fd (*Big* & *Little Harthill* 1733, *v.* heorot, hyll); Hatch Fd (*v.* hæcc); Hemp butt (*v.* hænep, butte); Hermit Fd (*v.* ermite); Hobback; Holly Bank; Horns Cottage 1777; Horse Pasture (cf. (*le*) *horse crofte* 1447, 1454, *v.* hors, croft); Intake (*the-* 1724, *Intack* 1710, *the Higher-* & *-Lower Intacks* 1786, *v.* inntak); (Far & Near) Light Oulers (*lighthollers* 1467, *the little light Owlers* 1637, *the two light Wollers* 1717, 'the light alder-trees', *v.* lēoht, alor (ME *oller*, ModEdial. *owler*)); Long Mdw 1788 (*the-* 1733); Lower Fd (cf. *Lowermost Field* 1786); Madge Fd (cf. *the four Madge Crofts* 1786, *v.* madge); Middle Fd (*the-* 1732); (Near) Nettle Wd, Nettlewood Lane & Mdw (*Netlewode* 1371, *-wood* 1581, *-wood(es)* 1627, *Netteleswode* 1433, *Netilwode* 1454, *Netill-* 1475, *Netel-* 1508, *Nettle Wood* 1690, (*-Lane*) 1710, *Farther-*, *Higher-*, *Lower Nettlewood* 1732, 'wood where nettles grow', *v.* netel(e), wudu); (The) New Croft 1703, 1750 (*New Croft Meadow* 1693); Odd Croft (1788, *v.* odde); Outcry Croft; Outlet (*v.* outlet); Over Yard 1733 (*v.* uferra, geard); Ox Grass (*v.* oxa, gærs); Pearl Mdw 1786 (*v.* pyrl(e)); Pease Croft 1786; Piece Hill; Pingle (cf. *The Pingoe* 1750, *v.* pingel, pingot); Polley's Croft (*Pollett's Croft* 1733); Poolefield 1710 (*the Pole* 1454, *v.* pōl¹); Far-, Second- & Third Ridd (*the Riddes* 1637, *v.* ryde 'cleared land'); The Ridding (cf. *le Loonge rudyng* 1371, *the Farther-* & *-Middle Riddings* 1717, *v.* lang, ryding); The Rowlands (*v.* rūh, land); the Royall Flatt 1700 (*v.* ryge, halh); Rye Croft; Sandy Fd & Flatt (*the Sandye Flatt* 1639, cf. *the Sandy Bank* 1717, *v.* sandig, flat); Saw Pit Fd (cf. *the Sawpit Croft* 1788, *v.* sawpytt); Long Shoot (*v.* scēat); Slack Yard 1733 (? for Stack Yard); Long Spring ('long plantation', *v.* spring); Ston(n)ey Rindle (*v.* stānig, rynel); Lower Stubbs 1703 (*v.* stubb); Three Quarters (*v.* quarter); Town Fd & Mdw (*the towne feld* 1566, *-filde* 1592, *-field(medow)* 1693, 1710, *þe Downefeld* 1468, *Townfields*, *Townfield Meadow* 1733, *The Town Meadow* 1750, *v.* toun, feld); Tup Fd (cf. *Tubcroftes* 1528); Wall Hill(s) (*Walls Hill* 1700, *v.* wælla, hyll); Washing Fd 1786; Way Fd (*v.* weg); Weir Bank & Fd (*Ware feild* 1693, *v.* wer); Well Bank, Fd, Mdw & Yard (*Well Bank* 1788, *-Medow* 1693, *-Feild* 1700, *v.* wella); Whitchurch Fd (1732, *the Higher-* 1683, probably after Whitchurch Sa, since a surname de Harecourt of *Quychurch* figures in a Chorley deed of 1435, *Chol* A 500); White Fd; the Witch Fd 1733 (*v.* wice); Wodey Medow 1703 (*v.* wudig); Wood Fd (cf. *le Caluerhey* 1447, *the Caluer heye or Wod Crofte* 1559, *Caluerhey or Woddecrofte* 1601, 'calves' enclosure', 'croft at a wood', *v.* calf (gen.pl. calfra), (ge)hæg, wudu, croft); Yeomans Croft.

(*b*) *the Bache Crofte* 1536 ('croft at a valley-stream', *v.* bæce¹, croft); *Baletyk Riddyng* 1454 (*v.* ryding); *the barlye feild* 1639; *le Boure* 1305 (p),

1325 (1619) (p), *the-* 1385 (1619) (*v.* būr[1]); *molendina de Chorlegh'* 1305 (*v.* myln); *le Cokshote field* 1447, *Cokshotte* 1454, *Kokshote glade* 1528 (*v.* cocc-scyte); *le Dousehouse crofte* 1447, *Duffehouse Crofte* 1454 (*v.* dovehouse, croft); *Fayrewethuracre* 1455 ('fair-weather acre', perhaps a selion liable to flood, *v.* æcer. The hitherto unrecorded ME adj. *fayre-wether* here antedates *fair-weather* NED (1736)); *Gay Riddyng* 1454 ('cheerful clearing', *v.* gai, ryding); *Goodmans field* 1645 (*v.* gōd-man; but perhaps a surname, *v.* Reaney 137); *le hegh fielde, le hiegh felde* 1447, *Hegh' felde* (*v.* hēah, feld); *Hova Feld* 1468 (from the ME masc. pers.n. *Hova* and feld); *the Kilne Croft* 1637 (*v.* cyln, croft); *Lumbardesfeld* 1371 (from a form of the ME (OFr) pers.n. *Lambert* and feld); *the Mawkins orchard* 1637, *Maukins-* 1639 (from malkin or the ME fem.pers.n. *Malkin* and orceard); *the meane brooke* 1693 ('the common brook', *v.* (ge)mǣne, brōc, cf. Maine Brooke 111 *supra*); *Ox hey* 1454, 1479 (*v.* oxa, (ge)hæg); *letull Podmore* 1457 ('toad marsh', *v.* pode, mōr[1], lȳtel); *Puleston* 1454; *magnum & parvum Rodd* 1467 (probably at a twiggy wood, *v.* rodd(e) 'a rod, a switch, a tender shoot'); *Schoklage howse* 1469 (a house-name, *v.* hūs, cf. Shocklach 326 *infra*); *Smalesiche* 1305 ('narrow watercourse', *v.* smæl, sīc); *Sponereshey* 1467, *the Spooners Hay*, *-hey* 1638, 1639 ('spoon-maker's enclosure', from spōnere, perhaps as a surname, and (ge)hæg); *(le) Stokkyng* 1447, 1454 (*v.* stoccing); *Yokkynge Feld Wodeles* 1468 ('wood-pasture at the yoking field', from wudu and lǣs, with feld and the verbal noun from *yoke* (OE geocian) 'to yoke'. *Yoking* is recorded from 1580 NED).

3. WOODCOTT (Ho & -HILL) (110–608485)

> *Wodecot(e)* c.1205 *Woll*, BM, E1 *AddCh et freq* with variant spellings *Wod(e)-, -cot(e), -cothe* to 1569 *AddCh, Wodecote iuxta Wrenbury* 1377 Orm², *Wod(e)co(o)tehill(e)* 1515 *MinAcct*, Orm², 1521 ChRR, Orm²
> *Wudecote* 1289 Court (p)
> *Woodcoke* 1570 Cre
> *Woodcoate alias Wooddcote* 1599 Orm², *Woodcott* 1602 ChRR *et freq* with variant spellings *-co(o)te, -cot, Woodcott Hill* 1609 Sheaf, *Woodcock hill* 1708 ib

'Cottage at a wood', *v.* wudu, cot, hyll, hūs. There has been popular confusion with wudu-cocc 'a wood-cock'.

YEWTREE HO.

FIELD-NAMES

The undated forms are 1841 *TA* 446.

(*a*) Ambleberry, -burry (*the lande in Ambelbary, Amblebury ground* 1685 Sheaf, cf. *Amblebury Meadow* 1845 *TA* 285 (104 *supra*). The final el. may be bearu 'a wood, a grove', or burh 'a fortified place', the first el. could be an OE pers.n. *Æmela* as in Amblecote St (DEPN), but this f.n. may also be an old p.n. OE **hamol-beorg* 'hill with its end cut off', analogous with the *hamol-dūn* type of Hommerton 1 167, *v.* hamol, beorg); Near Bullery (cf. 120 *infra*); Horse Pasture; Intake (*v.* inntak); Marl Fd; Outlet Fd (*v.* outlet); Penfold Fd (*v.* pynd-fald); Little Scratley (cf. 121 *infra*); Sweet Fd; Woodcote Fd.

4. WRENBURY CUM FRITH, 1708 Sheaf, *v.* Wrenbury, Frith *infra*.

WRENBURY (109–5947) ['renbəri, -bri]

> *Wareneberie* 1086 DB
> *Wrennebury* 1230 (1330) Ch, Dugd, 1284 ChF *et freq* with variant
>> spellings *-burye, -bure, -bur', -buri(e)* to 1510 Plea, *Wrenneburge* 1331 Dugd
> *Wrenebur(y)* c.1327 (p), 1328 Chol, *-ber'* 1488 *ib*
> *Wrenbury* 1327 Pat (p) *et freq* with variant spellings *-burye, -buri(e),*
>> *-bur(e), -bery(e), Wrenn-*; (*-Mill*) 1831 Bry
> *Wreynbery* 1404 Chol
> *Wenbyri* c.1536 Leland
> *Wrembury* 1554 Pat
> *Rhenbury* 1674 Dep, *Renbury* 1697 Sheaf, 1698 Wil

The first el. is probably **wrenna** 'a wren', but an OE pers.n. *Wrenna* is possible. The final el. is burh, 'a fortified place, a stronghold'. The meaning of the name is 'the wren's stronghold', perhaps from some old fortification haunted by the wren. Ekwall's suggestion **wrǣna** 'a stallion', (Studies[2] 67 and DEPN) seems unnecessary. No record of a fortification is known.

FRITH-HALL FM (109–575477), FRITH FM (109–577493), WRENBURY FRITH BRIDGE (109–584476)

> *Tereth* 1086 DB
> *Wrennebury Fryth'* 1340 *Eyre*, 1380 *ib*, *Wrenburifrith* 1441 *Chol*,
>> *Wrenbury Fryth* 1534 *ib*, *-Frieth* 1597 Orm[2], *-Frith* 1625 Sheaf,
>> 1842 OS, *-burie-* 1640 Sheaf
> *le Fryth* 1408 ChRR (p), (*the*) *Frith* 1646 Sheaf, 1682 Chol, 1708
>> Sheaf, *Frith Lane* 1708 ib, *-Farm & -Hall* 1831 Bry, 1842 OS
> *Malvon-Frythe* 1556–7 (1585) ChRR, *Malbon Frythe* 1557 Tab

'The woodland', *v.* (ge)fyrhðe, fyrhð. The DB form must be a miscopied *Fereth*. *Malbon* is the surname of William *Malbank*, tenant in 1086 DB (cf. Nantwich 30 *supra*). Frith was the area south and west of R. Weaver, about 109–5748. In 1831 Bry *Frith Farm* is marked at 109–564487, *Wrenbury Frith* 1842 OS is marked north of the bridge (a canal bridge over the Shropshire Union), cf. Yewtree Ho *infra*.

BANK FM (109–575486), *v.* banke. Bry calls this *Cholmondley Brook Farm, v. infra.* BLACK FIRS. BROOKLANDS. CHOLMONDLEY BROOK FM (109–562488), on a stream running from Cholmondeley Meres 326 *infra*. Bry marks this as *Heath Farm, v.* hǣð. Cf. Bank Fm *supra*. FAR CROFT. FIELD FM. THE HEALD, 1831 Bry, cf. *First-, Second Yeald*, etc., *Yeald Meadow, Yealds Field* 1841 *TA*, 'the hillside', *v.* helde. HILL FM, cf. *Hill Bank, Croft & Field* 1841 *ib*. LANE ACRES FM, *Leaneacre* 1560 Sheaf, *Lean Acres* 1831 Bry, 'poor ploughland', *v.* hlǣne 'lean', æcer. OLD COVERT, *Wrenbury Hill Gorse* 1831 ib, *v.* gorst. PORTER'S HILL, *Potters Hill* 1831 ib, *Porters Hall* 1842 OS, cf. *Porter's Hill Field* 1841 *TA*. SANDFIELD HO, cf. *Sand Field* 1841 *ib*. SHELFORD (LANE) (lost), 1841 *ib*, *graungia vocata Shefforde Graunge* 1547 *MinAcct*, 'shallow ford', *v.* sceldu, ford, grange. SPROSTONWOOD HO, the origin of this name is not known, cf. Sproston 2 254, *v.* Wrenburywood *infra*. WRENBURY BRIDGE. WRENBURY HALL, *the hall of Wrenbury* 1621 (1656) Orm[2]. WRENBURY HEATH, 1708 Sheaf. WRENBURY MILL, 1831 Bry. WRENBURYWOOD, *Wrenbury Wood* 1842 OS. This and Sprostonwood Ho are *Wrenbury Wood Farms* 1831 Bry, cf. foll. WRENBURY WOOD, cf. prec. and *Wrenbury Wood Cottage* 1842 OS, *Little- & Lower Wood, Wood Field & Meadow* 1841 *TA*. YEWTREE HO (109–570488). Bry calls this *Frith*, cf. Frith Fm *supra*, and puts *Yew Tree Farm* at 109–572495.

FIELD-NAMES

The undated forms are 1841 *TA* 450. Of the others, c.1536 is Leland, 1547 *MinAcct*, 1550, 1700 *Chol*, 1558 ChRR, 1568 Orm[2], 1569 *AddCh*, 1708 Sheaf, 1724 NotCestr, and 1831 Bry.

(a) Ayn(h)o 1724 (perhaps 'fenced-in hill', from hægen and hōh); The Bache (*v.* bæce[1]); Back Lane 1831; Bandock Mdw; Bean Fd (cf. *the long bean* 1700, *v.* bēan, feld); Black Cross (i.e. Black Cross Field, *v.* cros); Black Earth, Heath & Lake (*v.* blæc, eorðe, hǣð, lacu); Brimstone Fd (*v.* brynstān); Further Bullery (cf. Near Bullery 119 *supra*. Perhaps 'place where the bull is kept', from bula with ModE *-ery* (NED)); Carthouse Fd; Causeway Mdw (*v.* caucie); Chain Fd; Church Hatch Croft (*v.* cirice, hæcc); Coalyard mdw (*v.* col[1], geard); Cockshutt Croft (*v.* cocc-scyte); Cote Croft (*v.* cot); Crabtree Fd; Crooked Fd; Dale Fd (*v.* dæl[1]); Ferny Bank; Finger Post Fd;

Flatt Fd (v. flat); Footway Fd; Glade Fd (v. glæd[3]); Goose Fd; Gorsty Fd (v. gorstig); Hatch Fd (v. hæc(c)); Hattock Fd (v. hattock); Head Croft; Hob Fd (v. hobb(e) 'a tussock'); Hook Fd (v. hōc); Hulse Fd (*Hulsefeld* 1569, probably named after the *Hulse* family of Norbury 109 *supra*); Intake (v. inntak); Kiln Fd; Kellerns 1708 (probably from a surname); Little- & Ox Leasow (v. oxa, lǣs); Lidgate (v. hlid-geat); Long Shoot (v. scēat); Marbury Fd (cf. Marbury 106 *supra*); Marl Fd; Meadow Bache ('valley-stream at a meadow', v. mǣd, bæce[1]); Morras Acre, Morrars Mdw; Mosley's Head & Mdw (cf. Moseley 115 *supra*, v. hēafod, mǣd); Moss (Hey & Mdw) (cf. *the Mosses* 1724, v. mos, (ge)hæg, mǣd); Nib Fd (v. nib); Old House (site of old house); Outlett (v. outlet); Oven Croft (v. ofen); Park, Park Fd (*a parke* 1536, *Wrenbury Park(e)* 1558, 1568, v. park); Pease Croft (v. pise); Penny Patch ('a pennyworth of ground', v. peni(n)g, pacche); Pickles: Pingot (v. pingot); Platt Bridge Mdw, Platt Fd (v. plat[1]); Rhame; Big- & Little Ridding (v. ryding); Rose Fd (cf. Roseground 116 *supra*); Rough Moss (v. rūh, mos); Round Croft (v. rond); Rush Fd (v. risc); Rye Bank (v. ryge, banke); (Banky- & Near-) Scratley (cf. Scratley Fd 100 *supra*, Little Scratley 119 *supra*, probably 'devil's wood or clearing', v. skratti, lēah); Shawberries ('wood hills', v. sc(e)aga, beorg); Slang (v. slang); Swine House Fd (v. swīn[1], hūs); Turnbridge Mdw (named from a swing-bridge); Weesage.

(b) *Allekkefeld* 1550, *Allockefeild* 1569 (apparently from a pers.n. like *Alec*, a short form for *Alexander*, cf. the ME diminutive *Alekoc, Alecok* (ModE *Alcock*), v. feld); *Blackehey croft* 1569 ('dark enclosure', v. blæc, (ge)hæg); *lez Browne knolle* 1569 (v. brūn[1], cnoll); *Cedars Croft* 1569; *lez Oxe Hey* 1569 (v. oxa, (ge)hæg); *Shalfehurst* 1569 ('wood on a hill', v. scelf 'a shelf, a shelving terrain', hyrst); *Thomas feld* 1569 ('Thomas's field', from the ME pers.n. *Thomas* and feld).

xiii. Acton and Wrenbury

The township of Sound was partly in Acton parish proper, 126 *infra*, and partly in the Wrenbury chapelry, 113 *supra*.

SOUND (110–6148) [saund]

    Sond c.1208 (17) Sheaf (p), *Sonde* c.1220 *Chol*, 1274 Ipm *et freq* with variant spelling *Sond* to 1584 *Chol*

    Soonde 1377 *Eyre*, 1420 Rich, 1514, 1658 *Chol*, (*-in Fowleshurst*) 1408 Rich, *Soond* 1514 *Chol*, 1690 Sheaf

    Sonede 1392 ChRR, 1394 Rich (p)

    Sound 1403 ChRR, 1567 *Chol et freq* with variant spellings *Sounde, Soound*; (*Hall & Heath*) 1831 Bry, (*Lane*) 1841 *TA*

'Sand, the sandy place', v. sand, cf. Sandford Bridge *infra*. Sound demonstrates a typical NWMidl over-rounding (OE *sand* > *sond* >

sōnd > ME *sǫnd* > *sūnd* (spelled *sound*)) seen also in OE *land* > ME *lond* > *lound*, etc. Cf. Sunes *infra*.

FULLHURST HALL (110–622501) [ˈfuləːst]

> *Fougleshurst* H3 *AddCh* (p) *et freq* with variant spellings *Fough(e)l-*, *Foghel-*, *Fo(u)g(e)l-*, *Fuhgel-*, *Fuhegl-*, *Fugl-*, *Foghtl-*, *-es-*, *-is-*, *-us-*, *-hurst(e)*, *-erst*, *-hirst* to 1355 *AddCh*
>
> *Foulushurst* H3 *AddCh* (p) *et freq* with variant spellings *Fou(e)l-*, *Fow(e)l-*, *Fouwel-*, *Foull-*, *-(e)s-*, *-is-*, *-ys-*, *-us-*, *-hurst(e)*, *-hursth*, *-hurstes*, *-hyrst* to 1521 AD, *Foulesthurst* 1276 Ipm, *Fouleshurst in Soonde* 1464 Orm², *Fouleshurst Hall* 15 Rich, *Fowlesshurst* 1518 AD (p)
>
> *Fulishirst* 1307 *Eyre* (p), *-es-*, 1309 Pat, *-hurst* 1514 *ChEx* (p), *Fulshurst* 1311 MidCh (p), *-heurste* 1507 AD (p), *Folishurst* c.1322–8 *AddCh* (p), *Foles-* 1416 ChRR, *Fulles-* 1478 AD (p), *-ys-* 1558 Pat, *-is-* 1558–79 ChancP, (*-Hall*) 1831 Bry, *Fulse-* 1534 Cre (p), *Fulleschhurst* 1544 ib (p)
>
> *Fawelushurst* 1314–19 *BW* (p)
>
> *Fitchleshurst* 1323 Tab (p)
>
> *Foulerhurst* 1364 AD (p), *Fowler-* 1558–79 ChancP (p), *Fuller-* 1572 Cre (p)
>
> *Folehirst* 1309 Pat (p), *Foulehurst* 1402 ib (p), *Foulhurst* 1416 ChRR, *-herst* 1474 Pat (p)
>
> *Folneshurst* 1488, 1492 *Chol*
>
> *Foulecist* c.1536 Leland
>
> *Fulles otherwise callid Fulhers* 1545 Sheaf (p)

'Wooded hill frequented by fowl', *v.* **fugol**, **hyrst**, cf. Fulshaw 1 227 *supra*. For the collective sg. first el., cf. Bridgemere 53 *supra*.

APPLETREE FIELDS, 1841 *TA*.   BRIDGE FM, 1841 *ib*, named from a nearby railway bridge.   CORNER FM, 1841 *ib*.   FIELD'S FM, 1841 *ib*, *v.* feld.   HILL FM, *Hill House* 1831 Bry.   NEWTOWN. SANDFORD BRIDGE, *v.* 102 *supra*, cf. Sound *supra*.   SOUND HALL, 1831 Bry.   SOUND HEATH, 1831 ib, *bruer' de Sond* 1300 Sheaf, also known as *Sound Green* 1860 White, *le grene in Sonde* c.1230 *Chol*, *v.* grēne².   SOUND LANE, 1841 *TA*.   SOUND OAK, 1831 Bry, an oak tree.   WHITEGATE HO.

FIELD-NAMES

The undated forms are 1841 *TA* 361. Of the others, 1300 is Sheaf, 1537[2] *Sotheby*, 1831 Bry, and the rest *Chol*.

(a) Backe Bank (*v.* bæce[1]); Baddington Fd (cf. *Battington rowe* 1300 and Baddington 131 *infra*, *v.* rāw); Barn Lane Fd; Blake Fd (*v.* blæc); The Brockhouse (probably 'badger-holes', *v.* brocc-hol); Broomy Knowl (cf. *the Broome feild* 1656, *Big- & Little Brown Field* 1795, *v.* brōm, brōmig, cnoll, feld); Buckney Mdw; Chester Crofts 1729 (cf. *Chesters intacks* 1656 and Chesters Mdw 99 *supra*, *v.* inntak); Clover Croft 1795; Cow Heys (*v.* (ge)hæg); Five Daymath (1795, *v.* day-math); Ferney Flatt; Fossett; Glade Bank (*v.* glæd[3]); Hare Croft (*v.* hara); Hook Fd (*v.* hōc); Hop Yard (1831, *v.* hoppe); Intake (*v.* inntak); Kilmoreys Land (from the earls of Kilmorey, landowners); Lighton Fd (cf. Leighton 28 *supra*); Long Heys (*v.* (ge)hæg); Long Shoot (*v.* scēat); Malla Riddings c.1695 (*a certeyn Bache called Malaryddyng* 1537[2], *-riddyng* 1534, 1537, *-ridding* 1547, *Mallarriddinge* 1565, *a bache or wood called Malariddinge* 1612, *Mala Riddinge*, *-Rydding* 1634, 'dappled clearing', *v.* mǣle, ryding, cf. bæce[1]); Milking Bank (*v.* milking); Mill Mdw; Mistress's Fd (lit. *Mrs's*); The Moss; Nickle Heys; Outlett (*Far- & Near Outlet* 1795, *v.* outlet); Pavement Fd (*v.* pavement); Pease Fd 1795; Pinfold Fd (*v.* pynd-fald); Pingott (*v.* pingot); Rubbing Stake Fd (a field with a post or stake upon which cattle rub themselves); Rushye Mdw 1795 (*v.* riscig); Rye Croft; Sandhole Fd; Spinning Ridding (*v.* ryding); Sunes, Far Sunes, Sunes Mdw 1795 ('the sands', *v.* sand, cf. Sound *supra*); Swallows Steads (*v.* stede. The first el. may be a surname); Well Mdw; Whittening Fd (probably a field where cloth was bleached).

(b) *Alvastbury* 1300 (*v.* burh 'a fortified place'. The first el. is probably a pers.n. Dr von Feilitzen suggests ODan *Alfast* (OSwed *Alvast*; not recorded in WScand), and Professor Löfvenberg suggests OE *Ælfwald* as in Alvaston 28 *supra*); *Eglavescroft* c.1230, *Edelescroft* 1300 ('Ecglāf's croft', from the OE pers.n. *Ecglāf* and croft. The same pers.n., with the same development, appears in the adjacent Edleston 140 *infra*); *the Highe lane* 1575 (*v.* hēah, lane); *Holegrave* 1300 ('wood in a hollow', *v.* hol[1], grǣfe); *Irradelond* 1300 (a selion, *v.* land); *le Midelyort* 1300 (*v.* middel, geard); *Parkers Croft(e)* 1575; *Rylesgrene* 1542 (from grēne[2] and the surname *Ryle*); *Sadesvalle furlong* c.1230 (*v.* wælla 'a well, a spring', furlang. The first el. could be a pers. by-name from ME *sad* 'serious, grave', cf. Reaney s.n. *Sadd*; but Professor Löfvenberg suggests scēad 'a boundary', the p.n. being 'spring or stream on a boundary', *v.* -es[2]); *the Six-Crosse-Butts* 1656 ('the six headlands which lie athwart', *v.* cros, butte); *le Smalebroke* c.1298 ('narrow stream', *v.* smæl, brōc, Edleston Brook 1 22); *Sondehalc* c.1230 (from halc 'a corner of land', and Sound *supra* or sand 'sand'); *Westo Wylond* 1300 ('(selion at) west hillock', from west and hygel, with land).

xiv. Baddiley

The ecclesiastical parish of Baddiley is not mentioned in 1291 Tax. Orm[2] III 458 says it may have been originally a chapelry of either Wybunbury or Acton parishes. It is more likely to have been in Acton.

BADDILEY (109–6050) ['badili, bad]i]

Bedelei 1086 DB

Badileg' e13 (1244) Sheaf, *-le* 1287 Court, *Badyleye* 1291 Tax, *Baddil'* 1241 MRA, *Baddileg'* 1299 Plea (p) *et freq* with variant spellings *Bad(d)i-*, *Bad(d)y-*, *-legh*, *-ley(e)*, *-leigh*

Badeleg' 1298 Plea, *-legh* 1309 ChRR, and occasionally with variant spellings *-ligh*, *-le(e)*, *-ley* to 1576 ChRR, *Badelly* 1694 ChetOS VIII, *Baddeley* 1401 BM

Badlegh 1338 Plea, *-leigh* 1360 Orm[2], *-le(y)* c.1536 Sheaf, Leland

Badingley 14 (17) (1724) NotCestr

Budeley 1536 ChRR

Baduley 1574 Orm[2]

From lēah 'a wood, a clearing', and an OE pers.n. *Bæd(d)a* or *Bead(d)a*. The *-i-*, *-y-* spellings represent a reduced form of -ing-[4], fully represented in only one late copy in the spelling *Badingley*. Cf. Faddiley, Baddington 142, 131 *infra*.

BLACKHURST, *Blachurst* 1314 ChRR (p), (*le-*) 1371 *Chol* (p), *Blak-* 1359 BPR (p), *Black-* 1385 Comb (p), 1621 (1656) Orm[2], *Black(e)-hurste* 1576 ChRR, 1590 Sheaf, 'dark wooded hill', *v.* blæc, hyrst.

BADDILEY GORSE, *Baddiley New Covert* 1842 OS.   BADDILEY HALL, 1831 Bry.   BADDILEY HULSE, 1831 Bry, cf. *Baddiley Hulse Fox Cover* 1842 OS, perhaps 'the hills', from ME *hulles*, pl. of hyll, but cf. William *del Hules* of *Smethetonwode* (Smeatonwood 97 *supra*) 1359 ChRR, *v.* hygel 'a hillock', cf. also Hulse 2 185   BADDILEY LANE, 1831 Bry.   BADDILEY MERE, 1831 ib, *Badlemere* c.1536 Leland, a lake, *v.* mere[1], cf. Mere Ho *infra*.   BETHILLS BRIDGE, cf. *Far- & Near Bithells, Bithells Meadow* 1832 *TA*, probably from the surname *Bithel* and brycg.   CORNER FM.   CRABMILL FM, 1831 Bry, cf. *Crab Mill Bridge* 1831 Bry on the boundary with Ravensmoor 134 *infra*, *v.* crab-mill.   DAIRYHOUSE FM, *Dairy House* 1831 ib.   GREENFIELD BRIDGE, cf. *Higher-, Long- & Lower Green Field* 1832 *TA*, *v.* grēne[1], feld.   HALL'S LANE BRIDGE, *Hall Lane* 1832 ib, *v.* hall, lane.   HELL HOLE, 1842 OS, *v.* hell, hol[1].

HIGHFIELD FM, *The Fields* 1831 Bry, *v.* hēah, feld. HOLE HOUSE (lost), 1831 ib, *v.* hol². MERE HO, 1831 ib, *Meer House* 1860 White, named from Baddiley Mere *supra, v.* mere¹. SPRINGE LANE (HALL) [sprindʒ, spriŋ], *Spryng* 1537, 1540 Earw, *the Sprinke* 1556 *Chol, Springe-lane* 1781 Sheaf, *Springs Hall, Springe Hall Lane* 1831 Bry, *Springe-Lane-Hall* 1839 *TAMap*, from spring 'a young wood' with hall, lane. YEWTREE HO.

FIELD-NAMES

The undated forms are 1832 *TA* 32. Of the others e13 is (1244) Sheaf, 1394 Orm², 1536 is c.1536 Leland, 1831 Bry, 1842 OS, 1860 White.

(*a*) Acres Fd; Bean Yard (*v.* bēan, geard); Blake Fd (*v.* blæc); Box Fd (*v.* box); Brindley Orchard (cf. Brindley 133 *infra, v.* orceard); Bromley Fd (*v.* brōm, lēah); Butty Fd (*v.* butty); Catherine Ridding (*v.* ryding); Coat Fd (*v.* cot); Colt Ridding (*v.* colt, ryding); Cooks Pit (*v.* cockpit, cf. Cookspit 143 *infra*); Great Court (*v.* court); Coxet Fd (*v.* cocc-scyte); Glade Fd (*v.* glæd³); Grange Fd (*v.* grange. Combermere Abbey had land in Baddiley); Green Lane 1831; Handford Bache (Randle Brereton of *Handford* held Blackhurst *supra* in 1576 ChRR, *v.* bæce¹); Hodge Hey (*v.* hocg, (ge)hæg, cf. *Hodg Croft* 1 158); Hoo Fd (*v.* hōh); Intake (*v.* inntak); Larden Green Fd (cf. Larden Green 143 *infra*); Ley Fd (ModE *ley* 'a pasture', cf. lēah); Long Butts (*v.* butte); Long Lane 1860; Long Shoot (*v.* scēat); Loving Fd; Marl (Pit) Fd (*v.* marle-pytt); Milking Bank (*v.* milking); Mitch; New Heys (*v.* nīwe, (ge)hæg); Oat Fd; Ox Croft & Grass (*v.* gærs); Far- Middle- & Near Park (cf. *a parke* 1536, *v.* park); Pinfold Croft (*v.* pynd-fald); Pool Field Bank & Nook; Poolstead (*v.* pōl-stede); Pulley; Long Rake (*v.* rake); Ravensmoor Fd & Intake (*v.* inntak, Ravensmoor 134 *infra*); Ridding (*v.* ryding); Rusty Croft; Singe Croft; Sparsh (*v.* spearca); Sparth (*v.* sparð); Sprink (cf. Springe Lane *supra, v.* spring); Sprout Ridding (*v.* sprota, ryding; but Professor Löfvenberg notes that this name is more correctly derived from ME *sproute* (with ME *ū*), ModE *sprout* 'a sprout, a shoot, a young growth' (a.1300 NED), *v.* sproute); Stock Piece; Syche Mdw (*v.* sīc); Thompsons Loon (*v.* land); Treacle Mdw; Vine Yard; Wackers; Way Fd (*v.* weg); Well Fd (Bank & Bottom); Wet Rean (*v.* wēt, rein); White Fd; Wickstead's Gorse 1831 (from gorst and the surname from Wicksted 112 *supra*).

(*b*) *Dytteleymore* 1394 (probably for *Dycce-* and meaning '(waste-land at) the ditch clearing', from dīc, lēah and mōr¹); (*Little*) *Mersleg*' e13 (either 'clearing at a marsh' or 'at a mere', from mere¹ or mersc, and lēah); *Middle Mersh* e13 (*v.* middel, mersc); *Russiruding* e13 ('rushy clearing', *v.* riscig, ryding).

xv. Acton

The ecclesiastical parish of Acton contained the parochial chapelries of Church Minshull 154 *infra*, Nantwich and Wrenbury 28, 113 *supra*, parts of the townships of Newhall and Sound 101, 121 *supra*, and the following townships, 1. Acton (including a detached portion of Dodcott cum Wilkesley 92 *supra*), 2. Aston iuxta Mondrum, 3. Austerson, 4. Baddington, 5. Brindley, 6. Burland, 7. Cholmondeston, 8. Coole Pilate (including a detached part of Audlem parish 82 *supra*). 9. Edleston, 10. Faddiley, 11. Henhull, 12. Hurleston, 13. Poole, 14. Stoke, 15. Worleston (now a c.p. including part of Alvaston 28 *supra*). Baddiley parish 124 *supra* may have been part of Acton parish originally.

1. ACTON (110–630530) ['aktən, aktn̥]

> *Acatone* 1086 DB, *Aketon* 1287 Court, 1400 Pat, *Hakedon* c.1298 Chol (p)
> *Actune* 1086 DB, *-tun* (*-iuxta Wichum Malbanum*) c.1284 CASNS II, 113 *AddCh*, *-ton* c.1130 (1479) *Cott.* Faust. B. VIII, H3 (1331), 1253 Ch *et freq* with variant spellings *-tona*, *Hac-*; (*-iuxta*) *Wycum Malbanum*) 1295 ChancW, (*-Edlaston*) 1353 BPR, (*-Hurdeleston*) 1390 ChRR, (*-Mondrem*) 1421 Orm² III 420
> *Aghton* 1394 Sheaf, 17 (1724) NotCestr, (*Acton alias*) *Aighton* 1612 Sheaf, *Aughton* 1719 ib
> *Church Acton* 1671 *AddCh*

'Oak farm', *v.* āc (gen.pl. āca), tūn. The prefix *Church-* denotes the parish church, *v.* cirice, distinguishing the main hamlet from *Parva Acton* 1531 Chol, *Little Acton* 1671 AddCh, 1677, 1698 Chol, 1831 Bry, (*v.* lȳtel), a detached part of Dodcott cum Wilkesley 92 *supra*, which probably represents the carucate of land in the vill of Acton granted to Combermere abbey c.1130 (*Cott.* Faust. B. VIII 124–6). For *-Mondrem* cf. Aston iuxta Mondrum 128 *infra*. The other related places are Nantwich 30 *supra*, Edleston and Hurleston 140, 146 *infra*.

DORFOLD HALL (110–635524) ['dɔːrfəld] older local ['dɑːr-]

> *parcum de Derfald* H3 (1615) ChRR, Orm², *-fold* 1346 (1615) ChRR *et freq* with variant spellings *Dere-* from 1362 Plea, *-folde*, *-fould* to 1673 Sheaf, (*le-*) 1349 Eyre, *-forld* 1352 ChRR, 1456 Rich, *-feld* 1352 BPR
> *Dorfold* 1453 Cl, 1464 ChRR, 1706 Sheaf *et freq*, *-fould* 1633 Sheaf

Darford 1621 (1656) Orm², 1724 NotCestr
Darfould 1625 ChRR, *-fold House* 1643 Orm², *Darfold* 1666 Sheaf,
1724 NotCestr
'Deer-park', *v.* dēor-fald.

Bull's Wood, *Bulls Wood* 1841 *TA.*   Burford Ho (lost), 1831
Bry, *v.* 147 *infra.*   Crossroads Cottage.   Cuckoo Lane,
perhaps 'lane where the cuckoo haunts', *v.* cuccu, lane.   Dig
Lane (Fm), *v.* dīc, lane.   Dorfold Cottage & Dairy Ho,
Dorfold Dairy House 1831 Bry, 1842 OS, *Acton Cottage* 1842 OS,
cf. Dorfold *supra.*   Drake Lane, probably an aphetic form from
The Rake Lane with a reduced def.art., *v.* rake 'a narrow path, a lane'.
Haybays, *The Hay Bays Yard* 1841 *TA*, *v.* hēg, bay². Professor
Löfvenberg draws attention to ModEdial. *hay-bay* 'a place on the
ground-floor for keeping hay' (WO; EDD) and cites *bay* sb³ NED.
Madam's Fm, *le Brokehous* 1408 ChRR, *Brookhouse* 1719 Sheaf,
Brook House 1831 Bry, 1842 OS, 'house near a brook', *v.* brōc, hūs,
named from Ravensmoor Brook 134 *infra.*   Marsh Lane, 1831
Bry, *v.* mersc, cf. 39 *supra*, Ravensmoor Bridge *infra.*   Monk's
Lane, *venella quæ ducit versus molendina de Wich Malbank* 1359 Rich,
v. lane, probably named after the monks of Combermere Abbey, cf.
Little Acton supra, and *Monkyslone* (Nantwich) 35 *supra.*   Ravens-
moor Bridge, 1842 OS, *Marsh Bridge* 1831 Bry, *v.* mersc, cf. Marsh
Lane *supra*, Ravensmoor 134 *infra.*

FIELD-NAMES

The undated forms are 1841 *TA* 1. Of the others, H3, c.1302 *AddCh*, 1303–5
(1615) ChRR, 1349, 1438–9 Orm², 15 Rich, 1539 Plea, 1548 Pat, 1583
Sotheby, 1781 Sheaf.

(a) Brown Hill (*Brownehill* 1583, *v.* brūn¹, hyll); Butt Fd (*v.* butte);
Carlow Croft; Cathering Croft; Causeway Fd (*v.* caucie); Coney Greave
(*v.* coningre); the Cross-bank 1781 (*v.* cros 'a cross'); Deadman's Fd (the
burial place of the fifty men killed in a Civil-War skirmish, January 1644,
Sheaf³ 17 (4138)); Flagg Fd (*v.* flagge); Gorsty Fd (*the Gorstie felde* 1583,
v. gorstig); How Foot ('the foot of the hill', *v.* hōh, fōt); Kendale Croft; Lady
Fd (*v.* hlæfdige); Lawrence Fd; Long Shoot (*v.* scēat); Marl Fd; Park Fd
(cf. *le Parkefyldes* 1438–9, *v.* park, feld); Red Fd (*v.* rēad); Riddings Mdw
(*v.* ryding); Rushy Mdw (*v.* riscig); School Fd (probably part of the endowment of a school); (The) Shaws, Lower & Little Shaw (cf. *the Wetschawe*
1349, *v.* wēt, sceaga); Slang (*v.* slang); Studd Croft (*v.* stōd); Three Nooks;
Wild(e) Heath (*v.* wilde, hæð).

(b) *Acton pament* 15 (*v.* pavement); *le Chappell Crofte* 1548 (cf. 'a chantry in John de Wetenhale's chapel which was within the close of the manor of Acton' 1303–5, *v.* chapel); *Froggemulne* c.1302, *Frogghe Mulne* 1303–5 ('mill at a place infested with frogs', *v.* frogga, myln, cf. Welsh Row (Nantwich) 34 *supra*); *Gilloms Crofte* 1583; *le Marish lees* 1303–5 ('the marsh meadow', *v.* mersc, lǣs); *the newe Leisowe* 1583 ('the new meadow', *v.* nīwe, lǣs, cf. prec.); *Neuton* H3 ('new farm', *v.* nīwe, tūn, cf. *Newbold* 140 *infra*); *the Peas Flatte* 1583 (*v.* pise, flat); *Ravenescrofts* 1539 ('Raven's crofts', from the pers.n. OE *Hræfn*, ON *Hrafn* and croft, cf. Ravensmoor 134 *infra*, Ravens Croft 131 *infra*, *Ravenes croftes* 148 *infra*).

2. ASTON IUXTA MONDRUM (110–6557) [astn̥, ˈmɔndrəm]

Estone 1086 DB

Aston 13 AddCh 1276 Ipm *et freq* with variant spellings *-tona, -tun*; (*-iuxta Cholmundeston*) 1293 (1631) *Chol*, (*-Worleston*) 1296 Plea, (*-Sonde*) 1317 Orm², (*-Hurdeleston*) 1342 (1438) ChRR, (*-leghton in Mundrem*) 1347 ChFor, (*-Minshull*) 1621 ChRR

Aston subtus Mondrem 1290 *Chol*, *-sub-* 1323 *ib*, *-subter-* 1558 Orm², *-iuxte-* 1326 *Chol*, *-iuxta-* 1347 BPR *et freq*, *-ne(a)re-* 1586, 1633 *Chol*, *-in-* 1341 AddCh *et freq* with variant form *-en-* to 1597 Orm², *-in or neere-* 1630 *Chol*, all with variant spellings as for *Mondrem* 1 10 *supra*; *Aston et Mondrem* 1353 ChFor, *Aston Mondrem* 1474 (1630), 1694 *Chol*, *-Mondram* 1666 Orm²

Ashton 1347 ChFor

'The eastern farm', *v.* ēast, tūn. It adjoins Cholmondeston, Worleston, Church Minshull 136, 151, 154 *infra*, Leighton and Sound 28, 121 *supra*. Aston was within the old forest of *Mondrem* 1 10, cf. Wood *infra*. In 1356 AddCh 50860, a part of Aston was called *Mundrum*, cf. Mondrum 138 *infra*.

ASTON GORSE, 1831 Bry, *v.* gorst.   ASTON GREEN, 1694 *Chol*, *-Grene* 1497 *Chol*, *-Greene* 1594 *ib*, *v.* grēne². ASTON HALL, 1730 *ib*, *the mannor howse* 1630 *ib*, *v.* maner.   ASTON NEW FM. BRAYNE HALL, *Braynes Hall* 1831 Bry, 1842 OS, *a seat of the Braynes* 1621 (1656) Orm², named from the *Brayne* family, *de Bresne* 1238 P (p), *Breyn'* 1289 Court (p), *Brayn* 1417 ChRR (p), *v.* hall. BRICKYARD BRIDGE, cf. *Brick Kiln Field* 1842 TA, *v.* bryke-kyl, brick-yard.   GATE & HATCH (p.h.), *-Farm* 1831 Bry, *v.* geat, hæc(c).   HIGHFIELD FM.   LOWER HALL.   ROSE FM.

FIELD-NAMES

The undated forms are 1842 *TA* 24. Of the others, 13, 1275–82, l13, c.1300[2], 1307–27, 14, 1322[1], 1337[2], 1356, 1359, 1406, 1547 are *AddCh*, 1347 *ChFor*, 1831 Bry, and the rest *Chol.*

(*a*) Ash Fd; Barley Croft (*the barly croft* 1639); Barn Croft, Fd & Mdw (cf. *le bernelond* 1325, 'selion at a barn', *v.* bere-ærn, land); Further & Near Bodge Croft (*the Boose Crofts* 1683, *v.* bōs); Breach, Breech Mdw (*v.* brēc); Clock Croft (*the-* 1639); Common Fd & Piece; Cow Fd; Further, Little & Near Eddish, Eddish Fd (cf. *the oat Edishes* 1639 and *Ruyeedyhc, Ruyeedihc, Ruyedissch* 1322[1], *Ruycedyht* 1322[2], *v.* ryge, āte, edisc); Four Acres, Four Butts (*v.* fēower, æcer, butte); Goldhurst (*v.* golde, hyrst, cf. *le Hurst infra*); Higher-, Little- etc., Hall Fd (*the two Hall Feilds* 1683, *the Hall Feild* 1639, 1661, *v.* hall); Holms Croft; Hough Loom (*v.* hōh, loom); Husgate; Intake (*v.* inntak); Lawrence Mdw (*the three Lawraunce meadowes* 1639, 'Lawrence's meadows', from the ME pers.n. *Lawrence* and mǣd); Ley Hey (*Aston(e)legh'* 1335, 1337[1], *Leghheie* 14, *Le Legheheye* 1359, *le Lee Hey* (*lane*) 1594, *the Leehayes* 1639, *Leigh Hayes* 1694, 'enclosure(s) at a clearing', *v.* lēah, (ge)hæg); Mare Fd (*the mere feild* 1639, *the Meir(e) Feild* 1661, 1683, 'mere field' or 'boundary field', *v.* mere[2] or (ge)mǣre); Mill Fd (*the Miln Feild & Meadow* 1683, cf. *molendina de Astona* 1275–82, *via que ducit versus molendinum* 1295, *molendina super aquam de Weuere* c.1300[1], *le mulnewey* 1307–27, *le mulne* 1325, *v.* myln, weg, cf. R. Weaver 1 38); Moor Mdw (*v.* mōr[1]); Muck Fd (*v.* muk); Odd Croft (*v.* odde); Old Fd ((*le*) *Oldefeld* 1322[1,2], *v.* ald, feld); Patch (*v.* pacche); Pinfold Croft (*v.* pynd-fald); Ran; Rushy Mdw (*the russhie meadow* 1639, *the Russhy meadow* 1661, *the Rushey meddow* 1683, *v.* riscig); Small Thorns (*le Smalethornfeld* 14, *the Smallthornes* 1639, 1661, 1683, 'slender thorn-tree(s)', *v.* smæl, þorn, feld, cf. 138 *infra*); Spoon Stack ('a stack of shingles', *v.* spōn, stakkr); Staple(y) Fd (*the two Stapeley feildes* 1639, *the Little Stapley Feild* 1661, *the Stavly Feild* 1683, *v.* stapol, lēah, cf. Stapeley 71 *supra*); Stone Pasture; Stoney Hill (*v.* stānig); Thistle Hey; Tom Fd (*the Tom feild* 1639, 'town's field', *v.* toun); Triggers Lane 1831; Vawdridge (*the three Vawdrey Croftes* 1639, from the Cheshire surname *Vawdrey*); White Acres, Whittakers (*le quyteacres* 1322[1,2], 'white plough-lands', *v.* hwīt, æcer); Windmill Croft; Withens Fd (*Withynfeld* 14, *v.* wiðegn); Big, Little & Near Wd (cf. *boscus de Aston'* 1347, part of *Mondrem* forest 1 10 *supra*, cf. Aston *supra*, *v.* wudu).

(*b*) *Aldecrofte* 1322[1,2] ('the old croft', *v.* ald, croft); *le blakelond* 1322[1] ('black selion', *v.* blæc, land); *le Brok'* 1344 (*v.* brōc); *Cokshuteheie* 14 (cf. *quadam volatus in bosco de Aston* 13, 'enclosure at a cock-shoot', *v.* coccscyte, (ge)hæg); *le Coppedegreue* 1307–27 ('the pollarded wood', *v.* (ge)-coppod, grǣfe); *le Elrenegreuelond* 1307–27 ('(selion at) the alder-grove', *v.* elren, grǣfe, with land); *le Flecchereslond* 1344 ('the fletcher's selion', *v.* fleccher, land); *the Hillockie feild* 1639 (*v.* hylloc, -ig[3]. The adj. *hillocky* is first recorded 1727 in NED); *le Hulleshende* 1295 ('the end of the hill', *v.* hyll, ende[1]); *the Hulse Croft(s)* 1639, 1661 (perhaps from prec., or from

9

ME *hulles*, nom.pl. of hyll); *le Hurst* c.1300[1,2], 1336, 14, *Astonehurst* 1337[1] ('wood-hill', v. hyrst, cf. Goldhurst *supra*); *the Ithells Crofts* 1639 ('Ithell's crofts', from the Welsh pers.n. *Ithel* and croft); *Kel(e)rondesweye* 1297, *Kele-*, *Kilerondiswei* l13, *le Kelerondeswey* c.1300[1,2] (from weg 'a way, a road', with an obscure p.n. or pers.n.; *Kel-*, *Kilerond* could be a ME form for an aphetic *Mac-* patronymic from an OIr pers.n. such as *Gillurān* (CGH I 661) cf. the ModIr surname *Gilloran*, *Killoran* (Woulfe 376)); *le Kusnelond* 1307–27 (first el. obscure, v. land); *Long(e)hope iuxta villa de Stoke* 1307–27 ('long marsh-enclosure', v. lang, hop[1], cf. Stoke 151 *infra*); *Mabacres* 1547 (from *Mab*, a shortened form of *Mabel*, and æcer); *le Merssefeld* 14 (v. mersc, feld); *Mundrum* 1356 (v. Aston *supra*); *le Redebache* c.1300[1,2] ('reedy valley-stream', v. hrēod, bæce[1]); *le Ringisbache* l13, (*molendinum de-*), (*le-*), *Ring-*, *Ryngey(es)bache* 1295, c.1300[1,2], *le Ryggesbache* 1297 ('valley-stream at a meadow with a ring-fence', v. hring, ēg, bæce[1], cf. foll.); *The Ring Yards* 1683 ('enclosures at a ring', v. hring, geard, cf. prec.); *le Rouwebache* 1295, *le Rowebache* c.1300[1,2] ('the rough valley', v. rūh, bæce[1]); *le Soulondes* 1322[1] ('selions at a bog', v. sogh, land); *Sparrowes lane* 1594 (probably lane with the surname *Sparrow*); *Tibotesmulne* 14 (from myln with the ME pers.n. *Tibot* from *Tibald*, *Theobald*); *Tomasfeld* 1406 ('Thomas's field', from the ME pers.n. *Thomas* and feld); *Twen(e)brokes* 1337[1,2] ('between the brooks', v. betwēonan, brōc); *le Wallefeld* 1322[1,2] ('well or spring field', v. wælla, feld).

3. AUSTERSON (FM & (OLD) HALL) (110–6648) [ˈɔstər-, ˈɔːstərsən]

> *Afstaneston* l12 *AddCh* (p)
>
> *Allst'* l12 Rich, *Allston'* l12 (1786) ib, *Alstonestona* p.1266 (14) Chest, *Alstonoston* 1282 Court (p)
>
> *Alstaneston'* 1202–28 *AddCh* (p) *et freq* with variant spellings *-is-*, *-tona*, *-tone* to 1428 *Orm*[2], *Alstanston* 1301 ChancW (p), 1308 Ipm *et freq* to 1468 *Dav*, (*Over-*, *Nethir-*) 1454 ChRR, 1486 Orm[2]
>
> *Alstanton* 1335 *AddCh*, 1341 ChRR, 1393 Plea, (*Over-*, *Nether-*) 1487 Orm[2], *All-* 1347 ib
>
> *Allstaston* 1520 Comb
>
> *Austaston* c.1536 Leland, *Austerston* 1621 (1656) Orm[2], *Austerson* 1720 *Chol*, (*-Hall*) 1831 Bry
>
> *Asterson* 1550 *MinAcct*, *Asterton* c.1662 *Surv*
>
> *Ouesterton* 1673 Sheaf
>
> *Ostrason* 1699 *Chol*

'Ælfstān's farm', from the OE pers.n. *Ælfstān* and tūn, with uferra, neoðera, hall. This place and Edleston 140 *infra* have been identified with *Essetune* 1086 DB 265b, v. Tait 157, Orm[2] III 383, but

there is no identity of name, *Essetune* being 'ash-tree farm', *v.* esc
(æsc), tūn.

ASHTREE FM.   CHURCH HOUSE FM, *Churchhouse Field* 1841 *TA*.

FIELD-NAMES

The undated forms are 1841 *TA* 29.

(*a*) Bache (*v.* bæce[1]); Bakehouse Fd; Barkshaw ('birch copse', *v.* beorc,
sceaga); Bell Rough; Causeway Croft (*v.* caucie); Old Corn Fd; Cow Lane
Croft; Cross Fd (*v.* cros 'a cross'); Great Delight (*v.* 325 *infra*); Douve;
Drumble Bank (dial. *drumble, v.* dumbel); Eleven-, Five-, Four-, Three Day
Math (*v.* day-math); Fender Bank (*v.* fender, banke); Glazeley Fd; Hatchett
Fds; Kiln Fd; Kinsbury Fd; Marl Piece; Noman's Mdw (*v.* nān-mann);
Old Woman's Fd; Ox Grass (*v.* gærs); Pig Stye Croft; Pinfold Fd (*v.* pynd-
fald); Pingot (*v.* pingot); Ravens Croft (cf. *Ravenescrofts* 128 *supra*); Roade
(*v.* rod[1]); Little Rough; Sares Orchard; Shephay (*v.* scēp, (ge)hæg); Swine
Yard (*v.* swin[1], geard); Tinnings (*v.* tȳning); Weaver Bank (named from
R. Weaver 1 38 *supra*); Whole Grass; Wich-house Fd (*v.* wych(e)-hous(e),
cf. Wych House Bank 37 *supra*); Woodlane Fd (*v.* wudu, lane).

4. BADDINGTON (LANE) (110–6449)

Bedit' 1175–84 Facs (No. 3, p. 8; ed. reads *Beditona* and identifies
    with Bebington 325 *infra*)

Badington 1254 Pat (p), c.1536 Leland, *-yng-* 1520 Comb, *Badynton*
    1325 Plea, 1414 AD, ChRR, *Baddington Lane* 1643 Orm[2]

Batyntona (lit. *Cat-*) p.1266 Chest, *Batin-, Batynton* 1283 Ipm,
    1298 *Chol et freq* to 1490 ChRR, *-ing-* 1283, 1292 Ipm, *-yng-*
    1394 ChRR, 1428 *Chol*

'Beada's farm', from the OE pers.n. *Beada* and -ingtūn. Cf.
Baddiley 124 *supra*.

SHREWBRIDGE (HOUSE) (110–648509) ['ʃruːbridʒ]

Ssirardesbregge 1287 Chol, *pons Sscirardi* 1295 *ib*, *Schirardusbrugge*
    1298 *ib*, (mill of) *Shyrardesbrugge* 1348 Plea
(molendinum de) *Scrabruge* 1347 AddCh
Sherardesbrugge 1351 Eyre (p)
Sharebrugge 1355 BPR, *Sherabrugg(e)* 1355 ib, 1358 Eyre (p)
Schyrabreg, Chyrabrugge 1420 Rich, *Shyrabrugge* 1432 ib
Shryabrugge 1428 Rich
Shrewbridge 1557, 1621 Sheaf, 1831 Bry, (*-meadow(e)*) 1695 Chol,
    -brige (*Lane & Meadow*) 1579 Orm[2]

Shroebridge 1579 *AddCh*, *Shrowbridge* (*Meadow*) 1656, 1690 *Chol*, (*croft next*) *Shrowbridge* 1706 *Chol*, *-bridg* 1720 *ib*, (*-meadow*) 1736 *ib*

'Scīrheard's bridge', from the OE pers.n. *Scīrheard* and **brycg**. Cf. Baddington Bridge Fm *infra*, Shrewbridge Hall Fm 39 *supra*.

Baddington Bank 1831 Bry.   Baddington Bridge Fm, *Shrewbridge Farm* 1842 OS, cf. Shrewbridge *supra*.   Broomhall Gorse, *Baddington Fox Cover* 1841 *TA*, *v.* **gorst**, cf. Broomhall 114 *supra*.   French Lane, cf. *French Croft & Field* 1841 *ib*, probably named from the growing of french-wheat here.   Hack Fm, Green & House(s), *Hacke* 1520 Comb, *-Greene* 1594 *AddCh*, *-Green* 1831 Bry, *Hack House* 1842 OS, from **hæc(c)** 'a wicket-gate' as ModEdial. *hack* 'a hurdle, manger' (NED *hack* sb[2], EDD), with **grēne[2]** 'a green', **hūs**.   Stick Covert, *v.* **sticca**.

FIELD-NAMES

The undated forms are 1841 *TA* 33. Of the others, 1330 is Plea, 1650 Sheaf and the rest *Chol*.

(*a*) Arcars Wood 1720 (1695, *Arkars-* 1695); Bache (*v.* **bæce[1]**); Little Backshaw ('back-wood', *v.* **back, sceaga**); Baldthorn (perhaps 'polled thorn', from **polled** and **þorn**, but cf. **balled(e)**); Barn Fd (1729, *Barne-* 1690, *v.* **bere-ærn, feld**); Black Croft; Bridge Mere Mdw (probably called after Bridgemere 53 *supra*); Bye Flatt ('flat piece of ground in the bend of a stream', *v.* **byge[1], flat**); Catsford ('wild-cat's ford', *v.* **catt, ford**); Clover Bank; Coney Gree (*v.* **coningre**); Coppice; Cote Fd (*v.* **cot**); Cow Hay (*v.* (ge)**hæg**); Crab Tree Fd; Ten Days Math (*v.* **day-math**); Drovers Fd; Edleston Fd (*v.* Edleston 140 *infra*); Fair Water Croft & Fd; Frears Wood 1697; German Fd; Goose Croft; Green End (*v.* **grēne[1], ende[1]**); Hill Fd (1690); Hinsbury Fd; Horse Pasture Fd & Mdw; House Fd; Intake (*v.* **inntak**); Kiln Field; Ley Fd (*v.* **lǣge**); Lime Kiln (*v.* **limkilne**); Lodge Bank; Lodmore Hay (*v.* (ge)**hæg**, cf. Lodmore 97 *supra*); Long Fd (*the* 1650); Marl Fd; Near Mosley (*v.* **mos, lēah**); Newport Mdw; Old Acre; Orchard Bank; Ox Pasture; Park (Fd); Pear Tree Croft & Fd; Pinfold Fd (*v.* **pynd-fald**); Pingot (*v.* **pingot**); Plumpton Park ('plum-tree orchard', *v.* **plūme, tūn, park**); Pool Mdw; Long Range (*v.* **range**); Rough Fd; Long- & Round Row (*v.* **rāw**); Rush(y) Ridding (*v.* **risc, riscig, ryding**); Rye Bank; Salt Lake ('salty watercourse', *v.* **salt, lacu**); Spoil Bank; Swans Nest; Tankards Fd; Twisner; Walkerley, Walkerley Mdw (*Walcotele* 1330, *Wallcote Ley, Wall-cotte Hey* 1565, *Walker Lea* 1683, *Waukerley Field* 1690, 1729, '(clearing and enclosure at) a cottage near a well or spring', *v.* **wælla, cot**, with **lēah**, (ge)**hæg**); Wall Mdw (*v.* **wælla**); Whitefield; Witch Hazles; Far-, Little- &

Near Wd (*Little Wood* 1650, v. lȳtel, wudu); Far & Near Yard (cf. (*the*) *New Yord Meadow* 1656, 1690, 1718, 1729, v. nīwe, geard).

(*b*) *the Houghwayes* 1650 (apparently from hōh and weg, but the final el. might have been (ge)hæg); *Prestham* (v. 41 *supra*).

5. BRINDLEY (109–5854)

> *Burndelegh* 13 *Sotheby*, 1288 Court (p), 1324 *Chol* (p)
> *Birnedelegh* 1288 Court
> *Burendeleg* 1289 Court
> *Brundelegh, -ley* 1311 Plea, *Chol* (p) *et freq* with variant spellings
>   *-l(eghe), -lighe, Brundylegh, Brundley* to 1561 ChRR
> *Brinndeley* 1347 BPR, *Bryndeley* 1414 ChRR (p), *Brinde-* 1618 ib,
>   *Brindlegh* 1356 Tab, *-ley* 1584 ChRR, *Brynd-* 1520 ib, (*-alias*
>   *Brynley*) 1576 ib
> *Brynley* 1464 ChRR, (*Bryndley alias-*) 1576 ib, *Brin-* 1653 Sheaf
> *Broundeley* c.1490 *Surv*
> *Brenley* 1519 Orm²

'Burnt clearing', v. berned, brende², lēah. Cf. Brindley (Lea) Hall, Brindley Lea *infra*. The latter has a form *Bromleg-*, cf. *Broundeley supra*.

ASH HOUSE, 1831 Bry, v. æsc, cf. Highash *infra*.   BREECHES COVERT, v. brēc.   BRINDLEY BANK, 1831 Bry.   BRINDLEY FIELDS.   BRINDLEY HALL, 1842 OS, *Brindley New Hall* 1831 Bry, cf. Brindley Lea Hall *infra*.   BRINDLEY LEA, 1839 *TAMap*, *Bromleglegh* 1349 *Eyre* (p), v. lēah.   BRINDLEY LEA HALL, *Old Hall* 1831 Bry, *Brindley Old Hall* 1842 OS, cf. prec.   HIGHASH, 1785 Sheaf, *-Asshes* 1463–4 Tab, *Ash Hill* 1831 Bry, cf. *Asher Field, Ash Woods* 1841 *TA*, 'ash trees on a hill', v. hēah, æsc, hyll, wudu.   LONGLANE COTTAGE, cf. *Long Lane* 1842 OS, and Longlane Fm 135 *infra*.   RADMORE COVERT, 1842 ib, *Radmore Green Covert* 1831 Bry, cf. Radmore Green 316 *infra*.

FIELD-NAMES

The undated forms are 1841 *TA* 73. Of the others, c.1320, 1579 are *Chol*, 1400 ChRR, 1572 *Sotheby*, 1831 Bry, 1839 *TAMap* 73.

(*a*) Altery Fd; Little Bache (v. bæce¹); Bakehouse Croft & Fd; Bank Fd; Black Mdw; Blake Croft (v. blæc); Bootleys (v. bōt, lēah); Bottoms (v. botm); Bowers Bank, Croft & Mdw (*del Bour*' (p), *le bourus ville de Brundeleg*' c.1320, 'the dwelling-house, the residence', v. būr¹, hūs); Brant Orchard (*v.* brende²); Brindley Orchard & Mdw (cf. Brindley *supra*); Castle Hill (*v.* castel(l), hyll, though there is no recorded evidence for this); Chicken Fd & Graves (*v.* cīcen, grǣfe); Corn Moor Mdw ('crane marsh', *v.* cron, mōr¹); Cote Fd (*v.* cot); Coy Ducks (a decoy, *v.* decoy, dūce); Crooked Fd; Four Daymath (*v.* day-math); Deadmans Fd (perhaps analogous with the same name 127 *supra*, or named from the discovery of a corpse); Farthing Clay (*v.* fēorðung, clǣg); Fern Flax; Ferney Bank; Green Heads; Haly; Hard Lade (*v.* heard, lǣd); Hazzley (in Wind Mill Hazzley *infra*, 'hazel wood', *v.* hæsel, lēah); Hill Fd; Iron Fd (*v.* hyrne); Kettles Croft (*v.* keddledock); Long Platt (*v.* plat²); The Longley (*v.* lang, lēah); Madge Green (*v.* madge); Marl Fd; Moss Mdw; Nickall Fd (*v.* nicor); Oak Wd (cf. *the quyte okes* 1572, *v.* hwīt, āc); Oulery Fd, Owlery Croft (*v.* alor, -ig³); Outlett (*v.* outlet); Ox Pasture; Peas(e) Croft (*v.* pise); Penny Mdw (*v.* peni(n)g); Pike Fd; Ryders Green 1839 (from the surname *Ryder* and grēne²); Shore Fd (*v.* scora); Sprout Ridding (*v.* sproute, ryding); Stile Croft (*v.* stigel); Wall Fd (*v.* wælla); Weavers Fd (*Wievers fielde* 1579, 'the weaver's field', or from the occupational surname *Weaver*, or the surname from Weaver 163 *infra*); Wigs Green 1831 (cf. *Wiggs Croft* 1841 *TA*, 136 *infra*); Wind Mill Bank & Hazzley ('bank and hazel-wood near a windmill', *v.* wind-mylne, banke, Hazzley *supra*); Higher- & Lower Wd (cf. *le Wode* 1400 (p), *v.* wudu).

6. BURLAND (BRIDGE, FM, LOWER & UPPER GREEN, HALL) (110–6153), *Burlond* 1260 Court (p), *-land* 1288 ib, *et freq* with variant spellings *Bour-, Boor-, -londs, -londe, -lande, Burland Howse* 1602 Sheaf, *-Hall* 1831 Bry, *-Green* 1788 Sheaf, (*Upper-*) 1839 *TAMap* 32, (*Lower*) 1842 OS, 'peasants' land', from (ge)būr and land, with grēne², hall, hūs. This district is ancient common-land. Cf. Ravensmoor *infra*.

GRADELEY GREEN (FM) [greidli], *Grayley* 1417 ChRR (p), *Greleygreen* 1788 Sheaf, *Gradeley Green* 1831 Bry, either 'grey clearing' or 'badger clearing', from grǣg¹ or grǣg² and lēah, with grēne² 'a green'.

RAVENSMOOR (BRIDGE & BROOK) (110–620505) ['reivṇzmɔːr] older local ['ranmər, 'ramnər]

> *Raven(e)smor(e)* e13 (1244) *ChMisc*, 1216–72 (1331) Ch *et freq*, (*-in Acton*) 1394 ChRR, (*-bridge*) 1621 Sheaf, (*-vulgarly Ranmore*) 1621 (1656) Orm², *-moor* 1831 Bry
> *Raynmore* 1460 Chol, *Ranmore* 1514 *ChEx*, 1643 Orm², (*Common & Bridge*) c.1695 Chol, *Rane-* 1536 Sheaf
> *Tranmore Green* 1719 Sheaf

'Raven's waste-land or marsh', from the pers.n. OE *Hræfn*, ON *Hrafn*, and mōr¹, with brycg, brōc, and grēne². Cf. *Raven's Oak* 1831

Bry, 1842 OS, (v. āc), a lost hamlet or farmstead, and *Ravensmoor Bank* 1842 OS (v. banke), and *Ravensmoor Croft* 1841 *TA* (v. croft). Ravensmoor Bridge was formerly named from Marsh Lane, v. 127 *supra*, cf. Marsh Lane *infra*. Ravensmoor was ancient common, 'a very sweet and fruitful piece of ground...hitherto preserved for the relief of the poor neighbours to it, and others' (King, *Vale Royal* (1656) in Orm² III 292), cf. Burland *supra*, Swanley Hall *infra*. The brook becomes Edleston Brook 1 22.

STONELEY GREEN (110–617516) ['stounli]

> Stanleu 1086 DB, *Stanleg(ford)* e13 (1244) *ChMisc, Stanlegh* 1530 Plea, 1561 ChRR, *Stanley Grange* 1565 Cre
> *Stonlegh* 1319 ChRR (p), 1358 *AddCh*, *-leghe* 1518 Plea, *Stonley Green* 1831 Bry
> *Stoneley* 1407, 1536 ChRR, Plea *et freq, Stoonley* 1488 ChRR (p)

'Stoney clearing', from stān and lēah, with grange and grēne². DB 265b describes this as a berewick of *Westone* (Whitchurch Sa), v. Tait 161, cf. 112 *supra*.

SWANLEY HALL BRIDGE & COVER (110–615526) ['swɔnli]

> Swanle 1284 ChF, *-legh* 1530 Plea, *-ley* 1544 AD, 1842 OS, (*infra Badeley*) 1634 Orm², *Swanelegh* 1388 Earw (p)
> *Swoneley* 1365 BPR, *Swonlegh* 1375 *Eyre* (p)
> *Swynneley* 1486 *MinAcct*
> *Swanlowe* 1528–9 Orm², *Swanlow Cover & Hall* 1831 Bry

'Herdsmen's or peasants' clearing or wood', from swān² (gen.pl. swana) and lēah, with hall and (ge)hæg. Cf. Burland, Ravensmoor *supra*.

BROOK HO. COCK A BURLAND (lost), 1831 Bry, a house at Upper Green, probably named from an inn-sign, cf. Poolehill 150 *infra*. THE FOLLY, 1842 OS, cf. *Big- & Little Folley Field* 1841 *TA*, v. folie. GREEN FM GREENFIELD COTTAGE, cf. *Green Field* 1841 *ib*, v. grēne¹, feld. HEARN'S LANE, v. 143 *infra*. HICKEY HO, 1842 OS, *Ikey House* 1831 Bry, perhaps *Yekheth infra*. HOLLIN GREEN, (*Lane*) 1831 Bry, v. holegn, grēne². HURST FM, cf. *Hurst Meadow* 1841 *TA*, v. hyrst. LONGLANE FM, 1831 Bry, cf. Longlane Cottage 133 *supra*. MARSH LANE, v. 39, 127 *supra*. PINFOLD HO (lost), 1842 OS, *the Pinfould House of Burland Green* 1788

Sheaf, v. **pynd-fald.**   Ravensmoor Windmill, *Burland Mill* 1842
OS.   Sandy Lane.   Whitehaven   World's End (lost),
1831 Bry, v. 325 *infra.*

FIELD-NAMES

The undated forms are 1841 *TA* 84. Of the others, 1304 is Chamb, 1305,
c.1310, 1314 *Chol*, 1338, 1339, 1355 Plea, 1340, 1353, 1360, 1377, 1387 *Eyre*,
1348 *Indict*, 1391 *AddRoll*, 1831 Bry, 1842 OS.

(a) Ants Fd; Little Bank, Bank Fd; Black Bridge (v. brēc); Brindley (cf.
Brindley 133 *supra*); Brook Fd (cf. Ravensmoor Brook 134 *supra*); Bull Apple
Bank; Butter Fd (v. butere); Calfs Den, Calves Croft & Fd (v. calf, denn);
Clemley Park (v. clǣme, lēah, cf. Clemley 47 *supra*); Compass Fd; Eight-,
Five- etc. Daymath (v. day-math); Dirty Mdw; Drumble (dial. drumble 'a
wooded dell', cf. dumbel); Dunn Wd (v. dunn); Finney Greaves 1842 (v.
grǣfe, cf. Finney 240 *infra*); Big & Little Glade House Fd (*Gledehurst* 1304
(p), 1305 (p), 1331 (p), 1338 (p), 1348, 1353, 'kite's wooded-hill', v. gleoda,
hyrst); Hall Yard(s) (v. geard); Hanging Fd (v. hangende); Intake (v.
inntak); Island (v. ēg-land); Lads Land (v. ladda); Long Shoot, -Shute (v.
scēat); Loontons, Luntons; Lym Croft; Marl Fd; Milking Bank (v.
milking); Mud Croft; Big & Little Northern; Outlett (v. outlet); Oven Fd
(v. ofen); Owens Barn 1831; Plaster Croft (v. pleg-stōw); Rye Hulse ('rye
hills', v. ryge, hyll); Sand Fd; Saw Pit Croft; Scotch Croft; Silver Fd;
Snidley Croft (perhaps from a compound of sniþ 'cut off, separated', or OE
snid(e) 'cutting', and lēah, but Professor Löfvenberg suggests that *Snidley* is
more likely an adj. derived from ModEdial. *sniddle* 'coarse grass, rushes,
sedge', a Ch word in EDD. Cf. Snidley Moor in Frodsham 224 *infra*);
Springe Lane Fd (v. spring 'a young wood'); Swine (Stye) Croft (v. swīn[1],
stigu, croft); Town Fd; Long Tree Fd; Tynelds; Well Fd; Wiggs Croft (cf.
Wigs Green 134 *supra*); Williaw-, Will(i)ow Bed (v. wilig, bedd).

(b) *Yekheth* 1339 (p), 1360 (p), *Yeckehet* 1340, *Yekeheth* 1355, *yhecheth*
1377 (p), *ʒekeheth*' 1387 (p), 1391 (p) ('cuckoo heath', v. gēac, hǣð, cf.
Hickey Ho *supra*).

7. Cholmondeston Green & Hall (110–6358) ['tʃumstən, 'tʃum-
stən] older local ['tʃə:mstən]

> *Chelmundestone* 1086 DB, *-ton* 1294 Ipm, *Chel(e)mundiston* 13
> AddCh (p), 1272–90 ChFor, *-mondes-* 1295 Ipm, 1351 Chamb,
> *Chelmondeston* 1831 Bry
> *Cholmundistun* 13 AddCh, *-ton* 1290 Chol, *-mundes-* 1300 ChF
> *et freq* with variant spelling *-tone* to 1427 ChRR, (*-in foresta de
> Mondrem*) 1419 Plea, *Cholmondeston* 1347 ChFor *et freq*, (*-Hall*)
> 1831 Bry, *-monedeston* 1453 Orm², *Chomondeston* 1482 Rich
> *Cholmungeston* 14 (1615) ChRR

Cholmeston' 1343 *AddCh et freq* to 1646 Sheaf, *-us-*, (*in foresta de Mondrem*) 1417 ChRR, *Cholmston (Green)* 1677 Sheaf
Cholmunston 1417 Orm², *-monaston* 1435 VR, *-monston* 1542 ChRR
Chelmeston 1417 *Eyre*
Chomston 1531 *Chol*
Shelmonston 1547 *MinAcct*
Chamaston 1550 *MinAcct*
Chomaston (lit. *Thom-*) c.1662 *Surv*

'Cēolmund's farm', from the OE pers.n. *Cēolmund* and tūn, as in Chelmondiston Sf (DEPN). The same pers.n., and perhaps the same person, figures in Cholmondeley 325 *infra*, five miles distant. *v.* grēne, hall, cf. foll. and *Mondrem* 1 10.

WOOD GREEN LANE (lost, 110–629599 to 638602), 1831 Bry, cf. Woodgreen (Lane) 156 *infra*, and *boscus de Cholmundistun* l13 *AddCh*, *Cholmondestonwode* 1347 *ChFor*, and *le grene* 1347 *ChFor* (in *Cholmondestonwode*), '(lane to) the green in a wood', *v.* wudu, grēne², lane. This was part of the forest of *Mondrem* 1 10, cf. Mondrum *infra*, and since it is on a township boundary it is the most likely place for *Cholmundestoneuese* 1340 *ChFor*, *v.* efes 'the edge of a wood or forest'.

BOTTOM HO, *v.* botm. BROOK COTTAGES, named from Crowton Brook *infra*. CROSS BANKS, 1842 OS, *Cross Bank* 1831 Bry, perhaps 'bank with a cross', *v.* cros, banke. CROSS ROAD FM. CROWTON BROOK (Bankside Brook 167 *infra*), cf. *Crowton Field & Wood* 1843 *TA*, 'crow's enclosure', *v.* crāwe, tūn, brōc, wudu. DAISY BANK FM, *Stathams Farm* 1842 OS. *Statham* is a surname. FIRS BANK FM. GATES FM. GREENBANK FM. HAWTHORNE FM. HILL'S GORSE. THE HOLLIES. OAKFIELD HOUSE FM. OLD BARN, 1842 OS. ROSEBANK FM. SOUTH VIEW FM. STOKEGATE COTTAGES, on Stokehall Lane 151 *infra*, on the boundary of Stoke township 151 *infra*, *v.* geat 'a gateway'. TOP FM.

FIELD-NAMES

The undated forms are 1843 *TA* 107. Of the others, 1290 is *Chol*, 1353 *ChFor*, 1831 Bry.

(a) Little Abraham; Aspberry Croft; Black Fd & Mdw; Bradmore (*v.* brād, mōr¹); Breach, Breeches Fd (*v.* brēc); Sixteen Butts (*v.* butte); Chequer Lane Croft; Cocksheads (*v.* cocc-scyte); Eight- Eleven- etc.

Demath, Four Days Math (*v.* day-math); Deys Mdw (*v.* dey); Eddish Fd (*v.* edisc); Flatts; Flax Croft; Fosters Hey ('forester's enclosure', *v.* forester, (ge)hæg, cf. *Wood Green Lane supra*); Gill Sprink (*v.* spring 'a young wood'); Gorse Covert (*Chelmondeston Gorse* 1831); Green Leech (*v.* grēne[1], lece); The Hays (*v.* (ge)hæg); Hough (*v.* hōh); Intake (*v.* inntak); Marl Fd; Mean Mdw ('common meadow', *v.* (ge)mǣne); (Further & Near) Mondrum (cf. *Wood Green Lane supra, Mundrum* 130 *supra, Mondrem* 1 10); Hall Orchard (not near the hall, but supposed to mark the site of an ancient residence, cf. Orm[2] III 367); Outlett (*v.* outlet); Oxenon Fd; Ox Fd & Hey (*v.* (ge)hæg); Page Lane Fd & Plantation (cf. *Page Lane* 1831, a track near Cholmondeston Hall); Pinfold Croft (*v.* pynd-fald); Poole Fd (cf. Poole 148 *infra*); Rodgers Croft, Fd & Mdw (from the ME pers.n. *Roger*); Rye Eddish (*v.* edisc); Small Thorns (*v.* 129 *supra*); Sprink Weavers ('isolated saplings in a young wood', *v.* wæfre (dial. *waver*), spring); Town Fd; Wall Fd, (*v.* wælla); Well Fd; Water Pit Fd; Warri-, Worridon (perhaps 'outlaw's hill' from **wearg** and dūn).

(*b*) *le Halc* (an assart) 1290 ('the corner of land', *v.* halc); *Purturrydyng* 1353 ('clearing at a pear-tree', *v.* pirige, trēow, ryding. Professor Löfvenberg notes that *Pur-* here represents the reduced form of *pirige, pyrige* which also appears in OE *pirgrāf* 'pear-orchard' and the p.n. Purley Sr 54, DEPN).

8. COOLE PILATE (110–6546) [ˈkuːl ˈpailat]

Chouhul c.1130 (1479) *Cott.* Faust. B. VIII (Dugd V 323 reads *Cheuhall*), *foresta de Chouuyl* 12 (14) *Harl* 3868 (Orm[2] III 418 reads *Chouhyl*), *Chouall* 1385 Comb (p)

foresta de Couhull c.1130 (1479) *Cott.* Faust. B. VIII, *Couhull* 1266 (1333) Ch (Dugd V 324 reads *-hul*), 1330 Fine, *-hul* 1276 Ipm, *-hulle* 1330 ib

Cowele 1245 Sheaf, 1393 Plea, *Couele* 1356 BPR *et freq*, often lit. *Con-*, to 1485 Plea, *Coueley* 1379 (1574) ChRR (lit. *Con-*), *-lee* 1499 Orm[2]

wood of Couuel 1294, 1295 Ipm, *Cowel* e14 *AddCh*, 1325 Plea *et freq* with variant spelling *Cowell* to 1430 ChRR, *Couel in Wich-Malbank* 1350 ib (lit. *Conel*)

wood of Coule 1294 Ipm, *Coulewode* 14 Orm[2], *-wood* 1358 ChRR, *Coule* 1316 Chamb *et freq* with variant spelling *Cowle* to 1559 Pat, *Coulle(e)* 1355 BPR

wood of Cuvel 1295 Cl

Coul 1312 Plea, *Cowl* 1353 *Eyre*

Koole 1395 MainwB, *Coole* 1396 Plea, 1424 (1574), 1523 (1571) ChRR, 1590 Sheaf, 1609 ChRR *et freq*, *-pilate* 1707 Wil, *Coole or Coole Pilot* 1882 Orm[2], *Cool* 1397 MainwB

Cole 1404 MainwB, 1426 ChRR, 1514 *ChEx*, 1519 Plea, 1554 *AddCh*, *-Pilate* 1621 (1656) Orm[2]

v. Coole Lane *infra*, cf. foll. Barnes[1] 688 locates here a lost *Pilate-croft* 1327–77 *Rental* (p), 'croft where pill-oats grow', *v.* **pil-āte**, **croft**.

COOLE HALL FM (110–658458), *Cool Hall* 1831 Bry, *Coole Pilate* 1842 OS, *v.* **hall**, cf. prec., *v.* foll. This was in a detached part of Audlem parish in Coole Pilate township, 1831 Bry, and is shown as in Hankelow township by 6″ OS in 1912, cf. 90 *supra*, and cf. Hall o' Coole 102 *supra*, Old Hall *infra*.

COOLE LANE (110–652473 to 643435) [kuːl]

Cowlane 1529, 1550 ChRR, 1574, 1727 Wil
Colelanne 1549 Pat
Coole lane c.1550 *Surv*, 1590 Sheaf *et freq* with variant spelling *Cool-*; (*Cool(e) alias-*, *-alias Cowlane*) 1624, 1692, 1693 Wil, *Cool Lane within the parishes of Audlem and Wrenbury* 1749 ib
Colane 1560 *Chol*, 1562 Sheaf, 1566 ChRR
Coolane 1581 Sheaf, 1589 Wil *et freq* to 1760 ib, (*Coole alias-*) 1626 Sheaf, (*-in Wrenbury*) 1646 Orm[2]
Collone 1639 *Chol*

'Lane at Coole', from **lane** and Coole *supra*. Coole Pilate, Coole Hall Fm and Coole Lane comprise a district of about four square miles in this and Newhall townships, *v.* 102 *supra*, partly in Acton, Audlem and Wrenbury parishes. It would seem the whole area comprised the 'forest' or 'wood' of Coole in the earlier references under Coole Pilate *supra*. The p.n. Coole is 'cow hill', from **cū** and **hyll**, [kuːhyl, kuːhul] > [kuːil, kuːul] > [kuːəl] > [kuːl], with **lēah** 'a clearing, a wood', whence the old forms *Cow-*, *Cou(e)l(l)e(e)*, [ˈkuːəl ˈlɛi] > [kuːlɛi]. The suffix *Pilate* is **pil-āte** 'pill oats', presumably from their being grown there. It distinguishes that part of Coole which is not included in Newhall township.

BRINE PITS (FM), *Brinepits* 1831 Bry, named from a brine spring here, *v.* **brīne**, **pytt**. OLD HALL, 1838 *TAMap*, *Old Cool Hall* 1831 Bry, cf. Coole Hall Fm *supra*. TOP HOUSE FM, cf. Lower House Fm 104 *supra*. These are at the north and south ends of the Coole Lane district, at 110–649463 and 637439.

FIELD-NAMES

The undated forms are 1841 *TA* 130.

(*a*) Bank Side; Bell Rough; Bow Fd; Brockases; Chester Fd; Cockshutt (*v.* cocc-scyte); Cow Fd(s); Four-, Six- etc., Day Math (*v.* day-math); Fairwater; Goose Pasture; Gutter Fd (*v.* goter); Intack (*v.* inntak); Ireland and Scotland (*v.* 325 *infra*); Long Butts (*v.* butte); Marberry; Marl Fd; Megs Hayes (*v.* meg); Old Fd; Oracle Mdw; Patch; Pinacre Mdw; Platt Fd (*v.* plat²); Post Fd; Spoil Bank; Tinkers Croft (*v.* tink(l)ere); Tippers; Weaver Mdw (cf. R. Weaver 1 38); Wood Fd.

(*b*) *Ightfield Field* 1601 Sheaf³ 50 (cf. Ightfield 99 *supra*); *Onyoteshay* 1355 (p), 1356 BPR (p) (from (ge)hæg, probably with the same pers.n., OE *Wulfgēat*, as in Shocklach Oviatt 326 *infra*, with *Ony-* written for *Ouy-*. Feilitzen 419 shows the spelling *Ouiet* in DB for OE *Wulfgēat*).

9. EDLESTON (FM, HALL & HO) (110–6350) [ˈedǀstən]

   Eglauestun' c.1200 Facs (p)
   Heidlaston' 1280 AddCh (p), *Eidliston'* c.1320 Chol (p)
   Edlawiston c.1286 Chol, *Edelauston* 1288 Court (p)
   Edlagheston, (*grangia de*) *Edelaghston* 1288 Court (p)
   Edelaston 1288 Court, 1299 ChF, 1344 *Eyre* (p), *-tone* 1312 Plea,
      Edlaston 1298 Chol et freq to 1582 ChRR
   Edliston 1290 Court (p), *Edleston* 1367 Pat, 1462 ChRR, 1515
      MinAcct, 1683 Chol et freq, (*-Hall*) 1831 Bry, *Eddles-* 1640 Chol,
      Hedls- c.1690 ib
   Etheleston 1359 *Eyre*, *-aston* 1418 ChRR, Pat
   Elleston c.1550 Surv

'Ecglāf's farm', from the OE pers.n. *Ecglāf* and tūn. Dr von Feilitzen points out that, apart from the earliest spelling, the forms represent the OE pers.n. *Ēadlāf* (with *-laghes-* an inverted spelling reflecting the sound-change ȝ > w and representing a pronunciation *-lawes-*, not a form of the OE pers.n. *Ēadlāc* proposed by Ekwall in DEPN). His observation indicates that, either the name was changed from 'Ecglāf's farm' to 'Ēadlāf's farm', or the first el. of *Ecglāf* has undergone a reduction of *-cg-* [dȝ, g] to [d] before *l*. This change is also seen in *Eglavescroft* 123 *supra* in Sound, the next township. So the *Edl-* spellings could represent a form of *Ecglāf* rather than, or as well as, *Ēadlāf*.

NEWBOLD BY NANTWICH (lost), 1671 *AddCh*, *Neubold* 1319 Plea, *New-* 1348 ib *et freq* with variant spellings *Neu(e)-*, *New(e)-*, *-bold(e)*,

-bolt, -balt in Plea, *MinAcct*, ChRR, Orm², *Chol*, BPR and *Sotheby*; (*-iuxta Edlaston*) 1319 Plea, 1417 Orm², (*-by Wizmaubank, -iuxta Nantwich*, etc.) 1361 BPR, 1362 Plea, (*-in Acton by Hurleston*) 1440 ChRR, *le Newbolt* 1418 Orm², and cf. Edleston field-names *the Newbold(e) Me(a)dowe, Furnewbolde, the Hyer & the Lowere Newbold(e)*, (*le*) *Newbold bache* 1560, 1564, 1565 *Sotheby, Chol, the New Bales* 1640 *Chol*, *Farther-, Great- & Little Newballs* 1683 *ib*, *Farther- & Hither-* 1695 *ib*, *-Newbalds* 1741 *ib*. The name means 'the new house', from nīwe and bold (bōðl), with mǣd and bǣce[1]. This place may also be *Neuton* H3 AddCh, 128 *supra*. It was probably located in the eastern part of Edleston township about 110–6451. Orm² III 386 recites the inclusion in the manor in 1348 of a lane from Edleston *supra* to the rivulet of a mill at Shrewbridge 131 *supra*. There is an appropriate moated site at 110–638507, cf. Moat (Bank) *infra*.

FIELDS FM.   GREEN LANE (BRIDGE), *Dig Lane* 1831 Bry, *v.* dīc 'a ditch'.   MARSH FM & LANE, *The Marsh* c.1695 *Chol, Marsh Lane Farm* 1788 *ib, Marsh Lane* 1831 Bry, cf. 39, 127 *supra, v.* mersc. RAVENSMOOR BRIDGE, *v.* 134 *supra*.

FIELD-NAMES

The undated forms are 1841 *TA* 161. Of the others 1349–50, 1417 are Orm², 1515 *MinAcct*, 1532, 1554 *AddCh*, 1560 *Sotheby*, and the rest *Chol*.

(a) Aldersey's Fd 1788; Barn Croft (1741, cf. foll.); Barn Fd (1788); Breast of Veal Fd 1788 (perhaps named after its shape, *v.* 325 *infra*); (Far) Brickiln Fd (*Farther- & Nearer Brick Kiln Field* 1795, cf. *Farther- & Hither Brick Leasow* 1695, *v.* bryke, bryke-kyl, lǣs); (Little) Brook Fd (*two Brook Fields* 1698, *Big- & Little Brook Field* 1788, *v.* brōc); Brown Fd (*v.* brūn[1]); Cause Way Fd (1695, *v.* caucie); Six- Nine-, Ten Daymath (1788, 1795, *v.* day-math); Further Fd (*Farther-* 1706, 1726); Hill Fd (1729) Hither Fd (1695); Lady Lake Fd (1695, 'lady's watercourse', *v.* hlǣfdige, lacu, cf. foll.); Lady Mdw (1788, cf. *le Lady Feld* 1417, *Ladie-, (the) Lady feld(e)* 1563, *-field* 1571, *-feild(e)* 1564, 1631, 'the lady's field', *v.* hlǣfdige, feld, mǣd, cf. prec. and *le Ladylidiate* 1298, 'the lady's gate', *v.* hlǣfdige, hlidgeat. These names probably refer to dower-land or land held by a jointress); Litchfield (*Leech feild* 1683, *v.* lece); Long Rang 1729 (1683, *-Range* 1706, *v.* range); First-, to Fifth Moat, Moat Bank (1788, *the Motes* 1683, *-Moats* 1695, 1726, *v.* mote, cf. *Newbold supra*); Farther & Hither Newbalds 1741 (*v. Newbold supra*); Orchard Fd (1795, cf. *Hall Orchards & Yards* 1564, *v.* hall, orceard, geard); Otter Fd; Outlet (*v.* outlet); Big & Little Ox Pasture (1788, *Ox Pasture* 1695); Pool Fd ((*le Pole Feld* 1417, 1537, *-fild* 1548, *le-, the Poolefi(e)ld* 1565, *two Poole Fields* 1698, cf. *the poole meadowing* 1656, *v.* pōl[1], feld, meadowing); Rue Lane (Mdw) (*Roo Lane, Great & Little Roolane Field*

1690, *Rue Lane Meadow* 1795, probably 'rough lane' from rūh and lane, but Professor Löfvenberg suggests that the first el. could be the plant-name *rue*); Rutters Fd 1729 (1690); Shoulder of Mutton (-*Field* 1788, from its shape, *v.* 325 *infra*); Sound Mdw (cf. Sound 121 *supra*); Thistley Fd 1788; Three Nooked Fd (*v.* three-nooked); Way Fd 1729 (1690, *the way feild* 1683, *v.* weg); Weaver Mdw (cf. R. Weaver 1 38); Well Fd (cf. *Walfeld* 1537, *Wallfild* 1541, -*field*(*e*) 1563, 1564, *Great-* & *Little-* 1695, *Litlewall Field* 1741, *v.* wælla, wella, feld); Little Wd, Wood Fd (cf. *boscus de Edlaston*' 1298, þe *wood* 1695, Big & *Little Wood* 1795, *v.* wudu).

(*b*) *le Brunehul*(*l*) 1295, *Bromehull* 1417, (*the-*, *le-*) *Browne hill*(*e*)s 1541, 1563, 1565, 1640, *browne or bromehilles* 1565 ('the brown-, broomyhill', from brūn[1], brōm, and hyll, cf. Brown Hill(s) 40 *supra*); *Great Carsford* 1695 ('ford where cress grows', *v.* cærse, ford); *le Chirchefurlong* 1298 (*v.* cirice, furlang); *Clay Crofts* 1655 (*v.* clǣg, croft); *Evotts Croftes* 1563, *Eviotts Croft* 1564, *Evetts croftes* 1607 (from croft with the ME fem.pers.n. *Evot, Evet*, diminutive of *Eve, Eva*); *Flash Meadow* 1655 (*v.* flasshe); *Gorsty Field* 1655 (*v.* gorstig); *Edlaston Hay* 1417, 1634, -*haye* 1550, 1612, -*Hey*(*e*) 1560, 1565 (*v.* (ge)hæg 'a fenced-in enclosure'. This was the name of a wood); *Le Lee felde* 1417 (*v.* lēah); *Lewis*(*s*)*efeld* 1286, 1287 ('Lewis's field', from the ME (AFr) pers.n. *Lewis*, with feld); *Maylers Ryddynge* 1417 ('Meilyr's clearing', from the Welsh pers.n. *Meilyr* and ryding); *le Questhe* 1349–50 (possibly for *quesche*, i.e. queche 'a thicket'); *le Shypon croftes* 1417, *Shepyncrofte* 1515, *Shippon Crofts* 1532, *the Shippons croftes* 1554, *le Shippon croftes* 1573 (*v.* scypen, croft); *le Weteshagh* 1417 ('the wet wood', *v.* wēt, sceaga).

10. FADDILEY (109–5852) [fadili, fadəli, fadḷi]

> *Fadilee* c.1220 *Chol*, -*le* 1271 AD, *Fadileg*(*h*), *Fadyle* 1295 Ipm *et freq* with variant spellings *Faddi-* (from 1354 BPR), *Faddy-*, -*ley*(*e*), -*ly*
>
> *Faddelee* 1260 Court (p), *Fadelegh* 1288 ib (p) *et freq* with variant spellings *Fad*(*d*)*e*- -*ley*, -*leghe*, -*leigh*, -*lighe* to 1724 NotCestr
>
> *Fadyleng* 1297 Cl
>
> *Faduley* 1573–4 Orm[2]

'Fad(d)a's clearing or wood', from an OE pers.n. *Fad*(*d*)*a* and lēah, cf. Fadmoor YN 62, Vaddicott D 108. The -*i*-, -*y*- spellings probably represent a reduced form of -ing-[4], fully represented only by the inverted spelling *Fadyleng* for some such form as *Fadyngle*, cf. foll.

BOTTERLEY HILL (109–590517) ['bɔtəli], 1831 Bry, *Bottylegh* 1314 *Chol*, *campus qui vocatur Bottyleye* 1324 *ib*, The Botterley 1841 *TA*, cf. *Botteley's tenement…given by John Botteley* 1724 NotCestr, 'Botta's wood or clearing', from the OE pers.n. *Bot*(*t*)*a* and lēah. The

-y- spellings may represent a reduced form of *-ing*[4]-, as in Baddiley 124 *supra*, Faddiley *supra*. Other reductions of *-ing* in compounds to *-i-*, *-y-* may be seen in Fallibroome **1** 197 and possibly Ettiley **2** 270. But it must be observed that ME and ModE *-i-*, *-y-* spellings and ModE [-i-] pronunciations appear for the reduced forms and unstressed positions of OE *-an* inflexion (wk.dat.sg. or gen.sg.; ME *-en*, *-yn*) in Romiley **1** 292, Baguley **2** 12, Tabley **2** 60, Checkley 56 *supra*, Hankelow 89 *supra* and possibly Ettiley loc. cit.; for OE *-a* inflexion (gen.pl.) in Gatley **1** 244, Bulkeley 325 *infra*, Calveley 307 *infra*; possibly for OE *-en* suffix in Ettiley loc. cit.; and for the unstressed second syllable of **stapol** in Stapeley 71 *supra*; and it does not seem likely that these p.ns. would have had an alternative *-ing-*[4] form.

LARDEN GREEN (109–587516) ['lardən], 1700 *Chol, Laurthyn* 1341 ChRR (p), 1358 *Eyre* (p), 1367 *Sotheby* (p), *Lauurthyn* 1348 *Eyre*, *Laurdyn* 1372 *Chol* (p), *Lawrdyn'* 1448, 1457 *ib* (p), 'low enclosure or curtilage', from **lágr** (ME *lah*) and **worðign**, with **grēne**[2] 'a green'. The opposite p.n. is Hawarden Fl (NCPN 215) ['hardən], from **hēah** 'high'.

WOODHEY GREEN, HALL & CHAPEL (109–5752) ['wudɛi, 'wudi]

> *Wodehay* 13 *AddCh* (p), *Woodheye* 1331 *Adl* (Barnes[1] 703), *Wodhay* 1350 *Eyre* (p) *et freq* with variant spellings *Wo(o)d-*, *Wod(d)e-*, *-hay*, *-hey*; hall of *Woodhay* 1621 (1656) Orm[2], *chapel of Wodhay* 1536 Sheaf, *Woodhey Green, Hall & Chapel* 1831 Bry
> *Wodeye* 1307 Plea (p), *Wodey* 1320 *Chol* (p), *Woday* 1350 *Eyre* (p) *et freq* with variant spellings *-ey*, *Wodd-*, to 1536 Tab

'Fenced-in place at a wood', or 'enclosure of woodland', from **wudu** and **(ge)hæg**, with **grēne**[2], **hall**, **chapel**. Nearby is Woodhey Cross (6″), 'Ancient Cross' 1831 Bry, *v.* **cros**.

COOKSPIT FM, ['kukspit], *Cocks Pit* 1831 Bry, *Cookspit* 1842 OS, *Cook's Pit* 1842 *TAMap*. It is probably 'a cockpit', from **cocc**[2] and **pytt**, cf. cockpit, with a popular association of 'cock's pit' with 'cook's spit'. The name appears in f.ns., e.g. 125 *supra*, **2** 289. FADDILEY BANK, *Sidney Bank* 1831 Bry, *Sidney* 1841 *TA*, perhaps analogous with Sydney 24 *supra*, *v.* **banke**. FINGERPOST FM. HEARN'S LANE (109–587517 to 595524), 1842 OS, *Herons Lane* 1831 Bry, *Uriens Lane (End)* 1536 Sheaf[3] 17, 69, cf. *Arions Brook* 1831

Bry, 1842 *TAMap* (109–5852 to 110–6052), and *Arions Field* 1841 *TA*, 1869 *EnclA*, from the ME (MWelsh) pers.n. *Urien*, with lane, brōc, ende[1] and feld. The pers.n. el. has been confused with heiroun 'a heron'.   HOLLYWELL HO (109–577530), 1842 OS, *Holywell House* 1831 Bry, cf. *Big & Little Hollywell* 1841 *TA*, 'holy well', v. hālig, wella, from a nearby well now filled in (Sheaf³ 17 (4041)). The name was pronounced [hæli-] in 1879, Sheaf¹ 1, 242.   WILL BANK FM & HO, *Will Bank* 1831 Bry, cf. *Top Will Bank (Field)* 1841 *TA*, 'hill-side at a spring', v. wella, banke.

FIELD-NAMES

The undated forms are 1841 *TA* 167. Of the others, 13, 14, 1367, 1437 are *Sotheby*, 1271 AD, 1287 Court, 1295 Ipm, 1297 Cl, c.1300 *Dav*, 1326, 1536 ChRR, 1831 Bry, 1869 *EnclA*, and the rest *Chol*.

(a) Armsters; Bank Fd & Hey; Birches 1869; Blaggs Mdw, Bloggs Yard (*Blaggs Field & Yard* 1869); Higher & Near Brockhurst (*-Brockle-* 1869, *Le Brochurst* c.1300, 'badger's wooded-hill', v. brocc, hyrst, hyll); Butlands (v. butte, land); Chair Fd; Chapel Mdw (cf. Woodhey Chapel *supra*); Chicken Greave (v. cīcen, grǣfe); Cholmondeley Fd (cf. Cholmondeley 325 *infra*); Colts Hole; Colver Fd 1869 (v. calver); The Coppy (v. copis); Courtland Plantation 1869; Deep Lake (v. dēop, lacu); Farthing Mdw (v. fēorðung); Fernilos Croft 1708 (*The Fernilor Crofte* 1654, *The Ferniler croft* 1694); Folly Fd (v. folie); Golbornes Croft (cf. John de *Golborne* of Woodhey 1397 ChRR, *Chol*, named from Golborne 326 *infra*); Gorsty Nook (v. gorstig, nōk); Halfpenny Mdw (v. halfpeny); Hatch Fd (v. hæcc); Hill Fd (cf. the *Hillcroft* 1655, v. hyll, croft); Hob Fd (cf. *Hob Lane* 1831, v. hob); Hollin Lane 1831 (leading to Hollin Green 135 *supra*, v. holegn); Big Inckley 1869; Intake 1869 (v. inntak); Kate Croft; Kichen Fd 1869 (v. cycene); Lightmore (1536, *-moor* 1869, v. lēoht, mōr¹); Marl (Pit) Fd 1869 (cf. *Pitt Croft* 1583, v. marle, pytt); New Croft 1869 (*-Crofte* 1654, v. nīwe, croft); Outlet 1869 (v. outlet); Ox Pasture; Pavement Fd (v. pavement); Pills Moor Mdw (perhaps 'willow marsh', v. pill, mōr¹); Pingle (v. pingel); Priest Ridding (v. prēost, ryding, cf. foll.); Ridding 1869 (cf. prec. and *the fower-, -fowre Ridding(e)s* 1654, 1694, 1708, and *Ouwanis Ruding* 1271, from ryding, with fēower and the OWelsh pers.n. *Oue(i)n*, Welsh *Owen*); Rough Fd 1869 (cf. *Rowecroft* c.1310, v. rūh, croft); Stile Fd (v. stigel); Big Suckley; Swine Park (v. swīn¹, park); Townfield (*(the) Town(e)feild, -Field* 1654, 1694, 1708, v. toun); Wheat Croft 1869 (cf. *quatecroft* 13, *le Whetefeld* 1367, *le queteruding* 14, v. hwǣte, croft, feld, ryding).

(b) le-, la Boure 1287 (p), 1295 (p), 1297, 1326 (p) ('the bower', v. būr¹); *Brand(e) crofte* 1579, 1583 ('burnt croft', v. brende², croft); *Collyns Crofte* 1579, *Collins-* 1583 (from the ME pers.n. *Colin*, for *Nicholas*, and croft); *the common lane* 1583 (v. commun, lane); *Dunes Greffe* 1536 (the second word is probably *gresse*, for gærs 'grass'; the first is a surname or pers.n.); *le*

Haystou 1367 (perhaps 'fenced-in place', from (ge)hæg and stōw, but cf. hege-stall); *longacr'* 1391, *Longe Acre* 1579, *longeacer, -ar* 1583 ('long plough-land', *v.* lang, æcer); *le Lowefeld* 1391 (either 'low field', or 'field at a mound', from lágr or hlāw and feld); *(the) Sit(t)icrofte* 1677 (probably 'shitty croft', *v.* scite, -ig³, croft); *Sutcrofte* 1391, 1579 (*v.* sūð, croft).

11. HENHULL (BRIDGE & FM) (110–6453) ['henul]

> *Henul* c.1230 *Chol* (p), Whall (p) *et freq* with variant spellings *-ull* (from c.1290), *-ulle* to 1462 ChRR
> *Henhull* c.1230 Whall (p), 1304 *Chamb et freq* with variant spellings *-hulle, -hul*; (-*in Acton*) 1315 *AddCh, le Henhull* 1462 *Sotheby, Henhull Bridge* 1831 Bry
> *Henill* 1307 *Eyre* (p), *-yll* 1418 *Dav*
> *Henehull* 1367, 1372 (p), 1385 Plea
> *Hendull* 1410 *AddCh, Hendhull* 1553 Pat
> *Henwall* 1425 MidCh
> *Heynault* 1646 Sheaf

'Hen hill', *v.* henn, hyll, brycg. This probably alludes to wood-hens or some such wild fowl.

BLUESTONE, 1831 Bry, 'dark-coloured stone', from ME blew 'blue', and stān, cf. Gloverstone 326 *infra*. GREENBANK COTTAGE KINGSLEYFIELD FM, cf. Kingsley Fd 40 *supra*. WELSHMEN'S GREEN (110–641535), *Welschemanesgrene* 1531 *Chol, Welshman's Green* 1831 Bry, *Welchmans-* 1839 *TAMap*, 'the Welshman's green', *v.* Wels(c)h-man, grēne². Cf. *Welchmonis yarden* 1637 *Chol* (half an acre enclosed from the commons, *v.* gardin), and Welsh Row 34 *supra*. These place-names reflect the Welsh connexion of the Nant-wich salt trade. The green appears to have been a common, perhaps a camping-place for Welsh salters and packmen, cf. foll. and 1 48 (route XXV). WELSHMEN'S LANE, now named from prec., was *via que ducit versus Henull* c.1290 *Chol, Henullelone* 1338 *AddCh, Henhull lone* 1480 *Chol, Henhull Lane* 1553 *ChCert*, 1831 Bry, 'the lane leading to Henhull', *v.* lane, Henhull *supra*.

FIELD-NAMES

The undated forms are 1839 *TA* 201. Of the others, 13, c.1290, 1480 are *Chol*, 1312, 1336, 1359, 1423, 1466, 1579 *AddCh*, 1438–9 Orm², 1553 *ChCert*.

(*a*) Alms House Mdw; Breast of Veal (from its shape, *v.* 325 *infra*); The Nine Butts (*v.* nigon, butte); Causeway Fd (*v.* caucie); Ten Daymath (*v.*

day-math); Footway Mdw (v. fote-waye); Kiln Fd (cf. *le Kylne Crǫfte* 1553, *v.* cyln); The Meadow (cf. *le greate meydowe, Meydowfeld* 1553, *v.* mǣd (dat.sg. mǣdwe), grēat, feld); Shoulder of Mutton (v. 325 *infra*); Sooty Mdw (v. soti); Three Nook Croft (v. three-nooked); Wall Croft (v. wælla); The Withins (*le Wythynes, le Wythinis* c.1290, *v.* wiðegn); Bottom- & Top Wood (cf. *Lytle Henhull Wood* 1553, *v.* wudu).

(b) *Alflater* 1480, 1553; *le Barude* 1359 ('grove wood', *v.* bearu, wudu, cf. Big Barr 2 307); *le Blacke Croft* 1553 (v. blæc, croft); *Le Bruche* 1423 ('the breaking-in of land', *v.* bryce); *le Calde Wales croft* 1553 (probably 'cold spring', *v.* cald, wælla, but the second el. may be wēl² 'a deep pool'); *le Cleyefielde* 1423 (v. clǣg, feld); *Cresmore* 1480 ('marsh where cress grows', *v.* cærse, mōr¹); *Doggecroft* c.1290, -e 1438–9 ('dogs' croft', *v.* dogga, croft); *le grove* 1553 (v. grāf); *Halfeld* 1553 (perhaps 'field at a nook', *v.* halh, feld); *Ladye Croftes, lady meydowe* 1553 (dower lands, 'her ladyship's crofts and meadow', *v.* hlǣfdige, croft, mǣd); *Henhull lee* 1480 (v. lēah); *Marchumleyes crofte* 1579 (from croft and the surname from Marchamley Sa); *Reynaldescroft* c.1290, 1336 (from the ME pers.n. *Reynald* (OFr *Reinald*, OG *Raginald*, ON *Rǫgnvaldr, Ragnaldr*, cf. Fellows Jensen 213) and croft); *Ruccroft* 1312 ('rough croft', *v.* rūh, croft); *le Rye Croftes* 1553 (v. ryge, croft); *Sharpesfylde* 1466 (probably from the surname *Sharp* and feld, but cf. scearp); *le Snecchebrock* c.1290 (perhaps 'brook with a trap in it', *v.* brōc. The first el. appears to be ME **snecche* 'a trap, a snare, a catch', cf. ME *snacche* 'a hasp, a catch' (NED, 1342) or 'a trap, a snare' (NED, 14), ME *snekke* 'a latch, a catch' (NED, e14), ME *snecchen* 'to snatch' (NED, e13), *v.* snatch, sneck NED); *Swynscrofte* 1553 (v. swin¹, croft); *le Walkeriscroft* 13 ('the tanner's croft', *v.* walcere, croft); *lez Waybuttes* 1466 ('head-lands with a right of way', *v.* weg, butte); *Wheat Croftes* 1553 (v. hwǣte, croft).

12. HURLESTON (110–6255) [ˡ(h)ərlstən]

Hurdleston 1278 Ipm *et freq* with variant spellings *Hurdel(e)s-, Hurd(e)lus-, Hurdlis-, -ys-, Hurduls-, -ils-, -tone* to 1547 Orm²

Hyrdeleston 1305 ChF, *Hird(e)leston* 1347 BPR, *Herdeleston* 1391 AddRoll, *Hordeleston* 1419, 1425 ChRR

Hurleston 1325 Plea *et freq* with variant spellings *Hurl(e)ston(e)*; *Hurlestan* 1658 Wil

Herlaston 1328 Cl (p), 1390 ChRR, *Har-* 1390 ib, 1382 *Chol*, 1403, 1409 ChRR

Huldelston 1432 *AddCh*

Hurleton 1441 ChRR (p) *et freq* ib, AD, with variant spellings *Hurl(le)ton* to 1484, all (p), *Hurleton* 1545 Plea

Hurdelton 1442 ChRR (p), 1448, 1473 ib (p)

Hudleston 1506 AD

Hurdeston 1531 AD

'Endosure made of hurdles' or 'with a hurdle', v. hyrdel, -es[2], tūn, cf. Hurdsfield 1 106. Professor Löfvenberg suggests that the first el. in these p.ns. may be an OE *hyrdels (< PrGer *hurðislaz) 'a hurdle', which might have existed by the side of OE hyrdel like OE gyrdels beside OE gyrdel 'a girdle'. Ekwall (DEPN) is misleading upon this name. The spelling Hurdlaston 1325 in DEPN 258 is an error copied from BM 1 390, for Hurdleston 1325 (1420) AddRoll 6278, and should not be used as the basis of etymology.

(LITTLE) BACHE HO, BACHEHOUSE COVERT, MILL & POOL (110–614549) [batʃ], Great & Little Bache, Hurleston Fox Cover, Bone Mill 1831 Bry, Bach House (Covert) 1842 OS, cf. Bache House Field 1841 TA, Bache Cover & Pool 1880 Sheaf[1] 2, 181, 'stream in a valley', v. bæce[1].   BANK FM, Bank House 1831 Bry, The Bank 1842 OS. BURFORD (BRIDGE) (110–628539), BURFORD HO (lost, 127 supra) Burford in Acton 1461 Rich, Burford green 1719 Sheaf, -House, Burfords Green 1831 Bry, Burford Field 1841 TA, v. ford 'a ford' grēne[2], brycg, hūs. The place is on an unnamed stream between Hurleston and Acton 126 supra. The first el. is probably (ge)būr 'a peasant', as in Burland 134 supra, half a mile away.   CLATTER-DISHES FM, Clatterdishes 1842 OS. This may be a humorous modern name from some domestic noise. But if it is an old formation, the final el. would be edisc 'an enclosure, an enclosed park', and the first el. may be clater 'loose stones' as in Clatterwick 2 115, or clāte 'burdock, goose-grass'. The latter, with shortening of the vowel in composition would give *clat-edish ['klat ediʃ] which popular etymology would render clatter-dish.   CUCKOO LANE, 1831 Bry, v. cuccu, cf. 127 supra.   FIELDS FM, The Fields 1831 Bry. HENHULLBRIDGE FM, cf. Henhull Bridge 145 supra.   NEW FM. PARK FM, Hall Farm 1831 Bry, v. hall, park.   YEWTREE HO, Sycamore Tree House 1831 ib, Sycamore House 1842 OS.

FIELD-NAMES

The undated forms are 1841 TA 215. Of the others 1333, 1391, 1347 are AddCh, 1476 Rich.

(a) The Acres; Bakehouse Croft; Bone Fd (cf. bone-dust, v. bān); Bradley Lane Fd; Brindley Breach (v. brēc, cf. Brindley 133 supra); Butty Fd (v. butty); Cavendish (v. edisc, cf. Cavendish Sf (DEPN)); Cholmondeley Fd (named from the Cholmondeley family of Cholmondeley 325 infra); Coalpit Fd; Cross Fd (v. cros); Eight-, Three Day Math (v. day-math); Flooding Mdw; Green Flatt; Hall Flatt, Mdw & Yards; High Yard (v. geard);

Hinshall (cf. *Hinsall* 154 *infra*); Hurleston Hey; Kinsall; Big-, Middle- &
Lower Leas (cf. *Le Lee* 1333, *v*. lēah); Long Acre; Marl Croft & Fd;
Marsh Mdw; Moor Lane Fd (*v*. mōr¹); Top Moland Fd (*v*. mōr, land);
Moss Fd; Northridge (*v*. norð, hrycg); Oulery Fd (*v*. alor, -ig³); Overleys
(*v*. uferra, lēah); Ox Yard (*v*. geard); Great & Little Pavens; Picker (*v*.
pichel); Pinfold Fd (*v*. pynd-fald); Pingot (*v*. pingot); Pool Hill Fd (cf.
Poolehill 150 *infra*); Poole Fd (cf. Poole 148 *infra*); Wet Rean [*v*. wēt,
rein); Big-, Little- & Near Rid (*v*. ryde); Big-, Little & Long Ridding (*v*.
ryding); Sand Hole Fd; Stoke Fd (cf. Stoke 151 *infra*); Stone Wd; Sweet Fd
(*v*. swēte); Town Fd (Lane); Wet Wd; Wicksted's Yard (from geard, and
the surname from Wicksted 112 *supra*); Withy Croft (*v*. wīðig); Wobs (*v*.
cwabba 'a marsh, a bog'); Woodheys (*v*. wudu, (ge)hæg).

(*b*) *del Grene* 1391 (p) (*v*. grēne² 'a green'); *Heghurst* 1391 ('high wooded-
hill', *v*. hēah, hyrst); *le Hul* 1347 (p) (*v*. hyll); *Ravenes croftes* 1476 ('Raven's
crofts', from the pers.n. OE *Hræfn*, ON *Hrafn* and croft, cf. 128 *supra*);
Smythes parrek 1391 ('the smith's paddock', *v*. smið, pearroc).

13. POOLE (BANK, BRIDGE (lost), COVERT, FM, HALL & OLD HALL)
(110–6455) [puːl]

> *Pol* 1086 DB (twice)
>
> *Pulle* 13 *AddCh*, (1580) Sheaf, 1288 Court (p) *et freq* with variant
> spelling *Pull* to 1476 ChRR (p); *campus de Pull'* 1331 *ChFor*,
> *Pulle bridge* 1506 Sheaf
>
> *Polle* 1294 Ipm, c.1325 *Chol* (p)
>
> *Pullee* 1295 Cre (p)
>
> *Pole iuxta Wicum Malbanum* 1474 Orm², *Pole* 1542 Plea, 1562
> ChRR
>
> *Poole* 1559 ChRR, 1560 *Chol et freq* with variant spelling *Pool* from
> 1621 (1656) Orm²; *Poole Bridge* 1621 Sheaf, -*Hall* & -*Old Hall*
> 1831 Bry, *Pool Bridge* 1831 Bry, -*Hall* & -*Hall Farm* 1842 OS

'The pool', from pōl¹ and pull. The form *Pullee* 1295 may contain
a suffixed ēa 'a stream', or lēah 'a wood, a clearing', but it might be
a mistake for *Pulles*. The several manors in Poole township are
collectively known as *Pulles* 1544 Plea, 1559 Orm², *Pooles* 1544 AD,
three townships of the names of the Pooles 1621 (1656) Orm² III 293, cf.
Barrets-Poole, Warpoole and *White-Poole infra*. The name alludes to
some part of the stream 110–632550 to 110–663558 which traverses
the township, or to a pool near it, cf. *Pulewalle infra*.

POOLE GREEN (110–636556), *Pool Croft Heath* 1831 Bry, *Pulcroft* l13,
1325, 1331 *ChFor*, *AddCh et freq* with variant spelling -*crofte* to 1594
ChRR, (-*in Barettespull*) 1343 Plea, *Pulle Croft* 1544 ib, *Pullcroft* 1559

Orm², 'croft at a pool', from pull (cf. Poole *supra*) and croft. This may be *campus de Pull* 1331 *ChFor*, a part of Mondrem forest. Orm¹ places *Pulcroft* in Worleston, but it occurs as in *Barrets-Poole*, which was identified with *Pulcroft* by Orm² III 351 n. BM identifies *Pulcroft* in *AddCh* 50581 as 'Poole Croft in Worleston near Nantwich', following Orm¹. It now appears that the modern name Poole Green (from grēne² 'a green') represents both *Pool Croft* and *Barrets-Poole*.

BARRETS-POOLE (lost, *v.* prec.), 1609 ChRR, *Barrettispull* 1283–88 *AddCh*, 1288 Court *et freq* with variant spellings *Bar(r)e(t)t(e)s-*, *Bartes-*, *Barats-*, *Barrottes-*, *Barectes-*, *Baret(t)-* and *-pol* (1289 Court), *-pulle* (1303 Chamb), *-pool(e)* (1434 Plea, ChRR), *-pole* (1511 Plea), from Poole *supra* with a manorial affix from the surname of Richard *Baret* of *Barettespulle* E2 *AddCh* 49799.

WARPOOLE (lost), 1819 Orm² III 351

> *Horepull* 1296 Plea *et freq* with variant spellings *Horpull, Horepolle* (1417 *Eyre*), *-poole* (1488 Orm²), *Horpole* (1533 Plea), *Hoore Pull(e)* (1445, 1465 Comb), *Hoare-Poole* (1609 ChRR)
> *Horsepull(e)* 1399 ChRR, Sheaf
> *Whapulle* 1401–2 Orm²
> *Whorepulle* 1544 Plea, 1559 Orm², *-poole* 1626 Sheaf

If *Horse-* represents a genitive form, this p.n. might be 'Hoar's part of Poole', from Poole *supra* with a manorial affix from the surname of William *le hare* of *Pulle* 13 (1580) Sheaf³ 20 (4698), *v.* hār² 'grey, hoary'. Another member of this family is Richard *Canutus* of *Pulle* 13 *AddCh* 49787 (Lat. *canutus* 'having grown grey-haired'). Cf. foll. However, in view of the rarity of genitive forms as compared with *Barrets-Poole supra*, Dr von Feilitzen thinks the first el. is not a manorial affix. He suggests horu or horh, the p.n. being 'dirty, muddy pool' as contrasted with *White-Poole infra*, 'white, clean pool'.

WHITE-POOLE (lost), 1819 Orm² III 351, *Album Pull* c.1180 *AddCh*, (17) *Chol*, *Alba Pulle* 1303 Chamb, *Whyte Pulle* c.1260–70 (14) *AddCh*, e14 *ib et freq* with variant spellings *White-*, *-pull(e)* to 1559 Orm², (*Whytepulle iuxta Worleston*) 1355 Plea, (*Le Whitepulle*) 1405 ib, *Whitepole* 1474 (1630) *Chol*, *-Poole* 1588 AD, 1772 Sheaf, *Whitpole* 1534 Orm², *-poole* 1592 ib, 1609 ChRR, *Whitt-* 1609 ChRR. 'White Poole', from Poole *supra* and hwīt. The origin and significance of 'white' is debateable. It could be manorial, cf. *Barrets-* and *Warpoole* *supra*. There was a surname *White* in this district—William *Albus* of *Pulle* c.1395 Sheaf³ 22 (5295) (Lat. *albus* 'white')—and one Richard *Albus* witnesses a Nantwich deed 112 *AddCh* 43372. But these seem to be of the same family as the *le Hare, Canutus*, surnames under *Warpoole supra*. The 'white' in *Album-, Alba-* in the early references is rather an adj. than an affix (although translation into Latin may have affected the form). There is no trace of a genitive construction. The name appears with the def. art. in 1405 Plea. The evidence is against a manorial affix here. It may be that 'white' refers to some salinity of the water of the stream of Poole, *v. supra*, for the district is in the Nantwich salt-field, cf. Salt Brooks *infra*; on the other hand, 'white' may be contrasted with 'dirty', cf. *Warpoole supra*.

CHERRY ORCHARD, 1831 Bry.   OAKTREE FM.   POOLEHILL (HOUSE), *Pool(e) Hills* 1831 ib, 1842 OS, cf. *Poole Hill Field* 1842 *TA* and 148 *supra*, and *Cock up the Hill* 1831 Bry, *Cocapalle Hill* c.1662 *Surv, v.* hyll. The *Cock* was a public house, 'The Cock on Poole Hill', cf. Cock a Burland 135 *supra*.   POOLE HOUSE, *Alexanders* 1831 Bry.

FIELD-NAMES

The undated forms are 1842 *TA* 323. Of the others, 1283–88 is *AddCh*, c.1395 Sheaf, 1831 Bry, 1842 OS.

(a) Ash Bank (*v.* æsc, banke); The Banks (*v.* banke); Bone Dust Fd (*v.* bone-dust); Broom Fd (*v.* brōm); Two Butts (*v.* butte); Butty Fd (*v.* butty); Coney Grave (*v.* coningre); Drumbo Fd (*v.* dumbel); Fearn Hay (*v.* fearn, (ge)hæg); Fork Lane Fd (cf. *Fork Lane* 1831); The Fridays (*v.* Frīgedæg, cf. Saturdays *infra*); Heath Croft (*v.* hǣð, cf. Poole Green *supra*); Hemp Bank Fd (*v.* hænep, banke); Holmes Mdw (either from holmr, hulm, or the surname *Holme(s)*); Kitchen Croft (*v.* cycene); Intake (*v.* inntak); Kiln Fd (cf. *Culnehul* c.1395, *v.* cyln, hyll); Big Less (*v.* lǣs); Outlett (*v.* outlet); Pinfold Croft (*v.* pynd-fald); Poolstead ('place where a pool lies', *v.* pōl-stede); Salt Brooks ('salty streams', *v.* salt, brōc, cf. *White-Poole supra*); Sand Flatt, Sand Hole Fd, Sandy Foot (*v.* sand, sandig, flat, hol¹, fōt); Saturdays (*v.* Sætern-dæg, cf. Fridays *supra*); Shaw Fd (*v.* sceaga); Shirt Croft (*v.* scerde); Long Slangs (*v.* slang); Sprink Fd (*v.* spring 'a young wood'); Street Fd (*v.* strǣt); Weavers Fd; Wimbol Fd.

(b) *le Bruches* 1283–88 ('the grounds broken-in', *v.* bryce); *Hennelanda* c.1395 ('hens' land', *v.* henn, land); *Gamelesmeduwe* 1283–88 ('Gamel's meadow', from the pers.n. ON *Gamall*, ODan *Gamal* and mǣd, cf. Gamesley 151 *infra*); *Hedt medue* c.1395 (probably 'heath meadow', *v.* hǣð, mǣd); *Pulewalle* c.1395 ('spring at Poole or a pool', from pōl¹ or Poole *supra* and wælla); *le Withinis* 1283–8 ('the willows', *v.* wīðegn).

14. STOKE (BANK (FM), HALL (LANE) & PARK) (110–6256) [stɔːk]
older local [stɔːǝk], *Stok* 1260, 1288 Court (p), 1275, 1280 P (p),
Stoke 1270–1300 ChF (p), 1288 Plea (p), e14 *AddCh et freq, passim,*
(*-iuxta Cholmundeston*) 1339 Orm², (*-Hurdlestone*) 1369 Plea, *Stooke*
1513 ChEx, *Stoak* (*Hall*) 1694 ChetOS VIII, 'the hamlet', from stoc,
with banke, hall, lane and park. The township adjoins Cholmondeston and Hurleston 136, 146 *supra.*

BAR BRIDGE (110–614569), 1719 Sheaf, *Barbridge* c.1536 Leland, 1656
Orm², *Barr Bridge* 1621 Sheaf, 1643 Orm², 'bridge with, or at, a gate
or barrier', *v.* barre, brycg. The bridge is at the south-east end of
Watfield Pavement 323 *infra,* and the name may allude to this fact.
It crosses the now un-named stream on the boundary between
Wardle 322 *infra* and Stoke (*v.* R. Bar **1** 14), and gives name to a
hamlet Barbridge here. *Bar Mill* 1775 Sheaf, at Bar Bridge, is named
after R. Bar, *v.* myln.

BULLSGREEN FM, *Bulls Green* 1719 Sheaf, perhaps 'green where the
bull stands', from bula and grēne², but a surname *Bull* is possible.
GEORGE'S ROUGH, *v.* rūh.   THE ROOKERY.   SANDHOLE, *v.* sand,
hol¹.   VERONA, 1842 OS, *Marony Farm* 1831 Bry.

FIELD-NAMES

The undated forms are 1841 *TA* 371.

(*a*) Adder Fd (*v.* nǣddre); Barrow (*v.* bearu); Bath Croft (*v.* bæð);
Bithones (*v.* byðme); Bone Fd (*v.* bān, cf. bone-dust); Bradley (*v.* brād,
lēah); Carters Greece (*v.* cartere, grese); Dam Croft (*v.* damme); Flatt;
Gamesley (perhaps 'Gamel's wood or clearing', from the pers.n. ON *Gamall,*
ODan *Gamal* and lēah, cf. *Gamelesmeduwe* 150 *supra*); Gamford; Hough
(*v.* hōh); Low Moor; Mill Lees (cf. *Milnehey* 1467 *AddCh, molendinum de
Stoke* 1354 *Rental, v.* myln, lǣs, (ge)hæg); Moorsleys; Pingot (*v.* pingot);
Pool Mdw; Sand(hole) Fd; Wectainley Mdw; Well Croft; Will Mdw (*v.*
wella); Withy Fd (*v.* wīðig); Wobs (*v.* cwabba); Worthens Fd (*v.* worðign).

(*b*) le *Hache* 1286 Court (p), *Hatche* 1313 IpmR ('the gate', *v.* hæcc);
Lewynescroft E2 *AddCh* ('Lēofwine's croft', from the OE pers.n. *Lēofwine*
and croft).

15. WORLESTON (110–6656) ['wɔːrlstn̥]

Werblestune 1086 *DB* 265b (Tait 157 reads *Wereles-*)
Uerulestane in Wicesfeld 1096–1101 (1150), 1150 Chest, *Weruele-
stona in Wischefeld* 1096–1101 (1280) ib

Werflest' 1175 Facs 3, p. 8 (Chest 487 reads *Werrestona*)
Woruleston' 13 Dieul
Werleston 1216–50 Chest, 13 *AddCh et freq* with variant spellings
    -is-, *-as-*, *-us-*, *-tona*; (*-juxta Henhull*) 1367 Orm[2]
Worlaston 1274 Ipm, *Worleston* 1282 Court *et freq* with variant
    spellings *-as-*, *-is-*, *-us-*; (*-alias Wordelaston*) 1574 *AddCh*,
    Worlston 1521 *ib*, *Worleston Green* 1831 Bry
Wordliston 1288 Court (p), *-es-* 1424 Orm[2], 1538 Plea, 1542
    ChRR, *-as-* 1521, 1574 *AddCh*, *Wordeleston* 1440 Plea, *-as-*
    1544 *AddCh*, (*Worleston alias-*) 1574 *ib*, *Wordelston* 1482 Rich,
    -il- 1536 Sheaf
Worldeston 1417 Rich, 1515 *Dav*, 1524, 1545 Plea
Warlaston 1519, 1521 Plea, *-es-* 1526 ChRR

A difficult p.n. containing tūn 'a farmstead or an enclosure'. The
comparison with *Werlington* Sx in Sx 442, is irrelevant. Mr L. C.
Hector of the Public Record Office confirms that the form in *DB* (the
Exchequer original) is WERBLESTUNE with a rustic capital *B*. This
rustic *B* represents *b* for *v* in minuscule, but the capital *B* has been
mistaken for capital *E* by editors. The first el. in the p.n. is therefore
a form *Werfles-*, *Werv(e)les-* with an alternative form *Worv-*. Taking
this p.n. and *Wordesham* 318 *infra* to contain the same first el., and
noting the f.n. Trundle Moor in Tilstone Fearnall the same township
as *Wordesham*, the first el. might be identified as hwerfel 'a circle,
something round', but neither archaeology nor topography at these
places clearly proves this. The absence of *Wh-* spellings is unexpected
if hwerfel is the first el., and the alternative *Wer-*, *Wor-* spellings
suggest an original OE *weor-* form rather than (*h*)*wer-*. Ekwall's
derivation (DEPN) from the OE pers.n. *Wǣrwulf* would require a
contracted form *War-*, *Werulf* (gen.sg. *Werulfes*) with metathesis to
War-, *Werf(e)les-*, and the absence of even an occasional regular
Werulves- form alongside the irregular metathesised one is curious.
Professor Löfvenberg writes, 'Neither of the etymologies suggested
is satisfactory from a formal point of view. I would suggest the
following solution. The name consists of OE tūn and a compound
p.n. in the gen. case.' (*v.* *-es*[2]). 'The compound may be formally
identical with Warley Salop and Warley Wigorn Wo 302, derived by
Ekwall (DEPN, Studies[2] 63–4) from an OE **Weorfa-lēah*, **Weorfes-
lēah* "pasture for (draught) cattle", the first el. being the gen. pl. and
sg. of OE *weorf* "beast of burden, cattle". The gen. of the p.n. OE

Weorfa-lēah, -lēh may have been *Weorfa-lēas, -lēs*. The meaning would be "the farmstead by *Weorfa-lēh*" or "the farmstead of, called, *Weorfa-lēh*". For similar p.n. formations see Tengstrand 135, 281.' The el. **weorf** (*v.* EPN 2 254–5) also appears in Worsley Wo 74, Warracott D 200.

BEAM BRIDGE (110–652535) [biːm], BEAMBRIDGE (110–648536), *le Beem* E1 *AddCh*, 1340 *Eyre* (p), *le Bembrugg* 1302–6 *AddCh, le Beembrugge* 1344 *Eyre* (p), (*the*) *Beame Bridge* 1527, 1621, 1646 Sheaf, *Beam-bridge* 1643 Orm², (*-in Acton*) 1660 *AddCh*, cf. *le Beame medo(w)e* 1508, 1554 *AddCh, the Beam meadow* 1573 *ib, Beame Bridge Feild* 1639 Orm², *-Meadow* 1697 *AddCh*, 'bridge made of a beam, or of beams', *v.* **bēam, brycg**. The original structure seems to have been made of a single beam. The bridge crosses R. Weaver from Worleston into Nantwich township, 36 *supra*, and gives name to the hamlet in Worleston, to Beam St. and Beam Heath in Nantwich 32, 36 *supra*, and to the Nantwich f.n. (*The*) *Beame medowe* 1530, 1550 *AddCh*.

BROOK FM, *v.* **brōc**.   DAIRYHOUSE FM, *v.* **deierie, hūs**.   BIG & LITTLE EEL CAGE, *v.* **æl, cage**.   THE GRANGE.   HOLLOWS BRIDGE, 'bridge at the hollows', *v.* **holh, brycg**.   HOME FM, *v.* **home**.   MILE HOUSE, *The-* 1831 Bry, from **hūs** and **mīl** 'a mile', perhaps from its being one mile from Beam Bridge *supra*, but cf. foll.   REASE HEATH, REASEHEATH (OLD) HALL [riːs-], *Rease Heath Hall* 1772 Orm², 1842 *TAMap, Raseheath Hall* 1789 Sheaf, *Rees Heath* (*Hall*) 1831 Bry, 1842 OS, *Worleston Heath* 1326 Cre, *Werlestonheth* 1406 ib, *le Worleston heth* 1487 Rich, *v.* **hǣð**. The modern name may be 'heath where races were held', from **ras** (ModE *race*, dial. [riəs, riːs]), and Mile Ho *supra* might have been a distance-mark for competitors.   ROOKERY BRIDGE, *Worleston Bridge* 1842 OS, cf. foll.   ROOKERY HALL, 1831 Bry, *v.* **rookery**.   ROSEHEATH HALL.   WHITEGATE.

FIELD-NAMES

The undated forms are 1843 *TA* 449. Of the others 1216–50, p.1266 are Chest, 1297, c.1300, 1683 *Chol*, 1300 ChF, 1300 (18), 1439–40 Orm², 1340 *ChFor*, 1416, 1437, 1520, 1542 ChRR, 1487 Rich, and the rest *AddCh*.

(*a*) Annesey Fd & Mdw; The Bache (*v.* **bæce¹**); Barker's Heath (*v.* **barcere, hǣð**); Bellows Fd; Black-, Blake Fd (*v.* **blæc**); Black Lake Fd (*v.* **blæc, lacu**); Brock Mdw (*v.* **brocc**); Brook- & Lane Bar Fd (cf. Bar Bridge

151 *supra*); The Bury, Bury Fd (apparently from burh, but the significance is not known); the Buttey Landes 1683 ('selions held by butts', *v.* butty, land); Cockering; Colley('s) Croft, Colliery Mdw (*v.* colig, ModE *colliery*); Green Fd (*the Greene Feild* 1683, *v.* grēne[1]); Hanging Fd (*v.* hangende); Hill Fd (*the- -feild* 1683, *v.* hyll); Hitchen (perhaps from hiche); Howe Mdw (*v.* hōh); Kiln Fd; Kitchen Fd; Lordley's Heys (*le Lordes Weyhey* 1520, *Lord' Weyhey* 1542, 'the lord of the manor's enclosure near a road', from weg and (ge)hæg, with hláford, cf. foll.); Lord's Mdw (*the Lords Meddow* 1683, *v.* hláford, mǣd, cf. prec.); Mill Fd (cf. *molendinum de Werleston(a)* 1216–50, p. 1266, *molendinum aquaticum* 1391, *v.* myln); The Motts (*v.* mote); Oak Heys (*v.* āc, (ge)hæg); Ox pasture; Park Fd (cf. *parcum* (*de Worleston*) 1300, 1333, the old ditch near the park 1300 (18), *le Lyttyll Parke* 1487, *v.* park); Upper Pocket (*v.* poket); Lower & Upper Port (*v.* port); Salt Mdw (*v.* salt); Spurstow Flatt (*v.* flat, probably with a surname from Spurstow 315 *infra*); Stackyard Fd (*v.* stak-ʒard); Water Fd (*v.* wæter); Weir Fd (*v.* wer).

(b) *le Blakheth* 1478 (*v.* blæc, hǣð); *Hinsall* 1391 (cf. Hinshall 148 *supra*); *le hurst* l13, 1297, cf. *boscus de Mondrem in Worleston* 1320, *boscus de Werliston* l13, *-Worleston* 1297, *-Werleston* c.1300, 1340 (*v.* hyrst and wudu, cf. *Mondrem* 1 10); *New Fylde* 1520, 1542 (*v.* nīwe, feld); *the Skippon Crofts* 1573 (*v.* scypen, croft); *Whiteforlong(es Medewe)* 1300, *Qwytforlong(esmedwe)* 1301, *Quidforlong* 1302–6, *Whytfurlonge* 1416, *Whitfurlong* 1437, *-furlonge* 1439 (*v.* hwīt, furlang, mǣd).

xvi. Church Minshull

Church Minshull was formerly a chapelry of Acton parish 126 *supra*, and seems to have become a separate parish in the eighteenth century, *v.* Orm[2] III 336, 341.

CHURCH MINSHULL (110–6660) & MINSHULL VERNON (2 247) [ˈminʃəl]

Maneshale, Manessele 1086 DB

Mun(s)chulf(e) c.1130 (1230) (1331) Ch, 1266 (1331) ib *et freq* with variant spellings *Mun(e)sulf, Munsulcf, Munsulft, Mun(i)shulf, Munesschuf* to 1344 AddCh, *Chirchemunsulf* l13 AddCh

Muneshull c.1200 AddCh *et freq* with variant spellings *-is-, -ys-, -us-, -hul(l), Munihshull* to 1297 Chol (p), *Muns(c)hul(l), -hulle* 1260, 1287 Court, l13 AddCh, *Munsshull* 1360 Orm[2], *Munschehull* 1361 ChFor, *Munch(e)hul(l)* 1285 (17) Sheaf (p), 1311 ChRR, 1322 Chol (p), 1331 AddCh (p), (*le*) *Chirch(e)-munschull* 1289 Court, 1310 AddCh, 1416 ChRR, *Churche-* 1342 AD, 1360 BPR, *Chirchemunchul* 1315 AddCh, *Muns(c)hul(l)verno(u)n* 1308, 1311 *ib*, 1309 AD, 1351 Plea, 1391 AddRoll, 1394 AddCh, *Munshulle vernon* 1420 *ib*

Munsel 1244 *AddCh* (p)
Mun(e)shal(l) 1246 Orm[2] (p), 1272 (17) Chest (p), *Munshall Vernon* 1325 Plea
Mun(e)s(s)ul(l) 1259 Plea, 1260 Court, 13 *Chol* (p)
Munshil 1262 *AddCh*
Munessuhel c.1270-80 *AddCh* (p)
Moinshull (*iuxta Wermingham*) 1287, 1290 Court
Kirke-, *Chirchemonishull* 1288, 1289 Court, *Monishull* 1290 *Eyre* (p)
Munchalf 1309 Adl (p)
Min-, *Mynshul(l)* 1316 Plea, 1319 MidCh (p) *et freq* with variant
  spelling *Mynschull* from 1436 Tab; *Minchull* 1361 ChRR (p),
  Myn- 1435 *Chol* (p), *Minnishulle* 1421 AD (p), *Minshull Vernon*
  1394 ChRR, *-Varnon* 1607 *AddCh*, *Myns(c)hull Vernon* 1428
  (1551) ChRR, 1436 Tab, *Mynchull Vernon* 1527 Plea, *Church
  Minshull* 1396 ChRR, *Church(e) Mynshul(l)* 1428 (1521 & 1551)
  ChRR, 1460 (1471), 1498 ib, *Chirch(e)-* 1435 ChRR, 1460
  ChCert
Munhul' 1318 *Eyre*
Munhchull' 1322 *Chol* (p)
Munchnull 1323 *AddCh*
Mumshull 1334 ChRR (p)
Munskill 1346 Bark (p)
Muchel Vernoun 1353 BPR
Muschull 1357 *ChFor*
Chirchemynghull 1377 Plea
Minshall 1383 (1619) *Chol* (p), 1621 (1656) Orm[2], (*-Vernon*) 1425
  MidCh, *Mynshall Vernon* 1537 MidCh
Minchell 1660 Sheaf

'Mann's scylfe', from the OE pers.n. *Mann, Monn* and scylfe. The
second el. probably means 'shelf'. It has been confused with halh,
hyll and sele[1]. Church Minshull, on the west bank of R. Weaver,
occupies a broad shelving terrain between the river and the 150 ft.
contour, whereas the east bank at that point comes very close to that
contour. The affix is cirice 'a church', because this part of Minshull
contained a parish church.

DUTTON (lost, 110–665618), as in (*Far*) *Duttons* 1838 *TA*, cf. 'a
place of land in Church Minshull, bounded on one side by Richard
de Wettenhall's hedge, which is called *Dutton*' 113 *AddCh*, c.1303 *ib*,
'Richard de Wettenhall's *Dutton*'' 1325 *ib* (lit. *Richarddus Dutton*' de

Wetenale), *Greneduton* c.1230 *ib*, 'the lower half of *Duttone*' 13 *ib*, *Duttun* (a field, towards Wimboldsley) 1262 *AddCh*, 'farmyard or enclosure at a hill', from dūn and tūn, with grēne[1] 'green', cf. Dutton **2** 112.

LEE GREEN (HALL), *Legh Grene* 1550 ChRR, *Leigh Green(e)* 1598 AD, 1619 Sheaf, *Lee-* 1616 ib, *Lee-green Hall* 1724 NotCestr, cf. *le Leghemor* 1314, 1318 *AddCh*, '(green and moor at) the wood or clearing', *v.* lēah, grēne[2], mōr[1].

WADES GREEN (HALL), 1831 Bry, *Wades' Green* 1619 Sheaf, cf. *Wades Meadow* 1838 *TA*, named after the *Wade* family, resident here 1554–1754 (Sheaf[3] 17 (4110)), *v.* grēne[2].

WOODGREEN FM & LANE, 1831 Bry, *the woodgrene* 1567 AD, 'green at a wood', *v.* wudu, grēne[2], cf. 137 *supra*, and *boscus de Moneshull'* 113 *ChFor*, *-Munsul* 1278 *AddCh*, *Munshul(l)wod(e)* 1337 *ib*, 1340, 1347 *ChFor*, *boscus de Mu(n)schull* 1347, 1357 *ib*, one of the woods of the forest of *Mondrem* **1** 10, cf. *boscus de Mondrem* c.1304 *AddCh* (in Church Minshull) and Bricius *de Mondrem* 1360 Orm[2] (at Church Minshull). The forest's wood of Minshull included Wimboldsley **2** 257, and therefore probably Minshull Vernon also, cf. *manerium de Wymbaldesle in bosco de Moneshull'* 113 *ChFor*. Woodgreen Lane may be the same as *Wetenalewei* 1335 *AddCh*, 'way leading to Wettenhall', from weg and Wettenhall, cf. Wettenhall Wood 167 *infra*. Part of it, 137 *supra*, formed the boundary between Cholmondeston and Wettenhall.

ASHBROOK BRIDGE & TOWERS, *Astbrook bridge* 1621 Sheaf, *Ashbrook-* 1831 Bry, cf. Thomas de *Astebrok* 1329 Plea, from Ash Brook **1** 14 *v.* brycg.   CHURCH MINSHULL BRIDGE, *Minshall Bridge* 1619, 1621 Sheaf, cf. *le Bruggeheye* 1314 *AddCh*, *v.* brycg, (ge)hæg.   CORN MILL, *Mill* 1831 *TA*, cf. *le milneheye* 1391 *AddRoll*, *molendinum de Munsel* 1244 *AddCh*, and 'two water-mills in *Chirchemunshull*, one on the river next to the hall of *Hulgreve* (Old Hoolgrave **2** 248) and the other on a dam next to the hall of *Chirchemunshull* (Minshull Hall *infra*) 1343 *AddCh* 50840, *v.* myln, (ge)hæg.   DODD'S HOLLOW. HOME FM.   MANOR FM.   MINSHULL HALL FM, *Minshull Hall* (*Wood*) 1831 Bry, 'the hall of *Chirchemunshull*' 1343 *AddCh*, *the hall of Mynshull* 1575 Sheaf, cf. Minshull Fd *infra*, *v.* hall, mæd, (ge)hæg, lȳtel, wudu.   MINSHULL LANE, *Wood Green Lane* 1842

OS, cf. Outlanes Fm *infra*, Woodgreen Lane *supra*. NANNEY'S
BRIDGE. OUT LANES, 1842 OS, a farm, 'at the outlying lanes', *v.*
ūte, lane, cf. foll. OUTLANES FM, *Minshull Lane Farm* 1831 Bry.
This and prec. are taken from the road near them, probably the same
as *Astonewey* 1318 *AddCh*, 'outlying lanes', 'lane to Minshull', 'way
to Aston', *v.* lane, weg, cf. prec., Church Minshull *supra*, Aston
iuxta Mondrum 128 *supra*. PARADISE GREEN, 1831 Bry, from
paradis 'a pleasure garden, an enclosed garden' and grēne[2].
ROSALIE FM, *Tall Tree House* 1831 Bry. SANDICROFT WOOD, cf.
Sondicroft 13 *AddCh* and *Sand Croft* 1838 *TA*, *v.* sandig, croft.
WILLOWTREE FM. YEWTREE HO, 1842 OS.

FIELD-NAMES

The undated forms are 1838 *TA* 117. Of the others, 1323 is *Chol*, 1326, 1328,
1350[1] Adl, 1331, 1340, 1347, 1357 *ChFor*, 1350[2], 1353 *Eyre*, 1358 Plea, 1390
Orm[2], 1391 *AddRoll*, 1514, 1554 ChRR, 1567, 1579, 1598 AD, 1831 Bry, and
the rest *AddCh*.

(a) Avendrill Hill ('daffodil hill', *v.* affadille); Bear Croft (*v.* bær[1]);
Bended Eye Mdw (*v.* ēg); Birch (wood in *le Byrche* 1326, *v.* bryce); Black Fd;
Boroughs (*Burrowes meadowe* 1617, *v.* borow 'a burrow'); Bottoms (*v.* botm);
Brick Mdw (*v.* bryke); Bye Croft (*v.* byge[1]); Cade Croft; Church Fd;
Clappersongs; Coat Fd (*v.* cot); Cross Fd (*v.* cros); Davenports Fd (*-Lane*
1598, from the surname *Davenport*, cf. Davenport 2 301); (Four-, etc.)
Daymath (*v.* day-math); Denfords (*Derneford* l13, 'hidden ford', *v.* derne,
ford); Dowery Croft (*v.* dowarie); Great & Little Flatt; Green Fd (cf. *le
grenelond* c.1304, *le Grenacres* 1313, *v.* grēne[1], land, æcer); Hall Fd & Heys
(cf. *le heye* 1314, *le hallemedow* 14, *la Heye qest entour la manoir de Munschull*
1359, *v.* (ge)hæg, Minshull Hall Fm *supra*); Hemp Yard (*v.* hemp-yard);
Hetchells ((*le*) *Echeles* c.1304, 1313, *the echowes* 1567, *Etchus* 1617, *v.* ēcels,
cf. Etchells 1 239); Hillocks; Holy Mdw; Intake (*v.* inntak); Karry Croft
(*v.* kjarr, -ig[3]); Many Mdw; Marled Fd; Middle Fd (cf. *le middelfeld* c.1304,
-ul- c.1313, *Mydul-* 1320–40, *v.* middel); Milking Fd (*v.* milking); Minshull
Fd (cf. *Munshullheie* 14, Minshull Hall, Hall Fd *supra*, *v.* (ge)hæg); New
Hayes (*v.* nīwe, (ge)hæg); Outlett (*v.* outlet); Big- & Little Pale (*v.* pale);
Pavement Fd (*v.* pavement); Peacock's Fd (*pecokesfeld* 14, probably from a
pers. by-name *Peacock*); Pool Fd (cf. *Poolfield Cover* 1831, *v.* pōl[1], feld);
Priest Fd (*v.* prēost); Red Start Beech (*v.* bece[1]); Riddings (*the Ryddinges*
1579, cf. *de Assartis* 13 (p), *Bleytherudyng* 1325, from ryding with blīðe
'cheerful'); Royals Ground (cf. The Royals 102 *supra*); Shooting Butt Fd;
Sprink (*v.* spring 'a young wood'); Tom Fd, Town Fd & Mdw (*Town
Meadow* 1576, *v.* toun); Turf Cote Croft ('hut built of turves', *v.* turf, cot);
Twambrooks (*Twenebrok* 1331, 'between the brooks', *v.* betwēonan, brōc,
the later form means 'at the two brooks', *v.* twēgen (dat. twǣm), cf. Twam-
brook 2 195); Well Croft (cf. (*le*) *Wallecroft* 1324, *v.* wælla, wella, croft);

Wooden Bridge 1831 (a bridge over R. Weaver at 110–673630); Wood End (*v.* wudu, ende[1]).

(*b*) *Atterugge* 1347 (p) ('at the ridge', *v.* atte, hrycg); *Bacun* 113 ('at the ridges', from OE *bacum*, dat.pl. of bæc); *Blacsheche* c.1304 (p), *Blak-* 1312 (p) (*v.* blæc, sīc); *le brer'greve* 1320–40 ('the briar wood', *v.* brēr, grǣfe); *dil Brok'* 1323 (p), *les brokes* 1357 (*v.* brōc); *Byrusbrok(es)* 113, *Buresbrok'* 1317 ('brooks at a byre', *v.* bȳre, brōc); *Caluylegheway* 1343 'the way to Calveley', from weg and Calveley 307 *infra*); *Cleyforlond* 13, *-long* c.1304, *Cleifor(r)long'* 1307–27, *Cleyfurlong'* 1325 (*v.* clæg, furlang); *le Cnotelmor* 113, *Knotelmor* 1310 ('waste land at a hill', from cnotta and hyll, with mōr[1]); *le Cokschete* 1325 (*v.* cocc-scyte); *le Croftes* 1391 (p) (*v.* croft); *parcum de Dafahale* 1328, *maner' de Dayshale* 1350[1] (*v.* halh); *sichetum del Dene* 113 ('watercourse in a valley', *v.* sīc, denu); *le firefeld* c.1313 ('field where a fire burns', *v.* fȳr, feld); *le gatestok* 1310 ('the gate-stump', *v.* geat, stocc); *le grimebroc* 1277 ('goblin-brook', *v.* grīma[2], brōc); *le Haukesherd* 1357 ('the hawk's gap', *v.* hafoc-scerde, cf. Hawkers Head 2 249, the *Hawkesyord* 1 166); *Heghgreue* 1350[2] (p) ('high wood', *v.* hēah, grǣfe); *Helleclif* 1331 (the final el. is clif or klif 'a cliff, a bank'. The first el. may be helde 'a hill-side', but cf. hell, hella, hellir, hjalli, hjallr. Eel Brook 1 22 appears as *Hell Brook* 1831 Bry, and is probably associated with *Helleclif*); *le Heyehuyrne* 1358 (p) ('corner with an enclosure in it', *v.* (ge)hæg, hyrne); *le holm* 1317, *le holmmedwe* 1343 ('the island, the water-meadow', *v.* holmr, mǣd, cf. *Longey infra*); *le horestonele, le hor'stonele* 1310 ('(clearing at) the grey stone', from hār[2] and stān, with lēah); *le Hourselond* 1320–40 ('horse land', *v.* hors, land); *le hurtysbut* c.1270 (*v.* butte 'a head-land'); (*le*) *Hympe Wort, le Himpe-, Hympeʒort* 1317 (the name of an orchard, *v.* impa, geard, worð, impe-ʒard); *Lethenardeseye, Lethenardesewe* 113, *Leuenaldisheye* 1300–20, *Leuenardisheye* 1312, *Lethenardesheye* (*medue*) 1314, 1317, *Lethenhardesheye* 1357 (this was assarted meadow-land beside R. Weaver, and the final el. ēg 'an island, a water meadow' is replaced by (ge)hæg 'a fenced-in enclosure, *v.* also mǣd. The initial el. appears to be a ME pers.n. *Lethen(h)ard, Leuenard*, of obscure origin, also appearing in *Lethenardishustudes* 1 125, but not otherwise known. It appears to be OE *-heard*, OHG *-hard*, with a prototheme *Leðen-*, cf. the OSwed pers.n. *Lidhinvardh* (Lundgren-Brate 167), also Leavening YE 148. However, Dr von Feilitzen notes that *Lidhinvardh* is an unreliable form and observes that Leavening is differently explained in DEPN. He does not find an analogy for the *Lethen(h)ard* of the Ch p.ns. Professor Löfvenberg suggests that these p.ns. contain a ME pers.n. of French origin, and points to the Norman name *Lévenard* (a side-form of *Léonard, v.* A. Dauzat, *Dictionnaire des noms de famille et prénoms en France*, 382), and compares the interchange of *v* and *th* with the ME spellings of Earswick YN 12 and the examples in YW 7 92); (*le*) *light Aspes* 1340, 14, 1390, *leght Haspes* 1514, *Light Ashes* 1554 ('the bright aspens', *v.* lēoht, æspe); *Longey* 1310, *Longeylondus hende, Longeymedue* 1320–40 ('long island or water-meadow', *v.* lang, ēg, ēg-land, ende[1], mǣd); *Longe forlong'* 1304 (*v.* lang, furlang); *Le Lowe* 1353 (p) (*v.* hlāw); *le Markedeput* 1318 ('marked pit', from the ME pa.part. *marked* and pytt); *le Merstal'* 113 (perhaps 'site of a boundary-marker', from (ge)mǣre, stall, but, as in *le Merestal* 2 269, probably 'a pool, a pond of stagnant water' from mere-steall, or 'mare's stall' from mere², stall. In view of the frequency of this type, the derivation from OE mere-steall is the most likely one); *le Mormedewe* 13 ('marsh meadow', *v.* mor¹, mǣd); *Mos(e)-, Mouscote* 1347 ('cottage infested with mice', *v.* mūs, cot, cf. Muscoates YN 65, DEPN, Muscott Nth 27); *Northfordesheye* 1357 ('(enclosure at) the north ford', *v.* norð, ford, (ge)hæg); *Hormesrudyng* 1314, 1317 ('Orm's clearing', from the ON pers.n. *Ormr* and ryding); *le Pyndludehok* l13 (probably from āc, 'an oak'. The first el. appears to be pa.part. adj, perhaps related to *pindling* NED, and meaning 'withered, shrunken'; cf. ModEdial. *pindert* (pa.part., representing *pindled*(?)) 'shrivelled, dried up, burnt' EDS 42, 260, and *pinder* EDD); *Redecocyssuleyn* l13 ('Redcock's ploughland', from a ME pers.n. *Redecoc* with sulh, leyne); *Sycheforlonk* c.1270 ('furlong near a water-course', *v.* sīc, furlang); *Siwardesruding* 1300–20 ('Seward's clearing', from the OE pers.n. *Sigeweard* and ryding); *Tolkenheye* 1325, *le Tockenhaymedwe* 1343 (*v.* (ge)hæg, mǣd. The first el. appears to be OE *tācn* 'a sign, a token'); *Tunstaldich* 1335 ('ditch at the site of a tūn', *v.* tūn-stall, dīc); *le Twi-, le Twyssed hook* l13 ('the forked or double-stemmed oak', from āc and a ME pa.part. adj *twissed*, from (ge)twis 'a fork, branches of a common stem'); *le Wheteberne* 14 ('wheat barn', *v.* hwǣte, bere-ærn); *Wythynelache, Wythynesiche* 1317 ('stream growing with willows', *v.* wiðigen, lǣc(c), sīc); *Wlfrichilshale* 13, *Wlfrischishalc* c.1305 ('Wulfric's nook', from the OE pers.n. *Wulfrīc* and halh, halc); *le yatefeld* 14 ('field at a gate', *v.* geat, feld).

V. EDDISBURY HUNDRED

Eddisbury Hundred

Riseton(e)-, Risedon Hund', Roelau Hund' 1086 DB, *hundredum de Edesberi* 112 *Chol, -Edisbur(y)* 1260 Court *et freq* with spellings as for Eddisbury 213 *infra*

The meeting-place of this hundred was at Eddisbury 213 *infra*. This hundred did not exist in 1086, but was in existence by 1180–1200, the date of a deed (*Chol*, Box J) specifying the tenure of two bovates of land at Bunbury by the provision, for that township, at that hundred, of one *motsechindemon* ('a man who seeks, or goes to, the meeting' from OE (*ge*)*mōt*, ME *mot* 'a moot, a meeting' and ME *sechinde*, pres.part. of *sechen* (OE *sēcean*) 'to seek'). The territory of the later Eddisbury hundred was disposed in four of the DB hundreds of Cheshire, *Dudestan, Mildestuic(h)* (Northwich), *Riseton* and *Roelau*. In *Mildestuic(h)* (*v.* 2 184) was Weaver 163 *infra*. In *Dudestan* (*v.* 326 *infra*) were two districts, first, that of Alpraham, Little Budworth, Rushton, Over, *Alretone* (which seems to have been at the south side of Delamere, *v.* 211 *infra*) and presumably *Opetone* (*v. infra*), and second, the vill of Thornton le Moors. In *Roelau* hundred (*v.* Ruloe 196 *infra*), were the lost place *Done* (*infra*) and the remaining territory of Eddisbury hundred north and east of, and excluding, Barrow, Great Mouldsworth, Ashton, Kelsall, Willington and Utkinton and the first portion of *Dudestan* hundred. In *Riseton* hundred (*v.* Rushton 291 *infra*, itself in *Dudestan* hundred, *v. supra*) were the lost *Cocle* and *Ulure* and the rest of the southern part of Eddisbury hundred. The hundredal organisation of this area appears to have been already complex by 1086, and the afforestation of the great Forest of Delamere, which came to include virtually the entire hundred, might well have given the impetus for a simplification, whereby the administrative centre of the forest became that of the hundred. It may also be the result of afforestation and post-Conquest devastation, that there is a number of lost DB manors in the area. Since they cannot be precisely located, they are listed here.

Cocle (DB f. 266b, in *Riseton* hundred), probably 'cock wood', from cocc[2] and lēah, has had locations proposed in Kelsall township or

Over parish, *v.* Tait 189, n. 182. Kelsall is in *Riseton* territory; Over parish was partly in *Dudestan* and *Riseton* territory.

ULURE (DB f.265, in *Riseton* hundred). Tait 145 and Sheaf[3] 4, 132, suggest this was in Wardle or Calveley. The p.n. is difficult, for lack of any further instance. It may be 'wolf hill' from **wulf** and **ufer** (cf. Over 170 *infra*), but the name might also contain the lenited form of **bre** 'a hill', with an undetermined first el.

DONE (DB f.263b, in *Roelau* hundred and 'the earl's forest'), 'at the hill', *v.* **dūn**. This could be the same place as *le Donneswode* 1347, *le Dounewod* 1357 *ChFor* (PRO, Chester 33, 4, m.10, 6, m.23), a wood in the Forest of Delamere. The location of this wood has not been found. There is a lost *Duntun* in Little Budworth 187 *infra*, but that township is not in *Roelau* hundred. Gooseberry Lane 212 *infra* in Delamere was *Dan Town* 1831 Bry, but the earlier history of that name has not appeared, so a connection cannot be drawn. The DB place may have given surname to the *Done* family of Utkinton 298 *infra* (cf. Orm[2] II 243 n.). *Done* and Tarporley (294 *infra*, near Utkinton) were both held TRE by one *Ulviet* (OE *Wulfgēat*).

OPETONE (DB f.263b, in *Dudestan* hundred), 'the high(er) farm', from **upp** and **tūn**. Tait 109 observes that if this is not a lost vill in the detached part of *Dudestan* hundred, being listed between Rushton and Little Budworth, then it must be Upton by Chester. However, DB places Upton by Chester in *Wilaveston* (Wirral) hundred, though it is now in Broxton hundred. It may be significant that the other lost vill of *Dudestan* hundred within the bounds of Eddisbury hundred, *Alreton*, may be located in Delamere, *v.* 211 *infra*, and this *Opetone* may not have been far from it.

Geographically, Eddisbury hundred is bounded by the Mersey to the north, the R. Weaver to the east, Nantwich hundred to the south, and the R. Gowy and Broxton and Wirral hundreds to the west and north-west. This area contains the uplands of the sandstone Central Ridge, which runs from Frodsham and Helsby southwards to Beeston, and then on into Broxton hundred to Bickerton. This up-land, its central part occupied by the Forest of Delamere, consists of a series of broken sandstone plateaux, with a light covering of glacial drift, sloping down eastward towards the deep, wooded valley of the R. Weaver in a series of great fans of glacial sand and gravel. In pre-historic times, these districts appear to have supported a dry oak woodland on the plateaux with open tracts on the gravels. To the west, a steep, rocky, often precipitous and craggy escarpment descends from heights of between 400 and 700 feet to a shelf at between 200 and 300 feet. This shelf under the sandstone scarp is of variable soils, and is drained by the silted, once peat-bearing, marsh-lands of the Gowy and the wooded valleys of its tributaries. Its width varies greatly. It is narrow at Frodsham and Helsby, but north-westward from Mouldsworth it extends as far as Ince, a peninsula of low sandstone outcrops forming the firm ground which separates the Gowy marshes from those of Peckmill Brook and the R. Mersey. The south-east of the hundred is within the edge of the R. Weaver basin and its catchment area of glacial and alluvial gravels and marls. On this side, the hundred has no well-marked natural boundary.

LOST OR UNIDENTIFIED PLACE-NAMES IN EDDISBURY HUNDRED (the forms are *ChFor*, except where stated):

Alslees 1503; *Coluesdale* 1357, *Collesdale* 1503 (*v.* dæl[1]); *le Newe Copy*, *le Old(e)copy* 1503 (woods in the Forest of Delamere, *v.* nīwe, ald, copis); *Culuemonchegge* 1357 (*v.* hecg); *le Elbowe Oke* 1503 (*v.* elbowe, āc); *Hepelegh* 1357 ('wild-rose clearing', *v.* hēopa, lēah); *Hunterforde* 1503 ('hunter's ford', *v.* huntere, ford); *Longlake* 1503 ('long watercourse', *v.* lang, lacu); *Misden Slak* 1503 (probably '(hollow at) the mossy valley', from mēos and denu, with slakki); *Monythornefeld(e)* 1503 ('(open land at) many thorns', *v.* manig, þorn, feld); *Otter-*, *Otturbache* 1503 ('otter stream or valley', *v.* oter, bæce[1]); *le Pullehous* 1357 *Eyre* (p) ('house by a pool or creek', *v.* pull, hūs); *Rakedene(heued)* 1357 ('(the head of) the valley with a road in it', from rake and denu, with hēafod); *Randeletescrosse* 1357 ('Randelet's cross', from cros and a ME diminutive form of the pers.n. *Randle*, from *Randulf*); *Stanmere* 1503 ('stone pool', *v.* stān, mere[1]); *Tunstedehull*, *le Tunestudeslac* 1357 ('(hill and hollow at) the site of a farm or enclosure', from tūn-stede, -styde, with hyll, slakki).

i. Middlewich

One township of this parish, Weaver, is in Eddisbury Hundred, although it lay with the rest of the parish in *Mildestuic(h)* hundred DB, *v.* 160 *supra*. The date of transfer is not known, and is probably part of the post-conquest reorganisation of the hundreds. Weaver is now included in Darnhall township.

14. WEAVER (HALL) (110–6664) ['wi:vər]

Wevre 1086 DB, Weure c.1200 Dugd, 1225 VR (p), 1240 P (p) et
   freq with variant spelling Wevre to 1353 BPR (p), Wefre 1240 P
   (p), a.1271 MidCh (p)
Weueria 1205–15 Facs (p), Weuere e13 Cre (p), Wevere 1259
   Court (p) et freq with variant spellings Weuer(e), Wever, -ir to
   1724 NotCestr, le Weuere 1369 Tab (p), Weuerhe 14 Sotheby (p)
Weeuer 1250 MidCh (p) et freq ib, 1386 ChRR (p) et freq with
   variant spelling Weever to 1819 Orm², Weeuere 1330 MidCh (p),
   Weevor 1596 Orm², Weever Hall 1713 ib
Wewere c.1270–80 AddCh (p)
Wiuere 1278–82 AddCh, Wiure c.1284 VR, Wyure 1347 ChFor,
   Wyver 1400 ChRR (p), 1557 Pat, Wyuer 1492 MidCh (p)
Weauer 1484 MidCh (p), Weaver 1819 Orm², -or 1591 ib, Weaver
   Hall 1831 Bry

'Place on the R. Weaver', named from R. Weaver 1 38. Cf.
Weaverham 205 infra, Wivercot 327 infra. The form Weuerhe
probably has ēa 'river' suffixed to the r.n.

WEAVERWOOD FM (110–664635), 1831 Bry, Wood Farm 1842 OS, cf.
boscus de Weuere 1353 ChFor, Weuerewode 1367 AddCh, 'the wood
of Weaver', v. wudu, Weaver supra. This was part of the forest of
Delamere.

ASHBROOK BRIDGE & COTTAGES, Ashbrook Bridge 1831 Bry, v. 156
supra.   BADGER WOOD, v. bagga, wudu.   BOTTOM- & TOP
FLASH, v. flasshe. These are lakes caused by flooding of the R.
Weaver's valley after subsidence caused by salt workings, cf. 2 235.
HOP YARD WOOD, v. hoppe, geard.   NEW LANE, 1831 Bry, cf.
Weaverhall Lane infra.   OLD FARM (lost), 1842 OS, Pots House
1831 Bry, from the surname Pott, v. ald.   OWEN'S WOOD, Holding
Wood 1831 ib.   ROOKERY WOOD, Sheep Walk Wood 1831 ib,
1842 OS, v. scēp, walk.   SHAW'S WOOD.   SWANLOW LANE, v.
169 infra.   TRELFA'S WOOD, Rushey Wood 1831 Bry, v. riscig.
A family named Trelfa (i.e. Threlfall) lived at Weaver Hall in 1860
White.   WEAVER DAIRY HO, Dairy House 1831 Bry, v. deierie,
hūs.   WEAVERGROVE, 1842 OS, Grove House 1831 Bry v. grāf.
WEAVERHALL LANE, New Lane 1831 ib, v. New Lane supra.
WEAVER PARK FM, Barns Brow or School Bank 1831 ib, School Bank
1842 OS.

FIELD-NAMES

The forms are from *ChFor*, except 1671 Sheaf.

(*b*) *le Cleyerudyng* 1357 (*v.* clǣg, ryding); *le Dopeclowe* 1331 ('deep dell', *v.* dēop, clōh); *le grene* 1347 (*v.* grēne[2]); *Horestansich*, -*ston*- 1331 ('(water-course at) the old grey stone', from hār[2] and stān, with sīc); *Padokesmor* 1331 ('frog's marsh', *v.* padduc, mōr[1]); *pons de Weuere* 1357 ('bridge at Weaver', possibly Ashbrook Bridge *supra*); *Weever Mills Salthouses* 1671 (*v.* salt-hūs); *Wylmotteshurst* 1331 ('Willemot's wood-hill', from the ME pers.n. *Willemot* (ModE *Wil(l)mot(t)*), a diminutive of *William*, and hyrst).

ii & iii. Over & Whitegate

In addition to the Chapelry of Little Budworth 184 *infra*, Over parish appears to have contained originally the townships of Oulton Lowe, Wetten-hall, Darnhall, Over and Marton 165, 166, 168, 170, 182 *infra*. In Over township was the abbey of Vale Royal, with estates in Over parish and Weaverham parish. At the abbey gate was a church for the use of the abbey's tenants in these estates. After the dissolution of the abbey the church was made parochial (Statute 33 Henry VIII, cap. 32, *v.* Orm[2] II 145) and the newly created parish of Whitegate or New-Church consisted of Darnhall township, part of Over township (the demesne lands about the site of the abbey, shown as Whitegate township in 1831 Bry, together with Gavel Green, Salterswall, Brook Ho, *Sutton Grange* and Knights Grange 172, 173, 171, 179, 172 *infra*), and most of Marton township (all except a few fields about Marton hamlet and Marton Ho), and part of Weaverham township 202 *infra* (Hefferston Grange, Earnslow Grange, *Conewardsley*, Weaverhamwood and part of Sandiway 203, 207, 207, 210, 208 *infra*). The parish of Whitegate was divided into two parts (*v.* Orm[2] II 145, ChetOS VIII 264), Darnhall (containing only Darnhall township), and Newchurch (the rest). The follow-ing arrangement shows Whitegate parish integrated with the parent parish of Over, and avoids the confusion and fragmentation which would result from separating their parts.

Over and Whitegate parishes consisted of the following townships, 1. Oulton Lowe (Over parish, now included in Little Budworth c.p. 184 *infra*), 2. Wettenhall (Over parish), 3. Darnhall (included in Whitegate parish until 1876 when it reverted to Over parish, it is now a c.p. including Weaver 163 *supra*), 4. Over (Over and Whitegate parishes, included part of Marton *infra* and originally contained Whitegate *infra*. The townships of Over and Whitegate are now included in Winsford c.p., cf. Wharton **2** 202, 213, Winsford 173 *infra*, **2** 214), 5. Whitegate (originally part of Over township, described below by the boundaries given in 1831 Bry, cf. Over *supra*), 6. Marton (mostly in Whitegate parish, partly in Over parish), 7. parts of Weaverham township 202 *infra*.

1. Oulton Lowe (Cottage, Covert, Fm & Green) (110–6063)
['uːltən, 'oultən] older local ['uːtn̩]

   la Lawe 1225 VR (p), *Lawe* 1260 Court (p)
   (le) Lowe 1272–90, 1296 ChFor *et freq* to 1766 Wil, (*-iuxta Darnhale*)
      1294 ChF, (*-iuxta Buddeworth*) 1316 Plea, (*Olton et-*) 1357
      ChFor, 1611 ChRR, (*Oldynton et-*) 1382 *Chol*
   Oldyngton Lowe 1351 BPR, *Olton Lowe* 1353 ChFor *et freq*,
      (*Olton alias-*) 1526 ChRR, 1527 Plea, *-Low* 1671 Sheaf, *Oulton*
      Lowes 1480 ib, *-Low* 1687 Chol, *-Lowe* 1724 NotCestr, (*-Gorse*)
      1831 Bry, *Oultonlowe Green* 1845 *TA*
   Olton alias Haltonlawe 1557 Pat

'The hill (near Oulton)', from hlāw and Oulton 185 *infra*, with
grēne[2], gorst, cover. It is adjacent to Darnhall and Little Budworth
168, 184 *infra*. This manor has been identified with *Altetone* DB, *v.*
185 *infra*. Oultonlowe Green was *Cappars House* 1842 OS, probably
from a surname.

Darley Brook, Cottages, Gorse, Hall (110–607642) & Rough,
Derlegh'brok 1361 ChFor, *Derley* 1434 Orm[2], *Darlegh Brook* l15 ib,
Darley 1529 Tab *et freq*, (*the Hall of-*) 1613 Orm[2], (*-Hall*) 1666
Sheaf, (*-Gorse*) 1842 OS, *Darle* c.1536 Leland, 'deer glade', from
dēor and lēah, with brōc, gorst, hall, rūh. The Gorse was *The New
Gorse* 1831 Bry, *v.* nīwe. The brook becomes Ash Brook 1 14.

Adjuncts Covert, *Adjets Meadow* 1845 *TA*.   Ash Ho, 1831 Bry,
v. æsc.   Bawk Ho, *Bark House* 1831 ib, a tannery, *v.* bark(e).
Cocked Hat Covert, named from its shape.   Holmston Hall
(110–603627) ['houmstən], *Humpstones in Darley* 1671 Sheaf, *Holme-
stone Hall* 1831 Bry, 1842 OS, *Hulmeston Hall* 1845 *TA*, a p.n. which
occurs elsewhere in Ch, presumably meaning 'a hump of stones,
humped stones, stones on a hump or hillock', from hump and stān.
Old Lanes, *Dunns Lane* 1831 Bry, from a pers.n. *Dunn*, and ald,
with lane.

FIELD-NAMES

The undated forms are 1845 *TA* 307. Of the others, c.1300, 1449 are Bark,
1353, 1503 *ChFor*, 1428 (1551), 1435, 1437 ChRR, 1569 *AddCh*, 1831 Bry.

   (*a*) Black Croft; Butter Tree Fd; Done Flatt (from flat with the surname
Done); Haugh-, Hough Wd (*Oltonhagh'* 1353, 'hedged enclosure', *v.* haga);
Hockenhull (perhaps 'oak-hill', from ācen and hyll, but cf. Hockenhull 274

infra); Hook Fd (*v.* hōc); Intack, Intake (*v.* inntak); Milking Bank (*v.* milking); Oulton Lane 1831; Ox Pasture; Pinfold Fd (*v.* pynd-fald); Pingott (*v.* pingot); Rails (*v.* rail(e)); Ranford Mdw; Steans Fd; Swinners Moor (perhaps 'swine-hurst', *v.* swīn¹, hyrst, mōr¹); Ten Pound Fd (probably from a rent or purchase, *v.* 325 *infra*); Wheat Ridges (*v.* hwǣte, hrycg); White Fds (*le Witefeuld* c.1300, *Le Whitefeld* 1435, 1503, *-e* 1449, *v.* hwīt, feld).

(*b*) *le Marketmore* 1428 (1551), 1435, *Le Marletore* 1437, *Merledmore* 1569 ('the marled marsh-land', *v.* marlede, mōr¹).

2. WETTENHALL (GREEN & HALL) (110–6261 and 6262) [ˈwetɳɔːl] older local [ˈwetnə]

    Watenhale 1086 DB, 1121–9 (17) Chest, 1360 *Tourn* (p) (Barnes¹ 422), *-hala* 1175 Facs 3 (Chest 487 reads *Wentala*), *Watenhalle* 1389 MainwB (p), *-hall* 1581 ChRR, 17 (1724) NotCestr

    Wetenhale 1121–9 Chest *et freq* with variant spellings *Wetin-*, *-un-*, *-on-*, *-h(al)*, *-hal(a)*, *-(h)al(e)* to 1671 Sheaf, *Wetenhall'* 1238 P (p), 1270 Chest (p) *et freq* with variant spellings *-halle*, *-(h)all* to 1724 NotCestr, (*Wetenhall in forest of Mondrem*) 1414 ChRR, (*Wetenhall Hall*) 1724 NotCestr, *Wetenham* 1270 Chest (p) (*v.* ChetNS LXXXII, 559, n.1)

    Wethenhale 1121–9 (1285) Chest (p), 1259 Court (p), l13 AD (p), *Wethenal'* l13 *JRC* (p) (Barnes¹), *Wethenhall alias Watenhall* 1581 ChRR

    Suetenhala 1182 P (p)

    Wettenhal' 1238 P (p), *-hale* 1320 Cl (p), 1356, 1464 ChRR (p), *-hall* 1240–6, c.1300 MidCh (p), 1281 (17) Chest, 1291 (1338) VR (p), 1358 ChRR (p) *et freq* with variant spelling *Wettnall*; (*Wettenhall-hall*) 1671 Sheaf, (*Wettenhall Green*) 1831 Bry

    Werenh' 1267 Chest

    Wedenhal 1283 Pat (p), *-hale* 1290 CRV (p), 1291 P (p)

    Whetenhal 1283 Cl (p), *-hale* 1298 P (p), 1321 Cl (p), 1349 *Eyre* (p), 1415 ChRR, 1444 ib (p), *-hall* 1515 *MinAcct*, 1522 Orm²

    Witenhall 1284 ChF, *Witten-* 1406 ChRR (p), *Wytonhale* 1338 AddCh

    Whettenhull 1308 MidCh

    Wottenhull 1343 Cl (p)

    Waddenhalle 1389 MainwB (p)

    Wetenhull 1404 ChRR (p) (Barnes¹)

'Wet nook', from wēt (wk.dat. wētan) and halh (dat.sg. hale), with grēne² and hall. The first el. is sometimes confused with hwǣten 'growing with wheat', cf. Vale Royal 179 *infra*. The manor lay within the ancient forest of *Mondrem* 1 10.

ANKERSPLATT BROOK (Wettenhall Brook *infra*), *v.* brōc, cf. Wettenhall Lane Bridge *infra*. BANKSIDE (WOOD & BROOK), *Bank Side* 1831 Bry, *v.* banke, sīde. The brook joins Wettenhall Brook *infra*. BRIDGE FM, named from a nearby bridge over Wettenhall Brook *infra*. BROOKLANDS FM, near an un-named stream on the Cholmondeston boundary. BROOKSIDE FM, near Wettenhall Brook *infra*. THE CLAYLANDS, *v.* clæg, land. CORNER FM, *v.* foll. CORNHILL FM, *Cornhill* 1831 Bry, *v.* corn[1], hyll, cf. Cornhill 186 *infra*. Corner Fm *supra* is nearby, and the name may be identical in origin, though this farm may be named from its being round a sharp bend in a lane, *v.* corner. LONG LANE, 1831 ib, cf. 301 *infra*. MANOR FM, *v.* maner. TOWNFIELD FM, 1831 ib, cf. the surname *del Tonn* 1294 ChFor, *de To(u)n* 1382, 1384 Pat and Towns Green 293 *infra*, *v.* toun, feld. VILLAGE FM, *v.* village. WETTENHALL BROOK (Ash Brook 1 14), *v.* brōc. WETTENHALL LANE BRIDGE, *Ankers Plat* 1831 Bry, a bridge (*v.* plat[1]) giving name to Ankersplatt Brook *supra*. The first el. is either ancra 'a hermit', or the ME surname *Anker(s)*. WETTENHALL WOOD, 1831 ib, *boscus de Wetenhale* 1347 ChFor, cf. *Wood Green Lane* 1831 Bry, 1844 *TA*, *v.* wudu, grēne[2], lane, cf. Wood Green 137, 156 *supra*. WOODGATE FM, 1831 Bry, 1842 OS, *v.* wudu, geat. WOODSIDE, 1842 ib, -*Farms* 1831 Bry, *v.* wudu, sīde.

FIELD-NAMES

The undated forms are 1844 *TA* 422. Of the others, 1331, 1347, 1353 are *ChFor*, 1497, 1537 ChRR, 1671 Sheaf, 1831 Bry, 1842 OS.

(*a*) Ash Yards (*v.* æsc, geard); Banky Fd (*v.* banke); Barrows (*v.* bearu); Birchen Heys 1842 (*Birchin-* 1831, *v.* bircen[2]); Broad Marsh; Burnt Heys (*v.* brende[2], (ge)hæg); Long Butts (*v.* butte); Chapel Croft; Cinder Lane 1831 (*v.* sinder); Colley Croft (*v.* colig); Cook's Head (*v.* cocc-scyte); Two-, Three-, Four- (etc.) Day Math (*v.* day-math); Dudleys Lane 1831; Fastners; Finger Post Fd; Grannahs Croft ('grandmother's croft', a piece of dower land); Green Heys (*v.* grēne[1], (ge)hæg); Hall Fd & Mdw (*Hallfeld*, (a meadow called) *le Hall* 1497, *v.* hall, mæd, cf. Wettenhall Hall *supra* and *Hall Lane* 1831, *v.* lane); Hand Ridding; Headlands Croft (*v.* hēafod-land); Hemp Flatt; Hickers Fd; Hill Fd; Hinds-, Hynds Croft (*v.* hine); Homehurst Fd; Hynds Croft (*v.* Hinds *supra*); Jack Croft (*v.* jack); Kitchen Croft; Lapwing Fd (*v.* hlēape-wince); Loont (*v.* land);

Marl Bank & Fd; Marsh (*le Mershe* 1497, *v.* mersc); (Old) Milking Bank (*v.* milking); Mill Bank, Fd & Weir (cf. *Wettenhall Milnes* 1671, *-Mill* 1831 Bry, 1842 OS, *v.* myln, banke, wer); Muck'd Fd (*v.* muk); Outlet (*v.* outlet); Oven Croft; Palin(g)s Fd (*v.* palings); Pear Tree Bank; Pump Fd (*v.* pumpe); Ridding (*v.* ryding); Saw Pit Bank (*v.* saw-pytt); Shannons Wd; Shoemaker(s) Fd; Singlands; Big-, Further- & Middle Slip (*v.* slipe); Stiff Acre (*v.* stiff); Tippiter (perhaps *Typochurst* 1331, unintelligible unless *Typoc-* for *Typot-*, from the ME diminutive pers.n. *Tip(p)et*, (< *Tipp* < *Tibb* < *Theobald*), with hyrst); Tow Acres (*v.* twā 'two'); The Walletts (*v.* walet); Way Fd (*v.* weg); Wrong (*v.* wrang).

(b) *Crabtrefeld* 1497, 1537 (*v.* crabbe, trēow, feld); *Harewaieslond* 1497 (from land 'a selion' and a p.n., perhaps 'old way', *v.* hār², weg, but the first el. could be hara 'a hare' or hær 'a stone'); *le Oldehey* 1353 (*v.* ald, (ge)hæg); *Olrynesshawe* 1347 ('alder wood', *v.* alren, sceaga); *le Orewod* 1353 ('wood at a steep hillside', *v.* ōra¹, wudu); *Stokkeleymor* 1353 ('(marsh at) the clearing full of tree-stumps', *v.* stocc, lēah, mōr¹).

3. DARNHALL (ABBEY (site of), BRIDGE, HALL, MILL, PARK (lost) & WOOD) (110–6363) ['dɑːnɔːl] older local ['darnəl]

> *Dernhale* 1225 VR *et freq* with variant spellings *Derne-* 1275 Pat *et freq* to 1338 VR, *Derna-, -hal, Dernal(e)* to 1724 NotCestr, (*parcum de-*) 1239 Lib, (*vivarium de-*) 1251 Cl, (*abbey of-*) 1271 Pat, (*convent of St. Mary of*) 1276 Ch, (*abbey of Vale Royal alias-*) 1279 CRC, (*grangia de-*) 1334 VR, *Litledernal* 1334 ib, (*king's stew at*) *Ernhal'* 1239 Lib, (*abbot of-*) *Ernhale* 1275 P
>
> *Dernhall* 1237 P *et freq* with variant spellings *Derne- Derna-, -hall(e), Dernall* to 1845 ChetOS VIII, (*monasterium de-*) 1270 Orm², (*abbey of-*) 1270 CRC, *Dernhall Grange* 1656 Orm², *Dernhall Hall* 1724 NotCestr
>
> *Darnhal* 1237 P, *-hale* 1238 Lib *et freq* with variant spellings *Darne-, Darna-, -hal(e), Darnal(e)* to 1477 ChRR, (*parker of-, parcum de-*) 1238, 1241 Lib, (*king's chapel of-*) 1247 P, (*stagnum de-, vivarium de-*) 1251 Cl, (*mill of-*) 1252 ib, (*abbot of-*) 1275 P (*stagnum de*) *Arn(e)hal* 1250 ib, *Darnal-pool* 1656 Orm², *Barn-hale* 13 Misc
>
> *Darnhall* 1237 P *et freq* with variant spellings *Darne-, -halle, Darnall(e)* 1242 P to 1724 NotCestr; (*parcum de-*) 1237 P, (*abbot of-*) 1275 MidCh, (*grangia de-*) 1540 Dugd, *Darn(eh)all Parke, Woode & Pole* m16 AOMB 397, *Darnall Grange* 1606 ChRR, *the park side of Darnhall* 1656 Orm², *Darnhall Hall* 1831 Bry, *Badecok Darnhall* 1334 VR
>
> *Derhall* 1238, 1239, 1240, 1242 P

Dernhil 1239 P
Darenhal 1241 Cl, *-hale* 1342 AD, 14 Higden, *Derenhale* 15 Trev
Dornhall 1619 ChRR
Darnell 1682 Sheaf

'Secluded nook', from **derne** and **halh** (dat.sg. **hale**) with **abbaye, brycg, hall, park, myln, wudu** and **lȳtel**. Cf. Dingleside, Mill Lade & Wood, Park Wood, Poolhead, *Wro infra*, Vale Royal 179 *infra*. *Badecok* Darnhall was the name of a piece of newly approved land held by Adam *Badecok* 1334 VR, cf. *Badecok rudinges* 176 *infra*. The forms *Ern-*, *Arn(e)-* are due to metanalysis of *de Dern-*, *de Darn(e)-*, to *d'Ern-*, *d'Arn(e)-* in AN language or Exchequer record contexts. The *Barn-* form is a simple scribal error of *B-* for *D-*. Darnhall was anciently a manor of the earls of Chester—John le Scot, earl of Chester 1232–37, died here, Orm² 1 43.

HEBDEN GREEN (110–650629), 1842 OS, *Ebden Green* 1831 Bry, *Heppedene* 1225 VR, *-feld*, *Heppeden(feld)*, *Heppendenfeld* 1334 ib, 'hip valley', from **hēope** and **denu**, with **feld** and **grēne²**.

STOCKERLANE, *Stocker Lane* 1842 OS, *Stockrow Lane* 1831 Bry, probably associated with *Stokhall'* 1239 P (p), *Stochal* 1290 VR (p), 1334 ib (p), *Stokehale* (p), *Stokehalle* 1322 (1338) ib, *Stokhale* 1330 ib (p), 1348 *Eyre* (p), *Stoch'* (p), *Stochall'* 1334 VR, 'nook at a hamlet or dairy-farm', *v.* **stoc, halh**. Cf. *Stochale* 1 54.

SWANLOW FM & LANE (110–652635) ['swɔnlou], *Swanlowe* 1330, 1334 VR, 1409 Plea (p), 1540 AD, *-low* 1656 Orm², (*-in Over*) 1671 Sheaf, *Swanlow Lane* 1699 Dep, *Over Swanlow* 1819 Orm², 'herdsman's hill', *v.* **swān², hlāw**. This hamlet lay in Over and Darnhall townships, cf. Swanlow Ho 173 *infra*.

BANKSIDE FM. BEECH HO, *Beech House Farm* 1831 Bry, *v.* **bēce²**. BROOKSIDE WOOD. DINGLESIDE FM, DINGLE WOOD, *v.* **dingle** 'a deep dell', **sīde, wudu**, alluding to the valley of Ash Brook 1 14, whence also the township name. FIELDS FM, *Farm in the Fields* 1842 OS, *v.* **feld**. HALL WOOD, cf. Darnhall Hall *supra*. HANGING WOOD, *Had Bank* 1831 Bry, *Oldbrooks Wood* 1842 OS, *v.* **hangende**. HILLSIDE FM. KNOBS FM. THE LAKE, cf. Poolhead *infra*. LODGE WOOD, cf. *Lodge Bank* 1831 Bry, named from a park lodge. MILL WOOD, cf. Darnhall Mill *supra*. MOORS LANE (FARMS), *Moor Lane* 1831 Bry, *Moors Lane Farm* 1842 OS. PARK WOOD, 1831 Bry, cf. Darnhall Park *supra*. POOL-

HEAD, 1831 ib, 'the top end of a pool', v. pōl[1], hēafod, alluding to The Lake *supra* and the ancient fishpond and milldam recorded under Darnhall *supra*. PRIMROSEHILL, PRIMROSE WOOD. ROOKERY POOL & WOOD. SCHOOL GREEN, v. 175 *infra*, cf. *School Field* 1846 *TA*. SMITHY BANK, *Beauty Bank* 1842 OS, cf. *a smithy called Smythehous* 1395 Orm[2], v. smiðõe, hūs. *Beauty* is probably *booty* from botye 'shared profits', cf. bōt. SURRY'S HALL, *Sorrel House* 1842 OS. VALLEY WOOD.

FIELD-NAMES

The undated forms are 1846 *TA* 143. Of the others, 1395 is Orm[2], 1831 Bry, the rest VR.

(*a*) Cow Lane 1831 (*v.* cū, lane); Russams Clough 1831 (*v.* clōh).

(*b*) *Cunbbestyl* 1329 (*v.* stigel 'a stile'. *Cunbbe-* may represent *Cnubbe-*, an early form of ModE *knub* (NED from 1570) 'a lump, etc', cf. Dan *knub* 'a block, a log, a stump'. Professor Löfvenberg thinks *Cnubbe-* here may be a pers. by-name for a stocky person, cf. Swed dial. *knubbe* 'a stocky person', and that the eModE senses 'a small lump; a stag of the second year' (NED, loc.cit.) might also lend themselves to such a use. He cites Hellquist, *Svensk Etymologisk Ordbok*, s.v. *knubb*); *Dernaleness'*, *Darnalenes*, *Dernallenss'* 1334 (probably a bad copy for *Dernaleeues*, 'the wood-edge in Darnhall', from efes); *Munkesberne* 1395 ('monk's barn', *v.* munuc, bere-ærn, from the grange of Vale Royal abbey here, cf. *grangia de Dernehale* 1334 VR, etc., under Darnhall *supra*); *Wro* 1334, 1337 (p) (cf. John *del Wro*, bond tenant in Darnhall, 1338 VR, 'the nook', *v.* vrá, cf. the p.n. Darnhall *supra*); *Yatehous* 1395 (*v.* gate-hous).

4. OVER (HALL & LODGE) (110–6465) ['ouvə]

    Ovre 1086 DB, *Oure* 1237 P *et freq* with variant spellings *Ovre*, *Oure*, *Oura* to 1336 VR, *Owre* 1254 P, *Ouera* 13 Whall (p), *Ouere* 1246–77 Chest, 1247 P, *Overe* 1275 Misc *et freq* with variant spelling *Ouere* to 1538 Dugd, (*Great-*) 1284 Misc, (*Muchel-*) 1334 VR, (*Magna-*) 1350 Chamb, *Over* 1270 Dugd *et freq* with variant spelling *Ouer* to 1724 NotCestr, (*Great-*) 1311 VR, *Overee* 1475 VR, *Over Lodge* 1831 Bry

    Vfre 1096–1101 (1150), 1150 Chest, *Ufra* 1184 P, *Vuere* 1175 Facs, *Huure* c.1190 (1400) CASNS XIII, *Huuere* c.1232 (1246) Ch

    Ovuera (lit. *Ovn-*) 1157–94 Chest, *Ovuer* 1435 Dav, (*Litle*)*ouvere* 1275 Misc (p), *Ouvre* 1286 Court (p), *Owuer* 1435 Dav, 1555 Sheaf

    Ever 1278 Misc

'The hill', from ofer², ufer. The principal hamlet, *Great* Over, was distinguished from Littler *infra* by grēat, mycel, magna, and also may have been the *Chircheton* noted at Church Hill *infra*. Over is on a pronounced ridge parallel to the R. Weaver. The p.ns. Over and Littler are paralleled by Mickleover and Littleover Db 483, 478.

STREET-NAMES. CLOUGH ROW, 'row of houses near a dell', *v.* clōh, rāw, cf. Dean Cottages *infra*; DEAN ST., cf. Dean Cottages *infra*; DINGLE LANE, at the valley of Dene Brook *infra*, cf. Dean Cottages *infra*, *v.* dingle 'a deep hollow'; GRANGE LANE, *Knyghts yates, Knyghtys lone* 1475 VR, *v.* geat, lane, cf. Knight's Grange *infra*; HIGH ST., *Winsford Lane* 1831 Bry, (*-Field*) 1845 *TA*, *Over Lane* 1842 OS, cf. *Wynesfordstrete* c.1240 (1400) CASNS XIII 99 under Winsford (Bridge) *infra*; WELL ST., *v.* wella.

BLAKEDEN (GORSE & LANE) (110–622662) [blɛk-], *Blak(e)den(e)* 1304 Chamb, 1311 (1338), 1330, 1334 VR, *Blak(e)den(e) feld, Blackden (feld)* 1334 ib, *Blak(e)den grene, -heth, -heyes, -lone & mosse* 1475 ib, *Blakeden* 1842 OS, *Blackings Hall & Lane* 1831 Bry, 'dark, black valley', from blæc and denu, with gorst, lane, hall, feld, grēne², hǣð, (ge)hæg, and mos. Cf. Blackden 2 222.

BRADFORDWOOD (110–637676), *v.* Bradford Mill, Bradfordwood Cottage 178 *infra*.

BROOK HO (110–637679, a detached part of Whitegate, *v.* 164 *supra*), *þe Brookhouses* 1541–2 (1724), 1724 NotCestr (Orm² II 145 reads *Brock-*), *the Brokehowses* 1542 Sheaf, *Brooke-houses* 1632 ib, *the Brookhowses* 1637 ib, *Brookhouses* 1642 ChCert, (*-in Swanlow*) 1671 Sheaf, *Brockhouses* 1819 Orm², 'house(s) near a brook', after an un-named tributary of Bogart Brook 1 15, *v.* brōc, hūs. The context 'John Darlington of the Brookhowses' 1637 Sheaf² 1, 106 suggests that this may be the location of *John house Derlynton* 1475 VR 150, 'John Darlington's house'.

CHURCH HILL (FM) (110–650650), 1831 Bry, *Church Hill* 1669 Orm², named from St Chad's Church, (*ecclesia de Huure* c.1190 (1400) CASNS XIII, *church of Ovre* 1277 Pat, *Saint Chadde of Owver* 1526 Orm², *Overchurch* 1656 ib, *Over Church* 1831 Bry), and probably the location of *Chircheton* 1305 ChF (p), *Chirch(e)-, Chyrchton* 1334 VR, if this is not another name for Over *supra*, *v.* cirice, hyll, tūn.

GAVEL GREEN (110–631678, a detached part of Whitegate, *v.* 164 *supra*) [gavəl]

> the Gale (*feld*), *Galefeld* 1475 VR, *Gale* 1642 *ChCert*, 1724 NotCestr, 1819 Orm², (*-in Over*) 1671 Sheaf, *Galegreen* 1724 Orm²
>
> *Gavill* 1541–2 Sheaf³ 24 (5493), (1724) NotCestr (Orm² II 145 reads *-ville*), *Gavel Green* 1842 OS
>
> *Goale in Over* 1642 *ChCert*
>
> *Yale Green* 1671 Sheaf
>
> *Gaywell Green* 1751 Sheaf
>
> *Gravel Green* 1831 Bry

'Place where bog-myrtle grows', from **gagel** and **feld**, **grēne²**. The first el. has been confused with **gafol²** 'a rent, a tax'.

KNIGHT'S GRANGE (110–640670, a detached part of Whitegate, *v.* 164 *supra*)

> grangia de *Kyntes* 1326 VR
>
> grangia vocata *Beurepeyr* 1334 VR, grangia de *Bieurepeir* vel de *Knythtes* 1336 ib
>
> grangia de *Knythtes* 1336, 1340 VR
>
> manerium de *Knyghtes* 1360 ChRR, VR, 1395 Orm², graunge of-, grangia de *Kny-*, *Knight(e)s* 1535 VE, 1537, 1544 *Chol*, 1544 Orm², *Knyghtts* 1538 ib, *Knights alias Knights Grange* 1612, 1629 ib
>
> *Knyghtesgraunge* 1547 *MinAcct*, *Knightes-* 1554 *ib*, *-Grainge* 1555 Sheaf, *-Grange* 1560 ib, 1608 *Chol*, *Knight's Graunge* 1588 Tab, *-Grange* 1656 Orm², *Knyghts-* 1611 Sheaf, *Knights Grange* 1612, 1671 ib *et freq*, (*Knights alias-*) 1612, 1629 Orm², (*-Wood*) 1831 Bry, *Knightsgrange* 1631 ChRR
>
> manor of *Knighte* 1538 Dugd, *Knight Grange in Whitegat* 1553 Tab

'The retainers' or 'the young men', from the nom.pl. of **cniht**, ME *cnihtes*, *knihtes*, cf. Mottram 1 202 for an analogous type of name. This place was a grange of Vale Royal abbey 179 *infra*, *v.* **grange**, where it was obviously known as 'a pleasant resort', *v.* **bel²**, **repaire**. Cf. Childer Thornton 325 *infra*, for a social analogy, an estate supporting the youngsters of a community.

LITTLER (LANE) (110–633665) [ˈlitlər]

> *Parva Ov(e)re*, *-Ou(e)re*, *-Ouer*, *-Over* 1260 Court (p), Plea, 13 Tab, 1277 Dugd, 1281 Orm², 1284 *Chol* (p), 1285 Ch, 1299 Orm²,

Little Overe 1278 Misc *et freq* with variant spellings as for Over
supra, and *Lit(t)el(e)-, Lyttl(e)-, Lyt(te)l-, Lytil-, Lytel-, Littel(l)-,
Litt(i)l-, Lit(u)l-, Lut(t)el-, Lutle-, Lettel-, Lyttell-, Lyttull-,
Litell-* to 1553 Pat, *Little Ouere Lane* 1334 VR
Litlors 13 Tab, *Litlore* 1393 ChRR, *Lyttl-* 1398 Orm² (p), *Lytl-*
1400 ChRR (p), *Lyttel(l)-* 1402 ib (p), *Lytel-* 1405 ib (p),
Lyttull- 1421 AD (p), *Litell-* 1469 ChRR (p), *Lyttlelore* 1411
ib (p), *Littlelore* 1475 ib (p), *Lytulhore* 1429 Chol, *Lyttelor'* 1381
ib (p)
Leyttelehour' 1333 Tab (p), *Lutelour* 1336 VR (p), *Lytlour'* 1346
Chol (p), *Lytelour* 1353 Eyre, 1414 JRL
Litler (Farm) 1831 Bry, 1842 OS

'Little Over', from Over *supra*, with lȳtel, parva (and lane).
Hereabouts was *Netherton, Nethreton iuxta Littlover(e)* 1307 Plea,
(*Nethre-, Nether Litel Oure, -Ovre* 1277 Dugd, (1350) VR, 1299 Orm²,
Netherlitleovere 1285 Ch), *v.* neoðera, tūn.

SALTERSWALL (110–627670, a detached part of Whitegate, *v.* 164
supra), 1542 (1724), 1724 NotCestr, 1542, 1637 Sheaf, 1842 OS, *-well*
1831 Bry, *Salterwall* 1819 Orm², 'salter's well', *v.* saltere, wælla.
This place is on a route from Middlewich to Chester, *Saltereswey*
1334 Crump 94, *v.* saltere, wey, cf. 1 47–8 (route XXIII).

STOCK'S HILL (110–655654), *Stocks Stairs* 1842 OS, cf. *Stock Hill
Field* 1845 TA, and *le Stoc, Stocfeld, (le) Chirchestoc, Chyrchestok(e)*
1334 VR, from stoc 'a secondary settlement', with stæger 'a stair',
and hyll 'a hill' (there is a steep ascent here), feld, and cirice 'a
church' (St. Chad's Church, at Church Hill *supra*). Cf. Way's Green,
Welsh Lane, Hooterhall *infra*.

SWANLOW HO & LANE, cf. *Swanlow Field* 1845 TA, *v.* Swanlow Fm
169 *supra*.

WINSFORD (BRIDGE) (110–655663) ['winzfəd], (bridge of) *Wynisford*
1216–72 MainwB (p), *Wynesfordhet(h) & -strete* c.1230 (1400),
c.1240 (1400) CAS NS XIII, *Wines-, Wynesford* 1255 RH (p) (Barnes¹),
Winsford c.1350 BPR (Barnes¹), 1782 Sheaf, *Wynsfurth brigge,
-brygge* 1475 VR, *Winsford-bridge* 1656 Orm², *Wyneford bridge* 1334
VR, *Wynffordbrugge* 1400 ChRR, *Winteford Bridge* 1619 Sheaf,
'(bridge, heath and street at) Wine's ford', from the OE pers.n. *Wine*
and ford, with hæð, stræt and brycg. The ford gave name to a

hamlet, which now gives name to an Urban District and c.p., *v.* 164 *supra*. The 'street' is obviously the road leading to the ford, i.e. the road from Middlewich to Chester via Salterswall and High Street *supra*, and Stanthorne **2** 211, *v.* **1** 47 (route XXIII).

WOODFORD HALL & LODGE (110–627649), *Wodeford* 1217–32, 1225 VR *et freq* with variant spellings *Wod(e)-*, *Wud(e)-*, *-fordd*, *-forde*, *-fort(h)e* to 1500 ib, (pons de) *Woodford* 1338 ib, *Woodford* 1612 Orm[2] *et freq* with variants *-forde*, *-fort*; *Woodford Brook* 1671 Sheaf, *Woodford Hall* 1555 ib, cf. *Wodefordefurde* 1312–18 ib, *Wodefordfeld* 1373 ib, 187 *infra*, 'ford at, or in, a wood', from **wudu** and **ford**, with **brōc** (*v.* Poolstead Brook *infra*), **hall**, **ford**, **feld** and **loge**. Cf. Woodford Lane *infra*. Near Woodford, and, perhaps identical with it, was *the ford of Vernun* 1217–32 VR, from *Vernon* the surname of a great Ch family, landowners hereabouts.

BANKFIELD, cf. *Bank Field* 1845 *TA*, *v.* **banke**.   BOTTOM FLASH, *v.* **flasshe**, cf. 163 *supra*.   BRICK FIELD.   CROSSFIELD HO, cf. *Crosfeld* 1334 VR, 'field at a cross', *v.* **cros**, **feld**.   DALK HOUSES, cf. *Dawk Field* 1845 *TA*.   DARNHALL COTTAGE, *v.* Darnhall 168 *supra*.   DEAN COTTAGES, *Deans Cottage* 1831 Bry, *Dean Cottage* 1842 OS, cf. *Big & Little Dean*, *Deans* (*Meadow*) 1845 *TA*, *v.* **denu** 'a valley', cf. Clough Row, Dean St., Dingle Lane *supra*, Dene Brook, Overdene *infra*.   DENE BROOK (R. Weaver), cf. prec., Overdene *infra*.   GRANGE FM, near Swanlow *supra*, *v.* **grange**. GRANGE LODGE, *Grange Cottage* 1831 Bry, cf. Knight's Grange *supra*, *v.* **loge**   GREENFIELD COTTAGES, cf. *Green Field* 1845 *TA*. GROVE COTTAGE & MOUNT, *v.* **grāf**.   HOLLYHEAD FM (110–645651), cf. *Holloway Head Field* 1845 *ib* and *Holeweye-diche* 1334 VR, '(ditch at-, top end of-) the road in a hollow', *v.* **holh**, **weg**, **hēafod**, **dīc**. The 'hollow way' may have been part of Swanlow Lane, or an older road on the line of Gladstone St. in Over.   HOOTER-HALL, *Stock Stairs* 1831 Bry, *Stocks Hill* 1842 OS, cf. Stock's Hill *supra*.   KILNHOUSES, cf. *Kiln Field* 1845 *TA*, *v.* **cyln**.   LANE END FM.   MANOR HO.   MOORS LANE, *Moor Lane* 1831 Bry, *v.* **mōr**[1], **lane**.   MOSSBANK COTTAGES, *v.* **mos**, **banke**.   MOUNT PLEASANT.   OAK HOUSE (LANE), *Okewode* m16 *AOMB* 397, *le Oake* 1642 ChCert, *Oak House* 1831 Bry, *v.* **āc**, **wudu**.   OLD FM, *v.* **ald**.   OVERDENE, 'valley at Over', *v.* Over *supra*, **denu**, cf. Dean

Cottages *supra*. PARK HO, *v.* park. POOLSTEAD BROOK
(Chesterlane Brook 186 *infra*), *Woodford Brook* 1671 Sheaf³ 49
(stream and hamlet), cf. *Poolstead* 1845 *TA*, from pōl-stede 'site of
a pool', and brōc, cf. Woodford *supra*. ROEHURST LANE, 1842 OS,
Rohurst 1475 VR, *the-*, *le great(e)-*, *litle-*, *lytle-*, *mydle-*, *middel
Ro(o)hurst(e)* 1537, 1544 Chol, *Row Hurst* 1845 *TA* 310, perhaps
'rough wood', *v.* rūh, hyrst, but more likely the first el. is rā 'roe-
(buck)', as suggested by Professor Löfvenberg, hence 'roebuck
wood'. SANDHOLE, *Sand Hole Field & Loont* 1845 ib, *v.* sand,
hol¹, land. SCHOOL GREEN & LANE, 1831 Bry, *v.* scōl, grēne²,
lane. SMITHY BANK, *v.* smiððe, banke. SPRINGBANK, *v.*
spring, banke. TOWN FIELDS, *The-* 1831 Bry, *Town Field* 1842
OS, *v.* toun, feld. WAY'S GREEN (FM), *Waysgreen(e)* 1671 Sheaf,
Ways Green (Farm) 1831 Bry, from weg 'a way, a road', and grēne²
'a green'. Four or five ways met here to join the lost ford on Welsh
Lane *infra* by way of Stock's Hill *supra*. WELSH LANE (110–648648
to 658654), *Welch Lane* 1842 OS, cf. *Welch Pasture* 1845 *TA*, *v.*
Welisc 'a Welshman', lane. This lane led from Smithy Bank *supra*
(110–648647) to a now-submerged ford of R. Weaver at 110–658655
thence to 110–660656 near Rilshaw 2 214 in Wharton, cf. prec. It
probably marks a route used by Welsh salters trading with Middlewich, cf. **1** 47–8 (route XXIII). WOODFORD LANE, *Over Lane* 1831
Bry, *v.* lane, Woodford, Over *supra*.

FIELD-NAMES

The undated forms are 1845 *TA* 309. Of the others, 1278 is Misc, 1315 Plea,
1395, 1475² Orm², 1418 AD, 1426 ChRR, m16 *AOMB* 397, 1537, 1544 *Chol*,
1555, 1611 Sheaf, 1555² Tab, 1558–1603 *Surv*, 1642 ChCert, 1831 Bry, 1842
OS, and the rest VR.

(a) Bank Side; Black Mdw (cf. *the Blake crofte* 1475, *v.* blæc, croft);
Breach, Breeches Fd (*v.* brēc); Broadens Mdw; Brown Banks; Burnt Ground
Fd (*the Bonke* 1475, *Bank Ground* 1831, *Burnt Ground* 1842, *v.* banke,
brende², grund); Clemhunger (*v.* Clamhunger 2 52, cf. foll.); Clemley (*v.*
Clumley *infra*); Clough (*v.* clōh); Clumley, Clemley (*v.* clām, clǣme, lēah,
cf. Clemley 47 *supra*); Colley Croft (*v.* colig); Crabb Tree Fd (*Crabtre feld*
1475, *v.* crabbe, trēow, feld); Diperge; Doctors Fd; Dog Croft (*v.* dogga);
Edge Fd (*v.* ecg); Gallows Loont (*v.* galga, land); Grange Fd (*v.* grange);
Handl(e)y Hill; Hanging Hill (*v.* hangende); Head Butts (*v.* heved-butte);
Intake (1475, *v.* inntak); Kents Ash (from the surname *Kent* and æsc);
Kitchen Croft (*v.* cycene); Lang Fd (*v.* lang); Launds Fd (*v.* launde or land);
Lidgate (*Lydiate* 1642, *v.* hlid-geat); Loont (*v.* land); Marl Fd (cf. *le Marle-
pittes* 1334, *v.* marle-pytt); Small Marshall; Moss (cf. *Mosfeld* 1334, *v.* mos);

Muck Dish (*v.* muk, edisc); Oller Dale (cf. *Olreden(feld), Olredenfeld* 1334, 'alder valley', *v.* alor, dæl[1], denu, feld); Outlett (*v.* outlet); Pembertons Parlour (*v.* parlur, *Pemberton* is a surname, cf. 326 *infra*); Pig Cote Fd; Pingott (*v.* pingot); Poolstead (*v.* pōl-stede, cf. Poolstead Brook *supra*); Long Reaves (probably 'long greaves', *v.* lang, grǣfe); Row Butts (*v.* rūh, butte); Sandiway Fd (*v.* sandig, weg); Sand Lands (*v.* sand, land); Sheet Fd; Shorp Heys (*v.* scearp, (ge)hæg); Long Slang(s) (*v.* lang, slang); Stack Butts (*v.* stakkr, butte); Stone Fd ((*le*) *Stonfeld* 1334, *v.* stān, feld); Street Fd (*v.* strǣt, cf. Winsford, High St. *supra*); Sweet Fd (*v.* swēte); Tentry Fd (*v.* tentour); Thorney Croft (*v.* þornig, croft); Twices ('forks', *v.* (ge)twis); Water Doxes; Whit Fd (*v.* hwīt); Yaudless; Yell House Loont (*v.* land).

(b) *Albynesfeld* 1334 (from the ME (OFr) pers.n. *Albin* and feld); *Armetryding* 1426 (p) ('hermit's clearing', *v.* ermite, ryding 'cleared land'); *Asfe(i)ld* 1334 ('ash-tree field', *v.* æsc, feld); *Ayne crofte* 1475 (probably 'lamb croft', *v.* ēan, croft, but Professor Löfvenberg thinks the first el. could be an OE pers.n. **Æga* as in Aynho Nth 48, DEPN); *Badecok rudinges* 1334 an assart held by Randolph and Adam *Badecok*, cf. Darnhall 169 *supra*, *v.* ryding); *Barewe* 1334 ('the grove', *v.* bearu); *Barlowes Howse* 1558–1603 (from the surname *Barlow*); *le Brendewode* 1318, *-wood* 1475[2], (*le*) *Barndewode*, (*le*) *Berndewode* 1334 ('burnt wood', *v.* brende[2], berned, wudu); *the Beleawe* 1475 (perhaps 'beacon enclosure', from bēl[1] and haga); *Bentles* 1555, *Benteles* 1555[2] ('grassy clearings', *v.* beonet, lēah); *Berch', Berch(e)dench, Berchedenh', Bercdedench, Birchedench, Berch(e)den(e), Bircheden* 1334 ('birch valley', *v.* birce, denu. The *-den(c)h* forms indicate a contracted third el., but it is not possible to reconstruct it from these spellings in this source); *Bircheles, Birch(e)les(')nes, Birchele'nes, Burchel(es)enes,* (all with *-n-* for *-u-*), *Byrchlosheues* 1334 ('(the edge of (a wood called)) the little birches', *v.* bircel, efes); *Braden(h)al(e),* (*-land*) 1334 ('(selion at) the broad corner', from brād and halh, with land); *Bradestrete* 1334 ('broad street', *v.* brād, strǣt); *Bradwell feld* 1475 ('(field at) the broad spring', *v.* brād, wælla); *Brownfeld Knoll* 1475 ('(hillock at) the brown field', *v.* brūn[1], feld, cnoll); *le Bruch(e),* (*-land*) 1334 ('(selion at) the breaking-in of land', *v.* bryce, land); *Burifeld* 1334 ('manor-field', *v.* burh, feld); *Caldewalle* 1334, *Caldwall* 1475, cf. *Colewall'* 1334 (p) ('cold-, cool well', *v.* cald, cōl[2], wælla); *Chircheden(e), Chirch(e)denfeld* 1334 ('(field at) the church valley', *v.* cirice, denu, feld); *Chirch(e)feld* 1334 (*v.* cirice, feld); *Churnokfeldes* 1475 (from feld with the surname *Chernock* 1308, 1418 ChRR, cf. Charnock La 129, 130); *the grene att Ric' dor Coke* 1475 ('the green at Richard Coke's door', *v.* grēne[2]); *the Cokshote* 1475 (*v.* cocc-scyte); *Colewall'* (*v. Caldewalle supra*); *Col(l)escroft* 1334 ('Coll's croft', from the ME pers.n. *Coll* (ON *Kol(l)r,* ODan *Kol(l),* or a pet-form of *Colin*), and croft); *le Cowhous* 1395 (*v.* cū, hūs); *Croson Comons* 1611 (Sheaf[3] 2 (261), *v.* commun. The first el. may be a lost p.n. *Croston*); *Dal(l)es lane* 1537, 1544 (*v.* lane 'a lane'. The first el. may be an OE pers.n. **Dall,* cognate with OE *Dealla* (cf. Dalston Cu 131, DEPN s.n.)); *Denelden* 1334; *Deplach(e)* 1334 ('deep boggy stream', *v.* dēop, læc(c)); *El(l)wal(l)efeld* 1334, *Ellwall(s lone)* 1475 ('(field and lane at) the eel-pool', from ēl[2] and wælla, with feld, lane); *Fordlache* 1334 ('boggy stream with a ford', *v.* ford, læc(c)); *Grymvale* 1475 (*v.* vale. It is not possible to determine which of several possibilities is the basis of the theme *Grym-*); (*le*) *Hal(l)ewes* 1334 ('the nooks', *v.* halh); *le Hey(e)* 1334, *Heyez* 1475 ('the enclosure(s)', *v.* (ge)hæg); *Highewoode* m16 (*v.* hēah, wudu); *Holm(e)* 1334 ('the marsh', *v.* holmr); *Honde Ruding' Horne* 1334 ('Honde Horne's cleared land', *v.* ryding); *Hor(e)dich(e)gre(e)ues, Horddichgreues* 1334 (perhaps '(woods at) the old ditch', *v.* hār[2], dīc, grǣfe, but the first el. is probably horu, horh, hence 'dirty, filthy ditch'); *Horswallesich* 1334 ('watercourse at horse-well', *v.* hors, wælla, sīc); *Langwall aftyr Wever side, Langwallys* 1475 (a meadow, 'long meadow', *v.* lang or langr, vǫllr, the latter confused with wælla); *Litelhall* 1418 (a burgage, *v.* lȳtel, hall); *Litlemor(e)* 1334 ('the little marsh', *v.* lȳtel, mōr[1]); *Long(e)acre(s)* 1334 (*v.* lang, æcer); *Longen(h)al(e)* 1334 ('long corner of land', *v.* lang, halh); *Longe-rudings* 1334 (*v.* lang, ryding); (*le*) *Mers(s')*, (*le*) *Mers(s)lone* 1334 ('the (lane at the) marsh' *v.*, mersc, lane); *Mous(e)acre(s)* 1334 (from æcer and the nickname of Adam *le Mous*, tenant in *Litlemor(e) supra*); *Mulnefeld* 1334 ('mill field', *v.* myln, feld); *Murefeld* 1290, *Muryfeld* 1315, *Muriffeld* 1330 ('pleasant field', *v.* myrge, feld; Dr von Feilitzen observes, 'I suspect *myrge*, which is fairly common in p.ns., did not just mean 'pleasant', which seems very vague and abstract, but was used of localities where merry-making of various kinds took place—playing-fields, fair-grounds, etc.'); *Nick-rudings* 1334 ('cleared-land at a nick or valley', *v.* nick(e), ryding); *the Noonhowse* 1558–1603 ('the nun-house', *v.* nunne, hūs, perhaps alluding to property of the Nuns of Chester, who surrendered estates in Over and Weaverham for the endowment of Vale Royal); *Ouchden* 1334 (final el. denu 'a valley'); *Paxtons Crofte* 1475 (from a surname *Paxton* and croft); *Presterudings* 1334 ('priests' cleared-lands', *v.* prēost (gen.pl. prēosta), ryding); *Presteslye* 1334 ('priest's clearing', *v.* prēost, lēah); *Pypenlowe* 1334 (apparently from pīpe (gen.sg. *pīpan*) 'a conduit, a pipe' and hlāw 'a hill, a mound', but the first el. may be some unidentified pers.n.); *Sengles* 1334 (perhaps from sengel 'a bundle, a tuft', cf. Löfvenberg 182, DEPN s.n. *Singleton*); *Schot(e)wal(l)eden(e)* 1334 ('(valley at) the salmon pool', *v.* sc(e)ota, wælla, denu); *Smaldene* 1217–32 ('narrow valley', *v.* smæl, denu); *the Tewfeld* 1475; *Wallemor* 1334 ('marsh at a spring', *v.* wælla, mōr[1]); *Wallerudingg* 1334 ('cleared-lands at a spring', *v.* wælla, ryding); *Westeyedmor* 1334 ('marsh at west meadow', *v.* west, ēgeð, mōr[1]); *the Wether grene* 1475 ('green where wethers are kept', *v.* weðer, grēne[2]); *Wever side* 1475 ('the side of R. Weaver', *v.* sīde, R. Weaver 1 38); *le We(w)es* 1318, 1334 (the name of a grove belonging to Vale Royal abbey, probably 'the yews', *v.* īw, cf. *le Weueknoll* 1 58, and *yew, vew* NED); *Wyldemare-ford, -fort* 1225 ('wild-mare's ford', *v.* wilde, mere[2], ford. This p.n. may be associated with *Wyldemore Hey* 182 *infra*); *Wyneseyc* 1334 (a meadow, from the OE pers.n. *Wine* as in Winsford *supra*. The final el. is probably ēg 'a water-meadow' or ēgeð 'a small island', with *-eyc* for *-eye* or *-eyt*, cf. *Westeyedmor supra*); *Witesich, le Wytesyche* 1225, *Wyteschyche* 1278 ('white stream', or possibly 'watercourse where a penalty is paid', from hwīt 'white', or wīte 'a penalty, a punishment', and sīc. This was a boundary of Woodford *supra*).

12

5. WHITEGATE (Ho) (110–628694)

> *Whytegate* 1540 Dugd, *Whitegate* 1542 ib *et freq* with variant
> spellings *Why-*, *Whit(e)gat(e)*); ((altera) grangia de- 1540 Dugd,
> vicaria de- 1542 VE, parochia de- m16 *AOMB* 397, town &
> parish of-, rectory & church of- 1550 Pat)
> *Newechurch* 1612 Orm² *et freq* with variant spelling *New(e) Church*
> to 1831 Bry, (parish of *Whit(e)gate alias-*) 1612, 1629 Orm² *et
> freq* to 1812 Sheaf, *Newchurch or Whitegate* 1831 Bry
> *Newchurch or Whitegate church or Whitechurch* 1671 Sheaf

'The white gate', *v.* hwīt, geat, named from the outer gate of Vale
Royal abbey, where the church was situated, cf. 164 *supra*. The
alternative names are 'new church' and 'white church', *v.* nīwe,
hwīt, cirice, cf. Newchurch Common 183 *infra*. The original
structure was of wood and plaster, *v.* Sheaf³ 31 (6914). The site of the
gate itself is *locum illud ubi nunc porta exterior que barra abbatie
Wlgodr' situatur* 1338 VR 12, 'that place where now the outer gate or
bar of the abbey, *Wlgodr'*, is situated', cf. *þe Abbey-gate* 1724
NotCestr, *v.* abbaye, geat. The unintelligible *Wlgodr'* is identified in
Barnes¹ 435 with *Holdgore* 1216–72 MainwB. Dr Barnes derives it
from gor 'dirt, dung, filth', but the name is rather 'the old gore',
v. ald, gāra.

BRADFORD MILL (110–647687), BRADFORDWOOD COTTAGE (110–
639679), BRADFORDWOOD (110–637676) 171 *supra*, *Bradeford* c.1240
(1400) CASNS XIII (p) *et freq*, with variant *-forde* to 1467 *MinAcct*,
Bradford 1285 CRC (p) *et freq*, *Bradeford(e)wod(e)* 1275 Misc, Cl,
boscus de-, *wood of Brad(e)ford* 1278 Misc, 1284 Pat, 1326 VR,
grangia de-, *grange of Brad(e)ford* 1336 ib, 1542 Orm², wood called
Bradfordeshey 1395 ib, *le Brodeford* 1409 ChRR (p), *Bradford Wood*
1423 Morris, *Bradford Mylne* 1522 AD, 1542 Orm², *-mylle*, *-woode* &
-Graunge m16 *AOMB* 397, four mills called *Bradford Milles* 1642
ChCert, *Bradford Mill & Wood* 1831 Bry, '(mill and wood at) the
broad ford', from brād and ford, with myln, wudu, grange, (ge)hæg.
The material in printed sources is sometimes confused with Bradford
2 210, e.g. Orm² I 357, II 173. Cf. Newbridge Wood *infra*.

CATSCLOUGH, CAT'S CLOUGH, *Cats Clough (Wood)* 1831 Bry, *Catti-
scliue* c.1180 *AddCh*, 'wild-cat's cliff', *v.* catt, clif. The final el. has
been replaced by clōh 'a dell, a ravine'.

CONERSLEY (lost) may have been in this township, *v.* 207 *infra.*

SUTTON (lost), *Sutton* 1277 Dugd *et freq* to 1467 *MinAcct*, 1531 ChRR, 1629 Orm², *Sutton Grange* 1724 NotCestr, cf. *Sutton Felde* m16 *AOMB* 397, *Sutton Field* 1845 *TA*, cf. also 184 *infra*, 'south farm', *v.* sūð, tūn. Sutton, a grange of Vale Royal, was partly in Over and partly in Marton 182 *infra*. Sutton Field is at 110–634690.

VALE ROYAL (site of St. Mary's Monastery), VALEROYAL PARK, (110–6369)

> *Muncheniswra* 1276 Misc, *Munecheneswro* 1277 Dugd, (1350) VR,
>   1299 Orm², *Munesche(ne)swro* 1353 (1430) Pat, 1354 BPR,
>   *Muneschenewro* 1407–13 VR
> *Munchenewy* 1278 Misc
> *Munechenwro* 1279 Ch, *Munechen(e)wro* 1338 VR, *Munchenwro*
>   1311 Pat, 1312 Cl, 1330 VR
>
> *Hweteyhales* 1276 Misc
> *Whetenehalewes* 1277 Dugd, (1350) VR, *Wheten-* 1311 Pat, 1312
>   Cl, *Weten-* 1279 Ch, *-halewez* 1338 VR, *-haleues* (lit. *-nes*) 1724
>   NotCestr, *Whethenhalews* 1330 VR, *Quettennehalewes* 1338 ib,
>   *Wethenchalewes* 1353 (1430) Pat, *Wethenehalewes* 1354 BPR
> *Wetegoshalewes* 1278 Misc
> *Witerehalwes boscum* 1278 IpmR
> *Worthenhalowes* 1407–13 VR
>
> (abbey of-, abbot & convent of (St Mary's of)-) *Vallis Regalis* 1277
>   Pat, Dugd *et freq*, (-*alias Dernhale*) 1279 CRC, *-de Welle Regali*
>   1331 City, *-de Varl' Regal'* 1513 ChEx, *boscus vocatus de Valle*
>   *Regali* 1276 CRC
> (abbas de) *Loco Regali* 1278 IpmR
> (abbey of) *Vau Real* 1300 ChancW, *Vaureal* 1312 ib, *et freq* in
>   City, BPR, Pat to 1361 *ChFor*, *Vauriale* 1348 Pap, *Vaurialle* 1430
>   Cl
> *Valeryall* 1334 VR, *-Riall* 1530 Sheaf, *Valerviall* 1546 Dugd,
>   *Wall-Riall* 1649 ChetOS VIII, *Vale Reall* 1539–47 Dugd
> *Valreale* 1340 Sheaf, *-Real* 1351 BPR
> *locus vocatus Vallis Regalis vel Anglice Kingesdale* 1338 VR, *Vale*
>   *Royall or King's Dale* 1724 NotCestr.
> (*La*) *Vauroial(e)* 1357 *et freq* to 1360 BPR

le Valroyal 1357 *AddCh*
Vale Roiall 1407–13 VR, 1418, 1509–35 ib, *the-* 1537 Sheaf, *Vale
Roial* 1538 Dugd, *-Royall* 1407–13 VR, 1538 Dugd *et freq* to
1724 NotCestr, *the-* 1537, 1698 *Chol*, *Vale Royal* c.1536 Leland
et freq, (*-Wood*) 1831 Bry, (*-Hall*) 1845 ChetOS viii, *Vayle
Royall* 1559 Pat, *Valle Royal* 1430 ib, c.1536 Leland, *Vale Roall*
1446 Sheaf

'The nun's, or nuns' corner', from **mynecen** and **vrá**. 'Nooks
growing with wheat', *v.* **hwǣten, halh**. 'Royal valley', from **val,
vale** and **roial, real**, with **park**. 'King's valley', from **cyning** and
dǣl[1]. The abbey of Darnhall was re-established in 'a precinct of the
manor of Darnhall called *Whetenehalewes* and *Munecheneswro*', which
the founder, Edward I, 'caused to be named *Vallis Regalis*', cf.
Orm[2] ii 168. The first of the three names suggests that the place may
have belonged to the nuns of Chester, who had estates hereabouts,
cf. Orm[2] ii 161, para. xix, and cf. Nuns Grave *infra*. In 1338, VR 7,
the earlier names of the site were so interpreted, 'it was called
Munechenwro which means Monks' Wood...because *munechene*
means monk or nun, while *wro* means wood...the place was also
called *Quettennehalewes*, which means Holy Wheat or Wheat of the
Saints...for *quettene* is wheat and *halewes* saints' (cf. **halga**, 'a
saint').

ABBOT'S WALK, 1842 OS.   BARK HO, 1831 Bry, a tannery, *v.*
bark-howse.   BRICKHILL PITS, cf. *Brickkiln Field* 1845 *TA*, *v.*
bryke-kyl, pytt.   CHURCH-HILL WOOD, probably so named as
being near Whitegate church, *v.* **cirice, hyll**.   HEY'S WOOD, *the
Haywode* 1539 Orm[2], *Heywode* m16 *AOMB* 397, *Hey Wood* 1831
Bry, 'enclosed wood', *v.* **(ge)hæg, wudu**.   MAGPIE LODGE.
MEADOWBANK (HO), *Meadow Bank* 1831 ib, *v.* **mǣd, banke**.   MILL
COTTAGES & LANE, *Mill House & Lane* 1831 ib, cf. *Mill Field* 1845
TA, *Milnefelde* m16 *AOMB* 397, *v.* **myln, hūs, lane, feld**.   MONK'S
WELL, *v.* **munuc, wella**.   NEWBRIDGE (WOOD), *Bradford Woods*
1831 Bry, cf. New Bridge **2** 207, Bradfordwood *supra*.   NEW
POOL, 1656 Orm[2], *le Newe pole* m16 *AOMB* 397, *v.* **nīwe, pōl**[1].
NUNS GRAVE, 1842 OS, *the nun's grave* 1819 Orm[2], a burial from the
site of Vale Royal abbey. Whether this was in fact a nun is not
known, but cf. *Muncheniswra* under Vale Royal *supra*.   PARKSIDE
FM.   PETTY POOL, PETTYPOOL BROOK, FM & WOOD, *a poole...
cawllid Pety Pole* c.1536 Leland, *Petypole Dam & Hill* m16 *AOMB*

397, *Petty Poole Hill & Dam* 1542 Dugd, *Petty Poole* 1642 *ChCert*, *Petti-pool* 1656 Orm², *Petty Pool* 1819 Orm², *(House & Farm)* 1831 Bry, *(-Wood)* 1842 OS, 'little lake', from *pety* and *pōl*[1], with *brōc*, *damme*, *hyll*. The brook joins R. Weaver. QUESSE WOOD, 1842 ib, 'wood-pigeon wood', from *quist*. ROOKERY POOL 1831 Bry. SHERRATT'S ROUGH, cf. 183 *infra*. VALEROYAL CUT, part of the Weaver Navigation, *v.* cut. WOOD FM, named from Bradford-wood *supra*.

FIELD-NAMES

The undated forms are 1845 *TA* 310. Of the others 1334, 1375, 1475 are VR, 1361 *ChFor*, 1537, 1544 *Chol*, m16 *AOMB* 397, 1629 Orm², 1637 Sheaf, 1642 *ChCert*, 1831 Bry.

(a) Backside (*v.* ba(c)ksyde); Banking; Black Fd (cf. *Blakefeld* 1334, *the (her) Blak(e)fe(e)ld* 1475, *v.* blæc, feld); Boat House Mdw; New Bottoms 1629 (*the great(e)-, lytle-, mydle-, middell-, Bothoms, the Bothoms medowe, le Bothome medowez* 1537, 1544, *v.* botm, nīwe, mǣd); Breach Acre (*v.* brēc, æcer); Brew House Yard (cf. *Bishoppes or Brewers Croftes* 1642, *v.* brew-hous, brewere. This and *Bachous hey infra* were probably named after offices of Vale Royal abbey); Buckleys Moss; Bull Ring; Butty Moss (*v.* butty); Church Fds; Clay Flatt; Clough (*v.* clōh); Coney Grave (cf. *le Conyngrye* m16, *v.* coningre); Coxey Fd; Crab Tree Fd; Daffy Down Dilly Bank (*v.* affadille); Half- & Long Day Math (*v.* day-math); Double Ditch Wd 1831; Dove House Flatt (*Do(w)vehouseflatt(e)* 1537, 1544, *v.* dove-house, flat); Ferney Bank; Gale Fd (*v.* gagel); Greig Fd (*Gregge feld* 1475, *gryge fild* 1537, *Grygfeld* 1544, from lateME greg(g)e, 'a diminutive creature, a dwarf' and feld); Hanging Hill (*v.* hangende); Hillimoor Hey; Big & Little Holdness; Hough Mdw (*v.* hōh); Land Fd (*v.* land); Lees (*v.* lǣs); Great & Little March (*le mersshe* m16, *v.* mersc); Marl (Pit) Fd; Meadow Head (*v.* hēafod); Mere Stone Fd (*v.* (ge)mǣre, stān); Mill Fd (*Milnefelde* m16, *v.* myln, feld); Monkey Lodge 1831; Moor; Moss Lott ('a moss allotment', *v.* mos, hlot); Nicksons Wd 1831; Old Fd (cf. *Eldefeld* 1334, *v.* ald, feld); Old River; Ox Pasture; Pool Fd & Moss (cf. *Polfeld* 1334, *v.* pōl[1], feld, mos); Primrose Hill; Prison Bar Moss (*v.* prison-bars, mos); Red Hill (*Redhillfeld, Redhill medowe* m16, *v.* rēad, hyll); Riddings (cf. *le Rudinge, le Ruding(ge)s* 1334, *Ryd(d)yngges* m16, *v.* ryding); Rough Heys (*Roughehey* m16, 'rough enclosure', *v.* rūh, (ge)hæg); Row Hurst (*v.* Roehurst Lane 175 *supra*); Sand Fd (*Sandyfelde* m16, *v.* sandig, feld); Smithy Fd (*le-, the Smythe Croft(e)* 1537, 1544, *v.* smiððe, smið, croft, feld); Stanways Moss (*v.* stan, weg, mos); Big- & Three Cornered Twice (*v.* (ge)twis); Wall Croft (*the-* 1475, *le Wallecroft* 1334, 'croft at a well', *v.* wælla, croft); Way Fd (*v.* weg).

(b) Bachous hey m16 ('bakehouse enclosure', *v.* bæc-hūs, (ge)hæg); *the Barne croft, le Barnecrofte* 1537, 1544 (*v.* bere-ærn, croft); *Caldofyld, -feld* 1537, 1544; *Grette & litell Clay(e)feld* m16 (*v.* clæg, feld); *the Deanes* 1637 (*v.* denu); *le (litell-, Olde-) Intacke* m16 (*v.* inntak); *Starre medowe* m16

('sedge meadow', v. storr, mǣd); *Wettas* 1637, 1642; *Wyldemore Hey,*
Wildmerehey m16 (from (ge)hæg, probably with the first el. of *Wyldemareford*
177 *supra*); *Wright Eye* m16 (from ēg 'an island, a water-meadow', perhaps
with a surname); *the yerdes* 1537, *leʒ yardes* 1544 (v. geard).

6. MARTON (GRANGE (site of), GREEN, HALL & HO) (110–6267)
    Mertona l12 (17) Orm², *Merton* 1225 VR (p) *et freq* with variant
    spellings *-tone*, *-toun* to 1671 Sheaf, (*-alias Marton*) 1629 Orm²,
    Over Merton 1334 VR, 1642 ChCert, *grangia de Merton* 1336
    VR, 1542 Dugd
    Marton infra forestam de la Mara 1285 *Vern*, *Martona* c.1300 Bark
    (p), *Marton* 1531 ChRR, *Marton Graunge* m16 *AOMB* 397,
    Over Marton 1637 Sheaf, 1643 ChCert, *Marton Green, Hall &*
    Lane 1831 Bry, *-House* 1842 OS

'Farm by a mere', from mere¹ and tūn, with grange, grēne², hall,
lane, and hūs. Marton was a grange of Vale Royal abbey. The affix
Over- may be from uferra 'higher, upper', but seems to be more
probably the p.n. Over 170 *supra*, since part of Marton township is in
Over parish and seems to have belonged to Over township.

FOXWIST GREEN (110–625685), 1842 OS, *Foxwyste* 1475 VR *-wiste*
1487 ib, *-wist* 1488 MidCh, (*-iuxta Ouer*) 1503 ChFor, *Foxewist* 1542
(1724) NotCestr, *Fox's Green* (*Lane*) 1831 Bry, 'fox's lair', from fox
and wist, with grēne², cf. Foxtwist 1 194.

MARTONSANDS (110–625677) ['maːtṇ 'sæːnz], 1724 NotCestr (*the*
crosse at) *Merton sonde* 1475 VR, *Martin-Sands* 1666 Orm², *Merton*
Sands 1671 Sheaf, *The Sands* 1831 Bry, named from the beds of
glacial sand here, v. sand.

ABBOTS MOSS (HALL & WOOD), *Abbots Moss* (*Hall*) 1831 Bry, from
the abbot of Vale Royal, v. mos.   BALLSGATE, 1842 OS, *Baws*
Gate 1831 Bry.   BARK HO, v. bark-howse.   BEAUTYBANK, 1831
ib, v. botye, banke.   BLACKDOG, a house, perhaps formerly an
inn.   BROOKSIDE FM named from Bogart Brook 1 15, v. sīde.
CASSIA GREEN & LODGE [kɛːʃə], *Cassia Green* 1681 Sheaf, 1842 OS,
Acasia Lodge 1831 Bry, v. grēne², loge. Similar forms are Casha Bank
20 *supra*, Cassia Fd 325 *infra*. The origin may be a ME form
Catteshagh or *Catteshalgh* 'wild-cat's wood or nook', from catt,
catte and sc(e)aga or halh.   CHESTER LANE (FM), *Chester lone* 1475
VR, *-Lane* 1831 Bry, 'lane leading to Chester', v. Chester 325 *infra*,
cf. 186 *infra*, 1 48 (route XXIII).   CHURCH-HILL WOOD, v. 180

supra. CLAY LANE (FM), *Clay Lane (Farm)* 1831 Bry, *v.* clæg,
lane. COMMON FM, cf. *Common Croft, Field & Lot* 1846 *TA*, *v.*
commun, and hlot. COOKSTOOL, 1842 OS, *v.* cucke-stole 'a
cucking-stool'. DAISYBANK FM, *v.* dægesēge, banke. DALE-
FORDS (LANE), *Dale Fords (Brook)* 1831 Bry, 'ford in a valley', from
dæl[1] and ford, with brōc. DELAMERE FOREST (part of), cf. *Forest
Field* 1846 *TA*, *v.* forest, cf. 1 8. DONKEY LANE. HARES-
CLOUGH, *Hare-clough* 1846 *ib*, 'hare's dell', *v.* hara, clōh. HEAD-
LESS CROSS, *v.* 218 *infra.* HILLTOP, 1831 Bry, *v.* hyll, topp.
HOLLYBANK FM, *v.* holegn, banke. KAY'S FM, *Shays* 1831 Bry,
from a surname *Kay*, cf. Shay's Fm *infra.* LAPWING HALL, *v.*
hlēape-wince, hall. MARTON HOLE, cf. *Hole Field* 1846 *TA*, *v.*
hol[1]. This is the name of a large pit near Marton Grange. MILL
LANE, cf. *molendinum aquaticum* 1294 ChFor, *molend' de Merton* 1357
ib, *v.* myln, lane. NEWCHURCH COMMON, 1813 Orm[2], from an
older name of Whitegate 178 *supra*, *v.* commun. NOVA SCOTIA,
1842 OS. REEKING HOLE, *v.* rēcende, hol[1]. Whether the ancient
or modern sense of 'reeking' is implied does not appear. THE
ROOKERY, *Rookery Farm* 1831 Bry, *v.* rookery. SHAY'S FM &
LANE, SHAY'S LANE BROOK, *Shaw Farm, Lane & Brook* 1842 OS,
cf. *Shay Corner & Cover* 1831 Bry, *Big Shay, Shay Field & Meadow*
1846 *TA*, and Kay's Fm *supra*, from scaga, sceaga 'a copse', with
corner, cover, lane and brōc. The brook becomes Chesterlane Brook
186 *infra.* SHEMMY MOSS, 1846 *ib*, *v.* mos. SHERRATT'S
ROUGH, from the surname *Sherratt* and rūh. SNIPE ISLAND, *v.*
snype. SPRINGFIELD. THE SWALLOWS. VILLAVIEW, 1724
NotCestr.

FIELD-NAMES

The undated forms are 1846 *TA* 257, 259. Of the others, 1304 is Chamb,
1357, 1503 *ChFor*, m16 *AOMB* 397, 1831 Bry, 1842 OS, and the rest VR.

(*a*) Back Lane; Back oth House ('field at the back of the house'); Bake-
house Fd; Banks; Belle Vue; Birch Fd; Black Banks; Blackden Fd (cf.
Blakeden 171 *supra*); Bone Fd (*v.* bān, cf. bone-dust); Boors Mdw (*v.*
(ge)būr); Bowling Green; Braddock; Broom Fd (*v.* brōm); Cart House Fd;
Clarkes Fd (*Clerkes feld* 1475, 'the clerk's field', *v.* clerc, feld); Big & Little
Clough (*v.* clōh); Coppice Bank; Cow Lane; Cranberry Moss (*v.* cranberry);
Croming Bank; Dog Kennel Fd; Dunns Bank 1831 (from the surname *Dunn*
and banke); Eagle Fd (cf. dial. *eagles* 'hawthorn berries'); Fish Pit Fd
(*Fyschpitt feeldes* 1475, *v.* fisc, pytt, feld); Fletcher's Moss 1831; French Bank,
Croft & Fd (probably named after the crop french-wheat); Glade Fd;
Hanging Bank (*v.* hangende); Hatch Fd (*v.* hæc(c)); Haywood (*v.* (ge)hæg,

wudu); Hazlehurst (v. hæsel, hyrst); Heath Fd, Little Heath (cf. *Bruere*
1217–32, *del Heet* 1290 (p), *del Heth* 1304 (p), *dil Het* 1330, v. hǣð, bruiere);
Hemp Fd; (Big & Little) Holdings (perhaps *Holden* 1304 (p), *Holden(s)feild)*
1334, 'hollow valley', from hol² and denu, with feld, cf. The Holdings 2 199);
Hollins (v. holegn); Hopley Exchange Fd; Intake (v. inntak); Little Croft
(cf. *Litlecroft* 1334, v. lȳtel, croft); Marl Fd; Middle Fd (cf. *Middelfeld* 1334,
v. middel, feld); Moor; Big & Little Moss; Mountain; Paper Mill Wd
(1842); Pepper Hill (cf. Pepper St. (Chester) 326 *infra*); Pingott (v. pingot);
Pitracks (*Pykrakys* 1475, 'pointed strips of land', from rake with pīc¹ in the
sense 'a parcel of land running into a corner, a narrow pointed piece of land',
v. NED *pike* sb¹ 5, *pick* sb¹ 6, from 1585); Rough, Rough Bank(s), Ends &
Wd (v. rūh, ende¹); Rye Bank & Fd (cf. *the Rye crofte, the secund Ryefeeld*
1475, v. ryge, croft, feld); Saw Pit Bank (v. saw-pytt); Skin Pit Fd (probably
from a tanning-pit in which hides were immersed in oak bark, v. skinn,
pytt, cf. Bark Ho *supra*); Sky Fd; Sutton Fd (v. *Sutton* 179 *supra*); Far &
Near Yards (v. geard); Youth Fd.

(b) *Asshbrokschwa* 1357 ('(the wood at) Ash Brook', v. sceaga, cf. Ash
Brook 1 14); *le Erlesbroke* 1503 ('the earl's brook', v. eorl, brōc. The earls of
Chester owned the manors of Over and Darnhall before the foundation of
Vale Royal abbey, and Marton adjoins their ancient forest of Delamere); *le
Hey* 13 (v. (ge)hæg); *le Holrenbarwe* 13 ('alder wood', v. alren, bearu);
Merton Cop' m16 (v. copp 'a hill').

iv. Little Budworth Chapelry

Little Budworth was a free chapelry in Over parish, in the patronage of the
Nuns of Chester until the dissolution, and thereafter a parochial chapelry of
Over parish until the nineteenth century (Orm² III 211). It is now a c.p.
including Oulton Lowe 165 *supra*.

1. LITTLE BUDWORTH, locally [ˈbudəːþ] (109–5965)

Bodeurde 1086 DB, *Bodeworth* 1304 Chamb (p), 1329 Fine, 1357
    ChFor, *-wrth* 1328 (1338) VR, *Boddeworth* c.1300 Bark and 4
    examples to 1403 ib, *Bodworth* 1324 Bark, *-worthe* 1374 Tab
Buddeworth 1153–81 (1353–7) *ChFor et freq* with variant spellings
    Bu(d)d(e)-, -wr(th), -word, -worthe, -wurth(e) to 1456 ChRR,
    (*-iuxta Oure*) 1329 Plea, (*-Rushton*) 1350 Orm², (*-Ruysshton*)
    1359 ib, *Budworth* 1295 Orm² *et freq*
Buddew(o)r(th) in foresta (de Mara) 1290–1310 AD, 1311 Plea
Budworth en le Frith 1295 Orm² *et freq* with variant spellings as for
    Budworth and *-in le-, -in the-, -Frith(e), -Fryth(e), -Freth* to
    Budworth-in-the-Frith 1860 White, *Budworth in Frithe* 1534 Chol
Little Boddeworth 1353 BPR, *Little Budworth(e)* 1582, 1599 AD, *et
    freq*, *Budworth Parva* 1668 Sheaf, 1724 NotCestr

'Bud(d)a's enclosure', from the OE pers.n. *Bud(d)a* and worð. *Little-* (*v.* lȳtel) distinguishes this from Great Budworth **2** 107, which was a larger parish. It adjoins Rushton 291 *infra* and Over 170 *supra*. It was 'in the forest', *v.* in, en, forest, (ge)fyrhðe being within the Forest of Delamere **1** 8.

OULTON (LAKE & PARK (FM)) [ˈuːl-, ˈoultən] older local [ˈuːtŋ] (109–5964)

Altetone 1086 DB

Audinton 1180–1220 *Chol* (p)

Oldenton 1220–40 Whall (p), 1315 *AddCh* (p), 1326 Adl (p), -*inton* 1260 Court (p) *et freq* with variant spellings -*tona*, -*tun*, -*in*(*g*)-, -*yng*- to 1503 *Chol, Olton alias Oldyngton* 1397 Pat (p), ChRR (p)

Aldeton c.1230 Sheaf, 1259 Plea, 1260 Court (p)

Hold(e)ton 13 (17) Sheaf (p), 1287 MidCh (p), *Oldeton* 1272–90 *ChFor* (p), 1287 Court *et freq* with variant spellings -*tune*, -*ton(e)*, *Oalde*- to c.1536 Leland, *Oldton* 1343 *Chol* (p), 1370 AD (p), 1377 ChRR (p)

Olton 1275 MidCh (p), 1341 ChRR (p) *et freq* to 1656 Orm² , (*et* (*le*) *Lowe*) 1357 *ChFor*, 1381 ChRR, 1407 Pat, 1613 Orm² , (-*alias Oldyn(g)ton*) 1397 ChRR (p), Pat (p), *Oltowne* 1587 *JRC* (Barnes¹ 341)

Aulton 1335 Cl (p)

Oulton 1480 Sheaf, 1594 AD *et freq*, (-*in Little Budworth*) 1671 Sheaf, *Oulton Park* 1819 Orm²

This p.n. may be OE (**æt*) *aldan tūne* 'the old or former enclosure or farmstead', with ME reformation of -*an*- to -*en*- > -*in*- > -*ing*-. Dr von Feilitzen prefers an original -*ing*- formation with reduction of -*ing*- > -*in*-, -*en*-. This interpretation suggests that Oulton is 'Alda's farm, farm called after Alda', from the OE pers.n. *Alda* (WSax *Ealda*), in gen.sg. (*Aldan*-) or with -*ing*-⁴, and tūn. Tait 111 n.77, 209 n.220, identifies *Altetone* DB f.267b (*Riseton* hundred) with Oulton Lowe 165 *supra*, and *Alretone* DB f.263b (*Dudestan* hundred) with Oulton. But it looks as if *Alretone*, formally improbable for Oulton, is the name of a lost place near Harewood-Hill 211 *infra* in Delamere, whilst *Altetone* is the antecedent form of the p.n. Oulton rather than of *Lowe* (Oulton Lowe). Cf. Oulton Hall & Mill *infra*.

AKESMERE PLACE. AVENUE LODGE. BEECH HO, v. bēce².
BOOTH'S SMITHY, 1842 OS, *Booth Smithy* 1831 Bry, probably from
a surname *Booth* and smiðöe.   BROOKHOUSE FM, *Brook House* 1831
Bry, v. brōc, hūs.   BROOK SLACK 1842 OS, v. brōc, slakki, cf. *le
Brok* 1312–18 Bark.   BUDWORTH MILL, v. myln. There were two
mills, *Budworth Mill* 1831 Bry and *Walk Mill* 1831 ib, 1842 OS (v.
walke-milne), cf. 'a water-mill and a fulling-mill with ponds and
fisheries adjacent' 1370 Orm² II 212, cf. foll.   BUDWORTH POOL, *le
Walkemulnepoul* c.1300 Bark, *le Pol* 1357 ChFor, v. walke-milne,
pōl¹, cf. prec.   BUTT FM, *The Butt* 1831 Bry, v. butte.   CAB-
BAGE HALL.   CHESTER LANE, 1831 ib, v. 182 *supra*, I 48 (route
XXIII), cf. foll.   CHESTERLANE BROOK (> Ash Brook I 14), cf.
prec.   COMMON SIDE, 1842 OS, v. Little Budworth Common
infra.   CONEYGREAVES FM, *Coney Gree* 1794 Sheaf, 1831 Bry,
Coney Greave 1842 OS, 'rabbit-warren', v. coningre.   CORNHILL
FM, *Corn Hill* 1831 Bry, v. corn¹, cf. 167 *supra*.   FENNYWOOD FM,
1839 *TA*, *Le Fyney, or Finney* 1377–8 Orm² II 215, *Finnywood* 1543
Orm², *Fennywoodd* 1555 Sheaf, -*Wood* 1842 OS, 'rough-grass
enclosure', v. finn, (ge)hæg, cf. Finney 240 *infra*.   FOREST HO.
HEADLESS CROSS, v. 218 *infra*.   HILL FM.   HINDS GATE, v. 212
infra.   LITTLE BUDWORTH COMMON, 1842 OS, *Budworth Common*
1813 Orm², cf. *le Heth* c.1300 Bark, v. hǣð, commun.   LONG
STONE, 1831 Bry, v. lang, stān.   LOWER FM.   MANOR HO.
MILL COVERT.   OLD HALL, 1831 Bry, *aula in Buddeworth* 1373
Bark, v. ald, hall.   OULTON HALL, 1831 Bry, *Fernele(y)s, Ferne-
leghes iuxta Budworth in le Frith* 1503 ChFor, *maner' of Ferneleghes
otherwise cald the maner of Olton* 1537 Orm², *the Hall of Olton* 1564 ib,
-*Oulton* 1650 ChRR, 'ferny clearings', v. fearnig, lēah, later from
hall and Oulton *supra*.   OULTON MILL, v. 293 *infra*.   OUTSIDE
FM, *The Outside* 1831 Bry, *Outsides Farm* 1842 OS, 'outlying part',
v. ūt, sīde.   PARK FM, cf. foll.   PARK PLACE, 1842 ib, *Park Wall
Farm* 1831 Bry, from Oulton Park *supra*, v. park, wall, place, cf. prec.
POOL BANK, POOLHEAD FM, *Pool Head* 1831 ib, 1842 OS, cf. *le
Polforlong* c.1300 Bark, v. pōl¹, banke, hēafod, furlang, cf. Budworth
Pool *supra*.   ROBIN HOOD'S WELL, v. 325 *infra*.   SANDYFORD
BRIDGE, v. 211 *infra*.   SHAY'S LANE BROOK, v. 183 *supra*.   TOM'S
HOLE, 1842 OS, *Little Oulton Plantation* 1831 Bry.   TOP O' TH'
TOWN FM, *Top of the Town* 1831 ib, v. topp, toun.   WELLHOUSE
FM.   WHITE HALL, 1783 Sheaf.   WOOD COTTAGE.

FIELD-NAMES

The undated forms are 1839 *TA* 80. Of the others 1272–90, 1347, 1353, 1503 are *ChFor*, 1290–1310 AD, 1328 Cl, 1338 VR, 1393 ChRR, 1393², 1430, 1534 Orm², 1611, 1682 Sheaf, 1831 Bry, 1842 OS, and the rest Bark.

(*a*) Butty Piece (*v.* butty); Hewins Lane 1831, 1842 (cf. *le Huvyng* 1338 VR 44, a wood-name, 'the yew place', *v.* īw, -ing²); Thorn Ho 1831; Town Fd; Wanleys Lane 1842 (also 294 *infra*); Yew Tree Ho 1842.

(*b*) *Baldewelle* c.1300 ('Bealda's spring', from the OE pers.n. *Bealda* and *wella*); *le Berecroft* c.1300, 1449 ('barley croft', *v.* bere, croft); *le Blakeflotte* c.1300 (NRA 0406/31, probably a mistake for *-flatte*, 'the black plot of land', *v.* blæc, flat); *le Brodeokfeld* 1353, 1373 ('broad-oak field', *v.* brād, āc, feld); *boscus de Buddeworthe* 1347, *Budworthwode* 1393, *Bud(de)worth Wood, -Wode* 1393² (*v.* wudu); *le Caluerhey* 1353 ('calves' enclosure', calf, (ge)hæg); *Cleys* 1534 (*v.* clæg); *le Clovenlowe* c.1300 ('cloven hill or mound', *v.* (ge)clofen, hlāw, perhaps an excavated burial-mound); *le Dede Cherlischiche* 1290–1310, *le Dedecherlenche* e14 ('the dead peasant's stream', from dēad and ceorl, with sīc. The e14 spelling is unreliable, probably a mis-copy of *-enche* for *-siche*. The name probably alludes to the discovery of a corpse); *le Dichefeul* c.1300 (*v.* dīc, feld); *Doggruding* e14 ('dog's clearing', *v.* dogga, ryding); *le Drochurst* 1338 ('wood where beams were got', *v.* þroc, hyrst); *Duntun* e14 ('enclosure at a hill', *v.* dūn, tūn, cf. *Done* 161 *supra*); *le Halle-croft* c.1300 (*v.* hall, croft, cf. Old Hall *supra*); *Haskethay* 1353, *-hey* 1373 ('race-course enclosure', *v.* hestr, skeiδ, (ge)hæg); *le Haslond* c.1300 (*v.* land); *le Hayhous* 1312–18 (perhaps a barn, a 'hay-house', *v.* hēg, hūs); *le Hethilewes* c.1300, *Heytelegh* 1338, *le Hethelees* 1373 ('heathy clearing(s)', *v.* hǣδ, hǣδig, hǣδiht, lēah); *le Homappeltresseawe* c.1300 ('apple-tree copse', *v.* æppel-trēow, sceaga. The prefixed el. is hām 'home, the village' in the modern sense 'near the village, near home', cf. home); *le Parke* 1430 (*v.* park, perhaps Oulton Park *supra*); *le Shepcote* 1373, cf. *le Schepecroft* c.1300 ('sheep fold and croft', *v.* scēp, cot, croft); *le Solmhurstesflotte* c.1300 ('plot of land at a willow wood', *v.* salegn, hyrst, flat, cf. *Salynhill* 1503 *ChFor* (location unknown, Forest of Delamere), *v.* hyll, cf. Sallings Wo 42)); *landa de Stodle* 1272–90, *Stodleysiche* 1312–18, *Stodle* 1328 (p), *Oldestodeley* 1373 ('stud clearing', *v.* stōd, lēah, ald, sīc); *Wodefordefurde* 1312–18, *Wodeford-feld* 1373 ('ford and field towards Woodford', *v.* ford, feld, Woodford Hall 174 *supra*); *Wylmyscroft* 1324, *Wilymescroft* 1338 ('William's croft', from the ME pers.n. *William* (*Willelm*) and croft).

v. Witton Chapelry & Weaverham

The township of Hartford, here surveyed to the boundaries shown in Bry, is now partly included in Northwich c.p. with Castle Northwich 190 *infra*. It was partly in Witton Chapelry and Weaverham parish, cf. *Conersley* 207 *infra*.

1. HARTFORD (BANK, BRIDGE, COTTAGE, GRANGE, HALL, HILL, HO, LODGE & RD) (110–6472)

> *Herford* 1086 DB, 1349 Sheaf, 1425 Tab (p), 1557 Sheaf, (*-cum Horton*) 1581 ChRR, *Harford(bridg)* 1646 Sheaf, *Harford Green* 1684 ib
>
> *Hartford* c.1188–1209 MidCh (p), 1278 Misc, 1436 Tab, 1724 NotCestr *et freq*, (*-alias Hertford*) 1694 Orm², *Hartfurde* 1570 Chol, *Hartefourd* 1611 Sheaf, *Hartford House* 1799 *AddCh*, *Hartford Hall, Hill & Lane* 1831 Bry, *Hartford Lodge* 1842 OS
>
> *Hertford* 13 (17) Sheaf, 1291 VR (p), 1299 Plea *et freq* with variant spellings *- fford*, *-forde*, *-furde*, *Herteford* to 1694 Orm², (*-alias Herford cum Horton*) 1581 ChRR, *Hertefordbrygg'* 1353 *ChFor*, *Hertford Brigge* 1504 AD
>
> *Herdfer* 1537 MidCh

'Hart's ford', from **heorot** and **ford**, with **banke, brycg, grange, hall, hyll, hūs, loge, lane** and **grēne²**.

HORTON (lost, about 110–647724)

> *Horton* c.1200 Tab (p) *et freq*, (*-iuxta Hertford*) 1361 *ChFor*, (*-in-*) 1381 Orm², (*-and Hertford*) 1558 ib, (*Hertford alias Herford cum-*) 1581 ChRR, (*-alias Hartford*) 1639 Orm², *Hortona* 13 Tab, *Orton* 1541 Orm², (*-alias Horton alias Hertford*) 1584 ChRR, *Horton Meadow* 17 Chol, *Horton Field, Big & Little Horton* 1845 *TA*
>
> *Horston* c.1260 (p), 1436 Tab

'Dirty farm' or 'muck-yard', *v.* **horu, tūn**. The rare *Hors-* form appears in seventeenth-century copies only, and is obviously erroneous. The site is the park of Hartford Manor.

ASHBANK, 'ash-tree hill', *v.* **æsc, banke**.   BEACH FM & RD, BEACHFIELD, HARTFORDBEACH, [biːtʃ], *Beech Farm* 1831 Bry, *Beach House* 1845 *TA*, from **bece¹** 'a valley-stream', *v.* Beach Fm 206 *infra*.   CASTLE BANK, *v.* 190 *infra*.   CHESTER RD, *Chester Lane* 1845 *TA*, *v.* **lane**, Chester 325 *infra*, 'Watling Street' 1 40 (route VII).   CLOUGH WOOD, [klʌf], cf. *Lower Clough* 1845 *ib*, *v.* **clōh**.   GRANGE FM, cf. Hartford Grange *supra*.   GREEN-BANK WOOD, cf. Hartford Manor *infra*.   HARTFORDBEACH, *v.* Beach Cottage *supra*.   HARTFORD MANOR, *Green Bank* 1831 Bry, 1842 OS, cf. Greenbank Wood *supra*, *v.* **grēne¹, banke**.   HEYES-

WOOD FM, HEY'S WOOD, *Hey Wood* 1831 Bry, 1842 OS, *v.* 180 *supra*.
THE HEYSOMS. THE HOLLIES (FM), *Hartford Farm* 1831 Bry.
MANOR COTTAGE. MODEL FM. THE MOUNT. RED HO.
THE RIDDINGS, cf. *Ridding(s)* 1845 *TA*, *v.* ryding. RIDDINGS
LANE, *Jack Riddings Lane* 1831 Bry, cf. *Jack Riddings* 1839 *TA*,
'inconsiderable cleared-lands', *v.* jack, ryding. ROYALTY WOOD,
v. roialte. THORN FM, *Thorn House* 1724 NotCestr, *v.* þorn.
WALNUT COTTAGE, cf. *Walnut Croft* 1845 *TA*. 'WATLING STREET',
v. 1 40 (route VII), Chester Road *supra*. WEST HO. WOOD-
LAND COTTAGES, WOODLANDS, *The Woodlands* 1831 Bry, *Woodland*
1842 OS, cf. *bosc' de Hertford* c.1295 (17) Sheaf, *v.* wudu-land.

FIELD-NAMES

The undated forms are 1839 *TA* 416 (Weaverham parish) and 1845 *TA* 190
(Witton Chapelry). Of the others 13 (17), 1295 (17), 1671 are Sheaf, 1315–16
Orm², 1353, 1357 *ChFor*.

(a) Abbey (Lane) Fd (named from Vale Royal Abbey 179 *supra*, and a lane
leading to it); Bank Fd; Barnsley (*v.* lēah); Black Heys (*v.* (ge)hæg); Little
Bramleys (*v.* brōm, lēah); Breach (*v.* brēc); Broom Fd (*v.* brōm); Brown Fd;
Cajel Trees; Dragon Fd; Glede Fd (*v.* gleoda); Hatch Tree Hill; Hay Hill;
High Heaton; Hodge Lane Fd (*Hodge Lane* 1671, either 'hog's lane' or
'Roger's lane', from lane and either hocg or the ME pers.n. *Hodge* (*Roger*),
cf. foll. and *Hodg Croft* 1 158); Hodge Riddings (*Rogerrudyng* 1353, 'Roger's
cleared-land', from the ME pers.n. *Roger*, (pet-form *Hodge*) and ryding);
Kirk Acre (*v.* kirkja, æcer); Long Range (*v.* range); Milking Bank (*v.*
milking); Big & Little Moor (cf. *le Mores* c.1295 (17), *v.* mōr¹); Red Lion
Fd (named from the inn, *The Red Lion*); Rough Bank; Shippon Fd (*v.*
scypen); Sparrow Grove (*v.* spearwa, grāf); Town Fd; Twemlow Fd ('at
the two mounds', *v.* twǣm, hlāw); Well Fd; Whale Bone Fd; White Fd
(*v.* hwīt); Wood Hey (*v.* wudu, (ge)hæg).

(b) *Bernhull* 1353 ('barn hill', *v.* bere-ærn, hyll); *le bromhull* 1353 (*v.*
brōm, hyll); *Brounhull* 13 (17) ('brown hill', *v.* brūn¹, hyll); *le Ferneye* 13 (17)
('fern island', *v.* fearn, ēg); *le Fernylee*, *-legh* 1357 ('ferny clearing', *v.*
fearnig, lēah); *le Gatestode* c.1295 (17) ('place at a gateway', *v.* geat, stede);
Moseleyfeld 1353 ('(field at) the mossy clearing', *v.* mos, lēah, feld); *M.. solawe*
1357 (final el. hlāw 'a mound, a hill'); *le Mulnefeld* 1353 (cf. *a watermill in
Hertford* 1315–16, and *le Wynmulnefeld infra*, *v.* myln, feld); *Sydehale* 1353,
Si.. halawe 1357 ('wide nook', *v.* sīd, halh); *le Wynmulnefeld* 1353 ('windmill
field', *v.* wind-mylne, feld, cf. *le Mulnefeld supra*).

vi. Witton Chapelry

The Witton chapelry of Great Budworth parish (*v.* **2** 95) extended into Eddisbury hundred, including the townships 7. Castle Northwich, 8. Winnington and also part of Hartford 188 *supra*. Castle Northwich and Winnington are now included in Northwich c.p. *v.* **2** 185.

7. CASTLE NORTHWICH (110–655735)

> *Castellum* 1189–99 Orm² (p), c.1240 *JRC*, (*terra de-*) 13 (17) Orm², (*villa de-*), (*-prope Norwic*) c.1240 Tab, (*-juxta Northwycum*) 1356 *JRC, villa de Castell'* 1427 *ib, le Castel juxta Northwych* 1357 Orm², *villa del Castell iuxta Northwich* 1381 Plea
>
> *terra Castelli de Norwico* 1189–99 Orm², *castrum de Northwyc* 1361 ChFor, *Castrum Norweyci* 1347 *ib*
>
> Castle Northwich 1216–72 (17) Orm², 1303 Chamb *et freq* with variant spellings *Castel(l)-* and as for Northwich (**2** 192) to 1842 OS
>
> (*le*) *Castelton-, -Castleton* (*iuxta Northwich*) 1388 ChRR, 1491, 1536 ib, Orm², 1554 ib, 1724 NotCestr, *the Castell town of Northwich* 1574 Sheaf

'The township of the castle at Northwich', *v.* castel(l), tūn, toun, cf. Northwich **2** 192. The site of the castle was at CASTLE HILL, 1831 Bry, cf. Orm² II 2, *v.* hyll.

STREET-NAMES. CASTLE ST., 1842 OS, *regalis via* c.1240 *JRC, -que vocatur le Holewaye* 1301–3 *ib, le Hole waye* e14 *ib, Wynigton holeway* 1325–8 *ib, Wynintonholeway* c.1350 *ib, the Hollow Way* 1817 Orm² II 2, 197, 'road in a hollow, sunken road', from its course under Castle Hill *supra, v.* hol², weg. From the statement in *JRC* 845 and 846 that c.1240 the castle ditch was the Winnington boundary, and from the position of this boundary in 1831, Bry, it appears that part of this road lay in Winnington 191 *infra*, hence that p.n. is affixed to the road-name. This is part of 'Watling Street' **1** 40 (route VII); CHESTER RD, cf. 188 *supra*.

BURROWS HILL. CASTLE BANK, formerly on the boundary between Hartford 188 *supra* and Castle Northwich, 'hill in Castle township', *v.* castel(l), banke. FURY POND. HIGHFIELD HO. MOSS CLIFF & LANE, *v.* mos, clif, lane, Moss Fm 192 *infra*. TOWN BRIDGE, *v.* **2** 194.

FIELD-NAMES

(a) Lamprey Ditch 1819 Orm² 111 162, Sheaf¹ 2,114 ('ditch where lampreys are taken', v. lampreie, dīc. This was the boundary between a small part of Northwich which lay west of Weaver, and the township of Castle Northwich. It was covered with a plat in 1819. Helsby, the editor of Orm², quotes *Lampern, Lomrey, Lomon, Lomern* as other forms, but cites no references).

(b) *The New Swanne* 1641 Sheaf (a messuage, probably an inn).

8. WINNINGTON (HALL, LANE & PARK) (110–6474) ['winiŋtən] older local ['winitn̩]

Wenitone 1086 DB

Wyninton 1̄12 Orm² *et freq* with variant spellings -*tona*, -*tonn*, *Winin*-, *Wynyn*-, *Wynnin*- (from 1271–5 Chest), *Winnin*- (from 1354 Tab), *Wynnyn*- (from 1442 ChRR (p)) to 1527 AD, *Wininton iuxta Northwych* 1271–4 Chest

Wyneton 1190–1210 (17) Orm²

Wynington 1199–1216 Chest, c.1240 *JRC et freq* with variant spellings *Wyn*-, *Winington*, -*yng*-, -*thon* to 1673 ChRR, *Wynning*-, -*yng*- from 1271 (14) Tab, 1321 Plea, *Winning*- from 1399 ChRR *et freq*, *Wininctona* 1288 Court, *Wynygnton* 1535 AD (p), *Winnington Hall* 1831 Bry

Wynentona 1210–20 Chest, *Winenton* c.1270 *JRC* (p)

Winton 1238 (1580) Sheaf

Wynmington 13 (17) Sheaf

Wenyngton c.1260 *JRC*, 1325 Cl (p), and 10 forms with variant spelling *Wening*- to 1548 AD (p)

Weninton 1270 Sheaf, 1̄13 Chest, -*yn*- c.1300 JRL (p), 1320 VR (p), 1448 (p), 1495 ChRR

Winigton 1272–90, 1288 ChFor, 1287 Court (p), *Wyn*- 1292 Ipm (p), *Wynyg*- 1318 Eyre, 1332 Chol (p), 1526 AD, *Wynnyg*- 1389 ChRR (p)

Wyminton 1278 Misc, *Wim*- 1308 Tab (p), *Wymyn*- 1357 BPR (p), *Wymyng*- 1351 ib (p), 1540 AD (p), -*ing*- 1536 ChRR, *Wiming*- 1546 Dugd

Wymigton 1295 Fine (p)

Weynigton 1323 Chol (p), *Weynyngton* 1515 MinAcct

Wynyton 1430 ChRR (p)

'Farm called after Wine', from the OE pers.n. *Wine* and -*ingtūn*, with hall, lane and park. The same pers.n. occurs in Winsford 173 *supra*, five miles upstream on R. Weaver. Winnington is near Northwich 2 192, and formerly extended as far as the Town Bridge there, cf. Castle St. 190 *supra*.

WINNINGTON BRIDGE (110–642748), 1618 Sheaf, probably the location of *Wynintonnesforde* c.1278 *AddCh*, *v.* brycg, ford, cf. Winnington *supra*.

ABATTOIR COTTAGES.   AVENUE LODGE, *v.* loge, cf. Winnington Avenue *infra*.   BEACH LANE, cf. *Beach Moss* 1844 *TA*, *le Bache* c.1240 *JRC*, *Bachemosse* e14 *ib*, *Bachemoos* 1338 VR, *la Bachoe Mosse* 1399 ChRR, and Moss Fm *infra*, *v.* Beach Fm 206 *infra*, mos. BYEFLAT WORKS, *v.* works. *Byeflat* is 'flat plot of ground in a riverbend', *v.* byge[1], flat.   HILL VIEW FM, *Hill* 1831 Bry, *v.* hyll. THE LEY, *v.* lēah, dial. *ley* 'a pasture'.   MOSS FM & ROAD, *Moss Farm* 1831 Bry, *Moss Hall* 1842 OS. The road is known locally as *the* (*Golf*) *Links*. This district is probably *Bachemos*, cf. Beach Lane *supra*.   WINNINGTON AVENUE, *The Avenue* 1831 Bry, cf. *Avenue Moss* 1844 *TA*, after an avenue of Winnington Hall *supra*, *v.* avenue. WINNINGTON LODGE (lost), 1831 Bry, *v.* loge. The site is that of the Infirmary.   WORBOISE WORKS, *v.* works, cf. *Warburs Eye* 1844 *TA*, probably 'St Warburgh's island', from ēg and the OE fem. pers.n. *Wǣrburg*, the name of the patron-saint of Chester abbey, which owned half of Winnington, cf. Orm[2] II 200, 202.

FIELD-NAMES

The undated forms are 1844 *TA* 439. Of the others 13, 13 (17) are Orm[2], c.1278 *AddCh*, 1357 *ChFor*, 1536 ChRR, and the rest *JRC*.

(*a*) Lesser Azy (cf. *le Heseegclyf* 1357, '(cliff at) the island where brushwood grows', from hǣs and ēg, with clif); Beacle Fd; Broad Moss; Cawley Mdw & Moss; Gale Moss (*v.* gagel); Hales Hill; Holdings Moss ('mossland allocated in holdings', *v.* holding, mos); Island Mdw (*v.* ēg-land); Marl(e) Fd & Pit (*v.* marle, marle-pytt); Milking Bank (*v.* milking); Pinfold Fd (*v.* pynd-fald); Rock Pit Mdw (in local salt-mining terms, a rockpit is a mine of rock-salt, as distinct from a brine-pit or -well); Rushey Moss; Tankard's Eye (*v.* ēg); Westy Mdw (*Westey* 1272–1307, 'west island', *v.* west, ēg); Wheat Moss ('wet moss', *v.* wēt, mos); White Fd.

(*b*) *Agaslake* c.1240 ('Ēadgār s watercourse', from the OE pers.n. *Ēadgar* and lacu); *insula vocata Aldewareheye* c.1278 ('(island at) the old weir', *v.* ald, wer, ēg); *le Blakebottes* 1344 ('black selions', *v.* blæc, butte); *le Brothereye*, *-Brotheryee*, *-Brothirheye* c.1240, *le Broþerheye* 1272–1307 ('the brother's island', v. brōðor, ēg. If the first el. were taken as brōðra (gen.pl. of brōðor) the name would perhaps refer to the monks of Chester Abbey, cf. Warboise *supra*); *Caldacher, -yr* c.1240 ('cold acre', v. cald, æcer. For the *-ch-* spelling cf. Alsager 2 *supra*); *le cloyhg-, le cloc iuxta le Bache* c.1240 ('the dell near the valley-stream', v. clōh, bæce[1], cf. Beach Lane *supra*); *le Colhoppus* 1344 ('enclosures where charcoal is made', v. col[1], hop[1]); *le Conyngre* 1536 ('rabbit-warren', v. coningre); *Lorteborn, -burne* c.1240 ('dirty stream', v. lort(e), burna, cf. *Lothburne* 36 *supra*); *le More* c.1240, *mora* 1272–1307 ('marsh', v. mōr[1]); *Steynulvescroft, -ulsves-, Stainilliscroft* 13, 13 (17), *Staynuluescroft* 1301–3, c.1350 ('Steinulf s croft', from the ON pers.n. *Steinolfr* and croft).

vii. Weaverham

The ancient parish of Weaverham contained the townships 1. Acton, 2. Crowton (now a c.p. including Onston *infra*), 3. Cuddington, 4. Onston (v. Crowton *supra*), 5. Wallerscote (now included in Northwich c.p., v. 2 185), 6. Weaverham cum Milton (v. 202 *infra*), and also part of Hartford 188 *supra* and of Norley 249 *infra*.

1. ACTON (FORGE (lost), HALL, LANE & MILL (lost)) (109–5975)

> *Acton* e13 Tab, 1260 Court *et freq*, (*-iuxta Weverham*) 1314 Plea,
> (*-in foresta de Delamere*) 1400 ChRR, (*-iuxta Dutton*) 1420 Plea,
> *Actona* 1252 RBE, 1288 Court, *Akton* 1301 Chamb[1] (p), *Actonne*
> 1338 Orm[2], *Actun* 1545 Plea, *Acton Forge & Mill* 1831 Bry
> *Aketon* 1299 Tab (p).

'Oak farm', from āc and tūn, with forge, hall, lane and myln. *Aketon* may be from the gen.pl. āca, cf. Acton 126 *supra*. Acton adjoins Weaverham 205 *infra* and Dutton 2 112, and was within the Forest of Delamere 1 8.

ACTON BRIDGE (101–600760), *pons de Actona* 13 AD, *bridge of Acton* 1459 Pat, *Acton Brygge* 1486 BodlCh, *-Brugge* c.1500 Orm[2], *-Bridge* 1599 ChRR, *-bridg* 1646 Sheaf, v. brycg. The bridge gives name to a hamlet here. Orm[2] 1 645 states that a footbridge and a ferryboat were to be provided at a ford between Acton and Dutton in 1286. This may explain *Bridenefordclyf infra*. Acton Bridge carries an extension of *Peytevinnisty* (1 43 (route IX)) across R. Weaver into Little Leigh 2 115 to Street Lane 2 114 in Dutton.

ACTON BROOK (Cliff Brook *infra*), v. brōc.   ACTONCLIFF, THE CLIFF, CLIFF BROOK & LANE, *Acton Cliff* 1831 Bry, cf. *Cliff Field* 1839 *TA, Bridenefordclyf infra*, named from a steep bluff over

R. Weaver, *v.* clif. The brook was *Mill Brook* 1831 Bry, cf. Acton Mill *supra*, *v.* myln, brōc. DUTTON LOCKS, cf. *Lock Meadow* 1839 *TA*, on the Weaver Navigation. THE GRANGE. LOWER GREEN, 1831 Bry, *Actongrene* 1353 *ChFor*, *v.* grēne², cf. foll. HALLGREEN, 'green at a hall', *v.* hall, grēne², cf. prec. ISLAND FM, *Dutton Bottoms Farm* 1839 *TA*, cf. Dutton Bottoms 2 113, *v.* ēg-land. The new name arises from the creation of an island here between the old course of R. Weaver and *the New Cut* 1831 Bry (109–585770), *v.* cut. This location seems to be *Actonbothum* 1355, 1357 BPR, held by Thomas de Dutton, *v.* boðm 'bottom land, valley bottom', cf. Acton *supra*, Dutton 2 112. MANOR BROW & FM, *v.* maner, brū. MAYPOLE INN, *The Maypole* 1831 Bry, *v.* may(e)-pole. NOOK HO, 1831 ib, *v.* nōk. PIKENALL LANE, *the Picknall* 1656 Cre, (*Further-*) *Pickenall*, *Nearer Bickenall* 1839 *TA*, *Pikenow Lane* 1831 Bry, perhaps 'pointed cnoll', from pīc¹ and cnoll. STRAWBERRY LANE, cf. *Strawberry Croft* 1839 *TA*, *v.* strēaw-berige. WALLHILL COTTAGE, cf. *Wall Hill* 1839 *TA*, *v.* wælla, hyll. WEAVERHAM LANE, *v.* lane, cf. Weaverham 205 *infra*. WETTEN LANE, (*Long & Short Butty-*), (*Large-*) *Wetton* 1839 *TA*, 'wet enclosure', *v.* wēt, tūn. WOODFIELD, *Gorse Green* 1831 Bry, *v.* gorst, grēne². THE WOODLANDS. YEWTREE FM.

FIELD-NAMES

The undated forms are 1839 *TA* 416. Of the others, 13 is *LRO* Dx, 1289 (17) Orm², 1344 *MinAcct*, 1347 Plea, 1357, 1503 *ChFor*, 1831 Bry, 1842 OS.

(a) Acres (*v.* æcer); Acton (Big) Heath (cf. *bruera de Acton* 1347, *v.* hǣð); Adams Hill; Amster (*hamstal* 1357, also probably represented by *Hautestall* 1289 (17) Orm² II 121, a garbled copy, *v.* hām-stall); Backside (*v.* ba(c)ksyde); Barnshaw; Billinge Mdw (cf. Billinge 1 138); Blake Flat (*v.* blæc, flat); Bottom (*v.* botm, cf. Island Fm *supra*); Buttery; Carr Croft (*v.* kjarr); Chrimes Hey (*v.* cryme, cf. *le Crymbe* 2 171); Combs Croft (*v.* cumb); Cromford Lane 1831, Crum Fd (*v.* crumb, ford, feld. The *-ford* form may be a rationalization of feld); Crowstitches (from crāwe or cros and sticce); Drumbo (dial. *drumble* 'a wooded ravine', cf. dumbel); Eyes (*v.* ēg); Farding (*v.* fēorðung); Farrars Moor; Finney (cf. Finney 240 *infra*); Flay (*terra vocata Flayes* 1344, *v.* flage, cf. dial. *flay*); Fox Covert 1842 (*Acton Gorse* 1831, *v.* gorst); Gale Fd (*v.* gagel); Glade Hill; Hanging Hill (*v.* hangende); Kennards Gardens & Mdw (cf. *Kynardestonleye infra*. There is no evidence to show whether the places are identical. There is a modern surname *Kennard* derived from OE *Cyneweard*, *Cyneheard* or *Cēnheard*); Kenricks Moor; Locker (*v.* loca); Loont (*v.* land); Marl Fd; Mere Fd & Mdw (*v.* mere¹, cf. Mere Ho 205 *infra*); Milking Bank (*v.* milking); Mill Fd; Moor; Morley (*v.* mōr¹, lēah); Pingot (*v.* pingot); Prestow; Quarters Mdw (*v.* quarter); Royals, Royle(s) (probably from ryge and hyll 'rye-hill'); Royalty Wd, Cliff- & Nearer Royalty (*v.* roialte); Sand Hill (*v.* sand, hyll); Scotchats Fd, Lower Scotchats (perhaps associated with *Scottesbach* 210 *infra*); Springe (*v.* spring 'a young wood'); Stockton Mdw (*v.* stoc or stocc, tūn); Throstle Nest Banks (*v.* þrostle, nest, banke); Town Fd (*v.* toun); Try Trash Lot (*v.* hlot); Turnhill (*v.* trun, hyll); Two Fords (*le tuoforde clyf* 1357, *le toofordeȝ* 1503, '(cliff at) the double ford', *v.* twā, ford, clif); Wigan Acorn; Great & Little Wd (*v.* wudu).

(*b*) *le Barogreve* 1503 ('grove wood', *v.* bearu, grǣfe); *Bridenefordclyf* 1357 ('(steep hill at) the planked ford', from briden and ford, with clif, cf. The Cliff, Acton Bridge *supra*); *Helede* 1357 ('hillside', *v.* helde); *Kynardestonleye* 1357 ('(clearing at) Cyneheard's farm', from the OE pers.n. *Cyneheard* and tūn, with lēah, cf. Kennards Gardens *supra*); *le Rudinge* 1289 (*v.* ryding); *le Longerudyng* 1357 (*v.* lang, ryding); *le prete Rudyng* 1289 ('priest's cleared-land', *v.* prēost, ryding); *Thorstonessuice* 1357 (probably '(trap at) Þórir's farm', from the ON pers.n. *Þórir* (ODan *Thorir*) and tūn, with swice, but Dr von Feilitzen suggests that *Thorstones-* might represent the gen.sg. of an anglicized form (*Thurstan*) of the ON pers.n. *Þorsteinn*).

2. CROWTON (BRIDGE, HALL, MARSH FM & MILL) (109–5774) [krɔːtən],

> *Crouton* 1260 Court *et freq* with variant spellings *-thon*, *Crooton* to 1605 ChRR, (*-infra forestam de Mara*) 1439 Orm²
> *Crowton* 1330 VR (p), 1391 ChRR *et freq*, (*-Hall*) 1724 NotCestr, (*-Marsh*) 1780 EnclA, (*-Mill*) 1831 Bry, *Croweton* 1343 Tab (p), 1438 Pat, ChRR
> *Croughton* 1386 ChRR (p), *Craughton, or Crawghton* 1656 Orm²
> *Crawton* 1458 AD, 1499 Orm², 1536 ChRR
> *Croton* 1470, 1473 *Dav*, c.1602 *Chol*, 1609 ChRR, 1619 Orm², 1664, 1671 Sheaf, (*-Hall*) 1660 *Sotheby*

'Crow farm', from crāwe and tūn, with brycg, hall, mersc, and myln.

CREWOOD COMMON & HALL (109–568758 & 567762) ['kriwud]

> *Crewode* c.1240 Tab, 1287 Court, *Crewood* 1344 (19) Orm² *et freq* with variant spellings *-wo(o)d(e)*, *-wo(o)d(d)*; (*the Lower House... in Crewoode, the hall of Crewood*) 1619 Orm², (*Crewood Common*) 1778 EnclA, 1842 OS, (*Crewood Hall*) 1842 ib, *Crewd Hall* 1724 NotCestr
> *Cruwode* 1346 BPR, and 14 forms with variant spellings *Cru(e)-wo(d)d(e)* to 1549 ChCert

Cruwewode (wood called) 1353 *ChFor*
Crew Wood 1398, 1402 ChRR, 1635 Orm², 1671 Sheaf, *Crewe
Wood Common & Hall* 1831 Bry
Crown-wood 1651 Orm²
Creewood or Crew-wood Hall 1845 ChetOS VIII

An Anglo-Welsh hybrid p.n., from OE **wudu** 'a wood', with either
Welsh **cryw** (PrWelsh *crïu) 'a basket, a (wicker-work) fish-weir', as
in Crewe 9 *supra*, 326 *infra*, or the el. which lies behind ModEdial.
crew 'a hovel, a sty, a cote', described in EPN **1** s.v. **creu** Welsh,
corrected in JEPN **1** 45 to '*crou PrWelsh, PrCorn, PrCumb, **crau**
Welsh, **crow** Corn' although NED s.v. **crew²** cites 'earlier Welsh
creu, crau'. Crewood means 'wood where basket-materials were
obtained or where wicker-work was made', or 'wood where a pen,
hut or hovel stood', for the place is not close to a fishing-stream.

RULOE (109–583729) ['ruːlou], *Roe-loe* 1683 Orm², *Ruloe or New Hall*,
Ruloe Cob(b) 1780 *EnclA*, *Ruloe Hall* 1831 Bry, 1842 OS, *Ruloe
House* 1839 *TA*, *Ruelow* 1955 Index, 'rough mound', from **rūh** and
hlāw, with **cobb(e)**, **hall** and **nīwe**. This place is supposed the
meeting-place of the hundred of *Roelau* 1086 DB, cf. 160 *supra*, v.
Tait 99, Anderson¹ 190. The political importance of the place would
be eclipsed by the shift to Eddisbury in the twelfth century, but it
might account for the lost f.ns. *le Mareschaldesfeld, le Schyrreffeld*
1353 *ChFor*, 'the mareschal's, and the sheriff's field', from **feld** 'a
field, a piece of open ground' with **marescal** 'a master of horse, a
steward', and **scīr-(ge)rēfa** 'a sheriff'.

AINSWORTH LANE [einz-], 1780 *EnclA*, *Answort'* 1583–4 Orm² II 127,
Ansor(e) 1618–19, 1620–1 ib, *Ainsworth in Croton* 1671 Sheaf, from
worð 'an enclosure, a curtilage' and **lane**, with an unidentified first
el. Professor Löfvenberg suggests an OE pers.n. *Ægen* proposed in
DEPN s.n. *Eynsford* for Eynsford K 39, Eynsham O 258 (but see
Studies³ 46), Eynsworth Ess (*Ainsworth* Ess 517), Ainsworth La 53.
But the early spellings for the Ch p.n. indicate short *a* which tells
against the analogy.   BACK LANE, *v.* **back, lane**.   BENT LANE,
1831 Bry, 'coarse-grass lane', *v.* **beonet, lane**.   BIRCH HO.
BRATT'S BANK & LANE, from a surname *Bratt, Brett*, with **banke,
lane**.   BROOK COTTAGE.   CAMOMILE LANE.   CHEESE HILL
LANE, cf. Cheese Hill 249 *infra*.   COOKSONGREEN, probably from
the surname *Cookson* and **grēne²**.   CORNER FM, *v.* **corner**

CROWTON BROOK (Cliff Brook 193 *supra*), *Corleg'broc, ductus veniens de Corleg'* 1272–1307 *AddCh*, *v.* brōc, cf. *Cawley* 240 *infra*. DANE'S GUTTER, apparently the same as *Dingle Gutter* 1839 *TA*, cf. *the Dingle* 1780 *EnclA*, from dingle 'a deep dell', denu 'a valley', and goter 'a gutter, a watercourse'. DUTTON LANE, *v.* lane, cf. Dutton 2 112. GABRIEL BANK, cf. *messuage called Gabriel's* 1780 *EnclA*, and *Gabriels* 1839 *TA*, *v.* banke. HILLTOP FM, *Friars Farm* 1831 Bry, *v.* hyll, topp. HUNT'S HILL WOOD, *Hunt's Hill* 1831 ib, from hyll and the surname *Hunt*. MARSH LANE, cf. Crowton Marsh *supra*, *the Great Marsh Platt* 1780 *EnclA*, *Marsh Field, Lot & Meadow* 1839 *TA*, *v.* mersc, plat², lane, hlot. MOSS LANE, cf. *Moss Meadow* 1839 *ib*, *v.* mos. MOUNT PLEASANT, *Orchard Wood* 1842 OS, *v.* orceard, wudu. NEEDLESS BRIDGE. NORLEY BANK, *v.* 249 *infra*. OAKHILL, 1842 ib, *v.* āc, hyll. PEARTREE FM. PICKERING'S O' TH' BOAT 1860 White, -*the*- 1831 Bry, 1841 *TAMap* 153, *Pickerings of the Boat, Pickering's Boat* 1780 *EnclA*, cf. *Pickering's Intack* 1780 *ib*, *Pickerings Lot* 1839 *TA*, and Pickering's Bridge *& Cut* 2 114, from the surname *Pickering* and bāt, inntak, hlot, brycg and cut. There was a ferry here. PIN-GARD'S LANE, *Pingot Lane* 1780 *EnclA*, (*Big, Large & Little*) *Pingot(s)* 1839 *TA*, from pingot 'a little plot of ground' and lane. ROYALTY COVERT, *Royal Lot* 1831 Bry, *Royalty* 1839 *TA*, 'an allot-ment of crown land', *v.* roial, hlot, roialte. SANDHOLE FM, cf. *Sand Hole Field* 1839 *ib*, *v.* sand, hol¹. WOOD'S LANE.

FIELD-NAMES

The undated forms are 1839 *TA* 416. Of the others 1353 is *ChFor*, 1446 ChRR, 1503 *ChFor*, 1619 Orm², 1780 *EnclA*, 1831 Bry.

(*a*) Armshaw Mdw (cf. 201 *infra*); Bent (*v.* beonet) Black Croft Pit 1780 (*v.* blæc, croft, pytt); Bottom (*v.* botm); Broad Lane 1780; Butty Bottoms (*v.* butty, botm); Cale Green otherwise Earls Green 1780 (*v.* cauel); Carterage Fd (perhaps analogous with Cartlidge Wood 1 55, from kartr 'rough ground' and hrycg, but cf. Cartledge Moss 199 *infra*); Churchill; Clemly Park (*v.* park, cf. Clemley 47 *supra*); Big & Little Clough (*v.* clōh); Cockshoot (*v.* cocc-scyte); Big- & Little Common (*Crowton Higher & Lower Common* 1780); Cribb (*v.* crib); Dale's Bridge 1831; Dones Mdw 1780 (from the surname *Done*); Earls Green (*v.* Cale Green *supra*); Great Flaggor; Long & Top Friday (*v.* Frīgedæg); Golden Nook (*v.* golden, nōk, cf. 199 *infra*); Guild Fd; Hanging Fd (*v.* hangende); Hare Mills; High Fd (*v.* hēah); Hill Fd (*v.* hyll); Hollands Lot; the Hollins 1780 (a house-name, *v.* holegn); Honey Burn(s); Hurst Fd (*v.* hyrst); Intake (cf. *Turner's Intack* 1780, *v.*

inntak); Lime Kiln Fd (*v.* limkilne); Marrows Lot; Mickhow Wall 1780 (a house-name, 'great well', *v.* micel, wælla); Moat Croft (near Crowton Hall, *v.* mote); Morbund Fd; Moses Nooks; Pecks Bank (*Peck Brow* 1831, cf. *messuage called late Peck's* 1780, from the surname *Peck*, with banke and brū); Pichows Loont, Pickows (*v.* pichel, land); Pikenall (*v.* 194 *supra*); Plat Lot (*v.* plat², hlot); Poor Hill (*v.* 199 *infra*); Poors Land (*the Poors Field* 1780, land devoted to poor-relief, *v.* pouer(e)); Prison Bar Bank (*v.* prison-bars); Riddings (*v.* ryding); Rough Hayes Wd (*Rogh hey* 1503, *v.* rūh, (ge)hæg); Salt Ho (cf. *Salthouse Meadow* 1780, *v.* salt-hūs); Sheep Cote Fd (*v.* scēp, cot); Shethough 1780; Sleagoe, Slegoe Bottom; Stonehouse Croft (cf. *the Stone House* 1780, *v.* stān, hūs); Triangle Fd (*v.* 325 *infra*); Wallets (*v.* walet); Way Fd; Westons.

(*b*) *the Cockeswolds* 1619; *le Mareschaldesfeld* 1353 and *le Schyrreffeld* 1353 (*v.* Ruloe *supra*); *the Lower sparrhawke Cloughe* 1619 (*v.* spær-hafoc, clōh); *Throstylfeld* 1446 (*v.* þrostle, feld).

3. CUDDINGTON (HALL) (109–5972) older local ['ˈkuditn̩]

   Codynton c.1235 *Clif*, *Codington* 1270–1210 *Chol et freq* with variant spellings *Codin(g)-*, *Codyn(g)ton* to 1579 ChRR, (*Codynton iuxta Onston*) 1446 ib

   Cudinton 1260 Court (p), *Cudington* 1289 ib *et freq* with variant spellings *Cudin(g)-*, *Cudyn(g)ton* to 1508 ChRR, (*Cudynton iuxta Northlegh, -Norley*) 1339 Orm², 1473 Plea, (*-infra forestam de Mara*) 1347 *ChFor*, (*-in* (*hundred' de*) *Eddesbury*) 1440, 1460 ChRR

   Coodyngton 1322 *Clif*

   Cotynton 1390 ChRR

   Cuddyngton 1562 ChRR, *-ing-* 1585 Cre

   Coddington 1579 Dugd

'Farm called after Cuda', from the OE pers.n. *Cuda* and -ingtūn, with hall. It adjoins Onston and Norley 200, 249 *infra*, and was in the Forest of Delamere **1** 8. Cf. Cuddington 326 *infra*.

BRYN (FM) (110–6072), BRYNN BANK (203 *infra*) [brin], *le Brynne* 1391 Orm², *the-* 1779 Sheaf, *Brynnyl* 1467 ChRR, *Brinn Common* Jas 1 *Map* (*LRMB* 200), *Brinn* (*Chapel & Smithy*) 1831 Bry, *the bryn or Brandes* 1613 ChRR, *le Bryn* 1632 Orm², *Bryn* 1819 Sheaf, *Bryn* (*Smithy & Common*) 1842 OS, *Brin, Bryne in Cuddington* 1671 Sheaf, *the Brin* 1681 ib, *Brynn* 1721 *Chol*, 'the hill', from Welsh bryn (PrWelsh *brïnn), with hyll, commun, smiððe, chapel and banke. Part of this district is in Weaverham 202 *infra*, cf. 'messuages and lands called the bryn or Brandes in Kingsley, Cuddington,

Norley, Newton near Frodsham, Weaverham' 1613 ChRR (DKR XXXIX 101).

BAG LANE, 1831 Bry. BARRASTITCH LANE, perhaps 'barras-ditch', from barras 'a barrier' and dīc, with lane. BEECHFIELD. BROOK HO. BROOKLANDS. CARTLEDGE MOSS, *Cartlache mosse* 1503 *ChFor, Cuddington Moss* 1842 OS, cf. *Higher & Lower Cartlich, Cartlich Field* 1839 *TA*, and the surname *Cartelege* 1382, *Cartelache* 1385, 1417 ChRR, '(moss at) the boggy stream in stony ground', from kartr and læc(c), with mos, cf. *Cartelache* 1 17, Carterage 197 *supra*. CUDDINGTON BROOK, *v.* 1 20. CUDDINGTON LANE, *Ridding Head Lane* 1831 Bry, cf. Ravenhead *infra, v.* lane. CUDDINGTON LOWER MILL, *Mill* 1831 ib, *Lower Mill* 1842 OS, cf. *Cuddington Higher Mill* 1842 ib, *v.* myln. CUDDINGTON POOL, *v.* pōl[1]. CUDDINGTON WASTE, 1842 ib, cf. *Waste Flea Moss Pit* 1839 *TA, v.* wēste, flage, mos, pytt. DELAMERE HO, 1831 Bry, *Delamere Lodge* 1789 ChetOS VIII, 1819 Orm[2], *v.* hūs, loge, cf. Delamere Forest 210 *infra*. FORESTVIEW INN, on the boundary of Oakmere 217 *infra* and Delamere Forest. FOXEY HILL, *Foxy Hill* 1839 *TA*. GILL'S MOSS WOOD, *Gill's Moss* 1831 Bry, *Gillows Moss* 1839 *TA*. GOLDEN NOOK, *Goldenook* 1811 Sheaf, *v.* golden, nōk, cf. 197 *supra*. ERBACH CROSS (lost), *v.* 208 *infra*. MANOR FM, *v.* maner. MERLEWOOD. PEMBERTON COTTAGE, *Porto Bello* 1842 OS, *v.* 325 *infra*. POOR HILL, 1839 *TA* 416, 'hill of poor ground', *v.* pouer(e), hyll. RAVENHEAD, *Ridding Head* 1831 Bry, *Ravenhead Field* 1839 *TA*, cf. Cuddington Lane *supra*, The Riddings, Ravensclough *infra, v.* hēafod, ryding. RAVENSCLOUGH, *Rauensclogh* 1503 *ChFor, Ravens Clough* 1812 Sheaf, a valley at *Ravens Oake* Jas 1 *Map* (*LRMB* 200) a tree on the Oakmere boundary of Delamere Forest and Cuddington, cf. 218 *infra*. 'Raven's dell' and 'oak-tree', from hræfn, perhaps as a pers.n., and clōh, āc. THE RIDDINGS, *Higher & Lower Ridding* 1839 *TA, v.* ryding. SMITHY LANE, *v.* smiððe. STONYFORD (BROOK), *Stoney Ford House & Bridge* 1831 Bry, *Stonyford Brook* 1842 OS, from stānig and ford, with brōc, brycg, hūs. The brook joins Cuddington Brook 1 20, cf. Fir Brook 1 24. TOWN MOSS, 1839 *TA, v.* toun, mos. WASTE LANE, *v.* Cuddington Waste *supra*. WATERMILL FM, named from a nearby mill, *Paper Mill* 1831 Bry, *v.* water-milne. WOOD'S LANE. YEWTREE.

FIELD-NAMES

The undated forms are 1839 *TA* 416. Of the others, 1322 is *Clif*, 1353, 1503 *ChFor*, 1354 Sheaf, 1660 *Sotheby*, 1831 Bry, 1842 OS.

(*a*) Bank; Beeston Slack (*v.* slakki); Bottoms Wd (*v.* botm); Broom Fd (*the Broomfeilds* 1660, *v.* brōm, feld); Burnt Brows (*v.* brende², brū); Cranberry Fd, Mdw & Moss (*v.* cranberry); Dibdale, Diblake (*v.* dæl¹, lacu. The first el. may be dēop 'deep'); Filmo(r)t Hill (*v.* fulmard); Flam(m)ons Pit Fd; Gorsy Bank & Hill; Gransworth's, Near Gransworthe; Guild Fd (*v.* gildi); Hanging Hill (*v.* hangende); Heath Fd (*freq*) (cf. *del Heth* 1354 (p), *v.* hǣð); The Hollow 1842; Holmes (*Holme* 1353, *v.* holmr); Intake (*v.* inntak); Lands (*v.* land); Long Butts (*v.* butte); March Mdw; Marl (pit) Fd, Marled Hey, Marlers Hill (*v.* marle, marled, marlere, marle-pytt); Milking Bank (*v.* milking); Newlands (*v.* nīwe, land, from new enclosures of old forest land); Oat Hey (*v.* āte, (ge)hæg); Onston Fd (cf. Onston 200 *infra*); Pickows (*v.* pichel); Primrose Hill; Red Moss (*v.* rēad, mos); Reed (*v.* hrēod); Robin Hoods Butts; Rough Hill (*v.* rūh, hyll); Ruloe Fd (*v.* Ruloe 196 *supra*); Rutlands; Slack (*v.* slakki); Long Slang (*v.* slang); Slutch Mdw (*v.* slutch); Smales Hill; Tooler's Stone (*v.* 204 *infra*); Trough-hole Fd (*v.* trog, hol¹); Two Meres Fd (*v.* mere¹); Wall Fd, Hill & Moor (*v.* wælla); Washing Pit Fd; The Wood; Wrights Hill 1831.

(*b*) *Adderdale* 1322 ('heather valley', *v.* hæddre, dæl¹); *Ouercroft* 1503 ('higher croft', *v.* uferra, croft); *Pittfall Riddings* 1660 (*v.* pitfalle, ryding); *the Rough Hay* 1660 (*v.* rūh, (ge)hæg); *Rupelegh* 1322 (perhaps 'Hrypa's clearing', from an OE pers.n. *Hrypa* (cf. *Hryp*, Redin 31) and lēah); *Scheulebrod* 1322 ('shovel's breadth', the name of a narrow selion, *v.* scofl-brǣdu).

4. ONSTON (HALL & LANE) (109–5974), ONSTON MILL 204 *infra*, [ˈɔnstn̩] locally [ˈɔnssn̩]

Aneston 1182, 1183 P
Oneston 1184 P, 1305 VR (mill of), 1357 *ChFor*, 1534 (17) Orm², (*-or Honston*) 1671 Sheaf, *-tona* e13 (14) ChRR, *Oneston milne* m16 *AOMB* 397
Honeston 1185, 1186 P, 1280 Ipm
Honston 1292 Ipm, 1304 Chamb (p), (*Oneston or-*) 1671 Sheaf
Onston 1292 Ipm *et freq* with variant spelling *-tona*; *mill of Onston* 1338 VR, *Onston mille* 1446 ib, *-mylne* 1542 Dugd, *-Hall, Lane* 1831 Bry
Ouston 1304 Chamb (p) and seven forms to 1513 Plea
Ownston (*Millne*) 1446 VR, (*molend' aquaticum de*) *Ownston* 1540 Dugd
Onson 1665, 1682 *Chol*

Onson alias Auston 1666 *Chol*
Ongton 1724 NotCestr

'A single stone, a lonely stone, a stone by itself', from āna and stān, with hall, myln and lane. The first el. is confused with hān 'a stone'. The series of *Ouston* forms, and the *Auston* form, appear to be erroneous, either with *-u-* for *-n-*, or *Ous-, Aus-* for *Ouns-, Auns-* through loss of an abbreviation. The rock or stone which gave rise to the p.n. is no longer to be seen. The mill is in Milton 204 *infra*.

BAG LANE (FM), *Bag Lane* 1831 Bry, 'bag lane', *v.* bagga, lane, cf. Cuddington Brook 1 20 (*Bog Lane Brook* 1831 Bry). This might be 'badger's lane'. But the name-type *Bag Lane* may refer to a cul-de-sac, *v.* George St. (Chester) 326 *infra*. CHAPEL HOUSES, *v.* chapel(e).

FIELD-NAMES

The undated forms are 1839 *TA* 416. Of the others 1354 is Sheaf, 1357, 1503 ChFor.

(a) Acton Mdw (cf. Acton 193 *supra*); Arm(e)shaw (perhaps 'poor wood' from earm and sceaga, cf. Armshaw Mdw 197 *supra*); Broad Heath (cf. *Brawdeheth, le Brodeheth* 1503, *v.* brād, hǣð); Clays (*v.* clǣg); Court Mdw (*v.* court); Cross Heys ('enclosures near a cross', *v.* cros, (ge)hæg); Crow Fd (*v.* crāwe); Crowton Mdw (cf. Crowton 195 *supra*); Five Cornered Fd; Grange Ford (*v.* grange, ford); Headbutts ('a selion running down the ends of several others', *v.* heved-butte); Hemp Yard (*v.* hemp-yard); Marl Fd (*v.* marle); New Gate ('new pasturage', *v.* nīwe, gata); Pingot (*v.* pingot); Sneaps ('boggy pieces of ground', *v.* snæp); Sparks (*v.* spearca); Ston(e)y Butts (*v.* stānig, butte); Town Fd (cf. *Onston Feldes* 1503, *v.* toun, feld).

(b) *Arneweyesheth* 1357 (perhaps 'Earnwīg's heath', from the OE pers.n. *Earnwīg* and hǣð, but *Arnewey* 1285, 1290 Court is a surname in Macclesfield and John *Arnwey* was mayor of Chester 1268–78, so the p.n. may be 'heath belonging to one Arnewey'); *le Bronnegge* 1354 (perhaps 'brown ridge', from brūn[1] and ecg, with *-oun* written *-onn*, but the first el. could be bronn 'a hill, the breast of a hill'); *Le Cronerydyng* 1354 (probably 'crows' clearing', from crāwe (gen.pl. crāwena) and ryding, but the first el. may be cron 'a crane'); *le Gelderleyes* 1354 ('woods or clearings where traps or snares are set', *v.* gildri, lēah); *le Smythesrudyng* 1354 ('smith's clearing', *v.* smið, ryding); *Werlegh* 1354 (p) ('glade at a weir', *v.* wer, lēah).

5. WALLERSCOTE (110–635736) ['wɔləskout]

Walrescota 1185 P, *-cote* 1186 ib and 13 forms with variant spellings
Walris-, -cot(e) to 1475 AddCh, 1671 Sheaf
Wallerscote c.1185 (1400) CASNS XIII, 1277 Pat *et freq* with variant

spellings *Walleres-* (1354 VR, 1360 ChRR), *Wallors-* (1664 Sheaf), *-cot(t)*, *-coat(e)*, *-coite*, *-courte* (1639 Mere) to *Wallerscoat* 1831 Bry, 1839 *TA*, *-cote* 1842 OS
Warlischote c.1240 *JRC*, *-cote* 1272–1307 *ib*, *Warlescote* 1278 Misc
Wallescote 1588 *Bun*, *Wallascoat* 1843 *TA* 36
Walkerscote 17 Tab
Wallinge Court 1693 Mere

'Salt-boiler's cottage', *v.* wællere, cot. The form *Wallinge* is an -ing² formation, analogous with Wallange 2 212. The place is a mile from Northwich 2 192 and adjoins Winnington 191 *supra*, both places being notable for salt-making. There was a salt-works in Weaverham Lordship, cf. Salt Ho 198 *supra*, Salt House Mdw 209 *infra*. This small township, which belonged to the Nuns of Chester until 1360 (Orm² 1 346) and was 'but one house and a constablewick' in 1671 (Sheaf³ 49, (9923)), is now included with Winnington in Northwich c.p., and for the most part submerged in a reservoir.

BEACH LANE, *Beech Lane* 1831 Bry, *v.* 206 *infra*.

FIELD-NAMES

The undated forms are 1839 *TA* 416.

(a) Dock Ridding (*v.* docce, ryding); Dove House Fd; Intake (*v.* inntak); Plaster Fd (*v.* pleg-stōw 'a sporting-place'); Sand Fd.

6. WEAVERHAM CUM MILTON (110–6172), *Weuerham cum Mulneton* 1475 AddCh, *Weaverham, with Milton, Gorstich and Sandiway* 1819 Orm², *Milton cum Weaverham* 1831 Bry.

The township of Weaverham cum Milton contained the hamlets (1) Gorstage (including Hefferston Grange, a detached part of Whitegate parish 164 *supra*), (2) Milton, (3) Weaverham, (4) Weaverham Lordship (including Sandiway and Earnslow which belonged partly to Whitegate parish), (5) Weaverham-wood (a detached part of Whitegate parish). Gorstage is usually taken to be part of the hamlet of Weaverham Lordship, and Weaverhamwood part of Weaverham.

(1) GORSTAGE (GREEN, HALL & LANE) [gorstidʒ] (110–6173), *Gorstage grene* 1503 ChFor, *Gorstage (Green)* 1831 Bry, *Gorstitch* 1621 Orm², *Gorstich (in Weverham)* 1671 Sheaf, 1721 *Chol*, 1724 NotCestr, 'green at a place overgrown with gorse', from a term *gorstage*, which probably represents gorst and the ME, ModE noun-forming suffix

-age, but which may represent the assibilated form of an -ing[2] formation **gorsting. v.* grēne[2], hall, lane. Dr von Feilitzen objects that the absence of *-n-* makes derivation from OE **gorsting* unlikely; the development *-iŋ* (assibilated) > *-age* seems always to be associated with dissimilation (*n –n, m – n*), as in Lymage Hu (BdHu 270, PN-ing[2] 209), Wantage Brk (DEPN, PN-ing[2] 208), Hampage Ha (PN-ing[2] 207), Winterage K (PNK 435, PN-ing[2] 207), a condition not present in **gorsting*. Professor Löfvenberg suggests an alternative analysis, a compound name, the first el. **gor** 'dirt' or **gorst** 'gorse', the second el. **stycce** (ModEdial. *stitch* 'a small piece of land' EDD) with voicing of final [-tʃ].

HEFFERSTON GRANGE (110–603735) ['hefərsən]
A detached part of Whitegate parish.

Efferston 1272–90 ChFor (p), *grang' de-* 1545 (17) Orm[2], *grangia de Hefferston* 1331 VR, 1540 Dugd, *Hefferston* 1589 Sheaf, *Heffers-ton Grange* 1724 NotCestr, *-stone-* 1656 Orm[2], *Heffreston* 1327–77 ChFor, 1395 Orm[2], *manor of-* 1538 Dugd, *Heffreston Grange* 1542 ib, *Heffurstan* 1509 VR
grangia de Hefferton 1340 VR, 1508 ChRR, *Efferton* 1535 VE, *Heferton Grange* 1597 (1724), 1724 NotCestr
the Grange, nigh Weverham 1666 Orm[2], *Grange* 1673 Sheaf, *the house of Grange* 1819 Orm[2], *the Grange in the township of Weaver-ham in the parish of Whitegate* 1846 TAMap, *Grange Hall* 1831 Bry, 1842 OS
Heversham grainge 1630 LCWills
Hifferton Grange...called only Grange 1671 Sheaf
Hefferson-Grange 1745 Sheaf
Heiferson Grange 1846 TAMap

'Hēahfriþ's farm', from the OE pers.n. *Hēahfrið* and **tūn**, with **grange**, cf. Grange Lane *infra*. This was a grange of Vale Royal Abbey 179 *supra*. Here were *le Henshous, le Munkesberne, le Shephous* 1395 Orm[2] II 150, 'hen-house', 'monk's barn', 'sheep-house', *v.* **henn, scēp, hūs, munuc, bere-ærn**. Professor Löfvenberg notes that *Henshouse* may contain **hēns** 'poultry' found in Henbrook Wo 282 (*hensbroc* 770 (11th) BCS 204) cf. Swed *hönshus* 'a poultry-house', Hensington O 270.

ASHBANK, *v.* **æsc, banke**.   BRYNN BANK, cf. *Brinn Chapel* 1831 Bry, *Bryn (Smithy)* 1842 OS, *v.* **chapel(e), smiððe**, Bryn 198 *supra*.

CHURCH CROFT, v. cirice, croft.   GRANGE BROOK & LANE (FM),
Grange Brook & Farm 1831 Bry, *Grange Lane* 1842 OS, named from
Hefferston Grange *supra*. The brook joins Acton Brook 193 *supra*.
HANDFORTH BROOK & FM, (110–612733), 1831 Bry, cf. (*Further*)
Handfords 1839 *TA*. The material is late. The p.n. may be analogous
with Handforth **1** 254, either 'cock's ford' or 'ford marked by stones',
from hana or hān and ford, cf. Handbridge 326 *infra*. The brook
becomes Grange Brook *supra*.   THE HOMESTEAD.   HUNT'S
LANE.   MILLINGTON LANE.   OAKFIELD.   OAKLANDS.   SMITHY
LANE, cf. *Smithy Croft, Field & Meadow* 1839 *TA*, named from
Bryn Smithy, cf. Brynn Bank *supra*, v. smiðöe.   TOOLER'S STONE
(110–606714), 1839 *TA* 416 (cf. 200 *supra*), a boundary stone between Weaverham and Cuddington 198 *supra*, v. stān. The first el.
may be tollere 'a toll-gatherer' or one of its derivative surnames
Toller, Towler. Professor Löfvenberg notes, 'The modern form
points to a ME *tōler* "a maker or seller of tools". This word may be
found in Robert *le Toler* (La) 1246, included by Thuresson 141 under
tollere "a tax-gatherer"'. Cf. foll.   TOOLERSTONE (110–607713),
Stone House Farm 1842 OS, a farm named from Tooler's Stone
supra, v. stān, hūs.

(2) MILTON (BRIDGE, FM & HO) (109–595743)

 Milleton 1237, 1238 P (p)
 (*le*) *Mulneton* 1272–1307 AddCh, *Mulneton* 1305 VR and five
  forms to 1475 AddCh, (*-juxta Acton*) 1339 Plea, *le Mulneton* 1403
  ChRR (p)
 Mulleton 1290 VR (p), 1330 ib (p), 1353 BPR (p), *Muleton* 1334 VR
 Milnetoun 1316 Bark (p), *Mylneton* 1536 ChRR
 Multon 1454, 1466, 1488 ChRR
 Milton 1512 Plea *et freq* with variant spellings *Myl-, Mill-*; (*-in*
  Weverham) 1671 Sheaf, *Milton Bridge* 1831 Bry

'Mill farm or enclosure', from myln and tūn, with brycg. Cf. foll.

ONSTON MILL, 1831 Bry, v. 200 *supra*, cf. foll.   SANDFIELD SAW
MILL, *Milton Mill* 1842 OS, cf. *Sand Field* 1839 *TA*, v. Milton
supra, sand, feld.

FIELD-NAMES

The principal forms are 1839 *TA* 416.

(*a*) Castle Hill ('hill suitable for a castle', *v.* castel(l), hyll); Hanging Fd (*v.* hangende); Kiln Croft; Pad Fd (from dial. *pad* 'a path', *v.* pæð, or 'toad-field', *v.* padde, cf. Padfield Db 104); Rough Fd & Piece (cf. *Milton Rough* 1831 Bry, *v.* rūh); Sand Hole Croft, Fd & Mdw; Slack Fd (*v.* slakki).

(3) WEAVERHAM (110–6174) ['wiːvərəm] locally ['wɛːrəm, 'wɔːrəm]

    Wivreham 1086 DB, 1581 *AddCh, Wyver-* 1540 Dugd, *Wiver-* 1660 Sheaf

    Weueresham 1096–1101 (1280) Chest

    Weverham 1096–1101 (1280) (17) Chest, *Weuerham* 1150 ib *et freq* with variant spelling *Wever-, -ir-, -yr-, Wevere-* to 1724 NotCestr, (*-or Wareham*) 1671 Sheaf, *Weverhamme* 1546 Dugd *Weueram* 1150 Chest (lit. *-enam*), 1237 P, 1291 Tax (lit. *Wen'am*)

    Wauerham 1237 P, *Waver-* 1294 Court, 1295 Cl, 1579 ChRR, 1609 Sheaf, 1724 NotCestr

    Wewerham 1242 P

    Weeverham 1270, 1656 Orm²

    Woverham 1309 Pat, 1557 Sheaf

    Wereham 1420 Plea (p), 1514 Sheaf, 1540 *ChCert,* 1656 Orm², *Weram* 1505 Sheaf, 1539 Orm², 1611 Sheaf, *Wheram* 1505 ib, *Wareham* 1671 ib, *Wearham* 1695 ib

    Weaverham 1558–79 ChancP, 1767 Plea *et freq*

    'Village by R. Weaver', from hām and R. Weaver 1 38.

STREET-NAMES. CHURCH LANE & ST., cf. *Church Street Croft* 1839 *TA, v.* cirice, lane, strǣt; FOREST ST., *School Bank* 1831 Bry, 1842 OS, a hill near a grammar school, *v.* scōl, banke.

BURROWS HILL. CHURCH FM, *Back o' th' Church* 1831 Bry, cf. *Church Field (Lands)* 1839 *TA.* COPYHOLD, *v.* copyhold. GATE INN, *Weaverham Gate* 1831 Bry, *v.* geat. LAKE HOUSE FM, cf. *Lake House Field* 1839 *TA,* from lacu 'a watercourse'. MERE-BANK, MEREBROW, MERE HO (110–608748), *le-, la Mere* 1334 VR, *Meire in Weverham* 1671 Sheaf, *Mere Brow Farm* 1831 Bry, cf. Mere Fd 194 *supra,* 'the pool', *v.* mere¹, brū, banke, hūs, cf. *Lemerecloh* 210 *infra.* NEW ROOM, 'new allotment', *v.* nīwe, rūm¹. NOOK FM, *v.* nōk. OWLEY WOOD, *Roughs* 1842 OS, cf. *Rough Field, Land & Meadow,* and *Owlet Field* 1839 *TA, v.* rūh, owlet 'little owl'.

SANDY LANE.   SHADY BROOK LANE, cf. *Shady Brook Field* 1839 *ib*, probably *Schetingbroc* 1334 VR, 'brook which shoots forth', from scēotende 'shooting, gushing forth' (cf. OE *scēotan*) and brōc. WEAVERHAM BANK.   WELL FM & LANE, *v.* wella.   WITHEN'S LANE, *Withing Lane* 1831 Bry, *Withens* 1839 *TA*, cf. *a close called the Withings* 1692–3 (1860) White, *v.* wīðegn 'a willow'. WOODBANK, WOOD LANE, *v.* wudu, banke.

(4) WEAVERHAM LORDSHIP, 1831 Bry, *Manor of Weverham* 1275 Cl, *Weverham Alba* 1535 VE, *v.* lordes(c)hip. The significance of the suffix *Alba* 'white' is not apparent; the form may be a mistake for altera 'the other', i.e. the lordship as distinct from the township. Weverham, like Frodsham 221 *infra*, was anciently a manor of the duchy of Chester, and was similarly divided into the two parts, the town itself and the demesnes or lordship.

BEACH FM, HILL (WOOD), LANE & RD (110–6373), [biːtʃ], *Beech Hill Farm & Wood, Beech Lane* 1831 Bry, *Beach Croft & Hey* 1839 *TA v.* Beach Fm, Hartfordbeach 188 *supra*, Moss Cliff & Lane 190 *supra*, Beach Lane & Moss Fm 202, 192 *supra*. These names mark a district in Weaverham, Winnington, Hartford, Castle Northwich and Wallerscote, which is recorded as *le Bache* c.1240 *JRC*, c.1260 (1400) CASNS XIII 102, *Bachemosse* e14 *JRC*, *le Bach'* 1334 VR, *Bachemoos* 1338 *ib* (84, where a lawsuit decided land here was in Winnington not Weaverham), *la Bachoe Mosse* 1399 ChRR. The p.n. is '(moss at) the valley stream', from bece[1], bæce[1], with mos. The bece was probably the valley at 110–627733. *Catesbache infra* may be an ancient manor in which all these places were included, no doubt named from the same topographical feature.

CATESBACHE (lost), 1558–9 Orm[2] II 203, *Cotesbache* 1278 Misc, *Goddesbache* 1283 Pat, 1467 *MinAcct*, 1531, 1551 ChRR, *Godesbach(e)* 1298 P, 1299 Cl *et freq* to 1440 VR, (lit. -*lach*, -*lath*') 1299 P, *Godesbech* 1200 Fine (p), *Coddesbache* 1297 Cl, *Codesbach* 1307–27 VR, -*beche* 1327 Pat, 'stream and valley at a cot', *v.* bece[1], bæce[1]. The first el. is cot 'a cottage', as in Wallerscote 201 *supra*. *Catesbache* adjoined Wallerscote and must be associated with Beach Fm etc. *supra*. The first el. has been replaced with god[1] 'God', probably by the monastic owners of the place, which was given to Vale Royal Abbey in 1278 by the Nuns of Chester who owned the adjoining Wallerscote.

CONERSLEY or CONEWARDSLEY (lost, part of Whitegate parish)

Kenardeslie 1086 DB

Cholewardeleg' 1237 P

Conewardel' 1237, 1238 P, *Coneward'* 1291 VR, *Conwardleg'* 1238 ib (lit. *Cow-*), *aula de Conwardeley* 1278–82 AddCh, *Conwardale* 1291 Tax (lit. *Cow-*; Orm² II 172 reads *Conwardle*)

Cunewardesl' 1248 Cl, *-leye* 1276 ib, 1284 Ch, *Cunwardsley* 1284 CRC, *Cumwardesleye* 1277 Pat

Conewardislegh 1272–90 ChFor (p), *Conewardesley(e)* 1276 Ch *et freq* with variant spellings *Con(e)ward(e)s-*, *-le(gh)*, *-leg'* to 1361 ChFor, 1629 Orm² II 154, (*grangia de-*) 1336 VR

Conardeslee 1357, 1359 BPR, 1361 ChFor

Conerwardeslegh 1360 ChRR, BPR, *-ley* 1500 VR

Conwarsley 1538 Orm²

Conersley 1538 Dugd, (*the ferme of-*, *the grange of-*) 1542 Orm², *Conersleyhey* m16 *AOMB* 397

Conerley Grange m16 *AOMB* 397

Cuminsley alias Conwardesley 1629 Orm²

'Cyneweard's clearing or wood', from the OE pers.n. *Cyneweard* and lēah, with grange, (ge)hæg and hall (MedLat *aula*). This lost grange of Vale Royal, granted to that abbey by Edward I, who recovered it from Walter de Vernon for the purpose (1299 Orm² II 168), is included here because it was originally part of Weaverham manor (1237 P). It lay in Weaverham and Hartford townships 1357 BPR III 283, 263, which probably explains why part of Hartford 188 *supra* was in Weaverham parish. The location ought to be not far from Earnslow Grange *infra*, about 110–6371. The 1629 reference in Orm² II 154 appears in a list of manorial tenures in an Inquisition and does not prove the contemporary existence of the grange.

EARNSLOW GRANGE (110–625707, part of Whitegate parish)

Ernesley (House), *grange of Ernesley* 1542 Dugd, 1544–7 (17) Orm², *Ernesley Grange* m16 *AOMB* 397

Yenslow Grange 1724 NotCestr

Yarnsloue (lit. *Garnstore*) 1732 Sheaf³ 49 (9880)

Earnslow Grange 1819 Orm²

Earnshaw Grange 1846 *TA* 417

'Eagle's wood', from earn and lēah, with hūs and grange. The final el. has been confused with hlāw and sceaga. The *Y-* spellings are due to stress-shifting in the diphthong *Ea-*.

ERBACH CROSS (lost, 109–596704), 1699 Sheaf[3] 34 (7538), *Harebache* (*-sty, -cros, the water of-*) 1276 Ch, 1278 Misc, *Harebache Crose* 1336 VR, *Harebachescrosse* 1354 BPR, *Harebachecrosse, Harebachecrofte* 1359 VR, *Erbidge Crofte alias Herbach Cross* Jas 1 *Map* (*LRMB* 200), 'hare's valley or stream', from hara and bæce[1], with stīg 'a path', and cros 'a cross'. The *-crofte* forms are probably a misreading of *-crosse*. The cross marked the boundary between Cuddington township, the royal forest of Delamere and the abbot of Vale Royal's demesnes. It is called *Abbotts Cross* in Teesdale's map 1829–1830, cf. Sheaf[3] 34 (7538), *v.* abbat. The 'water' would be Blakemere *infra*. The stīg was probably 'Watling Street' 1 40 (route VII).

SANDIWAY (BANK, COTTAGE, FM & LODGE) (110–6070), *Sondeway* 1379 *Eyre*, 1435 VR, *Sondyway* 1503 ChRR, *Sandyway* 1499 Orm[2], 1615 *ChCert*, 1656 Orm[2], 1671 Sheaf, *Sandiway* 1721 *Chol, -Head* 1779 Sheaf, *-Bank, -Cottage, -Lane, -Lodge* & *-Three Houses* 1831 Bry, *Sandayway* 1671 Sheaf, *Sandaway Head* 1842 OS, 'sandy road', from sandig and weg, with banke, lane, loge and hēafod. This district was a hamlet partly in Whitegate parish and partly in Weaverham Lordship, and was named from 'Watling Street' (109–594703 to 110–622714), *v.* 1 40 (route VII).

BACKWOOD, *Beech Hill Wood* 1831 Bry, cf. Beach Hill Wood *supra*, *v.* back. BEECHTREE HO. BELLEVUE, 1842 OS. BISHOP LODGE, *Bishop's Lodge* 1831 Bry, *v.* loge. BLAKEMERE, cf. *Erbach Cross supra*, *v.* 217 *infra*. BLEAKLEY LANE (lost, 110–620737 to 633727), 1842 OS, *Blakely-* 1831 Bry, cf. the field of *Blakelowe* 1334 VR, *le Blakelowe* 1347 Plea, 'black mound', *v.* blæc, hlāw, perhaps associated with Gibbet Hill *infra*. BROOK FM, *Brook Field, Hey, Meadow* & *Piece* 1839 *TA*. BROWNHEATH, *-Farm* 1831 Bry, *v.* brūn[1], hǣð. BRYN COMMON (lost), 1842 OS, *Brinn* 1831 Bry, *v.* Bryn 198 *supra*. CHESHIRE KENNELS, 1846 *TAMap* 417, *the Foxhound Kennels* 1812 Sheaf, *Cheshire Hunt Kennels* 1831 Bry. FORESTHEY & HILL (FM), *Forest Hey* 1839 *TA* (*freq*), *Forest Hill* 1860 White, named from the adjacent Delamere Forest. GIBBET HILL (110–627727), 1839 *TA*, 'hill suitable for a gibbet', *v.* gibet. This is a tumulus, cf. Bleakley Lane *supra*. HEYESMERE, HEYESWOOD & HEYWOOD RESERVOIR, cf. Hey's Wood 180 *supra*. HODGE LANE (FM), *Hodge Lane* 1831 Bry, *v.* hocg, cf. *Hodg Croft* 1 158. HOLLY BANK. KENNEL LANE & WOOD, cf. Cheshire Kennels *supra*. LITTLEDALE'S GORSE. MOSS FM, 1831 Bry, *v.* mos.

OVERDALE, *v.* 218 *infra.*   PARK COTTAGE, cf. *The Park* 1839 *TA*, *v.* park.   PETTYPOOL (a house), PETTYPOOL PARK, *Vale Royal New Park* 1831 Bry, *New Park* 1842 OS, *v.* nīwe, park. These are in Whitegate parish, and are named from Petty Pool lake and Vale Royal abbey, 180, 179 *supra.*   SPEEDWELL COTTAGE, *Speedwell Lodge* 1831 Bry, cf. *Speedwell Hill* ib, from the plant-name *speedwell.*

FIELD-NAMES

The undated forms are 1839 *TA* 416. Of the others, 1276 is Ch, 1278 Misc, 1304 Chamb, 1334, 1338, 1352², 1359² VR, 1357, 1361, 1503 *ChFor*, 1359 BPR, 1399 ChRR, 1819 Orm², 1831 Bry.

(*a*) Ashtons Plantation 1831; Backside (*v.* ba(c)ksyde); Bank; Blake Hey (*v.* blæc, (ge)hæg); Brimmelow ('bramble mound or hill', from dial. *brimble, v.* brembel, hlāw); Brine Mdw (*v.* brīne 'brine', cf. Salt House Mdw *infra*); Broad Lane; Churns; Clough (*v.* clōh); Cook Stool Croft (*the cuckstool field* 1819, *v.* cucke-stole); Cote Fd (*v.* cot); Cribb ('manger field', *v.* crib); Cross (Lane) Fd (*v.* cros 'a cross'); Dial Hill (*v.* dial); Dunnocks Hey (*v.* dunnoc, (ge)hæg); the Two Eyes (*v.* ēg); Filence (*v.* filand(s)); Fill Barns (probably a prolific field, *v.* 325 *infra*); Flash Fd (*v.* flasshe); Flat(s) (*v.* flat); Fox Heys; Gravel Loont (*v.* gravel, land); Green Hill(s); Gurlings Fd; Gutter Fd (*v.* goter); Halloway-, Holloway Cross Fd ('(cross at) a sunken road', *v.* holh, weg, cros); Hammering Pits; Hanging Fd & Hill (*v.* hangende); Hares Clough (*v.* hara, clōh, cf. *Erbach Cross supra*); Hatch Fd (*v.* hæc(c)); Hay Hill & Holland ('high ground and land in a hollow, where hay grows', *v.* hēg, hyll, and hol², land); Hilledow ('hill allotment', *v.* hyll, dāl); Hitch Fd (*v.* hiche); Holloway Cross Fd (*v. Halloway Cross supra*); Hone Fd (*v.* hān); Howley (Wd) ('owl clearing', *v.* ūle, lēah); Hunger Hill (*v.* hungor); Jack Lake ('unimportant watercourse', *v.* jack, lacu); Kiln Hill; Lees (*v.* læs); Marl (Pit) Fd; Milk Knowl, -Knoll (from myln 'a mill' or meoluc 'milk' and cnoll); (Little) Netherwood (*v.* neoðera, wudu, cf. Big Nether Wd 210 *infra*); New Hey(s); Old Hollow (*v.* ald, holh); Pavement End (*v.* pavement, ende¹); Pingot (*v.* pingot); Pool Hey, Poughway ('pool enclosure', *v.* pōl¹, (ge)hæg); Red Hill; Riddings (*v.* ryding); Rudo (probably 'rough dole', *v.* rūh, dāl); Salt House Mdw (*v.* salt-hūs, cf. Brine Mdw *supra*, Wallerscote 201 *supra*); Sand Hey; School Loont (probably part of the endowment of a school, *v.* scōl, land); Shillbrows; Slack Fd (*v.* slakki); Slump Fd (*v.* slump (cf. *slumpy* NED) 'a boggy place', cf. Slum Wood 2 321–2); Soot Hill (*v.* sōt); Ston(e)y Fd; Tomb Fd, Town Fd (*v.* toun. *Tomb* is a variant of dial. *Tom* for *Town.* Cf. Weaverham Fd *infra*); Trafalgar (*v.* 325 *infra*); Wall Hill (*v.* wælla); Wall Spanish; Weaverham Fd (*campus de Weuerham* 1357, cf. Town Fd *supra*); Well Fd; West Hedge; Wood Hey (*v.* (ge)hæg).

(*b*) *Calfhull* 1399 (*v.* calf, hyll); *Cocshute* 1334 (*v.* cocc-scyte); *Crokehill* 1503 ('hill at a crook', *v.* krókr, hyll); *Cronkisnestisdale* (lit. *Crouk-*) 1278

14   DPN 3

('crane's-nest valley', from dæl[1] 'a valley', and a debateable first component, which appears to be 'Krókr's nest', from the ON pers.n. *Krókr*, but is here probably, 'crane's nest', with *Crouk-* for *Cronk-*, from cranuc and nest 'a nest'); *Cursed Oxegong* 1334 (*v.* cursed, ox-gang); *le Halchys* 1304 (p) ('the nooks', *v.* halh); *Harlescloh* 1276 ('(dell at) the gray wood', from hār[2] and lēah, with clōh); *Holleyeschart'* 1334 (perhaps '(gap at) the wood in a hollow', from hol[2] and lēah with scerde); *Lechemere brake* 1503 ('(a brake at) a pool near a boggy stream', from læc(c) and mere[1], with bræc[1]); *Lemerecloh* 1276 ('the dell with a pool in it', from mere[1] and clōh with the OFr def.art. This place may be at Merebank 205 *supra*); *Modrelake* 1399 (*v.* lacu 'a water-course'. Professor Löfvenberg proposes as first el. an OE **modor* (< PrGerm **muðra-*), corresponding to MLG, MDu *modder*, G *moder* 'mud, bog'. The name means 'stream at a bog'); *Olrinschawe, Orlesschawe* 1278, waste of (*H*)*oldreshawe* 1359, *Ollerschagh, -schawe* 1359[2], (*les Wastes de*) *Oldereshawe* 1361, 'alder copse', *v.* alor, alren, sc(e)aga); *Scottesbach* 1334 ('Scott's valley', from bæce[1], with either the OE pers.n. *Scot* or OE Scot(t) 'a Scot'. This may be associated with John *le Scot* (Johannes de Scotia), earl of Chester 1232–37, since Weaverham was a lordship of the duchy of Chester. Cf. Scotchats 195 *supra*, which may be the same p.n., or from the same first el.); *Sondiokes* 1276, *le Sondiokes* 1278 ('sandy yokes' referring to measures of land, *v.* sandig, geoc[1]); *Sortfeld* 1338 (perhaps 'short field', *v.* sceort, feld); *Thedrych Acre* 1334 (from the ME pers.n. *Thedrich* (OG *Theodric*), cf. *Thomas son of Thedrich of Weuerham* 1334 VR 111, *v.* æcer); *Tuin-, Twinwode* 1334 ('a double or twofold wood', probably two adjacent woodland estates, *v.* twinn, wudu); weir of *Warford* 1338 ('ford at a weir', *v.* wer, wær[1], ford. This place was on the Weaverham boundary).

(5) WEAVERHAMWOOD (110–619747, a detached part of Whitegate parish 164 *supra*), 1831 Bry, *Wyverham Woode* m16 AOMB 397, *v.* wudu.

FIELD-NAMES

The forms are 1846 *TA* 417.

(*a*) Birchen Heath (*v.* bircen[2], hǣð); Big Nether Wd (cf. Little Nether-wood 209 *supra*); Pale Fd (*v.* pale 'a palisade, a fence'); Way Fd.

viii. Delamere Forest

This parish was created in 1812 by Act of Parliament out of the last remaining part of the royal Forest of Delamere 1 8, as 'a parish to be known as Delamere Forest', *v.* Sheaf[3] 33 (7466), Orm[2] II 112. The parish contained the townships, 1. Delamere (now a c.p. including Eddisbury *infra*), 2. Eddisbury (*v.* Delamere *supra*), 3. Kingswood (now included in Kingsley and Manley c.ps. 239, 245 *infra*), 4. Oakmere. These townships appear first in the *EnclA* of 17 December 1819, 'we have divided the parish of Delamere into the Townships of Kingswood, Eddisbury, Delamere and Oakmere'.

1. DELAMERE (109–5567), ['deləmi:r] older local ['dæləmər], *v. supra.*
HAREWOOD-HILL, HARROW HILL (109–5467), *Harewod(edisc)* 1357
ChFor, Harewod(e) 1503 *ib, Harwood Hill* 1816 Sheaf, *Harewood Hill*
1842 OS, perhaps 'the grey wood', *v.* hār² (wk.obl. hāran), wudu;
but the first el. could be hara 'a hare' or even hær 'a rock'. Cf.
Primrose Hill *infra.* Harewood is also named *Olerton Harewod* 1357
ChFor, '*Harewod* at, or belonging to, *Olerton*'. *Olerton* is 'alder-tree
farm' from alor and tūn, which suggests that the lost *Alretone* 1086
DB 263b (*Dudestan* Hundred) might have been located here, cf.
Ollerton Mdw 300 *infra* in the adjoining township of Utkinton, *v.* 160,
185 *supra.*

SANDYFORD (BRIDGE), (109–573657), *Sondyford, Sondiford* 1347
ChFor, le Sondyforde, Sondefurth, le Sandyfforth 1503 *ib, Sanddi-,*
Sanddyford c.1536 Leland, *Sandyford* 1812 Sheaf, *-Bridge* 1831 Bry,
'the sandy ford', *v.* sandig, ford. Cf. Sandyford Brook 1 34.

ABBEY ARMS WOOD, named from the Vale Royal Abbey Arms hotel.
BIRCH HILL, 1831 Bry, *v.* birce, hyll. BLACKBANK WOOD, *Bothill,*
Bitthill 1503 *ChFor, Buttle or Black Hill Plantation* 1831 Bry, *Black*
Hill 1842 OS, 'black hill', 'hill with a mound on it' *v.* butt², blæc,
hyll, banke. BOOTHDALE, 1831 Bry, *le Bothes* 1347 *ChFor,*
Booths Dale 1813 Orm², '(valley at) the herdsmen's shelters', *v.*
bōth, dæl¹. CASTLEHILL, CASTLE YARD, *le Castell Hill* 1503 *ChFor,*
Castle Hill 1816 Sheaf, *v.* castel(l), hyll, geard, cf. Kelsborrow Castle
infra. CHURCH ALLOTMENT, cf. *Chyrcheheth* 1357 *ChFor,* 'heath
belonging to a church', *v.* cirice, hǣð. COLONEL'S HATCH, *v.*
hæc(c). DELAMERE FM, 1831 Bry. DICKS MOUNT, 1831 *ib, v.*
munt. DOG FALL, 'dog's felling-place', *v.* dogga, (ge)fall.
DOGMOOR WELL, 1831 *ib, Dogmore Well* 1812 Sheaf, cf. *Doggmare*
Lane Jas 1 *Map* (*LRMB* 200), *Dogmore Field* 1812 Sheaf, *Dogmoor*
Stile 1819 *EnclA,* 'dog's pool and marsh', from dogga and mōr¹,
mere¹, with wella, lane, stigel and feld. The well was on the Kelsall
boundary, cf. 278 *infra.* DUNGEON BANK, 'hillside with a hollow
in it', from dongeon 'a dungeon', and banke. FISHPOOL INN, cf.
the Fishpole 1480 Sheaf, *Fisshepole* 1503 *ChFor, the Fishpool* 1597
Dep, a mere, *v.* fisc-pōl. FOREST HO, 1816 Sheaf, *Rutters* 1813
Orm², *Rutter's Lodge* 1819 *EnclA,* 1831 Bry, 'house in the forest',
'hunting lodge belonging to the Rutter (*le Roter*) family', from
forest, hūs and loge with the surname of the hereditary foresters of

Delamere.   Foxhill Fm, *v.* **fox, hyll.**   Gooseberry Lane
(109–533671), *Dan Town* 1831 Bry, *v. Done* 161 *supra*, **toun.**
Gorselands.   Green Lane, *v.* **grēne¹,** lane, cf. 278 *infra.*
Harrow Hill, *v.* Harewood-Hill *supra,* cf. Primrose Hill Cottage
infra.   Heathfield.   Hindswell Gutter, named from *Hind's
Well* 1816 Sheaf, cf. Hinds Gate *infra,* 'hind's spring', from **hind**
and **wella,** with **goter** 'a gutter'.   Hollybank.   Kelsborrow
Castle (109–533676), 1842 OS, *Kelborow Castell* 1574 Sheaf,
Kelsborough Castle 1813 Orm², *Kel(l)sborrow* 1819 Orm², 'Kel's
stronghold', from the same ME pers.n. form, *Kel(l)e,* as appears in
Kelsall 276 *infra, v.* **burh, castel(l),** cf. Castlehill and Castle Yard
supra. The 'castle' is an earthwork, probably an Iron-age promontory
camp, *v.* Varley fig. 29 & schedule 6.   Kelsborrow Ho, cf. prec.
Kenmure   King's Gate, *v.* **cyning, geat.** An access to the forest.
Organsdale Fm, *v.* Organsdale Ho 215 *infra.*   Primrose Bank.
Primrose Hill (Cottage & Wood), *Primrose Hill* 1816 Sheaf,
Harwood Hill Lodge 1842 OS, cf. Harewood-Hill *supra.*   Quarry
Lane, *v.* **quarriere,** lane.   Rosebank Fm.   Sandybrow, 1842
OS, *v.* **sandig, brū.**   Sandy Mere, 1842 ib, *v.* **sandig, mere¹.**
Sandymere Wood, cf. prec.   Seven Lows (109–566672), *the vii
Loos* c.1536 Leland, *Seven Lowes* 1813 Orm², *the Seven Lows* 1819
Orm², a group of seven tumuli, *v.* **seofon, hlāw.**   Summer Bank,
v. **sumor, banke.**   Summertrees.   Tirley Hollow, *v.* Tirley
Lane 286 *infra.*   Urchins Kitchen, a ravine, 'hedgehog's
kitchen', *v.* **urchon, cycene.**   The Waste, Waste Lane, *v.* **wēste.**
Whistlebitch Well, 1812 Sheaf. An earlier form *Twisel-bache,* date
and source not stated, is reported in Sheaf³ 50 (10036). This would be
'valley stream with a fork', *v.* **twisla, bæce¹, wella.** Initial *T-* has
been regarded as a reduced def.art. The spring is on the boundary
with Willington 285 *infra.*   Willington Corner & Lane, *v.*
lane, cf. Willington (Corner) 285–6 *infra.*   Woodbine Lodge.

FIELD-NAMES

The undated forms are 1812 Sheaf³ 33 (7084, 7484–87). Of the others, 1819
is *EnclA,* 1347, 1357, 1503 *ChFor,* 1480, 1699 Sheaf, 1831 Bry.

(*a*) Abrams Well; Astmore Knowle 1699 (*Alstemerknoll* 1357, perhaps
'(hillock at) Ælfstān's pool', from **cnoll** and **mere¹** with the OE pers.n.
Ælfstān); Brock's Road 1819; Glead Brook (*v.* **gleoda, brōc**); Hinds Gate
(cf. *Hyndeheth* 1503 and Hindswell *supra,* 'hind's heath', *v.* **hind, hǣð.** The
gate was an access to the forest on the boundary of Little Budworth, cf. 186

supra); Masters Gate (*v.* geat); Padstocks Lake (*v.* lacu); Simpsons Hill; Stable End Lane 1819 (cf. Sidebottom Fm 299 *infra*); Walker's Lane 1819; Walley's Gate 1831 (*v.* 286 *infra*); Whittinghams Lane (named after one William *Whittingham*); Wimpenny's Gate (named after one John *Wimpenny, v.* geat).

(*b*) *Brokhull* 1347 ('hill near a brook', or 'badger hill', from brōc or brocc, *v.* hyll); *le Wharell iuxta Fisshepole* 1503 ('the quarry near Fishpool *supra*', *v.* quarrelle); *Wynsyche* 1480 (final el. sīc 'a watercourse').

2. EDDISBURY (HILL & LODGE) (109–5569) ['edizbəri] older local ['edzbəri, 'edჳbəri]

    æt Eades byrig 914 ASC(C), *-birig* (1130) FW, *Eadsbury* (1656) Orm², (1672) ib
    Edesberie 1086 DB, *-beri* 112 *Chol, -bery* 1671 Sheaf, *-bur'* c.1310 Chest, *-bury* 1331 Plea *et freq* with variant spelling *-buri* to 1666 Sheaf, (*-in foresta iuxta Cestriam*) 14 Higden, (*-hull*) 1365 *Tourn Edisbury* 1260 Court, and seven times with variant spellings *-bur(ye)* to 1813 Orm², (*-in þe forest bysides Chestre*) 15 Trev
    Eddingburie 1298 (17) *Harl.* 2115
    Eddisburgh 1307 *Eyre* (p), *-bury* 1404 ChRR, (*-Lodge*) 1817 *EnclA, Eddysbury* 1554 Sheaf
    Edersbury 1387 ChRR
    Eddesbury 1388 ChRR *et freq* with variant spellings *-byry, -burie* to 1819 Sheaf, (*-hill*) 1783 ib, (*-in the parish of Delamere*) 1819 ib
    Endysbury 1397 ChRR
    Edusbury 1468 *MinAcct*
    Elborough now called Edsbury 1574 Sheaf
    Erdesbury alias Edesbury 1650 *ParlSurv*
    Edsbury 1574 Sheaf, 1656 Orm², 1683 Sheaf
    Headberry Jas 1 *Map* (*LRMB* 200)

'Ēad's stronghold', from an OE pers.n. *Ēad* and burh (dat.sg. byrig), with hyll and loge. The pers.n. appears in Edgeley, *Edeshal(x)h* 309, 326 *infra*, Adisham K (DEPN, PNK 520). The p.n. is that of the Iron-age hill fort on Eddisbury Hill, which Æþelflǣd lady of the Mercians garrisoned in 914, cf. Castle Ditch *infra*. The place became the capital of a hundred in the twelfth century, *v.* 160 *supra*, and was the chief lodge of the Forest of Delamere 1 8, cf. Merrick's Hill *infra*. Cf. also notes 210 *supra*. The p.n. recurs at Eddisbury 1 139.

BARNBRIDGE GATES, *v.* 215 *infra*.   BATTLEAXE RD.   BLACK LAKE, a mere, *v.* blæc, lake.   BLAKEMERE MOSS, *Blakmere Mosse* 1503

ChFor, Great Blake Mere 1813 Orm², 1842 OS, '(moss at) black lake',
v. blæc, mere¹, mos, cf. Blakemere 249 *infra*, Blackmere Ford *infra*,
Small Brook² 1 35. *Great-* (*v.* grēat) distinguishes this from the
Blake Mere in Oakmere, cf. Barry's Wood 217 *infra*.   CASTLE
DITCH, cf. *the Castle Croft upon the top of the hill* 1652 Sheaf, named
from the ramparts of the Iron-age hill-fort and Anglo-Saxon *burh* of
Eddisbury, *supra*, cf. Varley 64–9, *v.* castel(l), dīc, croft.   EDDIS-
BURY HILL FM, *Eddisbury Farm* 1831 Bry, *Lower House* 1671 Sheaf,
the hous under the Chamber 1681 ib, cf. Eddisbury *supra*, Merrick's
Hill *infra*.   FOREST FM, 1842 OS, 'farm in old forest land', *v.*
forest, cf. Delamere Forest 210 *supra*.   GOVERNMENT COTTAGES.
GREY'S GATE, *v.* geat, an access to the forest enclosures.   HANGING-
STONE HILL, *Hanging Stones Hill* 1819 *EnclA*, named from over-
hanging rocks, *v.* hangende, stān, hyll.   HOLLYBANK.   HUNGER
HILL, *Hongur hill* 1503 *ChFor*, *v.* hungor, hyll.   KING'S CHAIR, a
rock at Hangingstone Hill, fancied to resemble a seat, *v.* chai(e)re.
LEA CROFT.   LINMERE MOSS, LINMER COTTAGE, *Linmere* 1813
Orm², cf. *Linmere Plat* 1819 *EnclA, Linmere Allotment* 1831 Bry, 'pool
where flax grows', *v.* līn, mere¹, plat¹ 'a footbridge'.   MERRICK'S
HILL, cf. *Merricks Road* 1819 *EnclA* (in Oakmere 219 *infra*), cf.
Thomas Merrick, d. 1683 (Sheaf³ 31 (6902)), and John Merrick,
tenant in 1812 when the forest was enclosed, Sheaf³ 33 (7460). The
hill is the south-eastern extremity of Eddisbury Hill *supra*, within the
Castle Ditch hill-fort, and the site was formerly *domus de La Mare*
1245 Lib, *the king's houses of La Mare* 1245 Pat, *camera infra forestam
de Mara* 1397 *MinAcct, The Chamber in the Forest* 1577 Saxton, 1656
Orm², 1690 Sheaf, *the Chamber or Headberry House* Jas 1 *Map*
(*LRMB* 200), *The Chamber olim Edesbury* 1610 Speed, *The Chamber
of the Forest* 1630 Sheaf, *The Chamber* 1681 ib, 1831 Bry, 1842 OS,
a royal hunting lodge, cf. Sheaf³ 31 (6902), *v.* chambre, cf. *Old
Chamber* 1 126. The name was also extended to Castle Ditch, Eddisbury Hill *supra*, and The Old Pale *infra*.   MOUNT PLEASANT.
NETTLEFORD WOOD, *le Netlyford* 1347 *ChFor, Nettle Ford Road* 1819
EnclA, 'ford where nettles grow', *v.* neteli, netel(e), ford.   (THE)
OLD PALE (109–5469), 1652 Sheaf, *Old Pale* Jas 1 *Map* (*LRMB* 200),
the Old Pale or Chamber of Forest 1671 Sheaf, *Old Pale Lodge* 1711
Chol, an ancient enclosed tract of the royal forest, 'the old park, or
fenced-in place', *v.* ald, pale, loge. The Old Pale is the area imme-
diately about Eddisbury Hill, cf. New Pale 216 *infra*, Merrick's Hill
supra.   ORGANSDALE HO, *Organs Dale* 1842 OS (109–547690),

'valley where organ grows', v. organa (ModEdial *organ(s)*) 'penny-royal, etc.', dæl¹, cf. Organsdale Fm 212 *supra*. Sheaf³ 31 (6931) reports a popular etymology from a row of trees like a range of organ pipes.   PALE HEIGHTS, high ground near The Old Pale *supra*, v. hēhǒu, ModE *height*.   SPY HILL, 1842 OS.   STONEY LANE. This is on the line of 'Watling Street' 1 40 (route VII).   WILLOW WOOD, 1842 OS.   THE YELD (FM), YELD CROFT, *le heldebonk* 1357 *ChFor*, *Yeld Marl Pit, Yeld Road, Marl Pit Road* 1819 *EnclA, Heald* 1842 OS, 'the declivity, the hillside', v. helde, banke.

FIELD-NAMES

The sources are, 1347, 1357, 1503 *ChFor*, 1813 Orm², 1819 *EnclA*, 1831 Bry.

(a) Antwis's Road 1819; Birchen Holt Moss 1831 (*le Byrchenhull* 1357, *Burchynholt* 1503, *Berchen Holt* 1813, 'hill' and 'wood growing with birch-trees', from bircen², and hyll, holt, with mos); Blackmere Ford 1831 (*Blakemere Ford* 1819, '(ford near) the black lake', v. ford, cf. Blakemere Moss *supra*); Marl Pit Road 1819 (v. The Yeld *supra*); Midgel Moss 1813 (*Megell mosse* 1503, probably 'big moss', from mycel and mos); White Moor 1831 (*le Qwytemor* 1357, *le Whitmore* 1503, 'white marsh', v. hwīt, mōr¹).

(b) le Brode Ook en Edesburyshawe 1347 ('the broad oak', v. brād, āc, cf. foll.); *Edesburys(c)hawe* 1347, 1357 ('the wood at Eddisbury', v. sceaga, Eddisbury *supra*).

3. KINGSWOOD (109–5372), 1819 *EnclA*, a division of the royal forest of Delamere Forest, cf. 210 *supra*, v. cyning, wudu.

HATCH MERE (WOOD), (109–553720), HATCHMERE (250 *infra*), *Hached(e)-, Hachemer(e)hurst* 1357 *ChFor, Hatchmere Hurst* 1780 *EnclA, Hachilmere* 1503 *ChFor, Hatchew Meare* 1597 *Dep*, 1598 Orm², *-Mear* 1739 *LRMB* 264, *-Mere* 1812 Sheaf, *Hatcher Mere* 1812 Sheaf, *Hatchen Mere* 1831 Bry, from hyrst 'a wooded-hill' and wudu, with the name of a lake, v. mere¹. The first el. is ME *hachede* 'with a hatch', cf. hæc(c), hec(c). The 'hatch' would probably be a fish-trap.

BARNBRIDGE GATES, *Barns Bridge* 1819 *EnclA*, v. bere-ærn, brycg, geat.   BIRCHDALE FM, 'birch-tree valley', v. birce, dæl¹.   BIRCH HILL (FM & HO), *Birch Hill* 1831 Bry, v. birce, hyll.   BLACK WOOD.   CASTLE COB (109–534734), 1813 Orm², *Castle Hill Cob* 1819 ib, a tumulus, v. cobbe, castel(l), cf. foll.   CASTLEHILL COTTAGE, *Castle Hill Allotment* 1816 *EnclA, Castle Hill* 1831 Bry, 'hill suitable for a castle', v. castel(l), hyll, cf. prec. There was no castle here. The tumulus may have been taken for a motte.   CLAIM FM, named from a claim made at the enclosing of the forest in 1813, v. Sheaf³ 34 (7560).   CLIFF VIEW.   FORESTGATE, cf. Forestgate Fm 242 infra, from a gateway at the boundary of Delamere Forest, v. forest, geat.   HONDSLOUGH FM (109–540725) ['hɔnslou, 'hɔnzlou], Wilkinsons 1831 Orm², Wilkinsons-Lodge 1819 EnclA, from loge 'a lodge, a hunting lodge', and the surname Wilkinson. The later name is that of a tumulus Hondslow 1842 OS, Honslow 1845 TA 244, 'Hund's mound' or 'the hound's hill', from hund or the OE pers.n. Hund, or 'Hond's mound' from the ME pers.n. (nickname) Hand, Hond, cf. Honde Cotrell 1288 Court 90 (Reaney 153), v. hlāw.   LORD'S WELL, & Hill 1812 Sheaf, 'lord's well', v. hlāford, wella, hyll, cf. Swan's Well infra.   MAIDEN'S CROSS, (a mere stone called-) 1812 Sheaf, Meadens-, Maydens Crosse 1614 ib, Maiden Cross 1831 Bry, an ancient cross demolished by reformers in the seventeenth century, cf. Sheaf³ 20 (4899), v. mægden, cros.   NEW PALE (FM) (109–5272), le Newepale 1503 ChFor, the New Palle 1637 Sheaf, the New Pale 1652 ib, 'the new enclosure', v. nīwe, pale, cf. foll., Old Pale 214 supra.   PUGH'S COTTAGES, New Pale Lodge 1711 Chol, 1831 Bry, 1842 OS, v. loge, cf. prec.   RAVENSLODGE FM. SUNNYBANK FM, v. sunny, banke.   SWAN'S WELL, 1812 Sheaf, 'peasant's well', v. swān², wella, cf. Lord's Well supra.   WANLOW'S WELL, 1813 Orm², Wandlow(s) Well 1812 Sheaf, Wanless Well 1831 Bry, from wella 'a well-spring'. The first component is a p.n. in hlāw 'a mound, a hill', with an unidentified first el.   WASTE FM, v. wēste. WATERLOO (GATE), Waterloo 1831 Bry.

FIELD-NAMES

The sources are 1347, 1357, 1503 ChFor, 1810, 1812 Sheaf, 1813, 1819² Orm², 1819 EnclA, 1831 Bry, 1842 OS.

(a) Burgess Stable 1831; Cockspool Gutter 1812 ('watercourse from woodcock's pool', from cocc² and pōl¹, with goter); Combey Slacks or Valley 1812 ('valley with enclosures', from cumb and (ge)hæg, with slakki, valeie); Fishpool 1819 (v. fisc-pol); Fleed Moss 1812 ('moss which has been "flayed"', i.e. stripped of peat', v. mos); a platt called Forrester 1810 ('the forester's bridge', v. forester, plat¹); Fox Cover 1819; Gills Quarry 1812; Glead Hill Cob 1842 (1813, '(tumulus at) hawk hill', v. gleoda, hyll, cobb(e)); Hengreave Quarry 1812 (v. henn, græfe); Hey Cliff 1842 (le Heghclyf, le Hegh' clyff 1357, Heghcliff 1503, 'the high cliff', v. hēah, clif); Hollin Hill 1831 (cf. Hollin Hill Road 1819, v. holegn, hyll); Linmere Plat 1819 (v. plat¹, and Linmere Moss

214 *supra*); Newton Gate 1812 (an access to the forest from Newton 248 *infra*, *v.* geat); Rough Hill 1842 (*v.* rūh, hyll); Seething Well 1812 (*v.* seoðinge, wella, cf. Seeding Well 244 *infra*); the Stone Benches 1812 (*le Stanberth in le Oldepark* 1357, *Stonebench* 1503, 'stone hill' from stān and beorg, the final el. replaced by benc); Wilkins Moss 1812 (from mos and the surname or pers.n. *Wilkin(s)*).

(*b*) *le Oldepark* 1357, *Oldeparke grene iuxta Manley* 1503, *v.* ald, park, grēne²); *Swappe lake* 1347, *Swaplake* 1503 (from lacu 'a watercourse'. The first el. may be either ON *svöppr* 'fungus', referring to vegetation about the water, or, as Professor Löfvenberg observes, it may be the OE pers.n. *Swæppa* (Redin 109)).

4. OAKMERE (HALL) (109–5769, 5970), older local [-mɛːr], *Oakmere* 1819 *EnclA*, *Oakmere Lodge* 1842 OS, *v.* loge, cf. foll., and 210 *supra*.

OAK MERE (a lake, 109–5767), OAKMERE COMMON (109–5768), a moor and stew called *Ocmare* 1277 Pat, *Okemere* 1347, 1503 *ChFor*, m16 *AOMB* 397, *Okemere Wo(d)de* 1503 *ChFor*, *Okemeyre* 1639 Orm², *Okmere* 1348 VR, 1517 AD, *-mer* 1499 Sheaf, *the pool of Oakmere* 1542 Dugd, *Oak Mere* 1813 Orm², 'oak lake', from āc and mere¹, with wudu and commun. This mere gave name to the township.

ABBOTSMOSS COTTAGE, *Abbots Moss Lodge* 1842 OS, named from Abbot's Moss 182 *supra*, *v.* loge. BARRY'S WOOD (109–595702), BLAKEMERE (a house), *Mr. Barrys Plantation* 1812 Sheaf, on and near the reclaimed site of a lake *Blakemere* 1359 VR, 1393 ChRR, *Little Black Mere* 1812 Sheaf, *Blake Mere* 1842 OS, 'black lake', *v.* blæc, mere¹. An older name was 'the water of *Harebache*', *v.* Erbach Cross 208 *supra*. *Little-* (*v.* lītel) distinguishes this water from that of Blakemere Moss 213 *supra*. BOWYERS WASTE, *v.* wēste. BURNT WOOD, *v.* brende². CORNER FM, *v.* corner. CRABTREEGREEN FM, *Crabtree Greene* Jas 1 *Map* (*LRMB* 200), *-Green* 1812 Sheaf, 'green at a crab-tree', *v.* crabbe, trēow, grēne². CUDDINGTON POOL, *v.* 199 *supra*. FIRBROOK, cf. Fir Brook 1 24. FOLLY FM, 1842 OS, *Folly House* 1831 Bry, *v.* folie. FOREST HO, 1816 *EnclA*, *Hornsbys Lodge* 1812 Sheaf, *Hornby's Lodge* 1813 Orm², 1819 *EnclA*, cf. Hornby's Rough *infra*, from the surname *Hornby* and loge, also 'house belonging to the forest', *v.* forest, hūs. FOX COVERT LODGE, cf. (*the*) *Fox Cover(t)* 1812 Sheaf, 1842 OS, *Small Brook Covert* 1831 Bry, cf. Small Brook² 1 35, *v.* cover. GALLOWS-CLOUGH COB (109–570713), a tumulus now named from foll., formerly *Geradeslowe* 1503 *ChFor*, *Garruslow* 1819 Orm², *Currus Low Cob* 1842 OS, from the ME pers.n. *Gerard* (OG *Gerard*) and hlāw, cobb(e).

Gerard was the surname of a family with estates in Kingsley 239 *infra* from before 1260 (Orm² II 131), and this may be the origin of the p.n. GALLOWSCLOUGH FM, HILL & LANE, [-klʌf], *Gallows Clough* 1819 *EnclA*, 'dell near a gallows', *v.* galga, clōh.   GIG HOLE, 'hole for a flax-drying fire', gigge, hol¹.   HALL WOOD, cf. Oakmere Hall *supra*.   HART HILL (BANK & HATCH), *Harthill Bank* 1842 OS, *v.* heorot 'a hart', hyll, banke, hæc(c) 'a gate'.   HEADLESS CROSS (109–583679), (a mere stone called-) 1812 Sheaf, a mutilated ancient cross on the boundary with Marton & Little Budworth 183, 186 *supra*, *v.* hēafod-lēas, cros.   HOGSHEAD LANE & WOOD, probably 'hawk's gap', from hafoc-scerde, analogous with Hogsheads I 191, *v. Hawkesyord* I 166.   HOOK HO, *v.* hōc.   HORNBY'S ROUGH, 1842 OS, *Forest House Allotment* 1819 *EnclA*, cf. *Hornby's Meadow & Road* 1819 *EnclA* and Forest Ho *supra*, *v.* rūh.   LOB SLACK (WOOD), *Lobs Slack* 1813 Orm², (*Plantation*) 1831 Bry, *Lob Slack* 1816 *EnclA*, (*Wood*) 1842 OS, *v.* slakki 'a hollow'. *Lob* may be dial. *lob* 'mud; a thick mixture', or ModE *lob* 'a lubber, a clumsy bumpkin; a kind of oafish goblin'.   LONG RIDGE, *Long Rige* 1503 *ChFor*, *Longridge* 1816 *EnclA*, 'long ridge', *v.* lang, hrycg.   MADDOCK LODGE, from loge and the surname *Maddock*.   MASSEY'S LODGE, 1812 Sheaf, from loge and the surname *Massey*.   NEWPOOL FM & WOOD, named from a former lake, *New Pool* 1812 Sheaf, 1813 Orm², *v.* nīwe, pōl¹.   OVERDALE, *v.* uferra, dæl¹, cf. 209 *supra*.   PLAGUE HOLE, 1813 Orm², *v.* plague, hol¹. This may be merely a derogatory name for a 'pestilent hole', but such a p.n. might indicate an old mass-burial site, as of plague-victims.   PLOVER'S MOSS, *Plouers Mosse* 1503 *ChFor*, *Plovers Moss* 1816 *EnclA*, *Plovers' Moss* 1816 Sheaf, cf. *Plovers Lodge* 1842 OS, *v.* plouer 'a plover', mos, loge.   RAVENSCLOUGH, *v.* 199 *supra*.   RELICKS MOSS, *Relicts Moss* 1813 Orm², 'left-over marsh', probably not allocated at the enclosure of the Forest of Delamere, *v.* relict, mos.   SANDYBROW COTTAGE, cf. Sandybrow 212 *supra*.   THIEVES MOSS, 1813 Orm², *v.* þēof, mos. 'WATLING STREET', *v.* I 40 (route VII).

FIELD-NAMES

The sources are 1503 *ChFor*, Jas I *Map* (*LRMB* 200), 1752 Sheaf, 1813 Orm², 1819 *EnclA*, 1831 Bry.

(a) Blakeford Moss 1831 (*Blakeforde* 1503, '(moss at) black ford', *v.* blæc, ford, mos. The ford was at 109–564693 on the line of the Roman road from Chester to Northwich, cf. 'Watling Street' *supra*); Blackmere Ford 1831 (*v.* ford, cf. Blakemere Moss 213 *supra*); Crap Moss 1813 (from mos and crappe either in its botanical sense 'darnel, rye-grass, etc.' or as 'chaff, residue, rubbish', cf. Crappilous Mdw 2 322); Merricks Road 1819 (cf. Merrick's Hill 214 *supra*); the Pedlar's Oak 1752 (*Pedlars Oake* Jas 1, 'oak where pedlars meet', *v.* pedlere, āc, a tree at 109–565695 on an old road from Eddisbury Hill to Crabtreegreen); Riley Moss 1813 (*Ryley mosse* 1503, '(moss land at) the rye clearing', *v.* ryge, lēah, mos); Rinney Moss 1813 (*v.* mos); Shipley Mere 1813 (*v.* mere[1]. *Shipley* is probably 'sheep pasture', from scēp and lēah); Stewards Well 1819 (*v.* stīg-weard, wella).

ix. Frodsham

The ecclesiastical parish of Frodsham contained the townships 1. Alvanley, 2. Frodsham (now a c.p. including Frodsham Lordship), 3. Frodsham Lordship (*v.* prec.), 4. Helsby, 5. Kingsley (now a c.p. including Newton *infra* and part of Kingswood 215 *supra*), 6. Manley (now a c.p. including part of Kingswood), 7. Newton by Frodsham (*v.* Kingsley *supra*), 8. Norley (part of this was in Weaverham parish 193 *supra*).

1. ALVANLEY (HALL) (109–500740) ['alvənli] older local ['ɔːvənli]

   Elveldelie 1086 DB
   Alualdeleh 1208–26 AddCh, *Alvaldeley* 1209 Tab, *-ley* 1292 Ipm
   Aluadeleya 1216–29 Chest, *-leg'* 1265–91 ib
   Aluedeleg' 1265–91 Chest, *Alvedelegh* 1346 BPR
   Alvandeley 1292 Ipm *et freq* with variant spellings *Alu-*, *Alvand(e)-*
       ley(e), *-legh* to 1724 NotCestr, (*capella de-*) 1468 *MinAcct*,
       Alvanley 1386 Sheaf, 1562 ChRR *et freq*, *-ly* 1724 NotCestr,
       Alvanley Hall, the chapelry of Alvanley 1831 Bry
   Aluendeleye 1294 ChFor, *Alv-*, *-legh* 1308 Misc, *-ley* 1729 *Chol*,
       Alvenley 1581, 1666 Sheaf
   Alvondelegh 1315 Orm[2], *Alvonley* 1503 ChFor, *Alu-* 1641 Orm[2]
   Alwandelegh 1330 Cl
   Olvendelegh 1369 Bark
   Almondelegh 1497 ChRR
   Albandelegh 1540 Dudg, *Abandley* 1553 Pat
   Alvenerley 1549 Sheaf
   Avantley 1611 *Chol*
   Aulmeley 1690 Sheaf

'Ælfweald's clearing', from the OE pers.n. *Ælfweald* and lēah, with hall. Alvanley was a chapelry of Frodsham parish, *v.* chapel. The p.n. probably recurs at *Aluandelegh* 2 50.

EDGIN COTES (lost), 1844 *TA*, *Huchenescote, Ichincote* 1265–91 Chest, *Hychenescote* c.1310 ib, *Ichyncote* 1440 *Rental*, *Edencote* 1539 Dugd, *-cot* 1579 ib, *Idencoate* 1546 ib, *-cote* 1579 ib, 1657, 1692 *Chol*, *Indecote* 1553 Pat. The first spelling indicates 'Huchon's cottage', from cot and the ME (OFr) pers.n. *Huchon*, diminutive of *Hugh*, but Professor Löfvenberg notes that the others indicate the ME pers.n, *Hychen*, diminutive of *Hich*, a pet-form of *Richard* (cf. John *Hychen* (Wa) 1332, v. Reaney s.nn. *Hitch, Hitchen*), and advises that the first spelling may be a scribal error. The place belonged to St Werburgh's Abbey, Chester, cf. Abbot's Clough *infra*, Addenda xvi *supra*.

ABBOT'S CLOUGH, 1842 OS, *Abbots Slough* 1831 Bry, cf. 246 *infra*, 'the abbot's dell', named from the abbots of Chester, cf. *Edgin Cotes supra*, v. abbat, clōh.   BOWLINGALLEY FM, *Bank House* 1831 Bry.

CHURCH-HOUSE FM, v. cirice, hūs.   CLIFF FM, ALVANLEY CLIFF, *le Clyffe* 1503 ChFor, *Alvanley Cliff* 1831 Bry, cf. *Black Cliff Hay* 1841 *TA*, v. clif.   COMMON SIDE, 1831 Bry, cf. *Common Field, Land & Lot* 1844 *TA*, v. commun, sīde, feld, land, hlot.   CRAB-TREE FM.   FOUR LANE ENDS.   THE GREEN, 1842 OS, v. grēne². GREENBANK FM, v. grēne¹, banke.   GREENGATE FM, v. grēne¹, gata 'a pasture plot'.   HORN'S MILL BRIDGE, cf. *Horns Field* 1844 *TA*, v. 237 *infra*.   MAIDEN'S CROSS, v. 216 *supra*.   PECK MILL, PECKMILL BROOK, *Peck Mill* 1831 Bry, 'a watermill in Alvanley' 1552 Orm² II 82, but cf. Horn's Mill 236 *infra*, for earlier references to mills. Both mills gave name to the same stream, cf. Hornsmill Brook 237 *infra*. The mill-name *Peck Mill* is discussed under Peckmill 2 84. QUEEN CHARLOTTE'S WOOD, *Alvanley Fox Cover* 1831 Bry, v. fox, cover.   RIDGEWAY, v. 224 *infra*.   ROSE COTTAGE.   WALNUT-TREE FM.   YARRANGALL GREEN, v. ȝar(n)wyndel 'a yarnwindle', grēne².

FIELD-NAMES

The undated forms are 1844 *TA* 13. Of the others, 1216–29, 1265–91 are Chest, 1307–24 *Chol*, 1309 Misc, 1347, 1357 *ChFor*, 17, 1812 Sheaf, 1831 Bry, 1842 OS.

(a) Antrobus (cf. 232 *infra*); Back Court (v. back, court); Backside (v. ba(c)ksyde); Barkers Moor (cf. *Barkers Pits* 1831 and Tan Pit Fd *infra*, v. barkere, mōr¹, pytt); Beesom Stail ('beesom's tail', after the shape of the field, from *besom* 'a broom' and tægl); Big- & Green Beaks (v. beak); Black Rook; Blanchetts ('fields with whitish soil', cf. NED s.v. *blanchet* 'white flour or powder', *blanchart* 'whitish', but the f.n. may be from the surname *Blanchett* (Reaney 35)); Bottoms (*v.* botm); Broad- & Broomy Hawks (*v.* Hawks *infra*); Church-mans Mdw; Clover Brow; Coal Field (*v.* col[1]); Cockspool Gutter 1812 (*v.* 216 *supra*); Coney Greaves (*v.* coningre); Cote Fd (*v.* cot); Dodwell; Eaves (*v.* efes); Farley; Fender Fd (*v.* fender); Fleed Moss 1812 (*v.* 216 *supra*); Hall Fold Gate (*v.* hall, fald, gata); (Broad-, Broomy-) Hawks (*v.* brād, brōmig, halc); Hengreave Quarry 1812 (*v.* 216 *supra*); Hill Hay, -Hey(s); Holly Well Dale (*v.* hālig, wella, dæl[1]); Hunger Hill (*v.* hungor); Intake (*v.* inntak); Long Folly (*v.* folie); Long Slack (*v.* Slack *infra*); Marl Fd; Mill Field Pingot (*v.* pingot); Mill Way(s) ('paths to a mill', *v.* myln, weg); Nook Croft (*v.* nōk); Northay, North Hay (*v.* norð, (ge)hæg); Old Woman's Lane 1831; Pikes (*v.* pīc[1]); Pingot (*v.* pingot); Pitstead ('site of a pit', *v.* pytt, stede); Pye Corner 1831 (*v.* pīe[2]); Rake Lane Croft (*v.* rake, lane, cf. Rake Lane 237 *infra*); Ree Fd; Riddings (*v.* ryding); Rough Slack (*v.* Slack *infra*); Royalty (*v.* roialte); (Long-, Rough- & Woods) Slack (*v.* slakki); Stone Heys; Tan Pit Fd ('field with a tan-pit in it', cf. Barkers Moor *supra*, *v.* tan-pit); Titles Croft; Toothill Croft (*v.* Teuthill 237 *infra*); Town Field or Loont (*v.* toun, land); Vilance (*v.* filand(s)); The Wall Moor (cf. *Hey More or Walls More* 17, *le Heymor* 1307–24, *le Heyemor* 1309 (227 *infra*), 'marsh at an enclosure and a spring', *v.* wælla, (ge)hæg, mōr[1]); Washing Brooks ('streams where washing is done', from ME *waschung*, cf. wæsce, *v.* brōc); Wigan Croft (from dial. *wiggen* 'mountain ash', *v.* cwicen, croft); Wood Lane 1842 (cf. *boscus de Aluadeleya* 1216–29, *-Alued'* 1265–91, *-Aluandeley* 1347, *v.* wudu); Woods Slack (*v.* Slack *supra*); Wormstool (*v.* wormstall).

(*b*) *Aluandelegh' yord* 1357 ('enclosure (or perhaps a fish-pound) at Alvanley', *v.* geard).

2. FRODSHAM (109–5177) ['frɔdsəm, -ʃəm] (older local ['frad-, 'fratsəm] obsolescent by c.1886)

Frotesham 1086 DB, 1581 *AddCh*, *-is-* c.1296 *Chol* (p)

Frodesham 1096–1101 (1280), 1150 Chest, 1184 P *et freq* with variant spellings *-is-*, *-ys-*, *Froddes-* (1270 Dugd to 1582 Sheaf), *Froddys-* (1580 *AddCh*) to 1619 Cre, *Frodessam* 1175 Facs, *Frodessham* 1535 VE, *Frodsham* 1211–29 Whall, 1282 Court (p) *et freq*, *Frodshum* e13, 1346 Tab, 1665 Sheaf, *Frodsam* 1527 Orm[2]

Fredesham c.1154 (1329) Dugd, 1216–72 *JRC* (p), *Fredesam* 1329 Cl

Frotheshamme c.1206 (1615) Dugd (p) (lit. *Froches-*), *Frothesham* 1238 P (lit. *Frochel-*), 1239 ib (lit. *Frothel-*), 1239 Lib

Frethesham 1237 P

Frodeham 1239, 1240 P, 1246 Lib

Fradesham 1245 Cl, *Fraddes-* 1556 Pat, *Fradsham* 1437 ib, 1557 Sheaf, 1640 Orm[2] *et freq* with variant spellings *Fradson*, *-som(e)*, *-sum(e)*, *-same*

Fordesham 13 Tab, 1297 Cl, 1312 Pat, 1324 Cl, 1434 Dugd, 1454 ChRR, 1560 Sheaf
Fordham 1325, 1328, 1338 Cl
Fridesham 1351 BPR
Fodersham 1351 BPR
Flettesham 1437 Pat

'Frōd's village', from the OE pers.n. *Frōd* and hām. The same pers.n. appears in the form *frodeshammespend* (*v.* hamm, pynd) BCS 335 for *Flotham* K, *v.* PNK 114, 118. Frodsham originally comprised both the town and the Lordship 228 *infra*. The town was made a borough by charter of Ranulph III (de Blundeville), earl of Chester 1181–1232, *v.* Orm² II 46, cf. *burgum de Frodesham* 1209–28 (1389) Ch, 1328 P, *Frodsham Town* 1656 Orm², *Frodsham Borough and Lordship, Frodsham Borough and Fee, or Frodsham Township* 1819 ib, *v.* burh, toun. That part of the original manor, which the earl retained out of the borough, continued to be called the Lordship of Frodsham, but in the earliest references that designation applied to the whole of the two townships and they continued always as part of one manor (Orm² II 46).

STREET-NAMES. CHURCH ST., 1844 *TA*, *le Kyrkstrete* 1272–1307 *AddCh*, (*le-*, *the-*), *Kirke-*, *Kyr(c)kestrete* 1300–7 *ib*, c.1300, c.1320 *Chol*, *Chirchestrete* 1429 Orm², 'street to the church', *v.* cirice, strǣt. Cf. Overton Hill 230 *infra*; MAIN ST., *le Heghstrete* 1429 Orm², 'the high street', *v.* hēah, strǣt; SHIP ST., 1844 *TA*, *le schypstrete* 1349 *Chol*, *le Shipstrete* 1363 *ib*, *le Shippestrete* 1404 *ib*, *le schipstrete* 1406 *ib*, *Shipstrete* 1429 Orm², *Shippstreete* 1680 *Chol*, cf. *Ship Lane Garden* 1844 *TA*, 'sheep street', *v.* scēp, strǣt, cf. Ship Fd, *Schiplendiggis infra*. This road leads down from the town on to Frodsham Marsh and to the R. Weaver. Vale Royal abbey grazed sheep on the marsh, cf. *le Shephous upon the Mersh* 1395 Orm² II 150, *v.* scēp, hūs; WATER ST., *v.* wæter. This adjoins Hale Pit *infra*.

FRODSHAM BRIDGE (109–530785), *pons de Wevere* 1308 Misc, *-Wewir* 1321 *Chol*, *Frodsham Brugge* 1447 *CoLegh et freq* with variant spellings as for Frodsham *supra*, and *-brygg(e)* 1527 Orm², *-Bridge* 1618 Sheaf, the origin of the Frodsham surname *de Ponte* 1240 P *et freq*, *del Brugge* 1305 Plea, *-Bruge* 1325 ChRR, *-Bridgg* 1341 Orm², and giving name to *le Bruggehousis* 1288 Court, *-es* 1358 ChRR (p), 1402 ib, *-howse* 1377–1399 Orm², *Bruggehous* 1446 ChRR, *Brugehouse* 1351 Chamb, *le Brugehoux* 1351 *MinAcct*, 1357 *ChFor* (p), *-hous* 1357 *ib* (p), *Brygehous* 1428 *AddCh* (p), *Brugge-*, *Briggehous* (*Mershe*) 1444 ChRR, *Chol*, *the Briggehous* 1496 Orm², and to *Bridge End House*

1708 *Chol*, from **brycg** and **hūs**, **ende**[1], **mersc**, cf. R. Weaver 1 38, Frodsham *supra*, Frodsham Marsh *infra*.

FRODSHAM MARSH (109–5078), *the marsh of Frodesham* 1308 Misc, *Le Merssh* 1348 BPR, *the Mersh* 1395 Orm[2], *lez Mershes* 1507 *MinAcct*, *Frodeshammersh* 1348 BPR *et freq* with variant spellings as for Frodsham *supra*, and -*merssh* 1355 BPR, -*marshes* 1580 *AddCh*, -*Marsh* 17 Sheaf, cf. *Lytelmersche* 1351 Chamb, *Litelmersh* 1365 ChRR, *the* (*Higher & Lower*) *Lit*(*t*)*le Mershe*-, -*Marsh*(*e*) (*Meadowe*) 1611 to 1719 *Chol, My Lady's Little Marsh* 1700 *ib*, and *Brigge*-, *Bruggehous Mershe* 1444 ChRR, *Chol, v.* **mersc**, **lȳtel**, cf. Frodsham, Frodsham Bridge *supra*, Lordship Marsh 231 *infra*. Frodsham Marsh & Lordship Marsh are part of the great tract of marsh between R. Weaver and R. Gowy and R. Mersey and the hills of Eddisbury hundred. This tract is described in 1348 (BPR 1 160) as 'waste and turbary in the forest of la Mare called *Le Merssh*, alias *Frodeshammersh, Eltonmerssh, Happesfordmerssh, Hellesbymerssh*, between Frodsham, Elton, Hapsford and Helsby', cf. 256, 257, 236 *infra*.

BRIDGE LANE (FM), cf. *Bridge Lane Garden* 1844 *TA* and *Bridgegate Field* 1691 *Chol, v.* **lane**, **gata** 'pasture', and Frodsham Bridge *supra*. BROOK FURLONG LANE, 1842 OS, *Sinaipool Lane* 1831 Bry, *Synypoole Lane* 1684 *Chol*, cf. *Sinepool infra, v.* **lane**. The modern name is from *Brook Furlong* 1844 *TA*, 1600 *Dep*, -*forlonge* 1593 *Dep*, -*furlongs* 1664 *Chol, Brookefurlonge*(*s*) 1665, 1690 *ib*, 'furlong(s) at a brook', *v.* **brōc**, **furlang**. The brook would be *Sinepool*.   FLUIN LANE, *Fluhen* c.1290 *Chol, the Fluen* 1630 *ib, the Fluin* (*in the townfield*) 1754 *Chol, Fluin* 1844 *TA freq*, 'the bushy land', from **llwyn** 'a bush', *v.* **lane**. FOXHILL (WOOD), *v.* **fox**, **hyll**.   FRODSHAM SCORE, 1842 OS, *The Score* 1617 *Chol et freq* to 1831 Bry, cf. *the Scorefield* 1729 *Chol, Score Hatch* 1743, -*Hatches* 1768 *ib*, 1844 *TA*, -*Meadow* 1844 *TA*, the name of a tract of pasture, now largely taken up by the Manchester Ship Canal, on the Mersey shore of Frodsham Marshes, cf. Score Bank *infra*. The origin is ON **skor** 'a cut, a ditch', probably a drainage ditch, with **feld**, **mǣd** and **hæc**(**c**) 'a hatch, a sluice'.   HARE'S LANE, *Hares Lane* 1831 Bry, from **hara** 'a hare' and **lane**.   LORDSHIP LANE, *v.* 231 *infra*.   THE LUM, 1842 OS, cf. *Lumb Meadow* 1844 *TA*, a marshy pit near R. Weaver in Frodsham Marsh, *v.* **lum**(**m**).   MARSH GREEN, 1729 *Chol*, cf. *Marsh Green Pingott* 1749 *ib, -Croft* 1768 *ib, -Common* 1797 *EnclA, Marsh Croft* 1699 *Chol,* 'a green on a marsh', *v.* mersc, grēne², commun, pingot, cf. Frodsham Marsh *supra.* MILL BANK (lost), 1831 Bry, *Windmill Hill* 1697 *Chol,* cf. *superior molendinum* c.1312 *Chol, le Mydelmullene* 1360 Chamb (a water-mill), *the Upper Mill, the Milles of Frodsham* 1611 *Chol, Frodesham Milnes* 1655 *ib,* and *le Milnefeld'* 1321 *AddCh,* 1349 *ib, le Mulnefeld* 1341, 1357 *Chol, Little Millmedow* 1700 *ib, Great Mill Pool* 1702 *ib,* from myln, wind-mylne, and banke, hyll, middel, feld, mǣd, pōl¹, and upper. MOORDITCH LANE, 1842 OS, cf. *le Meredyche* 1365 *Chol, -diche* 1365 ChRR, *Merletith* 1549 Pat, *Moore Ditch* 1687, 1699 *Chol,* 'ditch leading to a pool', from mere¹ and dīc, with lane. The first el. has been replaced by mōr¹ 'a marsh', cf. Frodsham Marsh *supra.* NEWTOWN, a hamlet at Frodsham Bridge *supra, v.* nīwe, toun. ORGAN LOT, *the-* 1797 *EnclA, a tenement...appropriated to the salary of an organist* 1819 Orm² ii 59, *v.* hlot. RED LANE, 1719 *Chol, Vicars Gate* 1719 *ib, higher end of red lane or Gate commonly called the Vicars Gate* 1752 *ib,* cf. *Re(e)dehull* 1377, 1378 *ib,* 'the red hill', 'red lane', 'the vicar's lane', *v.* rēad, hyll, lane, vikere, gata. The colour is that of the sandstone here. RIDGEWAY, *The-* 1831 Bry, 'road along a ridge', cf. (wood of) *Ruggis* 1309 Misc, InqAqd, *le Rugges* 1342 ChRR (p), *The Ridges* 1581, 17 Sheaf, *v.* hrycg, weg. This road forms the boundary with Frodsham Lordship 228 *infra* and Alvanley 219 *supra.* RILEY-BANK, [raili-], 1842 OS, a detached part of Frodsham lying in Frodsham Lordship, from ryge and lēah, with banke. THE ROYALTY, 1842 ib, a detached part of Frodsham within Frodsham Lordship, from roialte, alluding to some crown- or duchy-estate interest. SCORE BANK, 1842 ib, a bank in the Mersey estuary off Frodsham Score *supra, v.* banke. SHEPHERD'S HOUSES, 1831 Bry. SINEPOOL (lost), 1844 *TA, Sine Pool* 1844 *TA* 173, *Synnipole* 1629 *Chol et freq ib* with variant spellings *Si-, Sy(n)n(e)y-, Sini-, Syni(e)-, -pool(e), -pooll*; (*Little-, Great-*) 1636 *Chol et freq ib* to 1719, (*-Pasture*) 1653 *Chol et freq ib* to 1721, *Synipooles Pasture* 1667 *Chol, The Butty Sineypoole* 1757 *ib, Little Synypool alias Poore Pasture* 1636 *ib, Little Synnywood* 1689 *ib, Syninpoole pasture* 1690 *ib,* cf. Brook Furlong Lane *supra, v.* lȳtel, grēat, pasture, butty, pouer(e), wudu. The name recurs at Sinny Pool 2 182, cf. Siney Ditch Db 17. *Sinepool* was a stream in Frodsham Marsh. The final el. is pōl¹ 'a pool'. The first component seems to be 'drainage stream', from ēa 'a stream', and ModEdial. *sine* 'to drain'. SNIDLEY MOOR, 1844 *TA* 173,

Snedelmere 1503 *ChFor*, *Snudley Moor* 1797 *EnclA*, perhaps '(marsh at) a detached woodland', from mōr[1], mere[1], and a p.n. from snið and lēah, cf. Longmoss 1 119. But Professor Löfvenberg takes this and Snidley Croft (in Burland) 136 *supra* to contain ModEdial. *sniddle* 'coarse grass, sedge', and a derivative adj. *sniddl(e)y*, noting the Ch dial. *sniddle-bog* 'a marsh where *sniddle* grows'.   SOUTHBANK, *v.* sūð, banke.   TOWNFIELD LANE, cf. *Frodesham Towne Feild* 1630 *Chol*, *Frodsham Townfield* 1691 *ib*, *The Town Field* 1754 *ib*, *v.* toun, feld.

FIELD-NAMES

The undated forms are 1844 *TA* 172. Of the others, 1283, 1289, 1300–7, 1300–20, 1303, 1321, 1324[2], 1332, 1334[2], 1338, 1346, 1390, 1409, 1420, 1428, 1436, 1580 are *AddCh*, 1308, 1309 Misc, 1309[2] InqAqd, 1351 Chamb, 1355 *Indict*, 1353, 1357, 1503 *ChFor*, 1357[2] *MinAcct*, 1361 BPR, 1365 ChRR, 1394, 1656, 1819 Orm[2], 1495, 1579, 1581, 1582, 1671, 17 Sheaf, 1593, 1600 *Dep*, 1797 *EnclA*, 1831 Bry, 1842 OS, and the rest *Chol*.

(a) Acton Mdw (*freq*) ('oak farm', *v.* āc, tūn); The Alder Lane 1842 (*Alder Lane* 1831, *v.* alor); Ball Hill (*v.* ball); Ban Butt 1745 (*v.* bēan, butte); Barley Graves (*Barlow Greaves* 1667, cf. *Berlewe* 1289, -*legh* 1338 (a way called-), 1376, 1395 (way called-), '(woods at) barley clearing', *v.* bere, lēah, grǣfe); Bent (*le Bentte* 1348, *Little Bent* 1757, cf. *le Bentpole* 1373, 1380, from beonet 'coarse grass', with pōl[1]); The Bottoms 1709 (*le Botheum* 1289, *le bothym* c.1300, *le bothum* 1315, *le bothinn* c.1320, *le Bothom* 1350, *the Botomes* 1630, *the Bottomes* 1669, *Hollow Bottoms* 1690, *Bottoms* 1697, *Bowhills Bottoms* 1745, 'the valley bottoms', *v.* boðm); Bradley Fd (cf. Bradley 228 *infra*); Bridge Fd (1706, *le Brigffild* 1390, *Bridge Feild* 1695, *Bridgfield* 1697, *v.* brycg, feld, cf. Frodsham Bridge *supra*); Brownetts Marsh (*Brownettes Marsh* 1700, *v.* mersc); Buisey Pool (*Bosypull* 1378, *the Busipoole* 1684, 1692, 1700, *Busshy Poole alias Busypoole* 1729, 'pool near a cow-stall', from bōsig and pull, pōl[1]); Butterslake (also 232 *infra*, final el. lacu 'a watercourse'); Carvers Quarter 1819 (a meadow, from the surname *Carver* and quarter 'a fourth part'); Church Hole (also 232 *infra*, 'hollow at, or belonging to, a church', *v.* cirice, hol[1]); Cole Mdw (*freq*, *v.* 232 *infra*); the Copp 1684 (*the coppe* 1629, probably a sea-dyke, *v.* copp); Cow Pasture (1719); Cross Lane Mdw (cf. *Cross Lane* 1831, 'lane running across', *v.* cros, lane); Dale Acre (*v.* dæl[1]); Deep Moores (*v.* dēop, mōr[1], cf. 232 *infra*); Doubers Lot *freq* (*Daubers Pit* 1797, cf. Daubers-, Dobers Lot, 232, 248 *infra*, from dauber 'a plasterer, a dauber' with hlot and pytt); Dowles (*v.* dāl); Golden-heys (*Goudyehey Flattes* 1611, *Great & Little Goulding Hey* 1684, *Gouldin Heys*, *Gouldings Hey Meadow* 1745, *Goody Flatts* 1700, '(plots at) the golden enclosure', from goldy, golden 'golden' and (ge)hæg, with flat & mǣd, cf. golde 'a marigold', and *Goldyngforlong* 235 *infra*); Goldsmith's Acre 1757 (cf. *Goldsmythesruddyng* 1349, 'the goldsmith's clearing', *v.* gold-smið, ryding, æcer); Hale Pit 1842 (at Water St. *supra*, a pool fed by a watercourse

15

in a valley at 109–523782, *v.* halh (dat.sg. hale), pytt); Hard Hey 1700 (*v.* heard, (ge)hæg); Hewards Swath 1745 ('the hayward's *swathe* or strip of grass', *v.* hei-ward, swæð. The hayward would be an official of the royal manor of Frodsham); Hobhey (*v.* hobbe 'a tussock', (ge)hæg); Hoblane Croft (cf. *Hob Lane* 1842, and Hoblane Fd 233 *infra*, perhaps 'hobgoblin's lane', *v.* hob, lane); Hole Pool Mdw 1794 (*Holpulmedewe* 1351, *Howpoole Pasture* 1650, *-hey* 1695, *Hollpooll heis* 1657, *-heyes* 1672, *Holl Poole Hey* 1687, *Hollpool-Heys* 1712, *Holepoole Pasture* 1662, 1729, *-hey(e)* 1729, *Hole Pooll Hey* 1729, named from Hoolpool Gutter 1 29, *v.* mǣd, pasture, (ge)hæg); Hoome, Hulme (*le holme* 1428, 'the marsh-meadow', *v.* holmr); Horse Hey 1700 (*v.* (ge)hæg); Hulme (*v.* Hoome *supra*); Ladies Pasture (*Lower Ladyes Pasture* 1730, *v.* hlǣfdige); Lethwoods Croft (cf. *Lyth'wod, Lythwode* 1357, probably 'wood on a hillside', *v.* hliðᴵ, wudu); Long Hay 1757 (*v.* (ge)hæg); Lords Mdw (*v.* hlāford); Lydiate Mdw (*v.* hlid-geat); Manley Croft & Mdw (*Manleys Croft* 1745, from croft and the surname from Manley 245 *infra*); Mickle Mdw (cf. 233 *infra*); Moisdale (*v.* Moistdale 233 *infra*); Monks Mdw (*Muncks Meadow* 1749, cf. *terra de Munkis* c.1249, 'the monk's land and meadow', *v.* munuc, mǣd, probably alluding at first to the monks of St Werburgh's abbey, Chester, later to those of Vale Royal, cf. Ship St. *supra*); Netherlegh 1671 (*v.* neoðera, lēah); Over Mdw 1719 (*v.* uferra); Overton Hill (*v.* 230 *infra*); Overy Mdw (*v.* 234 *infra*); Perrinshey; The Pinfold 1691 (*v.* pynd-fald); Rapdowl(e)s (*Rapedoule* 1593, *Rapdowles* 1600, *Rappdoles* 1605, *Rapdalls* 1664, *-dow(e)s* 1680, 1719, *-dooles* 1694, *-dolls* 1699, *Rapdoles Meadow* 1747, *Rope Dale Pasture* 1749, 'allotments measured out with a rope', *v.* rāp (cf. NED *rope* sbᴵ, 2a), dāl, cf. Rope 68 *supra*, Smetherups 2 314, Rope Croft, -Field, Cyderope, 9, 16, 69 *supra*, Wandry, Long Rope(s) 327, 326 *infra*. An analogous name is Roper Lane K, *Roplande* 1278 PNK 120); The Rough 1695 (*v.* rūh); Ryding Gap 1745 (*v.* gappe); Server (*the Marsh brooke called the Server* 1630, presumably a tributary drain, *v.* server); Ship Fd (1729, *le Shepisfeld* 1321, *le Schep(pe)-feld(e)* 1338², 1347, (*le*) *Schip-, Schypfeld* 1349, 1380, *le S(c)hippe-* 1373, 1378, *le Scippe-* 1413, (*le*) *Shipfeld* 1420, 1428, *Shipp Feild* 1684, 'sheep field', *v.* scēp, feld, cf. Ship St. *supra*); Small Brook (*Smalbrok(e)* 1371, 1373, 1380, *Smalbrokeshed* 1378, *le Smallebrokwalle* 1399, *Small Brook outlett* 1749, '(the source of, the spring of, the "outlet" field at) the narrow stream', *v.* smæl, brōc, hēafod, wælla, outlet); Spittle Croft (1690, *le Spitell Croftes* 1556, cf. *le Spetelgrewes* 1338, *-grefus* 1395, 'crofts and woods at, or belonging to, a hospital', *v.* spitel, croft, grǣfe. This may allude to the lepers of Frodsham mentioned 1238 P, but the Knights Hospitallers of St John of Jerusalem owned land in Frodsham in 1435 Sheafᴵ 3, p. 77); Starkeyhey(s) (*Starkeys Hayes* 1611, *Starkis heay* 1700, *Further & Nearer Starkeys Heys* 1777, from (ge)hæg and the surname *Starky*); Stone Stile Fd 1754 (*Stonesteel(e) Fei(e)ld* 1667, 1670, 1681, *Stone Steel Field* 1743, '(field at) the stone stile', *v.* stān, stīgel); Stretches 1734 (*v.* strecche, though the surname *Stretch* is possible here); Thistley Hey (*v.* Thistle Hay 234 *infra*); Tong (*v.* tang); Turning But Flatt 1754 ('plot of land at a head-land where plough-teams were turned', *v.* turning(e), butte, flat); Tween Mills *freq* (*The Twene Milles* 1624, *Twine Millnes* 1627, *pasture called Twene Mills* 1629, *sluice at betwene Mills* 1633,

Twyne alias Tween(e) Mills 1677, 1692, *Tweens Mills* 1747, *Tween Mill Meadow* 1749, 'between the mills', *v.* betwēonan, myln, cf. Frodsham Mills *supra*); Widgrave 1671 ('wide copse', *v.* wīd, græfe); Windmill Hill 1697 (*v.* wind-mylne, hyll); Withins (*le Wethinez* 1420, *Wethynse infra forest' de Mara et Mondrem* 1503, cf. *Wethen mosse* 1503, 'the withins', *v.* wīðegn, mos); Wittersfield, Witters Pasture (from the surname *W(h)itter*); Yewcroft (*v.* īw).

(*b*) *Archforlong* 1428 (probably 'ploughed furlong', from ersc and furlang); *del Asshes* 1346 (p) (*v.* æsc); *the Bakehouse* 1611 (*v.* bæc-hūs); *Bloudlesacre* 1346² (probably a poor 'anæmic' piece of arable, from æcer and OE *blōd-lēas* 'bloodless'); *le Bugch* 1351 (perhaps 'the river-bend', from bycge 'the bend of a river', but the existence of the el. is contested by Ekwall NoB (1957), 142); *le Crufaughis* 1311 (the final el. is falh (ModEdial. *faugh*), 'fallow land', the first could be cryw 'a weir' (Pr Welsh *crĩu, cf. Crewe 9 *supra*), crūw 'a bend', or even a reduced form of crūc³ 'a cross')); *Cusers Feild* 1549 (perhaps from the ME occupational name *cosere* 'a dealer' (Fransson 55)); *Deyhouscroft* 1357² (*v.* dey-hus, croft); *Hare Haye* 1611 (probably 'hare's enclosure', *v.* hara, (ge)hæg); *Haybarne* 1549 (cf. *orreum de Frodesham* 1238 P, *grangia* 1351 Chamb, *v.* hēg, bere-ærn); *le Heyemor* (*v.* Wall Moor 221 *supra*); *þe Hyllehowse* 1495, *Hill* 1671, cf. Frodshum Hills 1656 (*v.* hyll, hūs); *Hundelessale infra forestam de Mara* 1355, *Hundeleshale* 1357, *moss' de Hundleshale* 1357² ('Hundolfr's nook', from the ON pers.n. *Hundolfr* and halh); *Le Legemor* 1308, *Le Ley(e)mor* 1309, *le Lewnore* 1309², *le Leghemor* 1353, *Lee More* 1579, *-Moore* 17, *Leymore* 1580 ('marsh at a wood or clearing', *v.* lēah, mōr¹, cf. *Lee Moore* 239 *infra*); *Leferuddynges* 1390 ('rushy clearings', *v.* lēfer, ryding); *le Leywode* 1307–24, *le Legewode* 1308, *-Leye-* 1309, 1357 ('wood at a glade', *v.* lēah, wudu, cf. *le Leyewode* 239 *infra*); *Lystaneshurst* 1359 (p), 1365 (p) ('Lēofstān's wooded-hill', from the OE pers.n. *Lēofstān* and hyrst); *le Longacre* 1378 (*v.* lang, æcer); *Long Meade* 1549 (*v.* lang, mǣd); *The Moores* 1624 (*v.* mōr¹); *le Mor(e)wall(e)* 1365, 1365² ('spring in a marsh', *v.* mōr¹, wælla); *Nedewood* 1549 ('wood for use in time of distress', *v.* nēd, wudu, cf. Needwood St (DEPN)); *Nedurgrewe* 1324 ('lower grove', *v.* neoðera, græfe); *le Netherfeld* 1311 (*v.* neoðera, feld); *le Nethergote* 1365 (a drain in Frodsham Marsh, *v.* neoðera, gote); *Holdemulnestude* c.1303, *le Oldemulnestede* 1409 ('former mill-site', *v.* ald, mylnestede, -styde, cf. Tween Mills, Frodsham Mills *supra*); *Orchardeflat'* 1390 (*v.* orceard, flat); *Pirlewalle* 1321 ('a purling spring', *v.* pyrl(e), wælla); *Seynt Marys Ye* 1549 ('St Mary's water-meadow', *v.* ēg. Saint Mary was the patron saint of Vale Royal); *Shadeway* 1363 ('boundary road', *v.* scēad, weg); *Shastlattes* 1549 (probably for *Shafflattes*, 'plots of land at a copse', from sceaga, flat); *Schiplendiggis* 1283, *le Schip lendynges* 1300–20, *le schiplendingis* 1315, *le schipplending* c.1320, *Schuplendyngis* 1346² ('the ship landings, places where ships are landed', from scip 'a ship' and lending. Frodsham was a haven of the port of Chester (*v.* 1324 Cl 183, 1342 Cl 486, 1351 BPR III 7). This provision for shipping has no doubt led to the adoption of the form *Ship* in Ship St. and Ship Fd *supra*); *Schirusmedow* 1350, *Shyresmedowe* 1365, *-medewe* 1365², *Schyresmedowe* 1378 ('the shire's meadow', perhaps a place where a district court met, or a meadow outside the jurisdiction of both the borough and the lordship of Frodsham, v. scīr¹, mǣd); *Shortforlong* 1300–20, 1371, 1376, 1420, (*le*) *schort(e)furlong* c.1310, 1332, 1334, 1436, *scortforlong* 1324, *-furlong* 1349, *Shortefurlong* 1413, *Schert(e)forlong* 1321, 1350, *-furlong* 1363, *Scheteforlong* 1353, *Schurtefurlong* 1324² (v. sc(e)ort, furlang); *Schowakyr* 1311 ('a plot of arable land near a wood', v. skógr, akr); *Stanidelf* c.1300, 1364, 1413, *Stany-* 1349, 1350, 1363, *Staindelf* 1333, *Standidelf* 1352, *Stanedelfe* 1436² ('stone quarry', v. stān, steinn, (ge)delf); *Stainfeld* 1334² (v. steinn, feld); *lez Three Foxefeild* 1549 ('the three fox-fields', v. fox, feld); a short flatt called *Three Quarters* 1662 (v. þrēo, quarter); *Tynkers Feld* 1549 (v. tink(l)ere, feld); *Wallesprung* c.1318, (*le*) *Wallespruge* 1338², *-spryng(e)* 1350, 1399, *-springe* 1373, 1376, *le Wellysspringe* c.1319, *le Vallespruge* 1338, *le Walspryng* 1395 ('well spring', v. wælla, wella, spring); *le Westmor* 1353, *Westmore* 1579, 1580, 1581, 1582, 17 ('the west marsh', v. west, mōr¹, cf. *Westmore* 239 *infra*); *Quabmore* 1361, *Whabbemor* 1365, 1365², *-more* 1396, *Whabmore* 1378, 1394, ('boggy marsh', v. cwabba, mōr¹); *Whetesplot* 1351 ('wheat patch', v. hwǣte, splott).

3. FRODSHAM LORDSHIP (109–5276), *dominium de Frodessam* 1175 Facs *et freq* with variant spellings as for Frodsham 221 *supra*, *Frodsham Lordship* 1581 Sheaf, *the lordship of Frodsham* 1750 ib, *manerium de Frodesham* 1185 P *et freq*, from lordes(c)hip, 'a lordship, the land belonging to a lord', v. 222 *supra*.

BEECH HO & MILL (109–535767), [biːtʃ], 1831 Bry, *Frodisham bache* c.1277 Chol, the wood of (*le*) *Bacheclowes, -is* 1308, 1309 Misc, *Le Bache* (a house) 1587 Orm², *Backehouse* 1640 ib, *Bradley-beach* 1671 Sheaf, *the Beach Farm* 1752 ib, cf. Beach 243 *infra*, 'valley with a stream in it', from bæce¹, bece¹, with hūs and myln. The *-clowes* (v. clōh 'a dell') are at 109–537767, called *Holly Wood* 1831 Bry, v. holegn or holh, wudu. Cf. Bradley *infra*.

BRADLEY (MILL, LANE (lost), ORCHARD) (109–5377)

   Braddele-Hee 1232–7 Tab, *Braddeley juxta Froddesham* 1599 Orm²
   Bradeley 1261–7 Whall (p) *et freq* with variant spellings *Bradi-, -leye, -leg(h), -lega, -le(e), -leghe, -leygh, -leigh* to 1546 Orm², (*Nether-*) 1275–90 Chol, (*Over-*) 1280–90 ib, (*-iuxta Frodesham*) 1280–90 ib, (*Inferior-*) 1285 ib, (*-Superior*) 1299 Plea, (*-Overe*) 1302 ib
   Bradleg' 1299 Orm², *-legh* 1384 AddCh, *-ley* 1388 Orm² *et freq*, (*Overe-*) 1299 ib, (*Over-*) 1387–8 ib, (*Nether-*) 1393 ChRR, (*Nethir-*) 1432 ib, (*-iuxta Frodesham*) 1435 ib, (*-Kyngesley*) 1441 ib, (*-beside Newton*) 1619 Chol, *watermill in Bradlegh* 1397 Orm²,

-ley 1435 *ib*, *Bradley Mills* 1831 Bry, *Bradley Orcharde* 1599 Orm², *-Orchard* 1602 *Chol*, *Bradley Lane* 1831 Bry, and cf. *Bradleghfelde* 1384 *AddCh*, *The Longe Bradley* 1668 *Chol*, *Bradley Meadow* 1796 *ib*

'Broad clearing', from brād and lēah, with ēa 'a stream', myln, orceard, lane, feld and mǣd, also neoðera, uferra, lang, inferior, superior, cf. Frodsham 221 *supra*, Kingsley, Newton 239, 248 *infra*. The name may also appear in *Bradlingselfe* 238 *infra*.

CASTLE PARK (109–515775), 1700 *Chol*, *le Park* 1351, 1357 *MinAcct*, *Parkhead* 1729, 1788 *Chol*, *Park Place* 1786 Orm², 1842 OS, *v.* park, hēafod, place, the site of a castle burnt down accidentally in 1654, *castrum (de) Frodesham* 1245, 1254 P, *the tower of Frodesham* 1355 BPR, *the Castell of Frodsham* 1624 *Chol*, *Frodsham Castell* 1615 *ib*, *-Castle* 1621 *ib*, 1671 Sheaf, cf. *Castle Moores & Orchard* 1700 *Chol*, *v.* castel(l), mōr¹, orceard.

GODSCROFT (109–503767), 1831 Bry, *Godcroft (-house)* 1671 Sheaf, 1687 *Chol*, *Gods Croft House* 1690 Sheaf, *Gilscroft alias Godscroft* 1729 *Chol*, *Godscroft alias Galescroft Hall* 1750 Sheaf, cf. a watermill called *Galdecroftemilne* 1386 *Chol*, 'boar's croft', *v.* galte, croft. The first el. became *god* through vocalisation of *t* and *l* and rounding of *a* > *o*, thus galte > *gald* > *gold* [goud] > *god*. *God* was seen as the *nomen sacrum* with gen. inflexion and religious delicacy gave rise to a meaningless alternative form.

MICKLEDALE (109–517757), *(le) Mukeldal(l)*, *Mulkeldal* 1351 Chamb, *MinAcct*, *Mukuldale* 1357 Chamb, *Mukel-* 1357 *ChFor*, 1358 Chamb, *le Mickeldale* 1351 *ib*, *Miccledale* 1614 *Chol*, *Micle-* 1663 Sheaf, *Mickle-* 1685 *Chol*, cf. *Big & Little Mickle Dale Field* 1794 *Chol*, 1844 *TA*, *Mekeldale (iuxta Frodesham)* 1503 *ChFor*, 'big valley', from mycel and dæl¹, influenced by mikill, dalr.

NETHERTON (109–513770), *Nethirton* c.1249 *Chol*, *Netherton* 1280-90 *ib* (p), 1288 Court *et freq* with variant spellings *Nethir-*, *-ar-*; *le Netherton* 1290–1300 *Chol* (p), 1404 ChRR (p), *Neithertowne* 1611, 1621 *Chol*, *-ton* 1671 Sheaf, *Nethertown* 1656 Orm², *Neatherton* 1666 *Chol*, cf. *the Greene in Netherton* 1676 *ib*, *Netherton Town Field* 1729, 1788 *ib*, *Netherton Hill* 1684 *ib*, *-Hall* 1819 Orm², 'the lower hamlet', from neoðera and tūn, toun, with grēne², hyll and hall. Cf. Overton *infra*.

OVERTON (HALL & HILL) (109–525770), *Overton* 1283 Cl *et freq*, (*le-*) 1351 Chamb, *Ower-* 1599 Sheaf, *Overtowne* 1611 *Chol, -town* 1656 Orm², *Overton Hill* 1684 *Chol, -Scar* 1819 Orm², 'the higher hamlet', from uferra, tūn, toun, with hyll, sker, hall. Overton was originally the hamlet at the parish church, and the hill ascended by Church St. 222 *supra* was *mons Sancti Laurentii Martiri* 1300–7 *AddCh*, 'St Lawrence's hill'.

PINMILL BROW (a road, 109–520773), *Pennell Yate* 1693, *Pimmel Brow*(*e*) 1729, 1785, *the Pennell Gate* 1731, *the Pinil Brow* 1766, *Pemmell Gate* 1773 all *Chol*, cf. *Pimhill Flatt* 1785 *ib*, *Pimmell Buts* 1844 *TA*, *v.* geat 'a gateway' (influenced by gata 'a road'), brū 'a brow, the ascent of a hill', flat, butte, with the p.n. *Pymmewalle* in *Pymmewallesyche* 1350 *Chol* (*v.* sīc 'a watercourse') from the ME pers.n. *Pymme* (Reaney s.n. *Pim*), and wælla 'a spring, a well'. Perhaps the same man, an unrecorded incumbent of Frodsham, appears in *Pymmefeld* 1280–90 *Chol, campus quod Pymme le parsun quondam tenuit* 1281 *ib*, *v.* feld, cf. Orm² II 57.

WOODHOUSE, WOODHOUSE FM & HILL (109–510760)

> *Wodehowse* 1272–1307 Orm², *le Wo*(*o*)*dehouse* 1351 Chamb, *Wood-house* 1543 ChRR, 1662 Sheaf, 1685 *Chol, -Green* 1579, 1581 Sheaf, cf. *Woodhouse-town-field* 1729, 1788 *Chol*, *Woodhouse Croft* 1768 *ib*, 1844 *TA*, *-Hill* 1842 OS
> *Wodehouses* 1304 Chamb (p), *le-* (*infra dominium de Frodesham*) 1444 ChRR, *Chol*, *Wodehwsis* c.1310 *ib* (p), *Woodhouses* 1581 Sheaf *et freq*, (*the-*) 1656 Orm², *-howses* 1611 *Chol*
> *Wodhousen* 1530 *Chol*

'House(s) in a wood', from wudu and hūs, with hyll, croft, and grēne². Woodhouses is described in 1581 Sheaf³ 5 (858) as 'a village adjoining to Woodhouse Green'. *Wodhousen* represents the eModE and ModEdial. nom.pl. form *-housen* (cf. *house* NED), from analogy with the OE, ME wk. nom.pl. in *-an, -en*.

BEACON HILL, BEACONHURST, (*The*) *Beacon Hill* 1797 *EnclA*, 1819 Orm², cf. *a high towering hill with a beacon on it* 1656 Orm² II 7, *v.* (ge)bēacon, hyll, hyrst, cf. *Belriding infra*.   CHURCHFIELD HO, *v.* cirice, feld.   THE CLOSE, *v.* clos.   CROW MERE, *Cromers Lake* 1797 *EnclA*, 1831 Bry, cf. *Crouemos* 1309 Misc (lit. *Crone-*), 'crow's lake and moss', from crāwe and mere¹, mos, with lake.   DUNSDALE

(HOLLOW), 1842 OS, *Dunsdale* 1797 *EnclA, Dungedale* 1684 *Chol, Dingdail* (lit. *Diny-*) 1729 *Chol*, 'muck valley', from **dynge** and **dæl¹**, with **holh, rūh**. FIVE CROSSES, *the-* 1699, 1729 *ib, the Fyve Crosses* 1578 ChRR, cf. *the five Cross Fields alias Old Marled hey and little Marled Hey* 1729, 1773, 1794 *Chol*, presumably there were five crosses here, *v.* **fīf, cros**, cf. Old Marled Hey *infra*. FIVELANES END, *Five Lane Ends* 1831 Bry, *v.* **fīf, lane, ende¹**. FOXHILL FM & WOOD, *v.* **fox, hyll**. FRODSHAM CUT, 1842 OS, *v.* **cut**, a part of the R. Weaver navigation. HARE'S LANE, 1831 Bry, from **hara** 'a hare' or the surname *Hare* and **lane**. HARROL EDGE, *Harrot Hedge* 1768 *Chol, Harrot Edge* 1842 OS, *Harrow Edge* 1844 *TA, v.* **ecg** 'hill-edge'. The p.n. could be *Eruesholt* 1503 *ChFor*, a place in the Forest of Delamere. This would be a metathesised form of *Euersholt*, 'wild-boar's wood', from **eofor** and **holt**, variant *Euerholt*, cf. *Euerholtclogh* 1 176. HATLEY (109–508771), 1671 Sheaf, 1831 Bry, *-Green* 1797 *EnclA, Hartley* 1842 OS, *v.* **lēah, grēne²**, derived from, or analogous with, Hatley Fm 241 *infra*. HAWTHORNE FM. HEMP GILL, 'valley where hemp grows', *v.* **hænep, hemp, gil**. THE HERMITAGE, 1831 Bry. HOWEY LANE, 1844 *TA*, cf. *Heyway Butts* 1672, 1687 *Chol, Hay-* 1722 *ib*, '(selions at) the road along which hay is carted', from **hēg** and **weg**, with **butte, lane**. IRON-DISH FM, *Iron Dish* 1831 Bry, 'eddish in corner', *v.* **hyrne, edisc**. LORDSHIP LANE, 1842 OS, *Marsh Lane* 1831 Bry, *v.* **lordes(c)hip, lane**, cf. foll. and Frodsham Lordship *supra*. LORDSHIP MARSH, 1651 *Chol, Lords Marsh* 1699 *ib*, the part of Frodsham Marsh belonging to Frodsham Lordship, containing *Lytelmersche, v.* Frodsham Marsh 223 *supra*. NETHERDALE, *v.* **neoðera, dæl¹**. OLD MARL PITS, cf. *a place called Marlepitt* 1694 *Chol, The Marle-Pitt in the lane going from Overton to Netherton* 1721 *ib, v.* **marle-pytt**. ORGAN LOT, *v.* 224 *supra*. RIDGEWAY, *v.* 224 *supra*. THE ROYALTY, *v.* 224 *supra*. SUCH PIT FM, '(farm at) the pit in a watercourse', *v.* **sīc, pytt**. SYNAGOGUE WELL, cf. *Synagogue Garden Lane* 1844 *TA*. TOWNFIELD LANE, cf. *Town Field* 1844 *ib, v.* 225 *supra*. TWIG BOWER, 1842 OS. WARRENHOUSE, 1797 *EnclA, the Warren* 1689, 1702 *Chol*, cf. *the Warrendale* 1736 *ib, Warren Dale* 1747 *ib*, 1844 *TA, Warrandale* 1797 *EnclA*, 'house and valley at a warren', *v.* **wareine, hūs, dæl¹**.

FIELD-NAMES

The undated forms are 1844 *TA* 173. Of the others, 1272–1307 (1338), 1338²
are VR, c.1300–7, c.1303, 1305, 1384, 1409, 1428, 1612 *AddCh*, 1308, 1309
Misc, 1347, 1357², 1503 *ChFor*, 1348² Orm², 1351 Chamb, 1351², 1357
1507 *MinAcct*, 1358, 1365², 1419, 1435, 1438, 1441, 1543 ChRR, 1549 Pat,
1593, 1600 *Dep*, 1637, 1671, 17 Sheaf, 1797 *EnclA*, 1831 Bry, 1842 OS, and
the rest *Chol*.

(a) Abbots Acre (*v.* æcer, probably named from the abbot of Vale Royal);
Antrobus Outlet 1729 (from the surname *Antrobus* (from Antrobus 2 127,
cf. Antrobus 220 *supra*) and outlet); Ashcroft 1785 (*v.* æsc, croft); Higher
Back Croft 1783 (1757, *Higher Black Croft, Lower Back Field* 1699, 1719,
v. back, croft); North & South Bank (cf. *le Bonks* 1349, *v.* banke); the Barn
Croft 1788 (1729, *Bernecroft* 1357, *the Barne Croft* 1677, *v.* bere-ærn, croft);
Barn Flatt 1729 (*v.* Lower Feilds *infra*); the Beane Croft 1731 (1677, *v.* bēan,
croft); Booths Yard (*Booth Yards* 1745, 'enclosures at a herdsman's shelter',
v. bōth, geard); Briary Fd (cf. *le Breryflatte* 1384, *v.* brērig, flat); Broadlane
Fd (*Broad Lane* 1831, *v.* brād, lane); the Brookfield Land 1768 (*v.* brōc,
feld, land); Brookley Moor (*v.* brōc, lēah, mōr¹); Burnd Croft 1666 (*v.*
brende²); Butterslake (*v.* 225 *supra*); the Calfcroft 1729 (*v.* calf, croft);
Calvers Croft (*Calverscroft* 17, *v.* calver, croft); Camp Slack (a valley near
a hill-fort site 109–510757, *v.* camp², slakki); Cheshire Tenement 1699
(from the surname *Cheshire* and tenement, probably associated with 'rent of
a field called Brook Furlong, left by Mʳ Chesshyre, of Stockham, in Runcorn
parish, to the poor householders of Frodsham', n.d. Orm² II 59); Chester
Lane Croft (1757, 'lane leading to Chester', *v.* lane); Church Hole (cf. 225
supra); Clock Croft 1712 (1657, *the Clock close* 1624, 'beetle, or cockchafer,
croft', from croft and dial. *clock* 'a beetle'); Cole Mdw (1629, (-*Flatt*) 1749,
Coal- 1741, (*Butty-*) 1747, *v.* col¹, mæd, flat, butty, cf. 225 *supra*); Cow Hey
(*Cow Hayes* 1617, -*heyes* 1686, *the Cow Heys* 1729, cf. *Netherton Cow Hey*
1729, 1752, *v.* cū, (ge)hæg, cf. Netherton *supra*); The Cracker 1787; Big-,
Further- & Little Cratchet (*the Booty Cratchet* 1729, 1788, perhaps from
cracche 'a hurdle, a fodder-rack', and botye); Cribbs (*Sythers-, Sydders
Hook alias Cribbs, -Crybbe* 1600, *Marle-* & *the Little Cribbes* 1668, (*the*) *Cribb*
1687, 1745, *the Two Crib(b)s* 1729, 1788, *v.* crib. The earlier name may be
from a pers.n. and hōc); the Crofts 1794 (1652, *le Croftes* 1351, cf. *the Croft*
1658, 1699, *v.* croft); Crooked Acre (*v.* croked, æcer); Dale (*acra de la Dale*
1290–1300, *Dale Flat* 1787, *v.* dæl¹, flat, æcer); Damberlane Fd (*v.* Damber
Lane 237 *infra*); Daubers Garden & Lot (*v.* gardin, hlot, cf. Doubers Lot
225 *supra*); Davies Mdw (*Davids Slack* 1729, 1757, from slakki and the
surname or pers.n. *David*); Deadmans Suck 1740 (1729, -*such* 1677, 'dead
man's watercourse', *v.* dede-man, sīc. This was the site of a mill-way for the
water mill in Bradley); Deep Moor (*v.* 225 *supra*); the Dogg Acre 1731
(-*Dagg-* 1677, *v.* dogga, æcer); Dunces Fd; Fender Fd ('field at a boundary
ditch', *v.* fender); Folly (*v.* folie); Frodsham Fd (probably a field in the
Lordship but belonging to the town); Galemoor (1637, 1842, *Gill Moss* 1831,
cf. *Galeyhey* 1503, 'bog-myrtle marsh', *v.* gagel, mōr¹, mos, (ge)hæg); the

Gorsty Fd 1729 (*v.* gorstig, feld); Gorsty Tang (*v.* tang); Gout Mdw (*v.* gote); (Little) Greens (*the Greenes* 1672, *the Greene* 1679, *the Greens* 1686, 1697, *v.* grēne²); Greeves (*v.* grǣfe); tenement called Grice's 1773 (1729, *Grices* 1691); the Grounds Lount 1694 (*v.* grund, land); Hankerchief 1796 (*v.* 325 *infra*); Hanging Fd (*v.* hangende); Hare Hill (*Harehill Land* 1787, *v.* hara, hyll); the Hassell Orchard 1668 (*v.* orceard); the Heire on the Hill 1701 (*Hea of the Hill* 1690 probably 'the high-point of the hill, the summit', from hēah² 'a high place, a height' and hyll); Hempyard 1839 (*Hemp Yardes* 1668, *v.* hemp-yard); Big-, Broad-, Farther- & Middle Heys (cf. *the Great Hay* 1699, *-Hey* 1719, 1783, *v.* grēat, (ge)hæg); the High Croft 1788 (1729, cf. *the Highfield* 1729, *v.* hēah, croft, feld); the Gorstye & the Higher Hobhaye 1668 ('tussocky enclosure', *v.* gorstig, hobbe, (ge)hæg); Hoblane Fd (*Hob Lane* 1842, *v.* 226 *supra*); Hockendale (*the Oakendale* 1699, *the Okendales* 1740, *Okendale* 1766, 1794, 'valley growing with oaks', *v.* ācen, dæl¹); Holbrook (*v. Holbrook* 1 28); Holly Wd (*v.* Beech Ho *supra*); The Hooles 1729 (1696, *the Holes* 1652, 1700, cf. *Arnaules Hooles* 1696, 'the hollows', *v.* hol¹. *Arnaules* represents the pers.n. or the surname *Arnold*, cf. *Harnaldeshok infra*); Hooley ('enclosure in a hollow', *v.* hol¹, (ge)hæg); Hoolpool (*v.* Hoolpool Gutter 1 29); Hooses Mdw 1794; Houghendale (cf. 248 *infra*); Hought Garden Spot 1747 (*Houghs-* 1736, from the surname *Hough, v.* gardin, spot); the Howlikys 1729 (*le Weuelace* 1357, 'yew-tree stream', *v.* īw, lacu); Hungerhill (cf. *Hangrills* 1757, from hangra or hungor and hyll); the Intacke 1768 (1702, *v.* inntak); Itch Fd (*v.* hiche); Jack Fd 1668 (*v.* jack); Kiln Fd (cf. *Kill Croft* 1668, *v.* cyln); Kitchen Fd; Ladyes Pasture 1658 (*v.* Nine Acres *infra*); Lane Croft (*le Lone Feild* 1549, *v.* lane, feld, croft); Longfield Flatts (*le longefeld* c.1300–7, *le Longfeld* 1341, *longfild* 1406, *the longfeild* 1690, *Longfield* 1745, *v.* lang, feld, flat); Long Furlong (*Lonk-* 1657, *Lank furlong(e)* 1672, 1712, *v.* lang, furlang); Long Headland 1787 (*v.* lang, hēafod-land); Long Odd Butts (*v.* lang, odde, butte); the Lower Feilds 1768 (1702, *the Lowfield* 1694, *the lower Field alias Barn Flatt* 1729, *v.* lower); Mare Heye 1668 (*v.* mere², (ge)hæg); Old Marled Hey 1794 (1729, *Old(e) Marle Hey* 1699, 1729, *the Marled Field* 1729, *the Old Marled Field alias Orchard Flatt* 1729, *the Marled Heyes* 1612, *Little Marled Hey* 1699, 1729, *v.* ald, marled, marle, (ge)hæg, cf. Five Crosses *supra*); Marsh Brows (*v.* mersc, brū); Martins Ley (1775, *-lay butte* 1630, 'selion at Martin's clearing', lēah, butte, with the surname or pers.n. *Martin*. The parish church is St. Martin's); Massey's Dale (1785, from dæl¹ and the surname *Massey*); Mickle Mdw (*Mukelmedewe* 1351, *Mikel-* 1351¹, *Micklethmeadow* 1593, *Mickle Meadow* 1600, *Micco Meadowe* 1605, *Micle Meadow* 1664, *Miclow-* 1667, *Miccle-* 1680, *Miccow-* 1686, *Mickow-* 1788, cf. *Butty Miccle Meadow* 1747, 'great meadow', from micel and mǣd, with butty); Mill Moors & Pool; Moistdale (Croft), Moisters Croft (*Moysty* c.1310, 1350, 1353, 1436, *Moisthill* 1630, *the-* 1729, *Moist Hills* 1690, *Moist Hill Flatt* 1754, *Moistdale* 1796, *Moisdale* 1844 *TA* 172, 'marshy, wet pathway', *v.* moist, stīg); Newhey (*Higher, Lower & Horse New(e) Haye* 1611, *the Newhayes* 1617, *Horse & Lower New Hey* 1636, *the Newe Haye* 1668, *Lower Newhey Meadow* 1691, *Loerneuhey, Hygher New Hey* 1700, *v.* nīwe, (ge)hæg, hors); Nickle Mdw (*v.* nicor); Nine Acres (*les Neneacres* 1438, *Nyne Acre Meadow* 1611,

Nyne Acres peece 1658, *Ladyes pasture or the Nine Acres peece* 1658, 1686, *the Nine Acres* 1661, *v.* nigon, æcer, hlæfdige); Oakhouse Flatt (*v.* āc, hūs, flat); Old Earthes 1668 (*v.* ald, erð); Old Orchard 1788 (1729); Old Wash (*v.* wæsce); Orchard Flatt 1729 (*v.* Old Marled Hey *supra*); Ovenhouse Croft 1729; the Over Feild 1768 (1702, *v.* uferra); Overton Town Fd (*v.* toun, feld, cf. Overton *supra*); Overy Mdw *freq* (*Overhey* 1351, (*le-*) 1438, *Overhey Meadow* 1665, 1747, *les Ouerhaies* 1507, *Overe Meadow* 1656, 1666, *Overy-* 1689, *Overley* 1671, 'the higher enclosure', *v.* uferra, (ge)hæg, cf. *Netherhey infra*); Oxehaye 1668 (*v.* oxa, (ge)hæg); Paddock Lake (*paddokislake* 1362, 'frog ditch', *v.* paddok, lacu); Litle- & the Longe Park 1668 (*v.* park); Pawsland, Powsland (*Pounds Land* 1785, *v.* pund, land); Pinfold Fd (*v.* pynd-fald); Pingot (*v.* pingot); Pool Mdw, Pool Stead Croft (cf. *the Poole Croft* 1699, *v.* pol¹, pōl-stede); Powsland (*v.* Pawsland *supra*); Ridding(s) (*v.* ryding); Ridges (*v.* hrycg, cf. Ridgeway *supra*); Roddy (cf. Rodey Lane 241 *infra*); Round Mdw (*the-* 1679, *le Round Mede* 1549, *v.* rond, mæd); Rye Croft 1796 (*Rucrof* 1317, *Ruycroft* c.1320, 1348, *Ricroft*(*e*) 1331, 1362, *Rycroft* 1338, 1394, *v.* ryge, croft); Sandfield (*v.* sand, feld); Score Hatches *freq* (*v.* hæcc 'a sluice', cf. Frodsham Score 223 *supra*); Sea Flatts (*Le See Flat* 1441, *Seaflat* 1600, *-Flatts* 1672, 'flats by the sea', *v.* sæ, flat. These belong to Frodsham Marsh); Sedge Mdw (*Sedgley Meadow*, *Sedghay Meadow* 1600, *Sedgye Meadowe* 1617, (*the*) *Sedggie Meadow* 1684, 1697, *v.* secg, -ig³, (ge)hæg mæd); Long & Short Shoots (*the Long Shutt* 1729, *v.* lang, sc(e)ort, scēat); Shrog Fd (*v.* shrogge); Sine Pool (*v.* *Sinepool* 224 *supra*); Snidley Moor (*v.* 224 *supra*); Sow and Pigs; Speakmans Mead; Spout Fd (*v.* spoute); Swinlake 1692 (1684, 'watercourse at a creek', swin², lacu); Tarforth Heys 1773 (1731, *Tarfootes Heys* 1662, *Sarfoot Heys* 1686, *Starfoot Heys* 1729, 1773, 'enclosures belonging to one *Torfote*', from the ME surname *Torfote* and (ge)hæg. *Chol* F813 records a grant of *Normonredyng* (*infra*) to Henry Torfote in 1349); Thistle Hay (1788, *Thessellnewhey* 1605, *Thisslenewhey* 1664, *Thissell New Hey* 1687, *the Thistle Hey* 1729, *-Thistley-* 1747, cf. Thistley Hey 226 *supra*, *v.* þistel, nīwe, (ge)hæg); Three Acres 1696 (*the-* 1688, 1694, *v.* prēo, æcer); Two Gates (1794, *v.* twā, gata); Warralls Garden & Lot (*v.* Worralls *infra*); Way Croft 1736 (1695, *v.* weg, croft); Wheat Reans (*v.* hwǣte, rein); Whitwalls (*Wetwall* 1785); Woodhay (*v.* wudu, (ge)hæg); Worralls Fd, Warralls Garden & Lot (cf. *Weralgrews* 1349, *Wyrallefelde* 1384, '(field and copses at) the bog-myrtle nook', from wir and halh, with grǣfe, feld, cf. Wirral 1 7); Yewcroft Meadow 1745 (*Yowe croft* 1351², *Yewe-* 1351, *le Yowcroftesdyche* 1365, *Yewe-* 1365², *two Yowcrofts* 1745, '(ditch at) the croft where ewes are kept', *v.* eowu (gen.sg. eowe), croft, dīc).

(b) Belriding syche 1348² ('watercourse at *Belriding*', *v.* sīc. The p.n. may be 'cleared land at, or belonging to, a beacon', *v.* bēl¹, ryding, cf. Beacon Hill *supra*); *le Cawayn*, *Cawaynmedowe* 1351 ('bare enclosure', from calu and hægen, with mæd); *Coppegrene* 1351, *Coppegreue* 1351² (perhaps 'pollarded copse', *v.* coppod, grǣfe, but the first el. may be an OE pers.n. *Coppa* as in Copgrove YW 5 90); *Cortisfeld* 1285, *Corttisfeld* 1324 (probably 'field consisting of a short piece of land', from cort(e) and feld, for this appears in documents to be associated with *le schortefeld infra*, but the first el. may be an OE pers.n. *Cort* as in *Cortes hamm* 955 BCS 917, *v.* Corton W 162, DEPN); *le Dychede3e* 1348 ('ditched water-meadow', from ME *diched* 'ditched', and ēg); *Foxrydyng* 1351² ('fox clearing', *v.* fox, ryding); *Goldyngforlong* 1441 ('furlong at a place where marigolds grow', *v.* golden, furlang); a water mill in Netherton called *Hallons Crofte* 1543 ('croft at the head-lands', *v.* hēafodland, croft); *Harnaldeshok(e)* 1351 ('Arnold's oak or corner', from the ME (OG) pers.n. *Arnald* with either āc 'an oak' or hōc 'a corner', cf. The Hooles *supra*); *le Haystoue* 1280–90 ('place with a hedge', *v.* hege-stōw, cf. hege, stōw, hege-stall and Hextells St (DEPN)); *Netherhey* 1351 (*v.* neoðera, (ge)hæg, cf. Overy Mdw *supra*); *Normonesriding* 1280–90, -*rudyng* 1300–7, *Normonisryding syche* 1324, *Normonredyng* 1349 ('Norman's cleared-land', from the ME pers.n. *Norman* (OE *Norðman*, cf. Norðman) and ryding, with sīc 'a water-course'. It is called 'the assart which Norman held' 1281 *Chol* F 799, 'the land of Bate Norman' c.1303 *AddCh* 50548, and 'the land of Bate son of Norman' 1305 *ib* 50552. This land may be the same as Tarforth Heys *supra*); *Peruswoderande* 1350 ('Piers's wood-outskirts', from the ME pers.n. *Piers*, with wudu and rand 'a border', cf. *a strothe rand* 'the edge of a brake', Sir Gawain 1710); *le Puchel* (lit. *Put-*) c.1319, *Pukkewile, Pukwyle* 1324, *Pycewalwey* 1324, *un' pucul'* 1349, *le Puhul* 1353, tertia pars unius *Pyghyll* 1399, *le Pughull* 1436 ('the little croft', from pighel, pichel, with weg 'a way'); *Pymmefeld* (*v.* Pinmill Brow *supra*); *Remershe* 1272–1307 (1338), -*mersshe* 1338², *le Re(e)mersche* 1351, 1351², *le Rowemarsh* 1358 (Professor Löfvenberg suggests 'roe-deer marsh', from ræge, rā 'roe', and mersc, cf. the forms of Rogate Sx 38); *Robertisruding* 1324 (from the ME (OFr) pers.n. *Robert* (OG *Rodbert*) and ryding. The land belonged to Master Robert de Frodsham); *Ride-, Rydefurlong* 1351 ('furlong at a place cleared of trees', *v.* (ge)rydd, furlang); *le Schortefeld, le Scherttefeld* 1280–90, *le Shortefeld* 1350 (*v.* sc(e)ort, feld, cf. *Shortforlong* 228 *supra*); *le Slyccheflatte* 1384 ('muddy plot', *v.* sliche 'slime, mud', flat); *Throwershaker* 1324 (from æcer and the ME occupational name *throwere* 'a thread-thrower', *v.* Fransson 84, Reaney s.n. *Thrower*); *le tungesarp* 1281 ('a pointed tongue of land', *v.* tonges(c)harp, cf. Tongue Sharp Wood 1 162); *Les Warthes* 1419, 1435 ('places on the shore', *v.* waroð. These were fishing places, cf. *Werewarth, Wylashebbe infra*); *Weremor* 1308, 1309, *le-* 1347 ('marsh near a weir', *v.* wer, mōr¹); fisheries in *Werewarth* and *Wylashebbe* 1351, 1351² ('shore near a weir', *v.* wer, waroð, and 'Wīglāf's ebb', from the OE pers.n. *Wīglāf* and ebba 'ebb, low tide', probably a tidal channel, cf. *les Warthes supra*).

4. HELSBY, (109–4975) [ˡhelzbi]

Helesbe 1086 DB, 1581 *AddCh*, -*by* 1217–29 Dieul, 1540 Dugd, *Helisby* 13, 1285, 1307–24 *Chol*, *Helysbi* 1240–9 Chest (p), *Helissby* 13 *CoLegh*

Ellesbi 1185 P (p), -*by* 1309 InqAqd, *Hellesbi* 1189–99 Orm² (p), -*by* 1200–10 Whall (p) *et freq* with variant spellings *Hellis-* c.1233 *Dow* (p) to 1512 *ChEx*, -*ys-*, -*bi(e)*, -*bye-*, -*bey* to 1656 Orm²

Hellesberi (lit. *Hellesb'i*) 1189–99 Orm² II 374 (p), *Hellesbury* 1357
    BPR (p), 1515 *ChEx*
Hallesbi 1208–29 Sheaf (p)
Helhesbi 1209–28 AD
Hellesorhee a.1245 MidCh (p)
Helleseby a.1297 MidCh (p)
Hellesley 1300 Plea (p), *-leye* 1309 Misc, *Helsly* 1546 Dugd
Helsbye 1539–47 Dugd, 1545 Plea, *-by* 1553 Sheaf *et freq*, *-bie*
    1599 ib, *-bey* 1684 *Chol*, *-be* 1692 ib, *Hellsbie* 1610 *JRC*, *Elsby*
    1780 Sheaf
Hillisbie 1553 Pat
Helshbye 1620 *Chol*

'Village on a ledge', from hjallr and býr, by. The village lies on
a narrow shelf between the foot of the precipitous Helsby Hill and
the edge of Helsby Marsh, cf. *Bradlingselfe infra*. The el. hjallr 'a
hut', is here used as in Norwegian p.ns. (cf. DEPN), with the sense
'a ledge on a mountainside', an extension of meaning doubtless
resulting from such features providing sites for mountain-pasture
huts in Norway. A few forms show confusion of býr and burh
(byrig).

HELSBY HILL (109–4975), 1831 Bry, *Hellesbytor* 1347, 1353 *ChFor*,
Hellesbyclyf 1353 ib, *Hellesby Torre* 1503 ib, *Helsby Tor(r)* 1656 Orm²,
1819 ib, *Helsbetower* 1692 *Chol*, *Elsby Hill* 1780 Sheaf, 'rocky hill at
Helsby', *v.* torr, hyll, clif.

HELSBY MARSH (109–4876), *mariscum de Hellesby* 1216–72 Orm²,
mora de Helisby 13 CoLegh, *le mor*, *Hellesbymor(e)* 1347, 1357 *ChFor*,
1543 Sheaf, *Hellesbymerssh* 1348 BPR, *the Marsh* 1665 *Chol*, *Helsbey-*,
Hellesby Marsh 1684, 1690 ib, cf. *the Milsh or Midest Marsh* 1719 ib,
and Frodsham Marsh 223 *supra*, *v.* mōr¹, mersc. *Milsh* is 'giving
milk', probably grazing for milch-cows, *v.* milce.

BANK HO, *þe Banckhowse* 1495 Sheaf, *v.* banke, hūs.   GORSEHILL,
v. gorst, hyll.   GREEN BANK, *v.* grēne¹, banke.   HELSBY HO,
Jas 1 Orm², *Hellesby-howse* 1495 Sheaf, *v.* hūs.   HELSBY LODGE
(lost, 109–485747), 1831 Bry, *v.* loge.   HELSBY QUARRY, *Mount
Skill* 1831 ib.   HORN'S MILL, 1831 ib, *molendinum de Hellesby*
1354 Sheaf, from horna or a surname *Horn(e)*, *v.* myln, cf. Horn
(Mill) 257 *infra*. Horn's Mill may be the site of the *molendinum de
Alualdeleh* (Alvanley 219 *supra*) in 1208–26 AddCh 40000, or the

watermills built c.1330 mentioned 1353 *ChFor*, but cf. Peck Mill 220 *supra*. HORN'S MILL BRIDGE, *pons de Hapusford* 13 *CoLegh*, *-Hapisford* 1307–24 *Chol*, *Happesfordbrugge* 1390 *CoLegh*, *Hapsford bridg* 1690 Sheaf, a bridge near Horn's Mill *supra*, on the boundary of Hapsford 257 *infra*, *v.* brycg.   HORNSMILL BROOK (> Hoolpool Gutter **1** 29), *Hapsford Brooke* 17 Sheaf, *v.* brōc, cf. Horn's Mill *supra*, Hapsford 257 *infra*.   OLD HALL, *le Halle* 1354 Sheaf (p), *Hellesby Halle* 1494 ib, *Helsby Hall* 1600 Orm², 1831 Bry, also *Motehowse* 1507 Orm², *þe mote house* 1653 Sheaf, *the Moat House, the Helsby demesne or Moatesteads* 1709 Orm², cf. *the Hall Green* 1788 *Chol*, from hall, mote, hūs, stede, grēne². ORCHARD CROFT.   RAKE HO & LANE, *þe Raykehouse* 1494 Sheaf, *þe Raikehowse* 1495 ib, tenement called *the Rayke* 1554 Orm², lane called *the Rake* 17 Sheaf, *Rakehouse* 1739 *LRMB* 264, *Rakehouse Lane* 1831 Bry, *The Rake Lane* 1797 *EnclA*, '(house at) narrow lane', *v.* rake, hūs, lane, cf. *Rak(e)-end pasture* 1681, 1686 *Chol*, *v.* rake, ende¹, pasture.   ROSE FM. SPRING FM.   SPRINGFIELD.   SPRING LODGE   TEUTHILL (109–500749), *Toothill Hill* 1831 Bry, 'watch-hill', *v.* tōt-hyll. This was on the boundary of Alvanley, cf. Toothill Croft 221 *supra*.

FIELD-NAMES

The undated forms are 1845 *TA* 199. Of the others, 13, 1407 are Bark, 13², 1390 *CoLegh*, 1265–91 Chest, l13, 1460, 1558–1603, 1581, 1882 Orm², 1318 *Eyre*, 1347, 1353, 1503 *ChFor*, 1354, 17, 1663, 1883 Sheaf, 1398 *AddCh*, 1797 *EnclA*, 1831 Bry, 1842 OS, and the rest *Chol*.

(a) Ackerleys Tenement 1790 (from the surname *Ackerley*); Three Acre (cf. *the six-, -seven Acres* 1790, *v.* æcer); Alder Greaves (*v.* alor, grǣfe); Ashbrooks 1729 (a tenement held by John *Ashbrook*); Bakehouse Pasture 1783; Barlows Moor & Pasture (cf. *Barlows* 1729, a tenement held by John *Barlow* 1576, *v.* mōr¹, pasture); Bean Fd; Big Pasture 1790; Blake Fd (*the-* 1719, *v.* blæc); Bog; Bottom Lane 1831 (*v.* botm); Broad Lane 1831; Brook Moor; Calvers Hey (*v.* calver); Cape Ridding (*the* 1665, *v.* ryding); The Clatch Hooks 1883 (the local name for a fissure in the face of Helsby Hill, cf. Sheaf¹ 3, 101. 'Clatch hooks' is a dial. expression for 'grasping hands; the clutch or grasp of the hand'); Cock Riddings (*v.* cocc², ryding); Comberbaches 1794 (*Cumberberches* 1690, after the family of Roger *Comberbach*, Recorder of Chester, 1719); Cotting Greaves ('copses where sheep are folded', from grǣfe and dial. *cott* 'to place sheep under shelter, to put them in a cote', cf. cot); Cottinghams Tenement 1729 (held by Peter *Cottingham* of London); Cow Hey (*the* 1719); Cunnary Rough (*The Coneries* 1882, *v.* coninger, rūh); Cutlers Croft 1652, 1729; Damber Lane 1831 (*Dam more lane* 17, *The Damber Road* 1797, cf. Damberlane Fd 232 *supra*, *v.* damme, mōr¹); Delights (*the Lord's meadow* 1630, *the Lords Pasture* 1622, *the Lords pasture alias the Little Delights* 1694, *v.* hlāford, mǣd, pasture); Densons Croft 1783 (named from Moses *Denson*, 1731); Doe Fd (*v.* dāl); Easter Greaves ('copses more to the east', *v.* ēasterra, grǣfe); Eller Greaves (*v.* elri, grǣfe); the Ends, the lower Endfield 1783 (*v.* ende¹); Five Butts (*the Five Buttes* 17, *v.* fīf, butte); The Five Pears Fd 1719; Forest Fd (probably named from the forest of Delamere 1 8); Fresh Mdw (*the-* 1719, *v.* fersc); Green Lane 1831; Greens (*le Grenes* 1393, *the Greens* 16, 1702, *the Greenes* 1626 to 1684, *the Nearer Green* 1788, *v.* grēne²); Gregs Mdw (*the Abbotts meadows* 1658 (leased to Robert *Gregg*), *Abbots Meadows or Greggs Meadows* 1710, probably named from the abbot of St. Werburgh's, Chester, *v.* abbat); Handley Lot (*v.* hlot); Hanging Fd (*v.* hangende); Hare Yards (*v.* hara, geard); Hill Fd, Green & Lot (*v.* hyll, grēne², hlot); Horse Pasture (*the-* 1783); Howpool (*v.* Hoolpool Gutter 1 29); Iron Dish Croft ('enclosure in a corner', *v.* hyrne, edisc, cf. Irondish 231 *supra*, Heronbridge 326 *infra*); Keys Croft; Knowles Mdw (cf. William *Knowles* 1563, *Knowles tenement* 16, *Knowlles-* 1620); Lane Ends (cf. *Three Lane Ends* 1831); Lee Ends, Lees (*v.* lēah); Marl Croft; Six- & Ten Measures Sowing; Moor Riddings (*v.* mōr¹, ryding); Mow Ridding (*v.* mūga, ryding); New Lot (*v.* hlot); New Mdw (1697, cf. *le Newe-* & *le Old medowe* 1390, *v.* nīwe, ald, mǣd); (The) Oakes (cf. *Okes mosse* 1503, *v.* āc, mos); Old Pole (*v.* pōl¹); Oval Fd & Mdw; the Over Fd 1783 (*v.* uferra); Overy Fd (cf. Overy Mdw 234 *supra*); Picken Lane Fd, Pickers Lane; Pickow (*v.* pichel); Pirrys Green (*Perry's quarter in the Greenes* 1665, *v.* quarter, grēne², cf. William *Perry*, living in *Perryes house* 1665, *-Howse* 1687); Far & Near Pool, Further Pole Pasture (*The Pool* 1788, *v.* pōl¹); Primrose Lane & Pasture (cf. *Primrose Tenement* 1699, home of Thomas *Primrose*); Pump Lot (*v.* pumpe, hlot); Robin Hood Fd; Rough Fd (*v.* rūh); Round Mdw 1719; Rushes (*v.* risc); Salt Mdw (*the-* 1719, 1783, *v.* salt, mǣd); The Sands 1842 (*v.* sand); Smut Fd; Springhole Mdw ('well-spring hollow', *v.* spring, hol¹, cf. *pratum iuxta fontem* 1307–24); Stew Yard (*v.* stuwe, geard); Stirrups Mdw (cf. *Stirrups Road* 1797); Stocks Brow 1831 (1797, *v.* stocc, brū); Townfield Flatt (*v.* toun, feld, flat); Twelve Flatts (*the Twelve Flatt* 1783, *v.* twelf, flat); The Twenty Roods 1783 (*v.* twēntig, rōd²); Well Fd (*v.* wella); Whitbye's Tenement 1699 (named from Jonathan *Whitbye* 1694, *v.* tenement); White Brook(s) (*v.* hwīt, brōc); Wilcocks Pasture (cf. *Wilcocks Tenement* 1749, named from Samuel *Wilcock* 1695); Windmill (cf. *molendinum ventricitum super Hellesbytor* 1347, 1353); Within Mdw (*v.* wiðegn, mǣd).

(b) *Blackeley* 1687 (*v.* blæc, lēah); the (*little*) *Bradlingselfe, -salfe* 1665 (the final el. is scelf 'a ledge, a shelving terrain, a shelf on a hillside', probably on the slopes of Helsby Hill *supra*, cf. Helsby *supra*. The name may be 'broad heather-shelf', from lyng and scelf, with brād, but it might also be OE *Bradleinga-scelf or *Bradling-scelf, 'shelf of land belonging to the men of *Bradley*' or '-called after *Bradley*', from a p.n. *Bradley* 'broad glade' (*v.* brād, lēah), with -ingas or -ing-⁴. This *Bradley* may have been in Helsby, but it could well be Bradley 228 *supra*, three miles east of Helsby, in the next township); *le Cnorvihurst* 1307–24 (CRO, *Chol* F*, 1. The form appearing as -*vi*- here may be -*Oc*-, in which case the name would be 'gnarled oak wood', from knorre, āc, hyrst; the palaeography of the -*vi*- letters is against a reading *Cnorri*- which could have been taken as an early instance of the adj. *knorry*, *knurry* 'full of knurs, knotty, gnarled' (1513 NED)); *the doore gapp*, 17 (a gateway, *v.* duru, gappe); *le Ermitesfeld* 13, *Ernutisfeld* 1265–91, *Ermitisfeld croft* l13, *le Ermetescrofte* 1398 ('hermit's field and croft', *v.* ermite, feld, croft); *Fluellens brooke* (*v.* 1 25); *Fynch Hill* 17 (*v.* finc); *le Hemlegh* 1393 (endorsed *Hemsleighe* 16, 'glade at the edge of a wood', *v.* hemm, lēah); *Hopplande* 1558–1603 ('selion where hops are grown', *v.* hoppe, land); *Horswelleruyding* 1307–24 ('(cleared-land near) the horse well', *v.* hors, wella, ryding); *The Intacke* 1665 (*v.* inntak); *Lee Moore* 17 (*v. Le Legemore* 227 *supra*); *le Leyewode* 1357 (*v. le Leywode* 227 *supra*); *Hellysby Lydʒate* 1318 (*v.* hlid-geat); *Lytelhurste medewe* 1354 ('(meadow at) the little wood', *v.* lȳtel, hyrst, mǣd); *Melne Aker* 1460 (*v.* myln, æcer); *le myllerlegh* 1558–1603 ('the miller's clearing', *v.* mylnere lēah); *Patfordissiche* 1307–24 ('(stream at) the muddy ford or the ford at a marsh', *v.* pat(t)e, ford, sīc); *Hellesbyredyng* 1407 (*v.* ryding); *the Ringyard of Helsbie* 17 (*v.* hring, geard); *pons Roberti* 1307–24 ('Robert's bridge', *v.* brycg); *Russels Well* 17 (a point on the Frodsham boundary, *v.* wella); *Rutters Mill* 17 (a mill near the Frodsham boundary, from the surname of a local family *Rutter* (*le Roter*)); *Stocwalhurst* 13² ('(wooded-hill near) the stock-well', *v.* stocc, wælla, hyrst); *Westmore* 17 (*v.* 228 *supra*).

5. KINGSLEY (109–5574) [ˈkiŋzli]

Chingeslie 1086 DB, -*leye* 1154–81 Chest (p), -*lee* 1153–60 Orm² (p)

Kyngesleya 1157–94 Chest, *Kinggesleia* 1175 Facs, *Kingeslega* 1178 ib (p) *et freq* with variant spellings *Ky*-, *Kinges*-, -*is*-, -*leh*(*e*), -*le*(*e*), -*ley*(*e*), -*leg*(*h*), -*ly*, -*leie*, -*leia* to *Kingesley* 1613 ChRR, *Kyngeslay* 1292 Ipm, -*lagh* 1369 Plea

Kingsley 1192–1208 Chest (p), 1217–32 VR (p), 1392 ChRR (p) *et freq* with variant spellings *Kyngs*- (1484 ChRR to 1599 Sheaf), -*leigh*

Kyngelegh c.1232 Fitt (p), *Kingeleg*' 1244 Chest (p), *King*(*e*)*l*' 1260 Court, and occasionally (43 examples) with variant spellings *Kyng*(*e*)-, *King*(*e*)-, -*legh*, -*ley* to *Kingley* 1693 Chol, *Kynggelegh* 1310 Plea, *Kyngelay* 1427 Pat

Keng(*esl*') c.1250–1316 Chest, *Kengeslegh*, -*ley* 1314 Chol

Kynchesleye 1351 BPR

'The king's wood or clearing', *v.* cyning, lēah. The spelling *Kynchesleye* suggests an assibilation of -*ng*- analogous with that in Altrincham **2** 7.

ALDREDELIE (lost) 1086 DB (*v.* Tait 107), the name of a lost manor of *Roelau* hundred, listed with the earl of Chester's manors of Frodsham,

Done (*v.* 161 *supra*) and Eddisbury, probably appears in *Alderlegh'-knolle* 1353 *ChFor, Alderdelegh*... 1357 *ib*, a place within the Forest of Delamere and in Kingsley. The p.n. is 'Ælfōryð's, or Æðelōryð's, clearing or wood', from the OE fem. pers.n. *Ælfðrȳð* or *Æðelðrȳð*, and lēah, with cnoll 'a hill, a knoll'. Cf. Alderley **1** 94.

CATTEN HALL (109–550769) [ˈkatṇɔːl]

> *Catenhale* 1129–48 Chest, 1260 Court *et freq* with variant spellings
>> *Katen-, -(h)ale, -hal* to 1446 ChRR, *K-, Catenhaleclogh* 1347
>> *ChFor, Catenalewod* 1353 *ib, Cattenale* 1306 Orm²
> *Tautenhall* 1206 CRC
> *Catnalwode* 1384 *AddCh, Catnall* 1467 ChRR, 1616 *ChCert et freq*
>> to 1671 Sheaf, *Catnell* 1671 ib, *Katnall Woods* 1641 *Chol*
> *Katenhall* 1391 ChRR, *Caten-* 1513 *ChEx et freq* with variant
>> spellings *Katten-* (1539 Dugd), *Cattne-* (1579 ib), *Catten-* (from
>> 1619 *Chol*), *-Halle* (1539 Dugd, 1619 *Chol*); *hall of Cattenhall*
>> 1596 ChRR, *Catenhall Wood* 1621 *Chol, Cattenhall Woods* 1622,
>> 1655 *ib*, 1831 Bry, *Little Cattenhall Wood* 1658 *Chol*
> *Cattenham* 1535 VE
> *Cattrall* 1599 Sheaf

'She-cat's nook', *v.* catte (gen.sg. cattan), halh (dat.sg. hale), with clōh 'a dell', and wudu 'a wood'. Cf. Belleair *infra*.

CAWLEY (lost, 109–557744), 1842 OS, *Corleg'* 1272–1307 *AddCh, Corley* 1371 AD (p), *Big- & Little Cowley* 1845 *TA*, cf. *a private foot-road in Norley called late Cawleys* 1780 *EnclA* and Crowton Brook 197 *supra*. The p.n. is probably 'clearing frequented by cranes', *v.* corn², lēah.

FINNEY HILL & HO, THE FINNEY (109–535741), [fini], *Feney-, -ay-, Fyneyhill* 1503 *ChFor, Finney Hill* 1780 *EnclA, Great & Little Finney* 1831 Bry, *Finny Hill* 1842 OS, 'enclosure growing with coarse grass', *v.* finn, (ge)hæg, hyll. The name-type *Finn(e)y* (discussed s.n. Fenay WRY **2** 258) appears in Finney Green **1** 222 (from the surname *Finney*), Finney Lane **1** 244, Finney's Lane **2** 245 (probably from the surname), and Fennywood 186 *supra* (influenced by fenn 'a marsh'), also in f.ns. as Finn(e)y (Fd, Mdw) 20, 194 *supra*, 250 *infra*, **1**, 222, 266, **2** 70, 317, Finney Greaves 136 *supra*, Finney Lee **1** 226. It influences the f.n. Finishaw **1** 65 (from fenn). The el. finn (cf. Problems 92) also appears in Finnacres 90 *supra*, and perhaps in Fenna's Fd 313 *infra*. At Finney was an ancient oak described by Webb in 1656 (Orm² II 11) as 'a stately old tree, which they call *the finny oak*...said to be derived from...the fort or castle of *Finborow*'. Orm² II 3 reports a form *Finborrow*. This is probably 'grass-grown fortification', from finn and burh, though the final el. could be beorg 'a hill'. This lost fortification is mentioned by the seventeenth-century antiquarian Erdswick (Orm² II 3) as the remains of a hill-top fort, like Kelsborrow Castle 212 *supra*, called *Finness*. This name appears as *Fynness* 1574 *Harl.* 473, Sheaf³ 22 (5234). It may be 'grassy headland', from finn and ness. Also in this vicinity was (*le*) *Brynk*, (*le Brynk subtus*) *le* (*H*)*oldecastel*(*l*) 1357 *ChFor*, 'the bank under the old castle', *v*. brink, ald, castel. Adjacent to Finney Hill are Castlehill Fm & Ho *infra*. It would seem that Finney Hill either was, or was supposed to be, the site of a fortification.

HALL O' TH' HEY (109–558758), [(h)ɛi], *le hey* 1420 Plea, 1433 ChRR, 1496 Orm², *Hall of Hay*, -*Hey* 1671 Sheaf, *Hall o' th' Heys* 1831 Bry, *Hall on the Hey* 1842 OS, 'the enclosure', from (ge)hæg, with hall, brū, wudu.

HATLEY FM (109–535763), *Hatteley*, -*legh iuxta Catenhaleclogh* 1347 *ChFor*, *Hatley Lane* 1780 *EnclA*, *Hartley Lane* 1842 OS, 'clearing at a hat-shaped hill', from hætt and lēah, with lane, brū and mǣd. Cf. Hatley 231 *supra*.

PEEL HALL (109–540755), [pi:l], 1780 *EnclA*, *quoddam Peele*, *pela* 1347 *ChFor*, *unum Pele* 1353 *ib*, *le Pele* 1370 Orm², *le Peele Ferme* 1631–2 *ib*, *the Peel Farm* 1656 *ib*, *Peele* 1671 Sheaf, 'the peel-house, the fortified house', *v*. pēl. Cf. *le Whytemore infra*.

RODEY LANE (109–554749 to 567745), [roudi], *Roodeye Lane* 1831 Bry, cf. *rodewayschewe* 1272–1307 *AddCh*, *rodewaysweth* 1359 *Chol*, *Rodaymor*(*e*), *pratum de*, *mora de Roday* 1279 *AddCh*, 1384 *ib*, *Rodeye* 1280–90 *Chol*, *Rodeymor* 1308 Misc, 1347 *ChFor*, *Rydemor* 1309 Misc, *Rodday* 1390 *AddCh*, *Rodhey* 1660 *Chol*, *Rody alias Rood Hey* 1668 *ib*, *Roddy* 1844 *TA* 173, '(copse, path and marsh at) the riding-way', from rodeway (cf. rād, weg), with sceaga, swæð, mōr¹, lane. For the form -*sweth v*. NED *swath*¹.

BALL LANE, *Bull Lane* 1831 Bry cf. *Ball Field* 1845 *TA*, *v*. bula, cf. Higher Heyes *infra*.   BANK TOP, *the Bankehouse* 1654, 1708 Orm², *v.* banke, hūs, topp.   BEECH FM & LANE, *the Beach House, Beach Lane, Norley or Kingsley Beach* 1780 *EnclA, Beech Farm* 1831 Bry, cf. Forest Lane *infra, v.* Beech Lane 249 *infra.*   BELLEAIR, *Cattenhall Wood or Bell-Air* 1780 *EnclA, Bellair* 1785 Sheaf, *Bellars* 1831 Bry, *Bellare* 1842 OS, cf. Catten Hall *supra.*   THE BELT, *Crewe Wood* 1831 Bry, cf. *Crewe Croft* 1845 *TA,* and Crewood Hall *infra.*   BIG WOOD, 1844 *ib, Hall o' th' Heys Wood* 1831 Bry, cf. Hall o' th' Hey *supra.*   BLAKELEES, BLAKE LEES HO, *Blake Leys* 1831 ib, 'black pastures', from blæc and ModE *ley* (cf. lēah, læs). BROOK HO, *þe Brokehowse* 1495 Sheaf, *the Brookehowse* 1654 Orm[2], *-house* 1668 Sheaf, from a family surnamed *del Broke* 1354 Sheaf (*v.* brōc) and hūs.   CASTLEHILL FM & HO (109–5374), 1831 Bry, 'hill suitable for a castle', *v.* castel(l), hyll, cf. Finney Hill *supra.* CLOUGH FM, *Clough Brow* 1842 OS, *v.* clōh, brū.   COMMONSIDE, cf. *Kingsley Common* 1780 *EnclA, Common Brow & Lot* 1845 *TA, v.* commun, brū, hlot, sīde.   CREWOOD HALL, cf. The Belt *supra, v.* 195 *supra.*   DEPMORE FM, *Depmore* 1503 *ChFor,* 1581 Sheaf, *Deep Moor* 1754 *Chol,* 'deep marsh', *v.* dēop, mōr[1].   DODGSLEY-(GATE) FM, *Dodsley Gate & Lane* 1831 Bry, *Dodsley Gate* 1842 OS, cf. *Dodgeley, Top Dodgeley, Dodgeley Meadow* 1845 *TA,* cf. *Dodds Croft* 1845 *TA, v.* docga 'a dog' (cf. *Hodg Croft* 1 158), lēah, geat 'a gate', lane.   FORESTGATE FM (*Perrin's House* 1831 Bry), FORESTHOUSE FM, and FOREST LANE (*Beech Lane* 1831 ib), are named from the Forest of Delamere, the surname *Perrins,* and Beech Lane *supra.*   GREEN BANK (FM), 1860 White.   HAREHEYS FM, 1831 Bry, *Higher Heys* 1842 OS, *v.* hara 'a hare', (ge)hæg, cf. foll. HIGHER HEYES, *Bull Lane Farm* 1831 Bry, cf. prec. and Ball Lane *supra,* cf. also *Hayes* 1845 *TA, v.* (ge)hæg.   KINGSLEY FORD (lost, 109–557764), 1842 OS, perhaps *Rowton ford in aqua de Wever* 1244–5 (17) Orm[2] II 89, 'ford at *Rowton,* or at an enclosure of rough land', *v.* rūh, tūn, ford.   KINGSLEY HALL, 1708 Orm[2], *le Hall of Kingsley* 1631 ib, origin of a surname *de Aula* 1272–1307 *AddCh, del Halle* 1357 BPR, *de*(*l*) *Hall* 1400 ChRR, *v.* hall.   KINGSLEY WATER-MILL, *molendinum de Kingisleye* 1257 *AddCh, Kingsley Mylne* 1484 ChRR, *Kyngesley miln, -Mylne* 1520 ChRR, AD, cf. *Oldemulnestude* 1365 Orm[2], *Mylne Heyes* c.1602 *Chol, v.* myln, styde, mylne-stede, (ge)hæg.   MILL LANE (FM & HO), *Mill Lane* (*Tenement*) 1780 *EnclA, Mill Lane* (*House*) 1860 White, *Croutonway* 1359 *Chol,* a road at 109–560752 to 570746, passing Kingsley Mill *supra,* leading to Crowton 195 *supra, v.* myln, lane, weg.   MOUNT PLEASANT.

OFFALPITS FM, *Occa Pits* 1831 Bry, *Offal Pits* 1845 *TA*.   PIKE'S
NOOK FM, *Pikes Nook* 1845 *ib*, *Pikes House* 1860 White, *Pykes
messuage or tenement*, occupied by William *Pyke*, 1658 *Chol*, v. nōk.
PROPHET'S HO, cf. *Profits Croft* 1845 *TA*, probably from the surname
Profit.   PROSPECT FM.   SILVER WELL (109–567767), a petri-
fying spring named from the colour of the deposit, v. seolfor, silfr,
wella.   SPRINGFIELD HO, cf. *Spring Field* 1845 *TA*, v. spring 'a
well-spring'.   STABLE MEADOW PIPE, a wooded bank beside
R. Weaver, from dial. *pipe* 'a small valley opening out of a larger'
(EDD), cf. pīpe.   TAN HO, *Westons Tan House* 1780 *EnclA, Tan
Yard* 1831 Bry, v. tan-hous, tan-yard.   WARBURTON WOOD.
WELL WOOD, v. wella.   WESTBROOK HOUSE (FM).   WIGANS
LAKE FM, *Wiggins Lake* 1780 *EnclA*, 1831 Bry, *Wigans Lake* (*Field*)
1845 *TA*, from cwicen, dial. *wicken* 'a mountain-ash', and lacu 'a
watercourse'.   WINDMILL TERRACE.

FIELD-NAMES

The undated forms are 1845 *TA* 224. Of the others, 1206 is CRC, 1272–
1307, 1279 are *AddCh*, E1 (17), 1446², 1586, e17, 1708–9 Orm², c.1277, 1314,
1359 *Chol*, l13 (n.d.), 1354, 1812 Sheaf, 1303, 1304 Chamb, 1347 Plea, 1347²,
1353, 1357, 1503 *ChFor*, 1371 (17) Tab, 1398, 1409, 1433, 1436, 1438, 1446,
1613 ChRR, 1780 *EnclA*, 1831 Bry, 1842 OS.

(*a*) Ash Furlongs (*v.* æsc, furlang); Ashurst Barn 1831 (*v.* æsc, hyrst);
Bale Fd; Barkers Lane 1831; Beach *freq* (*v.* bece¹, cf. Beech Fm *supra*,
Beech Ho 228 *supra*); Black Ground (*v.* blæc, grund); Bottom Fd (*v.* botm);
Briar Wd (*v.* brēr); Brickkiln (*v.* bryke-kyl); Brockaw (probably 'badger-
hole', *v.* brocc-hol); Broom Acre (*v.* brōm); Brow (*v.* brū); Browns Croft
(cf. *messuage called Browns* 1780, from the surname); Cale Fd (*v.* cauel);
Camp Fd, Castle Croft (*Camp* 1842, the site of an earthwork at 109–539768,
v. camp², castel(l)); Chapel Croft & Fd (cf. *Chapel Wood* 1831 and *capella de
Kingsley* 1371 (17), *v.* chapel(e)); Coal Pit Fd; Coney Graves (*le Conyngre*
1398, *v.* coningre); Cooks Yard (cf. *Cookes tenement* 1780, from the surname);
Crammers Fd; Crowton Stile (*v.* stigel, cf. Crowton 195 *supra*); Dale (*v.*
dæl¹); Day Croft (*v.* dey); Dingle (*v.* dingle); Dones Fd (from the surname
Done); Dovehouse Fd; Farthings (*v.* fēorðung), Fleets Fd (cf. *Beach Fleets
Lane* 1780, from dial. *fleet* 'a drain, a rivulet, a ditch', cf. flēot and Beech
Fm *supra*); Gale Moor 1780 (*v.* gagel, mōr¹, cf. *Wiremor infra*); Glade (cf.
glæd³); Guest Fd (*v.* Jessies Slack *infra*); Hand Croft; Handkerchief Fd;
Hanging Fd (*v.* hangende); Haverhill Fd (prob. 'daffodil field' from dial.
haverdril 'the daffodil', *v.* affadille); Heavy Leeches (*v.* læ(c)); Helsby Hey
& Mdw (*v.* (ge)hæg, mæd, cf. Helsby 235 *supra*); Hemp Croft (*v.* hænep);
Holdens Clough (*v.* hol², denu, clōh); Hollins (*v.* holegn); Holloway Knowl
(*v.* 250 *infra*); Holly Wd 1831 (*v.* Beech Ho 228 *supra*); Holt West (from

holt 'a copse', with wēste 'waste-land', or wist 'a lair', cf. Fox(t)wist 182 *supra*, I 194); Honslow (Lot) (*v.* hlot, Hondslough Fm 216 *supra*); Hop Ridding(s) (*v.* hoppe, ryding); Hovel Croft (*v.* hovel); The Hurst 1780 (e17, the old site of the manor of Kingsley, called *le Hurst* 1398 (DKR xxxvi 323), *Kingsley Hurste* 1708–9, 'the wooded-hill', *v.* hyrst); Jessies Slack (local, 109–545740) (*Guess's Slack* 1780, cf. Guest Fd *supra*, from slakki 'a hollow' and the surname *Guest*); Kiln Croft; Kingsfield (*v.* cyning); Kingsley Fd (cf. *Kyngesley hill* 1503, cf. Kingsley *supra*); Knabb ('hill-top', *v.* knabbe); Knowper Riddings; Lady('s)-, Ladies Hayes (*v.* hlǣfdige, (ge)hæg); Lands (*v.* land)! Lime Fd (*v.* lim); Long Lot ('long allotment', *v.* hlot); Long Shoots (*v.* scēat); Marl Fd, Flatt(s), Lot & Moor (*v.* marle, flat, hlot, mōr[1]); Marsh (Riddings) (cf. *del Mershe* 1354 (p), *v.* mersc, ryding); Meeting House Fd; Milk Knowl (perhaps 'hill on which a mill stands', *v.* myln, cnoll, but cf. foll. and milc, meoluc); Milking Bank ('hillside where cattle are milked', *v.* milking); Missack ('a boggy place', *v.* mizzick); Moor Bank; Moor Lane 1831 (probably *Neuton Way* c.1277, *v.* weg, cf. Newton 248 *infra*); Moss; Newton Dale (*v.* dæl[1], cf. Newton 248 *infra*); Oat Hay; Off Way (*v.* hōh, weg); Old Womans Mead; Oxhey (cf. *Ox Hey Wood* 1831, *v.* (ge)hæg); Peacroft; Pickow Hill (*v.* pīc[1], hōh); Pigeon Brow; Pingot (cf. *Pingot* (a cottage) 1842, *v.* pingot); Potatoe Brow; Ridding(s) (*le Ryddyng* 1409, *v.* ryding); Rough, Rough Lane & Moor; Royalty (*v.* roialte); Seeding Well (*the Seething Well* 1780, 1812, from wella and ME sēoþinge 'boiling, seething' cf. Exceeding Well 273 *infra*); Shaw Flatt (cf. *Shaw Plat Lane* 1831, *v.* sceaga, plat[2], flat); The Slack 1842 (*the Slack Ground* 1780, *v.* slakki grund); Smithy Moor; Snails Flatt; Spark Fd (*v.* spearca); Stanley Knowl (*Standrill Knowl* 1831, *v.* cnoll); Tanley Hill; Three Nooks; Tinkers Fd (*v.* tink(l)ere); Town Fd & Mdw; Wall Croft (the- 1780, *v.* wælla); Watery Lane Fd; Well Lot (*v.* wella, hlot); Wheat Hay; Whip Stile (*v.* stigel); Willow Moor Hill; Windy Harbour 1831 (*v.* windig, here-beorg); Wood (Fd) (cf. *Wood Lane* 1831, *boscus de Kingesleg'* 1206, -*Kyngeslegh* 1353, *v.* wudu, lane).

(b) *le Byrchenschawe* 1357 ('the birch wood', *v.* bircen[2], sceaga); *Birch-furlongesyate* 1347 ('(gateway at) the birch-tree furlong', *v.* birce, furlang, geat); *the Bryn or Brandes* 1613 (*v.* Bryn 198 *supra*); *le Cokshete* 1347 (*v.* cocc-scyte); *le Dernehurst* 1357 ('the secluded wood', *v.* derne, hyrst); *le Dodidac* 1272–1307 ('the pollarded oak', from āc and ME dodded, pa.part. of *dodden* 'to shave, to clip'); *Dygisturht* 1272–1307 (from storð 'a young wood, a plantation', with an unidentified first el.); *Le Flaxyordes* 1347 (*v.* fleax, geard); *Fleyeschepeshoc* 1279 (an oak, *v.* āc. The first el. looks like a surname or by-name 'Flay-sheep', from OE *flēan* 'to flay' and scēp 'a sheep'); *Glasshowse* E1 (17) (p), *Glassehws* 1272–1307 (p), *Glas(se)houses* 1303 (p), 1304 (p), *le Glashousez* 1354 (p), *le Glassehoux* (p), *le Glassehouxhull* 1357 ('(hill at) the house(s) where glass is made', *v.* glas-hous, hyll, cf. *Gleshousfeld* (1311) in Cholmondeley, 325 *infra*. There may have been another glass industry at Glass Fd 294 *infra*. The Kingsley and Cholmondeley p.ns. antedate the NED record (1385) of the compound *glas-hous* 'a glass-factory' and are the earliest instances of its use as a p.n. and surname that have been observed, cf. Glasshouses (1387) YW 5 149, *Glashouses* (1406) Cu 203, *le Glashows* (1479) in Wolseley St, and later examples Sx 136, Sr 192, 203, 225, Wa 174, Mx 97, Db 325, Gl 3 178, 188, YW 1 121, 2 70, 139, 145); *Le Hey Bernes* 1586 (v. hēg, bere-ærn); *le Holdefel* c.1277 (v. ald, feld); *Lyneymor* 1314, *Lynaymor(e)* 1354, 1359, *Lynamore* 1433, *Lene-* 1446, *Leni-* 1446[2] ('(marsh at) the flax meadow', v. lin, ēg, mōr[1]); *le Lowe* 1438 (p) (v. hlāw); *Mayoesmore* 1436 ('Mayowe's marsh', v. mōr[1], probably named after William *Mayowe* of Chester, for this land was owned in 1436 by one Barton who also owned property in Chester held by Mayowe, v. DKR xxxvii 232); *Pirlewall* 1347 ('bubbling well', v. pyrl(e), wælla); *Roughley-, -leghmor, Rouleyghmorheued* 1353 ('((the top end of) the marsh at) the rough glade', v. rūh, lēah, mōr[1], hēafod); *Rus(s)ibutes* li3 (n.d.) ('rushy selions', v. riscig, butte); *Le Sedemonnesbrok* 1347 (v. brōc 'a brook'. Dr von Feilitzen and Professor Löfvenberg point out that the first el. may be the OE pers.n. *Sidumann* in a variant form *Sede-* (from back-mutation *Sidu- > Siodu-, Seodu-*), but more likely the ME surname *Sedemon* 'dealer in seeds', cf. Alan *Sedemon* tenant in Kingsley 1260 Court 26, v. Thuresson 37, Reaney s.n. *Seedman*); *Le Shephonespert* 1398 ('spring near a shippon', v. scypen, spyrt); *Stanifordemor* 1314 ('(marsh at) the stony ford', v. stānig, ford, mōr[1]); *le Twychell'* 1353 (v. twychell); *del Walle* 1354 (p) (v. wælla); *le Wiremor* 1347[2] ('bog-myrtle marsh', v. wīr, mōr[1], cf. Gale Moor *supra*); *le Whytemor* 1347[2] ('white marsh', v. hwīt, mōr[1]. This was the locality about Peel Hall *supra*); *Yate* 1354 (p) (v. geat).

6. MANLEY (HALL & HO) (109–5071)

Menlie 1086 DB

Manl(eg), *Manleye* 1265–91 Chest, *-lee* 13 Tab, *-le* 1289 Court (p), *-legh* c.1270 Chol (*et freq* to 1385 Cl), *-ley* 1303 Chamb, *-ly* 1546 Dugd, *Manley Common & House* 1831 Bry, *Manley Hall* 1842 OS

Manlewe 13 CoLegh (p)

Manneley c.1310 Chest, *Manelegh* 1370 *Tourn* (p)

Mandeleye 1495 Sheaf, *Mandl(e)y* 1599, 1610 ib

'Common wood or clearing', v. (ge)mǣne, lēah. *Mannelegh* 1296 Plea, Orm[2] may belong to Monneley Mere 7 *supra*.

ARK WOOD (109–522713), 1842 OS, *the Dark Ark* 1812 Sheaf, 1831 Bry, 1838 *TA* 21 & 279 (269, 280 *infra*), a wooded valley on Ashton Brook 1 14. If the form *Ark* is analogous with that in Anglezark La 48, from erg 'a shieling', then this p.n. means 'gloomy shieling', and *le Erw..brok* 1347 ChFor might be identified with this part of Ashton Brook, v. erg, deorc, wudu, brōc. But *Ark* may simply be arke 'a box, a receptacle; a trap', cf. *Ele arke* 17 *supra*.   BUCKOAK,

1831 Bry.   DUNHAM HEATH, 1842 OS, *v.* hǣð, cf. Dunham 253 *infra.*   FOURLANES FM.   GARDEN WOOD.   HAZEL WOOD. INTAKE, 1842 OS, *Intack* 1831 Bry, *v.* inntak.   KENNEL WOOD. LORD'S WELL, *v.* 216 *supra.*   LOW FM, 1842 OS, *Dunham Lane Farm* 1831 Bry, *Dunham Farm* 1844 *TA*, cf. Dunham 253 *infra, v.* lane, lágr.   LOWERHALL FM, *Lower Hall* 1831 Bry, *Manley Lower Hall Farm* 1844 *TA, v.* lower, hall, cf. Old Hall *infra.*   MANLEY COMMON, 1831 Bry, cf. *communis campus de Manleg'* 1265–91 Chest, *v.* commun.   MANLEY LANE (109–497720 to 457715), 1842 OS. This road from Trafford Bridge to Manley may be on the line of *Salterestrete infra.*   MANLEY OLD HALL, *Mandeleye halle* 1495 Sheaf, *the halle of Manley* 1536 Orm², *Upper Hall* 1831 Bry, *Higher Hall* 1842 OS, *v.* upper, hall, cf. Lowerhall Fm *supra.*   MANOR FM, *The Gate* 1831 Bry, *v.* geat or gata.   THE MOSS, MOSS (LANE) FM, *le Manleymosse* 1353 ChFor, *Moss Plantation* 1831 Bry, *The Moss* 1842 OS, cf. *Mos(e)walle* 1265–91 Chest, *v.* mos, wælla.   NORTON'S LANE, *v.* 264 *infra.*   RANGEWAY BANK FM, *Rangers Bank* 1831 Bry, from banke 'a bank, a hillside', with ModE *ranger* 'a forest ranger' NED, probably connected with the forest of Delamere.   ROOKERY FM & WOOD.   SIDDALL'S HILL, *Syders Hill* 1831 ib, *Siddells Hill* 1842 OS, cf. *Siddalls Meadow* 1844 *TA*, from the surname *Siddall* and hyll, mǣd.   SIMMOND'S HILL, *Symondeshill* 1503 ChFor, *Simmons Hill* 1812 Sheaf, 'Simond's hill', from the ME pers.n. *Simond* and hyll.   SWAN'S WELL, *v.* 216 *supra.*

FIELD-NAMES

The undated forms are 1844 *TA* 250. Of the others, 1265, 1265–91 are Chest, 1347, 1353, 1357, 1503 *ChFor*, 1429, 1497 ChRR, 1610 Sheaf, 1819 Orm², 1831 Bry.

(a) Abbots Clough & Moss (named after the abbot of Chester, *v.* clōh, mos, cf. Abbots Clough 220 *supra*, The Moss *supra*); Barley Tongue (*v.* bærlic, tunge); Birchen Hey (*v.* bircen², (ge)hæg); Birchensuch (*Birchenhulsiche* 1347, '(watercourse at) birch hill', *v.* bircen², hyll, sīc); Chester Mdw (probably associated with the abbey of Chester, cf. Abbots Clough *supra*); Coal Pit Fd; Cote Mdw (*v.* cot); Cow Hey; Crab Tree Moor; Crib (*v.* crib); Dunge (*v.* dyncge); Elton Hey (*v.* (ge)hæg, cf. Elton 255 *infra*); Flash Croft (*v.* flasshe); Gills Quarry 1812 (*v.* 216 *supra*); Gorsty Banks & Heath; Gravel Moor (*v.* gravel); Big- & Little Hill, Hill Croft & Fd (cf. *Manley Hill* 1819, *v.* hyll); Hut Fd; Huxleys Lane 1831; Kitchen Fd; Knowl (*v.* cnoll); Marl Fd (cf. *the marlde haye* 1610, *v.* marled, (ge)hæg); Mow Ridding (*v.* mūga, ryding); Outlet(t) (*v.* outlet); Park Green; Pickos

(v. pichel); Pie Hey (v. pīe², (ge)hæg); Ridding (v. ryding); Road Fd; Rough; Rough Hey & Moor; Sandfield; Shaw Fd (v. sceaga); Short Acre; Soldiers Mdw; Standerly; Thorntree Fd; Tollgate Ho (v. toll-gate); Turnip Moor; Turnpike Fd; White Fd (v. hwīt); Wilkins Moss 1812 (v. 217 supra); Windmill Bank & Hill.

(b) Aleynes Haddelond 1265, -heuedlond 1265–91 (from the ME (OFr) pers.n. Alein and hēafod-land); Aspone(s)forlong 1265–91 ('(furlong at) the strip of ash-trees', v. æsc, spann¹, furlang); Bernullisleg' 1265–91 ('Beornwulf's glade', from the OE pers.n. Beornwulf and lēah); le blake lake 1265–91 ('the black watercourse', v. blæc, lacu); Brandwode 1503 ('burnt wood', v. brende², wudu); Cakebrok 1265–91 (v. brōc 'a brook'. The first el. may be the same as that in Cakeham Sx 88, Cakebole Wo 236, Cakemore Wo 293, Carick Nf (Wo 236) Kakewelle Wo 236, an OE pers.n. Cac(c)a (EPNS vols.) or the OE pers.n. Cǣfca (DEPN). The ME surname Cake (Reaney 57) is also possible); le Chircheweye 1265–91 (v. cirice, weg); Copenhaleeues(e) 1353, 1357 ('(edge of the wood at) Coppa's nook', from efes with a p.n. from an OE pers.n. Coppa and halh as in Coppenhall 22 supra, cf. 280 infra); the fore Aker 1610 (v. fēower, æcer); Foulesleeheued, Fouleleesheued 1265–91 ('(head of) the fowl's clearing', v. fugol, lēah, hēafod); Gerardesweye 1265–91 ('Gerard's way', from the ME pers.n. Gerard (OFr Gerart, OG Gerard) and weg. A family surnamed Gerard held land in Kingsley 239 supra from the thirteenth century); le Gosebuttes 1265–91 ('goose selions', v. gōs, butte); le Grenelawe 1265–91 ('the green hill', v. grēne¹, hlāw); Grenewalle 1265 ('the green well', v. grēne¹, wælla); Hoggeryddyng 1429, le Heggeriddyng 1497 (probably 'hog clearing', v. hogg, ryding. The Hegge- spelling may represent a phonetic confusion of hecg 'a hedge' and hocg the alternative form of hogg, cf. Hodg Croft 1 158); Hullesholm tre 1265–91 (a boundary point near Stonhul infra, either 'elm-tree at a hill', or 'tree at a marsh-meadow near a hill', from hyll and trēow with ulm or holmr (cf. hulm)); le Hullond 1265–91 (v. hyll, land); Lambelachelond 1265–91 ('(selion at) the lambs' boggy stream', v. lamb, læc(c), land); Ynumhoc 1265–91 ('hook-shaped piece of land, or oak-tree, at an intake', v. innām, and hōc or āc); la Lee 1265–91 (v. lēah); Le Leylond 1265–91 ('fallow land', v. lǣge, land); Leysigesmulnebroc 1265–91 ('Lēofsige's mill-brook', or 'brook at Lēofsige's mill', from the OE pers.n. Lēofsige, with myln and brōc); Manley Crosse 1503 (v. cros); The Oorsciheathes 1610 ('rushy heaths', v. riscig, hǣð); the Pouldsteelde 1610 ('the place where the pool is', v. pōl-stede); Salterestrete 1265–91, Salterstrete 1347 ('salter's road', v. saltere, strǣt. This suggests a salt-way from Northwich to Chester by way of Bridge Trafford, perhaps along Manley Lane supra. Such a route would avoid the toll-passage at Kelsall on the more direct 'Watling Street' road); Schadlond 1265–91 ('boundary selion', v. scēad, land); Siridac 1265–91 (an oak tree, v. āc. The first el. might be the ON fem.pers.n. Sigríðr); Stokenewalle 1265–91 ('well lined with logs, or well with a structure of tree-trunks', v. stoccen, wælla); Stonhul 1265–91 (v. stān, hyll); Teytesfeld 1265–91 (named from its former owner Punne Teyt, v. ChetNS LXXXII 710); Wetelache 1265–91 ('wet bog', v. wēt, læc(c)).

7. NEWTON BY FRODSHAM (109–530750), NEWTONBANK, NEWTON (OLD) HALL & LODGE

Neuton 1260 Court *et freq* with variant spelling *-thon* to 1520 AD, ChRR, (*-iuxta Frodisham*) 1287 Court, (*-Kyngeslegh*) 1296 Orm², (*-Alvandelegh*) 1396 Plea, (*-infra forestam de Mara*) 1398 Orm²

Neweton 1290 Ipm

Newton 1293 Plea *et freq*, (*-iuxta Kingesley*) 1293 ib, (*-in the forest*) 1297 ib, (*-iuxta Frodsham*) 1432 ChRR, *Newton Lodge* 1831 Bry

Nawton 1474 ChRR

Neowton 1538 Orm²

'The new farm', from nīwe and tūn, with banke, hall, loge, ald.

HILLTOP FM.   LOWERHOUSE FM.   NEWTON FIRS, *The Firs* 1831 Bry.   NEWTON HOLLOW, *Neuton Dale* 1503 ChFor, *Newton Dale* 1844 *TA*, v. holh, dæl¹.   OLD MANOR HO.   SPRINGSIDE. SUCH FM, 1831 Bry, *the Such House* 1780 EnclA, from sīc 'a water-course'.

FIELD-NAMES

The undated forms are 1844 *TA* 294. Of the others, 1297 is Plea, 1354 Sheaf, 1357, 1503 ChFor, 1613 ChRR, 1679 Chol, 1780 EnclA, 1831 Bry, 1842 OS.

(a) Backside (v. ba(c)ksyde); Barkers Lane 1831 (cf. 243 *supra*); Calvers Croft (v. calver); Chapel Lane 1842; Cock Shoot (cf. *Kocshetherudyng* 1354, 'cleared-land at a cock-shoot', v. cocc-scyte, ryding); Common Lot (v. commun, hlot); Coney Slack ('rabbit hollow', v. coni, slakki); Dobers Common Lot (cf. Common Lot *supra*, Daubers-, Doubers Lot, 232, 225 *supra*); Dones Fd (cf. *Dunnescroft* 1354, from the ME pers.n. or surname *Dunn* (OE *Dunn*), or from the ancient Cheshire family of *Done, Donne* and croft); Flashey Mdw (v. flasshe, ēg, mǣd); Hemp Yard (v. hemp-yard); Hough Riddings, Houghendale Hough, Houghow (cf. *Hough Moss* 1780, Houghendale 233 *supra*, v. hōh, ryding, dæl¹, mos); Jeffryes Feild 1679; Kiln Croft; Knowl Fd (v. cnoll); Lands; Marl Fd; Meeting House Fd; Milking Brow (v. milking); Moss (field) (v. mos); New Hay; Newton Common Lot (*Newton Common* 1780, cf. *supra*); Newton Gate 1812 (v. 217 *supra*); Newton Gutter 1831 (v. goter); Nixons Croft (*inclosure called Nicksons* 1780); Penny Croft (v. peni(n)g); Pickow (v. pichel); Pillow; Pingot Croft (v. pingot); Riders Fd; Riley (v. ryge, lēah); Salt Hill (v. salt); Slice (Head) (v. s(c)luse 'a sluice, a dam', hēafod); Sunday Fd (v. Sunnan-dæg); Townsend Croft (v. toun, ende¹); Wanlow's Well (v. 216 *supra*); Water Mdw; Well Mdw.

(b) *Neutonblakclyf* 1357, *Blakcliff*, *-clyff* 1503 ('black cliff', v. blæc, clif);
the Bryn or Brandes 1613 (v. Bryn 198 *supra*); *Roghull*, *R(o)ugh(h)ull* 1357,
Roghill, *-hull* 1503 ('rough hill', v. rūh, hyll); *Smaleshate* 1297 ('narrow projecting piece of land', v. smæl, scēat(a)).

8. NORLEY (BANK, GROVE, HALL & LANE) (109–5772)

> *Norl(o3')* 1239 *AddCh*, *Norley* 1239 (17) Sheaf, 1316 Chamb *et freq*
> with variant spellings *Nore-* (1270–1310 *Chol*), *-le(i)gh*; *Norley*
> *Bank* 1787 Sheaf (cf. *le Bonk* 1354 ib (p)), *-Hall* 1780 *EnclA*
> (cf. *the Old Hall* 1819 Orm²), *-Lane* 1831 Bry
> *Northleg'* 1239 (1580) Sheaf, *Nort-* 1259 Court (p), *-legh*, *Northe-*
> *leye* 1270–1310 *Chol*, *Northley(e)*, *-le(gh)* 1278 *ib*, 1287, 1289
> Court *et freq* to 1358 BPR

'Northern glade', v. norð, lēah, banke, hall, lane. Norley is north
of Eddisbury and Oakmere 213, 217 *supra*, in the forest of Delamere.

BLAKEMERE (109–555715), a hamlet near *Blackmere Ford* 1831 Bry,
perhaps the home of John Lestraunge of *Blakemere* 1363 Pat, named
from Blakemere Moss 213 *supra*.   BEECH LANE (FM), (109–560740),
le Bache feld 1270–1310 *Chol*, *Norleghbache* 1347 *ChFor*, *Norley-* 1503
ib, *Norley Beech Woods* 1831 Bry (109–560735), cf. *Beach Lot*, *Beach
Style* 1844 *TA*, Forest Lane *infra* and Beech Fm & Lane 242 *supra*,
v. bæce¹, bece¹, 'a valley-brook', feld, lane, hūs, wudu, hlot, stigel,
BIG WOOD, *Town Riddings Plantation* 1831 Bry, *Tom Ridding* 1844
TA, cf. *Town Field* 1844 *ib*, v. toun, ryding.   BREECH MOSS,
Beech Moss 1780 *EnclA*, 1842 OS, *Breach Moss* 1831 Bry, *Brick Moss*
1844 *TA*, from bece¹ 'a valley-stream' or brēc 'a breaking-in of land'
and mos.   BROWNMOSS FM, 1831 Bry, v. brūn¹, mos.   CHEESE
HILL LANE, cf. *Cheese Hill Lot* 1844 *TA*, *Chees Hill* 1780 *EnclA*, v.
196 *supra*.   COW LANE.   DARLEY COVERT, *Holwalls Plantation*
1831 Bry, cf. *Hol Walls* 1844 *TA*, 'springs in a hollow', v. hol²,
wælla, later named from *Darley Meadow* 1844 *TA*.   FERNLEA, cf.
Ferneleyforde 1503 *ChFor*, *Fearney Ley* 1844 *TA*, 'ferny clearing',
v. fearnig, lēah, ford.   FINGER POST FM & LANE.   FLAXMERE,
1842 OS, *Flaxmere Moss* 1780 *EnclA*, 1831 Bry, perhaps 'pool of
shallow water, pool at a swamp', v. flask, mere¹, mos, but Professor
Löfvenberg points out that the first el. could be fleax 'flax', and the
name could mean 'mere used for steeping flax', cf. *flex wer* MED 634.
FOREST LANE, *Beech Lane* 1831 Bry, v. Beech Lane *supra*.   GAZE-
BANK (a road, 109–568721), *Gad Bank* 1831 ib, *Gad Brow* 1844 *TA*,

perhaps 'hill where the goad was needed', from ME *gadd* 'a gad, a goad', with **banke** and **brū**. THE GORSE. GREENSLATE FM, *Green Slate* 1831 Bry, 'green pasture', *v.* **grēne¹, slæget**. HAMLETS HOLLOW, *Walken Lane* 1831 ib. HATCH MERE (lake), HATCHMERE (hamlet), *Hatchew Mere* 1844 *TA*, *v.* 215 *supra*. HOME FM, *The Whob* 1780 *EnclA*, *The Wab* 1831 Bry, cf. *Wob Orchard* 1844 *TA*, 'the bog', *v.* **cwabba**, home. LEIGH COTTAGE, on *Ley Lane* 1831 Bry, *v.* **lēah**. LOW FM. MOSS LANE, cf. 197 *supra*, *v.* **mos**. NEWPOOL WOOD, *v.* 218 *supra*. STANNEYBROOK FM, *Stanny Brook* 1780 *EnclA*, *Stanney Brook* 1842 OS, cf. *Stoney Brook* 1844 *TA*, *v.* **stānig, brōc**. TOWN FM, *v.* **toun**. WICKENTREE FM, *Wickentree* 1831 Bry, 'mountain-ash tree', *v.* **cwicen, trēow**.

FIELD-NAMES

The undated forms are 1844 *TA* 298. Of the others, 1270–1310, 1290–1310, 1362 are *Chol*, 1272–1307, 1300–20, 1314–18 *AddCh*, 1322 *Clif*, 1352 *Eyre*, 1357, 1503 *ChFor*, 1357² *Indict*, 1780 *EnclA*, 1831 Bry, 1842 OS.

(*a*) Ball Croft; Bank Ley (*v.* **banke, lēah**); Barrow Greaves & Mdw (*v.* **bearu** 'a wood', or **bearg** 'a pig', **grǣfe, mǣd**); Bell Fd (cf. *Bell's Lane* 1780); Blains Fd & Moss (cf. *messuage called Blain's* 1780); Blake Ridding (*le-* 1314–18, *-ruding* 1300–20, *v.* **blæc**, ryding); Bottoms (*v.* **botm**); Brook Bank Hill; Camp Fd (*v.* **camp²**); Cathrines; Cat Tail Mdw (*v.* **catt, tægl**); Clap Gate (1831, *v.* **clap-gate**); Clough Ridding (*v.* **clōh**, ryding); Crook Hill (*v.* **krókr**); Curved Fd; Deep Moor Leeke ('(watercourse from) the deep marsh', from **dēop** and **mōr¹** with **lece** or **lœkr**); Doctars Flatt (*v.* **flat**); Dungeon Lane 1831 (*v.* **dongeon**, here a deep hollow); Farthings (*v.* **fēor-ðung**); Finney Mdw (cf. Finney 240 *supra*); Firwood Moss 1780; Fleas ('turves', *v.* **flage**); Fleets Fd (*v.* **flight** 'a turf'); Folly (*v.* **folie**); Four Butts; Goosemere ('goose lake', *v.* **gōs, mere¹**); Hand Ridding (*Hounderudyng* 1322, 'hound's clearing', *v.* **hund**, ryding); Hankerchief (*v.* 325 *infra*); Hastows; Heifer Loonts (*v.* **hēah-fore, land**); Helsby Lot (*v.* **hlot**, cf. Helsby 235 *supra*); Holloway Knowl ('(hillock at) the hollow way', *v.* **holh, weg, cnoll**, cf. 243 *supra*); Kill Hen Fd; Kinseys Mdw (cf. *messuage called Kinseys* 1780); Knot(t) Holt (*Okenholt* 1357, *Knowcholt* 1503, *Knotholts Plantation* 1831 Bry, 'oak wood', *v.* **ācen, āc, holt, atten**, cf. Knockholt, Nackholt PNK 27, 386); Light Oaks ('light oaks, i.e. sparse oaks', *v.* **lēoht, āc**); Linemere (perhaps analogous with Linmere 214 *supra*); Lombars Fd (*Lambardesfeld, Lamberdesfeeld* 1300–20, *Lambardisfeld* 1314–18, 'Lambert's field', from the ME (OFr, OG) pers.n. *Lambert* and **feld**); Long Suit (*v.* **scēat**); Loonts (*v.* **land**); Lords (*v.* **hlāford**); Marl Fd; Mickle Hey & Mdw (*v.* **micel, (ge)hæg**); New Moss 1831 (1780); Nooked Fd; Norley Common 1780 (cf. *the Common House* 1780, *v.* **commun**); Old Riddings (*v.* **ald**, ryding); Oranges; Pickow Head (probably 'pointed promontory', from **pīc¹, hōh, hēafod**); Pool Flatt; School Bank 1842 ('hillside where a school stands');

Stall Moss 1780 ('peat-bog at a fish-pool', v. stall, mos); Such (v. sīc); Turnabout Hill 1831; Turners Lot (*messuage called Turners* 1780, v. hlot); White Pits.

(b) *Breccotes* 1357 ('huts on a hill-side', v. brekka, cot); *the Bryn or Brandes* 1613 (v. Bryn 198 *supra*); *Ganysmore* 1270–1310, *Gouynsmor* 1290–1310 (probably 'Gawain's marsh', from the ME pers.n. Gawain, Gawayne and mōr[1]); *le Godelesmer* 1357, *Godlesmere* 1503 (v. mere[1] 'a lake, a pool'. The first el. may be ME *gōd-les* (OE *gōd-lēas*) adj., 'devoid of good' i.e. useless or barren; alternatively it may be the gen. form of a p.n. from lēah and gōd[2] 'good' or the OE pers.n. Goda); *Grenlone* 1270–1310 (v. grēne[1], lane); *Longeshagh*' 1352 (p), *-schawe* 1357, *le Longeshawe* 1357[2], *Longshawe* 1503 ('long wood', v. sc(e)aga); *le Mere* 1357 (v. mere[1]); *Schortfurlong* 1322 (v. sc(e)ort, furlang); *Stanifurlong* 1322 (v. stānig, furlang); *Wolsalcroft* 1272–1307 ('(croft at) the wolf's nook', from wulf and halh with croft).

x. Ince

Part of the township belonged to Stoke parish 326 *infra* in Wirral. Ince now includes part of Little Stanney township 326 *infra* v. Holme Ho *infra*.

1. INCE (HALL & MARSHES) (109–4476) [ins]

   Inise 1086 DB, 1398 Orm[2], *Ynis* 113 Chest, *-ys* 1277 Sheaf, *Inys* 1312 Plea

   Ynes 1096–1101 (1280), c.1150 Chest *et freq* ib, Pat, Cl, Tax to 1311 Plea, *mariscum de-* 1249–1323 Chest, *Ines* 1271 *BW* (p) *et freq* to 1446 ChRR (p), *-merssh* 1357 BPR, ChFor, *Ynnes* 1320 AddCh

   Yns videlicet Ince 1096–1101 (17) Chest, *Yns* 1284 (17) ib, 1323 Misc, 1326 ChRR (p), *Ins* 1320 Plea *et freq* to 1446 ChRR, *Inns* 1584 Rental, *Insemersh* 1357 ChRR

   Ince 1096–1101 (17) Chest, 1415 ChRR (p) *et freq*, *-Marsh* 17 Sheaf, *-Hall* 1831 Bry, *Ynce* 1549 Sheaf

   Inssemersh 1357 *ChFor*

   Inchemore 1414 ChRR

'The island', from inis, ynys, with mersc, mōr[1] and hall. Ince marshes are also *le Mersh* 1440 Rental, *The Marsh* 1724 NotCestr. Ince occupies a low ridge standing amidst the marshland of the Gowy and Mersey estuaries. Cf. Ince La 103.

HOLME HOUSE FM (109–428753) [houm]

   Alrichesholm c.1184 Chest, 1209, 1279, 1310 ib, Whall, *Alfriches-* 1209 Bun, Whall, *Aldricheholm* 1279 ib, *Alwricheshulm* 1338 Sheaf

Holm e13 Chest, 1260 Court (p), *le-* 1250–1320, 1265–91 Chest, and
ten examples, with variant spellings (*le*) *Holm*(*e*) to c.1554 Whall
le Holmehous 1440 *Rental, the Holme House* 1584 *ib, Holmhouse* 1724
NotCestr, *Holme-house* 1784 Sheaf

'Ælfrīc's island or meadow', from the OE pers.n. *Ælfrīc* and
holmr, with **hūs**. This place is shown by 6″ OS (1912) as in Ince, by
Bryant (1831) as in Thornton-le-Moors 258 *infra*, but in 1844 *TA*
372 it is a district of Stoke parish (326 *infra*) lying in Eddisbury
Hundred. Anciently it was in Little Stanney township, Stoke parish,
Wirrall Hundred, the location of 'all the land of *le Holm* next to *the
mills of Ynes* (cf. Thornton Mill 258 *infra*)...as contained between
the water of Teruein ('Tarvin Water', *v.* R. Gowy 1 26) and the ditch',
cf. *villa de Staney cum le Holm* 1270–1316 Chest. The boundary
between Wirral and Eddisbury Hundreds appears to have followed
the new course of R. Gowy when the river was diverted from the east
to the west side of Holme Ho about 1279–1350 (*v.* ChetNS LXXXII
269–270, N⁰ 448 and addenda), thus removing the place from Wirral to
Eddisbury hundred. The adjacent Thornton Mill 258 *infra* appears to
have been equally within the forests of Wirral and Delamere in 1357.

BRICK KILN WOOD, *v.* **bryke-kyl.**   FOLLY BRIDGE & WOOD, *v.*
folie.   GOWYWOOD, cf. R. Gowy 1 26.   GREEN FM.   GRIN-
SOME FM, *Grymsholme* 1440 *Rental, Grinsoms Farm* 1831 Bry,
Grinsome 1842 OS, 'Grímr's island or meadow', from the ON pers.n.
Grímr (cf. **Grīm**) and **holmr.**   THE GROVE FM, *Lower Farm* 1831
Bry, *the lower towne* 1584 *Rental, Lower Ince* 1671 Sheaf, *v.* **lower,
toun,** cf. Old Hall *infra.*   HOLME FM, 1831 Bry, *v.* **holmr.**   INCE
BANKS, 1842 OS, a sandbank in the Mersey estuary.   INCE FERRY,
1842 ib, cf. *Ince Pier* 1831 Bry, formerly a Mersey ferry.   MARSH
LANE, 1831 ib, *v.* **mersc, lane,** Ince Marshes *supra.*   MILLHOUSE
FM, near the site of a windmill *Ince Mill* 1831 ib, *v.* **myln, hūs.**
OLD HALL, 1831 ib, *Manor House* 1842 OS, *the hier towne* 1584
Rental, Higher Ince 1671 Sheaf, cf. *the site of the Manor House of the
abbots of St Werburgh* 1819 Orm², and Grove Fm *supra, v.* **ald, hall,
higher, toun,** cf. Ince *supra.*   STANLOW POOL, 1842 OS, 'creek at
Stanlow', *v.* **pōl¹,** Stanlow 326 *infra.* This was a creek of Mersey
formed by the mouth of R. Gowy.   THORNTON MILL, formerly
Ince Mill, *v.* 258 *infra.*   WATER LANE, 1842 OS, *Mill Lane* 1831
Bry, leading to Thornton Brook 259 *infra* at Thornton Mill *supra.*
YEWTREE FM.

FIELD-NAMES

The undated forms are 1844 *TA* 372 and belong to the part of Ince which was in Stoke parish *v.* Holme House Fm *supra*. Of the others, 1249–1323, 1250–1320 are Chest, 1398 *AddCh*, 1440, 1584 *Rental*, 1671 Sheaf, 1831 Bry.

(*a*) Back House Marsh (*v.* back, hūs, mersc); Bank Mdw; Fish Hill 1831 (*v.* fisc, hyll); Nine Butts (*v.* nigon, butte); Pool Slidge (*v.* pōl¹, slicche).

(*b*) *le Amery* 1440 (a messuage, 'the ambry, the store-house', *v.* almarie, cf. *ambry* NED. This building belonged to the abbot of Chester's grange at Ince); *Daynescroft* 1440 (*v.* croft); *le Ermettescroft* 1440 ('the hermit's croft' *v.* ermite, croft); *Lokwodes yorde* 1440 (from the surname of William *Lokwode* and geard); *Mundayeslonde, Monendaieslond* 1398, *Monendayes londes* 1440 ('Monday's selion(s)', *v.* Mōnandæg, land. In 1398 *AddCh* 36764 these are separate selions, 'Richard le King holds one—, Elena wife of William Hoggeson holds one—'. The significance of the day-name is not clear. It may derive from some system of strip-rotation in a town-field or of day-work obligation in the lord's demesne); *Lyardesbruch'* 1440, *Liardesbruche* 1584, ('Liard's broken-in land', from the ME pers.n. *Lyard* (OG *Liuthard*, Forssner 179) and bryce); *Mucle Dich'* 1249–1323 ('the great ditch', *v.* mycel, dīc); *Muchele Medwe* 1250–1320 (*v.* mycel, mǣd); *Pepper Street* 1584, *Peper Street* 1671 (cf. Pepper St. (Chester) 326 *infra*); *Smalreod* 1249–1323 ('the narrow reed-bed', *v.* smæl, hrēod).

xi. Thornton le Moors

The parish of Thornton contained the townships 1. Dunham on the Hill, 2. Elton, 3. Hapsford, 4. Thornton le Moors, 5. Wimbolds Trafford.

1. DUNHAM ON THE HILL (109–4772) ['dʌnəm]

Doneham 1086 DB, *Donam* 1265–91 Chest, *Donham* 1310 Cl, and twelve examples with variant spelling *Done-* to 1559 Pat

Dunham 1283 Ipm *et freq*, (-*Hall*) 1724 NotCestr

Stony Dunham 1327 Pat *et freq*, with variant spellings -*Don(e)ham*, *Stone-*, *Staune-*, *Stanie-*; (-*iuxta Manlegh*) 1381 Plea, (-*alias Dunham on the Hill*) 1616 ChRR

Dunham de Hill' 1344 *MinAcct*, -*super Montem*, -*on the Hill* 1534 Plea *et freq* with variants -*up(p)on-*, -*Hyll*, -*on the Mount*; *Donham on the Hill* 1559 Pat, *Dunham o' th' Hill* 1860 White

Stanry Dunham 1348 Orm², *Stanredonham* 1410 Sheaf, *Stanre Dunham* (lit. *Staure-*) 1424 Plea *et freq* ib, ChRR, (all lit. *Staure-*) to 1444, *Stanredunham* 1427, 1452 Orm², 1428 Bark, -*dinham* 1438 ib, *Stonrydon(e)ham* 1421 Sheaf

Stanredinham (lit. *Staure-*) 1438 Bark, cf. *Dynhams Hough* 265 *infra*

'Village on a hill', from **dūn** and **hām**, with **hyll**. The affix, from the outcropping rock of the hill on which the village stands, is **stān**, **stānig** 'a rock', 'stony' and the ME adj. **stanry** (cf. *stannery* NED (from 1440), *stanners* NED, and **stæner**), which also enters into *le Stanryhurst* 1390, 259 *infra*.

BARROW LANE FM, cf. *Barrow Street* (*Field*) 1843 *TA*, 'road to Barrow' 261 *infra*, *v.* **strǣt, lane.** CORNHILL FM. DUNHAM HEATH, 1842 OS, *v.* 264 *supra*. DUNHAMHILL FM, *v.* **hyll**, Dunham *supra*. HOB LANE, 1831 Bry, perhaps 'goblin lane', *v.* **hob.** HORN'S FM, *Brook House* 1831 Bry, cf. *Horns Croft* 1843 *TA*, and Horns Mill 236 *supra*, *v.* **brōc.** HORN'S MILL BRIDGE, cf. prec. MANLEY LANE, *v.* 246 *supra*. MORLEY BRIDGE (COTTAGE), a railway bridge, cf. Morley Hall 263 *infra*. MOSS HO, 1831 Bry, cf. *Dunham Mosse* 1671 Sheaf, *v.* **mos.** RAKE LANE, 1831 Bry, cf. *Rake hey field, Rake way field* 1843 *TA*, *v.* **rake, lane,** (ge)hæg, weg. SQUAREHOUSE FM. TOWN FM, cf. *Great & Little Townfield, Town Wood Field* 1843 *TA*, *v.* **toun.** WOOD-HOUSE, cf. *Dunham wode* 1347 *ChFor*, and *Big Wood*, (*Town*) *Wood Field* 1843 *TA*, *brode wode* 1584 *AD* (Barnes[1] 359), *v.* **wudu, hūs, brād.** YEWTREE FM.

FIELD-NAMES

The undated forms are 1843 *TA* 151. Of the others, 1353 is *ChFor*, 1831 Bry, and the rest *AD* taken from Barnes[1] 359–360.

(*a*) Ashway Butts (*v.* **butte**); Boars Yard (cf. *Bores Yord*(*e*) (lit. *Bozco-*, *Borco-*) 1589, *v.* **bār[2], geard**); Broad Looms (cf. *Brodelounde, -launde* (lit. *-lonnde, -lannde*) 1584, *v.* **brād, land, loom**); Brook Field Hey (*Brookfeilde* 1584, *v.* **brōc, feld**); Bunting; Chester Way Croft (*v.* **weg**, cf. Chester 325 *infra*); Clay Fd; Coombhill Fd (*v.* **cumb, hyll**); Crib Fd (*v.* **crib**); Crosshey(s) (*v.* **cros, (ge)hæg**); Freeze Hay Fd; Gorsey-, Gorsty Fds; Green Ends ('pieces of land at the end of a green', *v.* **grēne[2], ende[1]**); Hanger Hill Fd (*v.* Hungerhill *infra*); Hayes (*v.* **(ge)hæg**); Long Hedge (*v.* **hecg**); Little Highon (*v.* **lȳtel, hyrne**, cf. Heronbridge 326 *infra*); Humpy Lane 1831; Hungerhill, Hanger-, Hungerhill Fd (probably 'barren hill' from **hungor** and **hyll**, influenced by **hangra**); Huzza (Fd); Intake (*v.* **inntak**); Kedlock Mdw (*v.* **kedlock** 'the colewort, or the common charlock'); Long Lands; Long Butt(s); Man Mdw (cf. Dunham Mans Mdw 257 *infra*); Martins Low (*v.* **hlāw**); Mean Part ('common portion', *v.* **(ge)mǣne, part**); Micco Furlong (*Mykofurlonge* 1589, *Muchelefurlong* 14, 'big furlong', *v.* **mycel, mikill**, furlang); Moorfield; Mowing Moss; Muck Fd (v. muk); New Bridge; New Hey Fd (v. nīwe, (ge)hæg); Old Fd (v. ald); Ox Hey Fd (v. oxa, (ge)hæg); Parsons Hey Fd (v. persone, (ge)hæg); Pavement Croft & Hayes, -Heys (v. pavement, croft, (ge)hæg); Peck Mill Woodfield (cf. Peck Mill 220 supra); Pike Fd; Push Plough Fd (v. push-plough); Great & Little Rough (v. rūh); Sidney Fd (Sydenhale 14, 'broad nook', v. sīd, halh); Three Butts (v. þrēo, butte); Three Nooked Moss (v. three-nooked); Two Foot Moss; Under Towns (v. under, toun); Wallway Fd (cf. Wallewaye 257 infra); Whitefield (v. hwīt, feld); Wickett Hill (v. wiket); Wishins Fd; Withens Fd (v. wīðegn).

(b) le Decheleys 14 ('ditch clearings', v. dīc, lēah); Donehamlee 1353 (v. lēah, cf. Dunham supra); Godyfield 1589 (perhaps 'goldy field', from goldy 'golden', feld); Heuwte Troffe 1589 (Barnes[1] 359 suggests 'hollow where trees had been felled', v. hīewet, trog); le Koubut 14 (v. cū, butte); le Kulnegreue 14 ('wood at a kiln', v. cyln, grǣfe); Meite-, Meytefyeld 1589 ('boundary field', v. mete, feld); the pyktheudlonde 1589 ('the sharp-cornered headland', v. piked, hēafod-land); Surapelton 14 (perhaps 'orchard on sour ground' or a p.n. Appleton with the affix 'sour', v. sūr, æppel-tūn; but Professor Löfvenberg (who compares Swed surapel, suräppelträd 'a crabtree') justly thinks this p.n. a compound of Surapel 'sour apple-tree (i.e. crab-tree)' and tūn. An OE cpd. sūr-æppel 'crab-tree', beside the OE adj.+ noun groups sūr apuldor 'crab-tree', sūr æppel 'crab apple', is suggested by the early forms of Appledore D 547 (Surapla DB, Surapple 1173–5 (1329), Sureapeldor 1242), v. sūr EPN 2 169, æppel EPN 1 3).

2. ELTON (GREEN & HALL) (109–4575)

Eltone 1086 DB, -tona e13 Chest, (-iuxta Petram) l13 ib, Elton e13 Chest, 1281 Court et freq, (-iuxta Ines, -Ynes, etc., as for Ince 251 supra) 1308 Cl, 1311 Plea et freq to 1497 ChRR, (-in the forest of Mara) 1343 Plea, Elton Hall 1671 Sheaf, -Green 1831 Bry, Helton 1307 Eyre, 1324 Chol (p)

Eldon 1356 BPR

Ealton c.1617 Sheaf

Elcton (Hall) 1742 NotCestr

'Eel-farm, farm where eels are got', from ēl[2] and tūn, with hall and grēne[2]. Elton lies next to Ince 251 supra on the low peninsula between the marshes of R. Gowy and R. Mersey. Elton 2 258, on R. Wheelock, has the same derivation. The invariable El-, rather than Elle-, in the spellings argues against the OE pers.n. Ella which DEPN proposes, whereas Ekwall's suggestion of 'eel-farm' for Elton Du, could well be accepted for the Ch Eltons, since both are places where eels might be taken. The addition -iuxta Petram alludes to Rock Fm infra.

CRYERS BRIDGE, *v.* 258 *infra.*   GREENBANK FM.   ELTON MARSH (lost), 1841 *TA*, *Eltonmos* 1292–1308 Chest, 1358 *ChFor*, *mariscum* l13 Chest, *Eltonmerssh* 1348 BPR, *mossetum de Elton* 1357 *ChFor*, *Eltonmosse* 1357 ChRR, 1360 Chamb, -*Moss* 1358 ChRR, *Elton Marsh* 17 Sheaf, cf. *Marsh Lane* 1831 Bry, *Top & Upper Marsh* 1841 *TA*, *v.* mos, mersc, cf. Frodsham Marsh 223 *supra.*   POOL LANE, 1841 *TA.*   ROCK FM (109–458755), cf. highway between Ince and Elton *iuxta Petram* l13 Chest, *Stanewaye* l13 ib, 'the road past a rock', *v.* stān, weg, rokke. The lost f.n. *Roggedelond infra*, may belong here. The road referred to is at 109–453760 to 460753.   SOUTH BANK.

FIELD-NAMES

The undated forms are 1841 *TA* 163. Of the others 1354, 1375 are *Eyre*, 1638 Mere, 1842 OS, and the rest Chest.

(*a*) Abbat(t)s Hay (*v.* (ge)hæg). The abbey of Chester held land in Elton); Ash Fd (*Aysefeld* c.1300, *Assefeld* c.1306, *v.* æsc, feld); Bare Fd; Bithoms (*campus qui dicitur Bothum* l13, 'the hollow(s)', *v.* bo̅m, by̅me); Broad Hay; Brosters Croft (1638, from the surname *Broster*); Cow Hay; Cunney (*v.* coningre); Fair Acre (*v.* fæger) Gorsty Hay (*v.* gorstig, (ge)hæg); Green Hay; Hapsford Moor 1842 (*v.* 257 *infra*); Hay Bay Heath; Heath Part (*Heath* 1842, *v.* hǣð, part); Heifer Long ('high furlong', *v.* heah, furlang, cf. Heifer Long(s) 257 *infra*); Hurst (*v.* hyrst); Intacke (*v.* inntak); Long Looms (*v.* loom); The Lunt (*v.* land); Marled Hays; Meer Fd (*v.* (ge)mǣre); Mill Hatch (*v.* myln, hæc(c)); Moat Fd (*v.* mote); Moor Hill (*Morhul* l13, cf. *Morfeld, -felt* l13, *v.* mor¹, hyll, feld); Nook Heath; Oakley(s) Hay; Ox Hay (*v.* oxa, (ge)hæg); Pingot (*v.* pingot); Roudish Hay ('rough enclosure', *v.* ruh, edisc); Shoe Bridge (*v.* sceo, brycg); Sour Looms (*v.* sur, loom, cf. Long Looms *supra*); Wheel Mdw & Way (*v.* hweol 'winding, curved', weg); White Fd (*Wyt-, Witfeld* 13, l13, *v.* hwit, feld); Wood Hay (*v,* (ge)hæg).

(*b*) *Brodelond* c.1306 (*v.* brād, land); *campus qui vocatur Brom* l13 ('broom field', *v.* brōm); meadow called *Bromihurst* 1354 ('broomy hill', *v.* brōmig, hyrst); *Crabbefurlong, Crabbelond* c.1300 ('crab-tree furlong and selion', *v.* crabbe, furlang, land); *Crowegraue, Crougreflont* l13 ('(selion at) crow wood', *v.* crāwe, grǣfe, land); *Dritegrauelond* c.1300 ('(selion at) the dirty wood', *v.* drit, grǣfe, land); *campus qui vocatur Egmundesheued* m13, *Egesmonde-sheued* c.1268–95 (17), *Egmundisheuede* c.1268–95 ('Ecgmund's hill', from the OE pers.n. *Ecgmund* and heafod); *Flahelond, Flaylont, Flayelond* l13 ('selion where turves are cut', *v.* land. The first el. is OE *flægen, flagen* 'flayed', pa. part. of OE *flean*, 'to flay', not recorded until 1634 NED in the sense 'to strip ground of turf'); *le Hoklone* l13 ('lane at a hook of land', *v.* hōc, lane); (*le*) *Longethorn* 13, l13 ('tall thorn-tree', *v.* lang, þorn); *Rogge-delond* l13 (this may be 'head-land at the rock', from rokke and heafod-land, cf. Rock Fm *supra*, but Professor Löfvenberg suggests this p.n. may contain an early instance of the adj. *rugged* in the sense 'broken, uneven' (1656 NED). ME *rogged* 'hairy' is recorded c.1330 NED. *Roggedelond* could mean 'broken, rough land', 'rugged selion', or figuratively, 'grassy selion', where *rogged* 'hairy' has some sense similar to feax 'hair; rough grass' EPN 1 166); *Seuenlond* 1268–95, *Seuenelondes* 13 ('seven selions', *v.* seofon, land); *Spertes Deynes* 1r3 ('hollows with springs', *v.* spyrt, denu); *Stubbes* 1375 (p) (*v.* stubb); *Wallewaye, Welle* c.1300 ('(way to) a well, a spring', *v.* wella, wælla, weg, cf. Wallway Fd 255 *supra*).

3. HAPSFORD (HALL) (109–4774)

> *Happesford* 1216–72 Orm² (p), 1302 Plea *et freq* with variant
> spellings *Hapes-* (13 Chest to 1365 Plea), *Hap(p)is-, -ys-, -us-,*
> *Apes-, Appis-, -forde* to *Happesford* 1641 Orm²
> *Heppysford* 13 AD (A 204, Barnes¹ dates it 14)
> *Apeford* 1316 ChRR, *Happeford* 1357 BPR
> *Harpesford* 1317 ChRR (p), and eighteen examples ib, *Eyre*, Plea
> with variant spellings *-forde, Harps-* to *Harpsford* 1671 Sheaf
> *Hape(s)feld* 1347 ChFor
> *Hapsford* 1348 ChFor (Barnes¹ 371), 1357 *ChQW* (loc. cit.), 1510
> ArlB, (*-Hall*) 1724 NotCestr, *Happsford* 1673 Mere
> *Hoppesford* 1384 AD
> *Heapsford* 1612 Orm²

'Hæp's ford', from an OE pers.n. *Hæp* and ford, cf. DEPN.

COMMON LANE, 1831 Bry.   HAPSFORD MOOR (lost), 1842 OS, *Hapesfordmerssh* 1348 BPR, *Hapesford mor* 1353 *ChFor, Hapsmore More* 17 Sheaf, *Harl.* 2079, cf. *Moor Lane* 1831 Bry, *v.* mersc, mōr¹, cf. Frodsham Marsh 223 *supra*.   MANOR FM, *v.* maner.   MERSEYBANK FM.   RAKE LANE, 1831 Bry, the boundary of Dunham, *v.* 254 *supra*.

FIELD-NAMES

The undated forms are 1838 *TA* 189. Of the others, 1407 is Bark, 1612 Orm².

(*a*) Backside (*v.* ba(c)ksyde); Bing (*v.* bing); Brick Kiln Common; Bridge Hays (*v.* (ge)hæg); Cash Fd; Dole (*v.* dāl); Dunham Mans Mdw (cf. Mans Mdw 254 *supra*); Elton Fd (cf. Elton 255 *supra*); Grimes Head; Hair Butts (*Harebuttes* 1407, *v.* hara, butte); Heath; Heifer Long(s) (cf. Heifer Long 256 *supra*); Hipping Stone Croft (*v.* hipping-stone 'a stepping-stone'); Middle-& Rough Horn (probably from hyrne or horna, but the surname *Horn(e)* is possible, cf. foll.); Horn Mill (*v.* Horn's Mill 236 *supra*); Kiln Croft; Long Acre; Milking Bank (*v.* milking); Moss Croft; New Hay (*v.* (ge)hæg); Old Fd; Oxen Doles (*v.* oxa, dāl); Peck Mill Stile (*v.* stigel, cf. Peck Mill 220

17

supra); Rush Hay (*v.* risc, (ge)hæg); Salt (Nook) Mdw (*v.* salt, nōk, mǣd); Snipe Lakes (*v.* snype, lacu); Town Mdw; Triangle; Wheat Hay (*v.* hwǣte, (ge)hæg); Under & Upper Yard (*v.* geard).

(*b*) *Carteresgreves* 1407 ('carter's woods', *v.* cartere, grǣfe); *Coumedewes* 1407 (*v.* cū, mǣd); *the parke leyes closse* 1612 ('(close at) the park pastures' *v.* park, lēah, clos); *Rouredyng* 1407 ('rough cleared-land', *v.* rūh, ryding).

4. Thornton le Moors (109–4474)

Torentune 1086 DB, *Thorent'* 13 Bun
Torinton' 1198–1216 Facs, MidCh, Dieul, 1272 Tab, *Thorinth'*, *Thorint(h)ona* c.1215 CoLegh, *Thorinton* 1260 Court (p), *-yn-* 1279 AddCh
Thorneton e13 Orm², Whall, 1260 Court *et freq* with variant spelling *-tun* to 1620 Sheaf, (*-le Mores*) 1291 Orm², (*-in le Moore*) 1299 ib, (*-in the Moors*) 1477 ChRR, (*-in the More*) 1553 Pat, (*-super* (*le*) *More, -Moor*) 1429 Plea, 1474, 1519 ChRR, (*-super* (*le*) *moras*) 1477 Orm², 1598 ChRR
Thornton e13, 1272 (17), 1284 Chest, 1289 Court *et freq* with variant spellings *-tona, -tone, -toun*; (*-on the Moor, -More*) 1299 Plea, 1391 Pat, (*-super Moram*) 1302 Cl, (*-super le More*) 1430 ChRR, (*-(up)on the Mores, -Moors*) 1439 Sheaf, 1591 ChRR, 1742 NotCestr, (*-iuxta Moram*) 1347 ChFor, (*-in the Moors*) 1730 Sheaf, 1842 OS, (*-le Moors*) 1831 Bry
Thurneton 1280 Ipm (p)
Thorton 1309 Misc (p), *-tun* 1314 Chol (p)

'Thorn-tree farm', from þorn and tūn, with in, on, le and mōr[1]. Thornton is beside the marshes of R. Gowy, cf. *The Moors infra*. It was a detached part of *Dudestan* hundred in DB.

Thornton Mill (109–439757), 1831 Bry, (*terra de la Holm iuxta*) *molendina de Ynes* 1265–91 Chest, *molendinum aquaticum super Inesmerssh*, (*-in Inssemersh*), *in tristera inter forestam de Wirhale et forestam de la Mare* 1357 ChFor, *molendinum aquaticum de Ince, le milnehous* 1440 Rental, *v.* myln, hūs, cf. Ince, Holme Ho 251, 251 *supra*. The *tristera* (*v.* trystor) appears to have been a hunting station common to both the forests.

Church Fm, cf. *Church Lane Field* 1841 *TA*, *v.* cirice, lane.   Cross Ho, 1831 Bry, *v.* cros, hūs.   Cryers Bridge, *Thornton Bridge* 1831 ib, *v.* brycg, identified ChetNS LXXXII 893 as *Fulford* 1284 Chest, 'dirty ford', *v.* fūl, ford, cf. foll.   Cryers Fm, *Criers House* 1831 Bry, cf. *Cryers Field* 1841 *TA*, from the surname *Cryer*.   Hob

LANE, 1831 Bry, v. 260 infra. THE MOORS (lost), 1842 OS, *Thorntonmore* 1353 *ChFor*, *le more uersus dominium de Frodsham*, *le Westmor* 1390 *CoLegh*, cf. *Moor Field* 1841 *TA*, v. mōr¹. *Westmor* was on the west side of the township, v. **west**. THORNTON BROOK (R. Gowy), 1842 OS, *Thornton Mill Stream* 1831 Bry, cf. Thornton Mill *supra*. THORNTON GREEN, *le Thorneton pasture alias Thorneton Grene* 1473 *CoLegh*, *Green House*, *The Green* 1842 OS, v. **pasture**, grēne². THORNTON HALL, 1831 Bry, cf. *situs manerii: quedam magna camerar' que est capitale messuagium cum quadam magna coquina* 1390 *CoLegh*. The site of the ancient hall remained in 1819, Orm² II 19.

FIELD-NAMES

The undated forms are 1841 *TA* 391. Of the rest, 1314–19 is *AddCh*, 1353 *ChFor*, 1390, 1473 *CoLegh*, 1831 Bry.

(a) Bear Fd ('bare field', v. bær¹); Berks Mdw (perhaps from birki 'birch-copse'); Black Butts (v. blæc, butte); Broad Lane Fd; Brook Wall Fd (v. brōc, wælla); Calves Croft; Coarse Way Fd ('field at a causeway', v. caucie); Goldings Hay; Hawks (v. halc); Hay Mdw (*le haymedo* 1473, cf. *le heymore* 1390, v. hēg, mǣd, mōr¹); Heath Fd (cf. *bruerium de Thornton* 1353, v. hǣð); Holme Fd (v. holmr); House Fd; Lordsfield, Lords Mdw (v. hlāford); Marled Fd; Mill Hill; New Hay (*Neuhagh* 1390, v. nīwe, haga); North Hill (*North Hill Lane* 1831); Old Mans Mdw; The Outlet (v. outlet); Ox Hay Bank (*le Oxheye* 1390, v. oxa, (ge)hæg); Pavement Hay (v. pavement, (ge)hæg); Pushed Plowed Mdw (v. push-plough); Riddings (v. ryding); Rough Acre; School Croft (probably part of an endowment, v. scōl); Shargreaves Hay; Thistley Green; Uncles Croft & Fd; Wall Fd (cf. *Huchecokewallefeld* 1390, from the ME pers.n. *Hichecok* (ModE *Hitchcock*) v. wælla, feld); Wood (Feild).

(b) *Benet(t)eshey(e)* 1390 ('Benet's fenced-in enclosure', from the ME pers.n. *Benet* and (ge)hæg. One *Benet*, or *Benedict*, de Salesbury was tenant in Thornton 1390); *Brodelondesende* 1314–19 ('(the end of) the broad selion', v. brād, land, ende¹); *Damesmedowe* 1390 ('lady's meadow', from ME (OFr) *dame* and mǣd); *le Fyuebuttes* 1390 (v. fīf, butte); *le greues* 1390 (v. grǣfe); a selion called *Houshald* 1314–19 (cf. *household* NED (from 1382). Here the significance is probably domestic, i.e. the land was appurtenant to the tenure of a particular house, or the maintenance of its inmates); *le lake* 1390 ('the watercourse', v. lacu); *le legh* 1390 (v. lēah); *lille hurste* 1390 (v. lytel, hyrst); *le New(e)-*, *le Neufeld(medowe)*, *le Newemedo*, *le Newerudmedowe* 1390 ('(meadow at) the new field', 'new meadow', '(meadow at) newly cleared land', v. nīwe, feld, mǣd, (ge)rydd); *le Persones hey* 1390 ('the parson's enclosure', v. persone, (ge)hæg); *le Polemedo* 1473 ('meadow at a pool', v. pōl¹, mǣd); *le Pyke* 1314–19 ('pointed hill', or 'field with a point', v. pīc¹); *le Shepcote* 1390 ('sheep shed', v. scēp, cot); *le Stanryhurst* 1390 ('stony wooded-hill', v. stanry, hyrst); *Tiffele Walle* 1390 (perhaps 'spring at (thorn-)bush glade', from þefel or þȳfel and lēah, with wælla); *le Wildrudyng* 1390 ('wild cleared-land', v. wilde, ryding).

5. WIMBOLDS TRAFFORD (109–4572) ['wimbɔ:lz, 'wimbḷz], *Troford* 1086 DB f.263b, *Wynebaldestrohcford* 13 Bun, and thereafter with variant spellings as for Mickle Trafford 326 *infra*, and *Wine-*, *Wyn(e)bald(e)s-, -is-* 13, 1295 Bun, 1272 Tab, 1388 Sheaf, *Wambaldes-* 13 Bun- Wimbaldes- 1288 ChFor, *Wymbaldes-* 1303 Chamb *et freq* with variant spellings *-bald(us)-* to 1514 ChEx, *Wynebales-* 1297 Court, *Wymboldes-* 1351, 1513 ChRR, 1514 ChEx, 1600 Sheaf, *Wymballes-* 1397 ChRR, *-is-* 1516 Mere, *Wymble-* 1533 Bun, 1535 Plea, 1626 Orm², *Wimble-* 1690 Sheaf, *Wymbold-* 1534 Plea, *Wynbalde-* 1539 Sheaf, *Wymbald-* 1589 ChRR, *Wimbles-* 1614 ib, 1662, 1671 Sheaf, *Wymbles-* 1626 Orm² (lit. *Wybles-*), *Wymboles-* 1624 ChRR, *Wimbolds-* 1819 Orm², 1842 OS. This is 'Winebald's part of Trafford', cf. Bridge Trafford, Mickle Trafford 261, 326 *infra*. The manorial affix is the gen.sg. of a pers.n., the rarely recorded OE *Winebald*, or the better evidenced OE *Wynbald*, or OG *Winebald* which would be the name of *Wynebaud* the sheriff mentioned 1121–c.1150 Chest after whom DEPN suggests this place was named.

FIELD FM.   HALL FM, cf. Wimbolds Trafford Hall *infra*. HEATH FM, *Thornton Heath* 1671 Sheaf, *Trafford Heath* 1831 Bry, v. hǣð.   HOB LANE (FM), 1831 ib, *Hob Lane* 1671 Sheaf, 'goblin lane', v. hob, lane.   MANOR FM   PARK FM, cf. *Park* 1834 TA. THE ROOKERY   SPRING FM, v. spring 'a spring'.   WIMBOLDS TRAFFORD HALL, 1831 Bry, *Trafford Hall* 1724 NotCestr.   WOOD FM, *Manor House* 1831 Bry.

FIELD-NAMES

The undated forms are 1834 *TA* 436. Of the others 13, 1295, 1322 are *Bun*, 1303, 1304 Chamb, 1831 Bry, 1842 OS.

(a) Bare Fd (v. bǣr¹); Broad Grove (v. grāf); Cart House Fd; Common Fd & Piece; Hallbrooke Flat (probably 'flat of land by a brook, belonging to a hall', from brōc and flat, with hall); Hall Greens (cf. *Hall Green Lane* 1831 Bry, *campus qui vocatur le Grenis* 1295, 'green places belonging to the hall', from grēne, with hall); Hurst (v. hyrst); Intake (v. inntak); Midding Street 1842 ('dirty street of houses', v. midding, strǣt); Moor Fd; Mouse Flatt (v. mūs, flat); New Heath; Pockets (v. poket); Quillet (v. quillet(t)); Sand Fd; Shaking Bridge 1831 (109–435725, crossing R. Gowy into Wervin, cf. Shakingbridge Mdw 326 *infra*, v. schakynge. Bryant puts this area in

Wimbolds Trafford); Shoulder of Mutton (*v.* 325 *infra*); Steefy Croft, Steefy (Lane) Mdw (*Steefy Lane* 1831, perhaps from dial. *stife, stif(e)y* 'suffocating, close, dusty (of an atmosphere)'); Town Fd; Waves; White Fd.

(*b*) *le Mulnemor* 1303, 1304 ('marsh at a mill', *v.* myln, mōr¹); *Quechul* 13 ('hill with a thicket', *v.* queche, hyll); *le Wallegreue* 1322 ('wood at a spring', *v.* wælla, grǣfe).

xii. Plemstall

One township of this parish lay in Eddisbury Hundred. The rest is in Broxton Hundred, *v.* 326 *infra*.

1. BRIDGE TRAFFORD (109–450710), *Trosford* 1086 DB f.263, *Bregetrouford* 13 *Bun*, thereafter with variant spellings as for Mickle Trafford 326 *infra* and *Brugge-* 1307–24 *Chol et freq* to 1493 Orm², *Brugges-* 1438 Plea, 1479 ChRR, *Bryge-* 1439 Sheaf, *Brigge-* 1535 VE, 1547 Pat, *Bruge-* 1539–47 Dugd, *Bridg-* 1546 ib, 1596 ChRR, (*Trafford alias-*) 1671 Sheaf, 1690 ib, *Bridge-* 1553 Pat *et freq*, *Brige-* 1562 Orm², 'the part of Trafford at the bridge', *v.* brycg, cf. foll. and Mickle Trafford 326 *infra*.

TRAFFORD BRIDGE (109–449710), *pons de Trofford* 1267–8 Chest, *the bridge at Troghford* 1391 ChRR, *pons de Troghford* 1410 ib, *pons de Troghford-Magna* 1454 ib, *v.* brycg, cf. prec. and Mickle Trafford 326 *infra*. The bridge crosses R. Gowy.

TRAFFORD HALL, 1671 Sheaf, *Bridge-Trafford Hall* 1724 NotCestr, cf. *the site of the manor of Trofford* 1304 Chamb, *v.* hall.

FIELD-NAMES

The undated forms are 1838 *TA* 71.

(*a*) Bridge Mdw; Cross Hay-, -Hey Looms (*v.* cros 'a cross', (ge)hæg, loom); The Flat (*v.* flat); The Hankerchief (*v.* 325 *infra*); Long Looms (*v.* loom); Moore-Lane Causeway 1693 Sheaf (*v.* mōr¹, lane, caucie); Morley Fd & Mdw (*v.* Morley Hall 263 *infra*); Moss Fd; Pocket Fd (*v.* poket); Sweet Nooks; Town Fld; Whitefield; Woodfield.

xiii. Barrow

GREAT & LITTLE BARROW (109–469684 and 470700) [ˈbarə]

Barue 958 (13) BCS 1041, KCD 473, (14) Chest, e13 Whall, (*Magna-, Parva-*) 1294 ChF, *Barua* e12 (17) Orm² (p), *Barwe* 1181–1232 Chest *et freq* with variant spellings *Barwa, Baruue* to

1445 ChRR (p), (*Parva-*) c.1200 *Chol*, (*Littel-*) 1332 *ib*, (*Luttel-*)
1333 Fine, (*Lytel-*) 1342 *Chol*, (*Litel-*) 1379 Pat, (*Lyttel-*) 1398
Chol, (*Magna-*) 1294 Misc, (*Mangna-*) 1324 *Chol*, (*Muke-*) 1389
Orm², (*Grande-*) 1390 *Chol*, (*Great-*) 1391 ChRR, (*Mykel-*) 1398
Chol, (*Mycul-*) 1420–50 *ib*

Bero 1086 DB

Barou 1154–60 (1329) Ch, *Baroue* 1208–29 Whall (p), *Barowe* 1318
ChRR *et freq* with variant spellings *Barow, Baro(o)* to 1555
Chol, (*Grant-, Petit-*) 1326 *ib*, (*Parva-*) 1369 *ib*, (*Lytill-*) 1397
ib, (*Magna-*) 1440 Plea, (*Great-, Little-*) 1527 ChRR, (*Mykell-*)
1555 *Chol*

Barewa 1202–17 *Chol*, *Barewe* 1208–29 Dieul, 1272–90 *ChFor*,
1282 CRV *et freq* to 1379 Pat, (*Magna-, Parva-*) 1296 *Chol*,
(*Littel-*) 1331 Cl, (*Luttel-*) 1333 Fine, (*Lytel-*) 1340 *Chol*,
(*Mukel-*) 1357 *ChFor*

Barrowe 1226 Whall (p), *Barrow* 1386 ChRR *et freq* with variant
spelling *Barro*; (*Mycul-, Lytul-*) 1420–50 *Chol*, (*Magna-, Parva-*)
1527 ChRR, (*Micle-*) 1534 *Chol*, (*Mich-*) 1534 (1666) Orm²,
(*Greate-, Lyttell-*) 1554 *Chol*, (*Little-*) 1668 *ib*, (*Great-*) 1724
NotCestr, (*Little*) *Barrow Green* 1700 *Chol*

Baruwe c.1260 *Chol*, 1295 Cl (p), (*Parva-*) c.1260 *Chol*, (*Magna-*)
c.1280 *ib*

Barawe 1294 Misc (p)

Parva Baruse 1302 Plea

Browe 1512 *Chol*

Over Barrough 1664 Sheaf

Berrow 1687 Sheaf

'The wood', *v.* **bearu**. The two hamlets, distinguished as Great &
Little, *v.* **magna, parva, micel, lỹtel, grand, petit**, represent distinct
manors. (*Little*) *Barrow Green* is from **grēne²** 'a green, a village
green'.

BARROW MILL (109–475683), 1831 Bry, *molendinum de Barou* 1154–60
(1329) Ch, -*Barowe* 1442 *Chol*, *Watercorn Mill called Barow-Mill* 1710
ib, cf. *Mill Croft(s), Field, Hay, Meadow & Moor* 1838 *TA*, *Milne
Hey* 1700 *Chol*, and Milton Brook *infra*, *v.* **myln**.

BROOM HILL, BROOMHILL (FM, HO, LANE & ORCHARD FM), (109–
475697), *Bromhull* c.1270 *Chol*, *Bromehull* 1393 *Surv*, *Brom(e)hill*
1512, 1560 *Chol*, *Bromhyll* 1564 *ib*, *Broomhill* 1598 Orm², *Broome-*

1610 Sheaf, *Broom(e)hill Rough* 1686, 1752 *Chol, Broom Hill, Broomhill House* 1831 Bry, *Bromehall* 1700 *Chol, Browne Hill* 16 Orm², 'broom hill', from brōm and hyll, *v.* rūh, hūs, lane, orceard. Here were *the Lower House Browne Hill estate* 16 (19) Orm², *the lower howse* 1615 *Chol* and *New House* 1831 Bry. Broomhill also gave name to part of Salters Brook² **1** 34.

HOLLOWMOOR HEATH (109–480687), 1842 OS, *Horymore* 1390 *Chol*, 1393 *Surv*, c.1400, 1443 *Chol, the hollyne moore meadow* 1615 *ib*, *Hollimore Heath* 1638 Sheaf, 1777 *Chol, Hallamoreheath* 1652, 1752 *ib*, *Hallo-* 1667 *ib*, *Hallow-* 1790 *ib*, *Halli-* 1676 *ib*, *Hali-* 1724 *ib*, *Hally-* 1731 *ib*, *Halemore Heath* 1774 *ib*, *Hallum Moor Heath* 1831 Bry, 'dirty marsh', *v.* horig, mōr¹, hǣð.

THE HOUGH (109–466700) [þə ˡhuf], *le Hoyh* c.1300, *le Hogheshed* 1342, *boscus del Hogh*' 1357, *le Hogh* 1364, *le Hoghwalle* 1369 all *Chol, Hughe House* 1610 Sheaf, *Hough House* 1671 *ib*, 1842 OS, *the Houghfeild* 1693 *Chol, Hough* 1724 NotCestr, *Houghhouse Farm* 1774 *Chol, Houghs Head* 1831 Bry, 'the end of a hill', *v.* hōh, hēafod, wælla 'a spring', hūs, and feld.

MILTON BROOK (BRIDGE & LODGE) (109–464679), *Milton Brook* (*House*) 1831 Bry, 1842 OS, cf. *Miltons Croft & Wood* 1838 *TA*, *Milstone Croft* 1747 *Chol, v.* brōc, brycg, loge, hūs, croft, wudu. These names derive from *Mulneton iuxta Barwe* 1353 *Indict, Mulneton* 1393 *Surv*, 'the mill hamlet', *v.* myln, tūn, probably at Barrow Mill *supra* from which the stream runs to R. Gowy, and which was probably established by John, Constable of Chester 1178–90, cf. *molendinum...et alter molendinum quod pater meus Johannes postea fecit in aggere eiusdem Barwe* 1190–1211 *Cott.* Nero C III, f.174.

MORLEY HALL (109–461709), 1690 Sheaf, *Morley* 1393 *ib*, (pasture called-) 1442 *Chol*, (farm place or capital messuage called-) 1590 *ib*, *Morley House* 1831 Bry, 1842 OS, *Morlay* 1724 NotCestr, *Maudley Hall* 1671 Sheaf, cf. *Morley Lane* 1796 *ib*, and *Morley Meadow* 1838 *TA, Moreles Meadowes & Heys* 1590 *Chol*, 'marsh clearing', *v.* mōr¹, lēah, with hūs, hall, lane, mǣd and (ge)hæg.

PARK FM & HALL (109–482682), *Park Hall* 1724 NotCestr, *the-*, or *Parker's tenement* 1766 *Chol*, named from *parcum de Barwe* 1253 Cl, *-Barowe* 1442 *Chol, v.* park, hall, (ge)hæg, mǣd. This was 'Hugh Despencer's park in his manor of Barewe' 1297 AD, a.1321 MRA 225.

SEINT PLEYMONDES WELL (lost), *fons vocata-* 1302 Plea (DKR XXVI 52, and Orm² II 339), 'well of the holy man Plegmund', *v.* wella, cf. Plemstall 326 *infra*. This well was in the manor of Little Barrow, presumably east of R. Gowy opposite Plemstall; but local tradition gives the name *St. Plegmund's Well* to a spring near Plemstall church, and the manorial interest may not have been territorial.

SWINFORD HO & -MILL FM (109–484698), (*molendinum de*) *Swyneford in Barue* 1208–29 Whall, Orm², (a watermill commonly called) *Swynford Mill* c.1400 *Chol*, (a heath called) *Swynford hethe* 1446 *ib*, *Swinford Mill* 1831 Bry, 'swine ford', *v.* swīn¹, ford, with myln, hǣð and hūs.

BACK BROOK, *v.* back, brōc, a flood-drain parallel to Barrow Brook. BARNHOUSE (LANE), *Barn House* 1831 Bry, *Barn Farm* 1860 White, cf. *gardinum domini coram hostio grangie* 1296 *Chol*, *v.* bere-ærn, hūs.   BARROW BROOK² (R. Gowy), *Lome Green Brook* 1671 Sheaf, *Ashton Brook* 1831 Bry, cf. *le Hee infra*, Long Green *infra*, Ashton Brook 1 14.   BARROW HALL, *the Hall in Great Barrow* 1685 *Chol*, *v.* hall. It is reported in 1272–90 *ChFor* that 'at Barewe a manorhouse (*unum manerium*) and several houses have been erected by Hugh Despencer's steward', cf. foll.   LITTLE BARROW HALL, 1831 Bry, *Aula* 1325 *Chol* (p), *v.* hall, cf. prec.   BARROW HILL, 1693 *Chol, Barrowhill Roughe* 1686 *ib*, cf. *Hill Lane* 1831 Bry, *v.* hyll, rūh. BARROW LODGE.   BARROWMORE FM, GORSE & HALL, cf. *the Greate-, the Little Mo(o)re* 1610 Sheaf, *Little-, Long- & Middle Moor Meadow* 1774 *Chol*, *v.* mōr¹.   FERMA LANE, *Ferny Lane Meadow* 1782, 1785 *Chol, Furmy Lane* 1831 Bry, 'ferny lane', *v.* fearnig, lane. GREENHEY LANE, cf. *the Green(e) Hey* 1685, 1719 *Chol*, *v.* grēne¹, (ge)hæg.   GREYSFIELD, cf. *Greys Croft & Moor* 1838 *TA, Grayes Mare* 1698, 1704 *Bun*, from the surname *Grey, Gray* and mere¹, mōr¹.   HOLLINSGREEN, *Hollin Green* 1831 Bry, *Hollin(s)-* 1838 *TA*, 'holly-tree(s) green', *v.* holegn, grēne².   IRONS LANE, 1831 Bry, *v.* hyrne, lane,⸗ cf. Heronbridge 326 *infra*.   LONG GREEN (HALL), (109–479702), (*the*) *Longe Greene* 1610 Sheaf, 1658 *Chol, Lome Green* 1671 Sheaf, *Long Green* 1693 *Chol*, *v.* lang, grēne². MANLEY LANE, *v.* 246 *supra*.   MANOR HO.   NEWHOUSE FM. NORTON'S LANE (109–503704 to 480718), 1831 Bry, probably named after Norton Priory (2 173) which had an estate in Barrow from 1190–1211 *Cott*. Nero C III, Dudg VI 314, to 1536 Dugd.   OAKLAND

COTTAGES, cf. *High Ooke lande* 1497 *Chol*, 'selion at a tall oak', *v.* hēah, āc, land. OLD FM. STAMFORD BRIDGE, *v.* 326 *infra*. 'WATLING STREET', *v.* 1 40 (route VII). WILDMOOR LANE, cf. *Wyldemore* 1442 *Chol*, *Wild Moores alias Allen's Moores* 1752 *ib*, *Wild Moors* 1831 Bry, 'desolate marsh', *v.* wilde, mōr¹. *Allen* is a surname.

FIELD-NAMES

The undated forms are 1838 *TA* 37. Of the others, 1208–29 is Whall, e13 (17) Orm², 1296², 1347 *ChFor*, 14 AD (Barnes¹ 359), 1360 BPR, 1389, 1437 ChRR, 1393 *Surv*, 1440 *Rental*, 1610, 1663 Sheaf, 1831 Bry, and the rest *Chol*.

(a) Abbots Croft (*v.* abbat, cf. Norton's Lane *supra*); Ague Hay; Banford Croft, Fd, Lane & Mdw (*Bamford* 1208–29, e13 (17), 1360 (p), *Baumford* 1437 ChRR, 'ford with a beam or tree', *v.* bēam, ford. The tree was either used as a footbridge or as a marker of the ford's position, cf. Bamford Db 39, La 54, and Beam Bridge 153 *supra*); Banks (cf. *le Lytill Banke* 1512, *v.* lȳtel, banke); Barley Fd (cf. *the barlie crofte* 1615, *v.* bærlic, croft); Batteridge Green 1704, 1754 (from the surname *Bettrich* 1574 *Chol* and grēne²); Bean Wd; Beckey; Bottoms (*v.* botm); Broad Acre Fd (*bradeacr'* 1393, *Higher-* & *Lower Broadacres* 1719, 1729, *v.* brād, æcer); Brook Croft & Fd (cf. *the brookesyde* 1615 and Barrow Brook *supra*, *v.* sīde); Butchers Hay (*v.* bocher, (ge)hæg); Butter Fd (*v.* butere); Big Butts (cf. *le Longebuttes* c.1260, *v.* lang, butte); Butty Mdw 1774 (*v.* butty); Chapel Wd (*Hy-*, *Higher* & *Lower Chap(p)el(l) Wood* 1700, 1745, 1759, *v.* chapel, wudu); Church Croft, Fd & Mdw; Cop(p)y (*the Koppy* 1702, *the Coppy* 1745, *v.* copis); Cordow Mdw (*Cardow Meadow* 1765, 'marsh allotment', *v.* kjarr, dāl); Cornell Mdw 1719 (*Cornel-* 1710); Cote Croft (*v.* cot); Crab Tree Loonts (*v.* crabbe, trēow, land); Cri(b)b (*the Cribb* 1695, 1719, 1752, *v.* crib); Croft (cf. *Crofts* 1700, *v.* croft); Cross Ways (cf. *lez Cros Hallandes* 1497, *v.* cros 'lying across, athwart', hēafod-land); Crow Gutter (*v.* crāwe, goter); Day Croft (*v.* dey); Four-, Six- & Nine Day Math (*the nine dayes mathe* 1610, *the Four-* & *the Six Day Math* 1783, *v.* day-math); Deacons Wd (cf. *Dyconscroft iuxta Stanford* 1440, from the ME pers.n. *Dicun, -on* (from *Dick* for *Richard*) and croft, cf. Stamford Bridge *supra*); Dig Lake ('ditch stream', *v.* dīc, lacu); Little Dowl (*the Dowlas* 1610, *v.* dāl); Down Suits (*Dounshuttes* (*meadow*) 1610, 'corners of land on a hill', *v.* dūn, scēat); Dranhams Moor (*Dranham Moor* 1784, *v.* mōr¹); Dry Mdw (*v.* drȳge); Dunham Clough 1729, 1754 (*v.* clōh, cf. Dunham 253 *supra*); Dunham Heath (*v.* hǣð, cf. prec.); Hough (cf. *the Houghfeild* 1693, *the New Heys called Dynhams Hough* 1752, 1782, *v.* (ge)hæg, hōh, cf. prec. and Dunham 253 *supra*); Eastingly (cf. Hasting Ley *infra*); Ellow Groves ('alder woods', *v.* elle, grāf); The Fatt; Faugh Fd (cf. *Faugh Flatt* 1663, *the Fough Feild* 1658, *v.* falh 'fallow', flat); Fearney Croft & Leys (cf. *le Ferneflatte* 1512, *v.* fearn(ig), croft, flat, ley); Flatt Cheese (cf. Cheese Hill 249 *supra*); Floss (*Floss(e) Meadow* 1710, 1719, *v.* flosshe 'a swamp'); Four Acres 1745 (1700, *Fawre akre* 1446, *v.* fēower, æcer);

Frog (the- 1783); Furrey Mdw; Golden Fd (v. golden); Gorsey Croft & Fd, Gorsty Hay, Gorsy Fd (the Gorsty Croft 1637, Gorsty Field & Meadow 1747, v. gorstig); Grantham's Mdw (1782, Granthorn 1497); Greenway (v. grēne[1], weg); Grow Ridding (v. ryding); Guttery Mdw (v. goter); Hasting Ley (cf. Eastingly supra, 'meadow where crops ripen early', v. hasting, ley); Heath Fd (v. hǣð); Hollin Bush (v. holegn, busc); Hollins Croft 1745 (le Hullond 1344, the Hullardes feilde 1610, Hollands Croft 1666, 'hill selion', v. hyll, land); Holly Hurst (Mdw) 1752 (1695, v. holegn, hyrst); New & Old Hood Hill; Horse Croft (Horscroft 1359, le Horse Crofte 1512, v. hors, croft); Hurst (v. hyrst); Hysons; Intake (the Intacke 1610, v. inntak); Kennery Croft (Kenny Crofts 1610); Kitchen Croft (the- 1610, v. cycene); Lady Hays (v. hlǣfdige, (ge)hæg); Lampits (v. lām, pytt); Land Frith Croft; Land Lakes (le Londlakes 1342, 'watercourses at, or separating, the selions', v. land, lacu); Lane Acres & Close; Lee's Doole 1729 (the Lees Dole 1574, 1702, from the surname Lee and dāl); Lightsfoots Fd (cf. Lightfoots Riding 1700, and Pool Ridding infra, from the surname of William Lightfote c.1400, George Lightefoote 1560, cf. 'Lightfoot's inheritance in Barrowe' 1570 ChRR, v. ryding); Little Barrow Lane; Little Barrow Mdw 1752 (1695, cf. les Medewes 1345, v. mǣd); Long Hay (the Long(e) Hey 1658, 1693, v. (ge)hæg); Loont(s) (v. land); Lower Field (the lower fielde 1615); Mare Lound 1745 ('mare's selion', v. mere[2], land); Margarets Fd; Marl Hay (v. marle, (ge)hæg); Meadow Hay (the Meadowehay 1610, v. mǣd, (ge)hæg); Mean Mdw ('common, shared, meadow', v. (ge)mǣne); Six-, Seven Measures Sowing; Meer Pit Croft (v. mere[1], pytt); Middle Goes (the Middle Gorse 1702, 1745, v. middel, gorst); Milking Bank (v. milking); The Missage (v. mizzick); Navigation; New Hay(s), New Hay Moor (the Newe Hay Moore 1610, Newhaies 1619, v. (ge)hæg, cf. Dunham Hough supra); Nine Butts (v. nigon, butte); Norley 1700 (le Nortley 1331, v. norð, lēah); Oat Hey (the Oate Hey 1658, 1693, v. āte, (ge)hæg); Old Mdw (Ould Meadowe 1610, v. ald, mǣd); Old Orchard; Olive Bush; Olle(r)ts Fd (v. howlet 'an owlet'); Oultons (the higher & the lowe Oultons 1610, v. ald, tūn, cf. Oulton 185 supra); Outlet(t) (v. outlet); Ox Hay (v. oxa, (ge)hæg); Oxley 1759 (v. oxa, lēah); Oxons Loont 1790 (probably from the surname from Oxton 326 infra and land); Pikes (cf. Pykes Wood 1710, Pikes- 1719, from a surname); Pingot (v. pingot); Pool Ridding (Pool(e) Ridinge-, -Rydyng-, -ing (alias) Lightfoot's Riding(e), -Ryding 1700, 1745, 1759, cf. Lightsfoots Fd supra, v. pōl[1], ryding); Poor Fd; Port Hills (pratum vocatum Portley c.1270, 'market clearing', v. port, lēah); Quillet (v. quillet(t)); Long Rangeley (Ranesley otherwise called Moregrene 1590, 'raven's clearing, or green at a marsh', v. hræfn, lēah, mōr[1], grēne[2]); Great Big Ridding (cf. the nearer Greate Ridding(e) 1658, 1693, v. grēat, ryding); Riddles Mdw; The Ridges; Ring Yard (the Ringeyardes 1610, v. hring, geard); Rough (Wd); Round Heath (le Rouneheth 1393, Litill Rowne Hethe 1512, 'rowan heath', v. raun, hǣð); Rye Croft; Sarrace Brow, Mdw & Rough (probably from the surname Sherratt); Shakers; Sheep Cote Fd; Sidders; Silver Mdw; Sitch Croft (v. sīc); (The) Slade, Big, Little & Long Slade (lez Slade, Slade lande 1497, Slade 1785, v. slæd); Sparks (v. spearca); Sprink (the- 1783, 'young wood', v. spring); Steads (v. stede); Stewards Bridge 1831 (cf. Stewards Field & Hey 1695,

1719, 1752, v. stīg-weard, (ge)hæg); Stonery Croft (v. stanry); Such (v. sīc); Swash Mdw (v. swash); Thieves Dale (*Theeuesdale* 1610, 'thief's valley, v. þēof, dæl¹); Thistley Fd (cf. *Thyslifeld* 1296, *le Thyslyfeld* c.1300, *le Thistelyfeld* 1352, v. þistlig, feld); Three Fd; Towers Fd; Townfield Crofts & Loonts, Town Mdw, Townsend (*the Towne feilde* 1610, *the Townefield*, -*feild* 1615, 1666, *Barrow Townfield* 1719); Turnpole; Wall Fd (*le Walle feld* 1342, v. wælla, feld); Wash Mdw (v. wæsce); Wet Mdw (v. wēt); Wheat Reans, -Reins (v. hwǣte, rein); White Fd (v. hwīt); Woodhill Croft; Yarn Croft (v. gearn, cf. Yarn Garth YW 7 193).

(b) *le Blakebrok* 1342 (v. blæc, brōc); *le Blakecroft* 1344, 1359 (v. blæc, croft); *blak grefe* (*lande*) 1497 ('black wood', v. blæc, grǣfe, land); *brere halland* 1497 ('briary head-land', v. brēr, hēafod-land); *le Brodewey* c.1270 (v. brād, weg); *le Carteway* 1364 ('way for carts', v. carte, weg); *Cortanefeld* 1296; *Cronmerfeld* 1442 ('(field at) the crane lake', v. cron, mere¹, feld); *Dunstawes* 1658 (v. tūn-stall); *the Edmondes Crofte* 1615 (from the pers.n. *Edmund* and croft); *Edriches lowe* c.1270, *Edrichelowe* 1296 ('Ēadrīc's mound', from the OE pers.n. *Ēadrīc* and hlāw); *le Forde* 1338, (-*de Lytelbarwe*) 1342, *le Forde ende & medewe* 1365 (v. ford, ende¹, mǣd); *Harestanfeld* 1338, *Harstan-* 1359, *le Horestonesmedewe* 1366 ('(field & meadow at) the hoar stone', v. hār², stān, feld, mǣd); *the lower healdes* (*meadow*), *the middle healdes* 1615, *Heyldes house* 1650 ('the hill-slopes, v. helde); *le Hee* c.1270, 1331 ('the stream', v. ēa, either Salters Brook² 1 34, or Barrow Brook² *supra*); *Hertonhirne* 1393 (probably 'nook at the herdsman's enclosure', v. heord, tūn, hyrne); *the highfeilde* 1590 (v. hēah, feld); *Hobryddyng* 1446 (from ryding with hob 'a hobgoblin', hobb(e) 'a tussock, a hummock', or the ME pers.n. *Hobb*, a pet-form of *Robert*); *Holowesfeld* 1342, *le Holo Weslond* 1344 ('field, selion, at the hollows', v. holh, feld, land); *Holkroft* c.1260, *Hul(le)-croft* 1325, *Hulcroft* 1329, 1342, 1366 ('croft in a hollow', v. hol², croft, the first el. confused with hyll); *lez Knoll* 1497 (v. cnoll); *longe lande* 1497 (v. lang, land); *Mallers Forlongs* 1497 (v. furlang); *le Morforlonges Wallelond* 1359 ('(selion at a spring in) the marsh furlong', from mōr¹ and furlang, wælla and land); *Moldeworthelane* 1512 ('lane to Mouldsworth', v. lane, cf. (*Great*) Mouldsworth 279 *infra*); *haia vocata Netherstokkes* (lit. -*stolkes*) 1393 ('tree-stumps', from stocc and neoðera 'lower', cf. *Wodestokke infra*); *le Oldedich* c.1260 (v. ald, dīc); *le Oldeheth* 1393 (v. ald, hǣð); *la Oldeyordes* 1393 (v. ald, geard); *le Rode medwe* 1329, *le Rotemedwe* 1342, -*medewe* 1366 ('meadow at a clearing', v. rod¹, mǣd); *the Rughehay* (*greene*) 1610 (v. rūh, (ge)hæg, grēne²); *mora que vocatur le Shaghteles* 1342 (a marsh, final el. lǣs 'a meadow'. *Shaghte*- appears to represent an OE *sceagiht sb., a derivative of sceaga 'a copse, a little wood', with the OE adj. suffix -iht. *Shaghteles* would be a marshy meadow broken up by *shaws*, patches of woodland, a 'copsed meadow'); *le Shertebuttes* 1359 (probably for *Shorte*-, v. sceort, butte, cf. scerte); *les tauels* 1497 ('two and a half lands in-'; from tæfl(e). This may mean 'disputed land', (cf. Tablehurst Sx 329) but it is probably 'square plots of land', from the original OE sense 'a chessboard'); a wood called *The Tolske* 1446 ('wood on which a toll is paid', v. toll, skógr); *Twisses Crofte* 1615 (v. (ge)twis); *Wallelond* (v. *Morforlong supra*); *le Walleway*

1369 ('way to a well', v. wælla, weg. This path led from Little Barrow *supra* to *le Hoghwalle* at The Hough *supra*); *Wari-, Warygreene land(s)* 1610 (perhaps 'felon's green', from wearg and grēne[2], with land); *Warstanisfeld* c.1330 ('Wǣrstān's field', from the OE pers.n. *Wǣrstān*, and feld); *Whitern-shuch* (lit. *Whiterushuth*), *Whytrensich* 1393 ('water-course at a white house', v. hwīt, ærn, sīc); *le Wodehousesmedewes* 1359, cf. *Barwe Wyduus* 14, *-wodehous* 1389 ('house at the wood of Barrow', v. wudu, hūs, mǣd, cf. foll.); *Barwewode* 1393, cf. *boscus de Barwe* 1296[2] (v. wudu, cf. prec.); haia vocata *Wodestokke* (lit. *-stolke*) 1393 (cf. *Netherstokkes supra*, v. wudu, stocc).

xiv. Tarvin

The ecclesiastical parish of Tarvin contained, in this Hundred, the townships 1. Ashton, 2. Bruen Stapleford (part of Stapleford in *Dudestan* (Broxton) Hundred, DB, cf. Foulk Stapleford *infra*), 3. Burton, 4. Clotton Hoofield (now a c.p. including part of Iddinshall 286 *infra*), 5. Duddon, 6. Hockenhull, 7. Horton cum Peel, 8. Kelsall, 9. Great Mouldsworth, 10. Tarvin, and, in Broxton Hundred, Foulk Stapleford 326 *infra*. Priors Heys 284 *infra* was anciently extra-parochial but is often taken as part of Tarvin township.

1. ASHTON IUXTA TARVIN (109–5069)

Estone 1086 DB
Achstone 1249–1323 Chest
Aiston 1272–90 *ChFor*, *Hayston* 1355 BPR
Ashtone 1289 Court, *Ashton* 1289 Plea *et freq* with variant spellings
    Assh-, Asch-; (*-iuxta Kelsale*) 1307 Plea, (*-Tervyn*) 1533 ChRR
Astone 1289 Sheaf
Assheton 1317 Plea *et freq* with variant spellings *As(s)che-, Ashe-*
    (from 1464 ChRR) to *Asheton alias Ashedon* 1580 Cre, (*-in(fra*)
    foresta(m) de la Mare, -de Mara) 1360 BPR, 1382 Plea, 1404
    ChRR, (*-iuxta Moldeworth*) 1362 Plea *et freq* to 1446 ChRR,
    (*-Kelshale*) 1369 Plea, (*-Horton*) 1377 *AddCh*, (*-Tervyn*) 1513
    Plea
Asshedon 1516 Cre, *Ashe-* 1580 ib
Asceton 1656 Orm[2]

'Ash-tree farm', v. æsc, tūn. This place is near Kelsall, Tarvin and Horton cum Peel 276, 281, 275 *infra*, and was within the Forest of Delamere 1 8.

ASHTON BROOK BRIDGE, cf. Ashton Brook 1 14.   ASHTONHALL FM,
Ashton Hall 1831 Bry.   ASHTON HAYES, *-Heys* 1787 Sheaf, a house
built in the eighteenth century, v. (ge)hæg.   ASH WOOD, 1842 OS,
cf. *Ashwoods* 1838 *TA*, v. æsc, wudu.   BECKETT'S WOOD, *Wood*

Acre 1842 OS, *v.* **wudu, æcer.** BLACK WOOD. BRICKBANK
COVERT, *v.* **bryke, banke.** BRINE'S BROW, cf. *Brans Green* 1831
Bry and *Brown Heath* 1838 *TA*, probably all from forms of the
surname *Bruen*, as in Bruen Stapleford 269 *infra*, with **brū, grēne²,
hǣð.** DALE COVERT, *-Cover* 1838 *TA*, *Dale Plantation* 1831 Bry,
v. **dæl¹.** GARDEN WOOD. HOLCROFT WOOD, cf. *Hoe Croft* 1838
TA, *v.* **hol², croft.** HOME FM. HORTON GATE, *v.* **geat** 'a
gateway', cf. Horton 275 *infra*. LILY WOOD, *Lilley-* 1838 *TA*,
v. **lilie.** LOWER LONGLEY FM, cf. *Longley Field & Meadow* 1838
ib, named from Longley 278 *infra*. SHAY LANE, 1831 Bry, *v.*
scaga, lane. 'WATLING STREET', *v.* **1** 40 (route VII). WOOD-
SIDE, 1831 ib.

FIELD-NAMES

The undated forms are 1838 *TA* 21. Of the others 1380 is *AddCh*, 1503
ChFor.

(*a*) *Alderley Fd* (*v.* **alor, lēah**); *Angle Cover* (*v.* **angle**); *Banks*; *Birchen Fd*
(*v.* **bircen²**); *Blade Fd*; *Brow Fd* (*v.* **brū**); *Butters Lake*; *Church Heath*;
Corn Hayes (*v.* **corn¹, (ge)hæg**); *Cotter Fd* (*v.* **cottere**); *Cow Hay*; *Coxey
Cover*; *Crib* (*v.* **crib**); *Cross Fd* (*v.* **cros** 'a cross'); *Dark Ark* (Cover) (*v.* Ark
Wd 245 *supra*); *Dove House Fd*; *Ferney Bank*; *Foot Riddings* (*v.* **fōt,
ryding**); *Forty Acre*; *Glade Hay* (*v.* **gleode, (ge)hæg**); *Hay Wd, Big & Little
Hayes* (*v.* **(ge)hæg**, cf. Ashton Hayes *supra*); *Holly Hill*; *Hongar Mdw* (*v.*
hangra); *Hovil Mdw* (*v.* **hovel**); *Hunger Hill* (*v.* **hungor**); *Intake* (*v.* **inntak**);
Kelsall Fd, Hay & Way (*v.* **(ge)hæg, weg**, cf. Kelsall 276 *infra*); *Laundry Fd*;
Long Hill; *Long Nooked Fd*; *Marl Fd*; *Meals Meat*; *Middlestays*; *Mossocks
Moor* ('marsh at the boggy places', *v.* **meōsuc, mōr¹**, cf. Missicke **2** 278);
Outlett (*v.* **outlet**): *Pindale* (cf. **pingel**); *Pingott* (*v.* **pingot**); *Little & Pool
Riddings* (*v.* **pōl¹, ryding**); *Ridge Hay* (*v.* **hrycg, (ge)hæg**); *Rye Croft*; *Shaw
Hay* (*v.* **sceaga, (ge)hæg**); *Sibbotts Heath*; *Slang Cover* (*v.* **slang**); *Stead
Croft* (*v.* **stede**); *Tarvin Mdw* (cf. Tarvin 281 *infra*); *Thorney Graves* (*v.*
þornig, grǣfe).

(*b*) *Assheton Comyns* 1503 (*v.* **commun**); *Huggecroft, Huggemese* 1380
(from the ME pers.n. *Hugge* (cf. Reaney s.n. *Hug*), *v.* **croft, mēos** 'a bog'.
Cf. Hug Bridge **1** 55).

2. BRUEN STAPLEFORD (109–4964), [ˈbruːən ˈsteipəlfəd], *Stapleford*
1086 DB, and spellings as for (Foulk-) Stapleford 326 *infra*; *Brune-
stapelford* c.1262 *BW et freq* with spellings as for Stapleford and
variant forms *Bruen-, -Bruen* 1288 Plea, 1304 Orm², 1724 NotCestr,
-Brun 1288 Court, *Bruyn-* 1313 to 1513 ChRR, *Bruyne-* 1316 Plea to
1485 ChRR, *Bryne-* 1563 ib, 'Bruen's part of Stapleford', from the
p.n. Stapleford and the surname of the *Bruen* family, lords of this
manor. Their ancestor is Robert *le Bru(i)n* of *Stapelford* 1222 *BW*,

Facs, 1208–29 Dieul, (brūn[1] 'brown'). This township originally formed part of the manor of Stapleford in *Dudestan* (Broxton) hundred DB, *v.* Foulk Stapleford 326 *infra*.

BROOKHOUSE FM & LANE, *Brook House* 1831 Bry, cf. Upper Brookhouse Fm 327 *infra*.   CROSSLANES FM, 1831 ib, at a cross-roads. FORD BRIDGE, cf. *Ford Meadow* 1838 *TA, v.* 326 *infra*.   OLD MOSS FM & LANE, *Old Moss Hall* 1831 Bry, cf. Old Moss 283 *infra*. ROUND HO, *v.* rond.   RYECROFT LANE, 1842 OS, cf. *Rye Croft* 1838 *TA, v.* ryge, croft.   STAPLEFORD HALL, 1831 Bry.   STAPLEFORD MILL, 1831 ib, *molendinum de Stepelford* c.1219 *BW et freq* with spellings as for Stapleford, cf. *Walkmill Meadow, Corne Mill Meadow, Mill House Meadow & Croft* 1692 *BW, Stapleford Lower Mill* 1787 *ib, v.* myln, walke-mylne.

FIELD-NAMES

The undated forms are 1838 *TA* 77. Of the others, c.1262, 1307, 1692 are *BW*, 1510, 1513 ChRR, 1671 Sheaf.

(a) Aldcroft 1692 (*v.* ald, croft); Barkers Fd (*v.* barkere); Briary Wd; Catheralls Moor 1692 (from the surname *Catherall*, and mōr[1]); Big-, Little-, Farther Combs, etc. (*the Combes* 1692, *v.* cumb); Coney Grave (*v.* coningre); Dale Loons, Dales (*the Dales* 1692, 'the allotments', *v.* dǣl[2]); Three Day Math (*Three Dayes Math* 1692, *v.* day-math); Dick Hill; Little England (*v.* 325 *infra*); Fat Pasture (*v.* fǣtt); (Little) Gale Moor (*Gale Moors* 1692, *v.* gagel, mōr[1]); Gleg Yate 1671 (from the surname *Glegg* and geat 'a gateway'); Goose Croft; Hall Fd (1692, *v.* hall); Hobbick; Houghs Wood 1692 (from the surname *Hough* and wudu); Intake (*v.* inntak); Kiln Croft, Mdw & Moor (*Kill Crofte & Meadowe* 1692, *v.* cyln, croft); Marl Field Loon (*v.* land); Moor Banks; Nedlow; Odd Croft (*v.* odde); Pool Dam, Fd, Mdw & Stead (*Pulmedowe* c.1262, *v.* pōl[1], damme, feld, mǣd, pōl-stede); Reed Mdws (*le Reddemede* 1510, *-medowe* 1513, *Reede Meadow* 1692, 'reedy meadow', *v.* hrēod, hrēoden, mǣd); Shaw Fd (*v.* sceaga); Stannidales ('stony allotments' *v.* stānig, dǣl[2]); Summers Wd 1831; Townfield Croft; Whitefield; Witters Moor (*three Witters Moores* 1692, from the surname *W(h)itter* and mōr[1]); Big- & Little Wood.

(b) le Bruggemor 1307 ('marsh with a causeway', *v.* brycg, mōr[1]).

3. BURTON (FM, HALL & HO) (109–510640)

Burtone 1086 DB f.263, *Burton* H3 (19) Orm[2] (p), 1282 Court *et freq*, (*-iuxta Stapulford*) 1426 ChRR, *Burton Hall* 1671 Sheaf
Birton 1280 P (p)
Brunburton 1282 Court 51
Borton 1291 Tax

'Farm or enclosure at a fortified manor', v. burh-tūn. The prefix
Brun- is only recorded once. It may represent an original form of the
p.n., later contracted to Burton. Brunburton could be 'the farm or
enclosure at Brūna's stronghold', from the OE pers.n. Brūna and
burh, with tūn, analogous with Bromborough 325 infra. But Brun-
may be a manorial affix, from the same surname Bruen (le Brun)
as in Bruen Stapleford 269 supra, the adjacent township. The
DB form may stand for the bishop of Chester's other manor at
Burton in Wirral 325 infra, cf. Tait 14–15, but that would suppose an
error in the DB hundred rubric.

FIELD-NAMES

The undated forms are 1838 TA 86. Of the others, 1831 is Bry, 1842 OS.

(a) Back Side (v. ba(c)ksyde); Bindle Moor (v. mōr¹); Bottoms (v. botm);
Clay Lands (v. clǣg, land); Cotgreaves (v. cot, grǣfe); Criggoes, Crighurst
(perhaps from PrWelsh crŭg 'a hill, a barrow', with hyrst or hōh); Drin-
stead (v. stede); Hatchew Mdw (perhaps analogous with Hatch Mere 215
supra); Homestead (v. hām-stede); In Mere; Long Fd; Marl Croft (v.
marle); Old Fd; Sandy Lane 1842 (Sand Lane 1831, v. sand(ig), lane); Sour
Fd, Sourley (v. sūr, feld, lēah); Stick Fd; Sullins ('ploughlands' v. sulh,
ME wk.pl. sulhene); Tapley Hill; Town Fd; Whilds Mdw (v. wilde);
Withins (v. wīðegn).

4. CLOTTON HOOFIELD (109–5263), Clotton et Hulfeld 1372 MidCh,
Clotton Hulfeld 1391 ChRR et freq with spellings as for Clotton,
Hoofield infra, Hulfeld-Clotton 1536 ChRR, Clotton com Highfeild
1663 Sheaf, -cum Hoofield 1724 NotCestr, -cum Hulfield 1819 Orm²,
v. Clotton, Hoofield infra.

CLOTTON COMMON, HALL & LODGE (109–525639) ['klɔtən]

Clotone 1086 DB, 1096–1101 (1280) Chest, -tona 1150 ib
Clottona 1157–94 Chest, Clottun 1185 Facs, Clotton 1246 Tab,
    1260 Court (p) et freq with variant spelling -tone; Clotton
    Common, Hall & Lodge 1831 Bry
Cloct' 1175 Facs, Clocton 1247 P, 1330 Plea
Clopton 1247 P, 1326, 1329 ChRR (p), 1348 Eyre (p), 1358 BPR
    (p), 1399 Pat (p), 1405 ChRR (p)
Coltton 1297 Ipm (p)
Clatton 1412 ChRR
Clutton 1512 ChEx
Cotton 1536 ChRR

Clooton 1549 *Surv*
Clitton 1560 Pat

'Farm at a dell', from **clōh** and **tūn**, with **commun**, **hall** and **loge**.

HOOFIELD HALL (109–515628)

Hulefeld 1282 Court (p)
Hulfeld 1284 Ipm (p) *et freq* to 1537 MidCh, *-field* 1297 Orm[2],
  1819 ib, *-felde* 1328 Plea (p), *-fyld* 1536 ChRR, *Hullfeld* 1300
  MidCh, *Hulle-* 1317 ChRR (p), 1353 *Eyre*
Holefeld 1286 *ChFor*, *Holfeld* 1317 ChRR (p)
Huffeld 1307 *Eyre* (p)
Hofeld' 1516 *ChEx*, *Howfield* 1549 *Surv*, 1656 Orm[2], *Hou-* 1671
  Sheaf, *Hoofeeld alias Howfield* 1586 Orm[2], *Hoofield Hall* 1831
  Bry
Highfeild 1663 Sheaf

'Open land at a hovel', *v.* **hulu**, **feld**.

BROOKHOUSE FM.   LADY HEYS FM, *Lady Hays* 1838 *TA*, *the litle
ladye hey* 1599 (1613) ChRR, *v.* **hlǣfdige**, **(ge)hæg**.   LOWER HO,
1831 Bry,   WOODLANE COTTAGE, cf. *Wood House* 1831 Bry, *v.*
wudu, **hūs**, **lane**.   YEWTREE FM.

FIELD-NAMES

The undated forms are 1838 *TA* 124. Of the others 1096–1101 (1280), 1150,
1157–94 are Chest, 1175 Facs, 1536 ChRR, 1831 is Bry.

(a) Back Lane 1831; Backside Bank (*v.* ba(c)ksyde); Bar Fd; Bird Fd;
Black Fd, Blake Land & Low (*v.* blæc, land, hlāw); Brindley Fd (*v.* brende[2],
lēah, cf. Brindley 133 *supra*); Burton Way (*v.* weg, cf. Burton 270 *supra*);
Chetter Pool; Cinder Head (*v.* sinder, hēafod); Clayland Mdw (*v.* clæg,
land); Clemly Park (cf. Clemley 47 *supra*); Cockshoot (*v.* cɔcc-scyte); Cote
Fd (*v.* cot); Crib (*v.* crib); Cuttings (Lane) (*v.* cutting); Four-, Sixteen-,
Three- & Twelve Da(y)math (*v.* day-math); Docky Flatt (*v.* docce); Forty
Acre; Four Shillings Croft (*v.* scilling, cf. 325 *infra*); Glad Lane Buts (*v.*
glæd[1], lane, butte); Gorsty Flat, Hey & Wd (*v.* gorstig, flat, (ge)hæg);
Great Hey (*v.* (ge)hæg); Hall Yard; Hasty Way; Hay-, Hey Brook (*v.* hēg);
Twelve Hollands (*v.* twelf, hēafod-land); Ho(l)me (*v.* holmr); Homestead
(*v.* hām-stede); Intake (*v.* inntak); Knowl; Big- & Little Land; Lane Croft
& Fd; Leggate Croft (*v.* hlid-geat); Long Moor; Mill Croft & Fd (cf.
molendinum de Clotone 1096–1101 (1280), *-Clotonae* 1150, *-Cloct'* 1175,
-Clottona 1157–94, *v.* myln); Moors, Moor Croft; Mow(ing) Croft; New
Bank, Fd & Heys; Nickows Moss (*v.* nicor); Oak Tree Fd; Out Lane 1842
(*v.* ūt, lane); Outlet (*v.* outlet); Ox Hey (*v.* (ge)hæg); Pickow (*v.* pichel);

Pingot (v. pingot); Pinnington; Pleck(s) (v. plek); Priest Flat (v. prēost); Ridley Moor (v. (ge)rydd, lēah); Ring Greaves (v. hring, græfe); Size Croft; Sunny Ford (v. sunny, ford); Taythe (v. tēoða 'a tithe', cf. Big Taythe Croft 274 infra); Town Fd; Wetchard Mdw (probably 'wet meadow' from dial. wet-shod (EDD) 'wet-footed' and mǣd); Wetmoor (v. wēt, mōr¹); Whip's Acre; Whitechurch Mdw; White Fd; Within Croft, Withy, Wythe (v. wīðegn, wīðig).

(b) Kendals Hey 1536 (from the surname Kendal and (ge)hæg); Lymme Greyve 1536 ('maple wood', v. hlyn, græfe); Le Rough Hey 1536 (v. rūh, (ge)hæg).

5. DUDDON (COMMON, (OLD) HALL, HEATH & MILL) (109–513647) ['dud(ə)n, 'dʌd(ə)n]

Dudedun 1185 Facs (p)
Duddon 1288 Court et freq, -e 1317 ChRR, Duddun 1357 ChFor, Dudon 1656 Orm², Duddon Hall 1671 Sheaf, Duddon Common, Green, Hall, Heath, Mill & Upper Hall 1831 Bry, Lower Hall, Duddon Old Hall 1842 OS
Dundon' 1307 Eyre, 1515 ChEx
Duddons 1317 ChRR
Doudon 1358 BPR
Dutton Hall 1719 Sheaf

'Dudda's hill', from the OE pers.n. Dud(d)a and dūn, with hall, commun, grēne², hǣð, myln, ald. Cf. Duddon Hill infra.

DUDDON HOOK LANE, Duddon Buts Lane 1831 Bry, Duddon Nook 1838 TA, v. butte, lane, nōk. DUDDON LODGE, Warren House 1842 OS, v. wareine. EXCEEDING WELL, 1831 Bry, cf. Seeding Well 244 supra, with which this is probably analogous, 'seething spring', v. sēoþinge, wella. FIRTREE FM.

FIELD-NAMES

The undated forms are 1838 TA 150. Of the others, 1317 is ChRR, 1348 Eyre, 1753 BW.

(a) Backside (v. ba(c)ksyde); Bank Fd; Big Moor; Black Croft (1753); Brickiln Croft (cf. Brekeyerd infra); Burton Croft (cf. Burton 270 supra); Chamber Fd; Clemley (cf. Clemley 47 supra); Cornery Flatt (Cornly Flatt & Meadow 1753, v. corn², lēah, flat, cf. foll.); Cornhill Flatt (cf. prec., v. corn², hyll); Duddon Hill (cf. Duddon supra); Goosecroft; Gorsty Fd 1753 (v. gorstig); Greenfield; Hall Yard(s); Hemp Yard Croft (the Hempyard 1753, v. hemp-yard); Houghlands (v. hōh, land); Hunters Mdw 1753; Inmere; Great & Little Marl Fd (1753); Little-, Mowing- & Old Moor (cf. the Moor

(*Meadow*) 1753); Big & Little Moss (*Higher & Lower Moss* 1753); Mount Pleasant (*v.* 273 *infra*); Outlet (*v.* outlet); Pinfold Croft (*v.* pynd-fald); Poolstead (*v.* pōl-stede); Primrose Hill; Redgate; Rendle Fd, Rindle Mdw, Rindlett (*v.* rynel); Round Bank (cf. *Round Meadow* 1753, *v.* rond, banke, mǣd); Sand Fd (cf. *Great & Less Sandy Fields* 1753, *v.* sandig); Shatt Flatt (*v.* scēat, flat); Sheep Cote Fd (*v.* scēp, cot); Soft Fd (*v.* sōfte); Sour Croft; Spark Mdw 1753 (*v.* spearca); Stocks Croft (*v.* stocc); Big Taythe Croft (*v.* tēoða 'a tithe', cf. Taythe 273 *supra*); Three Nooked Corner (*v.* three-nooked, corner); Townfield; Wasp; White Fd; Windmill Flatt; Big & Little Wd.

(*b*) Brekeyerd 1317 (p), -*yord* 1348 (p) ('enclosure where bricks are made', *v.* bryke-yard, from bryke and geard. This antedates *bryke, breke* 'a brick' , c.1440, 1465 NED, and *brick-yard* 1864 NED).

6. HOCKENHULL (HALL) (109–480660) [hɔk(ə)nul, -ʌl]

> Hokenull 1208–26 *AddCh* (p), *Okenul, Ocunul* 1208–29 Dieul, Hokenhull 1208–29 ib, 1272–90 *ChFor et freq* to 1538 ChRR with variant spellings -*yn*-, -*hul* (from *Hokynhul* c.1255 MRA), -(*h*)*ill* (1307 *Eyre* (p), 1327 ChRR (p), 1562 Orm²), -*hyll* (1453 *Sotheby*), -*el*(*l*) (1336 VR, 1380 *Eyre* (p), 1418 ChRR (p), 1430 *JRC*)
>
> Hokenale 1318 City (p)
>
> Hokenall 1418 ChRR (p), -*hall* 1539 Sheaf,
>
> Hockenhill 1314 ChRR, -*hull* 1331 (1586), 1563 ib *et freq*, (-*Hall*) 1842 OS, -*yn*- 1441–2 Orm², *Hokhenhull* 1385 (1619) *Chol*, Hockenhel 1656 Orm², *Hockhenell* 1663 Sheaf, *Hockenel Hall* 1783 ib
>
> Hogenhull 1333 *Dav* (*p*)
>
> Hokehull 1348 Plea (p)
>
> Hokynshull 1485 ChRR
>
> Hocknell 1549 *Surv, Hocknel*(*l*) 1658, 1663 Sheaf *et freq* ib to 1775, -*ill* 1719 Sheaf
>
> Hockenhall 1656 Orm², (*Hall*) 1831 Bry

'Hoc(c)a's hill', from the OE pers.n. *Hoc(c)a* and hyll. The hall was reported in 1347 *ChFor* as 'a certain *Peele* made by Richard de Hokenhull', which suggests a moated or stockaded site, *v.* pēl.

HOCKENHULL PLATTS, PLATTS LANE (109–476657), *le Plat* 1288 Court, *Hokenelplat* 1336 VR, *pont de Hokenhull* 1353 BPR, (*the bridge of*) *Hokenhall Platt* 1359 Sheaf *et freq* with variant spellings as for Hockenhull *supra*, and *Plat*(*t*), *Plot, Plate* to *Hockenhall Plats* 1831 Bry, -*hull*- 1842 OS, 'the bridge(s) at Hockenhull', *v.* plat¹.

Here a series of three pack-horse bridges carries Platts Lane across the R. Gowy and its marshes. A local name is *Roman Bridges* (Sheaf[3] 28, (6165)). About 1621, Webb (Orm[2] II 8) reported this as a passage on the main road from Chester to London, cf. I 42, 48 (routes VIII, XXIV).

BROOMHEATH LANE, cf. *Bromehey* 1453 *Sotheby*, v. brōm, (ge)hæg, hǣð, lane.

FIELD-NAMES

The undated forms are 1839 *TA* 203. The others are 1347 *ChFor*, 1453 *Sotheby*, 1539 *Vern*.

(a) The Acre; Billing's Mdw & Moor; Broad Hay (v. brād, (ge)hæg); Cock Croft; Cow Hay (v. (ge)hæg); Middle Fd; Mill Fd (cf. *Hockenhull myll* 1539, v. myln); Old House Fd; Pig Stead (v. stede); Platt Fd (cf. Hockenhull Platts *supra*); Reed Mdw (v. hrēod); Well Fd.

(b) *aqua de Hokenhull* 1347 (v. R. Gowy I 26); *le Mykell Feld* 1453 (v. micel, mikill, feld).

7. HORTON CUM PEEL, 1842 OS, *Peel cum Horton* 1831 Bry, *Horton et Parva Moldeworth* 1475 *AddCh*, *Little Mouldsworth* 1819 Orm[2], cf. Horton, Peel (Hall) *infra*. This was originally two townships, Horton and Little Mouldsworth, but in 1819 Little Mouldsworth township is said to consist of two estates, Horton and Peel, Orm[2] II 332.

HORTON HALL (109–494687)

> *Horton* 13 Whall (p), 1250 MidCh (p), 1296 *ChFor et freq* with variant spellings *Or-*, *-thon*; (*-iuxta Tervin*) 1326 Orm[2], (*-Molesworth*) 1327 ib, (*-Asshton*) 1357 *ChFor*, *Horton Hall* 1831 Bry
> *Arton* 1556 (1585) ChRR

'Dirty farm' or rather 'farm on muddy land' which is the interpretation for the type *Horton* in DEPN, v. horu, tūn.

PEEL (109–4969), formerly LITTLE MOULDSWORTH

> *Parva Mold(e)worth(e)* 13 Tab, c.1270 *Chol et freq* with forms as for (*Great-*) Mouldsworth 279 *infra*, and *Parva-* (to 1515 *ChEx*), *Lyttel-* (1357 *ChFor et freq* with variants *Litul-*, *Lytel-*, *Lit(t)el-*, *Liti(l)l-*, *Lit(t)le-*, *Lyttle-*) to *Little Mouldsworth* 1819 Orm[2]
> (*Horton iuxta-*) *Molesworth* 1327 Orm[2], *-Moldeworth* 1427 ib, 1497 ChRR
> *Peele* 1671 Sheaf *et freq* with spellings as for Peel Hall *infra*
> Cf. foll. and (*Great*) Mouldsworth 279 *infra*, v. lȳtel, parva.

PEEL HALL (109–498697)

Pele 1535 Orm², mannor or capital messuage called the Pele in Little
Moldesworth 1609 Chol
The Peele in Lyttle Mouldsworth 1582 Orm², 1591 Chol, the Peele in
the parish of Barow 1592 ib, the Peele 1610 Sheaf, Peele 1671 ib,
Peele Hall 1599 ib, 1845 ChetOS VIII, Peel 1615 Orm², the Peel
Hall estate in Little Mouldsworth 1819 ib
The Poole 1599, 1610 Sheaf, the Pool, or the Pile 1656 Orm²

'The peel-house', v. pēl 'a stockade'. An account of the original
fortification is given in Orm² II 332, cf. Bailey Fd infra. The Pool(e)
spellings are mistaken forms, -ee- read as -oo-, cf. Pooles Panns infra.

HORTON HO, The Cottage 1831 Bry, v. cotage.

FIELD-NAMES

The undated forms are 1846 TA 209. Of the others, 1353 is ChFor, 1522–3
Orm², 1610 Sheaf, 1637 Chol, 1831 Bry, 1842 OS.

(a) Ashton Fd (v. Ashton 268 supra); Big & Little Bailey Fd (Greate
Bealyfeild, Little Baylyfeild 1610 ('field at a bailey', v. baille, feld, grēat,
lȳtel, cf. Peel Hall supra); Booth Croft (v. bōth); Broad Acre (1831); Brook
Mdw (cf. the Brooke feild 1610, Brook House 1842, named from Ashton
Brook I 14, v. brōc, hūs); Coat Fd (v. cot); Coppice; Decoy; Big- & Little
Eller-, -Ellen-Suits (cf. Great & Little Elershawe 1610, v. ellern, ellen,
sceaga, scēat); Hall Fd (-feilde 1610, v. hall); Big & Little Hammers Fd
(Greate & Little Hammons Feild(e) 1610, from the ME pers.n. Hamon and
feld); Hop Yard (v. hoppe, geard); Hurst (v. hyrst); Kiln Croft; Lime Croft
(v. lim); Long Fd; Mill Mdw; Big Moor (Hortonmor 1353, v. mōr¹).

(b) Broade Meadowe 1610 (v. brād, mǣd); the Bromyfeild 1637 (v. brōmig,
feld); Fore Aker 1610 (v. fēower, æcer); Lady Croft 1610 (v. hlǣfdige,
croft); Mospitt Meadowe 1610 (v. mos, pytt, mǣd); the Muddy Croft 1637
(v. muddig); Pooles Panns 1610 (v. spann, cf. Peel Hall supra); Sellers Feilde
1610; Travors hamlet 1522–3 (v. hamelet 'a hamlet', an estate in Horton,
supposed to contain the surname Travis, v. Orm² II 332. Neither the original
document nor further record has been seen); Well Meadowe 1610 (v. wella,
mǣd); the Wheat Eddish, the two Wheat Feildes 1637 (v. hwǣte, edisc, feld);
the Rough Woody Groundes 1637 (v. rūh, wudig, grund).

8. KELSALL (HALL) (109–5268) ['kelsɔːl] locally ['kelsəl] older ['kelsə]
Kelsale 1257 (17) Chest (p), 1260 Court (p) et freq to 1581 Cre,
Kells- 1455 MidCh, Kelshale 1303 Chamb et freq to 1444 ChRR
(p)

Kelishal' 1272–90, 1288 *ChFor*, 1291 Court (p), *Keles-* 1292 ib (p),
   1295 Ipm, *Keleshale* 1281 (1338) VR (p), 1284 Misc *et freq* to
   1361 Fine, *Kelleshale* 1353 BPR (p)
Kilssale 1282 Court (p)
Keleshall 1295 Ipm, *Kelshall* 1346, 1352 Sheaf, 1355 Bark, 1398
   ChRR (p), 1444 ib, *Kells-* 1537 MidCh, *Cells-* 1656 Orm²
Kellesal 1300 Plea, *Kelsal* 1311 ChRR (p), 1441 ib, 1508 Orm²,
   1585, 1616, 1629 Cre, 1819 Orm², *Kelsall* 1358, 1398 ChRR *et
   freq*, (*-on the Hill*) 1812 Sheaf, *-alle* 1439 ChRR, *Kelsall Hall* 1831
   Bry
Kefeshale 1317 *InqAqd*
Kelsahale 1342–53 *ChAttorn* (p) (Barnes[1])
Keshale 1350 *Eyre*
Kelshales 1357 BPR (p)
Kelshill alias Ecclesale 1398 Pat (p)
Kelsoe 1590 Sheaf

'Kell's nook', from halh (dat.sg. hale), referring to the valley at
which the village stands, with a ME pers.n. *Kell* which also appears
in the adjacent Kelsborrow Castle 212 *supra*. No doubt the same
man gave name to both. The pers.n. form ME *Kel(le)* is adduced for
Kelsit Grange NRY 18, as a short form of an ON pers.n. in *-kell* <
-ketill. Reaney, s.n. *Kell(s)*, argues that the ME pers.n. and surname
Chel(le), *Kelle* is from an ON pers.n. *Kel* < *Ketill*, as OSwed *Kæl* <
Kætil (Lundgren-Brate 156). Feilitzen, 303 n.2, appears doubtful of
this possibility, in the simplex, at dates as early as DB, but he allows
it in the compound pers.ns. in *-ketill, Ketill-*. Professor Sørensen
conforms 'Neither as a simplex nor as the first el. of a p.n. or a pers.n.
can *Kell-* represent *Ketill* as early as DB'. He compares Kettles Croft
(Peckforton) 313 *infra*, still *Keteles-* in 1354, and cites Fellows Jensen
166–70 s.n. *Ketill*, esp. 170. DEPN takes Kelsall Ch, Kelsale Sf,
Kelsey Li, and Kelshall Hrt, to be from either an OE pers.n. *Cēl(i)* or
Cæl(i), or the OE pers.n. *Cēol* with *K-* from Scand. influence, or an
OE pers.n. *Cēnel* (gen.sg. *Cēnles*). DEPN and Hrt 159 also derive
Kelshall Hrt from an OE pers.n. *Cylle*. The explanation now offered
would remove Kelsall Ch from this series. A curious alternation of
forms for Kelsall appears in 'Thomas Andrewe alias Andrew *Kelshill*
of co. Chester alias Andrew *Ecclesale*' 1398 Pat 453, which suggests
a popular analogy between a surname form *o'Kelsall* and the p.n.-type
Ecclesall WRY, Eccleshall St, from eclēsia and halh. Kelsall com-

mands an important pass through the hills of the Forest of Delamere on the road from Chester to Northwich, and Kelsall Hill *infra* was the site of a medieval toll-passage.

BANK HO, 1831 Bry, *v.* banke.   BIRCH HO.   BROCK'S WOOD. BROOK HO, *v.* brōc.   BROOM'S LANE.   CHESTER RD, leading to Chester.   CHURCH LANE, *v.* cirice, lane.   (KELSALL) COMMON FM, *Common Farm* 1831 Bry, *v.* commun.   DEWSBURY HO, cf. *Dewsbury (Croft)* 1838 *TA*, probably from a surname.   DODD'S ROUGH, 1838 *ib*, cf. *Doddesrudyng* 1355 *Chol*, and *Dods Wall* 1812 Sheaf, from the pers.n. and surname ME *Dodd(e)*, ModE *Dodd*, *v.* rūh, ryding, wælla.   DOGMOOR WELL, *v.* 211 *supra*.   DUTTON'S LANE.   EARLSCROFT, EARLE'S LANE, probably from the surname *Earle*.   FLAT LANE, cf. *Flats* 1838 *TA*, *v.* flat.   FRODSHAM ST., *Ashen Knolls Lane* 1831 Bry, probably from æscen 'growing with ash-trees', *v.* cnoll, lane, but as the lane ran towards Ashton Hall 268 *supra*, *Ashen* may represent *Ashton*.   GREEN LANE, *v.* grēne[1], lane. GRUB LANE.   HALLOWSGATE, 1831 Bry, 'gateway at a valley or corner', *v.* halh, geat.   KELSALL HILL, 1831 *ib*, cf. *Kelsall on the Hill* 1812 Sheaf, and the pass of *Kelsal Hill* 1819 Orm[2] II 2, *passagium de Kelsale* etc., 1295 Ipm, 1300 Plea, 1317 Misc, InqAqd, etc., *v.* hyll.   LONGLEY FM, HILL & WOOD, HIGHER LONGLEY LANE (cf. LOWER LONGLEY 269 *supra*), *Langeleclif* 1338 Plea, *Longley* 1503 ChFor, 1831 Bry, -*Common* 1812 Sheaf, -*Farm & Covert* 1842 OS, 'long wood', *v.* lang, lēah, clif 'a steep slope', commun, hyll, wudu, lane.   ROOKERY FM, *v.* rookery.   SALTERSFORD BRIDGE (109– 498678), *Salters Bridge* 1831 Bry, carrying 'Watling Street' (*v.* Street Fm) over Salters Brook[2] 1 34, cf. Saltersbridge 283 *infra*, 'salter's ford', *v.* saltere, ford, brycg.   SPRING VALLEY.   STREET FM, 1842 OS, *Street House* 1831 Bry, *v.* strǣt. This refers to 'Watling Street' 1 40 (route VII), *alta via* 1347 *ChFor*.

FIELD-NAMES

The undated forms are 1838 *TA* 220. Of the others, 1347, 1353, 1503 are *ChFor*, 1363[2] *MinAcct*, 1503 *ChFor*, 1508 ChRR, 1812 Sheaf, 1819 Orm[2], 1831 Bry, 1842 OS.

(a) Ackerleys; Alderley (*v.* alor, lēah); Ashton Hill (*v.* hyll, cf. Ashton 268 *supra*); Barbers Lane (1831); Black Birch(es) (from blæc and birce or brēc); Branch Yard; Briny Fd; Broad Arm; Brook Spout (*v.* brōc, spoute); Caldy (*v.* cald, (ge)hæg); Crook Ridding (*v.* krókr, ryding); Corns End; Crib Croft

(v. crib); Cush Croft; Dog Lane Fd (v. **dogga, lane**); Done Hey (probably from the surname *Done* and (ge)hæg); East Ridding (v. **ēast, ryding**); Gorse Loonds, -Loonts (v. **gorst, land**); Hawk Ridding (from hafoc or halc and ryding); Hayes Mdw (cf. *le Heyes* 1353², v. (ge)hæg); Heath (Fd) (v. **hǣð**); Hick Fd; Hill Fd (cf. Kelsall Hill *supra*); Hough Tail (v. **hōh, tægl**); King Williams Croft; Kirkway (v. **kirkja, weg**); Marl Fd (v. **marle**); Meadow Flatt (v. **mǣd, flat**); Milking Bank (v. **milking, banke**); Nanny's Yacht; New Hey (v. (ge)hæg); Northward(s); Oaken Stile (v. **ācen, stigel**); Oathill (v. **āte, hyll**); Open Stiles (v. **open, stigel**); Padstocks Lake 1812 (v. 213 *supra*); Plenters Pits; Priest Loont (v. **prēost, land**); Prin Ridding; Quillet (v. **quillet(t)**); Ringsley Hey ('enclosure at a ring-fenced wood', v. **hring, lēah, (ge)hæg**); Rough Slate Holes; Slang (v. **slang**); Sowerly Butts (v. **sūr, lēah, butte**); Taggersley (v. **lēah**); Thick Fd (v. **þicce²**); Town Fd; Wall Moor (*Walmore* 1503, 'marsh at a spring', v. **wælla, mōr¹**); Whittinghams Lane 1812 (v. 213 *supra*); Wimberry Hill ('hill where winberries grow', v. **wīnberige**); Wimpenny's Gate 1812 (v. 213 *supra*); Worralls Way 1812 (v. **weg**); The Yolk, Yolk of Egg (v. 325 *infra*).

(b) *Laystall* 1508 (v. **lēah, stall**); *Riddyng* 1508 (v. **ryding**); *Kelsall Smethes* 1503 (v. **smið, smiððe**); *boscus de Kels(h)ale* 1347, 1353 (cf. *Woodside Brooke* s.n. Ashton Brook 1 14, v. **wudu**).

9. MOULDSWORTH (HALL) (109–5070) ['moulzwə:þ, 'mouldzwəþ]

Moldeworthe 1153–81 Chest (p), *Moldwyrt* c.1190 (17) Sheaf (p), *Moldewurth* 1230 CoLegh, -wrht c.1240 Chol, -worth 13 Tab, 1260 Court *et freq* with variant spellings *Mold(e)-, -wrth(e)*, *-worth(e), -wurth(e), -worte, -wrh(t), -worht, -werth, -word* to 1562 ChRR, (*Magna-*) 1288 ChFor, (*Mukel-*) 1357 ib, *Moldeworthes* 1280 P (p), *Muldeworth* 1304 Chamb (p), *Mowde-* 1564 Sheaf, (*the hall of*) *Mouldworth* 1526 AD

Moldesworth 1257 (17) Chest (p), 1565 Sheaf, (-*Hall*) 1622 ChRR, -*wrth* 1260 Court (p), *Moldsworth* 1372 MidCh (p), 1605, 1609 ChRR, (*Magna-*) 1425 MidCh, *Moulds-* 1275 ib (p), 1405 ChRR, 1582 Orm², 1627 ChRR, 1724 NotCestr *et freq*, (-*Hall*) 1831 Bry, (*Great-*) 1614 ChRR, 1656 Orm², *Mouldesworthe* 1566 ChRR, *Mowldes-* 1591 Chol

Maldeword 1307–24 Chol

Moleworth 1332 Fine (p)

Modelworth 1427 Cl, *Moddlesworth* c.1602 Chol

Magna Molesworth 1528 Orm²

'Enclosure at a hill', from **molda** 'the crown of the head' and **worð**, with **magna, mycel, grēat, hall**, cf. DEPN, and Peel formerly Little Mouldsworth, 275 supra. The *-es-* form represents a ME analogical gen.sg. inflexion. The discussion under Mildenham in Wo 112 is irrelevant, cf. Moxby NRY 29.

ASHTON BROOK BRIDGE, cf. Ashton Brook 1 14.   BEECHWOOD FM. CAT ROUGH, *Cats Rough* 1842 OS, *v.* catt, rūh.   LONG WOOD. MILL HO & WOOD, *Peel Mill, Mill Covert* 1831 Bry, *one Mulneplace in Great Moldeworth* 1397 Orm², *v.* myln, place, wudu, cover, cf. Peel 275 *supra*.   NORTON'S LANE, *v.* 264 *supra*.   POPLARGROVE FM. THE ROOKERY (a wood), *Shutts Sprout* 1831 Bry, cf. *Shuts* 1838 *TA*, 'young wood at the corners', *v.* scēat, sproute.   STONEHOUSE, 1842 OS, *v.* stān, hūs.   WRIGHT'S GORSE, *v.* gorst.

FIELD-NAMES

The undated forms are 1838 *TA* 279. Of the others 1353, 1357, 1503 are *ChFor*, 1355 *Chol*, 1610, 1739 Sheaf, 1831 Bry.

(*a*) Ark Fd, (Upper) Dark Ark (*v.* Ark Wood 245 *supra*); Backside (*v.* ba(c)ksyde); Bank Hay (*the Bancke Hay* 1610, *v.* banke, (ge)hæg); Boden's Hay (*the Bordens Hay* 1739); Broad Oak (*v.* brād, āc); Carter's Hay (*the Cart House Hay* 1739, *v.* carte-hows); Mouldsworth Common 1831 (*v.* commun). Cote Fd (*the Coates Field* 1739, *v.* cot); Cow Hay (*v.* cū, (ge)hæg); Crib (*v.* crib); Decoy (*v.* decoy); Finchet Fd (*the Fynchetts* 1610, *the two Finchett*s 1739); Foxhole Brow (*v.* fox-hol, brū); Gorsty Fd (*v.* gorstig); Higher & Lower Graves (1739, *the Greeves* 1610, *v.* grǣfe); Gungo (four examples, cf. *Gonger-, Gongo Lane* (local) 1937 Sheaf³ 32 (7182), perhaps from gang 'a path'); (Higher) Hay Fd (*the Higher & Lower Highfield, the High Field Meadow* 1739, *v.* hēah, feld); Hop Yard (*v.* hoppe, geard); Humpstone Field (*v.* hump, stān); Hunt's Mdw (1739); Lane Flatt (*v.* lane, flat); Leys (*v.* ley); Long Butts (*v.* lang, butte); Lower Lott (*v.* hlot); Marl Fd (*v.* marle); The Mickle Heath 1739 (*v.* micel, hǣð); Middle Fd (*v.* middel); Mule Hay; Purl (*v.* pyrl(e) 'a bubbling spring'); Ridding (*v.* ryding); Rough Hay (1739, *v.* rūh, (ge)hæg); Seven Measures Sowing; Shirat Fd (*Sarratts feilde* 1610 Sheaf, cf. John *Sarratt* ib); Sprinks Mdw (*Moldworth Spryng* 1503, *v.* spring 'a young wood'); Swiner's Dale (*Swenerd Dale* 1503, 'swine-herd's valley', *v.* swīn-hirde, dæl¹); Tithes Mdw 1739 (*v.* tēoða); Two Pets (*the Two Pits Fields* 1739, *v.* twā, pytt).

(*b*) Byrches Feilde 1610 (named from George *Berche* ib); *Brughells Meadowe* 1610 (named from William *Brughell* ib); *le Cambokes* 1353 ('oak-trees along a crest or ridge', *v.* camb, āc); *Chilriddinges* 1610 (perhaps 'cold cleared-lands', from ryding with eModE *chil* adj., (ModE *chill* NED) cf. OE *cele, cyle* 'coldness'); *le Cokshetehull* 1355 (*v.* cocc-scyte, hyll); *Copenhaleeues(e)* 1353, 1357 (*v.* 247 *supra*); *le Flaxlondes* 1355 ('flax selions', *v.* fleax, land); *le Horemerestall* 1353 (perhaps 'the old boundary-point', or 'the site of *Horemere* (the hoar pool)', from (ge)mǣre or mere¹ and stall, with hār²;

however Professor Löfvenberg proposes 'muddy pool' from horu and mere-
steall, which is a preferable interpretation); *Littlers Meadowe* 1610 (named
from George, Richard or William *Litler* ib); *le Penylondes* 1355 (probably
'selions worth a penny', *v.* peni(n)g, land); *Twisses Hay* 1610 (named from
John Twisse ib, *v.* (ge)hæg).

10. TARVIN (BRIDGE & HALL), (109–490670)

Terve 1086 DB, *Terue* 1239 P
Terne 1152, c.1234, 1246, 1249, 1255 MRA, 1242 Misc, 1296 Cl
Teruen 1185 Facs 5 (1) (Sheaf³ 46 (9403) reads *-uin*), c.1200 *Vern
    et freq* with variant spellings *Theru-* (1215 (1299) Chest), *Teru-*
    (to 1303 Chamb), *Terv-* (1287 Court to 1576 ChRR), *del Teruen*
    13 Whall (p), *Tereven* 1376 Pat
(aqua de) *Teruein* 1265–91 Chest
Teruin 1222 Facs, m13 Chest, *-vin* m13 Bark *et freq*, with variant
    spellings *-uin, -uyn, -vyn, -vyne, -vynn* to 1719 Sheaf, *Tervyn
    iuxta Barewe* 1319 Plea
Taruen 1220–40 Whall, *Tarven* 1287 Court, 1304 Chamb, 1611
    ChRR, 1656 Orm², 1669 Sheaf
Taruin 1250–78 Chest (p), *Tarvin* 1287 Court, 1326, 1411 ChRR
    et freq, (*-cum Oscroft*) 1724 NotCestr, (*-Hall*) 1831 Bry, *-vine*
    1599 Orm², *-vyn* 1359 Chamb, 1416, 1625 ChRR
Terney 1291 Tax
Treuyn 1324 *Fitt* (p), *Trevin* 1452 Pat
Terwyn 1328 MRA, 1496 Sheaf
Teruent 1347 *ChFor*
Tyrvyn 1411 InqAqd
Travine 1560 Sheaf

'At the boundary river', from (PrWelsh *terv̆ĭn, Welsh terfyn
v. JEPN **1** 51, **2** 74) 'a boundary', the old name of R. Gowy **1** 26
supra, v. brycg, hall. Tarvin was a manor of the Bishop of Lichfield,
and gives a name to a prebendal stall in his cathedral, cf. **1** 9 and
Park Fd, *Bisschopishaye infra*.

OSCROFT (BRIDGE & HALL FM) (109–505669) ['ɔskrɔft]

Ouuescroft 1272–90 *ChFor*, (lit. *Onnes-*) 1287 Court 65
Ouescroft (lit. *Ones-*) 1288 Court 153 (p), 1393 *Chol*, *Ouis-* (lit.
    Onis-) 1291 Court 170 (p), *Owescroft* 1314 ChRR, 1347 *ChFor*,
    Ovescroft 1506 Orm²

Ewescroft 1298 (17) *Harl.* 2115
Ouwescroft (lit. *Outhes-*) 1304 Chamb 69
Ousecroft 1305 Plea, 1317 ib (p), 1340, 1345, 1348 *Eyre, -e* 1333
    Plea, *Ouscroft* 1328 ib, *Hous-* 1343–4 Orm², *Owsecroft* 1355 *Indict*
Overescroft 1410 Plea, 1440 ib (p), *Overs-* 1426 ChRR, 1510 Orm²,
    (*-alias Auscroft*) 1514 ib, *-crofte* 1524 ib, *Orscrofte* 1517 ChRR
Overecroft 1443 ChRR (p), *Overcroft* 1510 ib
Oscroft in Tervyn 1503 Plea, *Oscroft* 1511 ib *et freq*, (*Tarvin cum-*)
    1724 NotCestr, *-e* 1517 ChRR, *Osscroft Farm* 1831 Bry
Auscroft (*Overscroft alias-*) 1514 Orm²
Ascroft 1594 Sheaf
Ostcroft 1663 Sheaf

'Sheep croft', from OE *e(o)we* (gen.sg. *e(o)wes*) 'a sheep' (*v.* BT,
cf. eowu), -es², and croft. Dr von Feilitzen points out that the masc.
variant is only recorded in the gen.sg. *eowes* (one example only, in the
Laws of Ine). The genitival -es² in this p.n. may be a ME construction. The form *Outhescroft* 1304 Chamb probably represents *Ouwes-*
with confusion of *p* (*w*) and *þ* (*th*). The *Ove-* forms represent *Oue-*,
and the *Over-* forms have an intrusive *-r-* [-wəːs-].

HOLME BANK, HOLME STREET (HALL) (109–480670) [houm]

> *Great Holme* 1298 (17) *Harl.* 2115, *Holme* 1439 Orm² (p), *the*
> *Holmes'* 1558 Sheaf, *Holms* (*Field & Meadow*) 1838 TA, *Holme*
> *Bank* 1831 Bry
> (highway called) *Holmestrete* 1396 ChRR, *-streete* 1611 *Crownmote*,
>   1671 Sheaf (a hamlet), *-street* 1656 Orm² (a farm), *-Street* 1658
>   ib (a hall), 1771 ib, (*-Hall*) 1819 ib, *Holm Street Field* 1838 TA
> *Hulme Street* 1663 Orm², (*-Hall*) 1740 ib

'Bank and road at a marsh', from holmr, with banke, stræt and
hall. The 'street' is the road from Stamford Bridge 326 *infra* to
Tarporley 289 *infra, v.* **1** 48 (route XXIV).

WEETWOOD COMMON, 1812 Sheaf, *Weetwood* 1831 Bry, *Weetewood*
Hey 1298 (17) *Harl.* 2115, *le Wet(e)wode* 1332 Cl, 1347 *ChFor*,
Westwood Common 1842 OS, 'wet wood', *v.* wēt, wudu, (ge)hæg,
commun.

AUSTIN HILL, *Austin's Hill* 1838 TA, *v.* hyll.   BROOKLANDS, *v.*
brōc, land.   BROOM BANK, *v.* brōm, banke.   BROOMHEATH
LANE, *Brown Heath* 1838 TA, *v.* brūn¹, brōm, hǣð.   CRIB

Cottage, v. crib.   Cross Lane (Fm), *Osscroft Lane* 1831 Bry, *Cross Lane Croft & Field* 1838 *TA*, v. cros, lane, cf. Oscroft *supra*.   Ducker's Well.   Duddon Heath (Fm), *Duddon Heath* 1831 Bry, v. hǣð, cf. Duddon 273 *supra*.   Field Ho, v. feld.   Hocken-hull Lane, 1831 Bry, cf. *Hockenhull (Hall) Field* 1838 *TA*, v. lane, hall, feld, cf. Hockenhull 274 *supra*.   The Limes, 1860 White, *Old Crow* 1831 Bry, 'the old shed', v. ald, crew.   Manor Fm, *Manor House* 1842 OS, v. maner.   Moss Hayes, *Moss Heys* 1831 Bry, 'moss enclosures', v. mos, (ge)hæg.   The Mount, v. munt. Mount Pleasant, 1838 *TA*, v. 325 *infra*.   Old Moss, 1831 Bry, cf. Old Moss Lane & Fm 270 *supra*, v. ald, mos.   Poolbank, v. pōl¹, banke.   Salem Cottage.   Saltersbridge (109–497678), a house at Saltersford Bridge, v. 278 *supra*.   Shay Lane, 1831 Bry, v. scaga, lane.   Tarvin Mill, 1831 ib, 'the mill of *Terven*' 113 MRA, *Milne-, Muln-, Mulnesfeilde* 1298 (17) Harl. 2115, *de Molendino* 1326 ChRR (p), 'the mill' 1327 Orm², *del Melne* 1347 *ChFor* (p), v. myln, feld.   Tarvin Sands, 1831 Bry, *The Sands* 1860 White, 'sandy places', v. sand, croft, feld.   Tithebarn, 1842 OS, *Tythe Farm* 1831 Bry, v. tēoða, bere-ærn.   Willington Corner, 1831 ib, v. 286 *infra*.

FIELD-NAMES

The undated forms are 1838 *TA* 384. Of the others, 1272–90, 1347, 1353, 1503 are *ChFor*, 1297 AD, 1298 (17) Harl. 2115, 1299 Pat, a.1321 MRA, 1447, 1599² Orm², 1551 ChRR, 1599 AD, 1638, 1663, 1690, 1708, 1914 Sheaf.

(a) Backside (v. ba(c)ksyde); Barn Fd (v. bere-ærn); Barrow Fd (v. Barrow 261 *supra*); Black Moss (v. blæc, mos); Bottom Moss (v. botm, mos); Breeches Croft (v. brēc); Byng Croft (v. bing); Calvers Croft (v. calver); Cherry Foot; Chester Fd; Collins (*the Collins field* 1708); Common Lot (v. commun, hlot); Coney Greave (v. coningre); Cotton Riddings (v. ryding, cf. Cotton 326 *infra*); Cow Gutter Fd (v. cū, goter); Cow Hey (v. cū, (ge)hæg); Crabssqueeze 1914 (perhaps the site of a cider press); Crab Tree Flatt (v. crabbe, trēow, flat); Cran Moor ('crane's marsh', v. cran, mōr¹); Crib (v. crib); Delamere; Dentists Fd; Dibbedell (*Dibblesdall* 1638, *Dibows-dale* 1663, v. dæl¹ 'a valley, a hollow'; Professor Löfvenberg suggests as first el. the ME pers.n. *Dibald* (< *Theobald* with voicing of initial consonant) or *Dibel* (diminutive of *Dibb*, a pet-form of *Dibald*) as in the surname *Dibble*, v. Reaney 94); Drift; Floss (v. flosshe); Gallows Hill (cf. *Gibbet Heath* 1690, v. gibet, galga, hyll, hǣð); Green Loons (v. grēne¹, land); Far- & Near Hatch (v. hæc(c)); Hercules Yard; Hills Heys (v. (ge)hæg); Hollin Hill (v. holegn, hyll); Hollow Moor Croft (v. holh, mōr¹); Horton Fd (cf. Horton 275 *supra*); Jointure (v. jointure); Kenilstone; Kiln Croft (v. cyln); Lodge

Hays, -Heys (*v.* loge, (ge)hæg); Loons, Loont (*v.* land); Marl Fd (*v.* marle); Millers Wish (*v.* mylnere, wisce); Miry Lane Croft (*v.* myry); Nook (*v.* nōk); Outfield (*v.* ūt, feld); Outlet (*v.* outlet); Ox Wd; Park Fd ('a certain park at *Teruen*' owned by the 'bishop of Chester' 1272–90, 'the bishop's park of *Terven*' 1297, a.1321, 'the imparked wood of *Tervyn*' 1299, 'park within the manor of *Teruent*', *Teruyn Wode* 1347, *Tervyn-, Tervin Park(e)* & *Warren* 1447, 1599², *v.* park, wudu, wareine, cf. Tarvin *supra*, *Bisschopishaye infra*); Pinfold (*v.* pynd-fald); Press Hill (*v.* pres, hyll); Quainter's Fd; Quillet (*v.* quillet(t)); Rails Fd & Mdw (*v.* rail(e)); Riddings (*v.* ryding); Shardsfield; Shoulder of Mutton (*v.* 325 *infra*); Six Butts (*v.* sex, butte); Smooth Wd (*v.* smēðe); Stone Hill Fd (*v.* stān, hyll); Stony Acre (*v.* stānig, æcer); Street Fd (*v.* strǣt, cf. 'Watling Street' 1 40, Holme Street *supra*); Town Fd; Woodsough ('bog at a wood', *v.* wudu, sogh).

(*b*) *Alstansfeld* 1298 (17) ('Ælfstān's field', from the OE pers.n. *Ælfstān* and feld); *Appletre* 1298 (17) (*v.* æppel-trēow); *Astwood* 1298 (17) (*v.* ēast, wudu); *Bisschopishaye* 1353 ('the bishop's fenced-in enclosure', *v.* biscop, (ge)hæg, cf. Park Fd, Tarvin *supra*); *Bromebeche* 1298 (17) ('broom valley', *v.* brōm, bece¹); *Crouchlake Holme* 1298 (17) ('water-meadow at a water-course by a cross', *v.* crouche, lacu, holmr); *Dedwoddes Hall* 1599 (from hall, and the surname (*del*) *Ded(e)wode* 1387 *Eyre*, 1390 ChRR *et freq* to 1480 ib, *Dedwod* 1426 AD, -*woode* 1450 ChRR, -*wodd(e)* 1488, 1489, 'dead wood', *v.* dēad, wudu); *Kayen acston* 1298 (17); *Maydenfield* 1298 (17) (*v.* mægden, feld); *Monygreves* 1298 (17) ('many woods', *v.* manig, grǣfe); *Moss Pitt Flatt* 1663 (*v.* mos, pytt, flat); *Newfield* 1298 (17) (*v.* nīwe, feld); *Potterfeilde* 1298 (17) ('potter's field', *v.* pottere, feld); *Sepeladmore* 1298 (17) ('(marsh at) the sheep-track', *v.* scēp, (ge)lād, mōr¹); *Synderhull* 1298 (17) (*v.* sinder, hyll); *Smallmore* 1298 (17), *Smalmere* 1503 ('narrow marsh and pool', *v.* smæl, mōr¹, mere¹); *Tervyn Hey* 1551 (*v.* (ge)hæg); *Teruynmor* 1347 (*v.* mōr¹).

xv. Prior's Heys

Prior's Heys was an extra-parochial liberty belonging to the bishop of Coventry and Lichfield, in Tarvin township, in the hamlet of Oscroft, *v.* Orm² ii 307.

PRIOR'S HEYS (109–513663), [praiəz, praiərz], 1842 OS, *Williamhaye le Prayers* 1357 ChFor, *Prayshayes* 1666 BW, *Pryars Hayes* 1692 *ib*, *Pryers-* 1721 *ib*, -*Heys* 1749 Sheaf, *Priorshays* 1724 NotCestr, *Pryor Heys* 1831 Bry, *Price Hall* 1656 Orm², 'William le Prayers's enclosure(s)', from (ge)hæg and the surname *Praers*, of an ancient Cheshire family (Orm² iii 299–301). William *le Prayers, de Preyers, de Prayers* was lord of half the nearby manor of Duddon (273 *supra*) in 1351 BPR, and it is alleged in 1353 *ChFor* that about 1339, near Tarvin, he 'fenced in an enclosure of sixty acres' (*inclusit unam hayam de lx acris*). This is the earliest allusion to Prior's Heys.

HOUGHLANDS HO (lost), 1708 Sheaf, the home of John *Houghland* ib, cf. *The Houghlands* 1692 *BW*, *v.* hōh, land.

FIELD-NAMES

(*a*) The Moor 1703 *BW* (*v.* mōr¹).

xvi. Willington

Willington was an extra-parochial liberty peculiar to Whalley Abbey La, (Stanlow Abbey Ch).

WILLINGTON (HALL, MILL (FM) & WOOD) (109–5466)

   Winfletone 1086 DB, *Wynfleton* 1233–7 (1347), 1347 *ChFor*, 1353–4 Orm², 1499 Sheaf

   Wynlaton 1208–29 Whall, and eight examples ib to 1308, *Win-* 1475 *AddCh*, (wood of) *Winlaughton* 1289 Cl

   grangia de Wymlaton 1291 Tax

   Wilanton 1303 Chamb, *Wy-* 1304 ib

   Wilaton 1304 Chamb, (*boscus de-*) *Wy-* 1318 Eyre, (*campus de-*) 1357 *ChFor*, *Willaton* 1307 Eyre, 1503 *ChFor*, (*boscus de-*) 1347 *ib*, (*-Wood*) c.1554 Whall, (*Willington or-*) 1819 Orm², *Wy-* 1537 *AddCh*

   Wolaton 1347 *ChFor*, 1357 Eyre, 1509 ChRR, (*boscus de-*) *Wollaton* 1353, 1357 *ChFor*, 1514 Orm², *Wollaton or Willington by Kelsall* 1671 Sheaf, *Wollaughton* 1547 *MinAcct*

   Willyngton 1526 Chol, *Willington* 1547 *MinAcct*, 1626 Sheaf, (*Willarton alias-*) 1632 Orm², (*Wollaton or-, -by Kelsall*) 1671 Sheaf, (*-or Willaton*) 1819 Orm², (*-Wood*) Jas 1 *Map* (*LRMB* 200), 1819 Orm², (*-Hall & -Mill*) 1831 Bry

   Willoughton 1554 *MinAcct*

   Willaston 1608 ChRR

   Willarton alias Willington 1632 Orm²

   Welleton 1663 Sheaf

'Wynflǣd's farm', from the OE fem. pers.n. *Wynflǣd* and tūn, with wudu, hall, and myln.

THE BELT, *v.* belt.   BENTLEY WOOD, *v.* 298 *infra*.   DICKINSON'S ROUGH, *Dicken-* 1842 OS.   THE DINGLE, *v.* dingle.   HALL WOOD.   HIGHERBARN FM.   JONES'S WOOD.   PEARL HOLE, 'spring hollow', *v.* pyrl(e), hol¹.   QUARRYBANK FM, *Quarry Bank*

1831 Bry.   ROCK FM.   THE ROOKERY.   ROUGHLOW FM, *Roghlawe, Rowe lowe* 1503 *ChFor*, *Rough Lowe* 1812 Sheaf, *-Low* 1831 Bry, 'rough mound', *v.* rūh, hlāw.   TIRLEY COTTAGE, COURT, FM & LODGE, *Tirley Farm* 1842 OS, cf. foll.   TIRLEY LANE, *Willington Doore* Jas 1 *Map* (*LRMB* 200), *Tyrly Gate or Willington Door*, *Willington Gate* 1812 Sheaf, *Tirley Gate* 1813 Orm², 1831 Bry, cf. prec., and Tirley Hollow 212 *supra*, from duru 'a door', and geat 'a gate', an entrance to the Forest of Delamere, with a p.n. *Tirley*, probably 'kindling-wood clearing', *v.* tyri, lēah.   WHISTLE-BITCH WELL, *v.* 212 *supra*.   WILLINGTON CORNER, 1831 Bry, at a corner of the boundary of the Forest of Delamere, cf. 212, 283 *supra*. THE WILLINGTONS, *Ley Farm* 1831 ib, *v.* lēah.   WOOD FM, 1831 ib, cf. Willington Wood *supra*, *v.* wudu.

FIELD-NAMES

The undated forms are 1849 *TA* 435. Of the others, 1503 is *ChFor*, 1537 *AddCh*, 1812 Sheaf, 1831 Bry.

(a) Abrams Well 1812 (*v.* 212 *supra*); Burnt Croft; Ellis Croft; Fox Holes; Glead Brook 1812 (*v.* 212 *supra*); Green Rough; Hall Yards; Intack (*v.* inntak); Long Wd; Marl Fd; Masters Gate 1812 (*v.* 213 *supra*); Moss Bank (*v.* mos); Old Falls (*v.* (ge)fall); Round Brow (*v.* brū); Simpsons Hill 1812 (*v.* 213 *supra*); Slack Fd (*v.* slakki); Smooth Wd; Utkinton Fd (cf. Utkinton 298 *infra*); Walleys Gate 1831 (1812, *v.* geat 'a gate'. This was an access to the Forest of Delamere on the boundary of Willington, cf. 213 *supra*, probably named from Whalley Abbey La, to which Willington belonged, *v. supra*); Long Woodend (*v.* ende¹, cf. Long Wd *supra*).

(b) *Monkeheth* 1503, *Monk's Heath* 1537 ('monk's heath', *v.* munuc, hǣð, part of Whalley Abbey's estate).

xvii. St Oswald's

The parish of St Oswald, Chester, had one township in Eddisbury Hundred. For the rest of the parish, *v.* 326 *infra*. Part of Iddinshall is now included in Clotton Hoofield c.p.

1. IDDINSHALL (HALL, ROUGH) (109–5362) [ˈidənʃɔː(l), ˈidinʃɔːl, ˈidn̩ʃɔː(l)]

   Etingehalle 1086 DB, (*H*)*edinchale* 1096–1101 (1280), 1150 Chest *Idighala* 1130–50 (1285) Chest, c.1150 (1285) Ch (p)
   Idinchale 1188–91 Chest *et freq* with variant spellings *Ydinchal(e)*, *Idyn-*, *Iden-*, *Idynchall* to 1671 Sheaf

Idinghale 1233–7 (1280) Chest, 1295 CRC, Ch, c.1380–90 ChRR
   (p), *Ydinghall* 1270–1 Chest, *Idinghal(l)* 1287, 1288 Court (p)
Idingham 1270 Tab
Idingehalle 1272–90 *ChFor* (p), *-hale* 1287 Court (p)
Ydonehale, Ydonekale 1291 Tax
Idynshaw 1535 VE *et freq* to 1819 Orm[2] with variant spellings
   *Eden-, Edin-, Iden-, Ithen- Idin-, -shaw(e), -shagh; (Edinshagh
   alias Edinshawe iuxta Tereton)* 1550 ChRR, *(Idenshaw alias
   Inenshagh neere Tarperley)* 1594 Orm[2]
Idenshall alias Idenshaw 1583 Orm[2], *Idinshall* 1644 Sheaf, (*-Hall*)
   1831 Bry

A further form of this p.n. may be the surname of Robert *Irynshall*
1497–8 Morris 189, at Chester. The p.n. Iddinshall is from OE halh
'a nook, a corner', and an -ing-formation, perhaps upon the OE
pers.n. *Ida*. DEPN makes it a pl. folk-name in genitival composition,
from -ingas, i.e. OE **Idinga-halh*, 'the valley of Ida's folk'. But this
p.n. is one of the series of Ch names with assibilated palatalized
medial *-ing-*, and the formation is probably halh added to a sg. -ing
p.n. in the palatalized loc.sg.-inflected form (EPN would call it an
-ing[2] form). This alternative prototheme, which looks more likely
than the pers.n. suggested in DEPN, would be OE **etting* 'a
grazing', an -ing-suffix derivative (-ing[1] in EPN) of OE *ettan* 'to
graze'. OE **etting* could be used as a p.n. el. meaning 'a grazing-
place, a pasture'. It is to be seen in the lost p.n. (usque) *Etinges hæle*
901 BCS 586, (in) *Etingesheles* 956 BCS 922 (at Chelworth in Crudwell
parish, W), with OE halh (dat.sg. *hale*, nom. and acc.pl. *halas*), *v.*
Karlström 155, Duignan 58. It appears with halh again in Ettingshall
St, Duignan 58, DEPN, (*Ettingeshale* 996, 1261, *Etynges-* 13,
Etinghale 1086, *Ettingehal* 1175), for which DEPN says, 'Perhaps
"Etting's halh". *Etting* is unrecorded, but would belong to *Atta*,
Etti. Possibly, however, the first el. is a verbal noun derived from OE
ettan and meaning "grazing"'. The St and W p.ns. show **etting* in
uninflected, and in gen.sg. and dat.sg. inflected composition. The Ch
p.n. does not show the gen.sg. inflected composition, but it does
reveal the assibilation from an old palatalized loc.sg. inflexion which
produces the 'pseudo-genitival' spellings *-yns-, -ens-*. The p.n.
Iddinshall ought to be taken as analogous with the Altrincham,
Wincham series (*v.* 2 7, 136), and construed as OE **Ettinge halh*, 'the
halh (called, at) *Ettinge*' where *Ettinge* is the loc.sg.-inflected form of

OE *etting 'a grazing', the loc.sg. form having become the nominative form of a p.n.

This exercise is shrewdly criticised by Professor Löfvenberg, 'The discussion is hardly convincing. I have no doubt that the etymology suggested by Ekwall in DEPN is the correct one. For the palatalization see the explanation given by Ekwall in PN-ing[2] 172–3', setting aside the hypothesis of my articles in BNF II 221–45, 325–96 and III 141–89; and by Dr von Feilitzen, 'Persistant initial *i* and medial *d* render derivation from *etting* rather doubtful; note that the St name has *Etting-* throughout and in the modern form. Are there any good Ch parallels to this unusual phonetic development?' On my assertion 'That the St and W p.ns. show *etting* in uninflected and in gen.sg. and dat.sg. inflected composition', he admonishes, 'This is not correct; both are of course ordinary genitival compounds: *Etinges hæle* 901, *Ettingeshale* 996. What are *dat.sg. compounds* supposed to be? The whole business of loc.sg. inflected forms becoming nominatives and taking a second el. strikes me as extremely hypothetical (to say the least)'. These objections are important and notable. Upon the etymology of Iddinshall, it would be prudent to resume Ekwall's position, and suppose as first el. the OE pers.n. *Ida*. Upon the assibilation of the medial *-ing-*, I cannot yet bring myself to abandon the thesis of my articles in BNF loc. cit., by which I suggest an alternative to PN-ing[2] 172–3. Cf. discussion of this etymology in BNF II (1967) 379 ff. *v*. Addenda.

WITHAN HO, *Within House* 1842 OS, *Little Iddinshall or Within House* 1831 Bry, *v*. wiðegn, hūs, lĩtel, Iddinshall *supra*.

FIELD-NAMES

Of the forms, 1360 is Sheaf, the rest are Chest.

(b) *le Blakesiche* 1265–91 ('black watercourse', on the boundary with Tiverton at 109–530618 to 536620, *v*. blæc, sīc); *Boteokweye* 1290–3 (the Iddinshall–Tarporley boundary at 109–536626 to 537620, probably '(road near) Bota's oak-tree', from the OE pers.n. *Bōta* and āc with weg, though the first el. might be bōt, alluding to some peculiar attributive of the tree, or to some legal rights attaching to it); *le Bradesunderlond in Colemon Leye* p.1270 ('the broad detached selion', *v*. brād, sundor, land, cf. *Colemon Leye infra*); *le Cokschutehauedlond in le Tounstede* p.1270 ('the head-land of the cockshoot', *v*. cocc-scyte, hēafod-land, cf. *le Tounstede infra*); *Colemon leye* p.1270 ('Coleman's clearing', from lēah, with a pers.n., either OIr *Colmán* or OG *Col(e)man*, cf. Feilitzen 218. In view of the occasional Scandinavian els. in this part of Ch (cf. 295 *infra*), the OIr name might be preferred); *le Derne-forde* 1290–3 ('the obscure ford', on the Iddinshall–Tarporley boundary, at 109–539626 or 537619, *v.* derne, ford); *Fildingeshurst* 1265–91 (from hyrst 'a wooded-hill' and an OE by-name *Felding*, or an OE **felding* 'one who lives in a field', cf. Reaney s.n. *Fielding* (*Felding* 1279)); *Flaxyord* 1290–3 ('flax enclosure', *v.* fleax, geard, cf. Flaxyards 290 *infra*); *le Gatebrugg'* p.1270 ('bridge at the gates', *v.* geat (pl. gatu), brycg); *Geylmaresiche* 1290–3 ('boundary stream growing with gale or bog-myrtle', at 109–536626 on the Tarporley boundary, *v.* gagel, (ge)mære, sīc); *le Hallecroftislond* p.1270 ('(the selion in) the hall croft', *v.* hall, croft, -es², land); *le Holefeld* p.1270 ('the field in a hollow', *v.* hol², feld); *Knolle* 1360 (p) ('the hill', *v.* cnoll); *Morichbuttes* p.1270 ('swampy selions' from butte with ME *moris(c)h* (cf. mōr¹, -isc), cf. *moorish* 'moor-ish, swampy, boggy', 1398 NED); *Netstallis* 1290–3 ('net-stalls, the places where the fishing-nets are placed', from stall in the sense 'a fishing pool' and OE nett 'a net'); *Penerlishurst* 1265–91 (ChetNS LXXXII 784 reads *Peu-*, which gives a more intelligible form, 'Peverel's wooded-hill', from the OFr pers.n. *Peverell* and hyrst); *le Sawe-heued* p.1270 (probably 'top end of the wood', *v.* sceaga, hēafod); *le Toun-stede* p.1270 ('the site of an enclosure or farmyard', *v.* tūn, toun, stede, cf. tūn-stede); *le Witokestonel'* 1290–3 ('the stone-hill at the white oak', from hwīt and āc, stān and hyll).

xviii. Tarporley

The ecclesiastical parish of Tarporley contains the townships 1. Eaton (cf. Rushton *infra*), 2. Rushton (now a c.p. including Eaton *supra*), 3. Tarporley, 4. Utkinton.

1. EATON (109–573634) [ˈiːtən, ˈɛitən]

> *Magna, Parva Eyton* 1240 P, c.1270 (1580) Sheaf, 1328 Cl, *Eyton*
> 1272–1307 *AddCh*, 1284 Pat *et freq* to 1671 Sheaf
> *Magna, Parva Eiton* 1240 P, *Eiton* 1569 Orm²
> *Magna et Parva Eton* 1240 P, 1241 Lib, *Eton* 1474 ChRR
> *Magna et Parva Eaton* 1240 P, *Eaton* 1418 Barnes¹ 398, 1442 ChRR,
> 1581 ib *et freq*, (*-or Ayton near Tarporley*) 1724 NotCestr
> *Ayton* 1304 Chamb *et freq* to 1724 NotCestr, (*-iuxta Torpurley*)
> 1415 ChRR
> *Aeton* 1417 *Surv*
> *Heyton* 1481 Tab, 1524 Barnes¹ 398

'Farm at a dry place', *v.* ēg, tūn. The village stands at the end of a spur running down between two streams. The topography suggests marshy valleys on either side of the site. Eaton adjoins Tarporley 294 *infra*. Eaton has been proposed for *Etone* 1086 DB f.267b, *v.* Hatton near Waverton, 326 *infra*.

FLAXYARDS (109–566625), (le) *Flaxyordes* 1337 *AddCh*, 1357 *ChFor et freq* with variant spellings *Flaxe-, -yordez, -yord(i)s, -ʒordes* to 1585 Cre, *Flaxehordes* 1356 *Indict* (p), *Flaxordes* 1457 AD, *Flaxeyerdes* 1345 *Eyre* (p), *Flax(e)-* 1540 Sheaf, *le Flaxyord* 1353 *ChFor*, *Flaxyord(e)* 1487, 1511 ChRR, *Flaxyardes* 1461 ib, *(the-)* 1781 Sheaf, *Flaxe-* 1537 MidCh, *Flaxyards* 1656 Orm², *(-in Eyton, -Hall)* 1671 Sheaf, 'enclosures where flax is grown', from **fleax** and **geard**, with **hall**.

ADAM'S WELL.   ARDERNE HALL, *Eaton Bank* 1831 Bry, *v.* **banke**. The hall is a nineteenth-century edifice named to commemorate the Ardern family, anciently landowners here.   BROOK HO, *v.* **brōc**. CROSSHILL LODGE, a gate of Arderne Hall park near a cross in the park, *v.* **cros, hyll, loge**.   EATONHILL FM, *Wind Mill Hill Farm* 1831 Bry, *v.* **wind-mylne, hyll**.   HILL HO, *Hell House* 1831 ib, *The Hill* 1842 OS, *v.* **hyll**.   LUDDINGTON HILL, *v.* 298 *infra*. ROYAL LODGE, cf. *Royals Lane* 1831 Bry, *Royal (Banks)* 1838 *TA*, probably 'rye-hill or -nook', from **ryge** and **hyll** or **halh**, with **banke, lane**.   SAPLING LANE, *Saplin Lane* 1831 Bry, 1842 OS, *(Higher-, Lower-) Sapling(s)* 1838 *TA*, 'lane at the saplings', from ModE *sapling* and **lane**.   STAGES PLATT [steidʒiz], *Stacio's Plat* 1831 Bry, cf. *Stacious Platt Field* (1840), 302 *infra*, and *Staysoes Yard* 1838 *TA*, *v.* **plat¹, geard**. The platt is a bridge over Wettenhall Brook at 109–580616. The first el. is hard to establish. It might be from the pers.n. *Eustace*, cf. Reaney s.nn. *Stacey, Stace* (ME and MedLat *Staci(us)*), but a reduced form of **sceaga** 'a wood', is possible. The location might suit a p.n. *Stayshaw* 'wood at a pond', from OE **stæg** and **sceaga**.   WINTERFORD FM & LANE, *Wynterford* 1500 AD, *Winterford Lane* 1831 Bry, 'ford usable in winter', or 'place which has to be forded, i.e. which floods, in winter', from **winter** and **ford**, with **lane**.

FIELD-NAMES

The undated forms are 1838 *TA* 158. Of the others 1270 is *Dav*, 1304 Chamb, 1356 *Indict*, 1360, 1508 ChRR, 1360², 1555, 1565 Orm², 1416, 1417 *Surv*, 1500 AD, 1831 Bry.

(a) Bab Field Bank; Birch Knowls (*v.* **birce, cnoll**); Black Croft; Blake Fd (*v.* **blæc**); Blindhurst ('blind wood', *v.* **blind, hyrst**, cf. Blindhurst La 166); Bottoms Bank (*v.* **botm, banke**); Broomy Low (*v.* **brōmig, hlāw**); Butts; Caukers Croft (cf. Cockers Fd *infra*); Clay Lake (*v.* **clæg, lacu**); Cockers Fd (*le Cokkersfyld* 1500, *Cockersfilde* 1565, 'the cocker's field', *v.* **cocker, feld**); Coney Grave (*v.* **coningre**); Cow Hey (*v.* **(ge)hæg**); Crook Fd (*v.* **krókr**); Cross Fd (*v.* **cros**); Edgrew Fd ('hedgerow field', *v.* **hecg-ræw**);

Gale Riddings (*v.* gagel, ryding); Hanging Fd (*v.* hangende); Big & Little Hile (*v.* hygel); Hinds Croft (*v.* hine); Homestead Yard; Hook Croft (*v.* hōc); Big & Little Hough (*le Hough* 1360, *v.* hōh); Knowl; Lightfield Lane 1831 (*v.* lēoht, feld); Long Shoot (*v.* scēat); Marl(ed) Croft; Maypole (*v.* maye-pole); Milking Bank (*v.* milking); Mill Lane 1831; Mistress's Mdw; Musk Croft; Nine Ends (*v.* nigon, ende[1]); Nook Croft; Old Hughs Mdw; Pingot (*v.* pingot); Riddall Heath (*v.* Rhuddall Heath 296 *infra*); Riddings (*v.* ryding); Rock Ho 1831 (*v.* rokke); Sein Butts ('seven selions', *v.* seofon, butte); Smiths Fd, Smithy Croft & Fd (cf. *Smithfilde* 1417, *Smith Crofte* 1416, *v.* smiδ, feld, croft); Sond Mdw (*v.* sand); (Hanging) Staypole (*Steple* 1417, from stēap and lēah or a contracted form of hyll, with hangende. Cf. *Stephul* c.1270 (p), *Stephull* 1304 (p), 1356); Stone Flatt (*v.* stān, flat); Such Lane 1831 (*v.* sīc); Town Flatt (cf. *townefilde* 1417, 'public field', *v.* toun, feld, flat); Villy Veeson; Way Fd (*v.* weg); Westmarsh (*v.* west, mersc); Wet Fd; White Fd; Winbury Hill ('hill where winberries grow', *v.* winberige); Woodhall.

(*b*) *Bo(u)ltons House* 1508, 1555 (from a surname *Bolton* and hūs); *Le Calverlegh* 1360 ChRR ('the calves' clearing', *v.* calf (gen.pl. calfra), lēah); *le Clogh* 1360[2] (p) ('the dell, *v.* clōh); *Marcallesland* 1417 (*v.* marescal, land).

2. RUSHTON (109–5863)

Rusitone 1086 DB

Riseton(e)-, Risedon Hund' 1086 DB, *Riston* 1237 Cl, *Rys-* 1284 Pat, *Ristone* 1287 Court (p)

Ruston 1154–89 Tab, 1240 P, Cl *et freq* with variant spelling *-tone* to 1359 BPR

Ruiston 1240 P, *Ruys-* 1254 ib

Rushton 1242 Ipm *et freq* with variant spellings *Rusch(e)-, Russ(c)he-, Russh-, -tun, -toun, -tonne; Russheton in Yevelegh, -by Yevele(y)* 1438, 1440 MainwB

Russeton 1297 Werb (p)

Rishton 1308 IpmR, 1311 Plea (p) *et freq* with variant spellings *Rys(s)h(e)-, Rysche-, Risshe-* to 1672 Cre, *Rysshton in Torperle* 1426 Sheaf

Ruysshton 1323 ChRR and eight examples ib, *ChFor*, BPR, Orm[2] with variant spellings *Ruy(s)sh(e)-, Ruissche-* to 1416 ChRR

Rusdon 1324 Cl

Risshteton 1471 *MinAcct*

'Rush farm', *v.* risc, tūn. Cf. Tarporley 294 *infra*, Yeanley *infra*. Rushton was the meeting-place of one of the DB hundreds of Ch, but was itself in the detached portion of another, *v.* 160 *supra*.

(Y)EANLEY (lost, about 109–575650 to 567654)

> *Geynle, Geinleg'* 1240 P
> *Yeynleg'* 1312 *CoLegh*
> *Yeyulegh, Yewelegh* 1353–7 *ChFor* (Barnes[1] 399), (*Russheton in-,*
>   *-by-*) *Yevelegh, Yevele(y)* 1438, 1440 MainwB, *Yeavley Wods*
>   1568 Orm[2]
> *Yemeleywode,* (watermill called) *Yemelemulne* 1353 *ChFor, molen-*
>   *dinum de Yemelegh* 1361 *ib*
> *molendinum de Eneley* 1357 *ChFor*
> *Yanelegh Mill* 115 Orm[2], *Yaynelegh* 1503 *ChFor*
> (*Y)Eanley Meadow* 1838 *TA*

'The lambing-glade' or 'glade where the lambs grazed', from ēan
'a lamb' (cf. Studies[2] 70–1) and lēah, with wudu and myln, cf.
Eanley Wood 2 173. However, Professor Löfvenberg adds that the
first el. may be the OE pers.n. *Eana* (*v.* Studies[2] loc. cit.). In some
forms *-v-* is for *-u-*, an error for *-n-*, and could cause confusion with
the forms of Isle Fm 326 *infra*, or even Yeaveley Db 619. The mill
appears to be Oulton Mill *infra*. Yeanley seems to have been quite as
considerable a place as Rushton in the thirteenth century.

BEECH LANE (FM), *Green Hill or Breach Lane Farm* 1831 Bry, *Breach
Lane Farm* 1842 OS, cf. *Green Hill Croft* and *Breach* (*freq*) 1838 *TA*,
v. grēne[1], hyll, brēc.   BOOTHOUSE FM, *Bothurste* 1416 *Surv*, *le
Bulthurst* 1500 AD, *Bowthurst* 1567 Orm[2], *Boote-house* 1671 Sheaf,
Boot House 1831 Bry, 1838 *TA, Boothurst* 1842 OS, *-or Booth House*
1882 Orm[2], 'wood-hill where a privilege to cut wood was exercised',
v. bōt, hyrst.   BROWNHILL, 1831 Bry, *Brounhill* 1507 Plea, *v.*
brūn[1], hyll.   COTE BROOK (109–5765), *le Brokh* 1360 ChRR,
Colbroke Mylne 1476 ChRR, *Colebrooke* Jas 1 *Map* (*LRMB* 200),
Cole Brook 1751 Sheaf, *Coatbrook* 1828 ib, *Cote Brook* 1831 Bry, now
the name of a hamlet on the Rushton-Utkinton boundary, near
Sandyford Brook 1 34, for which it may represent another name,
'cool brook', from cōl[2] and brōc, the first el. having been replaced by
cald 'cold'. The mill appears to be Oulton Mill *infra*.   DARLEY
GORSE & ROUGH, *The New Gorse* 1831 Bry, *Darley Gorse* 1842 OS,
v. gorst, cf. Darley 165 *supra*.   GARNERSHOUSE.   HAZELHURST
COVERT, 1842 ib, *Hasel-, Heselhurst, Aselishurst* 1304 Chamb (p), *Le
Haselhurst* 1360 ChRR, 'hazel wood', *v.* hæsel, hesel, hyrst.
HICKHURST LANE, 1831 Bry, *Haukeshurst* 1353 *ChFor*, 'hawk's wood-

hill', *v.* hafoc, hyrst. HILLHOUSE FM, *v.* hyll, hūs. HUNT'S
HILL. OAKTREE HO, 1831 Bry. OLD LANES, *Dunns Lane* 1831
ib, from the surname of the family *Done* of Utkinton 298 *infra, v.*
ald, lane. OULTON LAKE, cf. 185 *supra.* OULTON MILL, (109–
580650, on the Rushton side of Sandyford Brook), 1842 OS, 'one
mill and one mill-dam (*stagnum*) built in Oulton' 1272–90 *ChFor,*
Mylnecrofte 1416 *Surv, Olton myllne pole* 1497 AD, *a water miln in*
Russhton 1499 Orm², *a mylne in Russheton called the noow Mylne* 1531
ib, *le Olde Mylnefald* (a parcel of land on which a watermill is built)
1507 *MinAcct, Oulton or Nockinger Mill, Mill Lane* 1831 Bry (cf.
Nogginshaw *infra*), and also *Colbroke Mylne* 1476 ChRR (cf. Cote
Brook *supra*) and *Yemelemulne* 1353 *ChFor*, etc., (cf. *Yeanley, supra*),
v. myln, croft, pōl¹, nīwe, ald, fald, lane, mǣd. Cf. Oulton 185 *supra.*
OULTON PARK, *v.* 185 *supra.* OX HEYS, 1842 OS, cf. *oxhey* 1416
Surv, le Oxe Hey 1500 AD, 'ox enclosure', *v.* oxa, (ge)hæg. PARK-
WALL FM, adjoining the boundary of Oulton Park *supra, v.* park,
wall. PHILO COTTAGE & GORSE, *Wells Lew, Rushton Fox Cover*
1831 Bry, *Philo Gorse* 1842 OS. POOLHEAD, 1831 Bry, 'the top
end of a (mill-) pool', cf. *Pool Stead* 1838 *TA, v.* pōl¹, hēafod,
pōl-stede, cf. Oulton Mill *supra.* RUSHTON BANK, cf. *Bank Field*
1838 *ib, v.* banke. SANDYFORD BRIDGE, *v.* 211 *supra.* TOWNS
GREEN, 1831 Bry, cf. *le Toun* 1359 *Eyre* (p), 1399 ChRR (p), *Town*
Green Field 1838 *TA*, from a surname *Town*, from toun, with grēne²,
cf. Townfield Fm 167 *supra.* WITHEY BED, *v.* wīðig, bedd.

FIELD-NAMES

The undated forms are 1838 *TA* 158. Of the others, 1338 is VR, 1360, 1442
ChRR, 1416 *Surv*, 1500 AD, 1503 *ChFor*, 1598 Orm², 1711 Cre, 1831 Bry,
1842 OS.

(a) Ash Fd (*le Ashefilde* 1416, *Asschefyld* 1500, *v.* æsc, feld); Austin;
Barrow Yard (*v.* bearg, geard); Bottoms (*v.* botm); Boultocks (*Baltokkesfelde*
1416, *v.* feld. *Baltokkes* may be the genitive of a surname from Baldock Hrt);
Bradshaws Mdw (cf. *Bradshaw House* 1831); Broad Mdw (*brodmedow* 1416,
the broad meadow 1500, *v.* brād, mǣd); Calver Croft ('calves' croft', *v.* calf
(gen.pl. calfra), croft); Cats Croft (cf. *Catteshurst, Cattersfild* 1416, '(field at)
wild-cat's hill', *v.* catt, hyrst, feld, croft); Clammy Clough (*v.* clǣmig,
clōh); The Cole Fd 1711 (*v.* col¹); Coneygrave(s) (*v.* coningre); Cote Fd (*le*
Cotefild (lit. *Cete-*), *le Cotesfeld* 1416, *v.* cot); Cow Hey (*v.* (ge)hæg);
Cranbury Bank ('bank where cranberries grow', *v.* cranberry); Dogmoor
(*Dogemore medow* 1416, *v.* dogga, mōr¹); Dunstead (*v.* tūn-stede); Faddily
Dam (*v.* damme, cf. Faddiley 142 *supra*); Flatt (*v.* flat); French Fd (*v.*

french-wheat); Glade Fd; Glass Fd (*Glasfild* 1416, *v.* glæs[1]. There may have been a glassworks here, cf. *Glasshowse* 244 *supra*); Green Dale (*v.* dæl[1]); Hall Lane 1831; Hatch Ridding (*le Hakke* 1416, *v.* hæc(c)); Hickles Bank & Mdw (*v.* hicol); King Fd; Knowl(e); Lockinch Croft & Mdw (perhaps from loca and -ing[2]); Megs Yard (*v.* meg, geard); Moss; Nogginshaw (cf. *Nockinger Mill* 1831, Oulton Mill *supra*, 'at the oak wood', *v.* atten, ācen, sceaga); Niccobrook Mdw (*v.* nicor 'a water-sprite', brōc); Oak Wd; Pinfold Croft (*v.* pynd-fald); Pingot (*v.* pingot); Potters Croft (cf. *Potters-medowe* 1416, from pottere, perhaps as a surname, and mǣd); Riddings (*v.* ryding); Rough Wd; Ruffions Lake (probably 'watercourse at rough-corners', from ruh and hyrne, with lacu); Rushton Cross 1831 (*v.* cros); Shadywood (1831, 'shady wood', *v.* shady, wudu); Long Shoot (*v.* scēat); (Further, Middle & Nearer) Souche (*le Sowchus* 1500, 'the watercourses, the fields by a stream', *v.* sīc); Sprinks ('young woodlands' *v.* spring); Sycamore Bank 1831 (cf. Sycamore Hill 300 *infra*); Tinters Bank 1831 (*v.* tentour); Townfield; Wanleys Lane 1842 (*v.* 187 *supra*); Warren Fd (*v.* wareine); Way Fd (*v.* weg); Further & Nearer Wd (cf. *Wood Lane* 1831, 1842); Worlds End 1831.

(*b*) *Copthorne(lake)* 1503 ('(watercourse at) pollarded thorn tree', *v.* copped, þorn, lacu); *Eyrlondes* 1416 ('the heir's selions', *v.* eyr, land); *le Halle Knoll* 1416 ('hillock', *v.* hall[2], cnoll); *Housestilfilde* 1416 ('(field at) the stile near a house', *v.* hūs, stigel, feld); *Madynsfild* 1416 ('maiden's field', *v.* mægden, feld); *le owehwye* 1416 ('ewe enclosure', *v.* eowu, kví, the second el. being Professor Löfvenberg's suggestion); *the Pele* 1442 (DKR xxxvii 249, 'the site of the manor of Russheton, and all the timber &c of the houses within the said site except the soil and the bridge over the Pele', *v.* pēl 'a stake, a palisade, a pale', here used of the moat round a fortified house); *le Rauenehurst* 1338, (*Le*) *Raveneshurst, Ravenstrete in Ruysshton* 1360, *Ravenfeild alias Ranefeild, Ravenshursts alias Ravenscrofts house alias Wittar's tenement* 1598 ('raven's wood & field, street haunted by ravens', *v.* hræfn, hyrst, strǣt, feld; owned 1598 by John *Wittar*, cf. Witters Croft & Fd 297 *infra*); *Le Shephenses* 1360 (Professor Löfvenberg suggests that this is probably an error for *Shephouses*, *v.* scēp, hūs); *Westenehurst in Ruysshton* 1360, *Weste Nase* 1503 ('wood-hill at the waste-land', *v.* wēsten, hyrst).

3. TARPORLEY (109–5562) [ˈtarpəli] older local [ˈtarpli]

Torpelei 1086 DB, *Torpel'* 1198–1216 Facs, *-ll'* 1198–1216 MidCh, *Torpelegh* c.1208 (17) Sheaf, 1386 Pat, *-le* 1287 Plea (p), Court (p), 1357 Pat (p), *-ley* 1304 Chamb (p), 1549 Pat, (*Torpurley alias-*) 1581 ChRR, *-leye* 1307 *Eyre*, *-lee* 1328 Cl, *-les* 1664 Sheaf
Torplei 1086 (1380) IpmR, *-le* 1284 Cl, *-legh* 1298 (1724) NotCestr, 1348 *ChFor*, 1387 Orm[2], *-lighe* 1418 *Rental* (Barnes[1] 404), *-ley* l15 Orm[2], 1512 *ChEx*, 1560 Tab (p), 1578 *Chol*, 1618, 1653 Sheaf, *-leighe* (lit. *-leigse*) 1553 Tab (Barnes[1] 404)
Torperley 1198–1216 *MidCh et freq* with variant spellings *Torpor-*

(1281 Orm[2] to 1755 Sheaf), *Torpur-* (l13 Tab to 1665 Sheaf),
Torpir- (1328 MRA), *-leg'*, *-legh(e)*, *-l(y)*, *-le(e)*, *-ley(e)*, *-leygh*,
-lighe, *-leigh(e)* to 1781 Sheaf, *Torparley* 1441 ChRR (Barnes[1]
404)

Thopperlegh 1235 *Clif* (p)

Thorperleg(h), *-l(ey)*, *-le(e)* 1280–1300 *AddCh*, 1281 (18) Orm[2],
1282 Ch, 1284 Pat (p), 1287 *ChFine*, 1288 Court (p), 1293 (18)
Sheaf, and 12 examples to 1349 *AddCh*

Thorple 1282 CRC, 1344 Pat, *-leg'* 1295 *JRC* (p) (Barnes[1] 403),
Thorpeleg' 1289 MRA, *-ley* 1291 Tax

Torpereleye 1307 *Eyre* (Barnes[1] 404)

Toperlegh 1311 Ipm, *-ley* 1554 Pat (Barnes[1] 404)

Toprelegh 1355 BPR

Terperlegh 1369 Bark, *-ley* 1671 Sheaf

Tarporley 1394, 1402, 1663 ChRR *et freq*, *-ly* 1585 Cre, *Tarpurlegh*
1499 Sheaf, *-ley* 1522 Mere, 1715 LCWills, *Tarperley* 1568 Orm[2],
1578 *Chol*, 1593 LCWills, 1670, 1684 Sheaf, *-ly* 1660 ib

Turporley 1471 *MinAcct*, *-purley*, *-legh* 1508 ChRR

Tropley 1540 Sheaf

Tarpley 1665 Sheaf

This is a difficult name. DEPN suggests that this p.n. is 'pear
wood near a hill called *Torr*', from torr, pere and lēah, in which an
original p.n. *Perley* is modified by the prefixed hill-name *Torr*, as in
Tormarton Gl (DEPN, cf. Didmarton, Gl, ib). This type of p.n. is
not well attested, and Smith, EPN xxiii, doubts the correctness of the
analysis. An alternative analysis is available for the Gl p.ns., *v.* Gl 3
56. There is one for Tarporley, which avoids the formal difficulty,
but raises a more troublesome one of interpretation. The spellings
suggest OE **þorpera-lēah*, from lēah and a gen.pl. form **þorpera*
from OE **þorpere* 'a man who lives in a hamlet', *v.* þorp, -ere[1], cf.
ON *þorpari* 'a peasant, a cottager'. Although there is no p.n. in þorp
hereabouts, the form **þorpere* suggests a late-OE hybrid formed from
þorp. There may have been an ethnic minority of Scandinavians in
this district to whom English neighbours had given the nickname
'the Thorp-ers'. There is some Scandinavian influence observed in
the p.ns. of the neighbourhood, e.g. Kettles Croft, Whitegates, Scows,
Colemon leye 313, 316, 322 *infra*, 288 *supra*.

STREET-NAMES. HIGH ST., *v.* hēah, strǣt, cf. *Torperle...a long pavid village,
or thorough fare* c.1536 Leland v 26, and Road Street *infra*.

HERMITAGE (lost, 109–548630)

> capella Sancti Leonardi de Rode in Thorperl' 1287 ChFine, MRA,
> Chapel de-, -of-, Rood(e) (in Torperlee) 1301 (1724) NotCestr,
> (1819) Orm², 1496 ChRR, -la Roode 1507 Orm², Chapel of (the)
> Rode (of Torperle), (capella de (la) Rode) 1317, 1388 Orm², 1440
> ChRR, 1494, 1508 ChCert, cantaria del Rode juxta Torperlegh
> 1364 Orm²
>
> The Hermitage 1289 Court, Heremitorium 1290–3 Chest, capella de
> la Rode vocata le Ermitage 1338 Plea, capella heremet' juxta
> Torpurlegh 1385 Orm², capella vocata le Hermytes 1388 ib, þe
> Chappell called Le Hermitage 1389 (1724) NotCestr, Chapel of
> 'Hermitage juxta Torplegh' 1396 (1724) ib
>
> capella libera beate Marie Virginis et Sancti Leonardi heremet' de la
> Rode juxta Torplegh 1387 Orm²
>
> (libera) capella (siue) her(e)mitagium Sancti Leonardi de la Rode
> juxta Torplegh, -Torpurley 1388, 1397 Orm²
>
> a cottage called Le Ermytage 1564–5 Orm²
>
> Further, Middle and Nearer Hermitage 1838 TA

Orm² II 237 records the discovery c.1816 of the site, in *Hermitage Field* about half a mile NW of Tarporley church, of this, 'the free chapel of the Blessed Virgin Mary and St Leonard, of the hermitage of the Rood beside Tarporley', v. ermitage, rōd². The rood-cross probably gave name to Road Street *infra*, that road passing the hermitage. In 1290–3 Chest (ChetNS LXXXII 783) a road from the hermitage to Iddinshall was at the boundary of Iddinshall and Tarporley, 109–540634 to 540630.

RHUDDALL HEATH (109–560620), ['rudɔ:l], Red(h)aleheth' 1347, 1353 ChFor, Rudalheth 1393 Chol, Riddow Heath 1719 Sheaf, Riddal Heath 1831 Bry, 1838 TA 158, Rudhall Heath 1842 OS, 'heath at reedy nook', from hrēod and halh, with hǣð. The modern form is pseudo-Welsh.

ALPHA COTTAGES.   ASH-HILL, 1842 OS, *Ash Hill House* 1831 Bry, v. æsc, hyll.   THE ASH HO (lost), 1819 Orm², (messuage called) *Le Greate Asshe* 1564 ib, *the great Ashehouse, -howse* 1574, 1581 ChRR, *le Ashe* 1596 ib, *Ash Tree* 1719 Sheaf, v. æsc, hūs, cf. *le asslond* 1417 Surv, *Ash Field & Meadow* 1838 TA, v. land. The house was demolished e19, the materials were used to repair Haughton Hall 309 *infra*.   BACKLANES COTTAGES, v. back, lane.   BIRCH HEATH

(Ho), *Birch Heath* 1831 Bry, cf. *Burchewoode* 1564 Orm², *v.* birce, hǣð, wudu. The house was *Tan Yard* 1831 Bry, *v.* tan-yard. BOWMERE LODGE & RD, *Bowmer Lodge* 1842 OS, *Bowmoor Hill & Meadow* 1838 *TA*. COBBLERS CROSS, *Coblers Cross* 1831 Bry, *v.* cros. COMMON FM, *v.* commun. EATON RD, cf. Eaton 289 *supra*. FOREST RD, *New Road* 1831 Bry. FROG LANE, 1831 ib, *v.* frogga. HILL FM, *v.* hyll. MANOR HO, *v.* maner. MOSS COTTAGE, *Sour Butts* 1831 Bry, *v.* sūr, butte. PARK RD, leading to the park of Arderne Hall 290 *supra*, *v.* park. PORTAL (FM), *Portal Lodge* 1831 ib, 1842 OS. ROAD STREET, *v.* 1 48 (route XXIV), *Hermitage supra*. SALTERS WELL (HO) (109–552631), *Salters Well House* 1831 Bry, 'well used by salt merchants', *v.* saltere, wella. This is beside Road Street *supra* which was probably a salt-way. SPRING HILL, *v.* spring 'a well-spring', hyll. UTKINTON RD, cf. Utkinton 298 *infra*. WITHEY BED, *v.* wīðig, bedd.

FIELD-NAMES

The undated forms are 1838 *TA* 383. Of the others, 1287 is ChF, 1287² MRA, 1339 MidCh, 1360 ChRR, 1417 *Surv*, 1565 Orm², 1810 Sheaf.

(a) Blake Fd (*le blackfield* 1417, *v.* blæc, feld); Broom (Fd) (*v.* brōm); Calvers Croft (*v.* calver); Cockaynes Croft ('cockney's croft', *v.* cockaygne, cf. Cockaneys Croft 299 *infra*); Commanders Butts (*v.* butte. This ground may have belonged to a commandery of the order of the Knights Hospitallers, which had estates in Tiverton); Cooksey Mdw (cf. *Cooksey Lane* 1831 Bry); Cripplegate Nook (*v.* crypel-geat, nōk); Ten Day Math (*v.* day-math); Dean & Chapter Land (part of the Done inheritance claimed in 1715 by the Dean & Chapter of Chester, *v.* Orm² II 229, 249); Devils Bit (probably named after the plant); Diamond Hill (cf. 299 *infra*); Drumble Fd (dial. *drumble*, cf. dumbel); Fish Mdw; Flatt (*v.* flat); Gorsty Knowl (*v.* gorstig, cnoll); Long Hollands ('long head-lands', *v.* hēafod-land); Hollins Croft, Ardens Hollins (from holegn, croft, and the surname *Arde(r)ne*, cf. Arderne Hall 290 *supra*); Hop Yard (*v.* hoppe); Intack (*v.* inntak); Kiln Croft; Malkin Park (*v.* malkin, park); Mill Fd (*Le Millnefilde* 1565, *v.* myln, feld); Long Moss, Moss Bank, Croft & Mdw (*v.* mos); New Hay; New Town (*v.* nīwe, toun); Oat Hill (*othull* 1417, 'oats hill', *v.* āte, hyll); Palm Ridding (*v.* ryding); Big, Farther & Little Park, Park Mdw (*le parke, black parke, Lechesparch* 1417, from park, with blæc and the surname *Leche*); Priest Fd (*prist filde* 1565, *v.* prēost, feld); Rain Fd (*v.* rein); Round Fd; Royalty (*v.* roialte); Big & Little Shoot (*v.* scēat); Swan Park; Three Nooked Fd (*v.* three-nooked); Townfield; Wall Fd (*v.* wælla); Way Croft & Fd (*v.* weg); Welds Fd (from the surname *Weld*); Whippity Butts; White Croft; Witters Croft, Wittersfield (from the surname *Witter, Wittar*, as in *Ravenshursts* 294 *supra*).

(b) *Crocktridinge* 1417 ('clearing of crooked shape', v. croked, ryding); *Heydore* 1287 (p), *Haydor* 1287², 1360 (p) (perhaps 'gate through which hay is borne', v. hēg, dor, duru); *Heyfild* 1417 (v. hēg, feld); *Maleres rudyng* 1339 ('Meilyr's cleared-land', from the Welsh pers.n. *Meilyr* and ryding); *Shep(p)ard Ridinge* 1417 (from ryding and scēap-hirde 'a shepherd', here perhaps a pers.n.).

4. Utkinton (Hall, Ho, Mill) (109–5564) [ˈutkintən] older local [ˈutkitn̦]

>   *Utkinton* 1188 Tab (Barnes¹ 416), 1317 City *et freq* with variant spellings *-yn-* 1303 Chamb to 1584 AD, *-en-*, *Utknton*; *mill of Utkynton* 1517 Orm², *Utkinton Hall, Lodge & Mill* 1831 Bry, *Hutkynton'* 1349 *Eyre*
>
>   *Hudekintona* 1216–72 *AddCh* (p)
>
>   *Utkyngton* 1296 *ChFor*, and 3 forms in the fourteenth, 5 in the fifteenth century, *-ing-* 1386 IpmR, 1665, 1671 Sheaf
>
>   *Uckin(g)ton* 1304 Chamb (p), *Huckynton* 1321 MidCh
>
>   *Utkuton* 1324 Bark
>
>   *Otkynton* 1357 *ChFor*
>
>   *Uthinkton* 1390 ChRR
>
>   *Ulkynton* 1406 ChRR (p)

'Farm called after Uttoc', from an OE pers.n. *Uttoc* (diminutive of the OE pers.n. *Utta*) and -ingtūn, with hall, myln. The form *Hudekintona* indicates a thirteenth-century popular derivation from a ME pers.n., *Hudekin*, diminutive of *Hudde*, a pet-form of *Hugh* or *Richard* (cf. Bardsley, Reaney, s.n. *Hudd*). The pers.n. *Uttoc* also appears in the unidentified *Uttokishal* 1289 Court 144, 'Uttoc's nook or valley', v. halh, perhaps in Sa.

Hollins Fm & Hill (Fm), *le Holines* 1272–90 *ChFor* (lit. *Holmes*, PRO Chester 33/1/6), *Holyns* 1431 Plea (p), *le Holyns* 1503 *ChFor*, *Hollins Hill* 1842 OS, 'the hollies', from holegn, with hyll.

Luddington Hill, 1831 Bry, partly in Eaton 290 *supra*, may be the same as *Ludynton* 1396 ChRR (DKR xxxvi 54), and analogous with Luddington L (DEPN), Wa 235, from the OE pers.n. *Luda* and -ingtūn, with hyll.

Ash Wood, 1831 Bry, v. æsc, wudu.   Bank Ho, v. banke. Bentley Wood, cf. *Bentleys* 1838 *TA*, 'grassy glade', v. beonet, lēah, wudu.   High Billinge (Ho) (109–556659) [ˈbilindʒ], *High*

Billinge 1831 Bry, cf. *High-, Lower Billinge* 1838 *TA* and *le Belynge Mershe* 1503 *ChFor*, *v.* bil(l)ing, hēah, lower, mersc, cf. Billinge Hill
1 138.   BROADWAY.   FISHERSGREEN FM, *Fishers Green* 1831 Bry,
cf. *Fishers Field* 1838 *TA*, from the surname *Fisher* and grēne[2].
FOREST FM (109–563665), cf. *Forest Field, Further-, Lower Forest* 1838
ib, named from its proximity to the boundary of Delamere 211 *supra*,
v. forest. The spring adjacent to the farm is *Newfound Well* 1831
Bry, *the Newe found Welle* 1600 Orm[2] II 252, *the late new found well*
1656 ib 11, a therapeutic spring, said in 1600 (Orm[2] *loc. cit.*) to have
been anciently celebrated as *St Stephen's Well, in Delamere Forest.*
The reason for its name would seem to be the re-discovery of its
properties about 1600.   HALL WOOD, 1831 Bry.   HEATH GREEN,
1831 ib, *v.* hǣð.   HOLBITCH SLACK, 1838 *TA*, cf. *Dodds-, Higher-,
Lower-, Middle Holbitch* 1838 *ib*, 'deep valley', from hol[2] and bece[1],
with slakki.   HOLLINS FM (109–562660), *The Field* 1831 Bry, *v.*
feld; re-named from Hollins *supra*.   HOLLY BANK.   LIMETREE
Ho, *Lime Tree Farm* 1831 Bry.   MONARCHY HALL FM.   OX-
PASTURE WOOD, *v.* oxa, pasture.   QUARRYBANK, 1842 OS, *Ladies
Quarry* 1812 Sheaf, *v.* hlǣfdige, quarriere, banke.   RIDGEHILL
FM, *Ridge Hill* 1831 Bry, *Fox Holes* 1842 OS, *v.* hrycg, hyll, fox-hol.
ROAD STREET, *v.* 297 *supra*.   ROWLEY FM, 1831 Bry, *v.* rūh, lēah.
SHAW HO, *Shaw Farm* 1819 Orm[2], *v.* sceaga.   SIDEBOTTOM FM,
Sidebottoms Stables 1831 Bry, cf. *Stable Lane* 1812 Sheaf and Stable
End Lane 213 *supra*, from training stables here, associated with a
former racecourse in Delamere.   SUMMERHOUSE BANK, 1831 Bry,
'hill with a summer-house on it', *v.* somer-hous, banke.   WOOD
LANE (FM), *Wood Lane* 1831 Bry, cf. and *boscus de Utkynton,
Utkyntonwode* 1347 *ChFor*, *v.* wudu, lane.   YEWTREE FM, cf. *Yew
Tree House* 1831 Bry, *v.* īw.

FIELD-NAMES

The undated forms are 1838 *TA* 158. Of the others 1812 is Sheaf, 1813 Orm[2],
1831 Bry, 1842 OS.

(*a*) Barrel Head; Birch Gorst Hill (*v.* gorst); Bollands Hey; Bow Fd;
Brick Kiln Fd; Brock's Gate 1812, 1813 (a gate into Delamere township 211
supra, on the forest boundary); Buttercake (*v.* 325 *infra*); Coal Pit Fd; Cock
Pit Fd (*v.* cockpit); Cockaneys Croft ('cockney's croft', *v.* cokaygne, cf.
Cockaynes Croft 297 *supra*); Crib (*v.* crib); Diamond Hill (cf. 297 *supra*);
Dodds Pool (1831, *Dodds Pond* 1842, from the surname *Dodd* and pōl[1],
ponde); Domer Hill; Dry Pool Banks & Fd (*v.* drȳge, pōl[1]); Gorsty Bank,

Fd & Hill (v. gorstig); Gullet (v. golet); Hales Moor Lane 1831; Hanging Fd (v. hangende); Hare Hill 1842 (v. hara); Hawksmoor (v. hafoc, mōr¹); Hitch Fd (v. hiche); Holly Harbour (v. holegn, here-beorg); House Brooms ('broomy lands near a house', v. hūs, brōm, cf. Kiln Brooms infra); Iddingshall (cf. Iddinshall 286 supra, to which this may have belonged); Kiln Brooms (v. cyln, brōm, cf. House Brooms supra); Marl Wd; Mere Stone Flatt (v. (ge)mǣre, stān); Miry Wabs ('muddy bogs', v. myrg, cwabba); Nook Fd; Ollerton Mdw (v. alor, tūn, perhaps associated with Alretone 1086 DB, v. Harewood-Hill 211 supra); Pickaws (v. pichel); Pingot(s) (v. pingot); Priest Fd (v. prēost); Rogerdale; Sludge Fd (v. sludge); Stanley Hill; Big Stub Oak Fd (v. stubb, āc); Sycamore Hill (cf. Sycamore Bank 294 supra); Big Tushmarr (from marr 'a marsh', perhaps with ModE tush 'a tuft' (NED)); Top Twentemalls ('twenty rents', perhaps twenty rented selions, v. twēntig, māl¹, cf. NED s.vv. mail sb², molland); Warrans-, Warrent House Fd (cf. Warrant House Toll Bar 1831, Warren House 1842, v. wareine, cf. Wanner Hill 327 infra); Waterhole Fd; White Fd; Windmill Hill.

xix. Bunbury

The ecclesiastical parish of Bunbury contained the townships 1. Alpraham, 2. Beeston, 3. Bunbury, 4. Calveley, 5. Haughton, 6. Peckforton, 7. Ridley, 8. Spurstow, 9. Tilstone Fearnall, 10. Tiverton, 11. Wardle in Eddisbury Hundred and 12. Burwardsley 325 infra in Broxton Hundred.

1. ALPRAHAM (GREEN & HALL) (109–5859) ['ælprəm, 'ɔːprəm]

Alburgham 1086 DB, Albrugham 1581 ChRR
Alperam 1259 Court, Alpp- c.1300 Chol, Halperham c.1270 Tab, Alperham 1285 ChF (p), 1287 Court et freq with variant spelling -ir- to 1369 Orm²
Alpram 1259 Court et freq, (-alias Albrugham) 1581 ChRR, Halpram c.1260 (c.1340) Bun, Alprame 1555 Sheaf
Alpraham 1287 Court (p) et freq with variant spelling Alpre(h)am to 1400 ChRR, 1664 Sheaf, Alpraham Green 1831 Bry
Hulpram 1296 Dav (p)
Orpram 1719 Sheaf

'Ealhburh's village', from the OE fem. pers.n. Ealhburh and hām, with grēne², hall.

SOUTHLEY FM (109–578593), maner' de Soudlegh c.1305 Sheaf, Southleye 1357 BPR (p), -ley 1400 AD (p), 1671 Sheaf, (the hall of-) 1494 Orm², (-Common) 1831 Bry, Sowth(e)ley 1541 ChRR, 1557 Sheaf, 'the south wood or clearing', v. sūð, lēah. The place is near the south boundary of the township. The name is written Sautry 1675

Ogilby 46, pl. 23, 1719 Sheaf[3] 5 (381), *Sact*: 1727 Sheaf[3] 3 (513), which Crump 94 assumed to be ModE *saltery* 'a salt-works'.

ALLEY FM, 1860 White, *Bowling Alley Farm* 1831 Bry, cf. *Alley Field* 1840 *TA*.   ANTIGUA, *v.* 325 *infra*.   BARRETS GREEN, *v.* 308 *infra*.   BACK LANE, 1860 White, 1842 OS, *v.* back, lane.   BUN-BURY LOCKS, 1831 Bry, on the Shropshire Union Canal.   ELM COTTAGE.   THE GRANGE.   THE GROVE, 1842 OS, *v.* grāf. GRUB MILL HOUSE, 1842 ib, *Crab Mill House* 1831 Bry, cf. *Crab Mill Field* 1840 *TA*, *v.* crab-mill.   HIGHWAYSIDE, 1719 Sheaf, 'the side of the highway', a hamlet beside the main Chester road, *v.* hēah-weg, sīde.   HILL FM, 1840 *TA*, *v.* hyll.   THE HOLE 1831 Bry, *v.* hol[1].   LONG LANE, 1831 ib, *v.* lang, lane, cf. Calveley Fm 308 *infra*.   MOATHOUSE FM, *the moat-house* 1819 Orm[2], *Moat House* 1831 Bry, *v.* mote, hūs, named from the moat surrounding it. PAGE'S WOOD, 1831 ib.   PINFOLD HO, 1831 ib, *v.* pynd-fald. ROOKERY FM, (*The*) *Rookery* 1831 ib, 1842 OS, *v.* rookery.   TOLLE-MACHE ARMS (p.h.), 1840 *TA*, *Golden Lion* 1831 Bry.   WOOD LANE, 1831 ib, near Page's Wood *supra*, *v.* wudu, lane.

FIELD-NAMES

The undated forms are 1840 *TA* 10. Of the others, 1310 is Chest, 1312 *CoLegh*, 1347 *ChFor*, 1557 Sheaf, 1831 Bry, 1842 OS.

(*a*) Backside (*v.* ba(c)ksyde); Black Flatt; Boosey Pasture (*v.* bōsig); Braynes Lane 1831; Broom Knowl (*v.* brōm, cnoll); Brow Fd (*v.* brū); Butter Bache & Bank ('valley and bank where there is rich pasture', *v.* butere, bæce[1], banke, cf. Butter Bache 325 *infra*); Clam Croft (*v.* Clemley 47 *supra*); Clay Croft, Fd, Hey & Mdw, Clays ((*le*) *Cleyhis* 1312, 'clayey places', *v.* clǣg); Cockshutt (*v.* cocc-scyte); The Coombs (*v.* cumb); Cross Croft & Fd (*v.* cros); Daisy Lakes (*v.* lacu); Done Fd (probably named from the family *Done* of Utkinton); Forty Acres; French Fd (*v.* French wheat); Goblins Croft (*v.* gobelin); Green Fd (*the grene feyld* 1557, *v.* grēne[1]); Hall Yard(s); Heap Mdws (*v.* hēap); Hemp Yard (*v.* hemp-yard); Holly Bush; Intake (*v.* inntak); Kiln Fd, Kiln Lane (Croft), Kiln Tenement (*Kiln Lane* 1831, *v.* cyln); Knowl Fd; Marl Fd; Milking Bank (*v.* milking); Nook Croft; Oak Hill Flatt (*v.* āc, hyll, flat); Old Fd; Outlett (*v.* outlet); Ox Pasture; Pavement Fd (*v.* pavement); Pease Croft (*v.* pise); Pig Cote Croft; Plantation hard to do (*v.* 325 *infra*); Rabbit Burrow 1842 (*Warren* 1831); Ridding (*v.* ryding); Roadman Sheens Croft (cf. Sheens *infra*); Rose Hill; Rough Field Mdw (cf. *the rough-fyld* 1557, *v.* rūh); Rushy Mdw, Moor & Mugs (cf. *Rushet* 1347, 'a rush bed', *v.* ryscett); Russell Lane Fd; Saw Pit Fd (*v.* saw-pytt); Sheens or Sap Fd, Sheens Croft (cf. Roadman Sheens

Croft *supra, v.* Sheens Knowl Rough 319 *infra*); Slaughter House Fd; Spoon Studge (*v.* stycce 'a bit of ground', cf. Spoostitch, Spoon Slutch 326, 309 *infra*. In *Spoon Slutch* folk etymology has changed the second el., probably on account of some muddy characteristic of the ground there. The first el. in these f.ns. appears to be spōn 'a chip, a shaving of wood, a shingle' (*v.* EPN **2** 139, Spoonley Gl **2** 27), perhaps alluding to bits of ground as small as a shaving or as a shingle, or to corners where shingles were cut. But the ModE form *spoon* may be a rationalization to *spoon* 'a spoon', of a form *spon* from spann[1] 'a hand's breadth, a span', alluding to narrow bits of ground); Stacious Platt Fd (cf. Stages Platt 290 *supra*); Stoney Lake Fd (*v.* stānig, lacu); Swine Cote Fd (*v.* swīn[1], cot); Tennas Croft; Town Fd; Yearnstow (perhaps from hyrne and stall, cf. Iron Store Fd 305 *infra*).

(b) *le Dedelache* (*v.* 319 *infra*); *Erdeshurstes* 1312, *Erdeshawe* 1347 (probably 'herdsman's wood', from hirde and hyrst, sceaga, but cf. Yeardsley **1** 177); *sickettum de Otedische* 1312 ('the ditch of the oat enclosure', *v.* āte, edisc); *vetus molendinum aquaticum in Alpram* 1312 ('an old watermill in Alpraham').

2. BEESTON (HALL) (109–5458) ['biːstən, 'bistən]

  Buistane 1086 DB
  Bestan 1170 Facs, l12 *Chol* (p) *et freq* to 1353 BPR, -*e* 1296 Cl, *Beston* 1240 P, *et freq* to 1561 Pat, *le Beston* 1304 Chamb (p), *Bestone* 1308 Cl, *Bestun* 1277 P, *Bestoan* 1318 *Eyre* (p)
  Beeston 1188 (1819) Orm[2], 1237 P, 1290 Plea *et freq*, (-*Hall*, -*Brook*, -*Green*) 1671 Sheaf, *Beestan*' 1240 Lib, P, *Beestoun* 15 Trev, *Beestone* 1664, 1727 Sheaf
  Beustan' 1247, 1250 P (lit. *Ben*-), -*ston* 1297 (15) Werb, *Beueston* 1289 P (lit. *Bene*-), 1398 *MinAcct*
  Beystan' 1250 P, *Bieston* 1359 AD (p), *Byeston* 1447 Orm[2], *Beiston* 1536 ChRR, 1560 Sheaf
  Boeston 1280 Cl
  Bustan 1282 Court, *Buston* 1284 Ch, 1339, 1360 *Chol*, 1380 *Eyre*, 1398 *AddCh* (p)
  Beoston 1294 Ipm
  Biston 1398 *AddCh* (p), 1486 Orm[2], 1502 ChRR, c.1536 Leland, 1644 Sheaf, *Byston* 1560 *Chol*, 1562 (lit. *Sys*-), 1567 ChRR
  Borston 15 Trev
  Bishton 1672 BridgL

The final el. is stān 'a stone, a rock', cf. Beeston Castle *infra*. Since Beeston does not seem to be properly located for identification with *Bouio* (cf. 325 *infra* and DEPN) the first el. would appear to be byge[2] 'traffic, commerce', cf. Studies[1] 55. The p.n. probably means 'rock, or hill, where a market is held', inferring that the crag on which

Beeston Castle stands was a landmark at a notable commercial centre. Cf. Spurstow 315 *infra*. Morris 58 reports from Arch. Camb. I 59 a Welsh name for Beeston *Vel allt*, more correctly *y Fêl Allt* which, Professor Melville Richards advises me, is a translation by fifteenth-century Welsh court poets, of a popular etymology of *Beeston* 'bee rock'. *Y Fêl Allt* means 'the honey cliff, honey rock', from Welsh *mêl* 'honey' and allt.

BEESTON CASTLE (109–5359)

(*castrum-, castellum*) *Rupis* (*de Beston*) 1237, 1240, 1245 P, -*de Rupe* 1237 ib *et freq* ib, Cl, Pat, Lib to 1245 P, -*de Rupe Bestan* 1304 Chamb, *castella-, castellum de La Roche* (*de Beestan'*) 1238, 1240 Lib

castellum-, castrum de Bestan 1242 Lib, P *et freq* with spellings as for Beeston *supra*, *castell(e) of Beesto(u)n, -Borston* 15 Trev, *Biston Castel* c.1536 Leland, *Beeston Castell* 1646 Sheaf, -*Castle* 1656 Orm[2]

This castle was built c.1220 by Ranulph Blundeville earl of Chester and was last garrisoned in the Civil War. It stands on a precipitous crag commanding the road through a gap in the central ridge of hills at Tarporley, and was first named from this rock—*Beeston Castle Hill* or *The Rock of Beeston* 1819 Orm[2], *v.* roche[1], rokke, castel(l), cf. *le Beston* 1304 Chamb (p) and Rock Fm *infra*—which also gives name to Beeston itself, *supra*. The castle gave name to Richard *de Chastel* constable of Beeston 1347 BPR, to *Castle Field* 1846 *TA*, and to Castlegate and Castleside *infra*.

HORSLEY LANE (109–533583), *Hors(e)ley(e)* 1284 Ch, 13 Tab *et freq*

with variant spellings -*leg'*, -*legh(e)*, -*ly*, *Ho(r)sley* 1398 *MinAcct*, *Horlegh* 1311 Ipm, 'mill in *Horsleg*' 1297 Cl, *molendinum de Horsley* 1387 Eyre, *Horsley Mylne* 1476 ChRR, *Horseleywell* 1465 AD, *Horseley House* 1672 Sheaf, *the Horseley spring, Horseley Hill & Bath* 1819 Orm[2], *Horsley Bath, Hill & Lane* 1831 Bry, cf. *Broad & Long Horsely* 1846 *TA*, and *Horsseleghruding* 1313 AddCh. The p.n. is 'clearing where horses are kept', from hors (gen.pl. horsa) and lēah, with lane, myln, bæð, wella, spring 'a spring of water', hūs, hyll and ryding. Horsley was a subordinate manor of the lordship of Peckforton, and a hamlet in Beeston and Peckforton townships. *Horsley Hill* is the site of Peckforton Castle 312 *infra*. The Bath was an eighteenth-century spa which developed at *Horseley Spring, Horseley-well*. The mill was a watermill, and seems to have been in Peckforton. The house was a messuage in Beeston.

BEESTON BRIDGE, crossing R. Gowy.   BEESTONGATE, *Beeston Gate* 1831 Bry, beside a turnpike road, *v.* geat 'a gate'.   BEESTON MILL, 1842 OS, *Beeston Upper Mill* 1831 Bry, cf. *Beeston Lower Mill, Mill Lane* 1831 ib, *molendinum de Beston* 1295 Ipm, *v.* myln, cf. Brook Fm *infra*.   BEESTON MOSS, 1842 OS, cf. *Moss Lane* 1831 Bry, *Moss (Field & Garden)* 1846 *TA*, *v.* mos.   BEESTON SPA, a chalybeate spring half a mile from *Horsley Bath supra*, cf. Castleside Fm *infra*, *v.* spa.   BEESTON TOWER.   BOWLER'S MOSS. BROOK FM (109–5458), *Brook House* 1831 Bry, named from *Beeston Brook*, the R. Gowy, *v.* brōc.   BROOK FM (109–5559) named from R. Gowy. Near this farm is the site of the Upper Mill *supra*. CASTLEGATE FM, named from its position under the gate-way of Beeston Castle *supra*, *v.* castel(1), geat.   CASTLESIDE FM, *Spa Farm* 1831 Bry, cf. Beeston Castle, Beeston Spa *supra*, Rock Fm *infra*, *v.* castel(1), sīde.   COAL PIT LANE, 1831 Bry, cf. *Coal Pit Moor* 1846 *TA*, *v.* col¹, pytt.   CRIMES BROOK & LANE, 1831 Bry, cf. *(the) Crimes, Crimes Meadow* 1846 *TA*, *v.* cryme, cf. *le Crymbe* 2 171. The brook joins R. Gowy.   CUERDON COTTAGES.   DEAN BANK. ETTLEY HILL, perhaps 'heathy hill', from hǣðiht and lēah, with hyll.   FOXEY WOOD, 1831 Bry.   GREGORY'S WOOD, cf. William *Gregory* 1497 ChRR, Thomas *Gregory* 1672 BridgL, *v.* wudu. MOATHOUSE, *Moat House* 1831 Bry, *v.* mote, hūs.   PECKFORTON RD, cf. Peckforton 311 *infra*.   PENNSYLVANIA WOOD, *Pensylvania Gorse* 1831 Bry, *Pensylvania* 1842 OS, *v.* 326 *infra*.   (LOWER) ROCK FM, from the great rock at Beeston Castle, cf. *supra*, *v.* rokke. Rock Fm was *Castle Side* 1831 Bry, cf. Castleside Fm *supra*. WICKSON LANE.   WILLIS'S WOOD, *Cranberry Moss* 1831 ib, *v.* cranberry, mos.   YEW TREE HO.

FIELD-NAMES

The undated forms are 1846 *TA* 45.

(*a*) Badger Hills; Bigshaw Fd (*v.* sceaga); Black bands Fd; Bone Fd (*v.* bān, cf. bone-dust); Boose Fd (*v.* bōs); Bottoms (*v.* botm); Clemnley (*v.* Clemley 47 *supra*); Clenford; Crib (*v.* crib); Two-, Three- (etc.) Day Math (*v.* day-math); Earlam; Flatts (*v.* flat); Gailey Moor (*v.* gagel); Glade Birch (probably 'glade intake', from glæd³ and brēc); Hafodril Fd ('daffodil field',

v. affadille); Hass Lake; Hemp Yard (*v.* hemp-yard); Hick Heys; Hop Yard
(*v.* hoppe, geard); Horse Dale; Iron Store Fd (*v.* hyrne, stall, cf. Yearnstow
302 *supra*); Kettle Hill (*v.* keddle-dock); Marl Bache (*v.* marle, bæce[1]);
Oldershaw Fd & Mdw ('alder wood', *v.* alor, sceaga); Big Riddings (*v.*
ryding); Shallow Sough Fd (*v.* scealu, sogh); Stone Fd (cf. *Stonyfeld* 1398
MinAcct, *v.* stān, stāning, feld); Tom-, Town Fd ('town field', *v.* toun);
Turf Moss (*v.* turf, mos); Whit(e) Fd (*v.* hwīt); Well-, Will Croft (*v.* wella);
The Wood (*v.* wudu).

(*b*) *Dyssheresfeld* 1398 *MinAcct* (from ME *dischere* 'maker or seller of
dishes' (Fransson 185) and feld); *Fordesyde* 1476 ChRR ('beside the ford',
v. ford, sīde).

3. (LOWER) BUNBURY, BUNBURY BROOK, COMMONS & HEATH
['bunbəri, 'bunbri] older local ['bumbəri]

> *Boleberie* 1086 DB
> *Bonebury* 1135–54 (19) Orm[2], *Boneburi* c.1170 *Chol et freq* with
> variant spellings *Bonne-* (from 1170 Facs), *Bon-* (from 1282
> CRV), *-b(u)ry*, *-b(uri)*, *-byria*, *-bur(ia)*, *-bure*, *-b(i)r'*, *-bir(r)i* to
> 1674 Sheaf
> *Buneburi*, *-beri* 1180–1220 *Chol*, and occasionally, with variant
> spellings *Bunne-*, *Buni-*, *-bur(y)*, *-b'y* to 1368 Pap, 1387 Cl,
> *Bunburie* 1265–84 (17) Chest, *-bury* 1283 Ipm (p) *et freq* with
> variant spellings *-bur(i)*, *-burye*, *-ber(y)*, *-beri*, *-berye*, *-byre*, *-byri*,
> *-biri*; *Bunbury Brook* 1671 Sheaf, *Bunbury Heath* 1819 Orm[2],
> *Lower Bunbury, Bunbury Common* 1831 Bry
> *Banebar'* c.1240 *Chol* (p), *Ban(n)ebyr* 1273 *Dow*, *Bannebury* 1437
> *Dav*, *Babur* 1277 P (p), *Bambery* 1687 Sheaf
> *Bondburi* 1248 Rich (p)
> *Borneburie* 13 (17) Sheaf (p)
> *Bounbour* 1286 Tab (p)
> *Binneburi* 1294 Ipm, *Bim-*, *Bymburie* 1650 ParlSurv
> *Bumburye* 1318 *Eyre* (p), *-bury* 1354 BPR (p), and occasionally,
> with variant spellings *Bom(e)-*, *-bery*, *-berie*, *-buery* to 1694 Sheaf
> *Birnburie* c.1554 Whall (p)
> *Benbury* 1586 Cre

'Buna's stronghold', from the OE pers.n. *Buna* and burh, with
brōc, commun, and hǣð. The township contains two hamlets,
Bunbury Brook and Lower Bunbury, the former near the church
beside R. Gowy. The church dedication to St Boniface—*ecclesia
Sancti Bonefacii de Boneburi* 1180–1220 *Chol*—led to a popular
etymology *Bunbury, seu Boni-facibury* 1629 (1724) NotCestr.

PRIESTLAND (109–560587)

> *Presteland, -lond, -launde, -lont* 1180–1220 *Chol et freq* with variant
> spellings *Prest-* (from 1362 ChRR), *Preste-* (to 1444 Rich),
> *Presti-* (1362 ChRR), *-land(e), -lond(e)* to *Prestland* 1842 OS,
> *Prest Lande Poole* 1540 Sheaf, *Prestland Greves* 1595 ib, *Prestland
> Green* 1819 Orm²
> *Preslond* 1315 (1637) Rich (p), *-land* 1671 *AddCh*, 1831 Bry
> *Priestland Hall & House* 1860 White

'Priests' land', from prēost (gen.pl. prēosta) and land, with grēne²,
pōl¹, græfe, hall and hūs. A family with the local surname held the
place under the *de Calveley* family, who held of the prior of St John
of Jerusalem, (cf. 1408 ChRR (DKR xxxvi 81, 393) and *terra
Hospitalis Jerusalim* 1180–1220 *Chol*), but the Hospitallers would
hardly be called priests and the place-name probably alludes to some
earlier ownership.

WOODWORTH GREEN (109–576575)

> *Atwrthin* 1180–1220 *Chol*
> *Atwrthe* 1180–1220 *Chol* (p), *Ot(e)worth(e)* 1332 *ib*, 1341 *Eyre et
> freq* with variant spelling *-wrth* to 1629 Orm², *Oatworth* 1362
> (1637) Rich, *Oat(e)worth* 1640 *Chol*, 17 Orm²
> *Woodsworth Green* 1831 Bry
> *Woodworth Green* 1842 OS

'Oats enclosure', from āte and worðign, worð, with grēne². There
was a mill here, *molendinum de Oteworth(e)* 1332 *Chol*. The house was
Brertons farme at Oatworth 1640 *Chol*, from the Brereton family. The
W- spelling is the result of a stress-shift in the diphthong of *Oat-*.

BIRD'S LANE (FM), *Bird's Lane* 1842 OS, *Buds Lane* 1831 Bry, cf.
Bryddesmed in Bunebury 1398 *MinAcct*, *byrdes feylds* 1557 Sheaf, from
either bridd 'a bird' or the surname *Brid(d), Bird*, with mǣd, feld,
lane.   BOWE'S GATE, *Boars Gate* 1842 OS, *Bowesgate* 1860 White,
v. geat.   BROOKDALE.   BUNBURY BRIDGE (EAST).   BUNBURY
MILL, 1831 Bry, cf. *stagnum moline de Boneburia* 1180–1220 *Chol*,
molendinum de Bonebury c.1300 *ib*, and *Mill Field, Meadow & Moor*
1840 *TA*, *mullemore* 1398 *MinAcct*, *v.* myln, mōr¹, mǣd.   THE
CHAUNTRY HOUSE (lost), 1525, 1819 Orm², 1548 Pat, cf. foll., *v.*
chaunterie, hūs.   THE COLLEGE, COLLEGE LANE, *The (Old) College*
1860 White, *College Lane* 1842 OS, & *Wood* 1840 *TA*, the 'chantry
and college of one master and six chaplains in the church of Bunbury',

founded and endowed with two acres of land in 1387 by Sir Hugh de Calveley (Orm² II 256), cf. *the chantry & college of St Boniface at Bunbury* l14 MRA, *collegiata ecclesia de Bunbury* 1462 *Chol*, *the Colage of Bunbury* 1500 *ib*, *-Colledge-* 1547 Orm², *Bunbyri College* c.1536 Leland, *the capital house and mansion of the late college of Bunbury* 1549 Pat, *colledg of Bunbury* 1671 Sheaf, v. **college, lane.**
GOSLAND GREEN, 1840 *TA*, *Goslin Green* 1831 Bry, 1842 OS, probably a green where goslings were reared, v. **gōsling** (cf. YW 7 195), **grēne²**. THE GRANGE. HEATH FM, cf. *Heath Cottage* 1860 White, *Bunbury Heath supra*. WYCHE HO & LANE, *Witch Lane* 1831 Bry, *Wyche (Croft & Field)* 1840 *TA*, v. **wice** 'a wychelm'.

FIELD-NAMES

The undated forms are 1840 *TA* 83. Of the others, 1170 is Facs, 1180–1220, 1310–50, 1332, 1562 *Chol*, 13 *Bun*, 1240–50, 1248 Rich, 1255 Plea, 1260 Court, 1549 Pat, c.1550, 1557, 1671 Sheaf, 1700 Cre.

(a) Bache (v. **bæce¹**); Billington's Croft (cf. *Billinges Tenement* 1700); Bittersweet Croft (v. *325 infra*); Black Butt (v. **blæc, butte**); Brook Croft & Fd (cf. *Brook House* 1671 and Bunbury Brook *supra*); Buckland (perhaps **bōc-land**); Bunn Fd (cf. *Banefeld, Bone Croft* 1549, v. **bān** 'a bone'); Church Fd; Clatterbridge Fd (v. **clater, brycg**); Cow Hey (v. **(ge)hæg**); Dark Mdw (v. **deorc**); Ferrik Oak (v. *Ferret Oak* 310 *infra*); Fox Headland (v. **hēafod-land**); Halfpenny Croft (v. **halfpeny**); Haughton Stile (v. **stigel**); Gorsty & Higher Hellins 1700 (*a certen grave or wood callyd the Hollyns* 1562, v. **holegn**); Hill Fd; Intake (v. **inntak**); Knowl (v. **cnoll**); Long Arm Fd; Long Hays, -Heys (v. **(ge)hæg**); Marl Fd; Middle Heys (v. **(ge)hæg**); The Moors; Ox Heys (v. **(ge)hæg**); Pingle (v. **pingel**); Ridding (v. **ryding**); Riley ('rye clearing', v. **ryge, lēah**); Rough; Rye Grass Fd (v. **rye-grass**); Town Fd; Trundle Moor (v. 319 *infra*); Wardle Way (v. **weg**, cf. Wardle 322 *infra*); Withen Street Croft (v. **wīðegn, strǣt**, cf. a similar name at Withinstreet 2 261); Wood Mdw (cf. *boscus de Bonebyria* 13, v. **wudu**).

(b) *Accul* 1180–1220 (p), 1240–50, *Akchul* 1255 (p), 1260 (p) (lit. *Akthul*), *Hocul* 1248 ('oak hill', v. **āc, hyll**); *bellows fyld* 1557 (v. **belwes**, cf. foll.); *Frooge Poole* 1557 (perhaps 'frog pool' from frogga and pōl¹, but the first el. looks like forge 'a forge', cf. prec.); *Gorstanescroft* 1170 ('(croft at) the stone in a corner', from **gāra** and **stān**, with croft); *Haytelegh'* 1332 ('heathy clearing', v. **hǣðiht, lēah**); *Raymonde Croft* c.1550 ('Raymond's croft', from the ME pers.n. *Raymond* and croft).

4. CALVELEY (GREEN & HALL) (110–6059) [kɑːvəli]

Kaluileia, -leh, Caluilee, -leg' c.1180–1220 *Chol* (p) *et freq* with variant spellings *K-, Calvi-, Cal(l)vy-, -le(gh), -ley(e), -l(ay)* to 1474 ChRR

Keluileg' 1202–9 *Chol* (p)
Calueleg' 1233–9 Chest (p), *-lee* a.1240 MidCh, *Kalvelee* 1259
    Court, *Calveley* 1282 ib (p) *et freq* with variant spellings *Calue-*,
    -leg(h), *-le(e)*, *-le(y)ghe*, *-ly*, *-ligh*, (*Calveley Green*) 1671 Sheaf,
    1842 OS, (*Calveley Hall*) 1724 NotCestr
Caveleg' 1330 *BW* (p)
Calleye 1335 Pat, *Calley* 1440, 1473 ChRR, 1918 Sheaf, *Callay*
    1476 ChRR
Calverley 1475 VR (p), *Caverley* 1673 Sheaf
Caweley 1559 ChRR, *Cawley* 1918 Sheaf

'Calves' clearing', from **calf** (gen.pl. **calfra, calfa**) and **lēah**, with
grēne², **hall**. Cf. Green Fm *infra*. Court 223, 226 and index, confuses
this place with *Caluelegh* 1 52. For the *-i-* spellings cf. Botterley (in
Faddiley) 142 *supra*.

THE BANK FM, *v.* **banke**.   BARRETS GREEN, 1831 Bry, from
grēne² 'a green', with the surname *Barret(t)*, cf. 301 *supra*.
CALVELEY FM, *Long Lane End* 1842 OS, *v.* **ende¹**, cf. Long Lane 301
supra.   CALVELEY-HALL FM & LANE, *Hall Farm* 1831 Bry, *Dairy
Farm* 1842 OS, cf. Calveley Hall *supra*, *v.* **hall, lane, deierie**.
CROWTON BROOK, *v.* 137 *supra*.   THE ELMS FM, *Calveley House*
1842 OS, *v.* **hūs**.   THE FIELD FM, *v.* **feld**.   GREEN FM, *Dodds
Farm* 1842 OS, named from Calveley Green *supra* and the surname
Dodd.   HIGHBANK FM.   LADYACRE WOOD, *plantation in Lead
Acre* 1848 *TA*, cf. *Lady Meadow* 1848 *ib*, *v.* **hlǣfdige, æcer, mǣd**.
MODEL COTTAGE.   THE MOUNT.   OLD COVERT, *Old Fox Covert*
1842 OS, *Lower Gorse* 1831 Bry, *v.* **cover, gorst**.   PARKFIELD
HOUSE FM, PARKSIDE COTTAGE, *v.* **park**.   PLAT HO (lost), 1842 OS,
v. **plat¹**.   WARDLE BANK, *v.* 322 *infra*.   WATFIELD PAVEMENT,
cf. *Pavement Field* 1848 *TA*, *v.* 323 *infra*.

FIELD-NAMES

The undated forms are 1848 *TA* 90. The others are 1347, 1353 *ChFor*, 1831
Bry.

(*a*) Ash Fd; Beatrick; Great & Little Bentley, Bentley Wood Fd,
Bentleys Lane Close (*Bentelegh* 1347, 'grass clearing', *v.* **beonet, lēah**);
Black-, Blake Fd (*v.* **blæc**); Bottoms (*v.* **botm**); Breach (Mdw), Breeches
(cf. *Marybruche* 1353, from the ME pers.n. *Mary* and **brēc, bryce**); Burrows
Bank; Butty Fd (*v.* **butty**); Calf Croft; Cholmondeston Fd (cf. Cholmondes-
ton 136 *supra*); Church Fd; Clear Mdw; Coat Croft (*v.* **cot**); Coney Grey

Flatts, Corner Green Inclosure (*v.* coningre); Day Math (*v.* day-math); Dykes Fd (*v.* dīc); Forty Acre; Great-, Middle Gale, Gale Intake (*v.* gagel); Green Pit 1831; Hermitage Inclosure (*v.* ermitage); Horse Park (*v.* hors, park); Marl Fd; Mere Fd (*v.* mere¹); Milking Bank (*v.* milking); Old House Fd; Ox Pasture; Oxenhurst ('wooded hill where oxen are pastured', *v.* oxa, hyrst); Pavement Fd (*v.* Watfield Pavement *supra*); Great & Little Riddings (*v.* ryding); Rye Grass Fd (*v.* rye-grass); Slitch (*v.* slic(c)he 'slutch', cf. foll.); Spoon Slutch (*v.* slutch, cf. prec., *v.* Spoon Studge 302 *supra*); Town Fd; Wall Croft (*v.* wælla); Well Croft; White Fd; Wigley; Witton Croft.

(*b*) *Olrynbarwe, Olrynlegh* 1347 ('alder grove and wood', from alren and bearu, lēah).

5. HAUGHTON (HALL (FM), MOSS, THORN) (109–5856) ['hɔːtən]

   Halec(h)ton c.1180–1220 *Chol* (p), H3 *AddCh* (p), *Haleghton* 1311 *Chol* (p), *Halheton'* 1353 *Indict, Halug(h)ton* 1282 Fine, 1325 Pat *et freq* to 1452 AD, *Halunghton* 1418 Cre (p), *Halighton* 1477 ChRR (p)

   Haylton e13 *Bun*

   Halc(h)ton(ia) c.1240 *Chol,* Halhton 1282 Court (p), *Halghton* 1295 Ipm *et freq* with variant spellings *-tone, Halgton, Halx(h)-, Halxgton, Haglhton* to 1518 AD, *le Halghton* 1400 ChRR (p), *Haulghton* 1507, 1536 Plea

   Hauton' 1259 Plea, 1394 *Chol, Haghton* 1318 *ib,* 1518 AD, *Haughton* 1508 ChRR *et freq* with variant spellings *Ha(w)ghton* (to 1671 Sheaf); *Haughton Mosse* 1574 *Chol, Haughton Hall, Moss & Thorn* 1831 Bry

   Haleton c.1280 *Chol, Halton* c.1300 *ib*

   Hachton' c.1310–50 *Chol* (p)

   Ho(u)ghton 1346 *Chol* (p), 1517 ChRR, 1528 Plea, 1542 ChRR, 1584, 1662 Cre

   Holghton 1364 *Chol*

   Haighton 1656 Orm², 1671 Sheaf, *Hayghton* 1663 Cre

'Farm at a nook', from halh and tūn, with hall, mos and þorn 'a thorn-tree'.

EDGELEY LODGE (109–574562) ['edʒli]

   Edisleg' c.1300 *Chol, Edeslegh* 1333 ChRR (p) *et freq* all (p), with variant spellings *Eddes-* (from 1347 ChRR), *-ys-, Edis-, -leg', -ley, -lay* to 1480 ib (p), *Edesleg'-, Edeslag' clow(es)* c.1340 Sheaf *Hedelegh* 1359 BPR (p)

Eggesley 1398 ChRR (p), -*legh* 1404 ib (p)
Eggeley 1400 Pat (p), *Edgeley* 1839 *TA*

The p.n. *Edgeley*, origin of the surname which provides most of the material, was preserved as the *TA* f.n. from which the house took its name, *v.* loge. The p.n. is either 'Ēad's clearing', from an OE pers.n. *Ēad* (as in Eddisbury 213 *supra*) or 'clearing at an enclosed park', from edisc, and lēah, with clōh 'a dell, a clough'. For the development of the forms cf. Edgeley 1 248.

BACK-LANE FM, cf. *Back Lane* 1831 Bry, *Haughton Back Lane* 1842 OS, *v.* back, lane.   DAIRY FM.   FERRET OAK, *Ferrik Oak* 1840 *TA* 83, *Ferrit Oak* 1842 OS, a farmstead, presumably named from an oak on the boundary of Bunbury township, cf. 307 *supra*.   GREEN COTTAGE, named from *Hall Green* 1839 *TA*, 1842 OS, *Haughton Green* 1831 Bry, *Haighton Green* 1671 Sheaf, *v.* grēne². LONG WOOD.   MOSS FM, cf. *The Moss, Moss Croft* 1839 *TA*.   OAK FM.   RADMORE GREEN, *v.* 316 *infra*, cf. *þe longe Radmoore* 1598 Chol, (*Big & Little*) *Radmore* 1839 *TA*.   YEWTREE FM & HO.

FIELD-NAMES

The undated forms are 1839 *TA* 198. Of the others, e13 is *Bun*, H3 *AddCh*, 1297 City, 1307, 1357 *Eyre*, 1342, 1472 ChRR, 1372, 1665 Cre, 1503–4 Orm², 1530 Plea, the rest *Chol*.

(*a*) The Acres; Aud(h)am ('old enclosure', *v.* ald, hamm); Big & Little Beach (*v.* bece¹); Booths Mdw; Bottom Fd (*v.* botm); Broad Fd; Cleml(e)y (*v.* Clemley 47 *supra*); Coalman's Fd, (Near & Top) Colemans; Coat Croft (*v.* cot); (Big & Little) Cockshead (*the Cockeshote* 1574, *þe Cockshute* 1637, *v.* cocc-scyte); Cow Croft (*Cowe Crofte* 1598, *v.* cū, croft); Cow Lane & Yard (*v.* geard); Filcocks Fd (*Filcokesfield* 1372, 'Filcock's field', from the ME pers.n. *Filcock*, diminutive of *Phil*, a pet form of *Philip*, and feld); Old Folds (*v.* fald); Fox's Yard (*the fox yearthes* 1574, *þe Foxeyardes* 1637, 'fox's lair(s)', *v.* fox, eorðe); Gorsty Levy; Green Fd (*Greene Field* 1598, *v.* grēne¹); Hand Ridding; the High Field 1665 (cf. *the hier feild* 1599, *the Higher Meadow* 1665); Hodge (cf. *Hodg Croft* 1 158); Hollin Hurst (*le Holinehurst* 1310–30, (boscus vocatus) *le Holyn(e)hurst(e)* 1354, 1369, *the Hollinhurst Croft* 1599, 'holly-wood hill', *v.* holegn, hyrst); Kettle's Fd & Mdw (*Kettellesbache, field & meadow* 1598, *Kettles Crofte or Croftes* 1630, *Kettles Field* (*Meadow*) 1639, probably named from John *Ketull* of Larkton 326 *infra* who held land in Haughton c.1479 *Chol*, *v.* bæce¹, feld, mǣd, croft); Kiln Croft (*the-* 1630, *v.* cyln); Knowl (*v.* cnoll); Leys (dial. *ley*, cf. lēah); Liners Fd; Lower Mdw (cf. *the loer feild & meadow* 1599, *the Lower Ground & Meadow* 1665, *v.* lower); Big & Little Madge (*v.* madge); Main Fd (*v.* main); the Marled Field 1665 (*v.* marled); Middle Fd (*the midle croft &*

feild 1599, *v.* middel); New Hay (*v.* (ge)hæg); Outlett (*v.* outlet); Ox Heys (*v.* (ge)hæg); The Paddock (*v.* pearroc); Park Fd; Peacocks Fd; Peas Flatt (cf. *peason crofte* 1598, *v.* pise, pisen); Pingo(t) (*v.* pingot); Pitsteads (*v.* pytt, stede); Pointons Fd; Riddings (*v.* ryding); Robins Fd (*Robyns Fyeld* 1566, from the ME pers.n. *Robin*); the Round Field 1665; School Land; Six Butts (*v.* sex, butte); Smedley ('smooth clearing', *v.* smēðe¹, lēah); (Big & Little) Stony Hurst ('stony hill', *v.* stānig, hyrst); Tippers Fd; Topfield (*v.* top, feld); Wardel Mdw (cf. Wardle 322 *infra*); Well Butt; Welpland (*Whelp land* 1599, *v.* hwelp, land); Westfurlong, Westfurlong Croft & Head (*a fosse called Wister Long* 1503–4, *Westerlonge* 1574, *Westfurlonge* 1637, 'west arable-field', *v.* west, furlang); Within Croft (*v.* wiðegn); Big- Long- & Near Wd.

(b) *sepes de Acale* e13, *Othals(y)ord(e)*, *Ot(h)allemor*' c.1300, 1305, *sepes qui dicitur Othalesyord* 1310–30, *Atalehard* 1310–50, *campus-, fossata de Otal(e)* 1332 ('(moor and enclosure at) the oats nook', *v.* āte, halh, geard, mōr¹. The first instance has *c* for *t*. The place was at the boundary with Spurstow and Bunbury); *Aldhusebuttis* H3 ('selions belonging to an old house', *v.* ald, hūs, butte); *the bach* 1599 ('the valley', *v.* bæce¹); *Boredach*' 1310–50; *le Chirchewey* 1314 (*v.* cirice, weg); *crocke* 1310–50 ('a corner', *v.* krókr); *Esphalflond* H3 ('half-selion near an aspen tree', from espe and half-land); *Hautonhey* 1530 (*v.* (ge)hæg); *leya de Haylton*' e13, *Lee que vocatur Hach-toneslee*,...*illius Lee spectans ad villam de Ridleg*' 1310–50 (*v.* lēah, cf. Haughton *supra*, Ridley 313 *infra*); *Hiruichiscroft* H3 ('Herewig's croft', from ME (OG) pers.n. *Herewig* and croft); *Lawe* H3 ('the mound', *v.* hlāw); *Loninde* 1310–50 (perhaps 'the lane', cf. loning, and *loaning* NED; but more probably 'the lane-end', *v.* lane, ende¹, a cpd. noted from 1296 Löfvenberg 117); *Otal(e)* (*v. Acale*, *supra*); *Ouldford or Ouldfeld* 1619 (*v.* ald, ford, feld); *Pigenes ruding* 1332 ('pigeon's clearing', from ME pigeon 'a pigeon' (c.1390 NED) and ryding); *Platteneford* 1310–50 ('ford which has been bridged', *v.* plat¹, -en², ford); *Salteressich*' 1310–50 ('salter's stream', *v.* saltere, sīc); *þe shrewed crofte* 1598; *del Style, at Stele* 1357 (p) (*v.* stigel); *Wolueacres* 1372 ('wolf fields', *v.* wulf, æcer).

6. PECKFORTON (HALL, HILL, MERE, MILL (lost), MOSS, POINT & WOOD) (109–5356)

Pevreton 1086 DB

Pecfortuna 1096–1101 (1280), 1150 Chest, *-tona* c.1184 ib, *Pec(k)-forton* 1284 Ch, ChancW *et freq* with variant spellings *-tone*, *Pecke-*; (*the turbary & the wood of Pec-*, *Pekforton*) 1355 BPR, (*Peckforton Hall & Meare*) 1671 Sheaf, (*Hall Farm*) 1822 Cre, (*Peckforton Hill, -Mere, -Mill, -Moss & Point*) 1831 Bry, (*-Wood*) 1842 OS (cf. *Wood Lane* 1846 TA), *Pakforton* 1332 AddCh

Pecferton 1260, 1289 Court, *Pe(c)k(e)-*, *Pekferton* 1295 Ipm, 1550 MinAcct, 1560 *Chol*, 1561 Pat, 1571 Cre, 1583 ChRR, *Peckfarton* 1656 Orm²

Packfordton 1250–1300 (1637) Rich, *Peck-* 1305 (1637) ib, Orm², 1616, 1619 Cre, *Pecke-* 1332 *Chol*, *Pec-* c.1536 Leland *Peckforden* 1641 ChRR

'Farm at the ford by a hill', from tūn and the name of a ford '*pēac-ford*' from pēac and ford, with hall, hyll, mere¹, myll, mos and wudu. Peckforton Point is a prominence on a hill, *v.* point, cf. foll. The instance *Pec-*, *Pekford* 1288 Court 234, to which DEPN refers, is irrelevant to Peckforton, being a surname from some analogous p.n. in or near the forest of Macclesfield, probably towards the High Peak district of Db.

PECKFORTON HILLS, 1819 Orm², *Broxton Hylles* 1487 VR 155, *Buckley Hills, Peckfarton Hills, those mountains called Broxton Hills* 1656 Orm², *v.* hyll, cf. prec. and Broxton 325 *infra*. This is a 500–700 ft. range of hills comprising Peckforton Hill, Beeston Rock, Broxton Hill, Bolesworth Hill, Larkton Hill, Bulkeley Hill, Bickerton Hill and Burwardsley Hill, forming the southern part of the central ridge which extends northward to Frodsham Hill. This natural feature may lie behind the p.n. Broxton.

BRICKKILN WOOD, 1846 *TA*, *Brickhill Wood* 1831 Bry, *v.* bryke-kyl. FOUNTAIN COTTAGES, *The Fountain* 1831 Bry. HILL LANE. HILLSIDE FM, *Dairy House* 1831 Bry. MANOR HO. PARKGATE, 1842 OS, cf. *Park Fields Plantation* 1831 Bry and *the Park of Peckfordton* 1305 (1637) Orm², *parcum de Pekforton* 1320 *Chol*, *v.* park. PECKFORTON CASTLE, a nineteenth-century edifice, occupying *Horsley Hill* 1831 Bry, 1842 OS, *v.* Horsley Lane 303 *supra*. PECKFORTON GAP, a pass through the hills, between Peckforton Point & Bulkeley Hill, which carried an ancient salt-way *Welshman's Street* 1 48 (route XXV), *v.* gappe. PECKFORTONHALL LANE, *Bodens Lane* 1831 Bry. STANNER COTTAGES & NAB, *Stanner Hill* 1831 ib, *Stanner Nab* 1842 OS, 'stony hill', *v.* stæner, hyll, nabbi. STONE HO, 1842 ib, *Kinseys Farm* 1831 Bry. THE TABLE ROCK. WASTE HILL, 1842 OS, *v.* waste. WILLIS'S WOOD, *Cranberry Moss* 1831 Bry, *v.* cranberry.

FIELD-NAMES

The undated forms are 1846 *TA* 315. Of the others 1354, 1363 and 1398 are *MinAcct*, 1465 AD, 1819 Orm², 1831 Bry.

(a) Bache (*v.* bæce¹); Black Croft; Boat Mdw (*v.* bōt); Calveley's Lane 1819 Orm² II 304 (named from the *Calveley* family who had a hall here);

Daffodel Fd (*v.* affadille); Day Mdw (*le Deymedowe, le Deyemedew* 1354, *Deyemede* 1398, 'dairy meadow', *v.* dey, mǣd); Fenna's Fd (*Fynawes-, Fynowesfeld* 1354, *Fynoresfeld* 1398, probably a field at a hill, from fīn 'a heap' or finn 'coarse grass', with hōh or ōra[1], and feld); Glen Patch (*v.* glen); Hall Banks, Hays, Lane & Yards (cf. *Halleheth* 1398, 'heath near a hall', *v.* hall, hǣð; from the ancient hall of the Calveley family); Haylack Mdw; Hollin & Stubble Birch Moor (*Birchemore* 1363, 'birch-tree moor', from birce and mōr[1], with stubbil, holegn); Kettles Croft (*Ketelescroft* 1354, 'Ketill's croft', from the ON pers.n. *Ketill* (ODan *Ketil*) and croft); Knowl (*v.* cnoll); Marl Fd; Melon Garden; Nettledale 1831 ('valley growing with nettles', *v.* netel(e), dæl[1]); Ox Hays (*v.* (ge)hæg); Pool Fd, Poolstead (cf. *le polehede, le polesyde* 1465, *v.* pōl[1], hēafod, sīde, pōl-stede); Raddles Croft; Ridley Fd (cf. Ridley 313 *infra*); Rough Bank; Spath Mdw (*v.* sparð); Stocks Bank 1831 (*v.* stocc); Town Fd; Big & Little Western; White Fd; Windmill Fd; Within Yard ('enclosure growing with withins', *v.* wiðegn, geard); Wood Croft.

(*b*) *Asshefeld* 1354 ('ash-tree field', *v.* æsc, feld); *Gatlegh* 1354 ('goat clearing', *v.* gāt, lēah); *Mulnemedewe* 1363 ('meadow at a mill', *v.* myln, mǣd); *Torbokkes* 1398 (the name of an 'acre', from the surname *Torbok* (ModE *Tarbuck*), from Tarbock La, but *freq* in Ch records); *Walchmon-streete, le Walesmonwey* (*v. Welshman's Street* 1 48 (route XXV)); *Westefeld* 1354 (*v.* west, feld); *Wystaneshalgh* 1354 ('Wīgstān's nook', from the OE pers.n. *Wīgstān* and halh).

7. RIDLEY (FM, GREEN, HALL, POOL & WOOD) (109–5454)

   Ridle(i)a, -lee, -leh, -leg' 1180–1220 Chol (p), *-legh* 1265–84 (1640)
      Chest (p) *et freq* with variant spellings *Ryd-* (from 1331 ChRR),
      -le, -ley (from 1400 ChRR), *Ryddlgh'* 1310 Chol, *Ridle Hawlle
      Place, Ridle Parke & Poole* c.1536 Leland, *Ridley Pool* 1656
      Orm[2], *Ridley Farme* 1657 Chol, (*Higher & Lower*) *Ridley-greene*
      1671 Sheaf, 1677 Chol, *Ridley Hall* 1724 NotCestr, *Ridley Farm,
      Green & Wood* 1831 Bry
   Riddelegh c.1230 Chol (p), and 12 examples, with variant spellings
      Rydde-, -leg(h), -ley(e), -l(ee) to 1460 ChRR
   Ridele 1272 Chol (p), *-legh* 1288 Orm[2], 1290 Plea *et freq* with
      variant spellings *Ryde-, -leg', -ley, -lgh, -lee* to 1561 Pat, *Rydeleng*
      1297 Cl
   Redlegh 1297 IpmR, 1326 ChRR (p), *Reddeley* 1309 ib (p), 1336
      Orm[2] (p), *Redele(gh)* 1321 City (p), *Redilegh* 1378 *Eyre*
   Rudle 1320 Chol (p), *Rudylegh* 1349 Rich (p)

'Cleared glade', from (ge)ryd(d) and lēah, with hall, grēne[2], place, pōl[1] and wudu. Ridley Pool is the name of a tract of ground formerly covered by a mere, said by Leland c.1536 to be half a mile long by half a mile broad.

THE BACHE [bætʃ], 15 Rich, *The Beech* 1831 Bry, *Bache* 1840 *TA*, *Ridley Wach* 1842 OS, 'the valley stream', *v.* bæce[1]. The 1842 form, if not a scribal error, may arise from confusion with wæsce 'a washing-place'.   CHESTERTON WOOD.   GRANGE BRIDGE. THE MOSS, *Ridley Moss* 1831 Bry, *v.* mos.   RIDLEYBANK HO, *v.* banke.   RIDLEYHILL FM, *v.* hyll.

FIELD-NAMES

The undated forms are 1840 *TA* 336. Of the others 1250–1300 (1637), 1314 (1637) are Rich, 1536 is c.1536 Leland, 1831 Bry, and the rest *Chol.*

(a) Bake House Fd (*v.* bæc-hūs); Barley Hurst Wd (*v.* bærlic, hyrst); Barn Fd 1796 (cf. *Barne Yarde* 1677, *v.* bere-ærn, geard); Black Croft; Breretons Crofts 1677; Brew House Fd; Brickiln Fd (1796); Brin, (Big-, Little- & Middle-) Bryn (*Great-, Litle- & Midle Brins* 1677, *The Big-, Little- & Middle Brinn, -Bryn Field* 1796, 'the hill', *v.* bryn); Brook Lane Fd; Calf Pit Mdw; Cholmondeleys Mdw; Clay Riddings (*v.* ryding); Crab Tree Crofte 1677; One-, Fourteen Day Math, Twelve Demath (cf. *Five Days-, One Day-, Seven Day Math* 1796, *v.* day-math); Door House Fd; Dove House Fd (1796, *Doue House Field & Meadow* 1677, *v.* dove-house); Dunnes Fd 1677; Forty Acre (*the-* 1796); Glade Fd; Gorsty Fd (1677, cf. *Gorsty Hollands* 1677, *v.* gorstig, hol[2], land); Green Fd (1796, *Greene Field* (*Meadow*) 1677, *v.* grene[1]); Hakes Mosse 1677; Hall Lane 1831 (cf. Ridley Hall *supra*); Hillock Fd (*v.* hylloc); Hollins Wd (*v.* holegn); Horse Pasture (1796); Hubback Fd (*Habbocks Field* 1651, *Habbuck* 1677, *The Hubback, Hubback Field* 1796); Intack (*v.* inntak); Kiln Croft (*Kilne Croft* 1677); Knowle (*v.* cnoll); Lady's Mdw (*v.* hlǣfdige); Lee Green (*v.* lēah, grēne[2]); Long Croft (cf. *Long Crofte* 1677); The Long Mdw 1796; Marl Fd; Mart Fd; Litle Ollars 1677 (*v.* alor); Outlet (cf. *Outlet Field* 1796, *v.* outlet); Ox Pasture; Pear Tree Fd; Pease Fd 1677 (*v.* pise); Pool Fd, Fur & Near Pools (cf. Ridley Pool *supra*); Poor Fd; Ridley Fd 1729 (1651, 1695); Rough Close; Shoulder of Mutton (*-field* 1796, *v.* 325 *infra*); Long Slang (*v.* slang); Smithy Fd (1677); Square Fd 1796 (1677, *v.* squar(e)); Tomno Beach 1686 (1677, *v.* bece[1]); Way Fd (*v.* weg); Well Fd; White Fd; White Moore 1677 (*v.* hwīt, mōr[1]); Wind Mill Fd; Within Croft (1677, *v.* wiðegn); Wood Fd (1796); Woolgrass Fd.

(b) *the Barnedyche* 1314 (1637) ('ditch near a barn', *v.* bere-ærn, dīc); *le Lowe* 1454 (p) (*v.* hlāw); *Richinsford, Richimsfoorde* 1314 (1637) ('Richin's ford', from the ME pers.n. *Richin,* diminutive of *Rich,* for *Richard,* and ford); *Ridleyford* 1250–1300 (1637), *Ridley forde* 1314 (1637) (*v.* ford. This was at 109–538545 on the Bulkeley boundary).

8. SPURSTOW (HALL & LOWER HALL) (109–5656)

Spuretone 1086 DB

Sporstow 1180–1220 *Chol* (p) *et freq* with variant spellings *Spori-*
(e13 *Bun*), *Sporu-* (1308 Adl (p)), *-stowe*, *-stou(e)* to 1395 *Chol*
(p), *Sporstows* 1664 Sheaf

Spurestoa, -stou, Spuristou 1180–1220 *Chol* (p), *Spurstow(e)* c.1280
Misc, 1281 (17) Chest *et freq* with variant spellings *-stou, -staue*;
(*the Hall of Spurstowe*) 1584 ChRR, (*manors of Spurstow and
Spurstow Hall*) 1605 Cre, (*Spurstow Hall Farm*) 1806 ib,
Spurstow (Lower) Hall 1831 Bry

Spurtouwe 1282 Court (p)

Sprostowe 1287 Court (p), *Sproustou* (lit. *-ston*) 1313, 1434 Cre,
-stowe 1507 *MinAcct*

Spourstowe 1359 *Chol*, *-stow* 1366 MidCh (p)

Spirstowe 1400 Pat

Sperstou 1413 Cl (p) (lit. *-ston*)

Spurstall 1550 *MinAcct*, *-stoll* 1561 Pat

Ekwall (DEPN) derives this from **spor** 'a track, a footprint', here
possibly used in the sense 'trackway', and **stōw** 'a meeting-place',
perhaps in the sense 'hermitage', cf. EPN **2** 159 and Plemstall 326
infra. The p.n. might be interpreted, from **spor** and **stōw**, as 'meeting-
place on a trackway', as an allusion to the Roman road from Tarporley
to Whitchurch Sa, drawn by Webster (Atlas 13). Spurstow is near the
intersection, in Ridley township, of that road and the ancient saltway
from Nantwich to Farndon, *Welshman's Street*, *v.* **1** 48 (route XXV).
There could well have been some kind of venue near such a meeting
of routes, perhaps a market, cf. Beeston 302 *supra*. However, Dr von
Feilitzen observes that the forms point to a first el. with *-u-*. He
suggests OE *Spur-stōw from OE *spura* 'a spur' or *spure* 'a heel',
with a topographical sense, alluding to the hamlet's position on a
slight ridge, and as a possible alternative, a formation OE **spyrd-
stōw*, from OE *spyrd* 'a race-course' (with loss of interconsonantal *d*
and with WMidl *y* > *u* before *r* + consonant), analogous with OE
pleg-stōw 'a sport-place', *oret-stōw, winn-stōw* 'a wrestling-pitch'.
The topographical explanation is very likely.

BADCOCK'S LANE, 1831 Bry, from the surname *Badcock*.   BATH HO,
1842 OS, *Bath Farm* 1831 Bry, cf. Spurstow Spa *infra*, *v.* **bæð**.
BROWN HILLS, *Brown Hill* 1831 ib, 1842 OS, *v.* **brūn**[1].   BUNBURY

HEATH BRIDGE, cf. Bunbury Heath 305 *supra*.   CAPPER'S LANE
(FM), cf. *Cappers Lane Field* 1840 *TA*.   FIELDS FM.   GREEN
BUTTS, *Green Butt* 1840 *ib*.   HAYCROFT, 1831 Bry, *Hey Croft* 1842
OS, 'hay croft' or 'croft at an enclosure', *v*. hēg or (ge)hæg, croft.
LONG LANE, 1842 *ib*.   LOWERHALL GATE, *v*. geat, cf. Spurstow
Lower Hall *supra*.   NEWHALL FM.   PINFOLD COTTAGES, *v*.
pynd-fald.   RADLEYWOOD, *Radley Wood* 1786 Cre, 'red clearing',
v. rēad, lēah.   RADMORE GREEN (FM), *Rodmoregrene* 1372 AD,
Radnore Green 1745 Cre, *Radmore Green* 1831 Bry, cf. Radmore
Covert, Radmore Green 133, 310 *supra*. This was an ancient waste in
Brindley, Haughton and Spurstow, probably 'waste land at a
clearing' from rod[1] and mōr[1], with grēne[2].   ROOKERY FM, *v*.
rookery.   ROWE'S HO, 1831 Bry, from the surname *Rowe*.
SPURSTOW SPA, *Spurstow Spa Water* 1816 Orm[2], *Spa Well Field* 1840
TA, *Bath* 1831 Bry, 1842 OS, cf. Bath Ho *supra*. This is a saline
spring. Orm[2] II 295 reports that there used to be a bathing-pit here,
but it was disused by 1816, *v*. spa, bæð.   THORNYFIELDS, *Thorney
Fields* 1831 Bry, *Ferney Field* 1842 OS, *v*. þornig, feld.   WHITE-
GATES, *Spurstow Sketh* 1804 Cre, *Skirth* 1831 Bry, *Skith field* 1840
TA, apparently from skeið 'a course, a track, a race-course', cf. 295
supra.   WINDMILL BANK, cf. *Windmill Fields* 1840 *ib*, *v*. wind-
mylne, banke.

FIELD-NAMES

The undated forms are 1840 *TA* 363. Of the others, e13 is *Bun*, c.1340,
1500 Sheaf, 1372 AD, 1398 *MinAcct*, 1420 *Dow*, 1481 Plea, 1536 Leland,
1599 *Chol*, 1831 Bry, 1842 OS, and the rest Cre.

(a) Acorn Yard; Aldersey Rough 1842 (*v*. rūh 'rough place'); Ash Bank,
Ash House Fd (cf. *the Ashe grounds* 1658, and *Ash* 296 *supra*, *v*. æsc, banke);
Bache Fd, Big *&* Little Beach (*v*. bæce[1], bece[1]); Black Croft (cf. *Blacke
Flatt* 1599, *v*. blæc, flat); Bottoms (*v*. botm); Brandit (*v*. branderith); Butt
Land (*v*. butte); The Calvary (probably *Calverhey*, 'calves' enclosure', *v*.
calf (gen.pl. calfra), (ge)hæg); Chicken Grove (*Chekengreves* (*Fielde*) 1599,
'chicken woods', *v*. cīcen, græfe); The Copy (*v*. copis); Coxeys Croft (cf.
Coxhey's tenement 1807, from a surname *Coxhey*); Cross (House) Fd (*v*.
cros); Crow Wood Mdw (*the crow wood* (*meadow*) 1658, *v*. crāwe, wudu); The
Dam (*v*. damme); Dark Mdw (*v*. deorc); Three Daymath (*v*. day-math);
Dobb Mdw (cf. *Dob Lane* 1831 Bry, a lane running east from Spurstow
Lower Hall); Dunns Mdw (cf. *Done's Cottage* 1769, from the surname
Done); Embraws; Fox Holes (*v*. fox-hol); Gorsey Croft (*Gorstie Croft* 1599,
v. gorstig, croft); Gorsey Elling; the gostrey kiln 1658 (*v*. gorst-trēow 'a
gorse-bush', cyln); Long Grindley (*v*. grēne[1], lēah, cf. Grindley 326 *infra*);
Grow Hale; Hanging Fd (*v*. hangende); Heath Ho 1831 (cf. *Heath Croft*

1806, *v.* hǣ ð); the Hay Ridding 1658 (*v.* hēg, ryding); Hengleyse Croft ('steep pasture', *v.* henge, lǣs); the Hill Fields 1658; The Hollands ('selions in a hollow', *v.* hol², land); Horse Pasture; Intake (*v.* inntak); Kiln Coney Greave, Kiln Croft (*v.* cyln, coningre); Kinseys Croft; The (Little) Majesty; Marl Fd (*Marled fielde* 1599, *marled Feild* 1656, cf. *Marlecroftes* 1481, *v.* marle, marled, feld, croft); Milking Bank (*v.* milking); Mill Hallow (cf. *Spurstow Mill* 1831, *the two mill meadows* 1658, *v.* myln, holh); Moss Croft; Nib Croft (*v.* nib); Old Orchard 1776; Old Wd; Ox Pasture; Patch (*v.* pacche); Pingot (*v.* pingot); Platts (*v.* plat²); Pool Fd *&* Head, (The) Pools (*Newpoole* 1536, *the near(er) Pooles, the Poole field* 1658, *the Poole* 1776, *v.* pōl¹, nīwe, hēafod); Big *&* Little Rakings; Rileys (*Rileyfeld* 1481, *v.* ryge, lēah); Rotten Mdw (*v.* roten); Rushy Gale (*v.* riscig, gagel); Rye Eddish *&* Yard (*v.* ryge, edisc, geard); Swang (*v.* swang); Thompson's closes 1765 (cf. *Thompson's cottage* 1769); Well Croft (cf. *the wall croft* 1700, *v.* wælla, wella); the Whobs 1784 (*v.* cwabba); Withen-, Within Croft (*v.* wiðegn, croft); Woodfen's tenement 1699 (from a surname *Woodfin*); the Yards 1784 (*v.* geard).

(*b*) (sepes de) *Acale* e13 (*v.* 311 *supra*); *the Acres* 1599 (*v.* æcer); *Barnefielde* 1599 (*v.* bere-ærn, feld); *Buchewallehurst* (lit. *Bucbe-*), *Bocaldehurst* c.1340, *Bukkalhurst* 1420 (p), *Bokelurst* 1500 ('(wood-hill at) the buck's spring', from bucca and wælla, with hyrst); *Brerye croft* 1599 (*v.* brērig, croft); *Brownecrofte* 1481 (*v.* brūn¹, croft); *quercus que dicitur Crocke* e13 ('crooked oak', *v.* krókr); *Doddes Acre* 1599 (from the pers.n. or surname *Dodd* and æcer); *le Duffehowse medowe* 1481 (*v.* dove-house); *le Fynachis, le Finax* c.1340 ('grassy hooks', *v.* finn 'coarse grass, bent grass', haca 'a hook-shaped piece of ground, a corner'); *le Broc de Halickus* e13 ('brook at a place called "the little nooks"', *v.* brōc, halc); *Ladmor* c.1340 (p) (probably analogous with Lodmore 97 *supra*, 'moor with a track across it', from lād and mōr¹); *Lartonfeld* 1481 (*v.* feld, cf. Larkton 326 *infra*); *leya de Sporistoue* e13 ('the cleared woodland of Spurstow', *v.* lēah); *Mondaies Acres* 1599 (from æcer and Mōnandæg); *Schesewys* 1362, also (p), ('cheese dairy', *v.* cēse, wīc, perhaps the origin of the *Cheswis* family of Mickley Hall 114 *supra*); *Setebuck* 1284, *-bucke* c.1340, 1398 ('beech-tree near a fold', *v.* (ge)set, bōc¹); *Swynehey* 1481 ('swine enclosure', *v.* swīn¹, (ge)hæg); *Thorteleg* c.1340 ('troublesome or difficult wood or clearing', from þroht 'oppressive, grievous' and lēah); *Tomkynesfeld Jonessone* 1372 ('field belonging to Tomkin son of John', from the ME pers.n. *Tomkin*, diminutive of *Thomas*, and feld); *Watecroft* c.1340 (probably 'wheat croft' *v.* hwǣte, croft); *Woldscroftes* 1481 ('crofts in a woodland', *v.* wald, croft).

9. TILSTONE FEARNALL (109–5660), *Tilston Farnhale* 1427 Orm², *Tidleston et Farnall* 1475 AddCh, both *freq* with spellings as for Tilstone, *Fearnall infra*.

TILSTONE (HALL, HO, LODGE *&* MILL) [ˈtilstən]

Tidulstane 1086 DB, *-tan, -tona, Tyd-* e13, 13, 1310 Chest, 1260 Court (p), *Tidulestan* 1248 Rich, *Tidelstona* (*molendinum de*)

21

a.1208 Chest, *Tydelstan* 1311 Plea, *Tid-* 1321 City, *-is-* 1310–11 (17) Chest, *Tydeliston* 14 (17) *Bun, -es-* 1357 *ChFor, Tidd-* 1364 Plea, *Tidlistan* (*molendinum de-*) c.1260 (c.1340) *Bun, Tydleston* 1265–84 (1640) Chest, *Tid-* 1347 *Eyre et freq* to 1536 ChRR, *Tiddles-* 1369 Plea

Tideluestan 1096–1101(1280), 1150 Chest, *Tidil-* 1096–1101 (1280) ib, *Tidul-* 1188–91 ib

Tadeluestan 1096–1101 (1280) Chest

Tudelston(a) 1221–40, 13, c.1310 Chest

Tildeston 1265–84 (1640) Chest, 1380 *Eyre, Ty-* 1437 Orm², *Tildestan* 1318 Rich, (*-iuxta Bunbury*) 1364 Plea, *Ty-* 1353 *ChFor Tilleston'* 1398 *Add*

Tilstan 1440 *Rental, -ton* 1417 ChRR *et freq* with variant spelling *Ty-* to 1842 OS, *Hall of Tilston Fearnall* 1656 Orm², 1671 Sheaf, *-tone* 1459 (1594) ChRR, *-Hall, Lodge & Mill* 1831 Bry

'Tīdwulf's stone', from the OE pers.n. *Tīdwulf* and stān, with hall, hūs, loge, myln.

FEARNALL (lost) [ˈfəːrnəl]

Fornale (*Tyldestanmosse in-*) 1353 *ChFor, Fornall* 1565 Cre

Farnhale 1363 BPR *et freq* with variant spellings *Farn(e)hale, Farnale* to 1473 Plea

Farnhall 1438 ChRR, and 5 examples, with variant spellings *Farnall, Farnehall* to 1553 Pat, *Flarnhaw cum Idynshaw* 1535 VE

Fernehalle 1539–47 Dugd, and 6 examples, with variant spellings *Fern(h)all, Fernehall* to *Fernall* 1842 OS

Farnell (lit. *Faruell*) 1541 Dugd

Fearnall 1546 Dugd, *-hall* 1656 Orm²

Fernell 1579 Dugd

Fernhale 1671 Sheaf

'Fern nook', v. fearn, halh (dat.sg. hale). This appears to have been within Tilstone but a distinct manor. VE links it with Iddinshall 286 *supra*.

WORDESHAM (lost), 1544 Plea, *Worlisham* c.1260 (1340) *Bun, Werlesham* 14 (17) ib, *Worlesham* 1440 *Rental*, from hām 'a village, a homestead'. The first el. may be hwerfel 'a circle', or a p.n. hweorfa-lēah 'cattle pasture', v. Worleston 151 *supra*, cf. Trundle Moor *infra*.

THE CLAYS (109–590587), [klɛiz], *Le Cleyes* 1311 Plea, *-us* (lit. *Cleyns*) 1349 *Chol* (p), *Cleyes* 1400 AD (p), *le Cleys* 1392 ChRR (p), *the-* 1656 Orm², *Cleys* 1842 OS, *Clees Bridge & Farm* 1831 Bry, 'the clayey places', *v.* clǣg. In 1656 (Orm² II 9) 'a fair house' at the west end of Watfield Pavement 323 *infra*, this estate seems to have belonged to the Hospital of St John without Northgate, Chester, cf. DKR XXVII 100, XXVIII 40.

LOCK FM, named from Tilstone Lock on the Shropshire Union Canal.   STAGES PLATT, *v.* 290 *supra*.   TILSTONE BANK, 1831 Bry, cf. *Tidelstanlowe* 1321 City, *v.* banke, hlāw.

FIELD-NAMES

The undated forms are 1839 *TA* 395. Of the others, a.1208, 1265–84 (1640), 1310 are Chest, c.1260 (c.1340), 14 (17) *Bun*, 1353, 1357 *ChFor*, 1549 Pat, 1671 Sheaf, 1831 Bry.

(*a*) Amblers Eye (*v.* ēg); Barbers Lake (*v.* lacu); Birches (perhaps the same as *le Breches infra*); Black Butts (*v.* butte); Brook Bache (*v.* brōc, bæce[1]); Brook Fd; Bunbury Fd (cf. Bunbury 305 *supra*); Clay Flatt; Clemn Ley & Patch (cf. Clemley 47 *supra*); Coombs (*v.* cumb); Coppice; Dove Ho; Elm Hill; French Fd (*v.* French wheat); Big & Little Garden Fd (*v.* gardin); The Golden Mine; The Hill; Humpstones Mdw (*v.* hump, stān); The Huxleys; The Knowl (*v.* cnoll); Long Eye Mdw (*v.* ēg); Lucern Bank (*v.* 325 *infra*); Marl Fd; Marsh Flatt (*v.* mersc, flat); Mill Pool; Mud Fd (*v.* mudde); Out Fd (*v.* ūt); Outlett (*v.* outlet); Owlery Croft (*v.* alor); Ox Pasture; Patch; Pool Croft, Fd & Mdw (cf. *Tidulstan Pol* 1310, *v.* pōl[1]); Big & Little Ridding (*v.* ryding); Robinsons Croft & Knowl (cf. *land called Robynsons* 1549, *v.* cnoll); Sheens Knowl Rough 1831 (*v.* cnoll, rūh, cf. *Sheens or Sap Field*, etc. 301 *supra*. All these appear to be named from some locally notable road-mender surnamed *Sheen*); Big Shepherds Hey; Stoke Fd (*v.* stoc); Stone Wetch; Tilstone Heath (cf. *Tilston Heath Hall* 1671, *v.* hǣð); Town Fd; Trundle Moor (1840 *TA* 83, cf. 307 *supra*, 'moor at a ring', *v.* trendel, mōr[1], cf. *Wordesham supra*. The significance is not apparent); Wall Croft (*v.* wælla); Wash Pit Fd (*v.* wæsce, pytt); Well Mdw; Big & Little Winterfoot ('winter ford', *v.* winter, ford).

(*b*) *le Breches* c.1260 (c.1340), *le Bruches* 1265–84 (1640), 14 (17) (the name of an assart, 'land broken in for cultivation', *v.* brēc, bryce); *le Dedelache* 1310 (a watercourse forming the boundary between Tilstone and Alpraham, 'dead boggy-stream', *v.* dēad, læc(c). For the adj. 'dead' for a dried-up or sluggish (i.e. not flowing) stream, cf. *Dedhe, Dautha*, Dead Eye YW 4 252, 5 29, 6 28; ERN 115, NoB (1926) 149; and cf. Danish hydronyms in *Død*-by Sørensen in *Danske Sø- og Ånavne* I (1968) 353–4); *Henneshawe* 1310 ('hens' copse', *v.* henn (gen.pl. henna), sceaga); *Tyldestanmosse in Fornale* 1353 (*v.* mos, cf. Tilstone, *Fearnall supra*); *boscus de Northwode* a.1208 (*v.* norð, wudu); *boscus de Tydleston* 1357 ('Tilstone wood', *v.* wudu).

10. TIVERTON (FM & HALL) (109–5560) [ˈtivərtṇ] older local [ˈtiːərtṇ]

> *Tevreton* 1086 DB, *Teverton* e13 Orm² *et freq* with variant spellings
> Teuer-, Teuur-, -tona, -ten to 1819 Orm², (-alias Tearton) 1609
> Chol, (-Terton) 1613 AddCh, (-Teerton) 1671 Sheaf
>
> *Tiverton* 1253 Ch (lit. *Tibeton*), 1266 Dugd, 1316 Plea, 1347 Cl (p)
> (lit. *Tiber-*), 1396 ChRR (p), 1724 NotCestr, (-alias Tereton) 1694
> Sheaf
>
> *Taverton* 1360 BPR, 1548 Pat
> *Teyverton* 1519 Earw
> *Tybroughton* 1530 Sheaf
> *Taruton* 1550 *MinAcct*, *Tarveton alias Tarton* 1561 Pat
> *Tereton* 1550 (1569) ChRR, *Tarton* 1561 Pat, *Tearton* 1568 Orm²,
> *Teirton* 1575 Sheaf, *Terton* 1613 AddCh, *Teerton* 1656 Orm²

'Red-lead farm', from **tēafor** and **tūn**, with **hall**. The name may denote a red-painted building, or more likely a place where red-lead was available.

HULGRAVE FM (109–537607), *Hullgate Hall or Hortons House* 1831 Bry, cf. *Holegreue* 13 AddCh (p), -grewe c.1300 Chol (p), -greve 1322 ChancW (p), *Holle-* c.1300 Chol (p), *Hol-* 1311 Fine (p) *et freq* to 1387 ib (p), *Hulgreve* c.1306 (17) Sheaf (p) *et freq* to 1430 ChRR (p), *Halgreve* 1410 ib (p), a surname *freq* in this district, 'wood in a hollow', from **hol²**, **græfe**.

TIRESFORD (109–555616) [taiərz-]

> *Tirisford* 1180–1220 Chol (p), *Tyris-* 13 AddCh (p), *Tyres-* 1260
> Court (p) *et freq* to 1429 ChRR, *Tires-* 1348 Eyre
> *Tyrefford* 1208–29 Whall (p), 1348 ChRR (p), *Tireford* 13 Chest,
> 1357 BPR, 1560 Pat, -fordh l13 (n.d.) Sheaf, *Tyreford* 1513 Plea
> *Teyresforth* 1351 Chamb (p)

'Tīr's ford', from **ford** and an OE pers.n. *Tīr*, a short form for an OE pers.n. in *Tīr-*, *v.* Redin 37, DEPN s.n. Terrington Nf.

TIVERTON MOSS, 1831 Bry, 1839 *TA*, *Teverton Heath* 1819 Orm², cf. *Mosse Crofte* 1547 AddCh, *Moss (Bank & Croft)*, *Heath Field* 1839 *TA*, *v.* **hǣð**, **mos**. This is probably the location of *Moscote* 1303 Chamb, *le mos de Moscotes* 1313 AddCh, *moris de-* 1314 ib, *Moskote* 1343 ib, 'huts at a bog', *v.* **mos**, **cot**.

BANK FM, cf. *Bank (Field), Big & Little Banks, Banks Acre* 1839 *TA*, *v.* banke, cf. Simpson's Rough *infra.* BATE'S MILL BRIDGE, cf. Horton's Mill, *infra.* BEESTON BROOK (BRIDGE), *Beeston Brook Wharf* 1831 Bry, *Beeston Brook* 1842 OS, a hamlet beside R. Gowy, cf. Beeston 302 *supra.* BRASSEY GREEN (HALL), 1842 ib, *Bres(c)ygreene* 1671 Sheaf, *Bressie Green* 1819 Orm², cf. *Brasseys Hill* 1839 *TA*, named after the *Brassey (de Bresci)* family, from Wistaston 45 *supra*, resident in Tiverton since before 1406, Sheaf³ 17 (3935), *v.* grēne². CRIB LANE, 1842 OS, cf. *Crib Meadow* 1839 *TA, v.* crib. DAIRY FM. DAISYBANK, cf. *Daisy Field* 1839 *TA.* FERNEY LEES, *Fearny(e) Lees* 1595 *AddCh, Ferny-Lees* 1671 Sheaf, 'ferny pastures', *v.* fearnig, læs. FOUR LANE ENDS, 1719 ib, a crossroads. GARDENHURST. HAND GREEN, 1831 Bry, *-greene* 1671 Sheaf, *v.* grēne². HORTON'S MILL, 1831 Bry, cf. *Mulnehalgh* 1343 *AddCh, Mill Lane* 1831 Bry, *Mill Field, Hough, Meadow & Rough* 1839 *TA, v.* myln, halh. The location near Bate's Mill Bridge *supra* suggests that the surname *Bate* was once applied to the mill as well as that of *Horton.* NEWSTEAD. REDHILL COTTAGES. SIMPSON'S ROUGH, *Big Bank Woods* 1831 Bry, cf. Bank Fm *supra, v.* rūh. TOWN FIELDS, TOWNFIELD LANE, *Te'erton Townfield* 1643 Orm², *Town Field* 1839 *TA, v.* toun, feld, lane. WHARTON'S BRIDGE & LOCK, *Wharton Bridge* 1831 Bry, on the Shropshire Union Canal, probably from the surname *Wharton.*

FIELD-NAMES

The undated forms are 1839 *TA* 400. Of the others, 13, 1265–91 are Chest, 1253 Ch, 1266 Dugd, 1282 Court, 1313, 1314, 1343 *AddCh*, 1386 ChRR, 1388 *MinAcct.*

(a) Bakehouse Fd (*v.* bæc-hūs); Big Hills; Blake Fd (*v.* blæc); Broomhall Croft; Brown Pool (cf. *le barndepul* 1313, 1314, 'pool at a burnt place', *v.* brende², pōl¹); Buck a shee; Bytham, Bythom(s) (*v.* byōme); Cats Knowl (*v.* catt, cnoll); Clomnley Park (cf. Clemley 47 *supra*); Hospital Clover Croft (from clæfre and croft, with hospital, perhaps named after the Knights Hospitallers, landowners in Tiverton); Coffin Croft; Coney Greave (*v.* coningre); Dale Fd, Hoons & Rooms (*v.* dæl, land, rūm¹); Dean Yard (*v.* denu, geard); Dig Acre (*v.* dīc); Ewers; Flagg Fd (*v.* flagge); Flatt; Big & Little Grove; Hall Fd & Hill (cf. Tiverton Hall *supra*); Hanging Bank & Fd (*v.* hangende); Hollin-hurst ('holly wood', *v.* holegn, hyrst); Hook Fd (*v.* hōc); Horsewash Fd (*v.* hors, wæsce); Hunger Hill (cf. *Hungerhullesheth* 1343, '(heath at) the hungry hill', from hungor and hyll, with hǣð); Intake (*v.* inntak); Kiln Fd; King Fd; Lady Marsh & Oak (*v.* hlǣfdige); Big &

Little Moor(s); New Hey(es) (*v.* (ge)hæg); Old Wd (cf. *boscus de Teuerton* 1265–91, *Tevertonwode* 1386, 1388, *v.* ald, wudu); Old Yard Inclosure (*v.* geard); Orchard Fd; Ox Hey (*v.* (ge)hæg); Patch; Pinfold Croft (*v.* pyndfald); Poor House Fd (*v.* poor-house); Riddings (*v.* ryding); Rigger Fd; Road Hill (*v.* rod¹); Round Hill (*v.* rond); Scows (*Scales* 13 (14), 'the huts', *v.* skáli, cf. 295 *supra*, and *Hulam infra*); Long Shoot (*v.* scēat); Tarporley Mdw (cf. Tarporley 294 *infra*); Three Knook'd Fd (*v.* three-nooked); Walleys Hill; Way Fd (*v.* weg); Well Mdw; Wood (-head & Mdw) (*v.* wudu, hēafod, cf. Old Wd *supra*).

(*b*) *Barndeheth* 1343 ('burnt heath', *v.* brende², hǣð); *le birchenehul* 1313 ('hill growing with birch-trees', *v.* bircen², hyll); *horsseleghruding* 1313 ('cleared land at, or belonging to, Horsley or the horse-clearing', from hors and lēah or the p.n. Horsley 303 *supra*, *v.* ryding); *Hulam'* 1253, 1266, *Hulum* 1282 (p) ('at the sheds', *v.* hulu (dat.pl. *hulum*), cf. Scows *supra*); *Middelclif* 1343 (*v.* middel, clif); *le pauedelake* 1313 ('paved watercourse', probably a culvert, from ME *paved* (c.1374 NED) and lacu); *Sourebuttes* 1343 (*v.* sūr, butte); *Wolfputtes* 1343 ('the wolf-pits', *v.* wulf, pytt).

11. WARDLE (BANK, FM (BRIDGE), & HALL) (110–6057) ['wɔːrdl]]

Warhelle 1086 DB

Wardle 1184 Eaton B, 1383 ChRR, 1671 Sheaf, 1724 NotCestr *et freq*, (*-Hall*) 1671 Sheaf, (*-Bank, -Bridge*) 1831 Bry

Wardul e13 *Bun,* -*hul* 1278 Ipm, -*hull* 1290 ib, 1383 ChRR (p), 1663, 1681 Cre, (*-or Wardle*) 1671 Sheaf

Wordhull 1272–90 *ChFor,* 1287 Court *et freq* with variant spellings *Word(e)hull(e), Wordul(l)* to 1602 ChRR

Wordhill 1287 Court, *Wordehyll* 1560 *Chol*

Wardhill 1335 Pat, *Wardill* 1595 ChRR

Wordele 1317 Plea (p), c.1536 Leland

Wodhull 1351 Chamb (p), 1535 Orm², *Wode-* 1352 ChRR (p)

Wardeley 1437 ChRR (p), *Wardley* 1610 Speed, 1664 Sheaf

Wardell 1465 *ArlB,* 1557 Sheaf, 1577 ChRR, (*Wardall alias-*) 1561 Pat

Wordell 1485 ChRR

Wordhall 1523 Plea

Worldhull 1559 Orm²

Wardall alias Wardell 1561 Pat, *Wardall* 1663 Cre, 1673 ChRR, *Wardhall* 1656 Orm²

Wordle 1564 *Chol,* 1653 Cre, (*-alias Wordhall*) 1625 Orm²

Wordyhull 1594 Plea

Wardale 1664 Cre

'Watch-hill', from weard and hyll, with banke, brycg, hall.

Latchcote (lost, 109–591581), *Lachecote* 1180–1220, c.1280 *Chol*
(p), 13 *Bun* (p), 1288 Court, 1295 ChF (lit. *Lathe-*), 1302 Plea (p),
1353, 1358 *Eyre* (p), 1362 ChRR (p), *Lachcote* 13 (17) Sheaf, 1333
ChRR (p), *pasture called Lachot* 1492 Sheaf, *Latch Cote Field* 1840
TA, 'hut near a boggy stream', *v.* læc(c), cot, cf. Haughton Brook 1
28.

Watfield Pavement (110–614568 to 109–592587), 1698, 1719 Sheaf,
antiqua via 13 (17) ib, *la causey de Whetefeld* 1363 BPR, *via debilis de
Wetfield* 1413 Sheaf, *viae debiles-* 1413 Morris 351, *Edelfelde Pavmont*
1494 Sheaf (sic. for *Wet-*), *Wetfelt pavement* 1506 ib, *(the) Pauement*
17 MidCh, *the well-known pavements or stone causeway called Watfield-
Pavement so termed of the founder* 1656 Orm[2] 11 9, *W(h)eet(e)field
Pavement* 1667 Sheaf, *Whatfield Pavement* 1750 ib, cf. *Pavement
Field* 1592, 1595 ib, 1840 *TA*, also 301, 309 *supra*. King's derivation
of this road-name from some person may reflect an honest tradition,
but no evidence for it is available. The name appears to be 'wheat
field', from hwǣte and feld, with pavement and caucie. The road
runs straight, from Bar Bridge to Calveley, and forms the boundary
between Calveley & Wardle townships. It is part of a route from
Nantwich to Chester through Tarporley, *v.* 1 48 (route XXIV).

Bar Bridge, *v.* 151 *supra*.   Calveley Mills, cf. Calveley 307
supra, *v.* myln.   Goodwin's Bridge, on the Shropshire Union
Canal, cf. Wardle Old Hall *infra*.   Greenlane Fm (110–609573),
cf. *Green Lane (Gate)* 1831 Bry, a trackway from this farm, past
Wardle Hall (109–598572), to Bunbury, crossing the boundary,
Haughton Brook 1 28, about 109–587577, the probable site of
Wardle Ford infra, *v.* grēne[1], lane, geat.   Hill's Gorse, *Waltonson
Hill's Gorse* 1831 Bry, *v.* gorst.   Park Ho (lost, 109–599572), 1831
Bry, 1842 OS, cf. *Wordelp'ke* 1485 ChRR, *Wardall Park, Wardhull
Park Riddings* 1663 Cre, *v.* park, ryding.   Pinfold, *the-* 1702 ib,
Pinfold Croft & Wood 1840 *TA*, *v.* pynd-fald.   Rutter's Bridge
and Tweedale Bridge, bridges on the Shropshire Union Canal.
Wardle Covert, *Wardle Hall Gorse* 1831 Bry, *v.* gorst, cf. Wardle
Hall *supra*.   Wardle Old Hall, *Bridge House* 1831 ib, named
from Goodwin's Bridge *supra*, *v.* ald, hall, brycg.

FIELD-NAMES

The undated forms are 1840 *TA* 413. Of the others, 13 is *Bun*, 13 (17) Sheaf, 1287 Court, 1311 Plea, 1485 ChRR, 1614 Orm², 1663, 1668, 1702 Cre, 1831 Bry.

(*a*) Axe Yards; Bache (*v.* bæce¹); Bentley Lane (*v.* beonet, lēah); Bridge Fd (cf. *meadow at the bridge* 1668, *v.* brycg); Brinshill (*v.* bryn, hyll); Brock-hurst ((*the*) *Brockhurst* 1663, 1668, 'badger hill', *v.* brocc, hyrst); Cart House Croft; Castle Fd & Hill (*v.* castel); Church Fd; Clay Flatts; Coney Greave (cf. *Colligreaces Lane* 1702, *v.* coningre, lane); Crewe Fd (named from the *Crewe* family, of Crewe 9 *supra*); Dace Pitt Fd; Dry Piece; Big & Little Ewe; Four Acre (*the* 1663); Further & Near Furlongs (*v.* furlang); Greg Wd (*v.* greg(g)e); Hockenhull Fd (cf. Hockenhull 274 *supra*); Horse Wash Bank (*v.* wæsce); Kinsey Fd; Big & Little Lady Fd, Lady Mdw (*Great & Little Lady Field, Lady Field Croft & Meadow* 1663, *v.* hlǣfdige); Little Croft 1702; Long Croft; Long Land (*the long land, the higher & lower longland, the Long Lands Green* 1663, *v.* lang, land, grēne²); Milking Bank (*v.* milking); Mill Banks; New Mdw (cf. *the New Croft, the three new fields* 1663); Nine Butts (cf. *the five butts in the long land* 1663, *v.* fif, nigon, butte); Big & Little Palin (*v.* paling(s)); Podmores Wd; Priest Fd (*v.* prēost); Rakes (*v.* rake); Rough; Shaw Flatt (*v.* sceaga, flat); Sparrow Houses 1831; Stoke Green Fd (*the stoak green field* 1663, *v.* stoc, grēne², cf. Stoke 151 *supra*); Turnip Leasow (*v.* lǣs); Ward Fd; Withen Croft (*v.* wiðegn).

(*b*) *le Breres* 1485, *the Briars* 1663 (*v.* brēr); *the Brook(e) Meadow* 1663; *the Coat Meadow* 1663 (*v.* cot); *le Mos* 1287 (p), 1311 (*v.* mos); *Wordhullfield* 1614 (*v.* feld); cf. Wardle *supra*); *Wardhullisford* 13, *Wardle Ford* (13) 17 (*v.* ford, Wardle *supra*, cf. Green Lane Fm *supra*); *the Well Meadow* 1664 (*v.* wella).

INDEX OF CROSS-REFERENCES

References in Part III of *The Place-Names of Cheshire*, to names and topics contained in subsequent Parts. Township- and parish-names are cited simply; other names are followed by the name of the township or parish in which they lie. The **bold figure** indicates the Part in which the name or subject will appear.

INDEX OF PARISHES AND TOWNSHIPS
IN PART III